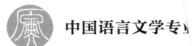 中国语言文学专业系列教材

丛书主编◎曹顺庆

语言学引论

主编◎董秀芳　张和友

编委◎宋作艳　林幼菁　乐　耀

YUYANXUE
YINLUN

北京师范大学出版集团
BEIJING NORMAL UNIVERSITY PUBLISHING GROUP
北京师范大学出版社

图书在版编目（CIP）数据

语言学引论 ／ 董秀芳，张和友主编. —北京 ： 北京师范大学
出版社，2017.8（2024.7重印）
中国语言文学专业原典阅读系列教材
ISBN 978-7-303-22495-1

Ⅰ．①语… Ⅱ．①董… ②张… Ⅲ．①语言学－教材 Ⅳ．①H0

中国版本图书馆 CIP 数据核字（2017）第 131361 号

教材意见反馈　gaozhifk@bnupg.com　010-58805079

YUYANXUE YINLUN

出版发行：北京师范大学出版社 www.bnupg.com
　　　　　北京市西城区新街口外大街12-3号
　　　　　邮政编码：100088
印　　刷：北京虎彩文化传播有限公司
经　　销：全国新华书店
开　　本：787mm×1092mm　1/16
印　　张：24.75
字　　数：480千字
版　　次：2017年8月第1版
印　　次：2024年7月第3次印刷
定　　价：45.00元

策划编辑：马佩林　周劲含　　责任编辑：赵媛媛
美术编辑：焦　丽　李向昕　　装帧设计：焦　丽　李向昕
责任校对：陈　民　　　　　　责任印制：马　洁

总 序

曹顺庆

《光明日报》2014年9月24日第1版刊登了叶小文的《民族文化基因是中国梦的魂与根》一文，文章指出：

在观摩北师大"国培"计划课堂教学后，习近平总书记强调要学习古代经典，语重心长。讲的虽是教材编辑要保留必要的中国文化经典，却涉及"把根留住"——民族复兴中国梦的文化根基和价值支撑……

纵览世界史，一个民族的崛起或复兴，常常以民族文化的复兴和民族精神的崛起为先导。一个民族的衰落或覆灭，往往以民族文化的颓废和民族精神的萎靡为先兆。文化是精神的载体，精神是民族的灵魂。

我认为，当代中国文化面临的最为严峻的问题，是中国古代文化经典面临失传的危险：现在许多大学生基本上无法读懂中国文化原典，甚至不知"十三经"究竟为何物。这种不读中国古代经典原文的现象，已经大大地伤害了学术界与教育界，直接的恶果，就是学风日渐浮躁，误导了大批青年学生，造就了一个没有学术大师的时代，造成了中国文化的严重失语，造成了当代中国文化创新能力的衰减。

造成这种局面的原因固然很多，但其中重要的一条是，我们在教育体制、课程设置、教学内容、教材编写等方面都出现了严重的问题。以教材编写为例，编写内容多为"概论""通论"，具体的"原典阅读"少，导致学生只听讲空论，只看"论"，不读经典；只读文学史，而很少读甚至不读经典作品就可以应付考试，以致空疏学风日盛，踏实作风渐衰。另外，许多教师所用的读本基本是以"古文今译"的方式来组织的，而并非让同学们直接进入文化原典文本、直接用文言文阅读文化经典与文学典籍，这样的学习就与原作隔了一层，因为古文经过"今译"之后，已经走样变味，不复是文化原典了。我认为应当要求学生直接阅读中外文原著，不用今译汉译，这也许是改变此种不利局面的有效途径之一。

正是基于以上的考虑，多年来，我大力倡导用古文（不用今译）读中国文化与文学典籍。我在本科生中开设了"中华文化原典阅读"课程，在研究生中开设了"中国文化原典：十三经"课程，要求学生阅读原汁原味的中国文化原典，教材直接用经典原文，不用今译本。开始时，同学们都读得很艰难，但咬牙坚持下来，一年后都基本能够自己查阅古代典籍，学术功底大大加强，不少学生进入毕业论文写作阶段后，才真正尝到原典阅读的甜头。我还开设了"中国古代文论"课程，要求同学们背诵《文心雕龙》《文赋》等中国文论典籍，同学们开始皆感到"苦不堪言"，但我要求严格，每个学生都必须过此关，结果效果非常好，无论是写文章，还是开会发言，同学们对中国文论典籍信手拈来，文采斐然。我也进一步加强了对西方文化与文学原典的教学，从1998年开始，我直接用英文教材给研究生开设"文学研究方法论：当代西方文论导读"课程，通过抽读的方式要求每位同学在课堂上用英文阅读西方文论著作。经过一番艰苦磨炼，虽然同学们感到太苦，但收获良多。我的用心，就是试图做一个教学改革尝试，让同学们能读到经典原文，读原汁原味的东西，学通中西，获得实实在在的知识与智慧，而不是大讲空论，凌空蹈虚，不是在岸上大讲游泳理论，而是让同学们跳下水去学游泳，教师只是从旁边给予必要的指导与点拨。

由此我发现，原典阅读是培养和训练学生文化根底、文化原创力的最重要、最具本原意义的途径。在专业学习中，对经典文本的研读和探讨能有效开阔视野并促进深度探究能力的形成，从而使学生真正成为适应性强的高素质人才。但在目前的中国语言文学教学中，原典阅读的缺席已成为一个培养优秀人才的明显障碍。长期占主导地位的教学方式，让学生始终同原典存在隔膜。针对这种情况，在教学中增加学生接触、研读、探讨原典的机会，就成了课程和教学改革的当务之急与必由之路。

针对现有的学生只听教师空讲"概论"，而不读经典原文，不会背文学作品的现状，我萌生了编写一套适应21世纪人才培养需要的高质量原典阅读教材的想法。我认为，编写一套好的教材也是学者的责任和使命。一位合格的学者，除了做好学术研究外，还负有传承文明、培养人才的神圣使命，一套优秀教材的影响力可能比学术专著的影响力还要大。目前，一些高校推行百本大学生必读经典书目的举措，立意甚好，但收效甚微，原因就在于学生课外不一定抽时间去读，所以必须将经典阅读和阅读评测放在课堂上进行。编写原典阅读教材，或许是课堂教学改革的有效举措。

本系列教材坚持体现"回到原典"这一总体思路，倡导读原典、讲段子，即课堂上抽查学生课外阅读原典的情况，进一步讲解原典，并且要讲精华，讲得有趣味，让学生由衷地喜欢经典原文。教材基本构架为理论概述加经典作品选讲。本系列教材一共10本，涵盖了高等学校汉语言文学专业的核心课程。它的特点是名家主编、点面结合、深入浅出，倡导特色鲜明、体例创新、名家把关、质量第一。非常感谢学界同人的大力支持，本次参加编写的主编皆为名家，其中有教育部长江学者特聘教授多名，还有国家级教学名师、国际国内重要学会会长等。为推进中国教育改革探索路径，教材的编写结构不以知识体系的完整性为唯一标准，而是以实际的课程时间和授课重点来安排内容和篇幅。每部教材均为知识面介绍与重点讲授的结合，原则上每部教材既有概述阐释，又有原典选读，概述阐释能让学生较为全面系统地掌握知识要点，而原典选读则为讲授重点。

作为"中国语言文学专业原典阅读系列教材"的主编，我认为这个工作是有重要意义的，要培养真正具有深厚文化底蕴、有大智慧、有审美感受力和创新能力的人，最重要的一条路就是返回文化的根，重新审视原典阅读对于青年学子的价值，为同学们打下坚实的学术基础，提高学生的学习积极性，巩固中国文化根底，增强学生的创新能力，加强中国文化自信。

党的十八大以来，习近平总书记在多个场合提到文化自信的问题，并多次将其认定为"一个国家、一个民族发展中更基本、更深沉、更持久的力量"。文化自信的一个重要方面就是要回到原典，回到民族文化的"轴心时代"，只有用文化传统的源头活水不断泽被精神家园，才能使国家、民族源远流长，生生不息。正如习近平总书记在文艺工作座谈会上的讲话所言："求木之长者，必固其根本；欲流之远者，必浚其泉源。"本系列教材以"原典阅读"为要旨，正是对文化自信的积极响应，同时也试图通过对世界各国原典著作的呈现、对比和解读，让中国学子真正认清民族文化的根脉所系，为每一位青年读者种下中华文明的种子。

本系列教材在整体规划上坚持马克思主义理论指导，积极推进习近平中国特色社会主义思想进教材，全面贯彻落实党的教育方针，通过原典再现充分展示中华文明的独特魅力和中国文化的软实力，并力求通过经典阐释和理论建构推动中华优秀传统文化的创造性转化，促进社会主义文艺事业繁荣发展。

感谢北京师范大学出版社马佩林先生的鼎力支持。本系列教材虽然立意甚高，但尚需教学实践的检验，希望学界及教育界广大师生不吝赐正。

写给读者的话

语言学引论，或曰纲要，是目前高校中文系中开设的语言学类基础课程，属于必修课。有的学校在大学一年级开设，有的学校在二年级开设。我们认为，从知识衔接和学生的接受能力上考量，这门课程最好安排在现代汉语课之后，学生如果能有一些基本的汉语史的知识更好。

语言学引论课是语言学的入门课程，涵盖的语言学知识比较宽，需要全面系统地介绍语言学各个分支领域的基本情况；其目的是将语言学的基本概念、基本理论和基本研究方法介绍给学生。因此，语言学引论课是本科阶段比较难的课程之一。这门课程的教学效果直接关系到学生能否对语言学产生兴趣并进入研究生阶段的学习。要保证语言学课的教学质量，一本好的语言学教科书是学生"登堂入室"的关键。

语言学学科的发展和更新是很快的，新的理论层出不穷。本教材的宗旨是：在传授基本知识的同时，注重视野的拓展。尽量较为全面地反映语言学各个领域的重要进展，把语言学前沿的并被学术界广为接受的观点吸收进来。为了强化和巩固学生对基本知识的掌握，给有余力和感兴趣的学生进一步学习和研究指出门径，我们在各章末尾给出了适量的思考题和拓展性阅读书目。

本教材有别于当前高校通行的语言学引论教材的突出特色是：着重通过鲜活的语言实例解释语言学概念与介绍相关理论的同时，在必要的部分增加语言学原典选读。由于很多语言学名著是英文的，因此选入的原典有不少是英文的。这部分原典的阅读可能会给学生带来一定困难，但是考虑到目前大学本科生英语能力的普遍提升，只要肯花些时间，理解这些英语原著也还是可以做到的。为了帮助学生理解，在原典之前配有简要的导读，概括了原典部分的主旨，并对其中的难点做了适当点拨。教师在使用本教材时，可以根据学生的程度灵活选讲其中的原典章节，也可以让学生在课外自己完成原典部分的阅读。如果教学时间允许，还可以在课堂上或课外辅导时组织一些相关的讨论。这本教材以本科生为主要对象，对于那些初入语言学领域的研究生来说，也有一定的参考价值。需要说明的是，为了保持原典的原貌，我们尽量使用照排文档形式，所以文字在形体上的一致性多少受到影响，但是不妨碍阅读。

本教材各章节的编写分工如下：张和友撰写第一章和第五章，宋作艳撰写第二章和第六章，林幼菁撰写第三章、第四章、第七章第二节语篇部分、第九章第三节语音演变部分以及第四节历史比较法与构拟部分，乐耀撰写第七章第一节语用部分和第八章、第十章，董秀芳撰写第九章除第三节以外的部分。统稿工作由董秀芳与张和友共同完成。

需要说明的是，本教材中所用的例子，有的是作者自拟的，有的是从语言学论著中摘引的，为了节约篇幅，没有一一注明。

这本《语言学引论》不仅要通过对语言学基础知识和基本研究方法的具体阐述，展示语言学之美，引领学生进入语言学大门，也要通过示范在复杂的语言事实中发现语言规律的科学求索过程，帮助学生建立严谨求实、追求真理的价值观和勇于探索、一丝不苟的精神品质，努力实现学科育人的目标，为国家的未来培养合格的建设者，并从教材建设的角度为构建中国特色哲学社会科学学科体系、学术体系和话语体系做一点基础方面的工作，为促进中国特色社会主义人文社会科学事业的繁荣发展尽一份微薄的力量。

要编写一部优秀教材，难度是非常大的。我们希望这部教材能为语言学的课堂教学带去一股清新的气息。当然，尽管我们尽了最大的努力，但限于能力和经验，缺点和不足在所难免，真诚地欢迎广大使用者提出批评意见。若有任何意见和建议，请来信给我们，不胜感激！

董秀芳（xdong@pku.edu.cn）

张和友（hyhm@bnu.edu.cn）

目　录

第一章

绪 论

　　语言是什么？语言从哪里来？犹如我们问自己：我是谁？我从哪里来？这是充满奇异幻想的问题，就像柏拉图问题一样，语言学家一直试图解答这些问题。本章首先从巴别塔的传说谈起，讨论语言的起源问题。在此基础上，还将涉及如下问题：语言的性质与功能、语言的机制、语言的内外之别与语言相对论、语言的多样性与语言共性、语言学的研究对象与任务。作为一门学科，语言学是如何登上历史舞台的，也是本章要介绍的内容。

　　本章的难点是语言的起源问题，这是一个至今无法解答将来也无法解决的"奥秘"。但是，这个问题可以引发我们对语言现象的思考。语言的性质与功能、语言的机制、语言的共性问题，是本章的重点。

引　子　巴别塔：关于语言的一个古老传说

　　人们运用语言就如同吃饭、穿衣、走路一样，是人类生活中司空见惯的行为。因为习焉不察，一般人从来不去考虑语言是什么以及语言从哪里来。不过，科学研究就是要对司空见惯的现象进行理性的思考，提供合理的解释，就像牛顿要思考和解释苹果落地的原因一样。对于语言现象，我们也需要进行思考和解释。

　　目前已知世界上有几千种语言。这些彼此不同的语言是怎么来的？《圣经》旧约第十一章所记载的巴别塔的古老传说对此提供了一个说法：

> 　　那时候，全地还是说一种语言，用一套词汇。人们向东迁移的时候，在示拿地看见一块平原，就在那里住下来。他们说："来吧，我们建一座城，造一座塔，塔顶通天，好显扬我们的名，免得我们分散在全地上。"
>
> 　　耶和华下来，要看看世人所建的城、所造的塔。耶和华说："看哪！他们是同一个民族，同说一种语言，如今做出这种事来，以后他们想做的，都没有做不成的。来，我们下去，在那里使他们语言混乱，彼此语言不通。"于是，耶和华把他们从那里分散到全地上，他们逐渐放下建城的工程。
>
> 　　那地方就叫巴别，因为耶和华在那里使全地共同的语言混乱了，耶和华又把人从那里分散到全地上。

　　《圣经》上的这段话表明人们很早就思考过语言的问题。暂且不管其中耶和华扰乱人类语言这个叙述，巴别塔传说显示了以下这样几个观点：①最初全地球上的人类都说一种单一的语言；②语言的分歧是后来产生的；③语言的作用巨大，可以使人们彼此沟通合作，共同成就一些大事。其中第三点是毫无疑问的，而第一点和第二点可以看作一个有趣的猜测。尤其是第一点，语言到底是单起源的（语言先在某个地方产生，然后扩散到其他地方）还是多起源的（语言在不同的地方独立出现）？要确定地回答这个问题，还需要很多探索。

　　语言究竟从哪里来呢？这个问题似乎是一个永远没有答案的奥秘。按照乔姆斯基（Noam Chomsky）学派的观点，人类在认识世界的过程中，会遇到两种情形：一种情形是有些事情现在搞不清楚，但是将来可以搞清楚；另一种情形是有些事情受人类认识能力的限制，可能永远搞不清楚。前一种现象可以称为"问题"（problem），后一种现象可以称为"奥秘"（mystery）。语言的起源问题似乎应该属于后者，是一个无法找到答案的奥秘。所以，19世纪中叶，巴黎语言学会一度在会章里明确提出不接受关于语言起源的任何报告。尽管如此，人类还是试图追寻有关这一问题的可能答案，这在中外都有比较有名的范例。

例如，德国的赫尔德（J. G. Herder）在他的著作《论语言的起源》中提出，"当人还是动物的时候，就已经有了语言"。这是赫尔德关于语言起源的经典主张，它至少包括如下三个观点：一是人与动物有某种共同的东西，二是动物也可以有语言，三是人类语言是从动物语言演化而来的。近年来的语言演化理论也很关心语言起源问题，有一些人用数学建模等手段来研究语言的涌现。美籍华人学者王士元（2001）就语言起源问题提出如下观点：语言的起源跟人类的起源密不可分；语言的起源是多源的，可用数学上的概率模型来证明多源说比单源说的可能性更大；语言起源于基因突变的说法站不住脚。语言作为人类区别于自然界其他动物的一个重要特征，其产生不能不说是一件"石破天惊"的大事。所以，对语言起源之谜的追问是很有意义的。

如今，人们试图重新找到失去的巴别塔，让人类再度回到"普天一语"的状态。当然，这也许只是个无法实现的乌托邦。不过，人类还是一直憧憬着这样的乌托邦，比如，属于计算语言学分支学科的机器翻译（Machine Translation）实际上就是希望能在不同语言之间实现自由转换，以便为操不同语言的人提供更便捷的沟通手段。

同时，大概正是这种"巴别塔"传说的昭示，人们对人类语言的共性（universality）问题发生了兴趣。比如，美国的乔姆斯基与格林伯格（J. H. Greenberg）分别从不同的角度研究人类语言的共性；我国清代的马建忠在他的《马氏文通》中也关注了语言的共性问题，他借鉴西洋文法来研究汉语，这本身就说明他坚持汉语与西方语言是有共通之处的。当代的语言学研究既关注语言的多样性，也关注语言的共性。在语言表面的纷繁复杂现象中隐藏着深刻的共性，这种共性不仅体现在共时的语言系统中，也体现在语言的演变中。

除了语言起源这样的"奥秘"之外，语言中值得探索的有趣"问题"也有很多，比如语言习得问题。儿童在习得语言的过程中，虽然接触到的语言材料（也就是输入大脑中的语料）很少，可是能在相对而言很短的时间内掌握语言。像汉语中的"把"字句、"被"字句、话题句等对于留学生而言比较难的语言现象，说汉语的儿童能很快在不知不觉间学会。语言习得问题实际上就是一个柏拉图问题。柏拉图问题的基本思想是：人类在极为有限的刺激环境下，如何获得那么多知识。柏拉图问题按照乔姆斯基的说法，跟罗素所说的人与世界接触之短暂有限与人类理论上所知无限的问题本质上是一致的，所以，柏拉图问题也称为罗素问题。对于柏拉图问题或者罗素问题的回答是乔姆斯基语言学理论的至高追求。乔氏给出的答案便是人脑中先天有一部语法，这就是通常所说的普遍语法（universal grammar，UG），简单来讲，普遍语法就是人脑中语法的初始状态，这对于说任何语言的儿童来讲都是一样的。儿童后天学习语言的过程其实是习得参数（parameter）的过程。"参数"是数学上的一个概念，也叫参变量，是一个变量。借用到语言学上就是不同语言在某些特征项目方面的差异。比如，人类语言中动词（V）和宾语（O）是普遍存在的现象，但是两者之间的线性位置则是一个参数。有的语言是动词在宾语之前，是所谓"VO型"语言，如现代汉语；有的语言是动词在宾语之后，是所谓"OV型"语言，如日语。不同的参数取值造成了语言的差异。不难看出，语言习得问题同语言的共性与个性也是密切联系在一起的。

此外，语言中值得探究的问题还包括语言的组成成分及其内部结构规则、语言为什么会变化又是如何变化的、语言与社会的关系等。可以说，对人类而言，语言至今仍是一座神秘的"巴别塔"。揭示语言的奥秘，也就是揭示人自身的奥秘，是非常有价值的。语言学就是致力于揭示语言奥秘的一门科学。

语言从本质上看，是一个复杂的符号系统，对于这个系统的方方面面的详细介绍，本书将在后面的章节中逐一展开。

第一节　语言是什么：性质及其功能

我们经常听到"人有人言，兽有兽语""食不言，寝不语""言必信，行必果""言者无罪"，等等。古诗里也有"不敢高声语，恐惊天上人"。从这里可以看出，"语"与"言"各有所用，实际上反映的是作为交际工具的"语言"的不同含义：一是指人类语言是一个符号系统，如"人有人言，兽有兽语"；一是指日常交际中个人的言语行为，如"言必信，行必果""言者无罪"等。这里所讲的"语言"是指作为符号系统的语言。

平常人头脑中"语言"一词只有模糊的、日常语言使用上的意义，只是将语言看作一种交际工具，没有科学研究的意义。瑞士语言学家索绪尔（F. de Saussure）提出，语言是一个符号系统，符号涵括能指（形式）和所指（意义）两个方面，这是结构主义对语言性质的一种认识。结构主义语言学所讨论的语言是作为交际的自然语言，有关语言符号系统的介绍，详见第二章。

值得注意的是，在以乔姆斯基为代表的形式语言学者看来，真正具有客观实体意义而值得语言学者去研究的，是大脑里的语言系统（所谓I-语言），而不是处于大脑以外的一些行为现象。我们需要区分"外部语言"（E-语言）与"内部语言"（I-语言），区分语言能力（ability）与语言运用（performance）。人类语言是自然之物，是遗传变异的产物。以研究人类语言的自然属性和生物遗传属性为目标的语言研究是自然科学。人类语言除了传统所认同的区别于动物交际的抽象转移性（displacement），也就是可以用语言来谈论不在眼前的事情，还具有离散性（discreteness）和递归性（recursiveness）。其中，递归性是人类语言的本质属性。离散性将在第二章介绍，递归性请参阅第五章。乔姆斯基等人还指出，语言是有限规则的无限利用，是句子的无限集合，语言最为重要的属性除了递归性，还有运算上的合并（merge），这一点将在第五章详细介绍。

一般认为，语言的两大主要功能是它的社会功能和思维功能。语言的社会功能主要是指其作为人类交际工具的功能。我们只要设想一下两个人在无语言状态下的情形，马上就会看到语言社会交际功能的重要性。不妨就像布龙菲尔德（Leonard Bloomfield）在其《语言论》中所做的那样拟想一下：吉尔和杰克两人在苹果园散步，吉尔又饿又渴，想让杰克翻过篱笆摘苹果给他吃。假如吉尔不用说话来达到这个目的，怎么办？杰克只有靠观察推测，才能明白吉尔的心思。比如看到吉尔流口水，眼睛不断向果园望去，又不时看看身边的杰克，杰克就可能心领神会，才会去做为吉尔摘苹果的事情。假如杰克没能领会吉尔的心思，就不会去为吉尔摘苹果。在这种情况下，没有语言恐怕就很难进行成功的交际了。

语言的另外一大功能是它的思维功能。在乔姆斯基等人看来，人类语言的第一位功能用于思维，而不是交际。作为交际工具的语言是"不完美的"，而作为思维工具的人类语言是"完美的"。有关语言的思维功能，一个有名的观点是"萨丕尔-沃尔夫"假说（Sapir-Whorf Hypothesis）。简单来讲，就是语言影响或决定思维。这方面的内容详见本章第三节介绍，这里主要谈谈思维与语言的民族性之间的关系。

传统的观点认为，语言是思维的外壳，思维是语言的内容。语言具有民族性，思维具有超民族性。需要注意的是，"思维具有超民族性"的真正含义应该是指，思维能力（ability to think）是全人类都有的，只要是正常的人，就具备一定的思维能力。但是，不同民族的思维方式（how to think）却是有差异的，也就是在如何进行思维方面，不同民族是存在一定的差异的。人类都具备思维能力，源于人脑的生理构造大致相同。可是，思维方式各民族有别，即"看世界的视角"不同。

思维方式不同，只能从语言上加以分析。语言的民族性其实就是思维方式的民族性。这方面可用一个经典的例子来说明。例如，汉语的颜色词与英语的颜色词不完全对等。汉语中有"赤橙黄绿青蓝紫"七种颜色，而英语里则只有"purple-blue-green-yellow-orange-red"六种颜色。这种语言上的差别跟汉英两种民族在认识颜色方面的思维方式的差异有关。语言学界曾有人提出，汉语是一种宽式语言，结果铸就的是一种宽式思维（轨迹）；西方语言（如英语）是一种严式语言，结果铸就的是严式思维（轨迹）。这跟说汉语是一种"人治的语言"和西方语言是一种"法治的语言"，本质上是一致的。撇开思维与语言谁决定谁的问题不论，可以看出，语言与思维方式紧密相关。在一定程度上，语言影响思维方式，而思维方式需要借助语言得以体现。

语言的社会功能是外在的，思维功能则是内在的。语言所具有的功能同它的内部运转机制不可分离，也就是跟语言是如何工作的紧密相关。下面就来看看语言的运转机制以及生理机制等问题。

第二节　语言机制问题

什么是机制（mechanism）呢？"机制"一词原本是指机器的构造与工作原理，也就是机器是由哪些部件构成的和机器是怎样工作的。比如，一部小汽车必须由一系列的零部件按照一定的程式组装，并按照一定的原理进行运作。就语言而言，同样需要一定数量的"零部件"（语言单位）和一定的"组装模式"（语言规则）来使语言正常运转，这就是语言的运转机制。在这一节中，我们首先介绍语言的运转机制，再介绍与语言生成及理解相关的生理、心理机制以及语言习得（acquisition）机制。

从构成要素上看，语言离不开一定数量的语音。这些语音就其在结构中的地位分为元音（又称母音）和辅音（又称子音），两者共同构成语音层。单独的元音或辅音本身一般是没有意义的（也有成音节的元音、辅音可以表达意义），必须结合起来，成为语素、词这样的单位才具有意义。词再进一步结合成为词组（又称短语）、句子，在层级上越来越高。语素、词、词组、句子这些单位都是有意义的。从数量上看，元音和辅音是有限的，单元音的数量更少，只有几个，辅音最多也就几十个。到语素和词这一级，数量渐增，但仍是有限的，到了词组和句子层面，数量就是开放的了。语言的各级单位及其层级关系、数量对比可以大致用下图表示：

句子（理论上无限）
⇑
（从句/小句）（某些语言中由显性标记引导的内嵌句，理论上无限）
⇑
词组（理论上无限）
⇑
词（有限）
⇑
语素（有限）
⇑
....................（有无意义的分界）
语音（有限）

图1-1　语言各级单位、层次关系及其数量对比

语言的运转机制包括静态和动态两个方面。静态上，无论是语音层，还是语法层，其中的各要素总是可以按照一定的标准归在一起，聚集成为一个集合或者一个类，这种关系是聚合关系（paradigmatic relation），相当于索绪尔所说的联想关系（associative relation），聚合关系有时也称为替换关系，因为可以在相同的组合位置上相互替换。动态上，语音层或语法层的要素还可以依照一定的规则组配在一起，这种关系是组合关系（compositional relation），相当于索绪尔所说的句段关系（syntagmatic relation）。这两种关系一纵一横，一静一动，使语言系统得以运转自如。关于这两种关系，本书后面有专门章节进行详细阐述。

语言还有其生理和心理机制。由于生理机制与心理机制紧密关联，所以，将两者放在一起介绍。语言的生理、心理机制与人脑的认知功能是分不开的，需要简要了解一下认知科学（cognitive science）。

20世纪60年代，认知科学诞生了。这种科学结合了心理学、计算机科学、语言学、哲学和神经生物学，试图解释人的智力活动究竟是怎么一回事。因为有了认知科学，人们对语言的认识发生了革命性的变化。按照认知心理学家的看法，语言是心理的官能（psychological faculty），是一个神经系统，也是一个计算模块（computational module），比较通俗的叫法就是"本能"（instinct）。"语言是一种本能"的观点达尔文早就已经提到，而关于"语言是一种本能"的理论系统阐述当归功于乔姆斯基。

乔姆斯基曾提出，不考虑个人之间的差异，人的头脑都具有某种固定的、全人类共同的心智状态。这是人类获得语法知识的基础，是人有别于鸟、猿等动物的特征。这种固有的心智就是前面提及的所谓的"普遍语法"。这个"普遍语法"让孩子从父母言谈中将（个别）语法提炼出来。下面是乔姆斯基曾经说过的一段话[1]：

> 过去几个世纪以来的人类文明，有一个很奇怪的现象，人们对身体和心智发展的研究，采取了完全不同的研究取向。好比说，没有人会对这样的说法重视：人类这个有机体是透过经验的学习才有手臂而不是有翅膀，或者说某一器官的基本结构来自一个意外经验的结果。大家都理所当然的认为，有机体的身体结构是由基因决定的，虽然在某些向度上会有些差异，例如身材的大小、发展的快慢等，是受外在的影响的……
> 而我们却从不同的角度来看待人格发展、行为形态，以及认知的结构。我们一般都认为，在这些范畴里，社会环境是最主要的影响因素。心智结构的长期性发展被认为是武断的、意外的，一般是把所发展的看成是历史的产物，而不认为有"人的本性"（human nature）存在……

1［美］史蒂芬·平克. 语言本能. 洪兰，译. 台北：商周出版社，1998：29–30.

但是假如我们好好地去研究认知系统，我们会发现它不比有机体的发展更逊色。那么，为什么我们不像去研究身体复杂的器官那样去研究认知结构的习得（好比说语言）呢？

乍看之下，这个提议似乎很荒谬，因为世界上有这么多种语言，但是仔细考虑一下，这些怀疑便站不住脚了。虽然我们对语言普遍性了解还不够深入，但我们已经知道语言的种类是非常有限的……每个人习得的语言都是个丰富而复杂的结构，不能只从儿童的片段证据就去限定它。每一个社区中的人，基本上都发展出同样的语言；只有假设社区的每一个人都使用非常有限的原则来规范他们的文法，才能够解释这个事实。

人所具备的这种固有的语法属性由一系列原则组成，每一条原则都有参数，允许在一定范围内变化。所谓获得语法知识及一切有关内容，就是在经验的基础上选定参数——取这一值或那一值。从这里可以看出，人类之所以有别于其他物种，根本原因在于人脑的生理结构以及由此而来的心智（mind）结构，这决定了人脑与其他动物的大脑有着不同的生理、心理机制，相应地决定了人类对于语言具有特定的习得机制。

乔姆斯基（Chomsky, 2005）对人类语言习得机制的三要素进行了归纳，认为有三个方面比较重要：一是人类所共有的、由遗传所得的语言机能，让人类能够以此为基础，从周围的环境中获取语言材料，并根据这种语言经验去设定自己语言规则的值；二是从外界取得的语言经验，可以依此构建各种不同的语言，由于各种语言的构建都基于遗传所得的语言机能，所以可能出现的差异数量和范围都十分有限；三是人类认知功能的普遍原则，即并非语言机能独有的那些原则。

从上面关于语言习得机制的三点归纳，可以做如下推论：人的差异性和共通性都是天生的，所谓"天性使然"。要研究人的心智，研究语言本能是一个最好的方法。

国外有研究表明，学习语法的能力受基因的控制。英国牛津大学威康信托人类遗传中心的安东尼·摩纳哥和西蒙·费希尔研究小组发现了人类第一个"语言基因"，其成果发表在2001年10月4日的《自然》杂志上，这个与语言能力有关的基因被称为叉头框P2（FOXP2）基因。假如语言的确是一种本能，那么，它们一定处在大脑的某一个部位，那些大脑的神经网络一定受到构建它们的基因的安排，基因会使大脑预备好它要扮演的角色。不过，研究大脑的困难很大，有些问题到现在还没有研究清楚，因此，遗传学和神经生物学方面至今还无法为基因控制语法这样的观点提供有效的证据，所以，语言的生物机制一直无法被彻底了解。尽管如此，科学研究表明，语言的机制在左脑。科学实验还发现，那些因脑伤而发生的病变，比如失语症，基本上都跟左脑西尔维亚裂沟的两旁区域有关，这个区域可以说是语言的器官（language organ）所在。

应该说，对于语言生理、心理机制的研究是当今应用语言学界一个热门的话题。

第三节　语言的内外之分及"萨丕尔-沃尔夫"假说

本章第一节谈论语言与思维的关系时已经提及，语言与思维方式之间有着紧密的关系。这一节来看看将语言的功能推到极致的一种假说，所谓"萨丕尔-沃尔夫"假说，通常也称为语言决定论。

"萨丕尔-沃尔夫"假说是美国语言学家B. L. 沃尔夫在继承其老师萨丕尔思想的基础上提出来的，其基本内容可简单概括如下：

> 人们对世界的看法，很大程度上受其所使用语言的制约。每一种语言都隐藏着一种对世界的看法。与其说语言帮助表达思想，不如说语言规定着我们的思想，帮助形成某种思想。
>
> 语言中只有一部分语法范畴有明显标记（overtly marked），其他范畴都是隐含的（covert）。这些隐含的范畴在很大意义上规定着我们对世界的看法。

应该指出，"萨丕尔-沃尔夫"假说尽管受到批判，但其关于语言与思维关系的认识若剔除极端的成分仍有一定的合理性。更值得注意的是，这个假说所说的语言是外部的自然语言，而批判者所谈的却是思想的语言（mentalese），大致就是内部语言（Internal language）。

语言学上经常提到I-语言，也就是内部语言；以及E-语言，也就是外部语言（External language）。搞清楚内部语言和外部语言，对正确认识"萨丕尔-沃尔夫"假说是很关键的。

I-语言是乔姆斯基语言学派的一个核心概念，除了将"I"理解为"内部的"之外，还有"个人的"（individual）和"内涵的"（intensional）两方面的意思。概括来讲，内部语言就是内在于（internal to）说话人与谈话人心智和大脑（mind-brain）之中的语言知识，而不涉及心智与外部世界之间的关系。内部语言是关涉特定说/听话人心理表征（mental representation）以及心理表征之间关系的，因而内在于心智/大脑的语言系统就能对提交给它的（外部）语言现象提供解释。相较而言，外部的E-语言是指"行为、话语或者与意义匹配的语言形式（词、句子）的集合或语言形式与事件的系统"。简单来讲，外部语言是一种外在于心智/大脑的言语行为。在乔姆斯基语言学派看来，外部语言是传统语法、结构主义语言学以及行为主义心理学研究的对象，但是不宜作为语言研究的对象。因为相对于内部语言而言，外部语言不是真实事件的客体，而是人为的存在，只有通过内部语言才能与物质联系起来，是派生的。

很显然，"萨丕尔-沃尔夫"假说所谈论的是外部语言，也就是日常所说的自然语言。这一假说的源头在德国语言学家洪堡特，洪堡特在《论人类语言结构的差异及其对人类精神发展的影响》一书中提出："一个民族怎样思维，就怎样说话，反之亦然，怎样说话，就怎样思维""每一种语言里都包含着一种独特的世界观"。萨丕尔在基于对美洲印第安语调查的研究中认为，语言是"社会现实"（social reality）的向导，人不是孤零零地生活在客观世界中，也不是孤零零地生活在我们通常所理解的那个社会活动的世界中，人在极大程度上是受着那种已经成为他们社会表达媒介的特定语言的支配。萨丕尔甚至指出，认为人本质上可以不借助语言适应现实，语言只不过是解决有关交际或思维（reflection）的特殊问题的偶然手段，这是一个大大的错觉；事实上，"真实世界"在很大程度上，是不知不觉地建立在人群集体的语言习惯上的。

沃尔夫关于语言决定论的极端表述如下[1]：

> 我们把自然依照我们的母语来切割。从世界万象中所分离出来的类别和形式，并不是因为我们看到它们；相反地，这个世界像个万花筒，有各式各样的影像，要靠我们的心智将它组合起来，而这个组合的能力，其实就是我们心中的语言系统。
> 我们把自然切割组成概念，因为我们大家都这样组织它，而这个一致性是我们的语言社区的每一个人所公认的，是跟我们的语言形态结合在一起的。这个一致性当然是内隐的、没有说出来的，但是它的条件却是每个人都要遵守的，只有透过这个相互同意的协定，人们才能沟通。

沃尔夫是在批判自然逻辑（natural logic）的荒谬的基础上提出这一假说的。他认为，自然逻辑是荒谬的，不认为不同语言的使用者遵循同一种"自然逻辑"。人类对世界的看法是相对的，有赖于所使用的语言。在沃尔夫看来，自然逻辑有两个谬误：第一，它没有认识到一种语言现象对于该语言的说话者来说是一种背景（background）。当自然逻辑学家在谈论推理、逻辑以及正确思维的规则时，他可能只与纯粹的语法事实相一致。这种语法事实在某种程度上具有自己语言或者语族（family of language）的背景特性，但绝不

1［美］史蒂芬·平克. 语言本能. 洪兰，译. 台北：商周出版社，1998：74.

是所有语言的普遍特性。第二，自然逻辑混淆了运用语言对问题达成的约定（agreement）与达成约定所运用的语言过程的知识（knowledge of the linguistic process）。

沃尔夫对于其假说进行了论证，比较经典的例子就是说英语的民族和说霍皮语（Hopi）的民族对于时间的反应不一样。究其原因，英语是"时态"（temporal）语言，而霍皮语是"超/非时间"（timeless）语言。在英语民族看来是时间上的差异，在霍皮语民族那里成了效力（validity）的差异。霍皮语时间的特殊属性在于，它随着每个观察者而变化，不允许同时性（simultaneity），存在零度空间（zero dimension），即不可能有大于"一"的数目度量。比方说，霍皮语不说类似"I stayed for five days"（我待了五天）那样的句子，要说成"I left on the fifth day"（我在第五天离开），与day对应的指称时间的词，不能有复数。

"萨丕尔-沃尔夫"假说在观点表述上有强弱的区分，强势的观点认为语言模造了思维，弱势的观点则认为语言在一定程度上影响思维。不管这种假说在语言与思维关系的表述上是强还是弱，有一点可以肯定：语言的不同对思维是有影响的，或者说，一种语言是一扇看世界的窗口。

对这一假说持肯定态度的不乏其人。赵元任1955年在《汉语语法与逻辑杂谈》里讲，美国一位前驻华大使纳尔森·约翰逊（Nelson T. Johnson）给他写过一封信，提出如下问题：汉语中不存在像英语里it rains（德语es regent，法语il pleut）中作体词主语的抽象的it，这一点不可等闲视之。赞同这位美国大使观点的人认为，由于科学的思维是以对中性的物质做客观的思考为前提的，语法上缺少了it，思维上也就缺少了考查客观的中性物质的能力。这也许是中国人没能在西方科学传入以前自己发展出一套自然科学体系的真正原因，这可以看作一种对李约瑟难题的尝试回答。科技史学家李约瑟曾经提出疑问：为什么中国古代有四大发明，而近代以来的自然科学技术却在西方产生？语言学界甚至还有一种认识：假如亚里士多德当初说的是汉语而不是希腊语，那么，他可能采取另外一种完全不同的逻辑，或者至少是一种完全不同的范畴系统。

当然，也有人对"萨丕尔-沃尔夫"假说持怀疑和批判的态度。不过，批判者多着眼于思考的逻辑与（自然）语言的差异来认识这一假说。反对者认为，人不是以英语、汉语这样的自然语言来思考的，而是以思想的语言（language of thought, mentalese）来思考的，而思想的语言应该是一样的，所谓普遍性的思想语言（universal mentalese）。

可以看出，批评者所说的"思想的语言"比较接近内部语言，而"萨丕尔-沃尔夫"假说是针对外部语言，也就是自然语言而言的。自然语言的不同究竟对人的思维有多大影响，目前似乎不再引起人们的多少关注。随着认知科学的兴起和发展，人们越来越注意从语言出发来探测人脑的"黑箱"之谜。

第四节　语言的多样性与语言共性

人类语言是多种多样的。据不完全统计，现存使用的语言大约有5000种（也有说6000种）之多。远的不说，即以中国大陆而论，除了汉语的几大方言之外，还存在为数众多的少数民族语言。据统计，中国的语言正在使用的就有80多种，已经消亡的古代语言更多。中国有55个少数民族，回族和满族一般使用汉语，其他少数民族都有自己的民族语言，有的民族还有两种以上的语言。与汉语一样，少数民族语言内部也有方言的差异，有的差异还相当大，比如彝语。

为什么世界上有这么多种语言呢？这个问题与语言从哪里来的巴别塔之谜一样，很难给出一个共识性的答案。达尔文在这个问题上曾经有一段富有启示的见解[1]：

> 不同语言和不同种族的形态，以及它们逐渐演化的证据，是非常地相似……我发现语言中明显的同源性（homologies）是源自同一演化群体，同功性（analogies）是因为它们有相同的形式处理过程（process of formation）……语言就像有机体一样，可以分成许多类，它们可以按照自然的分类，如依照它们一脉相承的语系，或是按人为的方式以特性来分。当强势的语言和它的方言分布得很广时，将造成其他语言的逐渐消失。语言就像物种一样，当它消失以后就不可能复生了。

从上面这段话可以看出，语言的多样化大概与生物体的分化过程相似，这跟历史语言学界的"谱系树"（family tree）假说的基本精神完全一致，达尔文甚至说他从语言中得到关于生物演化的一些灵感。

对于语言的多样性问题，美国语言学家史蒂芬·平克将其与生物的多样性进行比较，认为两者是相同的，都是三种处理过程经过长久的一段时间后所留下的结果，这三种过程分别是变异（variation）、遗传（inheritance）和隔离（isolation）。变异在生物学上称为"突变"（mutation），在语言学上叫作"革新"（innovation）。生物学上的遗传就是基因继承，对语言学来讲，遗传就意味着"语言习得"（acquisition of language）。隔离对物种而言就是地理因素、繁殖季节以及繁殖的生理结构，对语言来说就是迁移或社会阶层的隔离。要了解语言多样化的形成，需要详细了解这三种处理过程。读者可进一步阅读史蒂芬·平克《语言本能》第八章。

世界上如此繁多的语言呈现在我们面前，而普通人一般不会去问：这些语言真像它们

1［美］史蒂芬·平克. 语言本能. 洪兰，译. 台北：商周出版社，1996：286.

看上去那样差别很大吗？它们之间有共同之处吗？这样的思考只有语言研究者才会有。从语言学的角度讲，现存的各种自然语言之间除了自身的个性（particularity），彼此之间还有一些共享的特性，这就是通常所说的共性（universality）。

对人类语言共性的研究与语言的分类（classification）问题是连在一起的。语言分类可以有不同的标准，语言学上一般提到三种标准：生物学上的基因（genetic）分类、结构上的类型（typological）分类以及地理上的区域（areal）分类。基因分类就是历史语言学上所说的谱系分类（family tree），是从语言的起源上给语言分类；地域分类主要是从语言间的地理分布上给语言分类，这两种分类是对语言的一种外部分类。真正着眼于语言结构自身的分类是类型学的分类，这是一种内部分类。这里只从结构类型上来谈谈语言的共性问题。

从语言结构自身上讲，那些在所有语言中都出现的特性或模式，可以称为"绝对共性"（absolute universal），比方说，所有的自然语言都有名词（noun）与动词（verb）的区分。那些只在大多数语言中出现的特性或模式是一种"共性倾向"（universal tendency），比方说，大多数语言的元音系统都包含五个基本音素，就是一种共性倾向。语言的共性在语音、形态、句法上都有体现。

语音上的共性这里仅以元音为例。世界语言的元音系统最常见的是包含五个语音：两个高元音（i、u），两个中元音（e、o），一个低元音（a）。其中两个前元音（i、e）和低元音（a）是不圆唇的，两个后元音（u、o）是圆唇的。这个语音上的共性为世界上大约一半的语言所共享。

人类语言根据形态上的特点可分为孤立语（isolating language）、融合/屈折语（fusional/inflectional language）、黏着语（agglutinating language）和多式综合语（复综语）（polysynthetic language）四种。孤立语以汉语为典型代表，屈折语以俄语为代表，黏着语以土耳其语为代表，多式综合语见于北美洲的因纽特语（Inuktitut）、克里语（Cree）和萨尔西语（Sarcee）等。关于这四类语言各自的特点以及相互间的差异，后面有关章节将有详细介绍。

从形态上着眼，语言的分类还有一种做法，就是将人类语言分为综合性的（synthetic）和分析性的（analytic）。一般来说，分析性/型语言的语素多是自由的，缺少构形语素和词缀，语序和虚词的语法地位很重要，疑问词是不移位或者在位的（in-situ），并且可有非疑问用法，等等。纯粹的分析性/型语言就是孤立语，以汉语为典型代表。相比之下，综合性/型语言有形态变化，不自由语素（构形与构词语素）附着在自由语素之上，疑问词移位到句首。综合性/型语言有程度上的差别，可以细分为融合/屈折语、黏着语和多式综合语。分析性还是综合性，往往是相对而言的，例如，跟汉语相比，英语综合性凸显；

但跟印欧语系其他语言，如德语、俄语相比，则分析性凸显。

从句法上给人类语言分类目前比较有名的是美国语言学家格林伯格，他在20世纪60年代写过一篇很有名的文章《某些主要跟语序有关的语法普遍现象》（*Some Universals of Grammar with Particular Reference to the Order of Meaningful Elements*），就所调查的语言现象（30种语言样品）提出了45条普遍现象，其中大部分现象都是蕴含性的，也就是有X就必有Y。格林伯格在这篇文章中针对主语（S）、动词（V）、宾语（O）的相对顺序提出第一条普遍现象：带名词性主语和宾语的陈述句中，优势语序几乎总是主语在宾语之前。这样，在S、V、O构成的六种逻辑上的语序中，SVO、SOV、VSO 是优势语序，其他三种很少出现或根本不出现。

实际上，上面关于语言的共性是从某一标准出发对语言的一种分类，某些特性或模型涉及的语言自然具有共性。严格来讲，这并非共性的真义所在。人类语言所具有的共性应该是所有现存语言的最大公约数。以这样的标准看，只有绝对共性才是人类语言的共性。

语言共性的问题一开始就是乔姆斯基语言学派所关心的核心问题。但是，乔姆斯基有关"共性"的观点与格林伯格基于归纳的共性论有很大不同。乔氏对共性的一种认识是所有人类语言都运用相同的成分，比如元辅音、名词、动词以及句子等。但是，语言之间存在差异，比如，所有语言都有名词、动词，但只有某些语言有形容词和冠词，或者量词、语气词等。基于共性论的语言理论要对这样的现象做出合理的解释。不妨以语言中的照应现象为例来说明何为共性。语言中有一种现象，前面有一个名词性成分，后面再提及这个名词性成分时，往往用代词或者反身代词，这样，前面的名词性成分与后面的代词或反身代词形成一种"先行语-照应语"结构关系，这可以看作是语言中的一种共性现象。比如，John loves Mary and Tom also loves her. "约翰喜欢玛丽，汤姆也喜欢她。"其中的"her"与"她"分别与"Mary"和"玛丽"构成照应关系。再比如，"John likes himself"和"张三喜欢（他）自己"中的"himself"与"（他）自己"也分别与前面的"John"和"张三"构成照应关系结构。"先行语-照应语"的结构是一个共性，不过，共性之下也有差别。在"John said that Tom loved himself"和"张三说李四喜欢自己"之中，尽管"himself""自己"一定与前面的名词形成照应关系，但是，在与前面哪个名词指称相同方面有所不同，也就是受到不同的限制。"himself"严格受到局域限制（local constraint），只能就近指称"Tom"，不能指称较远的"John"；而"自己"既可在局域内指称"李四"，也可以突破局域限制，表现出非局域性（non-locality），指称较远的"张三"。

乔姆斯基语言学派看重的是语言的共性。为什么人类语言会有共性？他们认为人脑的初始状态是一样的，先天就有一部"语法"，这也是对前面一开始提及的柏拉图问题的回答。语言间的差异是外在的、后天习得的。大致说来，共性犹如一些固有的原则（principle），而差异就是通过学习获得的参数（parameter）。"原则"是共有的、内在的，参数可以各有不同，是外在的。打一个比方，有些地方汽车的驾驶座在左边（世界上大多数地方如此），有些地方驾驶座在右边（英国及其曾经殖民过的地方是这样），这是表面的差异。不过，这个表面的差异与另外一个差异相连：驾驶座在左边的汽车靠右行驶，驾驶座在右边的靠左行驶。差异的背后是共同原则：副驾驶座上的人能安全地下车到便道上。

正是因为语言各有差别，又共享一些特性，所以，在对待语言"个性"和语言"共性"的关系上应该采取不偏不倚的态度。在这一点上，王力关于汉语研究者需要具备两种素质的论述从另一个角度讲实际上也是强调正确处理语言个性与语言共性的关系（参阅《中国现代语法·自序》）：

> 中国语法学者须有两种修养：第一是中国语史学（Chinese philology）；第二是普通语言学（general linguistics），缺一不可。若只精于中国语史学（如所谓"小学"），而不精于普通语言学，就只知道从古书中大事搜罗，把若干单词按照英语的词类区分，成为一部"新经传释词"；若只精于普通语言学，而不精于中国语史学，就只知道运用若干术语，把中国的语法事实硬凑上去，成为别开生面的"削足适履"。

第五节 语言学的研究对象与研究任务

我们在前面详尽地介绍了语言是什么，那么，语言学是什么就很清楚了。简单来讲，语言学就是研究语言的科学。详细一点讲，语言学是对语言的科学研究，它以人类一切自然语言（natural languages）为研究对象，它的任务是描写和解释语言的内部结构规律，揭示语言的本质以及语言的存在和发展演变规律，并能够为人类其他方面所应用，为人类自身服务。根据索绪尔在《普通语言学教程》中的看法，语言学的任务可以总结为如下几方面：

（a）对一切能够观察到的语言进行描写并整理出它们的历史，即整理各语系的历史，尽可能重建（reconstruct）每个语系的母语；

（b）寻求在一切语言中永恒地普遍地起作用的力量，整理出能够概括一切历史特殊现象的一般规律；

（c）确定自己的界限与定义。

上述第三条其实是任何学科都需要做的，前两条概括起来就是：共时描写与历时溯源。就共时描写而言，一方面是对语言事实的搜罗呈现，另一方面是对事实的解释。就历时溯源来讲，一方面是要厘清语言在各个不同时期的演化路径，揭示其演化史；另一方面是要在共时语料观察与历时材料整理的基础上，尽量构拟语言的原始母语面貌，更为重要的是揭示语言演变的规律。下面透过语言事实来看看语言学的任务所在。

语言现象一

	ban	dan	gan
阴平	般	单	干
阳平	？	？	？
	pan	tan	kan
阴平	攀	贪	刊
阳平	盘	谈	？

（上述标音为汉语拼音）

针对上面的语言事实，语言学要对所观察到的现象进行直接描写，描写的结果是：汉语拼音的不送气声母b、d、g与前鼻音韵母an相拼时，在阴平调有相应的汉字，而阳平调无字。相应的送气声母p 、t、k在阴平调的条件下都有汉字，在阳平调的条件下有的有字，有的无字。对于这样的语言事实，如何解释？这就涉及语言的演变，也就是需要引入历时溯源。读者可以在本书后面关于语音演变规律的相关介绍中找到解决问题的切入口，真正要解决这个问题需要专门的音韵学知识。

语言现象二（标星号的句子不好，下同）

（1）你喜欢语言学吗?

（2）你喜欢不喜欢语言学?

（3）你可喜欢语言学?

（4）*你喜欢不喜欢语言学吗?

（5）*你可喜欢语言学吗?

（6）*你可喜欢不喜欢语言学?

上面的现象与前面所谈到的语音现象有所不同。撇开专业术语不论，从纯粹描写的角度着眼，读者可以看到这些都是疑问句，但是，有的成立，有的不成立，不成立的句子前面标了星号。更为细致一点的描写是：这些疑问句采用了三种基本手段，"吗"标记型、正反重叠标记型以及"可"标记型，分别如（1）-（3）所示。但是，这三种手段各自独立，不能两两合用，如（4）-（6）所示。基于这些共时观察，语言学需要进一步从中寻找规律，给出相应解释。

在观察语言事实的基础上进行描写，进而做出解释，这是普通语言学所要承担的任务，是一种理论性的探讨。当然，同样是理论探讨，着眼点可能有所不同。有的是从语言符号自身的组配关系上寻求解释，是一种形式主义的方法，以乔姆斯基学派为代表；有的是从语言所具有的功能出发，是一种功能解释，以韩礼德（M. A. K. Halliday）为代表。当然，功能学派内部还有其他各种细目，比如认知功能语言学。大致来讲，当今语言学界呈现出以形式主义语言学与功能主义语言学主流各领风骚的局面。需要指出的是，语言学家对语言事实的解释有不同的认识。生成语言学派认为，语言学家的任务就是要构建关于内部语言的语法，而在一定语料的基础上决定语法的形式以及选择形式合适的语法所依据的原则，称为"普遍语法"。对这种普遍语法的研究，其实就是对人类心智性质的研究。

任何一门学科都离不开应用，抽象的理论最终也可以转化为应用。语言学发展到今天，已经出现了各种应用语言学。不少大学的人文学科里有一门二级学科叫作"语言学及应用语言学"，这就是兼顾了理论和应用。

从应用上看，语言学可以与很多学科结合，形成各种各样的交叉学科，如社会语言学、文化语言学、心理语言学、计算语言学，等等。对于各种交叉语言学的介绍，不是本书要做的工作。读者只需要记住，这些"X语言学"仍属语言学的范畴，不过不是从语言本身出发而是从语言之外寻找对语言事实的解释。当然，这些"X语言学"也解决了一些实际问题。

这里不妨举一个经典的社会语言学方面的例子。20世纪80年代，美国语言学家魏茵莱希（U. Weinreich）和拉波夫（W. Labov）在他们那篇有名的文章《语言演变的经验基础》（*Empirical Foundations for a Theory of Language Change*，王洪君节译，载于《国外语言学》，1988年第4期）提出了一个新的语言理论模型，认为语言不是像索绪尔以来的结构主义语言学家一直到乔姆斯基学派所说的那样是一个同质的（homogeneous）系统，而是一个有序异质的（heterogeneous）结构。每个言语社团所说的语言都可以分为若干个子系统，每个子系统都相当于索绪尔所说的语言系统。使用双方言的人的头脑中同时存在着两个子系统，子系统之间是相互竞争的关系，说话人可以根据不同的语境、不同的交际对象而选择某一个子系统来进行交际。由于两个子系统在同一个人的言语能力中共存，一个子系统的成分会进入另一个子系统而成为变异成分。如果某一变异成分在人群中扩散、传播，就意味着演变的开始。如果使用这种变异成分的人群在社会中具有特殊地位，这种变异成分就可能成为其他社会人群的模仿对象，从而由一个人群扩散到另一个人群，完成演变的全过程。针对这种变异现象，魏茵莱希和拉波夫提出了一个变异规则的结构公式：$A \rightarrow g[B]/X[/z]Y$，$g[B]=f(C, D, E\cdots\cdots)$。这个公式的意思是：A在X[/z]Y的条件下变成g[B]，而g[B]的值由C、D、E来决定，C、D、E一般体现为年龄、风格、社会阶层等因素。比如，北京话里的汉语拼音声母j、q、x（相当于公式里的A）变成z、c、s（相当于公式里的g[B]），条件是在韵母i-和以i-为韵头的韵母之前（相当于公式里的X[/z]Y），决定g[B]值的因素是年轻的女性，就是相当于C、D、E的年龄、性别等。这篇文章提出了新的反映语言实际存在状况的模型，这一模型着眼于正在进行中的音变，运用变异规则对语言中的变异进行具体的分析。除了在共时和历时之间架起了一座桥梁，使我们可以从语言的共时差异中去考察语言的演变之外，更重要的是，它把年龄、风格、社会阶层等社会因素纳入语言结构中来，开阔了语言研究的视野，使语言研究迈入一个新的领域，引领了社会语言学的研究。

此外，心理语言学、计算语言学、文化语言学等都是应用语言学的范畴，读者可以通过专门性的著作获得详细的了解。这里的介绍旨在让读者明白，这些应用语言学在研究语言现象时是从语言与语言之外的其他现象之间的关系来寻找解释的。以心理语言学为例，顾名思义，心理语言学主要是研究语言的加工机制，具体来讲，就是研究词、句子和话语的意义在大脑中是如何表征和计算的。举一个句子语义加工方面的例子，"The horse raced past the barn fell"（跑过那个谷仓的马摔倒了）是语言学上经典的"花园幽径句"（garden path sentence）。这个句子语法上完全没有问题，但理解上容易出错。第五章的句法部分将对句子的句法结构进行详细介绍，这里只是从心理加工上看看哪里容易出问题。我们可以将心理对句子的加工过程比作一部句法分析器（syntactic parser）的句法分析过程。当这部句法分析器在进行语义加工时，很容易形成"the horse"、"raced past the barn"以及"the horse raced past the barn"这样几个心理模块，结果句子的主要动词"fell"无法进入加工过程。之所以出现这样的错误，原因在于"raced past the barn"不能作为独立的动词短语模块，而必须附接在模块"the horse"之上，而动词"fell"才是句子中独立的动词模块，是句子的谓语。汉语中也有类似的花园幽径句，比如"批评鲁迅的小说太晦涩"，读者可以自行进行心理加工测试。

我们从上面的介绍可以看到，无论是普通语言学，还是应用语言学，都以语言事实为研究对象，差别在于是基于理论的，还是基于应用的。普通语言学和应用语言学的内部都还需要做进一步的细致分类。

普通语言学离不开具体语言学，即以特定语言为研究对象的语言学，如汉语语言学。只有在对各种现存自然语言研究的基础上，才能提炼出一般的语言学理论。应用语言学也必须在普通语言学的指导下进行。在这样的认识下，"语言学引论"之类的课程应该是理论语言学的入门课程。我们可以用下面的简图来呈现"语言学引论"和"理论语言学"之间的关系：

一门学科达到成熟阶段，需要对其发展史做一个总结。在下一节里，我们将勾勒式地介绍一下语言学的发展历史。

第六节　语言学的发展历程：语言学史一瞥

任何一门学科只有达到成熟之后，其发展史的问题才会被关注。语言学作为一门独立的学科发展至今已有百余年历史。了解其自登上历史舞台以来的发展历程，对于语言研究自身是大有裨益的。

英国语言学家大卫·克里斯特尔（D. Crystal）曾经指出，唯有将语言研究当作终极的目标，语言学才能成为一门独立的学问。实际上，不仅语言学，任何一门学科之所以能独立存在，至少需要具备两个条件：一是明确的研究对象，二是具备属于自己学科特有的研究方法。以这两个条件为标准，19世纪以前语言学还没有作为一门独立的学科而存在。首先，19世纪以前，人们对于语言的关注只是基于读经解经的需要，并不是以研究语言本身为目的。西方社会的人们读《圣经》，阿拉伯民族读《古兰经》，印度人读《吠陀经》，中国人读"五经"。在读经书的过程中人们发现，对经籍的解读离不开对语言的了解，于是，对语言问题的关注引发了语言研究。

大致来讲，语言学的发展分为（规范）语法时期、语文学时期、现代语言学时期几个时期，其中语文学时期和现代语言学时期又可以根据研究侧重点不同进一步细分为几个小的时期。

第一个时期是语法时期，也称为规范语法（prescriptive grammar）时期。"规范"一词用的是"prescriptive"，其动词词基"prescribe"本意是"医生开药方"。显然，医生开的药方是不能违犯的，规定怎么做就必须怎么做。比方说，规范时期只能说"it is I"，而不能说"it is me"。语言使用者遵照规定使用就是了，不必问原因。规范语法时期所关注的是书面语言。

第二个时期是语文学（philology）时期，也称为传统语言学时期。索绪尔指出，语文学时期所使用的研究方法是考订式的，主要仍局限于书面语（经书典籍）。由索绪尔本人引发的语言学革命的贡献在于将关注点从书面语转移到口语。一般认为，语文学时期有三大传统，也可以看作语言研究的三个中心：印度、希腊-罗马、中国。

古印度宗教典籍，如《吠陀经》，是用梵文写的，这种语言在公元前5世纪就不再作为日常生活用语了，它只用于宗教典籍。由于传经需要准确，人们开始了对梵语的研究。公元前4世纪，古印度出现了一位伟大的语言大师巴尼尼，写了一部《巴尼尼语法》，全文由3996行诗文组成，对梵语的词法、语音进行了准确细致的描写分析。威廉·汤姆逊在《十九世纪末以前的语言学史》中说道："印度人在语言学上所达到的高度，那真是罕见的。欧洲的语言科学直到19世纪也尚未达到那样的高度，而且就是这样，也还有许多是从印度人那里学来的。"

古希腊-罗马学者对语言的研究是与逻辑哲学的研究结合起来的。他们不仅从哲学的角度认识语言实质，也从哲学的角度来解决语言问题，如希腊两次大辩论：一次是思维与词、事物与名称之间的关系，这些体现在柏拉图的《对话录》中；另一次是逻辑范畴与语言范畴是否一致的辩论，在亚里士多德的《诗学》中专门进行了讨论。

中国传统语言学就是所谓的"小学"传统，包括音韵学、文字学和训诂学。音韵学以隋代陆法言的《切韵》以及在此基础上形成的韵书系列为代表。文字学以东汉许慎的《说文解字》以及对《说文解字》的研究为代表，其中有名的是清代的"说文四大家"：段玉裁的《说文解字注》、桂馥的《说文解字义证》，王筠的《说文句读》《说文释例》、朱骏声的《说文通训定声》。其中，段玉裁的成就最大。以现代语言学的眼光看，训诂学相当于翻译学，但又跟语言学中的语义学尤其是词汇语义学接近。"训"就是通俗的解释词义，"诂"就是以今言释古语，"训诂"连用最早见于春秋时期鲁国毛亨的《毛诗故训传》，就是对《诗经》的注释。战国末期的《尔雅》被认为是最早的训诂学著作。作为一种小学传统，训诂学形成于唐代孔颖达的《五经正义》，国学大师黄侃则创立训诂学的现代观念。当然，语文学时期的传统语言学仍带有经学附庸的性质。

第三个时期是现代语言学时期。这一时期可大致分为历史比较语言学、结构主义语言学、转换生成语言学和各种语言学派的兴起几个不同阶段。

真正科学意义上的语言学是从19世纪历史比较语言学的诞生开始的。19世纪是历史比较语言学一统天下的时期，是现代语言学的第一个里程碑，也是希腊传统和印度传统结合的产物。历史比较语言学有时也称为"比较语文学""比较语法"，传统上一般还是称为"历史比较语言学"。这一时期的语言学是与英国东方学家威廉·琼斯（W. Jones）的名字连在一起的。

威廉·琼斯提出，梵语与希腊语、拉丁语在动词词根和语法形式方面有许多共同点，它们应有一个共同的来源，或者说有一个共同的原始母语。印欧语系假说就是在这个基础上提出来的。德国的葆朴（F. Bopp）（1816）所著的《梵语动词变位系统》，研究梵语与日耳曼语、希腊语、拉丁语等语言的关系。葆朴已经认识到，可以利用一种语言的形式去解释另一种语言形式，亲属语言关系的研究可以成为一门独立的学科。德国的格里姆（J. Grimm）也是杰出的比较语法学家，此外，还有丹麦的拉斯克（Rask）。

威廉·琼斯 （1746—1794）

历史比较语言学分为前后期或新老派。老派以施来赫尔（A. Schleicher）为代表，主张语言是一个有机体，像生物一样生长；新派（也称"新语法学派""青年语法学派"或"莱比锡语言学派"）反对将语言看作自我发展的有机体，以德国的布鲁格曼（K. Brugmann）、奥斯脱霍夫（H. Osthoff）、保罗（H. Paul）、雷斯琴（Leskien）为领袖，而发难者是美国人惠特尼（W. D. Whitney）。他在1875年著有《语言的生命与发展》，甚至提出语言是符号，是约定俗成的，但有系统，这在当时是先进的观念。

需要指出的是，新语法学派总是将语言现象分解为一个个孤立的、不相关的部分，分解为物理的、生理的、心理的东西，认为语言的变化也是彼此孤立的个别的变化，其根源在于个人的心理、生理深处。因此，新语法学派学者习惯于记录个别语言现象的历史，或者列举个别语音或形态的对应关系，建立一些局部的演变规律。这种方法被索绪尔讥为"原子主义"的研究方法。正是对这种"原子主义"研究方法的不满，才促使索绪尔从新语法学派中走出来，提出"语言是一个符号系统"，成为"现代语言学的鼻祖"。

结构主义语言学在现代语言学史上具有革命性的意义。这场革命是由瑞士语言学家索绪尔掀起的，现代语言学理论大都是在他的理论框架下进行的。在他的理论原则指导下诞生了三大语言学流派：哥本哈根语符学派、布拉格功能学派、美国描写主义语言学派。正是在这个意义上，索绪尔才被语言学界称为现代语言学的开山祖师。索绪尔的革命性主要在于他明确提出语言是一个同质的符号系统，从纷繁复杂的言语行为中提炼出"语言"。概括来讲，索绪尔的贡献主要体现在三个"转化"上：一是实现从新语法学派的"原子主义"研究方法向系统论研究的转化；二是由外而内的转化，从以前的关注语言外部因素进入到关注语言自身，从语言系统内部寻找答案；三是从历时（diachronic）研究向共时（synchronic）研究的转化。

索绪尔 （1857—1913）

其中，第三个转化是前两个转化的必然结果。他认为，语言研究需要在一种系统匀质的状态下进行，这种系统匀质的状态就是一种共时态。共时态犹如一棵树的横切面，历时态则如一棵树的纵切面。不妨认为，历时态（纵切面）是由共时态（横切面）叠加而成。对语言系统的研究必须在共时态下进行，系统性存在于共时态之中。共时态与历时态的关系有点儿像静止与运动一样，先研究静态，再研究动态。索绪尔的这些思想对后来的结构主义语言学派影响很大，结构主义中以美国描写主义语言学派最为有名。

美国描写主义语言学是20世纪20年代美国语言学者在调查美洲印第安语的基础上逐步形成的，以注重对语言结构形式的描写而著称，并因此而得名。在20世纪30年代至50年代，美国语言学界是描写主义占主导地位。在基本理念上，美国描写主义语言学主张行为主义，反对心灵主义。在实际操作方法上，运用分布分析和替换分析。这一学派的先驱是萨丕尔（E. Sapir）和博厄斯（F. Boas）。此二人既是语言学家，又是人类学家。他们在对美洲印第安语进行人类学调查的基础上发现这种语言不同于欧洲语言，需要采用不同的分析方法，从而奠定了美国描写主义语言学研究的传统。

这一学派前期的核心人物是布龙菲尔德。其基本的理念及操作规程集中体现在1933年出版的《语言论》中，甚至有人称这一学派为"布龙菲尔德学派"。后期的美国描写主义学派在做法上越来越极端，完全采用数学的方法来描写自然语言，以哈里斯（Z. S. Harris）为代表，称为"后布龙菲尔德时期"。关于美国描写主义语言学派的一些分析方法，本书将在专门章节（词法、句法部分）进行介绍。

布龙菲尔德 （1887—1949）

作为对结构主义语言学的反叛，美国麻省理工学院的乔姆斯基掀起了一场革命，有评价甚至认为，"乔姆斯基革命"的结果才真正诞生了现代语言学。这场革命以乔氏（1957）在荷兰摩顿出版公司（Mouton Company）出版的《句法结构》（*Syntactic Structures*）为发端。

乔姆斯基 （1928— ）

正如索绪尔是从新语法学派走出来，奠定结构主义语言学基础一样，乔姆斯基是从结构主义阵营里走出来，创立了转换生成语言学派。乔氏的老师是著名的后结构主义大师哈里斯。理论界有人认为，乔姆斯基革命的最大贡献是引入了一个星号，对于句子的好坏，母语者可以凭借自己的直觉进行判断，母语者认为不好的句子在前面加上星号。乔氏想要弄清楚：使说话人能够运用语言的那种直觉的、无意识的知识的本质究竟是什么。

从发展阶段上看，转换生成语言学先后经历了古典理论（Classic Theory）、标准理论（Standard Theory）、扩充的标准理论（Extended Standard Theory）、修正的扩充的标准理论（Revised Extended Standard Theory）、管辖与约束理论（Government and Binding Theory）以及最简方案（Minimalist Program）几个阶段。确切地说，转换生成语言学理论没有最后的阶段。所谓最简方案，只是一种基于"奥卡姆剃刀"精神的方案而已，包括实体上的最简和方法上的最简，前者要求语言的实体项目尽量地少，后者要求方法上达到最简。转换生成语言学理论一直处于动态更新过程之中，这是由它所采取的演绎式研究方法决定的。演绎式的研究方法在语言学上的运用大致是：在一定量的语言材料的基础上，经过观察，提出相应的假设，再将这个假设放到更广的语言事实之中加以验证，得到验证的作为规则、原则接受，没有得到验证的需要加以修正，形成一种"小范围观察→提出假设→大范围验证→修正假设的某些部分→再验证→……"循环往复的模式。正是这样的演绎式方法使得理论处于动态更新之中。

当今语言学界俨然已形成多派纷呈的景象。除了经久不衰的转换生成学派之外，还有从这个阵营里走出来，自成一派的认知语言学派，以雷可夫（G. Lakoff）、兰盖克（R. W. Langacker）等人为代表。认知是人脑的一种功能，从这个意义上讲，认知语言学也是一种功能语言学。功能语言学除了认知派之外，还有韩礼德的系统功能语言学派。学术界有人认为，语言学界形成乔姆斯基与韩礼德"二分天下"的格局，可见其影响。韩礼德是英国著名的语言学家，其语言学理论集中体现在《功能语法导论》（*An Introduction to Functional Grammar*）一书中。韩礼德创建的系统功能语言学，主要由系统和功能两个部分组成，两者融为一体。系统是由一系列语言功能选项组成的集合，功能则是系统中体现的语言意义和价值。

韩礼德 （1925— ）

该理论以语义为核心，建立在一个基本假设之上，即在最底层上，一切语言都离不开交际中的语言运用本质：语言用于形成大脑中对外部世界的基本概念（概念/经验功能），与他人进行互动（人际功能），使语言运用者的信息连结成一个有机的整体，以达到有效的交际目的（语篇功能）。概念功能、人际功能以及语篇功能是所谓的三大元功能或纯理功能（meta-function），三位一体。韩礼德的语言学理论是一个广博精深的系统，有兴趣的读者可以通过专门的学习去掌握。

☯ 思考题

1. 根据你的了解，你认为语言最初是如何产生的？语言的发生与儿童获得母语的过程有什么不同？

2. 语言对思维真的有影响吗？"萨丕尔-沃尔夫"假说的基本内容是什么？你认为这个假说是否合理？

3. 什么是机制？你认为语言的运转机制和生理/心理机制是什么？

4. 什么是内部语言与外部语言？

5. 你是如何看待语言的共性与个性的？这样的区分对于语言研究有什么意义？

6. 在语言学发展过程中，你认为哪些人物对推动学科研究发挥了巨大作用？

📖 拓展性阅读书目

▢ Noam Chomsky. 1968/1972. *Language and Mind*. (enlarged edition). Harcourt Brace Jovanowish, Inc.

▢ Noam Chomsky. 2005. Three Factors in Language Design. *Linguistic Inquiry*, Vol. 36,

No. 1, pp.1-22.

☐ David Crystal. 人类心智的桥. 连金发, 译. 台北: 三山出版社, 1974.

☐ Marc D. Hauser, Noam Chomsky, W. Tecumseh Fitch. 2002. The Faculty of Language: What Is It, Who Has It, and How Did It Evolve? *Science*, Vol. 298, No. 22.

☐ Neil Smith. 2004. *Chomsky: Ideas and Ideals*. Cambridge: Cambridge University Press.

☐ Steven Pinker. 1994. *The Language Instinct*. New York: William Morrow and Company, Inc. 中译本: [美] 史蒂芬·平克. 语言本能. 洪兰, 译. 台北: 商周出版社, 1998.

☐ 赫尔德. 论语言的起源. 姚小平, 译. 北京: 商务印书馆, 2014.

☐ 王士元, 柯律云. 语言的起源及建模仿真初探. 中国语文, 2001 (3): 195-200.

☐ 乔姆斯基语言哲学文选. 徐烈炯, 尹大贻, 程雨民, 译. 北京: 商务印书馆, 1992.

第二章
语言是符号系统

　　语言学的研究对象是语言，那么，语言是什么呢？这个看似简单的问题，直到20世纪初才由语言学家索绪尔做出了回答。他提出语言是一个符号系统，并区分了语言和言语、语言的共时态和历时态、语言的内部要素和外部要素。语言符号是听觉符号，具有任意性，音义之间的关联是没有理据、不可论证的。语言符号还具有线条性，体现为一个线性长度。语言符号系统中最重要的两种关系是横向的组合关系和纵向的聚合关系，不管是区别意义的音系层，还是表达意义的语法层，都由这两种关系来组织。当我们学习某种语言时，最重要的是不断扩大词汇量并掌握这种语言的语法，因为词库和语法是语言系统的两大组成部分。

第一节　符　号

一、语言与言语

语言不等于说话。"你平时说哪种语言，汉语还是英语？""这句话用英语怎么说？"，这些说法已经隐含了语言与说话的区别与联系：语言是说话所使用的工具，而说话是运用语言的活动。说话是一种言语活动，说话所使用的语言是一套符号系统，由语音、词汇、语义、语法等子系统构成；说出来的话，则是言语或言语作品。我们说某个人会说英语时，是说他掌握了英语这种工具，包括英语的发音、词汇以及组词造句的规则。这些规则对英语母语者来说是共同的。语言是用来说的，语言的存在以说话为前提，而说话是个人行为，语言如果没有人说就会消亡。我国某些少数民族的语言，都不再作为母语使用，已经成为死语言（dead language），如鲜卑语、契丹语。梵语、拉丁语、赫梯语、吐火罗语等也已经成为死语言。需要注意的是，某些死了的语言，如拉丁语，在宗教等一些场合还会使用。

语言也不同于言语。语言是从社会众多成员的言语里提炼出来的社会共同的语言单位及组词造句的规则，具有社会性、全民性和抽象性；言语是个人在特定情景中对语言的具体运用，具有个人性和具体性。每个人说话都有自己的特点，对于熟人，即使我们未见其人，只闻其声，也能分得出谁是谁。老人和孩子说的话不一样，男人和女人说的话也有差别，贩夫走卒与文人雅士说的话也各有特点，但是并不妨碍他们之间进行日常交流。那是因为他们有共同的语言，只是有的人善于运用语言，有人不太擅长。就好比有人作文写得好，妙笔生花，文采卓然，而有的人作文写得平淡无趣，跟白开水似的。但互相能看明白，原因就是他们所运用的语言是一样的。语言是进行言语活动的工具，言语是言语活动的产物。语言好比是简谱，说话好比是用简谱谱曲，言语就是所谱的曲子。每个人谱曲（相当于说话）的风格不同，谱出的曲子（相当于言语）质量参差不齐，但用的简谱（相当于语言）是一样的。作家的写作也是言语活动，写作可能用不同国家的语言，写作的成品属于言语作品。

语言和言语有区别也有联系。首先，二者互为前提。言语的理解需要语言，语言的存在需要言语。如果你没有学过意大利语，听到意大利语是完全无法解码的，因为你没有解码的工具，不知道意大利语的词汇，也不知道它的语法。而要描写、建立一种语言的系统，则需要调查、研究个人的言语。如果没有文字记录下来的古代文献这些言语作品，我们就无从知道某个语言在过去某个时期的词汇和语法规则。语言是一种抽象的系统，存在于全体言语社团成员的大脑里。语言是人人心中皆有，但人人都说不清楚的东西。语言学家的任务就是从纷繁复杂的言语中来寻找语言。其次，从历时的角度看，言语的事实总是在前，言语促使语言演变。像"草根""宅男""雷"（使震惊）这样的新词最初只在网络和口语中由部分人使用，尤其是年轻人，后来迅速普及，目前已经被收入《现代汉语词典》（第7版），成功"转正"。"N的V"（春天的到来）这样的表达最初是一种欧化形式，现在也已经合法化了，成了汉语中很常见的表达方式。20世纪五六十年代，美国英语car、door、four等词中的r有的人发卷舌音，有的人不发，同一个人有时候发卷舌音，有时候不发，这时候还属于言语现象，带有个人化色彩。而现在美式英语中的r都要发卷舌音，这一规则已经进入美式英语语言系统。

总之，语言是从大量言语事实中抽象出来的，这样抽象出来的语言是个符号系统。用符号和符号的配列构成的系统，是人类最重要的交际工具。言语则是人们运用一整套语言规则和语言要素表达个人意愿的行为和产物，带有个人意志和风格特征。

二、符号与符号的类型

语言是个符号系统，在了解语言符号之前，我们先来看看什么是符号。其实，生活中充满了符号：走在马路上，我们会看到直行、左转弯、右转弯、掉头等路标指示符；在十字路口，会看到指示"停"的红灯、指示"通行"的绿灯或者交通警察指挥交通的手势；在机场，会看到指示卫生间、饮水处、直梯、扶梯、饭店等的符号；在学校，会听到上课、下课的铃声；打开电脑，会看到桌面上指示回收站、文件夹等的符号；打开电脑中的Word，会看到数字、运算符、字母、文字、标点等形形色色的抽象符号。可以说，符号无处不在。

那么，究竟什么是符号呢？符号由形式和内容两部分构成。可以用感官感知的物质形式是符号的形式。从形式的角度来分类，常见的符号包括视觉符号、听觉符号和触觉符号。比如红绿灯是用视觉可以感知的颜色作为形式；上下课铃声、裁判的哨声、轮船的汽笛声是用听觉可以感知的声音作为形式；盲文是用触觉可以感知的凸点作为形式。内容是符号所代表的事物或意义，如"红灯"这个符号所代表的意义就是"停"。符号是形式和内容的结合体，二者就像一枚硬币的两面，是不可分割的，缺一不可。没有无形式的符号，也没有无内容的符号。

根据形式和内容之间的关系，可以将符号分为三类：图像符号（icon）、指示符号

（index）和标志符号（symbol）。图像符号的形体与其所代表的对象之间存在相似性，人们可以通过其形式感知其内容。比如，肖像就是人的图像符号，与真人极为相似；地图与真实的地形之间也存在相似性。指示符号与所指涉的对象之间具有时空上或因果关系上的关联，符号的形体能够指示对象的存在。比如，门能指示建筑物的出口；水银柱的升降能指示温度的变化。标志符号的形式与内容之间没有相似性或因果等必然联系，它的形式和内容的关联是约定俗成的结果。图腾、旗语等都属于标志符号，语言符号也属于标志符号，"人"的意义与rén这个声音之间的关系完全是约定俗成的。

根据符号的形式和内容之间有无联系，符号又可以分为象征性符号和非象征性符号。象征性符号的形式和内容之间有内在联系，形式由内容决定。图像符号和指示符号都属于象征性符号。校徽、院徽、园徽、会徽等各种徽标都是象征性符号。比如2008年北京奥林匹克运动会的会徽：近似椭圆形的中国传统印章上刻的是一个向前奔跑、舞动双手迎接胜利的运动员的图案，刻画了运动员冲向终点、迎接胜利的情景，又象征着中国人民对世界各地朋友的热烈欢迎；人物造型是一个用篆体书写的新"京"字，寓意新北京、新奥运；这个"京"字又酷似汉字的"文"字，取意中国悠久的传统文化；汉语拼音"Beijing"和"2008"的字样，象征2008年北京奥运会；奥运五环象征奥林匹克运动精神。此外，表示禁止烟火的符号，表示左转的符号，指示男女卫生间的符号都是象征性符号。形式与内容之间的联系有强弱之分，联系比较紧密、明显的能让人一目了然，如左转标志；联系比较隐蔽的则需要一些解释才能明白，如会徽。

非象征性符号的形式与内容之间没有内在的联系，用什么样的形式代表什么样的意义是人为规定的。红绿灯、数学运算符号、数字、标点、逻辑运算符号、文字、莫尔斯电码、军号、上下课铃声、旗语等都是非象征性符号。比如为什么用"+"表示加法，用"−"表示减法，是没有道理可言的。最早的交通信号灯用的是红色和蓝色，同样可以起到指示交通的作用。

语言是一个符号系统，语言符号属于非象征性符号。语言符号的形式是声音，内容是意义。语言符号是听觉符号，是音义结合体。"音"是语言符号的物质表现形式，"义"是语言符号的内容，只有音和义相结合才能指称现实现象，构成语言的符号。比如，汉语的符号"火"的形式是huǒ，意义是"物体燃烧时所发的光和焰"。英语的eat的语音形式是［iːt］，意思是take in solid food（摄入固体性的食物）。日语的符号はな的语音形式是［hana］，意思是"花"。声音、意义和客观事物之间的关系如图2−1所示：一定的声音表示一定的意义，意义反映的是客观世界中的事物，声音与意义、意义与事物之间是直接的联系（以实线表示），但声音与事物之间通过意义间接联系在一起（以虚线表示）。声音和意义构成语言符号，通过语言符号中的意义，声音可以代表客观世界中的事物，从而描述世界。关于语言符号的形式和意义，可进一步参考本章原典选读一。

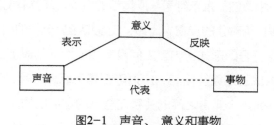

图2-1　声音、意义和事物

三、自然语言符号与人工语言符号

我们通常所说的语言指的是自然语言。"旗语""数学语言""计算机语言"这样的说法说明这些符号系统与人类的自然语言符号系统有相似之处，属于广义的语言，我们称之为"人工语言"。自然语言是在人类演化的进程中自然形成和发展起来的一套符号系统，言语社团把它作为母语来使用和学习。人工语言则是依照一定的原理人工设计出来的，有专门的用途，不能作为母语使用。人工语言主要有三类。第一类是模仿自然语言而创制的人工语言，在特殊情况下发挥自然语言的作用。比如，波兰医生柴门霍夫为消除语言隔阂于1887年设计的世界语。电影《阿凡达》中纳维（Navi）族人说的纳维语也是一种人造语，由南加州大学语言学家保罗·费洛莫（Paul R. Frommer）教授创造，有1000多个单词，有自己的语法规则和语言结构。目前全世界有很多纳维语爱好者在学习这种语言。第二类是为某种特殊用途而设计的语言代码，如通信上使用的莫尔斯电码、音乐上使用的五线谱和简谱，数学上使用的运算符等。第三类是依照语言原理而设计的用于人与计算机之间进行通信交流的符号系统，如C语言、JAVA等计算机编程语言。计算机语言是人与计算机之间传递信息的媒介，由字符和语法规则组成计算机能理解的各种语句（各种指令）。人工语言在当代社会生活和科学技术的发展中起着重要的作用，并与自然语言有许多相似、相通，甚至相同的地方。不过，语言学的研究对象主要是自然语言。

自然语言与人工语言都是符号系统，但二者不是一回事。与人工语言相比，自然语言符号有如下几个特点[1]：

第一，自然语言符号是人类在漫长的演化进程中自然形成和发展起来的，不是某个个人

---

1 参考：［苏联］兹维金采夫. 普通语言学纲要. 伍铁平，等，译. 北京：商务印书馆，1981.

创造的，使用范围超过任何一种人工符号；人工符号是人类为了某种目的而专门创制的，发明者往往是一个或几个人，只用于特定的领域。比如，英国数学家欧德莱发明了"×"号，瑞士人哈纳创制了"÷"。简谱是法国人苏埃蒂发明的，用于音乐。莫尔斯电码是由美国人莫尔斯发明的，用于无线通信。C语言是由美国计算机专家丹尼斯·里奇发明的，用于编程。

第二，自然语言符号是开放的，可以自然发展变化，不仅声音可以发生变化，而且意义也可以发生变化。比如北京话中的"鸡"原来读 [ki]，现在读 [tɕi]。feet原来读 [feːt]，现代英式英语中读 [fiːt]。"河"原来指黄河，现在可以泛指一般的河。人工语言符号都是封闭的符号系统，可以根据需要修改、废除，但都需要正式宣布，不会自然发展变化。

第三，自然语言符号的形式和意义之间不一定是一一对应的关系，一个形式可以有多个意义，如多义词；一个意义也可以由多个形式来表示，如同义词。人工语言符号的形式和意义之间通常是一对一的关系，一个形式只表示一个意义，一个意义只用一个形式来表示。

第四，除了理性意义，自然语言符号还可以表达感情意义，比如"团结"是好的，"勾结"则带有贬义。人工语言符号只表达理性意义。

第五，自然语言符号的意义具有模糊性，比如究竟多大为"大"，"早晨"是几点到几点，并没有明确的规定。人工语言符号的意义是有明确规定的，比如加减乘除的意思非常清晰。

文字也是一种符号系统，是记录语言的符号，是符号的符号。语言符号是第一性的，文字符号是第二性的。文字也可能会变，但文字的变化与语言的变化不一定是同步的，前者往往会滞后。比如，英语中表示"光"这个意思的语言符号是 [lait]，但记录这一语言符号的文字符号light却保留了不发音的gh。

第二节　语言符号的性质

一、语言符号的任意性与理据性

语言符号是音义结合体，语言符号的任意性是指其声音与意义之间的联系是任意的，没有理据的，没有内在或必然的联系，用什么声音表示什么意义是约定俗成的。正因为语言符号具有任意性，所以，世界上才会有那么多种语言，因为同一个意义在不同的语言中可以用不同的声音来表示。比如同样指"人身最上部或动物最前部长着口、鼻、眼等器官的部分"，汉语用tóu这个音来表示，英语用head［hɛd］，日语用あたま［atama］，法语用tête［tɛt］。反过来，同一个音在不同的语言中也可以表示不同的意义。［bolna］在印地-乌尔都语（Hindu-urdu）中意思是"说"，在俄语中是"疼痛的"；［tɑkɑ］在日语中的意思是"鹰"，在盖丘亚语（Quechua）中是"拳头"，在祖鲁语（Zulu）中是"一种小鸟"，在孟加拉语（Bengali）中是"钱"。[1]英语face（脸）的发音与法语fesse（屁股）的发音非常相似；汉语的"岁"与英语的sway（摇摆）也很像。赵元任先生曾经讲过一个故事：

> 听说从前有个老太婆，初次跟外国话有点儿接触，她就稀奇得简直不相信。她说："他们的说话怪，嘎？明明儿是五个，法国人不管五个叫'五个'，偏偏要管它叫'三个'（Cinq注：法语五的音像中文的"三"）；日本人又管十叫'九'（ジュウ）；明明儿脚上穿的鞋，日本人不管鞋叫'鞋'，偏偏儿要管鞋叫'裤子'（クツ）；这明明儿是水，英国人偏偏儿要叫它'窝头'（water），法国人偏偏儿要叫它'滴漏'（de l'eau），只有咱们中国人好好儿的管它叫'水'！咱们不但是管它叫'水'诶，这东西明明儿是'水'嚜。"[2]

这个故事形象地描述了不同语言的同音异义现象。如果把音义关系看作有必然的联系，就会产生上述疑惑，觉得不可思议。

不仅不同语言中的音义之间没有关联，并非一一对应的关系，同一语言内部也存在同义不同音和同音不同义的现象，前者表现为同义词，后者表现为同音词。比如汉语中"嘴"和"口"、"脚"和"足"是两组同义词，"公、弓、功"是同音词。英语中present与gift是同义词，meat与meet是同音词。这种音义的任意结合有时候会很有意思，在下面的句子中，三个can实际上是同音词，第一个是能愿动词"能"，第二个是词汇动词"将……装入"，第三个是名词"罐头"。

（1）Can you can a can?

　　"你能装罐头吗？"

任何一种语言的音和义从古到今都在变化，这也说明音义之间的关联是任意的。如果

1 引自：Victoria Fromkin, Robert Rodman, Nina Hyams. 2013. *An Introduction to Language* (10e). Michael Rosenberg, p. 3.
2 引自：赵元任. 语言问题. 北京：商务印书馆，1980：3.

音义之间的关联是有理据的，就不可能发生变化。比如right在当代英语中读［rait］，gh不发音，但以前gh是发音的。

　　关于语言的任意性或约定俗成性，古代的思想家、哲学家在名实关系的讨论中都曾经论及。比如，在《克拉底鲁篇》里，柏拉图的朋友赫谟根尼（Hermogenes）说过：

> Any name which you give is the right one, and if you change that and give another, the new name is as correct as the old. （无论你起什么名字，都是对的；如果你想改名，起一个新的，也和旧的一样是对的。）

柏拉图也同意这一观点。大约处于同一时代的我国古代思想家荀子表达了相似的看法：

> 名无固宜，约之以命，约定俗成谓之宜，异于约则谓之不宜。名无固实，约之以命实，约定俗成谓之实名。——《荀子·正名》

上述关于名实关系的讨论说明了语言符号的语音形式与其意义之间并没有必然的联系，是任意的、约定俗成的。当然，语言并不是一个简单的分类命名集，各种语言不是简单地给已经存在的范畴命名，它们都创造自己的范畴（详见原典选读一）。所以，不同的语言对世界的分类是不一样的，一个语言中的词可能在另一个语言中无法找到完全对等的词。比如，英语的sister对应汉语中的"姐姐"和"妹妹"。

　　语言符号在创制的最初，音义之间的联系是任意的、不可论证的。可是一旦投入使用之后就具有强制性，所有讲这种语言的人都不能随意改变这种音义关系。对于个体的人来讲，一出生就被置于某种语言环境中，就必须遵守这一语言的规约，不能随便更改，汉语母语者不能突然把"书"改叫book。从这个意义上说，语言类似于社会契约和法律制度。不同的是，契约和法律制度都可以人为地打破或更改，而语言是人们自觉地在遵守的规则，一般只能自然而然地慢慢发生变化。

　　那有没有违反任意性原则的符号呢？经常提到的反例是拟声词、叹词和对父母的称呼语。拟声词，顾名思义就是模拟声音的词。既然如此，声音和意义之间应该是有联系的。比如mōu（哞）模仿的是牛的叫声，shāshā（沙沙）模仿的是风吹树叶声、雨声等。可是，不同语言中模拟同一种声音的拟声词并不完全一样。同样是模仿公鸡的叫声，汉语是"喔喔"，英语是cock-a-doodle-doo，法语是法cocorico，意大利语是coccodè，俄语是kukareku，日语是こけこっこー（kokekokkoo），南美洲印第安人的瓜拉尼语是kõrõrõ。在英语中，猪的叫声是oink，在日语中则是boo-boo。从表2-1可以看出，英语和汉语中有关动物叫声的拟声词有些比较相像，如moo-mōu；有些差别比较大，如模仿鸭子叫的

quack-gāgā。不仅使用的语音材料不同，而且语音的组合方式也不同，英语中有长元音，有复辅音tw，汉语中没有。这说明，拟声词不等于真实的声音，只是对声音的模仿，受具体语言语音系统的制约。

英语	moo	woof	tweet	cluck	baa	quack
汉语	哞哞mōumōu	汪汪wāngwāng	啾啾jiūjiū	咯咯gēgē	咩咩miēmiē	嘎嘎gāgā

表2-1 英语与汉语中的拟声词比较

叹词在不同的语言中也不完全一样。比如英语的oh常用来表示惊讶、指责、痛苦、称赞、懊恼等，译成汉语不一定是"哦"，还可以是"哎呀""啊""哎哟"等。英语的good heavens对应汉语的"天哪"。

再来看对父母的称呼语。世界上多数语言中关于"父母"的称呼很像，第一个音常常是唇音，比如普通话中的"爸爸、妈妈、父亲、母亲"，英语中的mama、mummy、father、mother。之所以会这样是有原因的，婴儿吃奶靠吮吸，因此唇部最发达，唇音往往是婴儿最早会发的辅音。但是也有些方言和语言中称呼父母不用唇音，比如有些汉语方言中称呼爸爸为"大大、爹、爷"，称呼妈妈为"娘"，英语中的daddy也没有唇音。

退一步说，就算拟声词、叹词、对父母的称呼语是反例，它们在语言系统中所占的比例非常小，影响也是有限的。加拿大马更些（Mackenzie）河上的阿萨巴斯根（Athabaskan）部落是美洲最原始的土著部落之一，他们的语言里几乎没有拟声词。[1]

与符号的任意性有关的是关于人类语言的起源假说。德国学者马克斯·米勒（Max Mueller）提出的"汪汪说"（the bow-wow theory）与拟声词密切相关。"汪汪说"声称语言产生于人类对自然界里各种声音的模仿。听到狗的声音就模仿说"汪汪"，听到鸭子的声音就模仿说"嘎嘎"，听到猫的声音就模仿说"喵呜"。这些模仿的声音不断被重复，时间一长逐渐固定下来，开始代替被模仿的自然界的真实声音，进而抽象为指代那种声音的名字，最后成为发出那种声音的自然现象或动物的名字。也就是说，名称乃是对它所表示的事物声音的模仿，起名字的人总以声音来模仿他所称呼的事物。比如，"布谷"本来是对布谷鸟叫声的一种模仿，后来被用来指称这种鸟，英语中的cuckoo（布谷鸟）也是如此。同样，英语中的bow-wow最初只是对狗的叫声的模仿，现在可以用来指狗。有人认为，"猫""鸡"分别是从拟声词"喵""叽"来的。这种用声音指发出声音的事物的方法

---

1 引自：［美］萨丕尔. 语言论——言语研究导论. 陆卓元，译. 陆志韦，校订. 北京：商务印书馆，1985：7.

在大人对婴儿说话时也常常用到，比如，有些方言会用拟声词gougou来指"鸡"。《山海经》中也有这样的记载：

> 北二百里，曰发鸠之山，其上多枯木，有鸟焉，其状如乌，文首，白喙，赤足，名曰"精卫"，其鸣自詨。

"其鸣自詨"的意思是"它的叫声像是在呼唤自己的名字"，"精卫"也许就是从它的叫声而得名。柏拉图在《对话集》中也提出过类似的看法，认为人类语言起源于拟声。"汪汪说"较好地揭示了拟声词的由来，但并不能由此否定语言符号的任意性。即使最初的音义之间有一定关联，后来这种关联也已经消磨了。除了"布谷鸟"这样的词，不经提示，很多人并不知道"鸡""猫""蟋蟀"这样的名称与其叫声相关。

有时候，一般词汇中的有些音看起来与一定的意义相关联。比如很多以m开头的词带有"女性"这一语义成分，如mammy（妈妈）、madam（女士）、maternal（母系的）、miss（小姐）、matron（女警卫）、maid（女仆）、mistress（主妇）。一种语言中的词汇有数万甚至数十万，在意义上有所关联可能只是偶然。我们也可以列举很多反例，比如man、mini、many这些词与女性没有任何关系。另外，有些词之间有意义上的衍生关系。比如"婚"就是从"昏"来的，因为古代女子出嫁都在黄昏时候。这种情况是利用已有的符号创造新符号，因此新符号与原有符号之间有一定的意义关联。

符号创制的最初阶段是否有一定的理据性，无从知晓；即使有，也是偶然的，并且不同的语言理据也不一样。而且，这种理据性大都随着时间的流逝逐渐被人类遗忘了。所以，从根本上来说语言符号是任意的，任意性是语言符号的根本特性。

需要注意的是，语言符号的任意性是就单个符号而言的，不同于造词的理据，符号与符号的组合是有理据的，不具有任意性。比如"电脑"和"计算机"指同一种事物，但组词的理据不同，一个强调与人脑的相似性，有一定智能；一个强调其强大的计算功能。

二、语言符号的线性与非线性

任何语言都具有线性特征。说话时，语言符号只能一个跟着一个依次出现，在时间的线条上绵延，顺着时间的线条前后相续，好像一根链条，一环扣着一环，绝不可能在同一时间说出两个符号。比如"我爱北京天安门"是由"我-爱-北-京-天-安-门"依次出现组合而成的。英语的bye-bye [bai-bai] 也不会一次性发出，要发两次。表现在书面语上就是文字从左到右或从上往下依次出现。[1] 线性还体现在非符号的语音层面，比如，"天"的语音形式是由t-i-a-n四个音素依次出现组合而成的。语言的线性特征有别于其他一些符号系统，比如音符就可以叠加在一起同时出现，构成和弦，造成和声效果。

语言符号的线性特征是一目了然、不言而喻的。然而，语言符号除了其表面上的线性特征之外还具有非线性特征。这一点在语调和重音上看得很清楚。语调和重音都是叠加在音段成分之上的。另外，音义之间的结合可以是非线性的，比如，阿拉伯语中动词的词根是辅音组合，元音组合提示其形态变化，如katab的词根是k-t-b（写），a-a表示主动态、过去时，这个词相当于英语里的wrote。符号之间的语义关系也常常呈现非线性，相邻的单位之间关系可能很远，不相邻的单位之间关系可能很近，也就是说，单位的线性排列顺序不一定反映其组合顺序。比如，"美丽的中国姑娘"并非"美丽的"与"中国"先组合成"美丽的中国"，而是"中国"与"姑娘"先组合成"中国姑娘"，即"美丽的"并非修饰与之相邻的"中国"，而是修饰与之不相邻的"姑娘"。再比如，"游了一小时的泳"是"游"和"泳"关系更密切，"将你的军"是"将"和"军"关系更密切，"一小时的泳""你的军"反而没有意义。

三、语言符号的离散性

我们说话时声音似乎是连续不断的，形成一个语流，实际上，看似连续不断的语流可以切分为许多离散的单位。语言符号的离散性是指语言符号之间的界限是清楚的、可以分开的。在口语中，我们可以分辨组成短语的词，以及组成词的音节，比如上文的"我爱北京天安门"可以切分成"我-爱-北-京-天-安-门"这几个符号。从书面语上看，英语的单词之间都是有空格的，说明英语母语者对于词的界限是比较清楚的。汉语词之间没有空格，但是同样也有词的概念，中文信息处理要先分词。正是因为符号具有离散性，才可以从链条上拆卸下来，重复使用，与其他符号进行多种组合，用有限的语言符号表达无限的意义。

符号是离散的，而世界上有些事物或现象却是连续的，这种矛盾就造成了语言符号意义的模糊性。比如彩虹的颜色是个连续统，颜色的变化是渐进的，不同颜色之间的界限是模糊的。而每个语言中的颜色词是有限的几个，汉语中常用的颜色词包括"红、黄、蓝、白、黑、绿、灰、紫、棕、褐、橙"等，这些颜色词的意义是模糊的，参见第六章。

---

1 语言符号能指的线性特征在文字上也可能得不到体现，比如"瓩"表示"千瓦"，是两个符号能指的合写。

四、语言符号的区别性

语言符号是声音和意义的结合体。语言是个符号系统，系统里的各符号之间互相对立、互相制约。所有的符号都处于与其他符号之间的关系当中，因为与其他符号不同而具有存在的价值，这就是语言符号的区别性。语言符号的区别性可以从音和义两个方面来看。

我们每个人的发音都不一样，同一个人每次说话时发的音也不完全一样。比如汉语拼音b，同一个人的每次发音以及不同人的发音可能都不同，但是这并不影响我们交流，别人都能听明白，为什么呢？声音是一种物质要素，是语言符号的材料，但声音本身不属于语言。准确地说，语言符号的形式并不是声音本身，而是声音与声音之间的差别。语言只要求有区别，而不要求每个人发出的音是一模一样的，也不要求每一次发出的音一模一样。换句话说，重要的不是声音本身，而是使一个语言符号区别于其他语言符号的声音上的差别，带有意义的正是这些差别。所以，即使同一个人每一次发的汉语拼音的b都不同，不同的人发音也不完全相同，只要发出的b与其他语言符号的声音保持足够的差别，就不影响听话人理解。比如，只要说话人能区分b、p、t、l等声母，就可以保证不会混淆"爸""怕""踏""辣"。所谓有区别，是指区别于同系统的其他成员。如何区别取决于具体的语言系统，系统不同，成员不同，要求也不一样。北京话中的 [w] 是个半元音，但是很多人发成浊音 [v]，比如"为人民服务"中的"为 [wei^{51}]"读成 [vei^{51}]，但这并不影响交流。因为北京话中并没有 [v] 这个音，不会造成混同。普通话中"河南"的"南"与"荷兰"的"兰"发音不一样，一个声母是n，一个声母是l，讲普通话的人认为二者差别很大。可是有些说四川话的人会把这两个词都听成"荷兰"，因为在四川话中n、l并不区别意义。

从意义的角度看，一个语言系统中彼此关联的符号因为互相区别而获得意义，系统不同，意义也不同。比如book与books处于对立关系中，s的有无造成形式上的差别，而这一差别又对应意义上的单复数差别。汉语中的"书"没有这种形式上的差异，自然也就没有单复数的区分。又比如，汉语中表示同胞的词有"姐姐、妹妹、哥哥、弟弟"四个，彼此之间可以通过年龄和性别来区分。"姐姐"指的就是年长的女性同胞。而英语中表示同胞的只有sister和brother，二者只有性别差异，而无年龄差异。sister与"姐姐"的意思也就不同。类似地，汉语中的"借"与英语中的borrow和lend都不相当，而是包含了两者的意义，既指借入，也指借出。可见，符号的意义是由它与语言中其他要素的关系和差别决定的。一个符号的意义受制于其他符号，因此，系统中符号数量的变化会引起符号意义的变化。比如古代汉语中的"口、嘴、喙"分别指人的嘴、兽的嘴和鸟的嘴；到了现代汉语中，"口"和"喙"不再单用为词，"嘴"的意义就扩大了，还可以用来指人的嘴和鸟的嘴。再比如，英语中的指人的疑问代词有两个，who是主格形式，whom是宾格形式，例如（2）-（3）。

（2）Who likes you?

"谁喜欢你？"

（3）Whom do you like?

"你喜欢谁？"

但随着格在英语中消失，whom逐渐开始退出，其结果是whom原来的意义转移到了who上，导致who的意义发生了变化，不仅表主格，还可以表宾格，例如（4）。

（4）Who do you like?（语义同（3））

使一个符号区别于其他符号的一切要素就构成该符号，差别造成特征。语言符号的意义（价值）由系统中其他要素来决定。它们最确切的特征是：它们不是别的东西。有关符号的区别性，详见原典选读三。

第三节　语言符号系统

离散的语言符号并非杂乱无章，任何一种语言都是一个组织严密的符号系统。语言一直处于变化之中，但又是相对静止的。我们说语言是个符号系统时，指的是它相对静止的共时状态。准确地说，共时的语言才自成一个系统，比如现代汉语是一个系统（有关语言的共时与历时的区分参见原典选读二）。

这个系统的有效运转得益于以下三个因素：第一，系统具有二层性；第二，系统中的要素处于组合关系、聚合关系中；第三，语言系统主要由词库和语法两部分组成。以下我们对这三点分别进行说明。

一、语言系统的二层性

语言符号系统分为两层：底层的音系层和上层的语法层。音系层只能构成符号的形式，只能区别意义而不能表达意义。语法层才是音义结合的层面，能够表达意义。每一层都有自己最小的单位，单位与单位按照一定的规则可以组成更大的单位，两个层面的规则具有一定的平行性。

音系层的最小单位是音位，音位按一定的规则组合成更大的单位——音节。音节与音节组合成音步。音步之上还有停延段、语调段等。音位和音节只能构成语言符号的形式，因此音系层是不能表达意义的。比如汉语普通话中用拼音表示的b、p、m、f、d、t、n、l、a、o、e、i等都是音位，它们本身并不承载任何意义，但是能区别意义。比如b和p可以区别"爸"与"怕"，zh和z可以区别"支"与"资"，a和o可以区别"怕"与"破"。

语法层最小的单位是语素，语素是最小的音义结合体。语素与语素组合成词，词与词组合成词组，词组和词组还可以组合成更大的词组，词或词组带上一定的语调就构成句子。比如"上"和"课"都是语素，既有语音形式也有意义，这两个语素可以组合成词"上课"。"上课"与词"在"组合成词组"在上课"，"在上课"与词"学生"组合，并加上一个陈述语调，就构成了一个完整的句子"学生在上课"。

一个语言系统的音位通常只有几十个，比如现代汉语普通话的音位是30个左右，英语的音位是50个左右。音位和音位组合成音节有几百个，普通话中的基本音节约为400个。音节再与声调配合，就可以得到1600多个音节。当然，不是每个音节都有四个声调（比如汉语中没有fò），所以，现代汉语只有1300个左右的音节。这些音节就是语素的语音形式，因为在现代汉语中一个音节大致对应一个语素、一个汉字。考虑到同音字，再考虑到多义字，语素（汉字）的数量会上万。只是很多字不常用，常用字只有几千个。语素与语素可组合成词，现代汉语中以双音节词（往往同时也是双语素词）居多，词的数量至少是语素的几倍。1994年出版的《中华字海》收字85000个，但很多字并不常用，甚至几乎不用。1988年出版的《现代汉语常用字表》收录了常用汉字2500个，次常用汉字1000个；2008年的《现代汉语常用词表（草案）》收录了现当代社会生活中比较稳定的、使用频率较高的汉语普通话常用词语56008个。《现代汉语词典》（第6版）共收单字13000多个，收词条约69000个。从这些工具书中就可窥见现代汉语语素和词的数量。

词和词按一定的语法规则可以组合成无限数量的词组和句子。从最初的几十个没有意义的音位，到成千上万的音义结合的语素、词，凭借有限的语法规则，就可以随心所欲地说出无限个句子。一级一级，不断地翻番增量，这就是语言符号系统的奥秘之所在。二层性大大提高了语言系统的效率，达到了以简驭繁、以少驭多、以有限生成无限的效果。

二、组合关系与聚合关系

音位、语素、词等都只是语言的备用材料，如果只是杂乱地堆放，毫无章法，不成系统，语言这个双层分级的装置也就不可能正常运转。语言系统的有序运转是以关系为基础的，最重要的两种关系就是组合关系和聚合关系。这两种关系使语言中的各级单位在不同的维度上彼此关联，互相依赖、互相制约，从而建构了语言这个系统。

组合关系是单位与单位横向联接的关系，联接的结果是形成更大的单位或结构。这里的单位既可以是没有意义的音位，也可以是有意义的语素、词、词组等。比如"北"的语音形式是bei（暂不考虑声调），b-e-i三个音位之间就是组合关系。"北京"这个词中的语素"北"与"京"也是组合关系。"北京大学到了"中的"北京大学"与"到了"，"北京"与"大学"，"到"与"了"之间都是组合关系。

单位之间的组合是有规则、有条件的。汉语普通话中有bei这样的组合形式，却没有*eib这样的组合形式。可以说"我正在吃苹果"，不能说"我正在苹果吃"。组合对顺序有要求，"雪白"与"白雪"意思不同，"蜂蜜"与"蜜蜂"意思也不同，"我打你"与"你打我"意思截然相反。组合成分之间的关系不同，意思就不同，"进口设备"可能是修饰关系，也可能是支配关系，一个意思是"进口的设备"，一个意思是"进口某种设备"。

组合关系存在于现成的结构中，是已经实现了的关系。比如"我吃香蕉"中的"我"、"吃"和"香蕉"都是可听或可见的，它们之间是组合关系，组合成一个主谓宾结构。假设我们来仿造句子，把其中的某个词去掉，来做完形填空题，"＿＿吃香蕉"中"＿＿"的位置能填入哪些词呢？

$$\left.\begin{array}{l}\text{我}\\\text{老师}\\\text{小王}\\\text{猴子}\\\vdots\end{array}\right\}\text{吃香蕉}$$

在"＿＿"可以填入"我""老师""小王""猴子"，等等。为什么我们会想到要填入这些词，而不是"大、小、红、走、打"这样的词呢？因为后面这些词与"我"并不属于一类，前面那些词才与"我"属于一类，具有共同的特点，都是指人或动物的体词或体词性短语，它们聚为一类，它们之间的关系称为"聚合关系"。同样地，"吃"的位置还可以换成"切、分、买、卖、扔"等动词，它们之间也是聚合关系；"香蕉"的位置还可以换成"苹果、梨、橘子、米饭、馒头、饼干、红烧肉、排骨、芹菜、菠菜"等名词，它们之间也是聚合关系。

概括地来看，同一结构中某个位置上能相互替换的单位具有相同的功能，自然聚集成群，彼此之间的关系就是聚合关系。聚合关系反映的是"类"的关系。这种关系是潜在的，是一种联想关系。我们在做替换的时候，其实就是在联想。不仅词类的成员之间构成聚合关系，同义词、反义词、类义词（如亲属词、颜色词）等的内部成员之间也都构成聚合关系。不但语言符号（词、语素）处在这种关系之中，而且构造符号的音位也处在这种关系之中。比如"bā"中的"b"还可以替换为p、m、f、d、t、n、l，等等，这些音位之间也构成聚合关系，属于同一类音，都是辅音。可见，组合关系与聚合关系在音系和语法两个层面都存在。

横向的组合关系与纵向的聚合关系彼此联系，前者向后者提出要求，后者为前者提供可选项。比如"＿＿吃香蕉"要求空格位置的成分应该指能吃东西的人或动物，而不能是植物名词和无生命的名词。每个母语者都掌握着自己母语的组合规则，头脑中分类储存着大量的聚合群，在说话时，根据组合规则的要求，从聚合群中提取符合组合规则要求的单位，来进行拼读或者组词造句，达到交际的目的。如果只了解一种语言的语法规则而没有丰富的词汇积累，或者只掌握了丰富的词汇而不了解语言的规则，都不能很好地运用这种语言。

三、语言系统的两大组成部分：词库与语法

语言是个符号系统，是个二层性装置，其中的要素通过组合关系和聚合关系联系在一起。那么这个符号系统是如何工作的呢？换句话说，作为一种言语交际工具，这个系统是如何实现自己的功能的？或者说，我们是如何使用这个工具来生成言语，表达我们的想法，进而与人交流的呢？

对于母语我们已经驾轻就熟，好像从来没想过我们是怎么说出一句话的。想一想我们在刚开始学习英语时，要说一句英语，比如"我们是学生"。我们通常会想"我们"是we，"是"是are，"学生"是student。如果不知道这三个词，就无法说出正确的英语句子。但只知道这三个词还不够，还要对这三个词进行正确排序，而且还要知道we是主格形式，are是复数形式，student要加复数标记s。最后才会生成正确的句子"We are students."如果是日语，那么所用的词，以及词的排列顺序都会发生变化，如（5）所示。

（5）私たちは 学生 です。

　　　我们　　学生 是

　　　"我们是学生。"

在日语中，宾语是放在动词前面的。"は"表明前面的"私たち"是被说明的话题。从中可以看出，我们运用语言系统的过程简单来说就是个遣词造句的过程。搜肠刮肚找词的过程实际上是在从我们的心理词库中调取合适的词，然后像拼字游戏一样按照一定的语法规则对这些词进行排列组合，并根据要求适当改变词的形式。可见，语言系统有两大组成部分：词库和语法。这也是为什么学习一门外语最重要的两件事就是背单词和学习语法。

（一）词库

每个人的脑海里都有一个心理词库，那么，这个心理词库里装的究竟是什么呢？我们一般说词库里装的是词，这里的词指的是能够造句的最小的语法单位。虽然这些词可能是通过构词规则产生的，比如worker由work和词缀−er组合而成。但在语法上worker却是不可分割的一个单位，表现在语法的规则不能进入其内部。比如可以对句子"He is a worker."中的worker进行提问："What is he?"但是不能对work或者er进行提问。词可以由部件根据规则组合而成，词组和句子可以根据规则由词组合而成，但两种规则不同，前者称为词法，后者称为句法。广义的语法包括词法和句法，狭义的语法专指句法。

另外，心理词库还收录意义不可预测的固定用语，比如"守株待兔""坐吃山空"这样的成语，"磨刀不误砍柴工""拍马屁""翘辫子"这样的俗语，"北京师范大学""十二届三中全会"这样的专名。英语中的习语也是需要收录到心理词库中的，比如，kick the bucket（去世、死亡）、out of the blue（出乎意料，突如其来）；lick the boots（拍马屁）；love me, love my dog（爱屋及乌）。这些短语的共同特点是与一般的词一样，其意义并非字面义，无法靠规则得出，具有任意性，是需要专门记忆的。就像迪休洛（Di Sciullo）和威廉姆斯（Williams）（1987）所说：The lexicon is like a prison—it contains only the lawless, and the only thing that its inmates have in common is lawlessness.（词库就像一个监狱，里面装的都是违法的犯人，这些犯人的唯一共同点就是目无法纪。）[1]

研究表明，"蓝天白云""大风大浪""由此可见""简而言之""换句话说"这样比较固定的词组也常常作为词汇储存在词库里，在组词造句的时候直接调用。

简而言之，词库里的东西都是需要记忆的，不是靠规则临时组合而成的，包括词和固定用语，它们就像是盖楼用的砖块和预制板等材料。巧妇难为无米之炊，没有大量词汇的积累，是不可能自如地运用一种语言进行交流的。

那么，一个人的心理词库里到底可以装多少个词呢？统计表明，莎士比亚的十四行

---

[1] 引自：A. M. Di Sciullo, E. Williams. 1987. *On the Definition of Word*. Cambridge: MIT Press，p. 3.

诗和戏剧中所用的词大约是15000个。通常我们认识的词比我们所用的要多得多。心理学家威廉姆·纳吉（William Nagy）和理查德·安德森（Richard Anderson）调查发现，美国的高中生认识大概45000个词，比莎士比亚用的多了两倍。[1]语言学家郑锦全提出了著名的"词涯八千"的说法。[2]古往今来，旧词消失，新词产生，词语不能无限积累，只能新陈代替。郑锦全统计发现，记载各个朝代社会、政治、帝王、世家、游侠、经济、经籍、艺文各方面活动的二十五史各本书，不管全书总字数是几万字还是几百万字，所用的不同的字种，只有四五千，很少超过八千。比如《史记》约53万字，用字约5100个；《红楼梦》约73万字，用字约4500个。只有《清史稿》用了八千多个字种，但这部书是集体编写，不代表一个人的心理词库。古代汉语以单音节词为主，一个字大致等于一个词。英文过去伟大的著作也一样，把单数、复数、过去式等各种语形变化排除，每本著作用词也不超过八千个。

（二）语法

只有语言材料是不够的，一个博闻强记的人即使背下了整部词典，也不一定能造出合法的句子。因为这些材料必须按照一定的规则来排列组合。"人""狗""咬"这三个词，如果排列组合的话，有六种可能，如（6）所示。

（6）a. 人咬狗。

b. *人狗咬。

c. 狗咬人。

d. *狗人咬。

e. *咬人狗。

f. *咬狗人。

只有第一种和第三种组合在汉语中是合语法的句子，这说明语言是有规则的。我们能够判断一个汉语句子是否正确，说明我们拥有语法知识，虽然有时候我们自己并不能说得很清楚。如果是日语，第二种、第四种句子语序就是合法的，因为日语中宾语出现在动词前面。

---

1 转引自：Steven Pinker.1997. *The Language Instinct: How the Mind Creates Language.* Harper Perennial Modern Classics. 中译本：［美］史蒂芬·平克. 语言本能：探索人类语言进化的奥秘. 洪兰，译. 汕头：汕头大学出版社，2004：162.

2 引自：郑锦全，苏新春，张秀英. "词涯八千"与汉语词汇的扩展性. 第四届汉语词汇语义学研讨会，2003.

如果译成英语，要考虑名词的单复数、动词的时态等问题。这说明不同的语言规则是不一样的。这也是为什么"好好学习，天天向上"不能一个词一个词地译成"good good study, day day up"。语法规则是有限的，可以列出清单，比如学习英语需要知道英语的单复数变化、时态、语态等，学习法语还需要知道阴性、阳性等。一本语法书大致可以讲清楚一个语言的语法。

　　词库里的单位是有限的，组词造句的规则也是有限的。语言的奇妙之处在于，我们可以利用有限的词汇和有限的规则生成无限的句子。随便打开一本书，你几乎找不到完全相同的句子。我们每个人一生都可以讲出无数不同的句子，但用到的规则是有限的。同一个规则可以反复使用，造出无限结构相同的短语或句子。比如，婴儿有个阶段什么都咬。我们可以说"婴儿咬苹果，婴儿咬手指头，婴儿咬衣服……"，"咬"后面可以出现很多指具体物体的名词。这些句子跟上面的"狗咬人"一样都是"主-谓-宾"结构。儿童在语言习得的某个阶段就是像做游戏一样，不断地仿造句子，下面是英语的例子。

（7）a. This is a green ball.

　　　b. This is a blue ball.

　　　c. This is a yellow ball.

　　　　⋮

　　相同结构的重复可以产生并列结构，比如"左手一只鸡，右手一只鸭"，这样的联合式重复并不会增加句子的层次。（8）-（9）是古汉语中的例子：

（8）孔子曰："不知命，无以为君子也；不知礼，无以立也；不知言，无以知人。"

（9）鱼，我所欲也；熊掌，亦我所欲也。二者不可得兼，舍鱼而取熊掌者也。生，亦我所欲也；义，亦我所欲也。二者不可得兼，舍生而取义者也。

这样平行的三联句、两联句在《论语》《孟子》等诸子散文中比比皆是。这样的句式不仅朗朗上口，具有语言的对称美，而且在表义上也互相呼应。《三字经》《弟子规》等古代启蒙读物里也有大量类似的例子，例如，"玉不琢，不成器；人不学，不知义"以及"父母呼，应勿缓；父母命，行勿懒；父母教，须敬听"，等等。

　　同样的语法结构可以层层嵌套，同一条结构规则可以重复使用而不致造成结构上的混乱，这就是递归性（参见第五章）。当然，因为记忆的限制，我们通常说的句子都不会太长。但是，理论上，一个句子可以是无限长的，只要合规则，比如（10）。

（10） a. 我父亲

b. 我父亲的父亲

c. 我父亲的父亲的父亲

d. 我父亲的父亲的父亲的父亲

e. 我父亲的父亲的父亲的父亲的父亲

⋮

后面再出现"的父亲"，整个词组也是合法的，而且其中只涉及一种结构——偏正结构。这种"中国套娃式"的句子会不断增加句子的层次。下面是英语中的一个句子，用了12个that定语从句，每个定语从句都修饰前面的名词短语。

（11） This is the farmer sowing the corn,

That kept the cock that crowed in the morn,

That waked the priest all shaven and shorn,

That married the man all tattered and torn,

That kissed the maiden all forlorn,

That milked the cow with the crumpled horn,

That tossed the dog

That worried the cat

That killed the rat

That ate the malt

That lay in the house that Jack built.[1]

目前吉尼斯世界纪录中最长的句子是福克纳（William Faulkner）小说《押沙龙，押沙龙！》（*Absalom Absalom!*）里的一句话，有1300个词。它是这样开头的：They both bore it as though in deliberate flagellant exaltation...（他们俩以宗教自律而受鞭笞的自得心情来承受它……）。这个句子还可以变得更长：Faulkner wrote，"They both bore it as though in deliberate flagellant exaltation..."。进一步地，还可以加长，变为：Pinker wrote that Faulkner wrote，"They both bore it as though in deliberate flagellant exaltation..."。纪录可以一次次被打破，句子越来越复杂，但是基本结构类型没变，这就是递归性的真谛。

---

1 引自：Victoria Fromkin, Robert Rodman. 1983. *An Introduction to Language*（3e）. New York: Holt, Rinehart & Winston，p. 219.

运用有限的单位和规则生成无限的句子，演绎出美妙的语言的篇章，这就是人类语言符号系统的奇妙之处。

📑 原典选读

一、符号、所指和能指

[瑞士]费尔迪南·德·索绪尔. 普通语言学教程. 高名凯，译. 北京：商务印书馆，1999. 本章的三个选文都取自这部著作。

【导　读】

语言符号连结的不是事物和名称，而是概念和音响形象，即符号的所指和能指。概念和音响形象都是心理层面的。音响形象不是我们实际发出或听到的声音，而是这一声音在我们大脑里留下的心理印记。比如默读的时候，我们其实并没有发出声音，而是唤起了这些音响形象。事物是客观存在的，而与事物对应的概念则是心理活动的结果。符号是所指（概念）和能指（音响形象）的结合体，符号的所指和能指就像一张纸的正反面，不可分割。索绪尔所说的"所指"和"能指"大致相当于符号的意义和形式。

§1. 符号、所指、能指

在有些人看来，语言，归结到它的基本原则，不外是一种分类命名集，即一份跟同样多的事物相当的名词术语表。例如：

这种观念有好些方面要受到批评。它假定有现成的、先于词而存在的概念（关于这一点，参看以下第157页）。它没有告诉我们名称按本质来说是声音的还是心理的，因为arbor"树"可以从这一方面考虑，也可以从那一方

: ARBOR

: EQUOS

etc.　　etc.

面考虑。最后，它会使人想到名称和事物的联系是一种非常简单的作业，而事实上决不是这样。但是这种天真的看法却可以使我们接近真理，它向我们表明语言单位是一种由两项要素联合构成的双重的东西。

我们在第33页谈论言语循环时已经看到，语言符号所包含的两项要素都是心理的，而且由联想的纽带连接在我们的脑子里。我们要强调这一点。

100

语言符号连结的不是事物和名称，而是概念和音响形象①。后者不是物质的声音，纯粹物理的东西，而是这声音的心理印迹，我们的感觉给我们证明的声音表象。它是属于感觉的，我们有时把它叫做"物质的"，那只是在这个意义上说的，而且是跟联想的另一个要素，一般更抽象的概念相对立而言的。

我们试观察一下自己的言语活动，就可以清楚地看到音响形象的心理性质：我们不动咀唇，也不动舌头，就能自言自语，或在心里默诵一首诗。那是因为语言中的词对我们来说都是一些音响形象，我们必须避免说到构成词的"音位"。"音位"这个术语含有声音动作的观念，只适用于口说的词，适用于内部形象在话语中的实现。我们说到一个词的声音和音节的时候，只要记住那是指的音响形象，就可以避免这种误会。

因此语言符号是一种两面的心理实体，我们可以用图表示如下：

这两个要素是紧密相连而且彼此呼应的。很明显，我们无论是要找出拉丁语 arbor 这个词的意义，还是拉丁语用来表示"树"这个概念的词，都会觉得只有那语言所认定的联接才是符合

① 音响形象这个术语看来也许过于狭隘，因为一个词除了它的声音表象以外，还有它的发音表象，发音行为的肌动形象。但是在德·索绪尔看来，语言主要是一个贮藏所，一种从外面接受过来的东西（参看第35页）。音响形象作为一切言语实现之外的潜在的语言事实，就是词的最好不过的自然表象。所以动觉方面可以是不言而喻的，或者无论如何跟音响形象比较起来只占从属的地位。——原编者注

101

实际的，并把我们所能想象的其它任何联接都抛在一边。

这个定义提出了一个有关术语的重要问题。我们把概念和音响形象的结合叫做符号，但是在日常使用上，这个术语一般只指音响形象，例如指词（arbor 等等）。人们容易忘记，arbor 之所以被称为符号，只是因为它带有"树"的概念，结果让感觉部分的观念包含了整体的观念。

如果我们用一些彼此呼应同时又互相对立的名称来表示这三个概念，那么歧义就可以消除。我们建议保留用符号这个词表示整体，用所指和能指分别代替概念和音响形象。后两个术语的好处是既能表明它们彼此间的对立，又能表明它们和它们所从属的整体间的对立。至于符号，如果我们认为可以满意，那是因为我们不知道该用什么去代替，日常用语没有提出任何别的术语。

这样确定的语言符号有两个头等重要的特征。我们在陈述这些特征的时候将同时提出整个这类研究的基本原则。

二、共时与历时的区分

【导　读】

索绪尔先通过两个比拟形象地说明了语言的共时态与历时态之间的关系：二者就像物体在平面上的投影与物体之间的关系；也像树干的横面与断面之间的关系。然后将语言的运行比之于下棋：二者都有共时态和历时态。从共时的角度看，语言中的各项要素因为彼此之间的对立关系而获得价值，就像棋子之间因为彼此之间的相对位置而获得价值；下棋有规则，共时的语言系统也有规则。从历时的角度看，一个棋子的移动可能会影响整个棋局，就像语言中一个要素的变化可能会引起整个系统的变化。二者的不同之处在于，棋子的移动是有意的，而语言要素的变化通常是无意的、偶然的。

§4. 用比拟说明两类事实的差别

为了表明共时态和历时态的独立性及其相互依存关系，我们可以把前者比之于物体在平面上的投影。事实上，任何投影都直接依存于被投影的物体，但是跟它不同，物体是另一回事。没有这一点，就不会有整个的投影学，只考虑物体本身就够了。在语言学里，历史现实性和语言状态之间也有同样的关系，语言状态无异就是历史现实性在某一时期的投影。我们认识共时的状态，不是由于研究了物体，即历时的事件，正如我们不是因为研究了，甚至非常仔细地研究了不同种类的物体，就会对投影几何获得一个概念一样。

同样，把一段树干从横面切断，我们将在断面上看到一个相当复杂的图形，它无非是纵向纤维的一种情景；这些纵向纤维，

127

如果把树干垂直切开，也可以看到。这里也是一个展望依存于另一个展望：纵断面表明构成植物的纤维本身，横断面表明这些纤维在特定平面上的集结。但是后者究竟不同于前者，因为它可以使人看到各纤维间某些从纵的平面上永远不能理解的关系。

但是在我们所能设想的一切比拟中，最能说明问题的莫过于把语言的运行比之于下棋。两者都使我们面临价值的系统，亲自看到它们的变化。语言以自然的形式呈现于我们眼前的情况，下棋仿佛用人工把它体现出来。

现在让我们仔细地看一看。

首先，下棋的状态与语言的状态相当。棋子的各自价值是由它们在棋盘上的位置决定的，同样，在语言里，每项要素都由于它同其它各项要素对立才能有它的价值。

其次，系统永远只是暂时的，会从一种状态变为另一种状态。诚然，价值还首先决定于不变的规约，即下棋的规则，这种规则在开始下棋之前已经存在，而且在下每一着棋之后还继续存在。语言也有这种一经承认就永远存在的规则，那就是符号学的永恒的原则。

最后，要从一个平衡过渡到另一个平衡，或者用我们的术语说，从一个共时态过渡到另一个共时态，只消把一个棋子移

128

动一下就够了，不会发生什么倾箱倒箧的大搬动。在这里，历时事实及其全部细节可以得到对照。事实上：

（a）我们每下一着棋只移动一个棋子；同样，在语言里受变化影响的只有一些孤立的要素。

（b）尽管这样，每着棋都会对整个系统有所反响，下棋的人不可能准确地予见到这效果的界限。由此引起的价值上的变化，有的是零，有的很严重，有的具有中等的重要性，各视情况而不同。一着棋可能使整盘棋局发生剧变，甚至对暂时没有关系的棋子也有影响。我们刚才看到，对语言来说，情况也恰好一样。

（c）一个棋子的移动跟前后的平衡是绝对不同的两回事。所起的变化不属于这两个状态中的任何一个；可是只有状态是重要的。

在一盘棋里，任何一个局面都具有从它以前的局面摆脱出来的独特性，至于这局面要通过什么途径达到，那完全是无足轻重的。旁观全局的人并不比在紧要关头跑来观战的好奇者多占一点便宜。要描写某一局面，完全用不着回想十秒钟前刚发生过什么。这一切都同样适用于语言，更能表明历时态和共时态之间的根本区别。言语从来就是只依靠一种语言状态进行工作的，介于各状态间的变化，在有关的状态中没有任何地位。

只有一点是没法比拟的：下棋的人有意移动棋子，使它对整个系统发生影响，而语言却不会有什么予谋，它的棋子是自发地和偶然地移动的——或者无宁说，起变化的。由 hanti 变为 Hände "手"，gasti 变为 Gäste "客人"的"变音"（参看第

129

122页）固然造成了一个构成复数的新方法，但是也产生了一个动词的形式，如由 tragit 变为 trägt "搬运"等等。要使下棋和语言的运行完全相同，必须设想有一个毫不自觉的或傻头傻脑的棋手。然而这唯一的差别正表明语言学中绝对有必要区别两种秩序的现象，从而使这个比拟显得更有教益。因为在有意志左右着这类变化的时候，历时事实尚且不能归结到受自己制约的共时系统，如果历时事实促使一种盲目的力量同符号系统的组织发生冲突，那么情况就更是这样了。

三、语言的价值

【导 读】

在这里，索绪尔强调语言的价值源自语言的系统，准确地说，是由系统中语言符号的差别性造成的。语言没有先于语言系统而存在的概念或声音，只有由系统发出的概念差别

☯ 思考题

1. 说说语言与言语的区别与联系。

2. 下面这段话出自莎士比亚的《罗密欧和朱丽叶》，从中可以看出语言的什么性质？

What is a name? That which we call a rose, by any other name would smell as sweet.

—Shakespear

3. 考察自己方言和普通话的词汇差异，或者与同学比较各自方言之间的词汇差异，证明语言符号的任意性。

4. 试从语言符号形式和意义的角度分析"指鹿为马"中的语言学问题。

5. 举例说明什么是语言符号的聚合关系和组合关系。为什么说二者是相互依存的？

6. 找一段中英文对应材料，比较汉语和英语，说说两种语言用词和语法规则的差异，比如肯定句变否定句的规则。

7. 试着造一个具有递归性的句子。

▯ 拓展阅读书目

▢ Steven Pinker. 1997. *The Language Instinct: How the Mind Creates Language*. Harper Perennial Modern Classics.中译本：［美］史蒂芬·平克. 语言本能：探索人类语言进化的奥秘（第四章、第五章）. 洪兰，译. 汕头：汕头大学出版社，2004.

▢ P. H. Matthews. 2003. *Linguistics: A Very Short Introduction*. Oxford: Oxford University Press. ［英］P. H. 马修斯. 缤纷的语言. 戚焱，译. 南京：译林出版社，2008.

▢ ［美］萨丕尔. 语言论. 陆卓元，译，陆志韦，校订. 北京：商务印书馆，1985.

語

第三章

语音与音系

语音学（phonetics）所关心的是语音的构造、数量、性质以及类别；音系学（phonology）则探究语音的组织规律，为了达到这个目的，必须先找出语音分布环境的特性，进而预测语音在帮助辨别词义的同时，如何随环境而变化。

本章先介绍语音学（第一节），再介绍音系学（第二节）。语音学的内容如下：语音的标音和基本单元（一）、语音类别——辅音和元音（二）、语音特征（三）、超音段（四）。音系学部分则包含了：音位与音位变体（一）、最小对立组和互补分布（二）、语音层面与音位层面的转写记音（三）、音系规则（四）、音位组配制约（五）、蕴含定律（六）、如何进行音系分析（七）。

第一节　语　音

语音学（Phonetics）所关心的是语音的构造、数量、性质以及类别。音素（phones 或speech sounds）是构成语言的最小形式。与"声音"（sounds）不同的是，音素承载着语言表达的功能。音素可以分为辅音、元音、音高和韵律。人类语言的语音数目庞大，但不是无限大，因为人类的发音器官构造还是有其限制的，而且有一些音人类虽然能够发出，却不用来承载语言功能。理论上，人只要生理健康，不论其种族或社会背景，都有条件能发出世界上所有的语音。语音学可以从三个方面进行研究：发音语音学（articulatory phonetics）研究语音发音生理机制，声学语音学（acoustic phonetics）研究语音的传递以及物理原理，听感语音学（auditory phonetics）研究语音的感知。本章的讨论将着重在发音语音学，但也会部分提及语音的声学原理。

一、语音的标音和基本单元

（一）国际音标（IPA）

本章的语音皆以国际音标符号标注。之所以不是用目前现有的语言文字系统，主要是考虑到文字系统的一些限制。既然是标音的系统，如果不是全由反映语音的符号或部件构成，就不纳入考虑。在此要求下，形音义皆表的汉字就先被剔除在名单之外了。但即使是以拼音为原则的系统（如英文、韩文、藏文、希伯来文等），内部呈现的形音对应也不一致。例如同样是 [f] 这个音，在英文father和enough两个词里却分别用f和gh表示；反之，同一种拼写组合也可能对应不同的语音，如house "房子"和enough "足够"中的ou，一个读成 [aw]，一个读成 [ʌ]。再者，就算一种语言使用拼音文字，且形音对应整齐一致，也不见得能使用同一套系统记录拼写另一种语言。比如说，英语look和Luke这两个词的元音不同，而且混淆的话就无法准确分别语义，但在汉语的拼音方案中就不区别这两种元音。

目前语言学界普遍使用的标音符号系统是从1888年发展至今的国际音标（International Phonetic Alphabet，简称IPA）。这一套记音系统的原则是为每一个语音派定一个专属的符号，这些符号用方括弧（[　]）加以标记，表示该记音是语音层面的，而且不是任何一种语言专属的文字系统。例如，英语在this这个词中用th拼写的音，在IPA中用的是 [ð] 这个符号，而根据IPA的使用原则，不论哪种语言出现这个音，一律都以 [ð] 这个符号标记。例如，西班牙语也有 [ð] 这个音，那么不论是英语或西班牙语，都一律用同一个符号 [ð] 来标记。

语言	文字拼写	IPA书写	释义
英语	this	[ðɪs]	"这"
西班牙语	hada	[ɑðɑ]	"仙女"

使用IPA记音，可以让不同的语言学家在记录并呈现语音的时候有统一的符号标准。一个人只要知道每个IPA所代表的语音，就可以阅读任何语言学家用IPA转写的语言材料，了解其语音的系统和性质；同样地，使用IPA记录一种语言，就可以使其他语言学家认识这种语言。

（二）音段

音标的字母是用音段（segment）的形式来体现人的说话。音段也就是个别的语音，如 [t]、[z]、[n]，等等。当我们第一次听到一种全新的语言，并且想将连续的语流切分成一个个单独的音时，往往会发现极其困难；而当我们聆听自己的母语时，我们其实比较关切词义，放在单个语音的注意力比较少。不过，即使如此，任何语言的使用者都可以识别出自己母语的语音，这是因为人对自己的母语语音的变化和组合样式有充足的知识，所以可以将连续的语流拆解成一个个基本单元，也就是音段。

二、语音类别：辅音和元音

音段可以下分为两大类：辅音（consonant）和元音（vowel）。这两类音可以从发音、感知及功能这三方面来区别。

从发音方面说，发辅音的时候，人的声道会因为发音器官的调节，形成气流的阻塞，这样的阻塞可以是部分阻塞或者完全的闭塞；换句话说，气流可能必须从缩小的紧窄处穿过，或者暂时完全被阻挡。而发元音时，声道形成的阻碍极其微小。辅音可以是带声的（voiced，可称为浊辅音），即发音的时候声带振动；也可以是不带声的（voiceless，可称为清辅音），也就是发音的时候声带不震动；元音则一般是带声的。

从感知上来说，元音的响度比辅音大，所以元音听起来比辅音大声，而且持续时间较长。

而从功能上来说，响度较大的音段容易成为音节的核心（nucleus）。"音节"（syllable）在这里的定义是最响的音段配上周围响度较低的音段的组合，像cat [kæt] "猫"，awe [ɔ] "敬畏"都是一个音节的词（awe [ɔ] 只有一个音节核心，周围没有响度较低的音段与之搭配组成这个音节）；children ['tʃɪldrən] "儿童（复数）"有两个音节；battery ['bætəri] "电池"有三个音节。实际上当我们在数音节数的时候，我们在数的是元音的数量。不过有些语言中，也有响度较大的辅音作音节核心，例如，分布于中国西南的永宁纳语就会以浊辅音［v］作音节核心。

不过要注意的是，以上辅音及元音的区别有一个灰色地带，处于这个灰色地带的是滑音（glide）（见后面讨论"通音"的部分）。滑音在成阻程度及响度方面都与元音相仿，但是在功能定义上是辅音。所以，滑音是介于辅音和元音两大类之间的一类音。

（一）辅音

辅音可以用发音部位（places of articulation）及发音方式（manners of articulation）来加以描写、界定和分类，以下分别介绍发音部位及发音方法。

[1] 发音部位

发音部位是人能加以调节造成气流受阻，因而发出不同的音的部位。双唇、口腔、咽壁及声门都是可以进行调节的区域，如图3-1所示。

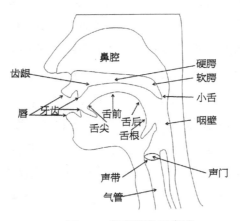

图3-1　发音部位示意图

以下介绍的语音类别就是利用这些发音部位的调节运动所发出的。

唇音（labial）：在发音的时候，嘴唇如果闭合或几乎闭合，就是发出唇音。如果发音时牵涉到两片嘴唇的运动，发出的是双唇音（bilabial），而使用下唇与上排牙齿的音则是唇齿音（labio-dental）。汉语普通话既使用双唇音，也使用唇齿音。例如，"把"［pa²¹⁴］使用双唇音［p］，而"发"［fa⁵⁵］则使用唇齿音［f］。

齿音（dental）：发齿音的时候，舌尖顶住牙齿或接近牙齿，也可以置于上下齿之间发出齿间音（interdental）。汉语普通话没有齿间音，但英语有。英语的this［ðɪs］"这"、though［ðow］"虽然"、thing［θɪŋ］"事情"、thaw［θɔ］"解冻"等词中用th拼写的音［ð］

和 [θ] 就是齿间音。

齿龈音（alveolar）：齿龈是在上排门牙后方突出的一小块隆骨。齿龈音，又称"舌尖前音"，就是将舌头顶住或靠近齿龈所发出的音。以下几个汉语普通话的例子就是齿龈音开头的："搭" [ta⁵⁵]、"他" [tʰa⁵⁵]（辅音右上方的h是送气符号，下同）、"撒" [sa²¹⁴]。

腭龈音（palato-alveolar）：腭龈音，又称"舌叶音"，其发音部位有一部分是硬腭，也就是齿龈后方一块陡然升高、呈圆顶状的区域。腭龈辅音在英语中的例子有show [ʃow]"秀"中的 [ʃ]、measure ['mɛʒəʳ]"测量"中的 [ʒ]、chip [tʃʰɪp]"晶片"中的 [tʃ]、judge [dʒʌdʒ]"法官"中的 [dʒ]。

卷舌音（retroflex）：发卷舌音的时候，舌尖朝向硬腭和齿龈隆骨的交界方向向后卷。卷舌音又称"舌尖后音"，汉语普通话有不少卷舌辅音（还有一个卷舌元音）。卷舌辅音的例子有："这" [tʂɤ⁵¹]、"撤" [tʂʰɤ⁵¹]、"社" [ʂɤ⁵¹]、"热" [ʐɤ⁵¹]，其中的卷舌辅音以下划线标示。

龈腭音（alveo-palatal）：龈腭音，又简称"舌面前音"，成阻的方式是舌前向齿龈隆骨靠拢。龈腭音的符号有 [ɕ]、[ʑ]、[tɕ]、[dʑ] 等。波兰语有 [ɕ]、[ʑ] 两个龈腭音。汉语普通话"切""街"的第一个音是典型的龈腭音，IPA的转写是 [tɕʰɤ⁵⁵]、[tɕæ⁵⁵]。

硬腭音（palatal）：如果舌是顶住或接近硬腭，发出的音就是硬腭音，又简称"舌面中音"。英语yes [jɛs] 的第一个音就属于硬腭音。汉语客方言中，"妇人"的"人"发音是 [ɲin²¹]，是以硬腭鼻音开头，不可读成齿龈鼻音 [nin²¹]。

软腭音（velar）：口腔内圆顶的后缘有一块柔软的区域，称为"软腭"（velum）。以舌后抵住或接近这个区域所发出的音就是"软腭音"，又称"舌面后音"或"舌根音"。普通话的"刚" [kaŋ⁵⁵]、"康" [kʰaŋ⁵⁵]、"航" [xaŋ³⁵] 等词都以软腭音开头和结尾。

小舌音（uvular）：在软腭后缘正中悬垂的小圆锥体叫作悬雍垂，俗称"小舌"（uvula）。舌后顶住或接近这个部位所发的音就是小舌音。法文用r这个字母书写的音在法国的法语中读成小舌音，国际音标记为 [ʁ]，如法语的"红色"rouge [ʁuʒ]。

咽音（pharyngeal）：在小舌与喉头（也就是声带所在位置）之间的管腔叫作咽腔（pharynx）。发咽音的时候，舌根后缩使咽腔空间缩小，气流从该狭窄的通道经过。最为人知的带咽音的语言应该是阿拉伯语。例如，[ħæ:l]"条件"，就是一个以咽擦音开头的词。

声门音（glotttal）：两条声带之间的空间就是声门（glotis）。借助于调节声门开合所发的音就是声门音（带声与不带声的区别除外），国内习称"喉音"。英语的hot [hat]"热"以及hay [hei]"干草"两个词就是以声门擦音开头的。

[2] 发音方法

嘴唇、舌、软腭和声门可以用不同的方式调节气流，以发出不同种类的音。换句话说，若发音器官成阻的位置相同，但调节气流的方式不同，所造成的音质就会有变化。这些不同的调节方式就叫作"发音方法"。

口腔音（oral）和鼻音（nasal）：发音方法的最基本的一个区别是分出口腔音和鼻音。发口腔音的时候，气流只从口腔通过。发鼻音的时候，软腭降下打通咽腔和鼻腔，如此气流便能从鼻腔通过。辅音和元音都能有口腔音及鼻音的区别。

塞音（stops）：发塞音的时候必须在口腔的某个部位有短暂的完全闭塞。鼻辅音虽然在鼻腔有气流通过，但在口腔需完全闭塞成阻，因此也属于塞音。在世界语言中，塞音的发音部位囊括了双唇、齿、齿龈、卷舌、硬腭、软腭、小舌及声门。在汉语普通话中，塞音的发音部位包括双唇、齿龈和软腭。以下的例子除了"桑"之外，全都以塞音开头。汉语普通话没有以软腭鼻音开头的字，软腭鼻音只能出现在末尾。

双唇
爸 [pa⁵¹]　　　　怕 [pʰa⁵¹]　　　　慢 [man⁵¹]
齿龈
大 [ta⁵¹]　　　　踏 [tʰa⁵¹]　　　　南 [nan³⁵]
软腭
尬 [ka⁵¹]　　　　卡 [kʰa²¹⁴]　　　　桑 [saŋ⁵⁵]

在汉语普通话中，塞音进一步区别送气与不送气，送气是辅音除阻后元音开始前一个释放气流的空档，过程中听得见呼气声，例如，"爸" [pa⁵¹] 和"怕" [pʰa⁵¹] 就是靠送气与否分辨的，前者不送气，后者送气。送气（aspiration）在国际音标用小号字符 [ʰ] 来表达。

擦音（fricatives）：发擦音时，口腔发出持续的气流。持续的气流元音和滑音也有，但是发擦音时口中要形成极窄小的间隙，这样空气从其间通过时就会制造出摩擦的噪音。英语的擦音有几对是呈清浊差异的，如表3-1所示。

	清（不带声）		浊（带声）
f	fast [fæst] "快的"	v	vast [væst] "广阔的"
s	sip [sɪp] "啜饮"	z	zip [zɪp] "拉链"
θ	thigh [θaɪ] "大腿"	ð	thy [ðaɪ] "你的"
ʃ	ashore [aˈʃor] "在岸上"	ʒ	azure [ˈeʒɚ] "蔚蓝"

表3-1 英语擦音的清浊对立

和英语的情形不一样，汉语普通话的擦音中，只有卷舌擦音有清浊的区别，如表3-2所示。

部位	清（不带声）		浊（带声）	
唇齿	f	[fa⁵⁵] 发		
齿龈	s	[sa⁵⁵] 撒		
腭龈	ɕ	[ɕi⁵⁵] 溪		
卷舌	ʂ	[ʂuo⁵⁵] 说	ʐ	[ʐuo⁵¹] ¹若
声门	h	[ha⁵⁵] 哈		

表3-2 汉语普通话的擦音

塞擦音（affricates）：发塞擦音的时候，声道首先完全闭塞，但在除阻时并不像塞音一样马上完全放开，而是在一开始先逐渐形成狭窄的间隙，然后才完全除阻。正如其名称"塞擦音"所显示的那样，塞擦音有塞音的完全闭塞与初始除阻，但在完全除阻前形成的狭窄间隙则会有气流通过产生摩擦声，摩擦阶段的时长比单独的擦音短。汉语普通话的塞擦音有齿龈和腭龈两个部位，分为送气与不送气，"擦"和"掐"都是送气塞擦音（aspirated affricates），请看表3-3。

部位	不送气		送气	
齿龈	t͡s	[t͡sa³⁵] 杂	t͡sʰ	[t͡sʰa⁵⁵] 擦
腭龈	t͡ɕ	[t͡ɕa⁵⁵] 家	t͡ɕʰ	[t͡ɕʰa⁵⁵] 掐

表3-3 汉语普通话的两组塞擦音对立情况

闪音（tap/flap）：闪音是肌肉快速收缩一次松开，使发音器官瞬间接触后即分开。美式英语的t和d在非重音音节常会读成闪音，例如，letter "信"的发音是 [ˈlɛɾəl]。闪音的原文有tap和flap两种名称，其区分原则为齿龈闪音称为tap，其他部位的闪音则称为flap。闪音和塞音最大的区别是前者不会在闭塞部位后方积累气压，所以除阻时也没有爆开的效果。

颤音（trill）：颤音在发音时，发音器官不是接触即分开，而是保持在一个位置上，通过气流的作用而颤动。西班牙语rosa [rosa] "玫瑰"的第一个音就是齿龈颤音。

通音（approximants）：通音在发音的时候，一个发音器官向另一个发音器官靠近，但制造的间隔并没有狭窄到气流通过时会产生摩擦声。根据IPA的分类，通音可分为一般通音和边通音（详见下面"边通音"的讨论）。一般通音传统上称为滑音（glide）。英语有

---

1 本章中以[ʐ]标注的音在汉语拼音以"r"标注，其他语音学研究也有将其性质认定为卷舌通音[ɻ]。本章以蔡莲红与孔江平（2014）《现代汉语音典》之声学分析为基础，统一将汉语拼音标注为"r"的音处理为卷舌浊擦音[ʐ]。

三个一般通音：[ɹ]、[j]、[w]。[ɹ] 是齿龈通音，例子有red [ɹɛd]“红的”；[j] 是硬腭通音，是yes [j̱ɛs] 这个词的第一个音；[w] 是英语的water [w̱ɑtəɹ]“水”开头的音，在发这个音时，除了舌后向软腭隆起，双唇也同时噘起作圆唇状“圆唇软腭音”，因为涉及两个发音部位，所以 [w] 被称为唇软腭（labio–velar）通音。

边通音（lateral approximants）：简单地说，以 [l] 为基础调节带声与否和发音部位的通音都属于边通音。在发边通音的时候，空气从舌头放低的两边逸出，所以当我们保持 [l] 的音姿不除阻，同时倒吸一口气的时候，会感觉舌的两边凉凉的。当舌尖抬高顶到齿龈或门齿后时，就是齿龈边通音或齿边通音，两种都可以转写成 [l]。因为边通音一般是带声的，所以“边通音”这个词单独使用时通常是指“浊边通音”。当然，边通音也可以不带声，清边通音的转写方式是在 [l] 这个符号下方加一个圈作附加符号（在IPA中称为“变音符”（diacritic））。在许多藏语方言中，西藏首府“拉萨”的“拉”读成 [l̥a]，其开头就是一个清边通音。

表3–4是将龈腭音纳入的国际音标辅音表，以2005年IPA颁布的辅音表为基础。

国际语音学会描写辅音的参数顺序为：清浊—送气与否—发音部位—发音方法；国内的描写顺序则是：发音部位—送气与否—清浊—发音方法。例如，[p]，根据国际语音学会的描写顺序为：清—不送气—双唇—塞；根据国内的描写顺序则是：双唇—不送气—清—塞。

Consonants (Pulmonic)	Bilabial	Labio-dental	Dental	Alveolar	Palato-alveolar	Retroflex	Alveo-palatal	Palatal	Velar	Uvular	Pharyngeal	Glottal
Plosive	p b			t d		ʈ ɖ		c ɟ	k ɡ	q ɢ		ʔ
Nasal	m	ɱ		n		ɳ		ɲ	ŋ	ɴ		
Trill	ʙ			r						ʀ		
Tap, flap		ⱱ		ɾ		ɽ						
Fricative	ɸ β	f v	θ ð	s z	ʃ ʒ	ʂ ʐ	ɕ ʑ	ç ʝ	x ɣ	χ ʁ	ħ ʕ	h ɦ
Lateral fricative				ɬ ɮ								
Approximant		ʋ		ɹ		ɻ		j	ɰ			
Lateral Approximant				l		ɭ		ʎ	ʟ			

在此表中，在一个格子中若有两个音，则左边的音为不带声，右边的音为带声。用阴影标示的区域是被认为不可能发出的音。

表3–4 国际辅音表

（二）元音

[1] 元音的性质与描写方式

元音是有响度、能成音节的音，在发的时候声道的开度比辅音大。调节舌头的摆放位置以及双唇的形状可以发出不同的元音。口腔的形状可以进一步通过噘起双唇的方式来改变，发出圆唇元音；若双唇没有噘起，则发出展唇元音；或者也可以通过降低软腭，发出鼻元音。

元音要如何掌握呢？发元音的时候，声道不像发辅音时那么狭窄，所以不容易一下子就感觉到发音器官的作用。要熟悉元音的发音，可以先交替地发“一”[i] 和“啊”[ɑ] 两个字，这样可以感觉到舌头从一个前高的位置移动到一个比较后、比较低的位置。舌头的位置大约如图3-2所示：

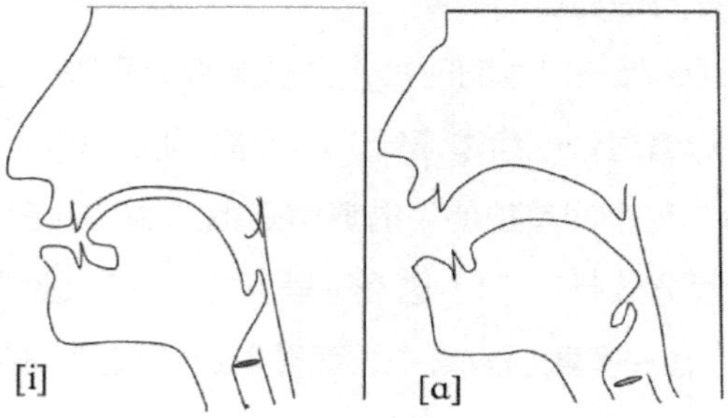

图3-2　[i] 和 [ɑ] 发音对比图

当我们交替地读“一”[i^{55}] 和“五”[wu^{214}] 这两个字时，就会发现舌头在前高及后高的位置来回移动，除此以外，在发 [u] 元音的时候，双唇是噘起来的，如图3-3所示：

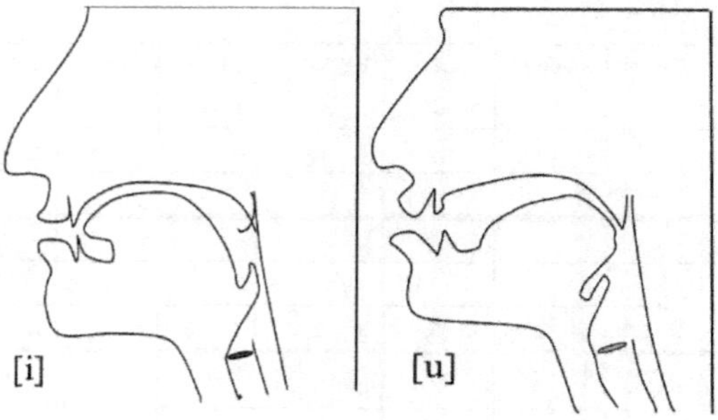

图3-3　[i] 和 [u] 发音对比图

如果一个元音在发音的时候，舌头没有抬高或降低的话，就会发出“中元音”。汉语的“给”[kei^{214}]、“被”[pei^{51}] 里面的核心元音 [e] 是前中展唇元音；“欧”[ou^{55}] 这个字的核心元音 [o] 则是后中圆唇元音。[ei]、[ou] 都是复元音，也就是在单一音节中发音位置改变的元音。对复元音的发音描述是以核心元音的舌位为主（见下文对复元音的讨论）。表3-5汇总描写汉语普通话元音的基本参数。按照国内的惯例，这些参数的顺序是：前后—高低—圆唇/展唇。

汉字与拼音	元音（音标）	语音描写
力　lì	[i]	前高展唇
路　lù	[u]	后高圆唇
绿　lǜ	[y]	前高圆唇
乐　lè	[ɤ]	后中展唇
辣　là	[ɐ]	央低展唇
类　lèi	[ei]	前中展唇
漏　lòu	[ou]	后中圆唇

表3-5　汉语普通话主要元音及其语音描写

图3-4为国际音标的元音总汇。这个倒梯形大致对应到舌头移动的空间，在口腔的上部比较大，底部比较小。这个图将前后分成三个区域：前（front）、央（central）、后（back）；高低则四分：闭（close，表示口腔开合度最小）、闭中（close-mid）、开中（open-mid）、开（open，表示口腔开合度最大）。同一个点出现成对儿的元音，左边的是展唇，右边的是圆唇。注意［ɪ］、［ʏ］、［ʊ］不落在图中的任何点上，传统上将它们分析为"松"元音（lax vowels）。与［i］、［y］、［u］相比，松元音［ɪ］、［ʏ］、［ʊ］的舌位较低，且朝中央靠拢。

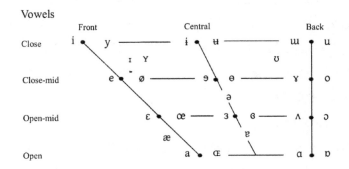

图3-4　国际音标元音

（其中央低展唇的 ［ɐ］ 在国内的转写惯例是以 ［A］ 标示）

[2] 单元音与复元音

汉语普通话的元音和英语一样，可以分为两大类：单元音（simple vowels）和复元音（diphthongs）。单元音是指在发音的过程中音质（quality，这里指的是舌位及声道形状）没有明显转变的元音。"车"［tʂʰɤ⁵⁵］、"莫"［mo̠⁵¹］、"辣"［lɐ⁵¹］、"肚"［tu̠⁵¹］、"西"［ɕi⁵⁵］、"徐"［ɕy³⁵］、"儿"［ɝ³⁵］这些词的元音都是单元音。复元音是在一个单一的音节中呈现音质改变的元音，也就是舌头从一开始的元音发音位置移到另一个元音或者一个滑音（一般是［j］或［w］）的位置。这种音质的改变在以下汉语普通话的字里可以清楚听到："来"［lai³⁵］、"画"［huɐ⁵¹］、"快"［kʰuai⁵¹］、"岁"［suei⁵¹］、"小"［ɕiɑʊ²¹⁴］。

单元音			二合复元音			三合复元音		
汉字	拼音	音标	汉字	拼音	音标	汉字	拼音	音标
怕	pà	［ɐ］	排	pái	［ai］	萧	xiāo	［iɑʊ］
破	pò	［o］	配	pèi	［ei］	酒	jiǔ	［iou］
特	tè	［ɤ］	跑	pǎo	［ɑʊ］	快	kuài	［uai］
力	lì	［i］	漏	lòu	［ou］	贵	guì	［uei］
鲁	lǔ	［u］	加	jiā	［ie］			
吕	lǚ	［y］	列	liè	［ie］			
耳	ěr	［ə］	挂	guà	［uɐ］			
			拓	tuò	［uo］			
			月	yuè	［yɛ］			

表3-6　汉语的单元音和复元音

英语的复元音一般是被分析为"元音—滑音"的组合。例如，house "房子"的复元音会标记成［aw］，而gate "大门"这个词的复元音则是［ej］。有关复元音的界定，语言学家还有许多工作可做。英语的元音如果在音质上有变化，并且音质的改变是发生在核心元音之后，就会被定为复元音。但是像yet［jɛt］和wet［wɛt］这样的词就被视为开头是一个滑音辅音，而不是与［ɛ］构成［滑音—元音］这样的复元音。然而，在对其他语言（如芬兰语）的元音分析中，［jɛ］和［wo］的组合就被当成复元音。复元音在跨语言的研究中是否能达到统一的转写，还有待更深入的分析。

［3］鼻元音（nasal vowels）

鼻元音和鼻辅音一样，在发音的时候都会把软腭降下来。空气同时从口腔及鼻腔逸出。英语、法语、葡萄牙语、北印度语以及不少汉语方言都有鼻元音。这些鼻元音在国际音标系统中用一个放在元音符号上方的波浪符号［~］来转写。

英语：　　　　　　　　pan　［pæ̃n］　　　　　　　　"平底锅"
葡萄牙语：　　　　　　grande　［grã̃di］　　　　　　"大的"
法语：　　　　　　　　pain　［pɛ̃n］　　　　　　　　"面包"
波兰语：　　　　　　　zomb　［zɔ̃p］　　　　　　　　"牙齿"

三、语音特征

语音可以按不同特征来分类。本节依次介绍：几种常用来给语音分大类的特征、发音部位特征、发音方式特征、一些常用来为元音分类的特征。

（一）常见的主要特征

[辅音性]（[consonantal]）：具有辅音性的语音发出时，在口腔中形成的阻塞比元音所需的阻塞大。阻塞音（obstruents，包含塞音、擦音及塞擦音）、边通音以及鼻辅音都是[+辅音性]。通音，如[j]、[w]等，虽然也是一种辅音，但是发音时口中阻塞极小，与元音相仿，也因此[j]、[w]在部分文献中被称为"半元音"或"半辅音"，而且在[辅音性]这个特征上被视为带负值，即[−辅音性]。

[音节性]（[syllabic]）：这个特征是针对语音能不能作音节的核心来说的。音节性为正值的语音并不只有元音，边通音、鼻辅音和浊擦音都可以具有音节性。英语的dazzle"耀眼"这个词本来音标可以标注为['dæzəl]，但实际上快读的时候不需通过中间的央元音[ə]，而是直接从[z]连接边通音[l]，这样，[l]就担负了音节核心的功能：['dæzl̩]（在辅音下的一小竖是国际音标[音节性]的标记）。中国有许多方言都有鼻辅音单独成音节的词，例如，闽南语的"黄"就读成[ŋ³⁵]。阻塞音和通音都没有音节性，因为它们永远伴随元音出现，由元音担任音节的核心。

[响音性]（[sonorant]）：所有噪音较低（即没有摩擦所产生的不稳定气流）而且可以在某个音高上持续发出的音都具有响音性。有这个特征的音包括元音、通音（[j][w]等）、边通音（[l]）和鼻音（如[m] n [ŋ]），发音的时候共鸣可以持续。阻塞音没有这个特性，所以是[−响音性]。擦音也是阻塞音，虽然可以持续发出，但发音时噪音较高，所以也没有响音性。鼻辅音虽然在口腔有完全的闭塞，但是空气仍持续从鼻腔出来，持续在鼻腔发出共鸣，所以也是响音。

[鼻音性]（[nasal]）：无论是辅音、元音或是通音，只要发音的时候软腭降下使气流从鼻腔通过，就是[+鼻音性]的辅音。

将这些二元的特征组合起来，就可以让我们描述以下的音类：阻塞音、元音、通音、成音节的辅音等。一个特征若标示为 ±，表示该音类可带也可不带该特征。

	阻塞音	元音	通音	成音节的辅音
[辅音性]	+	−	−	+
[音节性]	−	+	−	+
[响音性]	−	+	+	+
[鼻音性]	−	±	−	±

表3-7　音类的语音特征二元表示法

（二）发音部位特征

下面是以发音部位为依据的语音特征。

[唇音]（[labial]）：只要发音时需要唇部的参与就带唇音的性质。有唇音性的音包括双唇音 [p]、[b]、[m]，唇齿音 [f]、[v] 和唇软腭音 [w]。

[龈前]（[anterior]）：龈前音是齿龈及其之前的部位成阻发出的音，包括双唇音 [p]、[b]、[m]，唇齿音 [f]、[v]，齿间音 [ð]、[θ]，齿龈音 [t]、[d]、[s]、[z]、[n]、[l]、[ɹ]。不在这个部位成阻的音包括软腭音、喉音、龈腭音、腭龈音和元音。

[舌冠]（[coroal]）：舌尖与舌前上抬而发出的音属于舌冠音。舌冠音包括齿间音 [θ]、[ð]，齿龈音 [t]、[d]、[s]、[z]、[n]、[l]、[ɹ]，腭龈音 [ʃ]、[ʒ]、[tʃ]、[dʒ]，卷舌音 [tʂ]、[dʐ]、[ʂ]、[ʐ] 以及龈腭音 [ɕ]、[ʑ]、[tɕ]、[dʑ]。

[高]（[high]）：舌位比中性位置高的音都具有 [+高] 的特征，硬腭及软腭辅音以及高元音都是这样的音。

[低]（[low]）：发音时舌位比中性位置低，且在口腔中发出的音就具有 [+低] 的特征，此特征描述低元音以及小舌辅音等。

[后]（[back]）：所有在口腔中硬腭后方所发的音都具有 [+后] 的特征。在汉语普通话中，软腭音是 [+后]。

以上 [高]、[低]、[后] 三个特征都说到口腔中成阻的位置，而声门塞音 [ʔ] 和擦音 [h] 这两个音因为是通过调节声带形成阻塞，不是在口腔中成阻，所以 [高]、[低]、[后] 三个特征都带负值。

（三）发音方式特征

语音特征还可以从发音方式上进行分类。

[连续性]（[continuant]）：这个特征是指在口腔中没有完全闭塞的音。在这个条件下，塞音和塞擦音因为都在口腔形成完全闭塞，所以是 [−连续性]。擦音虽然在口腔中成阻，但是没有完全闭塞，所以就可以算是 [+连续性]。至于鼻音，虽然空气一直连续从口腔逸出，但是口腔有完全的闭塞，所以不是连续音。

[延缓除阻]（[delayed release]）：这个特征描述这样一种情形：从塞音的完全闭塞逐渐除阻，缓慢到足以产生一个类似擦音的音之后才完全除阻。所有的塞擦音都是 [+延缓除阻]。

[咝音性]（[sibilant]）：辅音还可以按照声学性质分出"咝音"这个类。发咝音的时候，发音器官趋近摩擦，发出频率很高的咝咝声。常见的咝音有 [s]、[z]、[ʃ]、[ʒ]、[tʃ]、[dʒ]、[ts]、[dz]。

[**带声**]（[**voice**]）：这个特征指的是声门的状态。如果声带振动的话，以[+带声]表达；如果声带不振动，就以[−带声]表达。

[**送气**]（[**aspirated**]）：辅音会有送气和不送气辅音的区别。例如，汉语的"爸"[pa⁵¹]和"怕"[pʰa⁵¹]的区别就在于前者的辅音不送气，而后者送气。

[**边音**]（[**lateral**]）：这个特征可以用来区别边通音（也就是[l]这一类的音）和一般通音（如英语的[j]一类的音）。[l]和[j]在英语中都是[+连续性]的音，所以用[边音]这个特征区分开，也就是[l]是[+边音]，[j]是[−边音]。

音段（元音或辅音）可以用一组语音特征来表述。综合上面介绍的语音特征，下面通过几个例子来呈现音段如何用语音特征加以表述。

语音特征	p	pʰ	f	m	d	kʰ	tʃ	l	j	h
[辅音性]	+	+	+	+	+	+	+	+	+	+
[音节性]	−	−	−	−	−	−	−	−	−	−
[响音性]	−	−	−	+	−	−	−	+	+	−
[鼻音性]	−	−	−	+	−	−	−	−	−	−
[龈前]	+	+	+	+	+	−	−	+		−
[舌冠]	−	−	−	−	+	−	+	+	+	−
[高]	−	−	−	−	−	+	−	−	−	−
[低]	−	−	−	−	−	−	−	−	−	−
[后]	−	−	−	−	−	+	−	−	−	−
[连续性]	−	−	+	−	−	−	−	+	+	+
[延缓除阻]							+			
[咝音性]	−	−	−	−	−	−	−	−	−	−
[带声]	−	−	−	+	+	−	−	+	+	−
[送气]	−	+	−	−	−	+	−	−	−	−

表3-8　辅音语音特征矩阵图

（四）元音的其他发音特征

元音的发音是用舌头在口腔中做成不同形状，所以上面用来描述辅音的几个特征——[高]、[低]、[后]——都可以用来描述元音。此外，还有一些上面没提到，但也常用来描述元音的特征。

[**圆唇**]（[**round**]）：需要噘起嘴唇作圆唇发出的元音，如[o]、[u]等，都是[+圆唇]。

[**紧**]（[**tense**]）：这是指如英语元音[i]—[ɪ]、[ej]—[ɛ]、[æ]—[ɑ]、[u]—

[ʊ]、[ow]—[ɔ] 之间的分别。传统上认为，相较于 [ɪ]、[ɛ]、[ɑ]、[ʊ]、[ɔ]，在发 [i]、[ej]、[æ]、[u]、[ow] 的时候声道的肌肉比较紧张，所以是 [+紧]；而与它们相对的元音就是松元音，舌位较低，且向中央靠拢，用 [−紧] 来表示。

　　下面是针对一部分汉语普通话元音的特征所建立的矩阵。因为所有的元音都是 [+音节性]、[−辅音性]、[+响音性]，所以不列在矩阵中。复元音的特征所标示的是核心元音的音质。在这个矩阵中，所有的元音用同样一套特征表述，并且因为每个元音所带的特征正负值不同，因此可以彼此区分开。例如，[i] 和 [y] 在 [高]、[低]、[后] 这三个特征上取值相同，但在 [圆唇] 这个特征上，[i] 带负值，[y] 带正值，所以就区分开了。而 [u] 和 [o] 两个元音都是后圆唇元音（[+圆唇]、[+后]），也都不是低元音（[−低]），然而 [u] 是高元音，所以带 [+高]，而 [o] 是中元音，所以是 [−高]，因此 [高] 这个特征区分了二者。

	i	y	ei	ɐ	u	o	ɤ
[高]	+	+	−	−	+	−	−
[低]	−	−	−	+	−	−	−
[后]	−	−	−	−	+	+	+
[圆唇]	−	+	−	−	+	+	−

表3-9　汉语普通话元音特征矩阵

四、超音段

　　到目前我们已经讨论了辅音的发音部位和发音方法；元音的舌位高低、圆唇展唇等；也讨论了语音的分类依据、各种语音特征等。这些都是属于"音段"（segmental）层次的特性。这一节来介绍其他的语音特征：音长、语调、声调和重音。这些特征被归为"超音段"（suprasegmental）特征，因为其表现是"覆盖在音段之上"的。我们只要听见单单一个音段，就足以开始描述这个音段的语音特性；但是，如果要从这个音段析出某个超音段特征，则几乎是不可能的。要掌握超音段特征，必须将不同的音段拿来比对。有些超音段特征甚至可以覆盖到数个音段上，在这种情况下就需要比对不同的语段。

（一）音长（Length）

　　辅音和元音都有可能用较长或较短的音长来发，也就是发得长一些或短一些。要注意的是，这里的"音长"并不是指随着情绪、互动需要或是否赶时间等生理、社会及环境因素而随意调节成可长可短的语音时长。在火车离站时对送行的朋友急促地说话，音段都比较短；将英文词里的字母一个一个拼给学生听，音段都拉长了。像这样的长短并不是固定伴随音段出现的。要确认一个语言的辅音或元音是否分成长短两类，就必须在音段之间作比较。世界上有不少语言，会在同一个（辅音或元音）音段上调节音长，并造成语义的不同。在这些语言中，音长变化所代表的意义，是和元音调节舌位高低前后一样重要的，长元音和短元音的差别，就和 [i] 相对于 [a] 一样承载着辨别词义的功能。因此如果将一个词中的短元音替换成一个音质一模一样，只是比较长的元音，其结果可能是说成了一个完全不同的词。

区别元音音长的语言众多，比如，意大利语、匈牙利语、德语、希伯来语、日语、芬兰语等就是这样的语言。首先来看日语的例子。在表3-10中，左列的元音 [i]、[a]、[u] 拉长之后，即使周围的音段组合都不变，也变成了另外三个语义完全不同的词（右列所示）。在下面的语料中，长元音和长辅音后面都以尖端上下相对的迷你三角标示 [:]；短元音和短辅音则不带这个符号。

短元音		长元音	
[ozisaɴ]	"叔叔"	[ozi:saɴ]	"爷爷"
[obasaɴ]	"阿姨"	[oba:saɴ]	"奶奶"
[tuki]	"月亮"	[tu:ki]	"气流"

表3-10 日语长短元音辨义实例

芬兰语也有元音长短的对立。下面芬兰语的例子中，短元音 [u]、[a]、[e]（左列）拉长了之后（右列），语义也变了，如表3-11所示。

短元音		长元音	
[muta]	"泥土"	[mu:ta]	"另外的"
[tapan]	"（我）杀"	[tapa:n]	"（我）遇见"
[tule]	"来（命令式）"	[tule:]	"（他）来"

表3-11 芬兰语长短元音辨义实例

辅音以长度区别的语言也不罕见，芬兰语、土耳其语、日语、意大利语和匈牙利语都已证实在辅音音段上有长短的调节。下面的例子是意大利语以辅音长短区别对立的词汇。左列和右列是截然不同的词汇，但它们在语音上的差别仅为辅音 [t]、[s]、[n] 的长短。

短辅音		长辅音	
fato [fatɔ]	"宿命"	fatto [fat:ɔ]	"事实"
casa [kasa]	"房子"	cassa [kas:a]	"盒子"
fano [fanɔ]	"小树林"	fanno [fan:ɔ]	"（他们）做"

表3-12 意大利语长短辅音辨义实例

（二）音高（Pitch）

音高是基频（fundamental frequency）在心理层面的联系，基频高低取决于声带的振动速度，速度越快，基频越高。声带振动的速度是通过控制声带的紧张程度以及调节通过声门的气流量达成的。在发元音或响辅音时，如果声带拉紧、气压较大，会使音段听起来有较高的音高；如果声带较不紧绷、气压较低，则音高就降低了。人不管说什么语言，都有能力控制自己说话的音高。在世界的语言中，有两种超音段的语音特征是通过音高的变化来体现的，那就是声调和语调。

在许多语言中，一个词用什么音高呈现会造成词义的差异，因此声调（tone）的基本定义是有区别性的音高。如果一种语言在区别词义的时候是通过音高来实现的，这种语言就被称为"声调语言"（tone language）。声调语言遍布全球各地，亚洲有泰语、越南语、中国境内各种汉语方言、部分藏语方言以及其他汉藏语系语言、苗语、瑶语，等等；新几内亚的语言，如斯构语；非洲的祖鲁语、卢干达语、修纳语、伊博语、约鲁巴语，等等；北美及南美的印第安语言，如阿帕奇语、纳瓦霍语，等等。

声调语言和非声调语言的音高变化在功能上是非常不同的。一个英语的使用者可以用扬升的音高说water，也可以用一个平平的音高曲线读出water这个词，这样的变化并不会改变water"水"的基本词义。但是在汉语普通话中，如果将"水"所带的低降升调替换成高降调，就变成了另一个词："睡"。在非声调语言中，如法语和英语，不存在音高别义现象。对汉语普通话的母语者来说，声调改变词义是系统性的，例如，"妈""麻""马""骂"。表3-13是大家经常用到的一个例子。如例子所示，一模一样的音段组合用不同的声调读出来，语义也就不同。

汉字	音段（音标）	调型
妈	[ma]	高平
麻	[ma]	升
马	[ma]	低降升
骂	[ma]	高降

表3-13 汉语普通话四声别义实例

声调按音高曲线走势可以分为两种：平调（level tone，又称为"音域调"（register tone））和曲拱调（contour tone）。所有的声调语言都有平调，也就是能在一个相对稳定的音高上发出一个音节。平调按照音高的高低可分为高调、中调和低调等。曲拱调是在一个音节内从一个音阶滑到另一个音阶的调型。例如，从低调滑到高调的是一种升调（当然也可以从低滑到中，或从中滑到高）；而从高调滑到低调（也有可能从中滑到低，或从高滑到中）是一种降调。汉语普通话只有一个平调，也就是高平调，如"妈"的声调，其他都是曲拱调，其中"马"带了一个低降然后升高的音高曲线，所以这是一个"低降升"的曲拱调。

声调的标记方式有很多种，使用哪一种标记方式，关键看语言需要划分出几种声调的对立，以及记录材料的用途为何。音系学上习惯将音段及超音段（这里指声调）分在两层，然后将音高与音节核心用线连接起来。上面提到的汉语普通话的四个声调，就可以这样表示：

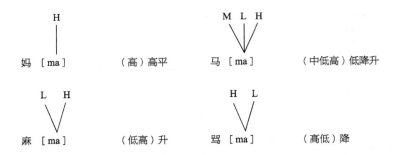

当然，汉语普通话的材料在标声调的时候，常使用赵元任提出的"五度标调法"（five-scale system），也就是把声调的相对音高分为低、半低、中、半高、高五个等次，并分别用1、2、3、4、5表示。

五度制符号	相对音高
1	低
2	半低
3	中
4	半高
5	高

表3-14　赵元任的 "五度标调法"

按此原则，汉语普通话的声调调值可以呈现如下：

汉字	音段（音标）	调值	调型
妈	[ma]	55	高平
麻	[ma]	35	升
马	[ma]	214	低降升
骂	[ma]	51	高降

表3-15　汉语普通话调值与调型对应

另外，也可以使用类似标记重音那样的符号，在音节元音上加标记来体现声调。例如，汉语拼音就有一套标记声调的简易符号：

声调标记（普通话）	调型
[ˉ]	高平
[´]	升
[ˇ]	低降升
[`]	高降

表3-16　汉语普通话声调简易标示法

类似的标记在克雷威语（分布于坦萨尼亚的班图语支语言）中，标示的是不同的调型，这一套标记与国际音标的声调标记相符。

重音标记	调型
[´]	高调
[ˉ]	中调
[`]	低调
[ˇ]	升调
[^]	降调

表3-17　克雷威语调型标记

以下的克雷威语例子都是动词：

例子（音标）	调型	释义
[kùsàlà]	低-低-低	"疯狂愚蠢"
[kùsálà]	低-高-低	"切肉"
[kùʃǐːngà]	低-升-低	"得胜"
[kùkālâaːngà]	低-中-降- 低	"炸"

表3-18　克雷威语动词调型标记

需要注意的是，声调调值虽然取决于音高，但在一定程度上是看声调间相对的高低，而非绝对的差异。换句话说，一个声调只要能跟另一个声调区别开来即可。例如，一个说汉语普通话的人用低沉的声音所发出的高平调，其音高客观而言就会低于一个嗓音尖而高的女性所发出的高平调。因此，要确定一个音节是高调还是低调，需要比较同一个人所说的各种音节及其声调；当然，同一个人在不同时候也可能发出不同音域的音高。所以，声调的音高曲线在调查记录的时候必须严谨地考虑个人差异等因素。

声调语言一般都会使用声调来区别词义。在为数不少的声调语言中，声调的功能更强大，可以被当作语法标记。许多分布于非洲的声调语言都广泛地使用声调表达不同的语法范畴。在中国境内也有这样的声调语言，例如，在嘉戎语（四川境内汉藏语系语言）里，声调可以标示动词不同的语法范畴。如下面的例子所示，同样的音段组合（torjap）带上不同的声调调型，就分别表示命令式（"站起来！"）和完整体（"（他）站起来了"）的语义。

（命令式）　torjap　"站起来！"　　　（完整体）　torjap　"（他）站起来了"

　　与音高相关的另一个超音段特征是语调。如果音高的变化在语流中发生，而且不会造成词义的差别，那就是语调（intonation）。例如，在英语中用扬升或下降的音高曲线来读seven这个词，都不会造成语义的差别。请试着用不同的音高变化来读下面的英语句子，看看会得到什么结果。我们可以在末尾的地方用扬升的音高或下降的音高读，或者用任何可以想到的语调模式来读：

　　You walked all the way home "你一路走了回来"

　　当前针对语调有五花八门的分析方式，最为普遍接受的一个假设是：有两个韵律参数在语调调型的形成上起着关键的作用，这两个参数分别是韵律重音（prosodic accents）和边际调（edge tones）。

　　韵律重音通常涉及一段话语中基频、音量和音长的显著变化。带韵律重音的词可能会比周围的词都要高、长或响亮，所以在听感上是一段话语中非常显著的部分。一个语段中并不是所有的词都能带韵律重音。请朗读下面的例子，带韵律重音，也就是特别显著的词，用大写字母加以标示。你会发现可以用同一个句子回答不同的问题，关键在于让不同的词带上韵律重音。

　　Juliana ate THE PEAR. （可能情况：有一个梨和一个苹果，Juliana吃掉梨，没吃苹果。）

　　JULIANA ate the pear. （可能情况：有几个人都看见了梨，但最后是Juliana把它吃掉的。）

　　边际调指的是出现在一个语句结尾处的音高变化。在英语中，最常见的边际调是在语段末尾扬起来或降下来，而且往往随着对话参与者的互动而调节。例如，Fred parked the car这句话结尾如果带有下降的音高曲线，通常表示这个语段结束。因为这个缘故，在一个语段末尾下降的语调被称为终止语调调型（final intonation contour）。至于扬升或平的语调则通常表示语段尚未终止。用英语读清单和电话号码，一项接着一项读的时候，会在每一项末尾听见扬升或平的语调，一直到最后一项，才会以下降的音高曲线结束。英语的问句也常带末尾扬升的语调，这也可视为一种未终止，因为说话者在等待被问的人回答，所以互动尚未告一段落。当然，我们也知道在英语中带who、what、when、how等疑问词的问句一般不以扬升的语调结尾。有一个可能性是疑问词本身已经足够传达对答案的期待，不需要未终止的语调来提示听话者。

（三）重音（Stress）

本章要介绍的最后一个超音段特征是重音。在任何语段中，有些音节就是听起来比其他音节显著。在psychological［sajkəladʒəkəl］"心理学的"这个词里面，有两个核心元音（［aj］和［a］）比其他的显著。听起来比较显著的音节就是带重音的音节。重音和声调一样，是整个音节的特征，不属于单个的音段。它是一个涵盖了音高、响度（loudness）和音长三个不同参数的统称，这三者加总的结果就是音节的显著性。

在不同的语言中，这些重音参数的比重也不同。大致来说，在英语中与不带重音的音节相比的话，带重音的音节体现出较高的音高、较长的音长、较大的响度。但并不是非这样不可。比如，在psychological这个词中，带重音的音节可能有时候读出来在音高方面比不带重音的低。换句话说，重音音节可能会完全满足音高、音长和响度这三个参数的要求，但也可能只满足其中一个或两个，无论如何只要比周围的音节显著就可以了。

在英语以外的语言中，上面提到的体现音节显著性的参数可能在使用上与英语不同。例如，现代希腊语，音节的长度都一样，所以重音不用音节长度体现，只用音高和响度来表达。另一方面，声调语言不用音高的曲线变化来标示重音，很多都是以增加元音音长或将原有音高曲线的调域加宽（也就是音高最高点和最低点之间的差距加大，曲线的幅度也变大）等手段来表达重音。

在语音的转写系统中，标示重音的方式很多。北美的转写通常把上标重音标记［'］放在音节前来表示最显著或者主要的（primary）重音，同时把一个下标重音标记［ˌ］放在另一个音节前表示第二显著或者次要的（secondary）重音。例如，psychological这个词的主要重音和次重音可以这样打标记：

$$［ˌsajkə'ladʒəkəl］$$

另外还有一种标记法，是在带重音的元音上方标数字，1标示主要重音，而2标示次重音。所以psychological这个词的重音用数字表示，就会是这样：

$$［\overset{2}{sa}jkəl\overset{1}{a}dʒəkəl］$$

和上面讨论语调时介绍的韵律重音不同的是，重音是有区别意义的作用的。例如，下面的两个英语词的音段组合一模一样（export［εksport］），但是将主要重音放在不同音节上，就造成了词义（词类）的差异：

ex'port　　　　［εks'pɔrt］　　　　"出口　（动词）"

'export　　　　［'εksport］　　　　"出口物　（名词）"

第二节　音　系

　　语音学和音系学研究的对象都是语音，但是关心的层面是不一样的。语音学关心的是语音是如何发出来的、语音的物理特性以及相关的生理机制。音系学则探究语音的组织规律，这牵涉到人类运用这些规律时所参照的语言知识。受具体的语言系统制约，语言在日常使用的时候会出现丰富的语音变化。有的变化是语言以外的情况导致的，例如疲劳、兴奋、感冒，甚至咀嚼食物都会导致发出的音有差异。这种差异不是音系学所关心的差异。另一方面，许多语音的变化是呈系统且有规律的，它们通常是由音段所处的语音环境所制约。换句话说，有些语音会受到邻近语音特性的影响而发生改变。每一个语言的使用者都有能力析出这种系统性的变化，以便掌握一个语言重要的对立区别。音系学家一直致力于能清楚且准确地表述语音在一种语言中的组织分布，找出其分布环境的特性，进而预测语音在帮助辨别词义的同时，如何随环境而变化。

一、音位与音位变体

　　"音系学"一词中的"音系"是"语音系统"的简称。在音系的研究中，语言学家致力于将语音之间不同的关系梳理清楚，并按照所确认的条理为一种语言的语音分门别类。每一类所囊括的语音或许音质有异，但母语者都会判定为"相同"的音。例如，［p］和［pʰ］在英语被归成同一类的音，但是［pʰ］和［b］就隶属于不同的类，因为后面这一对儿有辨义的功能。也就是说，如果将一个英语词里面的［pʰ］抽出来，以［b］替换，有可能引起语义的改变，例如 bike［bajk］"自行车"相对于 pike［pʰajk］"梭鱼"，只有开头的辅音不一样，但是语义就相去甚远。但另一方面，对汉语普通话的母语者来说，［p］和［pʰ］就有辨义作用，如"爸"［pa4］和"怕"［pʰa4］的差别只在辅音一个是［p］，另一个是［pʰ］，就是两个不同的词。这个事实就引出了"音位"的基本定义：最小的能区别语义的语音单位。

　　如果有两个以上的语音在音质的层面上类似，而且呈现互补分布（也就是一个语音的分布环境和另一个语音的分布环境从不重复），这些语音是音位变体（allophones），而这些音位变体的集合单位叫作"音位"（phonemes）。音位不只是用来归纳音位变体的一个方便的符号，它更体现了语言知识。我们从来不会念出一个音位，我们所发出的都是音位变体。但是有许多证据显示，语言使用者在认知系统中归纳语音时，其脉络大致上反映出音位的格局。音系学的一个主要内容就是要论证一种语言有哪些音位，这些音位的变体有哪些，各自出现的环境和条件是什么。

　　在美式英语中，用t来拼的音其实有以下几种不同的读法：

two ［tʰu］ "二"	stew ［stu］ "炖菜"
kitty ［kɪɾi］ "猫咪"	eaten ［iʔn̩］ "吃（过去分词）"

从上面这些例子我们可以观察到，two中的t是送气的，这个在国际音标中我们用［tʰ］来表示；但是到stew这个例子的时候，我们会发现t不送气：［t］。而在kitty这个词中，t的发音其实是闪音（flap），在国际音标中用［ɾ］标示。而在eaten这个词，t的发音其实是喉塞音［ʔ］。这里所介绍的［tʰ］、［t］、［ɾ］、［ʔ］都是英语的/t/这个音位的音位变体：

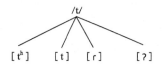

由上可知，音位符号是放在两条斜线中间，而其音位变体置于方括弧中。

　　在英语中［t］和［tʰ］是同一个音位/t/的音位变体；但是在汉语普通话中，［t］和［tʰ］就不属于同一个音位了。普通话的使用者无法将两者视为同一个音的不同变化，因为这两个音具有辨义功能。从以下的表3-19，就可以看出在普通话中有不少例子读起来几乎一样，差别只在于开头的辅音是否送气：

杜［tu⁵¹］	大［ta⁵¹］	地［ti⁵¹］
吐［tʰu⁵¹］	踏［tʰa⁵¹］	替［tʰi⁵¹］
对［tui⁵¹］	逗［tou⁵¹］	到［tao⁵¹］
退［tʰui⁵¹］	透［tʰou⁵¹］	套［tʰao⁵¹］

表3-19　汉语普通话中送气与不送气辅音对立实例

由此可见，在汉语中，[t] 和 [tʰ] 并不是同一个音位的音位变体，而隶属不同的音位。

音位与音位变体的分析要成立，必须凭依在一个基础上，那就是要假定一个个语言的音系有两个层面：比较具体的那一层牵涉到语音音段的物理实现层面，也就是音位变体；另一个层面上的音位，则比较抽象。有的语言学家根据这个假定，进一步将音位视为语音储存在人脑里的形式。换句话说，音位是心理层面的抽象概念，它们无法在言语中直接被感知到或观察到，我们能观察到的只有音位变体。

二、分析音位和音位变体：最小对立组和互补分布

（一）最小对立对儿、最小对立组

音位是具有区别词义功能，彼此对立的语音。要确认两个音是不同音位或者同是某音位的变体，最小对立对儿（minimal pair）的呈现是最基本有效的方式。如果两个词其他环境一模一样，仅仅是在同一位置上（比如开头或者结尾），有一个音不同，而且两个词表达的是不同的语义，这两个词就构成了最小对立对儿。像上面列出的"地"[ti⁵¹] 和"替"[tʰi⁵¹] 就是最小对立对儿。这两个形式有相同的元音、相同的声调，音段的排列顺序也相同，唯一不同的是声母（音节开头的辅音）：一个是 [t]，一个是 [tʰ]，因此，我们可以说两个词的语义对立主要是由这两个对立的音造成的。

以下列举一些反映汉语普通话中辅音对立的例子。这些最小对立对儿有相同的元音和相同的声调，唯一的不同是做声母或韵尾的辅音。以这些最小对立对儿为依据，我们可以说以下划线所呈现的辅音在汉语普通话都属不同的音位：

不 [pu⁵¹]	铺 [pʰu⁵¹]	/p/ vs. /pʰ/
毒 [tu³⁵]	图 [tʰu³⁵]	/t/ vs. /tʰ/
搞 [kao²¹⁴]	烤 [kʰao²¹⁴]	/k/ vs. /kʰ/
麻 [ma³⁵]	拿 [na³⁵]	/m/ vs. /n/
脚 [tɕiao²¹⁴]	巧 [tɕʰia²¹⁴]	/tɕ/ vs. /tɕʰ/
早 [tsao²¹⁴]	草 [tsʰao²¹⁴]	/ts/ vs. /tsʰ/
蒸 [tʂəŋ⁵⁵]	曾 [tsəŋ⁵⁵]	/tʂ/ vs. /ts/
森 [sən⁵⁵]	深 [ʂən⁵⁵]	/s/ vs. /ʂ/
生 [ʂəŋ⁵⁵]	深 [ʂən⁵⁵]	/ŋ/ vs. /n/

现在来观察下面这一对普通话的例子：

  住 [tʂu⁵¹]   卒 [tsu³⁵]

这两个字在"辅音—元音"的组合上呈现了最小对立，但是另一个语音环境——声调没有被满足（一个是降调一个是升调），因此"住"[tʂu⁵¹]和"卒"[tsu³⁵]只能算是"近似最小对立对"（near minimal pair）。在找不到最小对立对的时候，适当地使用近似最小对立对，还是可以帮助确立对立的音位。

  呈现音位对立的相同环境，有可能不只呈现两个对立的音位，而是能扩大范围，让许多对立的音都在相同的语音环境出现。这种两个词以上的语音对立被称为"最小对立组"（minimal set）。表3-20这个庞大的最小对立组确定了以下几个音位：/p/ vs. /pʰ/ vs. /t/ vs. /tʰ/ vs. /k/ vs. /kʰ/ vs. /m/ vs. /n/ vs. /l/ vs. /ʐ/ vs. /f/ vs. /h/ vs. /tʂu/ vs. /tʂʰ/ vs. /ʂ/ vs. /tsʰ/ vs. /s/ vs. /w/。

/p/	/pʰ/	/t/	/tʰ/	/k/	/kʰ/
不 [pu⁵¹]	铺 [pʰu⁵¹]	杜 [tu⁵¹]	吐 [tʰu⁵¹]	顾 [ku⁵¹]	酷 [kʰu⁵¹]
/m/	/n/	/l/	/ʐ/	/f/	/h/
慕 [mu⁵¹]	怒 [mu⁵¹]	路 [lu⁵¹]	入 [ʐu⁵¹]	复 [fu⁵¹]	护 [hu⁵¹]
/tʂu/	/tʂʰ/	/ʂ/	/tsʰ/	/s/	/w/
住 [tʂu⁵¹]	处 [tʂʰu⁵¹]	树 [ʂu⁵¹]	醋 [tsʰu⁵¹]	速 [su⁵¹]	误 [wu⁵¹]

表3-20　最小对立组实例

  在第二节第一部分已经提过，语音对立的格局是因语言而异的。我们已经知道 [t]和 [tʰ]之间的对立在汉语普通话极其重要，把 [t] 误读成 [tʰ]很有可能造成语义的不同（如"递上"读成了"替上"）。但是，普通话这种清塞音送气和不送气的的对立，在其他的语言不一定有。我们如果将英语的 [t] 和 [tʰ] 互换，比如 ['stʌdi] 读成了 ['stʰʌdi]，听的人还是会知道读的是study"研究、学习"这个词，只是发音比较奇怪而已。因此，我们可以说英语中 [t] 和 [tʰ] 之间不存在对立关系，它们都属同一个音位/t/：

为语言建立彼此对立、具有辨义功能的音位系统是音系分析的第一步。当然，每种语言都会有许多语音是彼此之间不存在对立关系的，不具有辨义功能的语音变化在所有的语言中都非常普遍。接下来我们要讨论这样的语音变化，看看音系学如何处理并掌握这些变化。

（二）互补分布

如果仔细记录英语母语者的l这个字母的发音，我们会发现至少有两种区别较为显著的发音方式。比对一下下面两列l的读法，我们会发现左边一列的l是带声的，而右边一列的l是不带声的（想发不带声的l，可以用说悄悄话的气音，以l的发音方式和部位来发）：

"吹"	blow	[blow]	"犁"	plow	[pl̥ow]
"高兴的"	glad	[glæd]	"拍手"	clap	[khl̥æp]
"翻转"	flip	[flɪp]	"请"	please	[pl̥iz]
"滑动"	slide	[slaɪd]	"云"	cloud	[kl̥aʊd]
"笑"	laugh	[læf]			

右边一列的之所以不带声，是其语音环境使然。它的变化非常规律，只要前面紧邻清塞音，l就毫无例外地会以不带声的形式出现，因为在这个环境里，只会出现不带声的 [l̥]，而带声的 [l] 则出现在其他的语音环境中，所以我们可以说 [l] 与 [l̥] 呈现出互补分布（complementary distribution）：

> [l̥]： 在清塞音之后
>
> [l]： 其他的环境

所谓"其他的环境"指的就是带声的 [l] 所出现的应用环境更广、更多样化。如上所示，带声的l出现的环境包括了词首的位置以及浊塞音、清擦音之后。

尽管在语音的体现上有所不同，但是英语的母语者将两个英语的l视为同一个辅音，因为：①它们的语音性质相仿；②两者之间的差异是有条理且可预测的。在英语中，两种l从来没有被用来造成语义的对立。所以，我们可以说，对英语的使用者来说，两种l在语音的层面不同，但是在音系的层面是一样的。换句话说，[l] 和 [l̥] 都是音位/l/的音位变体。

（三）自由变体（free variation）

最小对立组和近似最小对立组可以帮助我们为一种语言建立语音对立格局；语音的相似性以及互补分布可以帮助我们决定哪些音是同一个音位的不同变体。不过，不是所有的语音变化都可以用这些分析方式迎刃而解。

有些语音彼此相似，但既不呈现互补分布，也不会引起语义的差异。当然，还是有可能将它们归纳为同一个音位的音位变体，词尾的清塞音就是这样的情况。像wait "等待"这个词中的t，有时候说话者会做一个明显除阻的动作，t还可能伴随明显的送气，读成 [wejtʰ]；有时候则不除阻，一直停留在成阻的姿势上，读成 [wejt̚]（加一个不除阻的标记）。这样的语音差异既不造成语义的不同，出现环境都一样，但又在语音层面上是类似的，因此我们说这两个不同的t是同一个音位的音位变体，这种变体是一种自由变体。

三、语音层面与音位层面的转写记音

因为语音可以用两个层次（语音及音系）来分析，所以在符号的表现上需要让这两个层次的语音记录有所区别。语音层次的记音将音标放在方括弧（[ ]）中，记音标载实际读音的特点，这个层面的标音一般称为"严式标音法"（narrow transcription）；音位层次的记音则将音标放在两条斜线中间，记录的是音位的信息，称为"宽式标音法"（broad transcription）。表3-21中的例子以前面对英语l及t的分析为基础，演示语音层面及音系层面标音在转写上的异同。

	语音标音	音位标音	英文拼写	释义
1	[pl̥ow]	/plow/	plow	"犁"
2	[blaɪnd]	/blaɪnd/	blind	"盲的"
3	[kl̥æp]	/klæp/	clap	"拍手"
4	[tʰu]	/tu/	two	"二"
5	[stu]	/stu/	stew	"炖菜"
6	[ˈkɪri]	/ˈkɪti/	kitty	"猫咪"
7	[ˈiʔn̩]	/ˈitən/	eaten	"吃（过去分词）"

表3-21 严式记音与宽式记音

读者若逐项对照两种标音，会发现在"语音标音"这列中第1个词的边音清化（[l̥]）、例4的塞音送气（[tʰ]）、例6的闪音（[r]）以及例7的喉塞音（[ʔ]）都没有在"音位标音"中被表现出来，因为这些特征的出现都是规律可预测的：边音/l/在清塞音后会清化（例1）、/t/在词首会送气（例4）、在两个元音间变闪音（例6）、在元音后鼻音前则变喉塞音（例7）。

依据上面的讨论，我们大致已经知道何为"语音的分布"。简单地说，一个语音的分布就是其出现环境的总和。语言学家分析语音的分布时，就是在归纳其出现的环境的各种特性。两个音之间的关系若是对立的，我们便很可能发现它们出现在一模一样的语音环境中，而且造成词义的不同，这样的环境帮助我们确定它们隶属不同的音位。两个音也可能呈现互补分布，其中一个音能出现的环境，另一个音无法存立，于是，我们能推定它们应该是同一个音位的音位变体，不过有一个重要前提，那就是两个音必须是相似的。具有自由变体关系的语音也可以出现在一模一样的环境中，但是不会造成语义的差异，它们也是同一个音位的变体。语音如果出现在最小对立组或自由变体的环境，我们无法通过分析语音环境来预测哪个音会出现；但如果语音呈现互补分布，那么，什么条件下出现哪一个音就是可以预测的。

四、音系规则

我们先来看以下几个前缀un-在不同语音环境里的变化，如表3-22：

拼写	音位标音	语音标音	释义
<u>un</u>bind	/ʌnˈbaɪnd/	[ʌmˈbaɪnd]	"解开"
<u>un</u>clear	/ʌnˈklɪr/	[ʌŋˈklɪr]	"不清楚"
<u>un</u>tomb	/ʌnˈtum/	[ʌnˈtʰum]	"发掘"
<u>un</u>ambitious	/ʌnæmˈbɪʃəs/	[ʌnæmˈbɪʃəs]	"没有野心的"
<u>un</u>fortunate	/ʌnˈfɔrtʃənɪt/	[ʌɱˈfɔrtʃənɪt]	"不幸的"

表3-22　前缀un-中n的分布环境

综合以上的分布，我们可以列出前缀un-中的n的分布：

> [n]在　　　　　[b]前　　　　　　　[m]
> 　　　　　　　[k]前　　　　　　　[ŋ]
> 　　　　　　　[t]前　　　　　　　[n]
> 　　　　　　　[æ]前　　　　　　　[n]
> 　　　　　　　[f]前　　　　　　　[ɱ]

可以看出，前缀un-中的n在变化后还是保持为鼻音，但是有一些例子里，[n]的发音部位会趋同于后面那个音的发音部位。归纳之后，我们得到以下的布局：

> [n]在　　　　　双唇音之前　　　　　　[m]（双唇鼻音）
> 　　　　　　　唇齿音之前　　　　　　[ɱ]（唇齿鼻音）
> 　　　　　　　软腭音之前　　　　　　[ŋ]（软腭鼻音）
> 　　　　　　　其他环境　　　　　　　[n]（腭龈鼻音——不变）

接下来我们将以上的观察整理成音系规律。需要注意的是，音系规律包含了三个部分：①受规律影响的音；②规律起作用的环境；③规律应用后的结果。在上面这个例子中，受到影响的音是/n/。当/n/的后面接的是双唇音、唇齿音、软腭音时，音系规律就会发挥作用。这条音系规律作用后的结果，就是/n/会采用后面相应那个音的发音部位。这样的规律可以用以下的格式表达出来：

$$X \rightarrow Y / A \underline{\quad\quad} B$$

在以上的规律表达中，X是受影响的语音（也可以称为目标音），箭头"$\rightarrow$"表示变化，Y则是规律作用后变化的音。斜线"/"的意思是"在……环境条件下"，斜线后是导致变化的环境条件。空白下划线"____"指的是受影响的音（也就是X）出现的位置，A是出现在其前的音，B则是出现在其后的音。这个规律用文字表述出来就是："X会变成Y，条件是它出现在A后以及B前。"所以，当我们掌握这样一条音系规律，又看见AXB的序列时，我们知道按照音系规律这序列会变成AYB。

拿上面/n/的变体来说，我们可以这样写规律：

[n] $\rightarrow$ [m] / ____双唇辅音

[n] $\rightarrow$ [ɱ] / ____唇齿辅音

[n] $\rightarrow$ [ŋ] / ____软腭辅音

[n] $\rightarrow$ [n] / ____其他环境

现在看看上面的语音形式如何从抽象的音位派生出来，如表3-23：

音位形式	/ʌnbaɪnd/ "解开"
规律应用：[n] $\rightarrow$ [m] / ____双唇辅音	ʌmbaɪnd
语音形式	[ʌmbaɪnd]
音位形式	/ʌnklɪr/ "不清楚"
规律应用：[n] $\rightarrow$ [ŋ] / ____软腭辅音	ʌŋklɪr
语音形式	[ʌŋklɪr]
音位形式	/ʌnfɔrtʃənɪt/ "不幸的"
规律应用：[n] $\rightarrow$ [ɱ] / ____唇齿辅音	ʌɱfɔrtʃənɪt
语音形式	[ʌɱfɔrtʃənɪt]

表3-23　音位、规律与语音关系例示

（一）音系特征的概念与应用

因为音段是由特征（features）组合而成的，所以，我们可以用特征这样一个概括的方式来呈现音位对立。所有的特征都有其语音学的基础，并且在变化发生的时候可以只由一个特征独立引起变化。换句话说，说话者可以调节好几个特征造成语音的变化，也可以只调节一个特征。下面的例子显示，汉语普通话的/p/和/pʰ/是对立的，可用特征表述如下：

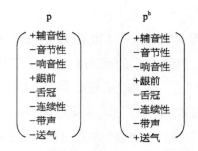

由以上的呈现可以看到，与音段呈现相比，特征体现看上去复杂许多。但是，就音系学的分析来说，这个呈现的方式是有优势的，因为两个音差别的远近也可以通过特征的比较来界定；而语音的变化，特别是音位变体的变化，可以用特征的增加、脱落或替换来表达，同时也能将制约环境的影响因素清楚地呈现出来。由汉语普通话/p/和/pʰ/的例子可以看到，两个音几乎一模一样，只有最后［送气］这个特征的值不同。在汉语普通话里与这种特征值差异（［+送气］vs.［−送气］）关联的对立音位就有好几对儿，可以系统性地归纳如表3−24：

［−送气］	［+送气］
p	pʰ
t	tʰ
k	kʰ
ts	tsʰ
tʂ	tʂʰ
tɕ	tɕʰ

表3−24　［送气］在汉语普通话的特征对立

同理，其他特征描述在汉语普通话里也都能造成对立，表3−25是靠［连续性］造成对立的音：

［−连续性］	［＋连续性］
p	f
t	s

表3-25　［连续性］在汉语普通话的特征对立

从上面这些例子可以看出，在特征呈现音段的时候，我们所使用的是音段的区别性特征（distinctive features），这些不能再分解的语言成分可以用来有效地表述一种语言的音位系统。这些特征的选取会随语言而有不同的考量，例如在英语中，用特征表述音段时，就不会用［送气］来描写塞音和塞擦音，也不会把［鼻音性］列入元音特征。这是因为在英语中，送气和元音鼻化都是音位变体的特征，因此在音位的系统中不会列入。

（二）自然类

在"（二）互补分布"一部分的开头，我们看到英语的l在不同的环境中会体现为带声的［l］或不带声的［l̥］两个变体。其分布环境归纳为：/l/在清塞音前变为［l̥］，在其他环境中则体现为［l］。这个分析以音系规则形式呈现如下：

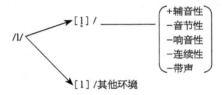

然而，若是深入观察，我们会发现在英语中，这个规则不仅能用在边通音/l/上，还能用在其他的语音/ɹ/、/w/、/j/上：

/ɹ/

"新娘"	bride	［bɹaɪd］	"自尊"	pride	［pɹ̥aɪd］
"绿色"	green	［gɹin］	"奶油"	cream	［kɹ̥im］
"自由"	free	［fɹ̥i］			
"切碎"	shred	［ʃɹɛd］			
"红色"	red	［ɹɛr］			

/w/

"人名（女）"	Gwen	［gwɛn］	"皇后"	queen	［kw̥in］
"缩小"	dwindle	［'dwɪndl̩］	"双胞胎"	twin	［tw̥ɪn］
"汗"	sweat	［sw̥ɛt］			

"湿的"	wet	[wɛt]			
/j/					
"美"	beauty	[ˈbjuɹi]	"纯净的"	pure	[pjuɹ]
"你的"	your	[juɹ]			

有没有可能用一条规则对英语的 /l/、/ɹ/、/w/、/j/ 加以归纳：这些音都会因为前面有清塞音而变为不带声（清音）？为什么这四个音都会遵从同一条音系规则？是巧合吗？要回答这些问题，我们首先要看这四个音的发音描述：

/ɹ/	腭龈通音
/w/	唇软腭通音
/j/	硬腭通音
/l/	齿龈边通音

这四个音不只都是通音，而且它们还是英语中所有的通音。因此，我们可以把其中的一些特征表述移除，用一个更概括的范畴把所有四个音都吸纳进来：

/ɹ/、/w/、/j/、/l/	通音

在英语中，提到"通音"就等于说到 /ɹ/、/w/、/j/、/l/。所以，它们这些通音形成了一个自然类（natural class）。如果在一个语言中有一群语音共享一个或多个发音或听觉特征，而除了这群语音之外再没有其他语音具备这个或这些发音或听觉特征，那么，这群语音就组成一个自然类。从另一个角度说，如果一群语音形成一个自然类，这个类一定包括所有共享一个或一组特征的语音，并且排除不带有该特征的语音。对英语来说，/ɹ/、/w/、/j/、/l/ 这个自然类可以用以下区别特征来表达：

$$
\begin{bmatrix}
-\text{音节} \\
+\text{响音} \\
-\text{鼻音} \\
+\text{带声}
\end{bmatrix}
$$

　　音系描写的一个主要目标就是提出语音规律，而且该规律越概括化、能解释越多的事实越好。自然类的概念，可以帮助我们达到这个目的。自然类所反映的就是我们做音系概括所能推展的范围。之所以如此，是因为人们早已发现音位及其音位变体并不是随机任意生成规律的；相反地，音系规律会以自然类为其运行范围。

　　在上面的描述中，造成英语通音产生 [−带声] 变化的环境也是一个自然类：清塞音。清塞音 [p, t, k] 是英语全部的清塞音，所以，在英语中它们组成了"清塞音"这个自然类。因此，我们可以用自然类的概念来陈述英语通音变成清音（不带声）的这条音系规则：

$$\begin{bmatrix} -音节 \\ +响音 \\ -鼻音 \\ +带声 \end{bmatrix} \longrightarrow [\,-带声\,]\ / \begin{bmatrix} +辅音性 \\ -音节性 \\ -响音性 \\ -连续性 \\ -带声 \end{bmatrix} \underline{\qquad}$$

上面的特征符号表述可以用文字叙述如下：

　　　通音会变成清音（不带声），条件是处于清塞音后。

　　有时用音系特征为语音分群时，除了界定单个音的特征外，还必须用到一些其他特征。例如，在汉语普通话中只有一个唇齿辅音，而且是一个擦音/f/，而双唇这个发音部位没有擦音，只有塞音、鼻音和通音。在许多情况下，将唇齿的/f/和双唇的/p，pʰ，m，w/归到一个自然类是有帮助的，这个自然类可以用"唇音"［labial］这个特征来概括。

　　另外一个常用来描述自然类的特征将音段分为两个群：阻塞音（obstruents）和响音（sonorants）。阻塞音在发音的时候，会形成气流的阻塞。这个类包括塞音、擦音和塞擦音。响音则是在发音的时候，气流通道相对比较无阻隔。响音音段包括鼻音、通音、边通音和元音。所以在英语中，齿龈阻塞音这一类包括［t，s，d，z］，而齿龈响音这一类则有［n，l，ɹ］。齿龈辅音这一类包括［t，s，d，z，n，l，ɹ］，若能进一步用［响音性］将其分为阻塞音和响音，对陈述音系规则是很有用的。

（三）常见的音系规则

[1] 同化

　　在同化（assimilation）的语音变化过程中，一个音会在某些语音性质上趋同于邻近的音。如果同化规则在一个音上面起作用，表示这个音接受了一个邻近音的特性，而变得比较像那个邻近的音。造成同化的语音性质可以用特征呈现，而这些特征可以是发音部位的同化，也可以是发音方法的同化。

　　同化是非常普遍的语音变化，例如英语的元音如果后面接着一个鼻音，元音就会带鼻音的性质，例如Sam"山姆（人名）"用美式英语的口音读一定会带鼻音：［sæ̃m］。这种增加鼻音性的同化被称为"鼻化"（nasalization），用文字表述为：

　　　元音会鼻化，条件是后面的音是鼻音。

用音系规则符号表述，就是：

　　V → ［+nasal］/ _____ ［+nasal］

在这个符号表述里，"V"代表"元音（vowel）"。在呈现语音环境的时候，不需要明确标出造成变化的环境是辅音，因为这个环境条件的关键是目标音之后是否为鼻音，所以，只要将关键的特征标出就可以了。

还有一种常见的同化现象是"腭化"（palatalization）。在这个变化中，一个音因为后面邻接硬腭音，所以也带了硬腭的性质，例如英语的Would you？如果说得比较自然、比较快，发音不会是［wʊdju］，而是将would这个词最后与［j］邻接的［d］腭化，读成腭龈音［dʒ］，所以上面这个Would you？的读音是［wʊdʒu］。

有时候一个语音在发音部位上的同化不是专指某个特定的部位，而是随着后面语音的发音部位作出改变，前面提到的英语前缀un-的例子（表3-22及以下）中［n］的发音就是这种部位同化，先将其规律重复如下：

［n］ ➝ ［m］ /_____双唇辅音

［n］ ➝ ［ɱ］ /_____唇齿辅音

［n］ ➝ ［ŋ］ /_____软腭辅音

［n］ ➝ ［n］ /_____其他环境

如果要用规则的符号表述来表达，就不需要将双唇、唇齿、软腭等部位特征都写入，而是可以这样写：

［n］ ➝ ［α发音部位］ /_____［α发音部位］

使用"α"这个符号的意思是语音环境（也就是［n］后面的音）呈现什么发音部位，［n］也会采用同样的发音部位（所以改变后的音和语音条件都带有α，互相参照）。

［2］异化

异化（dissimilation）与同化相反，经过异化，两个邻接的音会变得彼此相异。在这个情形下，有可能是一个音发生改变，也有可能是两个音都作出改变拉大彼此的距离。在英语中，fifth"第五"本来的语音是［fɪfθ］，但是在自然说话中，常被说成［fɪft］。这个变化的过程就是［θ］前面已有一个擦音［f］，所以变成了一个接近部位（由齿间到齿龈）的塞音［t］，拉大了它和［f］的差异。汉语普通话中，比较常见的异化的例子是两个上声相连时，前一个上声听起来像阳平，比如，"雨水"听上去像"鱼水"，"土改"像"涂改"。

［3］插入

在语音插入（insertion）的变化中，一个本来不存在的音段会被加到一个词的语音形式里面去。英语最常见的一个插入的例子，就是当复数标记/-z/加在一个咝音结尾的名词后时，央元音/ə/会插入咝音和复数的/z/后缀中间。这个规则用文字表述为：

将元音/ə/插入表示复数的后缀/z/之前，条件是名词是以咝音结尾的。

以符号形式表达如下，表述中/∅/是零，意思是原来是没有语音的：

∅→ə/ [+咝音性]_____z

［4］删除

语音的删除（deletion）是指一个原本存在于音位层次的音，到语音的层次被删掉了。在英语中，不带重音的音节或比较弱的元音和辅音较容易被删除。例如，restaurant "餐厅"这个词本来在音位层次的标音应该是/ˈɹɛstəˌɹɑɹt/，但是非重音音节的 [ə] 在口语使用的时候被删除，现行的标音已经是 [ˈɹɑʊɹzɑɹ] 了。

［5］换位

有一种音系规律是改变语音在序列中的排列顺序，这个变化称为"换位"（metathesis）。有些人说英语ask 这个词的时候，常常说成 [æks]；还有animal 应该读成 [ˈænəml̩] 却读成 [ˈæmənl̩]，等等，都是常见的换位现象。

［6］强化

语音如果应用"强化"（strengthening）这个音系规则，就会变得比较强，听起来也比较显著。英语清塞音的送气就是一例。例如/pope/ "主教"这个词读成 [pʰowp]，第一个/p/就是一个强化的送气的 [pʰ]，第二个/p/则一般不送气，除非在强调读音的时候，才会送气。

［7］弱化

弱化（weakening，又作lenition）是使语音变弱的音系规则。在英语中，/t/或/d/在非重音音节经常被闪音 [ɾ] 所取代，例如better "更好"这个词在美式英语常常读成 [ˈbɛɾɚ]，这就是一个语音弱化的过程。之所以说被闪音取代是弱化，是因为和 [t] 与 [d] 相比，[ɾ] 阻隔气流的时间比较短。

五、音位组配制约

音位组配制约（phonotactic constraints）所关切的是音位可以在哪个位置出现，以及如何与其他音位组配成序列。在介绍音位的组配原则之前，先对"音节"的概念作一个基本的讨论和界定。

（一）音节的界定

音节的组成是指一个音节核心（syllabic nucleus）——通常是元音——配上非音节性音段。一种语言的母语者可以毫无困难地数算任何词的音节数，这个事实证明人对音节这个音系结构单元是有意识的。英语的母语者应该会毫不迟疑地说accident这个词有三个音节，将其切分为/æk.sə.dənt/。音节结构的组成方式与音位组配法（phonotactics）关系密切。母语者在切分一种语言的音节时，不会违反这种语言的音位组配法。像extract /ɪkstɹækt/ "提取"这个词，母语者就不会切分为/ɪ.kstɹækt/，而是会遵守英语的音位组配法则，该法则禁止英语用kstɹ这样的序列，但可以允许stɹ，也允许元音后带辅音，所以可以切分为/ɪk.stɹækt/。

（二）音位组配的方式和原则

每一种语言对哪一种音位、哪一些音位序列会在一个音节的哪些位置出现，甚至哪些音位可以组配成序列，等等，都会有限制。这些限制都可以用音位组配制约（phonotactic constraints）的概念来阐释。最常见的音节组合是由一个辅音（C）后面接一个元音（V）组成，但是有些语言允许音节以一个以上的辅音开头。例如，英语就有词开头和（或）结尾最多有三个辅音的；不仅如此，英语还可以只用一个元音作音节的唯一成分。所以音节组成样式在英语中是相当丰富的，如表3-26所示：

V	VC	VCC	VCCC
awe /ɔ/ "敬畏"	itch /ɪtʃ/ "痒"	apt /æpt/ "合适的"	asked /æskt/ "问（过去）"
CV	CVC	CVCC	CVCCC
tea /ti/ "茶"	pot /pɑt/ "锅"	land /lænd/ "土地"	lamps /læmps/ "灯（复）"
CCV	CCVC	CCVCC	CCVCCC
flee /fli/ "逃走"	speed /spid/ "速度"	cramp /kɹæmp/ "痉挛"	crafts /kɹæfts/ "载具"
CCCV	CCCVC	CCCVCC	CCCVCCC
spree /spɹi/ "狂欢"	spread /spɹɛd/ "展开"	strength /stɹɪŋθ/ "力量"	strengths /stɹɪŋθs/ "力量（复）"

表3-26 英语的音节组配模式

不过，其他的语言可能就没有数目这么大的音节结构种类，先观察表3-27中汉语普通话和希伯来语的音节组配样式，注意这里的V包括了单元音和复元音：

汉语普通话	希伯来语
V	CV
CV	CVC
CVC	CVCC
	CCV
	CCVC#

表3-27　汉语普通话与希伯来语音节组配模式

如上所示，汉语普通话就没有辅音序列；而希伯来语则不允许元音单独作一个音节，并且CVCC这样的组合只能出现在词尾（#标示词的边界），而且最后的辅音必须是/t/。

　　上面表3-27同时反映了音位组配制约的另一项特性，就是它不仅规定元音和辅音的数量及位置，还会进一步限制哪些音或哪种音是可以组配、放在什么位置的。例如，在汉语普通话中，鼻音只有/n/和/ŋ/可以出现在元音后面，而/ŋ/不能出现在音节首。至于英语，则是除了 [ʒ] 和 [ŋ] 以外，所有的辅音都可以出现在音节首。这一点是专指英语的本土词而言，借词则不一定会遵从其组配原则。另外，英语还有为数众多的复辅音组合可以出现在音节首，其组合部件规定是一个塞音或擦音后面跟着通音（一般通音及边通音）。

塞音加通音		擦音加通音	
/gɹ/	green "绿"	/fɹ/	free "自由的"
/bl/	blue "蓝"	/sl/	slide "滑梯"
/bj/	beauty "美"	/hj/	humor "幽默"
/tw/	twice "两次"	/hw/	where "哪里"

此外，/s/后面也可以接清塞音和鼻音（如spy [spaj] "间谍"、snail [snejl] "蜗牛"），还可以接f和v（如sphere [sfɹ] "范围"）。/ʃ/后面可以接鼻音或通音/l/和/ɹ/，但是只有/ʃɹ/是英语的本土组合（如shrink [ʃɹɪŋk] "缩小"）。

　　最后，我们来看音位组配制约对英语最长的复辅音CCC在音节首的限制。先看表3-28中的几个例子：

例子	音标	音节首序列
spring "春天"	[spɹɪŋ]	[spɹ]
strip "长条"	[stɹɪp]	[stɹ]
squeak "吱吱作响"	[skwik]	[skw]
skew "歪曲"	[skju]	[skj]

表3-28　英语节首CCC式复辅音组配限制

这些例子反映出一个事实，在英语三合复辅音构造里，第一个音段永远是/s/；第二个音段必须是一个清塞音（在英语中就是/p/、/t/、/k/）；而第三个是通音（英语的四个通音/l/、/ɹ/、/w/、/j/）。这个组配方式可以表达如下，其中"$"是音节边界标记，放在三合辅音的左侧，表示这个三合辅音的位置在音节首。

$$\$ \quad s \left\{\begin{array}{l} p \\ t \\ k \end{array}\right. \left\{\begin{array}{l} l \\ ɹ \\ w \\ j \end{array}\right. V$$

（三）以音位组配制约原则划分音节

本部分开头的例子extract /ɪkstɹækt/ "提取"为什么要切分成/ɪk.stɹækt/而不是/ɪks.tɹækt/？这两种组合方式其实在表3-26的英语音节组配样式中都看得到，/ɪks.tɹækt/是VCC加上CCVCC。是什么原因让我们选择一种切分而放弃另一种呢？答案是音位组配制约原则。下面我们就来介绍以音位组配制约原则划分音节的手续。

每一种语言对音节结构的组成都有自己的要求，但是，会有一些大原则和具体语言专属的要素产生交互作用。这里以英语为例，演示大原则与语言专属的要素交互作用的情况：

第1步：每一个带音节性的音段（通常是元音）组成一个音节核心（用N来代表）。现将/ɪkstɹækt/中音节核心ɪ、æ用线连接到它上面的N，然后将N连到上面的音节符号"σ"。

第2步：从音节核心最左边开始找，只要辅音序列不违反该语言的音位组配法，就可以放在音节核心前作这个音节的节首（onset，以O代表）。将这些作节首的辅音连于O，并且让O和位于其右的音节核心连于同一个音节符号。

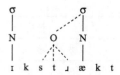

这一步在考量的时候，除了音节核心前的辅音数量（英语最多只有CCC）要纳入考量之外，另一个要考量的是词首CCC的组成音段的性质。从表3-28的讨论我们知道，英语的

CCC第一个辅音一定是s，第二是清塞音，第三是通音，所以将/stɹ/划为作节首的CCC复辅音是恰当的。

第3步：其他剩下的辅音就被归到音节核心的后面。辅音若位于音节核心后面，就被视为一个音节的"节尾"（coda，用C代表）。作节尾的辅音连到C，然后和位于其左的音节核心连于同一个音节符号。

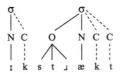

通过这个手续，我们就可以知道为什么extract要切分成/ɪk.stɹækt/，而不是用其他的组合方式了。如果切分成/ɪks.tɹækt/，步骤2没有被满足；如果切分成/ɪ.kstɹækt/，组成第二个音节节首的，是一个英语的音位组配制约所不允许的复辅音序列：第一，英语最长的复辅音必须以/s/开头，但是/kstɹ/以/k/开头；第二，英语的复辅音最多只能是三合，而/kstɹ/却有四个组成成分。根据音节划分手续以及英语音位组配制约的限制，extract要切分成/ɪk.stɹækt/。

六、蕴含定律

蕴含定律（Implicational Laws）是指用"如果X，那么Y"的概括性方式陈述的定律。在音系层面的蕴含定律所陈述的是较普遍的音与罕见的音之间的蕴含关系。

如果我们花点时间了解数种世界不同语言的音系，会发现人类在语言中所使用的语音呈现着非常大的变异性。不过，即使如此，我们还是能观察得到，有些音相较于其他音，出现在比较多种的语言中。我们会看见几乎所有人类的语言都有塞音［p］、［t］和元音［a］，不过像阿拉伯语中使用的咽擦音/ħ/和/ʕ/（发音的时候好像把喉咙挤着说话）以及非洲语言的喷音（clicks，中文写成"啧啧"的音就是一种喷音）等就不那么常见了。所以［p］、［t］在人类语言中比较普遍，而咽擦音、清元音和喷音是比较不普遍的语音。接下来从语音总藏、频率与分布、语音的习得和语音演变四个方面来呈现人类语音系统的蕴含定律。

（一）语音总藏

第一个要检视的范围是每个语言的语音总藏（sound inventory）。这里说的"语音"实际上专指有辨义作用的"音位"，而不是"音位变体"。所以针对语音总藏中的蕴含定律，确切的陈述是这样的：如果一个语言的音位总藏（inventory of phonemes）里存在一个较不常见的音，那么一个较常见的相对音（counterpart）一定也存在于这个语言里。

"相对音"的概念包含着这样一层意思：每一个较不常见的音都会对应一个较常见的相对音，两个音几乎一样，只是在一个或两个语音特征上出现差异。例如，一个语言有清元音（[带声]的特征为负值），这是不常见的，而与之相对的就会是一个舌位前后高低、展唇圆唇的值都一样，但是[带声]的特征为正值的浊元音。一个语言的语音系统里若有不常见的清咽擦音/ħ/，那么，与它相对的音（可能是清软腭擦音/x/），就应该存在于这个语言中。

需要注意的是，所谓的"常见"和"不常见"都是相对的概念。在一个音系中，/s/和/x/相比，/s/比较常见，但是和/t/比较的话，/s/就比较少见了。这说明，在一个蕴含关系（implicational relationship）中使用"比较常见"和"比较少见"的概念来界定一个音的时候，我们并不是主张一种绝对的标准，而是在相对的概念下界定。因此我们会说：[s]比[t]较少见，但是比/x/较常见。

蕴含定律所蕴含的事实是不可逆转的。比方说，如果蕴含定律陈述"任何一个使用/x/的语言也会使用/k/这个较常见的相对音"，表示/x/存在的事实蕴含着其相对音/k/也存在于同一个系统中的事实；但是，反过来说就不行了，像英语中/k/的存在就不蕴含英语有/x/的存在。

不仅个别的语音适用蕴含定律，语音的自然类也能体现蕴含定律的作用。例如，清辅音这个类比浊辅音常见。所以，如果一个语言存在浊擦音，那么，这个语言也有清擦音。但是，反过来说就不成立，因为的确存在只有清擦音而没有浊擦音的语言。因此，浊擦音的存在蕴含了清擦音的存在，但是清擦音的存在并不表示浊擦音也存在。

语音自然类体现蕴含定律的另一个例子是塞音和擦音之间的关系。擦音在音位系统中的出现会蕴含与该擦音同部位的塞音的存在。所以，如果一个语言有/s/，那这个语言一定也有/t/，因为与/s/这个齿龈清擦音相对的同部位塞音就是/t/。

（二）频率与分布

蕴含定律还可以在语音的使用频率和分布中观察到。较常见的音，在一个语言里面的分布较广，它们出现的语音环境比较之少见的音要多样化。比如，在一个有咽擦音的语言中，咽擦音在词汇项的出现频率会比其较常见的相对音软腭擦音要低。也就是说，带咽擦音的词会比带软腭擦音的词少。在分布的位置上，较少见的音也会比其较常见的相对音受限制。例如，在闽南话的语音总藏中有塞音和擦音，但是擦音较少见，而且只能出现在声母的位置；塞音较常见，而且分布较广，可以作节首，也可以作节尾。

（三）语音的习得

第三个关于蕴含定律的观察与语音习得的顺序有关：孩子在学语言的时候先学会使用较常见的语音，然后才学会较少见的语音。因此，还没有掌握完整语音总藏的孩子会用比较常见的语音来代替其较少见的相对音。比如，一个汉语普通话还在发展中的孩子，可能会将"小蝴蝶飞呀飞"说成"小蝴蝶杯呀杯"。很显然，他的策略是用较常见的塞音/p/来代替较不常见的擦音/f/。这说明这个孩子还没有完全习得/f/这个音，但是其相对音/p/则已经掌握得相当好了。一个孩子的语言发展从牙牙学语期启动之后，一直到发展完成，都会遵循一个特定的习得顺序，这个顺序在全世界的儿童习得各种语言的过程中是相当稳定的。因此，我们可以说蕴含定律也适用于语言习得的过程：一个较少见的语音被习得时，蕴含着其较常见的相对音已经被习得了。

（四）语音演变

第四个对蕴含定律的观察是关于语音演变的。较少见的语音没有较常见的语音稳定。所以，在语言演变的过程中，经常可以观察到较少见的音被较常见的音所取代，而常见的音却很少被较少见的音替换。例如，在茶堡嘉戎语中保留了软腭塞音/k/和小舌塞音/q/的对立，但在四土嘉戎语中，这样的对立已经消失了，较少见的小舌塞音/q/已经被较常见的软腭塞音/k/所取代，/q/和/k/两个音位在四土嘉戎语中已经合并为/k/一个音位。

七、如何进行音系分析

结合上述所论，这里对音系分析内容进行简要归纳，读者会发现这对于解决音系方面的问题很有帮助。

第一，一开始的时候先找最小对立对儿，这个工作可以厘清哪些音段是对立的。

第二，一个音位的音位变体通常在语音上是彼此相似的。寻找语音性质相近的音，查验它们是否呈现互补分布。进行这一步时，可以一边审视语料，一边将观察到的语音环境逐条列出来。

第三，如果有两个或两个以上的音被初步假定为音位变体，然后在语音环境上发现它们呈现互补分布，这时就可以合理地确认它们是同一个音位的音位变体。试着使用自然类的概念为它们的分布作一个概括的表述。这样，我们就有材料可以做一个音位及其变体的关系表。

第四，将其中一个音位变体选为底层形式，通常是能出现的语音环境种类最多的那个变体。

第五，在第四点的基础上，写一条音系规则来解释其他音位变体是在什么环境下由底层形式变来的。如果你的规则能用自然类的概念提出一个比较普遍的语音变化过程，能解释一个自然类的语音如何与相邻的音段以及音节结构互动，那你提出的规则很有可能是正确的。

第六，如果两个音段找不到最小对立对儿，或者无法观察到呈现互补分布，那这两个音段可以先直接分析为两个独立的音位。

📑 原典选读

一、辅音音姿（consonantal gestures）

Peter Ladefoged, Keith Johnson. 2011. *A Course in Phonetics*. Boston：Wadsworth.

【导　读】

本章语音学的原典选读，选取的内容是Ladefoged and Johnson（2011）的第七章"辅音的音姿"。从这份阅读材料中，读者可以进一步认识世界语言辅音的特点，有不少音是英语或者汉语普通话所没有涵盖的。本章首先介绍"发音标的"（articulatory targets），相当于我们所介绍的"发音部位"（places of articulation）。本章也说明了为何不用"发音部位"而是用"发音标的"这样的概念。在本章后半部分介绍了"发音音姿"（articulatory gestures），相当于我们所介绍的"发音方式"。每一种发音标的和音资在本章都有详细的介绍，读者可以按照文中的指示，用自己的口、舌、齿、鼻等发音器官演练一番，同时也能认识一些特殊的语言发音分布在世界的哪些区域。原书还附光盘，里头提供习题以及书中提及的各种语音现象，某个音或某些音若有音频演示，都会在旁边标注有光盘标记，方便读者查找，有兴趣的读者可直接参阅原典及原典光盘。

ARTICULATORY TARGETS

Many of the possible places of articulation that are used in the languages of the world were defined in Chapter 1. Figure 7.1, which is similar to Figure 1.5, shows three additional places that will be discussed below. The terms for all the places of articulation are not just names for particular locations on the roof of the mouth. They should be thought of as names for the numbered arrows. Each term specifies where the arrow starts (the articulator on the lower surface that makes this particular gesture) and where it ends (the part of the vocal tract that is the target of the gesture).

A large number of non-English sounds are to be found in other languages. Many of them involve using gestures in which the target, or the place of articulation, is different from any found in English. For others it is the type of gesture, what is traditionally called the manner of articulation, that is different. We will illustrate the different targets by considering how each place of articulation is used in English and in other languages for making stops, nasals, and fricatives. The numbers in the following paragraphs refer to the numbered arrows in Figure 7.1.

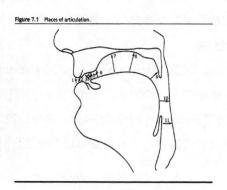

Figure 7.1 Places of articulation.

(1) The **bilabial** gesture is common in English, which has bilabial stops and nasals [p, b, m]. But bilabial fricatives in English are simply allophones of the labiodental sounds [f, v]. In some languages (for example, Ewe of West Africa), bilabial fricatives contrast with labiodental fricatives. The symbols for the voiceless and voiced bilabial fricatives are [ɸ, β]. These sounds are pronounced by bringing the two lips nearly together, so that there is only a slit between them. In Ewe, the name of the language itself is [èβè], whereas the word for *two* is [èvè]. Try to pronounce these contrasting words yourself. Ewe also contrasts voiceless bilabial and labiodental fricatives. Contrasts involving all these sounds are shown in Table 7.1.

We should also note here some other labial sounds not shown in Figure 7.1. A few Austronesian languages spoken in Vanuatu have **linguo-labials**, in which the tongue touches the upper lip. V'enen Taut has nasals, stops, and fricatives made in this way. The diacritic for indicating a linguo-labial articulation is [̼], a shape like a seagull, placed under the coronal symbol. The V'enen Taut for "breadfruit" is [t̼atei], and for "stone" is [naθ̼at]. These and other V'enen Taut sounds are on the CD.

TABLE 7.1	Contrasting bilabial and labiodental fricatives in Ewe.		
Voiceless bilabial fricative	éɸá 'he polished'		éɸlè 'he bought'
Voiceless labiodental fricative	éɸá 'he was cold'		éflé 'he spit off'
Voiced bilabial fricative	èβè 'Ewe' (the language)		éβló 'mushroom'
Voiced labiodental fricative	èvè 'two'		évló 'he is evil'

(2) Many languages are like English in having the **labiodental** fricatives [f, v]. But probably no language has labiodental stops or nasals except as allophones of the corresponding bilabial sounds. In English, a labiodental nasal, [ɱ], may occur when /m/ occurs before /f /, as in *emphasis* or *symphony*. Say these words in a normal conversational style and see if your lower lip ever contacts your upper lip during the nasal.

Some languages have affricates in which the bilabial stop is released into a labiodental fricative. Practice these sounds by learning to say the German words *Pfanne* [ˈpfanə] "bowl" and *Pflug* [pfluk] "plough."

(3) Most speakers of both British and American English have **dental** fricatives [θ, ð] but no dental stops, nasals, or laterals except allophonically before [θ, ð], as in *eighth, tenth, wealth* [eɪtθ, tɛnθ, wɔlθ]. Many speakers of French, Italian, and other languages typically have dental stops, nasals, and laterals. In these languages, [t̪, d̪, n̪] are not just coarticulated allophones that occur only before [θ, ð], as in English. However, there is a great deal of individual variation in the pronunciation of these consonants in all these languages. According to a careful palatographic study, around one-third of Californian English speakers have dental stops, and many French speakers have alveolar rather than dental consonants—well over half of them in the case of the lateral /l/. Say words such as *tip, dip, nip, lip* and try to feel where your tongue touches the roof of your mouth.

Some languages, such as Malayalam, a Dravidian language spoken in southern India, contrast dental and alveolar consonants. Examples of contrasting Malayalam nasals are shown in Table 7.2. The table also includes other consonantal gestures that are used in Malayalam but not in most forms of English. We will discuss these in subsequent paragraphs.

(4) **Alveolar** stops, nasals, and fricatives all occur in English and in many other languages. They need no further comment here.

(5) **Retroflex** stops, nasals, and fricatives do not occur in most forms of English. The outstanding exception is the English spoken in India. Retroflex sounds are made by curling the tip of the tongue up and back so that the underside touches or approaches the back part of the alveolar ridge. The symbols used by IPA for retroflex sounds include [ʈ, ɖ, ɳ]. Remember that, just as *dental* is a gesture that can be defined as an articulator (the tip of the tongue) and a target (the upper teeth), so also *retroflex* describes a gesture involving the underside of the tip of the tongue and a target, the back of the alveolar ridge. Students sometimes imagine that the term *retroflex* describes a manner of articulation, but in fact it is a place of articulation like dental and alveolar. At each of these places of articulation, it is possible to produce stops, nasals, fricatives, and sounds made with other manners of articulation. As we saw in Tables 6.2 and 6.7, the languages Sindhi and Hindi contrast several types of retroflex stops. Malayalam (Table 7.2) contrasts three coronal gestures—dental, alveolar, and retroflex. In addition, Malayalam has bilabial, palatal, and velar sounds, so that it contrasts nasals with six basic types of gesture, six places of articulation, all of which are exemplified in Table 7.2.

(6) The **palato-alveolar** gestures for [ʃ, ʒ] differ from retroflex gestures in the part of the tongue involved. A palato-alveolar gesture is one in which the target on the upper surface of the mouth is about the same as for a retroflex sound—at the margin between the alveolar ridge and the front of the palate. But unlike retroflexes, in this gesture, the front of the tongue is slightly domed, as opposed to being hollowed. (以下省略)

Another way of distinguishing between retroflex and palato-alveolar sounds is to call them both post-alveolar and, in addition, name the part of the tongue involved. Sounds made with the tip of the tongue may be called **apical**, and those made with the blade may be called **laminal**. Thus, the term *retroflex* is exactly equivalent to *apical post-alveolar*, and *palato-alveolar* is equivalent to *laminal post-alveolar*.

The IPA chart puts palato-alveolars into the post-alveolar column. A section labeled "other symbols" also mentions **alveolo-palatals** and provides the symbols [ɕ, ʑ]. These symbols are used for voiceless and voiced fricatives in Polish and Chinese. (以下省略)

(7) **Palatal** sounds can be defined as being made with the front of the tongue approaching or touching the hard palate, and for many speakers, with the tip of the tongue down behind the lower front teeth. There is no clear-cut distinction between these sounds and palato-alveolar sounds. The only true palatal in English is /j/, which is usually an approximant but may be allophonically a voiceless fricative in words such as *hue*. The symbol for a voiceless palatal fricative is [ç], so this word may be transcribed phonemically as /hju/ and phonetically as [çu]. Voiceless palatal fricatives occur in German in words such as *ich* [ɪç], meaning I,' and *nicht* [nɪçt], 'not.'

Say [ç] as in *hue* and then try to prolong this sound. Add voice so that you make a fricative something like the [j] as in *you*, but with the front of the tongue nearer the hard palate. The symbol [ʝ], a curly-tailed *j*, is used for a voiced palatal fricative. Say [ççjjjççjjj], making sure that the tip of the tongue is down behind the lower front teeth. Now change the fricative [ç] into a stop by raising the front of the tongue still more, while keeping the tip of the tongue down. The symbols for voiceless and voiced palatal stops are [c, ɟ]. Say sequences such as [aca] and [aɟa], making sure that the front of your tongue touches the hard palate but that the tip of the tongue is down. Then try making similar sequences with a palatal nasal (for which the symbol is [ɲ], reminding one of [n] and [j] combined).

Palatal nasals occur in several languages, including French, Spanish, Italian, and many non–Indo-European languages. Try saying French words such as *agneau* [aɲo] "lamb" and Spanish words such as *Señor* [seɲor] "Mr."

(8) **Velar** stops and nasals [k, g, ŋ] occur in English. But unlike other languages such as German, we no longer have velar fricatives. They are not, however, hard to make. Starting from a syllable such as [ak], build up pressure behind the velar closure, and then lower the tongue slightly. The result will be a voiceless velar fricative, which we write as [x]. The symbol for the corresponding voiced sound is [ɣ]. As with other fricatives, learn to say [xxxyɣɣxxx]. Then produce sequences such as [axa, exe, oɣo, əɣə].

Examples of words in other languages containing velar fricatives are Lakhota, as shown in Table 6.1; German *Achtung* [ʔaxtʊŋ] 'warning'; *Bach* [bax] 'Bach' (proper name); and Spanish *jamás* [xaˈmas] 'never' *ojo* [ˈoxo] 'eye' *pago* [ˈpaɣo] 'I pay' and *diga* [ˈdiɣa] 'speak.' The Spanish [ɣ] is often not very fricative, and may be more accurately transcribed using the symbol for a voiced velar approximant, which is [ɰ]. The part of the tongue involved in making velar sounds, the back of the tongue, is called the **dorsum**; these sounds are referred to as *dorsal sounds*.

(9) **Uvular** sounds are made by raising the back of the tongue toward the uvula. In a broader grouping of sounds, they, like velar sounds, can be called dorsal. They do not occur at all in most forms of English. But in French, a voiced uvular fricative—[ʁ]—is the common form of *r* in words such as *rouge* [ʁuʒ] 'red' and *rose* [ʁoz] 'rose,' more like an approximant. The voiceless uvular fricative, [χ], also occurs in French as an allophone of /ʁ/ after voiceless stops, as in *lettre* [lətχ] 'letter.' French differs from English in that it often has perseverative assimilations in which, for example, the voicelessness of one sound continues on through the following sound.

Uvular stops, written [q, ɢ], and nasals, written [ɴ], occur as idiosyncratic pronunciations in English and as part of the regular sound systems of Eskimo, Aleut, and other Native American languages.(以下省略)

One way of learning to produce uvular sounds is to start from a voiceless velar fricative [x]. While making this sound, slide your tongue slightly farther back in your mouth so that it is close to the uvula. The result will be the voiceless uvular fricative [χ]. Learn to make this sound before and after vowels, in sequences such as [aχa, oχo, uχu]. You will find it easier to use back vowels at first; then go on to sequences such as [eχe, iχi]. Next, add voice to this sound, saying [χχχʁʁʁχχχʁʁ]. Practice saying [ʁ] before and after vowels.(以下省略)

Once you have mastered the pronunciation of uvular fricatives, try changing them into uvular stops. Say [aχa], then make a stop at the same place of articulation, saying [aqa]. Now produce a voiced uvular stop [aɢa] and a uvular nasal [aɴa]. Practice all these sounds before and after different vowels.

(10) and (11) The gestures for **pharyngeal** and **epiglottal** sounds involve pulling the root of the tongue or the epiglottis back toward the back wall of the pharynx. Many people cannot make a stop gesture at this position. Furthermore, it would be literally impossible to make a pharyngeal or epiglottal nasal. Closure that deep in the vocal tract would prevent the airstream from coming through the nose. But pharyngeal fricatives, shown by the symbols [ħ, ʕ], can be made, and they do in fact occur in Semitic languages such as Arabic and Hebrew. The Arabic word for 'bath' is [ħammaam], for 'uncle' is [ʕamm]. The articulation varies considerably in the Semitic languages, some speakers using

epiglottal and others pharyngeal gestures. These sounds also vary considerably with regard to the degree of constriction. For many speakers, there is little or no actual friction, so that approximants rather than fricatives are discussed. The voiced fricative made in this region usually has a great deal of laryngealization (creaky voice), perhaps because the necessary constriction in the pharynx also causes a constriction in the larynx. Neither Hebrew, Arabic, nor any of the other Semitic languages distinguish between pharyngeal and epiglottal fricatives; but some of the languages of the Caucasus contrast these two possibilities.(以下省略)

At a first stage in learning phonetics, it is sufficient to be able to produce either pharyngeal or epiglottal fricatives. If you try to constrict your pharynx as much as possible, you will probably be doing so by retracting the epiglottis. Try to produce the voiceless sound [ħ]. Now, if you can, produce this sound before a vowel. Next, try to make the voiced sound [ʕ], not worrying if it turns out to have creaky voice. Produce these sounds in the Arabic words cited above.

Before finishing this section on gestures at different places of articulation, we must note that some sounds involve the simultaneous use of two gestures. The English approximant [w] has both an approximation of the lips (making it a bilabial sound) and of the back of the tongue and the soft palate (making it a velar sound). Sounds that involve these two gestures are called **labial velars**, or, in some more old-fashioned books, **labiovelars**.

Yoruba, Ewe, Tiv, and many other languages spoken in West Africa have labial velar stops. Some of the languages spoken in this area also have labial velar nasals. As in the case of nasal and voiced clicks, we can symbolize two co-occurring articulations with a tie bar joining two symbols. The Yoruba for 'arm' is [akp͡á] and for 'adult' is [àg͡bà]. In these words, the two closures occur almost simultaneously. One of the best ways of learning to say these sounds is to start by making a bilabial click (a kissing sound, but with the lips being simply compressed and not puckered) between vowels. Say [a] 'kiss' [a] at first slowly, and then as fast as you can. Then weaken the suction component of the kiss, so that you are making little more than a labial velar articulation between vowels. The result should be a labial velar stop much as in the Yoruba word [akp͡á], 'arm.' (以下省略)

TYPES OF ARTICULATORY GESTURES

Stops

We can begin our consideration of the different manners of articulatory gestures that occur in the languages of the world by reviewing what has been

TABLE 7.4 Symbols for nasals, stops, and fricatives. As in all consonant charts, when there are two symbols within a single cell, the one on the left indicates a voiceless sound.

	bilabial	labiodental	dental	alveolar	retroflex	palato-alveolar	palatal	velar	uvular	pharyngeal	labial velar
nasal	m	ɱ	n̪	n	ɳ		ɲ	ŋ	ɴ		ŋ͡m
stop	p b		t̪ d̪	t d	ʈ ɖ		c ɟ	k g	q ɢ		k͡p g͡b
fricative	ɸ β	f v	θ ð	s z	ʂ ʐ	ʃ ʒ	ç ʝ	x ɣ	χ ʁ	ħ ʕ	

said already about stop consonants. Table 7.5 illustrates a number of different types of stops, most of which were discussed earlier in this book. The first seven possibilities were discussed in Chapter 6. Make sure you understand all these terms and know what all these stops sound like, even if you cannot make them all yourself.

The only comment on the first seven sounds that it is necessary to add here—where they are all listed together—is that no language distinguishes between (5), an implosive [ɓ] and (6), a laryngealized (creaky-voiced) [b̰]. Certain languages have the one sound, and others the other. In a few languages, both sounds occur as allophones or as free variants of the same phoneme. They have not been found in contrast with each other.

Stops with nasal release, the eighth possibility listed in Table 7.5, were discussed in relation to English in Chapter 3. Nasal plosion occurs in English at the ends of words such as *hidden* and *sudden*. In some languages, however, it can occur at the beginning of a word. Try to say the Russian word for 'bottom' which is [dno].

The next possibility listed in Table 7.5 is the prenasalized stop [nd], which is in some senses the reverse of a nasally released stop. In a prenasalized stop, the oral closure—in this case an alveolar gesture—is formed first, while the soft palate is lowered. Then there is a short nasal consonant, after which the soft palate is raised so that there is a stop. This stop is released by removing the oral closure (in this case by lowering the tongue tip) while the soft palate remains raised. Prenasalized stops occur in many African languages. Say the Swahili words *ndege* [ndege] 'bird, airplane,' *ntu* [ntu] 'wax.' (Swahili is a language in which the orthography itself is equivalent to a broad IPA transcription.) When

you make these sounds, be careful not to make the initial nasal component into a separate syllable. Make it as short as possible.

TABLE 7.5 Examples of stop consonants.

Description	Symbol	Example	
1. voiced	b	banu	(Sindhi 'forest')
2. voiceless unaspirated	p	panu	(Sindhi 'leaf')
3. aspirated	pʰ	pʰaṇu	(Sindhi 'snake hood')
4. murmured (breathy)	bʱ	bʱaṃu	(Sindhi 'manure')
5. implosive	ɓ	ɓani	(Sindhi 'field')
6. laryngealized (creaky)	b̰	b̰aʈàː	(Hausa 'spoil')
7. ejective	k'	k'aʀàː	(Hausa 'increase')
8. nasal release	dn	dno	(Russian 'bottom')
9. prenasalized	nd	ndizi	(Swahili 'banana')
10. lateral release	tl	tlàh	(Navajo 'oil, ointment')
11. ejective lateral release	tl'	tl'éeʔ	(Navajo 'night')
12. affricate	ts	tsaɪt	(German 'time')
13. ejective affricate	ts'	ts'áal	(Navajo 'cradle')

Stops with lateral release (see (10) in Table 7.5) were previously discussed in relation to their occurrence in English (for example, in *little*, *ladle*). In other languages, they can occur initially in a word. Sometimes, as indicated by (11) in Table 7.5, laterally released stops can occur with an ejective airstream mechanism. On these occasions, the stop closure for [t] is formed, the glottalic egressive (ejective) airstream mechanism is set in motion, and then the stop is released laterally by lowering the sides of the tongue. The examples in (10) and (11) in Table 7.5 are from a Native American language, Navajo. (Listen to examples on the CD in the performance exercises for chapter 11.)

The only affricates that can occur initially in most forms of English are [tʃ, dʒ]. Some dialects (for example, London Cockney) have a slightly affricated stop of a kind that might be written [tˢ] in words such as *tea* [tˢoi]. Alveolar affricates also occur in German, as shown in (12) in Table 7.5. In addition, German has a bilabial affricate [pf], as in *Pflug* [pfluk] 'plough.' Affricates can also occur with an ejective airstream mechanism. Example (13) in Table 7.5 is from Navajo, which, in addition to the ejective [ts'], also has the affricate [ts] made with a pulmonic airstream mechanism as in German.

Nasals

We will now consider the other manners of articulation used in the languages of the world. Little more need be said about nasals. Like stops, they can occur voiced or voiceless (for example, in Burmese, which can be found in the chapter 11 performance exercises on the CD). As voiceless nasals are comparatively rare, they are symbolized simply by adding the voiceless diacritic [̥] under the symbol for the voiced sound. There are no special symbols for voiceless nasals.

Fricatives

There are two ways to produce the rough, turbulent flow that occurs in the airstream during a fricative. It may be just the result of the air passing through a narrow gap, as in the formation of [f]. Or it may be because the airstream is first speeded up by being forced through a narrow gap and then is directed over a sharp edge, such as the teeth, as in the production of [s]. Partly because there are these two possible mechanisms, the total number of different fricatives that have been observed is larger than the number of stops or the number of nasals. Table 7.4 shows ten pairs of fricative symbols, compared with seven pairs of stop symbols and eight nasal symbols.

So far, we have classified fricatives as voiced or voiceless and as made with a number of different articulatory gestures. But we can also subdivide fricatives in accordance with other aspects of the gestures that produce them. Some authorities have divided fricatives into those such as [s], in which the tongue is grooved so that the airstream comes out through a narrow channel, and those such as [θ], in which the tongue is flat and forms a wide slit through which the air flows. Unfortunately, not enough is known about fricatives to be sure how this distinction should be applied in all cases. It is also clearly irrelevant for fricatives made with the lips and the back of the tongue.

The sound patterns that occur in languages often arise because of auditory properties of sounds. We can divide fricatives into sibilant and nonsibilant sounds only by reference to auditory properties. We need to divide them into these two groups to show how English plurals are formed. Consider words ending in fricatives, such as *cliff, moth, kiss, dish, church, dove, lathe, maze, rouge, judge*. Which of these words add an extra syllable in forming the plural? If you say them over to yourself, you will find that they are all monosyllables in the singular. But those that end with one of the sounds [s, ʃ, z, ʒ]—that is, with a sibilant fricative or an affricate containing a sibilant fricative—become two syllables in the plural. It seems as though English does not favor two sibilant sounds together. It breaks them up by inserting a vowel before adding a sibilant suffix to words ending in sibilants.

Trills, Taps, and Flaps

The most common pronunciation of the sound written with the letter "r" in the languages of the world is the trilled [r]. This is why the IPA uses the common letter [r] for **trill** and the typographically unusual symbol [ɹ] for the phonetically unusual rhotic approximate found in English. Some languages contrast a long and short trilled [r].(以下省略)

（省略） So, even in the case of a very short trill in which there is only a single contact with the roof of the mouth, the movement is different from that in a tap, or a flap. In a trill, the tip of the tongue is set in motion by the current of air. A **tap** or a **flap** is caused by a single contraction of the muscles so that one articulator is thrown against another. It is often just a very rapid stop gesture.

It is useful to distinguish between taps and flaps. In a tap, the tip of the tongue simply moves up to contact the roof of the mouth in the dental or alveolar region, and then moves back to the floor of the mouth along the same path. In a flap, the tip of the tongue is first curled up and back in a retroflex gesture, and then strikes the roof of the mouth in the post-alveolar region as it returns to its position behind the lower front teeth. The distinction between taps and flaps is thus to some extent bound up with what might be called a distinction in place of articulation. Flaps are typically retroflex articulations, but it is possible to make the articulatory gesture required for a flap at other places of articulation. The tongue can be pulled back and then, as it is flapped forward, made to strike the alveolar ridge or even the teeth, making alveolar or dental flaps. Flaps are distinguished from taps by the direction of the movement—from back to front for flaps, up and down for taps—rather than by the exact point of contact.

Some forms of American English have both taps and flaps. Taps occur as the regular pronunciation of /t, d, n/ in words such as *latter, ladder, tanner*. The flap occurs in words that have an *r*-colored vowel in the stressed syllable. In *dirty* and *sorting*, speakers who have the tongue bunched or retracted for the *r*-colored vowel will produce a flap as they move the tongue forward for the non-*r*-colored vowel.

Trills are rare in most forms of English. The stage version of a Scottish accent with trilled /r/ is not typical of most Scots. In Scottish English, /r/ is more likely to be pronounced as a tap. The American pronunciation of *petal* with a voiced alveolar tap in the middle will sound to a Scotsman from Edinburgh like his regular pronunciation of *pearl*.

The distinction between trills and different kinds of taps and flaps is much more important in other languages. But before this point can be illustrated, we must review the symbols that can be used for different types of *r* sounds. In a broad transcription for English, they can all be transcribed as /r/. But in a narrower transcription, this symbol may be restricted to voiced alveolar trills. An alveolar tap may be symbolized by the special symbol [ɾ], and the post-alveolar (retroflex) flap by [ɽ]. The approximant that occurs in most Americans' pronunciation of /r/ may be symbolized by [ɹ], an upside-down *r*. If it is important to show that this sound is particularly retroflex, the symbol [ɻ] may be used.

TABLE 7.6	Specific symbols for types of *r*, and for bilabial trills. Note the use of [*] as a special symbol that can be defined and used when there is no prescribed symbol.		
r	voiced alveolar trill	[pero]	(Spanish 'dog')
ɾ	voiced alveolar tap	[pero]	(Spanish 'but')
ɽ	voiced retroflex flap	[bárɽaː]	(Hausa 'servant')
ɹ	voiced alveolar approximant	[ɹed]	(English 'red')
ɾ̃	voiced alveolar fricative trill	[rɛk]	(Czech 'rivers')
ʀ	voiced uvular trill	[ʀuʒ]	(Provençal French 'red')
ʁ	voiced uvular fricative or approximant	[ʁuʒ]	(Parisian French 'red')
ʙ	voiced bilabial trill	[mʙulim]	(Kele 'your face')
*	voiced labiodental flap	[bə́*ú]	(Margi 'flying away')

Most speakers of American English do not have a retroflex approximant, but for those who do, [ɻ] is an appropriate symbol in a narrow transcription. All these symbols are shown in Table 7.6.

As illustrated in Table 7.6, Spanish distinguishes between a trill and a tap in words such as *perro* [pero] 'dog' and *pero* [pero] 'but.' Similar distinctions also occur in some forms of Tamil, a language of southern India. This language, like Hausa (Nigeria), may also distinguish between an alveolar tap and a retroflex flap. Trills may also have accompanying friction, as in the Czech example in Table 7.6, which uses the IPA diacritic [̝], meaning raised (and thus more fricative).

Learning to make a trill involves placing the tongue, very loosely, in exactly the right position so that it will be set in vibration by a current of air. The easiest position seems to be with the tongue just behind the upper front teeth and very lightly touching the alveolar ridge. If you get the tongue in just the right position and relaxed, you can blow across the top of it, setting it vibrating in a voiceless

trill. Many people find it easier to start with a voiceless trill and then add voicing once they can make steady vibrations. The jaw should be fairly closed, leaving a space of 5 mm between the front teeth. Check this by inserting the top of a pencil between your teeth, and then removing it before making the sound. The problem experienced by most people who fail to make trills is that the blade of the tongue is too stiff.

Most people can learn to produce a voiced tap by adopting the typical American English pronunciation of words such as *Betty* (which can be transcribed as [ˈbɛɾi]). You should also be able to produce a retroflex flap. As we have seen, many speakers of American English use this type of articulation in sequences such as *herding* [hɚ-ɽɪŋ], in which the tongue is curled up and back after the *r*-colored vowel, and then strikes the back part of the alveolar ridge as it moves down during the consonant.

When you have mastered all these sounds, try saying them in different contexts. You might also learn to say voiced and voiceless trills, taps, and flaps. Try varying the place of articulation, producing both dental and post-alveolar trills and flaps. Some languages, such as Malayalam and Toda, spoken in southern India, contrast alveolar and dental trills. The word for 'room' in Malayalam is [ara], whereas the word for 'half' is [aɾa]. The Toda rhotics on the CD illustrate an even more complex situation in which three kinds of trill are contrasted.

The tongue tip is not the only articulator that can be trilled. Uvular trills occur in some dialects of French, although, as we have noted already, most forms of French have a uvular fricative in words such as 'rose' [ʁoz]. The symbol for a uvular trill is [ʀ]. There is no symbol to distinguish between uvular fricatives and approximants because this phonetic difference is not used to distinguish words in any language. Both sounds are symbolized by [ʁ].

Trills involving the lips occur in a few languages. The IPA symbol for these sounds is a small capital [ʙ] (just as a small capital [ʀ] is used for a uvular trill). In Kele and Titan, two languages spoken in Papua New Guinea, bilabial trills occur in a large number of words. The Titan for 'rat' is [mʙulei]. To pronounce the first part of this word you need to hold the lips loosely together while making [m], and then blow the lips apart. Some people find it easier to trill the lips than the tongue tip. If you are having difficulty making an alveolar trill [r], see if you can get the sensation of making a trill by making a bilabial trill [ʙ]. Kele and Titan bilabial trills are included on the CD.

Laterals

In Chapter 1, we regarded the term *lateral* as if it specified a manner of articulation in a way comparable to other terms such as *fricative*, or *stop*, or *approximant*. But this is really an oversimplification. The central–lateral opposition can be applied to all these manners of articulation, producing a lateral stop and a lateral fricative as well as a lateral approximant, which is by far the most common form of lateral sound. The only English lateral phoneme is /l/ with, at least in British English, allophones [l] as in *led* [lɛd] and [ɫ] as in *bell* [bɛɫ]. In most forms of American English, initial [l] has more velarization than is typically heard in British English initial [l]. In all forms of English, the air flows without audible friction, making this sound a voiced alveolar lateral approximant. It may be compared with the sound [ɹ] in *red* [ɹɛd], which is for many people a voiced alveolar central approximant. Laterals are usually presumed to be voiced approximants, unless a specific statement to the contrary is made.

Try subtracting and adding voice while saying an English [l] as in *led*. You will probably find that the voiceless lateral you produce is a fricative, not an approximant. When the vocal folds are apart, the airstream flows more rapidly, so that it produces a fricative noise in passing between the tongue and the side teeth. The symbol for this sound is [ɬ], so in alternating the voiced and voiceless sounds you will be saying [lɬlɬlɬlɬlɬ]. It is possible to make a nonfricative voiceless lateral, but you will find that to do this you will have to move the side of the tongue farther away from the teeth. The alternation between a voiced and a voiceless lateral approximant may be symbolized [ll̥ll̥ll̥ll̥]].

To summarize, there are four lateral sounds under discussion: voiced alveolar lateral approximant, [l]; voiced alveolar lateral fricative, [ɮ]; voiceless alveolar lateral approximant, [l̥]; and voiceless alveolar lateral fricative, [ɬ]. No language uses the difference between the last two sounds contrastively. But some languages make a phonemic distinction between three of the four possibilities. Zulu, for example, has a three-way contrast, as shown in the first row of Table 7.7. As you can see in the second set of Zulu words in Table 7.7, after a nasal, the voiceless fricative may be an ejective. And the final Zulu word in the table illustrates an initial voiceless velar lateral ejective affricate, using the symbol [ʟ] for a velar lateral. Listen to this sound on the CD, but don't worry if you can't produce it in your first year of phonetics. Voiceless lateral fricatives can also be exemplified by Welsh words such as [ɬan] 'church' and [ˈkəɬəɬ] 'knife.'

二、曲折音段（contour segment）

Bruce Hayes. 2009. *Introductory Phonology*. West Sussex：Wiley-Blackwell.

【导　读】

在这段选读的原典中，Hayes讨论了一个制定音位系统时比较棘手的问题：曲折音段是单音段还是音段序列（3.4.1节）？"曲折音段"指的是像复元音、塞擦音或带前鼻音的塞音等在语音音质上为序列，但是在音系的层面则被视为一个音段。文中还讨论了汉语普通话复元音［ei］和［ou］的音位化处理方式，虽然其观点在我国国内并没有被广为接受，但仍不失为一种简洁有效的方式。

3.4.1 *Contour segments and the segment/sequence problem*

Sounds like diphthongs ([aɪ]), affricates ([t͡ʃ]), and prenasalized stops ([m͡b]) are often called **contour segments**: they have two phonetic qualities in sequence, but are often treated phonologically as a single sound. The recognition of the contour segments is often an analytic difficulty faced in phonemicization. For example, given a sequence like [ai] in the data, we need to decide whether it should be treated

56　　　　　*More on Phonemes*

as a diphthong (that is, as a single phonemic unit), or as a sequence of /a/ + /i/. The same issue arises for [t͡ʃ] (is it the affricate [t͡ʃ], or is it /t/ + /ʃ/?) and for [mb, nd, ŋg] (prenasalized stops or *nasal + stop* sequences?). This analytical issue might be called the **segment/sequence problem**.

The problem is easy to solve if there is an actual contrast between segment and sequence. For instance, the analysis of [t͡ʃ] as an affricate in Polish is uncontroversial, because this sound contrasts with the stop + fricative sequence [tʃ]. The following minimal pair illustrate this:

[t͡ʃɨ] *trzy* 'three'
[t͡ʃi] *czy* 'if, whether'

[tʃ] and [t͡ʃ] are phonetically different; in particular, [tʃ] is noticeably longer than [t͡ʃ]. The affricate [t͡ʃ] must be analyzed as a single segmental unit in Polish, since otherwise we could not express the contrast between monosegmental /t͡ʃ/ and bisegmental /tʃ/. Similarly, in other languages diphthongs contrast with two-vowel sequences (English *boing* [bɔ͡ɪŋ] vs. *sawing* [sɔɪŋ]), and prenasalized stops contrast (for example in Sinhala) with nasal + stop sequences. In Turkish, long vowels contrast with identical vowel sequences, as in [daː] 'mountain-nom. sg.' vs. [da.a] 'mountain-dat. sg.', which leads to the clear conclusion that the long vowels must be single phonemic units in Turkish.

Sometimes phonologists choose between segments and sequence on the basis of the overall pattern of the language. Suppose that a language has five monophthongs /i, e, a, o, u/, and that moreover any one of the 25 logical possibilities for putting any two of these vowels together occurs in the language; that is, we observe:

[iː]	[ie]	[ia]	[io]	[iu]
[ei]	[eː]	[ea]	[eo]	[eu]
[ai]	[ae]	[aː]	[ao]	[au]
[oi]	[oe]	[oa]	[oː]	[ou]
[ui]	[ue]	[ua]	[uo]	[uː]

In this case, we would be sensible to opt for a sequence analysis, in which these putative "diphthongs" are not phonemes, but merely sequences of the independently existing vowel phonemes /i, e, a, o, u/, as follows:

/ii/	/ie/	/ia/	/io/	/iu/
/ei/	/ee/	/ea/	/eo/	/eu/
/ai/	/ae/	/aa/	/ao/	/au/
/oi/	/oe/	/oa/	/oo/	/ou/
/ui/	/ue/	/ua/	/uo/	/uu/

The two criteria just given do not always suffice to determine an analysis. The apparent diphthongs of Mandarin Chinese are a classical example; they have been

More on Phonemes　　　　　57

treated by some analysts as monophonematic diphthongs and by others as sequences. To consider just a subset of the Mandarin problem, observe that Mandarin has the following sounds: [ə], [i], [u], [ei], and [ou]. [e] and [o] never occur alone, but only as part of the diphthongs [ei] and [ou]. One possible phonemicization is the following:

/ə/	/əi/	/əu/	/i/	/u/	
—	ei	—	—	—	Vowel Assimilation I: ə → e / ___ i
—	—	ou	—	—	Vowel Assimilation II: ə → o / ___ u
[ə]	[ei]	[ou]	[i]	[u]	surface forms

The appeal of this analysis is that we can get by with just three phonemes (/ə/, /i/, /u/) to derive five sounds. Moreover, the rules make sense as **assimilation** rules; the vowel /ə/ is assimilated to [i] or [u], become phonetically more similar to its neighbor; and assimilation is a very common process in phonology. However, not all phonologists would necessarily agree that this is an iron-clad argument – in principle, we want to know not just a convenient and elegant way to symbolize Mandarin sounds, but the way that actually is found in the internalized grammars of native speakers. In general, the issue of how to segment the speech stream into its phonemes is an unsettled one in phonology.

三、特定环境下的对立

Bruce Hayes. 2009. *Introductory Phonology*. West Sussex：Wiley-Blackwell.

【导　读】

下面这段选文出自上述文献第3.6节。作者介绍了一种在普通话的音系中也存在的现象，也就是只在特定环境下呈现的对立（contextually limited contrasts）。在分析相关现象时，本书诉诸音位组配制约来避免使用音系规律所产生的缺陷。

3.6 Contextually Limited Contrasts and Phonotactics

Phonemic contrast is often not an across-the-board matter, but is confined to particular contexts. For instance, in Toba Batak (Austronesian, Sumatra), there

is a general contrast between voiced and voiceless stops and affricates, as the following near-minimal pairs attest:

[pinoppar]	'descendant'
[biaŋ]	'dog'
[dukkar]	'let out'
[tuak]	'palm wine'
[korea]	'Korea'[6]
[garut]	(name of town in Indonesia)

Many words of Toba Batak also end in voiceless stops:

[sukkup]	'adequate'
[hotop]	'fast'
[dohot]	'with'
[surat]	'letter'
[rappok]	'steal'
[halak]	'man'

However, no word in the language ever ends in a voiced stop: hypothetical words like *[sukkub], *[dohod], or *[rappog] sound "un-Batak" to native speakers.

Thus, we have a phonological contrast of voicing, but it is a **contextually limited contrast**. A full description of Toba Batak must include a characterization not just of the contrasting phonemes, but also a characterization of where the contrast is allowed.

3.6.1 *Analyzing phonotactics and contextually limited contrast*

Two formal approaches have been taken to contextually restricted contrast. In one, we write rules that would have the effect of eliminating the contrast. For the Toba Batak case given above, a suitable rule would be the following:

Final Devoicing (Toba Batak)
[+stop] → [−voice] / ___]$_{word}$
Stops are devoiced at the end of a word.

This approach may seem slightly counterintuitive, since one wonders: what are the forms to which the rule applies? There is no reason to set up any underlying forms in Toba Batak that would qualify. The idea behind positing such a rule is

---

[6] A caution: /k/ is a borrowed phoneme in Toba Batak, so that this (unlike /p/–/b/ and /t/–/d/) is a marginal contrast.

to say, "even if Toba Batak *did* have final voiced stops in its underlying forms, they would be pronounced as voiceless in surface forms." The result is in fact a correct prediction, as no Toba Batak word can end with a voiced stop.

A different approach to contextually limited contrast posits that phonological theory involves not just rules but also **constraints**. A constraint is a formal characterization of a structure that is illegal in a particular language. In the constraint below, the asterisk may be read "is illegal" or "is ill-formed."

Constraint against Final Voiced Stops (Toba Batak)
$$*\begin{bmatrix} +stop \\ +voice \end{bmatrix} / \underline{\quad} \,]_{word}$$
It is illegal to have a voiced stop in word-final position.

Such constraints are sometimes called **phonotactic constraints**, "phonotactics" being a general term for the principles (however stated) of phonological well-formedness in a particular language. Phonologists debate what are the roles and relative importance of rules and constraints in phonology. Some theories make use only of rules, some use both, and some theories use only constraints.

3.6.2 *Contrast with zero*

The notion of phonological contrast can be broadened to include **contrast with zero**. For instance, English allows contrasts like *tax* [tæks] vs. *tack* [tæk], where the [s] of *tax* is said to be in contrast with zero. The following diagram illustrates this; Ø is the symbol representing the null string.

```
t   æ   k   s
t   æ   k   Ø
```

Contrast with zero can also be contextually limited. Thus, for instance, Toba Batak has no contrasts like the one just given, because it never permits two consonants to occur at the end of a word. Consonants do contrast with zero in other environments of Toba Batak, for example in the context / V ___]$_{word}$. One of many examples would be [laŋa] 'empty' vs. [laŋan] 'pale'. In fact, Toba Batak falls into a very widespread phonological pattern whereby consonants may contrast with zero only when they are adjacent to a vowel.

To ban the CC vs. C contrast in final position, we formulate either a rule or a constraint, as shown below. Note that "X → Ø" is the usual notation in phonology for deletion.

Rule: Cluster Simplification
C → Ø / C ___]$_{word}$
Delete a word-final consonant if a consonant precedes.

In comparing these two approaches, we see one possible objection to the rule-based theory: it often forces us to make arbitrary analytic decisions. In particular, given the data we have, there seems to be no reason to delete the second consonant rather than the first (C → Ø / C ___]$_{word}$); both rules would suffice to enforce the one-consonant limit.[7] Often, there is further evidence from the language that tells us which rule is correct; see chapter 6. In addition, one should bear in mind that it is perhaps not so bad to have two possible analyses available, when both of them happen to work.

☯ 思考题

1. 请看以下的音标符号，写出其语音特征，包括发音部位与发音方式。例如：

[k]：清、软腭、塞音

符号	特征	符号	特征
[t]		[θ]	
[b]		[dʒ]	
[m]		[ə]	
[ɲ]		[o]	
[ð]		[e]	
[ts]		[d]	
[g]		[ɔ]	
[l]		[ɹ]	
[w]		[ʐ]	

2. 使用语音特征将第一题的语音划分为不同的自然类（同一个语音可能出现在不同的自然类中）。

3. 以下是一首中文流行歌的歌词，呈现的方式是IPA记音，没有声调标注，将记音朗读出来，看看能不能辨认出是哪首歌。

/ni tə wan mei tʂu ji tʰai tʂʰə ti

ʐaŋ wo lian hən tou nan ji ɕia pi

tɕiaŋ tʂən ɕin tʂʰou li ɕie tʂʰəŋ ʐ̩ tɕi

ɕiaŋ ʂ̩ ji tʂʰaŋ mo jy

ni tə wan mei tʂu ji tʰai tʂʰə ti

fən ʂou tə hua ɕiaŋ jan jy pao li

wo ji wu nəŋ wei li tsai tʰi tɕʰi

tɕue tiŋ tʂoŋ tuan ʂou ɕi/

提示：作曲、演唱为周杰伦

4. 以下的记音是第3题的歌在唱片中的原唱记音（严式）（如果能取得mp3自己转

写一次更好），请比较两份记音，思考在本题中的语音变化可以用什么音系规律来分析。

注意 [ʔ] 这个符号是喉塞音，是在声门的部分成阻的塞音。

[ni tə wan me tʂu ʔi tʰai tʂʰə ti

zaŋ wo lian gən tou na~ʔi ɕia pi

tɕiaŋ tʂɤ̃ ɕin tʂʰo li ɕie tʂʰən ʐɻ tɕi

ɕiã ʂɻ ji tʂʰən mo jy

ni tə wan me tʂu ʔi tʰai tʂʰə ti

fɤ̃ ʂo lə wua ɕia ʔy ʔian pao li

ʔuo ʔi wu nə wei li tsai tʰi tɕʰi

tɕue tiŋ no nuan ʂo ɕi]

5．在汉语普通话的音系中，[u]（汉语拼音符号"u"）和 [y]（汉语拼音符号"ü"，在有些环境是"u"）是不同的音位，还是同一音位的音位变体呢？请详细列出两者的分布并加以讨论。

📖 拓展性阅读书目

- Robert Mannell, Felicity Cox, Jonathan Harrington. 2014. *An Introduction to Phonetics and Phonology*. Department of Linguistics, Macquarie University. 线上阅读：http://clas.mq.edu.au/speech/phonetics/index.html

- Elizabeth C. Zsiga．2012. *The Sounds of Language：An Introduction to Phonetics and Phonology*. West Sussex: Wiley-Blackwell.

- Peter Ladefoged. 2001. *Vowels and Consonants：An Introduction to the sounds of languages*. Oxford：Blackwell.

- Peter Ladefoged, Ian Maddieson. 1996. *The Sounds of the World's Languages*. Oxford：Blackwell.

- 蔡莲红，孔江平．现代汉语音典．北京：清华大学出版社，2014．

第四章
词　法

　　"词法"的原文是"morphology"，直译是"形态学"，意指所研究的是词的形态样貌，包括词的结构与构成，构词的规律，以及调整词的形态的方式。

　　本章首先介绍构成词的基本单位："语素"（第一节），内容涵括语素的"自由"与"黏着"、语素变体、词根与词干、词缀以及依附词；之后讨论派生与屈折这两种词的成形方式（第二节）；第三节介绍语言构造词的规律（构词法），内容涵括加缀、复合、**重叠**、交替、异干交替；第四节从类型学的角度，讨论依形态划分的语言类型，首先将语言分为分析型与综合型，再对综合型语言进行细致区分；最后一节（第五节）简单说明分析词法时如何辨识语素。

第一节　语　素

语素（morpheme）又称"形位"，是表达语义的最小形式单位。例如，英语的cats这个词就有两个语素：cat以及-s。其中cat体现这个词的主要语义内涵："猫"；而-s则表达复数的语义。无论是cat"猫"或复数-s都无法进一步分解成更小具有语义内涵的单位，因此两者都是语素。必须注意的是，最小的形式单位并不是只通过音段来体现，也可以是超音段的成分。例如，在嘉戎语中，有一种名词的格位标记——呼格（vocative case，用于对人、动物等的称呼）的语素就不是一个音段或一串音段的组合，而是声调调型。下面表4-1中的例子显示，无论人名原来是否在最后一个音节带降调，其呼格都是一律带降调（在方括弧［ ］中的L代表音高为低，H代表高音，HL是下降的音高）：

	人名	呼格
a.	kraʃes	kraʃês
	［L–H］	［L–HL］
b.	ptsesmôn	ptsesmôn
	［L–HL］	［L–HL］
c.	mtsʰomoscit	mtsʰomoscît
	［L–H–H］	［L–H–HL］
d.	kraʃismôn	kraʃismôn
	［L–H–HL］	［L–H–HL］
e.	kraʃitamo	kraʃitamô
	［L–H–H–L］	［L–H–H–HL］

表4-1　嘉戎语呼格的声调调型表示法

以下几个小节（一至五小节）将讨论几个跟语素相关的类别以及语法特征。

一、自由语素与黏着语素

自由语素（free morpheme）不需要接在其他语素上，就可以单独成词；而黏着语素（bound morpheme）则不能单独成词，必须接在其他语素上才能出现在语流中。黏着语素不一定都是词缀（affix），也可能是依附词（clitic），甚至词根（root）也有可能不是自由语素而需要黏着在其他语素上。例如，西班牙语的cant-"歌唱"这个动词词根就必须带屈折标记才能成词：cant-ar是不定式，cant-amos是"我们唱（现在时）"。另一方面，英语的cat"猫"则可归为自由语素，因为它不需要接在其他语素上就可以单独成词。关于"自由"和"黏着"，读者可以进一步阅读第五章原典选读一。

二、语素变体

语素变体（allomorph）又称"形位变体"。"音位变体"是音位在不同语音环境的实际体现，同样，"语素变体"是语素在不同语音环境中的变化形式，也就是语素的实际体现。从表4-2的例子可以看出，英语的复数语素（一般以-s代表）至少有三种不同的语素变体：

释义	拼写	音标	复数标记形位变体	语音环境（词根韵尾）
农场	ranches	[ræntʃɪz]	[ɪz]	咝声音
岩石	rocks	[rɑks]	[s]	其他清辅音
狗	dogs	[dɔgz]	[z]	其他浊辅音

表4-2 英语复数语素{S}的变体形式

此外，英语还有几个不同的复数形态标记，像goose [gus]"鹅"的复数是geese [gis]，是靠词根的元音从 [u] 替换成 [i] 这样的手段达成的。在这样的例子中，我们不能说 [i] 是复数形式/-s/的语素变体，因为geese [gis] 并不是goose加上复数后缀-s，并在语音环境的制约下变化而成的。像goose [gus] 和geese [gis] 这样的单复数表现形式，采用的是一种叫"交替"的手段，关于"交替"在下面第三节会有更详细的说明。

三、词根与词干

词根表达一个词最基本的词汇语义内容，而且在形式上不能再切分为更小的单元。需要注意的是，这并不表示只要是词根就能单独成词，有时候词根必须与屈折标记结合之后才能成词。如前面所提，西班牙语的cant-"歌唱"是一个词根，但是不能单独出现，必须加上表示人称及时体、情貌等范畴的屈折标记才能成词。此外，像英语就有不少源于拉丁语的词其词根是无法单独出现的，例如（1）中的词都共享 ceive这个词根。

（1）　deceive　　　"欺骗"

　　　　receive　　　　"接受"

　　　　conceive　　　"怀孕"

　　　　perceive　　　"察觉"

对原来使用拉丁语的人来说，ceive 是有清楚的意义的；但是对现代英语的使用者来说，它已经没有独立的意义了。我们必须看加了前缀后的整个词，借助其词义来推敲这个词根的可能意义。

　　词干（stem）最少要包含一个词根，但可能要再进一步切分为词根和派生语素。在英语中，defrost"解冻"是一个词干，它可以像其他动词一样带屈折标记，例如（2）。

（2）　过去时：　defrost-ed

　　　　第三人称现在时：　defrost-s

不过，defrost又可以进一步分析为词根frost"使结霜"加上派生前缀de-（派生与屈折标记在第二节有更详细的讨论）。

四、词缀

　　词缀（affixes）是附在词根或词干上的黏着语素。根据词缀相对于词根/词干的位置，可以将词缀分为前缀、后缀、中缀、环缀等。

（一）前缀

　　前缀（prefix）附在词干或词根的前端。英语的uncomfortable"不舒服"，就是un-这个表示否定的前缀接在comfortable这个形容词词干上。嘉戎语表示第二人称的标记也是一个前缀：tə-，ɳǝk是"跑"的词根，而tə-ɳǝk则是"你跑"的意思。

（二）后缀

　　后缀（suffix）附在词根或词干的末端。英语的名词复数标记-s（如"狗"dog（单）vs. dogs（复）、过去时-ed（如"走路"walk vs. walked）、现在分词 -ing（如"走路"walk vs. walking），以及将动词变成名词的 -er（如write"写"vs. writer"作家"），等等，都是常见的后缀。

（三）中缀

中缀（infix）是插入词根之中的词缀，在世界的语言中比较罕见，而且有时容易误判。例如，有些人可能会因为wonderfully"奇妙地"可以拆解成wonder-ful-ly，便将其中的-ful-当成一个中缀，因为-ful-看起来像出现在词的中间。但是，这是不正确的，因为前、后、中缀的分别主要在于词缀相对于词根/词干的位置，而相对于词根来说，ful还是一个后缀，如（3）所示。

（3）词根：wonder

加缀：wonder+-ful

加缀：wonder+-ful+-ly

真正的中缀是像他加禄语（菲律宾）里的-um-。它插入词根内部，将词根切成两半，如表4-3所示。

动词词根	非限定形式	注释
bili	b-um-ili	"买"
kuha	k-um-uha	"拿取"
sulat	s-um-ulat	"写"

表4-3　他加禄语动词的非限定形式

他加禄语的例子中有三个双音节词根（bili、kuha、sulat），就像上面英语的wonder一样，已经不能再拆分为更小的、承载语义的单元。非限定形式中缀-um-是插入词根的哪个位置呢？插入第一个辅音的后面。所以，bili"买"这个词根就被中缀拆分为b和ili两个部分，而-um-置于两个部分之间。

（四）环缀

环缀（circumfix）是一个环绕着词根或词干的不连续黏着语素，通常分成两个部分：一部分接在词根或词干前端，另一部分接在其末端。德语的过去分词（past participle）有一种构成方式就是使用环缀：在动词词干前加ge-，词干后加-t或-et，例如（4）。

（4）　ge-spiel-t　　　　　"玩"

　　　　ge-arbeit-et　　　　"工作"

　　　　ge-sag-t　　　　　"说"

　　　　ge-hört　　　　　"听见"

马来语也有丰富的环缀，有不少的功能是将名词变成具有相关词义的动词。如表4-4所示，以 pasang "（一）对；（一）双"为例，在词根之前加"ber-"，在词根之后加"-an"，构成环缀。

名词	动词
pasang "（一）对；（一）双"	**ber**-pasang-**an** "成为一对"
guna "用处"	**memper**-guna-**kan** "使用"
sakit "苦痛"	**di**-sakit-**i** "被……伤害"

表4-4　马来语中的环缀

在形态分析中，一般用连字符"-"来联结词缀与词干，"-"一端是词缀本身，另一端是词干或其他词缀。例如，上述英语表示否定的词缀un是前缀，所以将连字符置于词缀后：un-，连字符另一端是词干；而英语表示名词复数的标记是后缀，词干在前，所以用-s表示。

五、依附词

依附词也是黏着语素，但是运作的范围不是词，而是短语或小句。换句话说，依附词所黏着的对象不是一个特定词类的成分，而是某个短语或小句的组成成分。依附词的黏着性体现在音系的层面上，受到宿主（host，也就是依附词黏着的对象）的制约。英语的冠词（定冠词the及不定冠词a/an）就是典型的依附词，以下举不定冠词为例。英语不定冠词如果依附在辅音开头的宿主上，要读成 [ə]（书写为a）；如果依附在元音开头的宿主上，则读成 [ən]（书写为an）。表4-5显示了英语不定冠词的依附对象是其后的名词短语：

例子	翻译	依附对象
an apple	一个苹果	短语中心语
a good apple	一个好苹果	定语
an incredibly good apple	一个好得不可思议的苹果	状语

表4-5　英语不定冠词为依附词

从表4-5的例子可以看出，英语的不定冠词会随着后面所接的词开头为辅音或元音而变化，这显示不定冠词在音系上是受约束的，必须依附于名词短语的第一个成分。从例子中我们看到，名词（apple）、形容词（good）、副词（incredibly）等都有可能担任不定冠词的宿主，因为它们都有可能作名词短语的第一个成分。

在词法的分析中，依附词与宿主一般用"="分隔开，所以英语的不定冠词在语法分析里应以a=/an=来表示（当然目前英文的书写并不这么要求）。

不同依附词的运作范围也不同，有的可能比短语还大，大至整个小句。若以小句为运作范围，依附词一般会依附在小句最开头或最后一个成分上。如果是依附在最开头的成分，有可能黏着在该成分的前方或后方。如果是黏着在该成分的后方，一般称这样的依附词为"第二位置"（second-position）依附。（5）中的例子来自塞尔维亚-克罗地亚语。第三人称单数的量词既可以置于整个名词短语的后面（5）a，也可以插入开头的名词短语之间，将自己置于小句第一成分的后方，成为名符其实的"第二位置"依附词，如（5）b。

（5） a. Taj　　　　　čovek=je　　　　　video　　　　　Mariju

那　　　　　男人=**量词：三单**　　　看见：过去时　　　玛丽

b. Taj=je　　　　　čovek　　　　　video　　　　　Mariju

那=**量词：三单**　　　男人　　　　看见：过去时　　　玛丽

"那个男人看见玛丽。"

第二节　派生与屈折

当我们在描写语言并论到词是如何"成形"时，可以从两方面来说，第一方面牵涉到一个词根以及以该词根为基础形成的新词，它们之间成系统的联结方式我们称之为"派生"（derivation）；另一方面涉及一个词和这个词为适应不同语法环境要求，作出相应调节变化的形式，我们称之为"屈折"（inflection）。

一、派生

派生的结果是造成新词，这个新词有可能词类改变（例如词根是动词，但是派生后的新词是名词）；也有可能词类不变，但是词义改变了。英语中改变词类的派生标记相当丰富，例如，许多动词加上后缀-er，就会变成是施行该动作的人（名词），如表4-6所示。将其它词类的词变成名词的过程是"名词化"（nominalization），具有这个功能的派生标记就是"名词化标记"（nominalizer）。

动词		名词	
help	"帮助"	helper	"帮助者，帮手"
teach	"教导"	teacher	"教师"
drive	"驾驶"	driver	"驾驶员"
sing	"唱"	singer	"歌手"

表4-6　英语动词+派生后缀 （-er） ➡名词

书面藏语的名词化标记相当丰富，以下列举一些，如表4-7所示。

动词		名词	
byed	"作"	byed-po	"创造者"
ston	"指引"	ston-pa	"导师、佛陀"
slob	"学习"	slob-ma	"学生"
lta	"看"	lta-mkhan	"观众"
nyan	"听"	nyan-mkhan	"听众"
sprod	"给（现在时）"	sprod-byed	"给的工具或方式"
sprad	"给（将来时）"	sprad-bya	"给的东西"
thos	"听见"	thos-byed	"耳朵"
		thos-bya	"所听到的内容"

表4-7　藏语名词化标记

词缀加于词根之上，不仅会改变词类，还会带来语义上的变化。下面列出一些在英语中会使新词改变词类的后缀及其构成新词后的语义，词根意义在这里以X代表，表4-8清晰地显示了词缀在派生构词中对词类与语义所起的作用。

词类转换	后缀	语义	例子	注释
名词→形容词	−al	与X有关	bridal（bride+−al）	"新娘的"
	−ial	与X有关	presidential（president + ial）	"总统的"
	−ian	与X有关	Singaporian（Singapore + ian）	"新加坡的"
	−ic	有X的特质	classic（class + −ic）	"上等的"
	−ful	有X	wonderful（wonder + −ful）	"奇妙的"
	−less	没有X	speechless（speech + −less）	"无言的"
	−ous	有X的特质	marvelous（marvel + −ous）	"神奇的"
名词→动词	−ize	变成X	crystalize（crystal + −ize）	"结晶"
	−fy	变成X	mummify（mummy + −fy）	"成木乃伊"
动词→形容词	−able	可以被X	perishable（perish + −able）	"易腐烂的"
	−ive	有做X的性质	active（act + −ive）	"活动的"
	−ate	擅于X的	considerate（consider + −ate）	"体贴的，深思熟虑的"
动词→名词	−ation	实施X的过程或结果	examination（examine + −ation）	"检验，测试"
	−ion	实施X的过程或结果	creation（create + −ion）	"创造"
	−er	从事X的人或物	writer（write + −er）	"作家"
	−ment	实施X的过程或结果	measurement（measure + −ment）	"测量，尺寸"
形容词→动词	−ize	使成为X	legalize（legal + −ize）	"合法化"
形容词→名词	−ity	X的状态	stupidity（stupid + −ity）	"愚蠢"
	−ness	X的状态	happiness（happy + −ness）	"快乐"
形容词→副词	−ly		sadly（sad +−ly）	"令人遗憾地"

表4-8 英语派生词缀及其词类、语义变化

派生的结果有可能词类不变，但词汇的基本意义变了。英语中具有派生功能的前缀大

抵都是这样的，如表4-9所示。

前缀	词根	派生结果	词类
re-	play "播放"	replay "重复播放"	都是动词
in-	considerate "体谅的"	inconsiderate "不体谅的"	都是形容词
un-	happy "快乐"	unhappy "不快乐"	都是形容词
	do "做"	undo "取消"	都是动词

表4-9 英语派生词缀及其语义变化 （词类不变）

一个词也可以带一个以上的派生词缀，例如（6），以play "播放"为词根，依次添加前缀re-、后缀-able与后缀-ity，每次加缀都带来语义上的变化，词类可以不变（replay），也可以变化（replayable、replayablity）。

（6）play 播放
replay 重复播放 （加re-）
replayable 可重复播放的 （加-able）
replayability 可重复播放性 （加-ity）

二、屈折

屈折是同一个词适应不同语法环境的要求而调节形态的手段，并不会造成新词，也不改变词的基本意义。比如说，一个名词的屈折标记会表示名词的数、格位、类别等信息，而动词的屈折标记或手段则经常为该词义标定地点、时间和参与者。以下讨论几个常见的屈折范畴。

（一）数（名词）

名词的数我们在英语中就能观察到。许多英语名词都可以带复数标记-s，而与之相对不带标记的名词形就表示单数，如表4-10所示。

单数	复数	释义
cup	cup-s	"杯子"
skirt	skirt-s	"裙子"
boy	boy-s	"男孩"

表4-10 英语名词单复数

英语复数形式表示所指涉的名词数量是两个或更多，只要比一个多就是复数。但另一方面，世界的语言中有不少还要进一步在复数的概念上区别"两个"和"多于两个"的数，也就是双数与复数。中国四川境内的嘉戎语，就在名词的数标记上区分单数（无标记）、双数（后依附词=ndʒês）以及复数（后依附词=ɲê），如表4-11所示。

单数	双数	复数	释义
pak	pak=ndʒês	pak=ɲê	"猪"
câ	câ=ndʒês	câ=ɲê	"麝"
rdəgə̂	rdəgə̂=ndʒês	rdəgə̂=ɲê	"盘羊"

表4-11　嘉戎语名词数的差别与标记

（二）类别（名词）

名词类别（noun class）存在于许多形态丰富的语言中。不少印欧语系语言有名词"性别"（gender）的分类方式。例如，西班牙语的定冠词就分成阳性名词专用的el，以及阴性名词专用的la。但这样的名词分类格局与班图语系的斯瓦特语（Swati）相比就是小巫见大巫了。斯瓦特语将名词分为十数类，表4-12仅列举其中的几类。

前缀	类别	例子	释义
um（u）-	人	um-fana	"男孩"
li-	身体部位；果子	li-dvolo	"膝盖"
in-	动物	in-ǰa	"狗"
s（i）-	器具	si-tja	"盘子"
pha-	处所	pha-ndle	"外面"
bu-	抽象性质	bu-bi	"邪恶的"

表4-12　斯瓦特语的名词类别

很多时候，这些名词的分类并不是由名词所指涉对象的客观性质来决定的，而是社会约定俗成的结果，例如，澳大利亚的迪尔巴尔语（Dyirbal）将名词分为四类，其中第一类是"男人及有生命的活物"，第二类则将"女人、火、危险的事物"划为一类。这样分类很显然不是根据客观的外在性质，更可能的是反映出使用这个语言的族群对人和事物的主观认知。

（三）格（名词）

还有一个常以名词屈折手段表示的是"格"（case），这是一种为名词的语法关系角色（如主语、直接宾语等）信息编码的语法范畴。拉丁语的名词格标记可为典型代表，表4-13以"主；主人"这个阳性名词来呈现单数的格位变化。

格	屈折形态	后缀	功能
主格 nominative	dominus	-us	标示主语
呼格 vocative	domine	-e	称呼时用
宾格 accusative	dominum	-um	标示直接宾语
属格 genitive	domiňī	-ī	标示领属者
与格 dative	dominō	-ō	标示间接宾语
从格 ablative	dominō	-ō	标示"从（某处）离开"的意思

表4-13　拉丁语阳性名词 "主； 主人" 格位与格标记

接下来的几个小节将简单介绍常见的动词屈折标记，包括人称与数、时、体和情态。

（四）人称和数（动词）

在动词上可以标示其主语或宾语，并且可以指明是第几人称，单数或是复数。印欧语系语言有许多都呈现了这样的形态变化，以西班牙语的"说（某种语言）"的现在时为例，就可以观察到动词的形态标记能标示主语是第一、第二、第三人称，以及单数或复数，如表4-14所示（"说"的词根为habl）。

hablo	我说
hablas	你说
habla	他说
hablamos	我们说
hablais	你们说
hablan	他们说

表4-14　西班牙语的 "说" 义动词形态变化与人称、 数对应关系

我国境内的嘉戎语的动词标记也相当复杂。在嘉戎语中，动词的人称标记区分人称、数（单、双、复）以及语法关系角色。以mtô"看见"为例，在完整体的语境中，第一人称及第二人称分别作主语及宾语的动词形态如（7）所示。嘉戎语的动词有两种词干变化，完整体采用第二词干，例句中在词干后标为2。

（7）a. na-　　　　　　　ta-　　　　　mtô　-n
　　　　完整体- 第一人称主语: 第二人称宾语- 看见: 词干2- 第二人称单数
　　　　"我看见了你。"

b. na-　　　　　　　ta-　　　　　mtô　-ɲ
　　　　完整体- 第一人称主语: 第二人称宾语- 看见: 词干2- 第二人称复数
　　　　"我看见了你们。"

从（7）a可以看出，嘉戎语使用动词前缀ta-表示主语是第一人称、宾语是第二人称；同时，还使用动词后缀-n，表达第二人称宾语为单数。在（7）b中，动词后缀替换成了-ɲ，表示作宾语的第二人称为复数。

（五）时

时（tense）范畴所表达的是所描述情况发生的时间，其参照点一般是说话的当下。若是情况发生得比说话时间早，标为过去时；若是情况发生得比说话时间晚，则用将来时标记；与说话处于同一个时间段的事件或状态则带现在时的标记。需要注意的是，这里提到的"时范畴"是一个语法的范畴，也就是有专属的语法标记表达的语法功能范畴。汉语也能表达发生在过去、现在和未来的情况，但是并没有相应的动词语法标记，一般是通过状语的使用将情况发生时间标明出来，例如（8）。

（8）a. 我们家明天吃炸酱面。
　　　　b. 我们家昨天吃炸酱面。
　　　　c. 我们家今天吃炸酱面（一边吃着炸酱面，一边向人说明）。

从上面的例子我们可以看出，无论"吃炸酱面"这个事件发生在未来（a）、过去（b），还是现在（c），汉语的动词形态不变（都是"吃"）；时范畴的语义由状语"明天""昨天"和"今天"承担。据此，我们可以说汉语的动词本身并没有表达"时"的语法范畴。

在有动词时范畴屈折变化的语言中，最常见的划分是过去时与非过去时相对的格局，如英语的-ed表达过去时，而无标记的动词就是非过去时。

（9） a. I walk to school. （非过去时）

     b. I walked to school. （过去时）

     "我走着去上学。"

读者可能会问：英语不是还有将来时吗？可以说"I will walk to school."。在传统的英语教材中的确是这样分析的，但请注意walk、walked相对于will walk有一个重大差别，那就是walk和walked的调节对立都在词的层面，而will walk则是用一个自由语素（will）来表达将来时，因此是个词和词组合成的短语。因为在（9）这个例子中所呈现的是词的"屈折形态"的格局，所以以自由语素构成的短语就不在这个格局内。

西班牙语就是一个以动词屈折变化表达将来时的语言。表4-15的例子呈现了"说"这个动词的不定式、现在时以及将来时形态。

不定式	hablar
现在时	habla
将来时	hablará

表4-15 西班牙语的 "说" 义动词的形态变化， 主语为第三人称单数

（六）体

体（aspect）所描述的是事件或状态内部的时间结构，可以分为完整体和非完整体两大类。两者的区别就像将镜头拉远拉近，呈现出不同的视野。完整体（perfective）呈现的是完整的情况，所以情况的边界（起始点和终端）会出现在视野内。与动态动词一起使用的时候，完整体标记常常将终端带入视野中，但不交代起始点为何。例如，在（10）中，一个个带"了"的事件是连续发生的，但是我们只知道其终端。

（10）他回到家， 自己烤了披萨当晚餐吃。 吃过饭， 他刷了盘子、 擦了厨房，

     然后洗了个澡。 上了床后他拿起书看， 看了没一会儿就进入了梦乡。

与表达状态的词连用时，完整体经常表达状态的改变，特别是状态的起始。汉语普通话的完整体"了"和表达状态的词"红""绿"一起用，就有这样的语义功能，例如（11）。

（11）花红了、草绿了

在（11）中，花进入了"红"的状态，经历了从"不红"到"红"的状态改变；同样地，"绿"加上完整体"了"也算是进入了"绿"的状态，而不是"绿"的状态的终端、结束。

完整体经常指涉过去的时间，有一些语言（如希腊语）的完整体只能与过去时的语义一同使用。不过，在不少语言中，完整体并不限于过去时，也可用于将来时。汉语普通话就可以这样使用完整体"了"，例如（12）。

（12）你先别急，现在店门还没开，开门了你再去。

在（12）中，说话的当下"开门"这个事件还没有发生，完整体"了"还是呈现一个事件（开门）的终端，因此我们可以说汉语普通话的"了"不专属过去时，还可以用于将来时。

非完整体（imperfective）则是将镜头拉近到事件或状态的一部分，不交代其起始或终端，例如，英语的He is driving（他在驾车）就是表达一种非完整体的语义，并没有指示"驾车"的开始或结束，而是两端之间的一个部分。需要注意的是，这个be V-ing的结构在英语中归为"进行体"（progressive），而进行体并不等同于非完整体，只是非完整体的一个次类。非完整体同时包含"进行体"和"习惯体"（habitual）这两类。如果有一个语言在表达"他正在驾车"和"他每天驾车"时，动词都带同样的语法标记，那么这个语言所使用的动词标记就是"非完整体标记"。

鉴于完整体经常与完成体（perfect）发生混淆，因此有必要介绍完成体的特点及分析方式。完成体的定义牵涉到三个时间：说话时间（speech time）、事件时间（event time）以及参照时间（reference time）。如果一个事件是简单过去时或简单将来时，事件时间与参照时间重叠，则两者或都发生在说话时间之前即过去时，或都在说话时间之后即将来时。（13）中的图呈现的是简单过去时，请仔细观察三个时间之间的关系。

（13）简单过去时的时间结构

至于完成体所表达的时间结构，则是事件时间永远先于参照时间。英语、法语、西班牙语等分布于欧洲的语言都有专门表达完成体的结构（也就是像英语的"have 加上过去分词"这样的表达方式），但是在表达的时候必须同时标明时范畴，因此有现在完成体（present perfect）、过去完成体（past perfect，英语语法俗称pluperfect）和未来完成体（future perfect）的区别。在以时范畴区分完成体标记时，是以参照时间与说话时间的相对关系来决定的。也就是说，如果参照时间等同于说话时间，由现在完成体来表达；如果参照时间先于说话时间，则由过去完成体来表示；如果参照时间后于说话时间，则由未来完成体来表示。下面用数轴逐一说明三种完成体。现在完成体的例子请看（14），其中的事件时间先于参照时间（完成体的基本界定），而且参照时间与说话时间重合（现在时的界定）。

（14）现在完成体的时间结构

例句：I have seen three lions. "（到说话的这会儿）我已经看见三头狮子了。"

如果事件时间还是先于参照时间，但参照时间先于说话时间，则由过去完成体来表示，如（15）。

（15） 过去完成体的时间结构

例句：I had seen three lions when they found me.

"他们找到我的时候（过去的一个时间点），我已经看见三头狮子了。"

如果事件时间先于参照时间，而参照时间后于说话时间，则由未来完成体来表示，如（16）。

（16） 未来完成体的时间结构

例句：I will have seen many lions when they find me.

"等他们找到我的时候（未来的一个时间点），我都已经看见好多狮子了。"

（七）情态

情态（modality）标记所表达的是说话的人对一个情况或事件的立场或态度，包括其对事件真实性的确定度，或者对事件或情况与自己的关联的评估。在情态范畴的次类中，传信（evidentiality，又称"示证"）是一个常用动词屈折标记来表达的语法功能，其主要作用是交代所描述事件或状态的信息来源，包括说话者自己经历的、看见的、从他人那里听见的，或是依据眼见的事实推论出来的，等等。嘉戎语会使用动词的屈折手段表达"间接传信"的范畴。试比对以下两个例子，两个小句的主要含义都一样（"饭熟了"），只

是（17）a的信息是说话者本来就知道的（可能他是煮饭的人，而且一直在锅边看着），而
（17）b是说话者在饭熟了以后才发现的。

（17）a. khri   ko-   smen

       饭   完整体-煮熟₂

     b. khri   ka-   â-   smən

       饭   完整体： 间接传信-间接传信-煮熟₁

       "饭熟了。"

藏语拉萨话用异干交替的方式表达所描述的事件或状态对说话者来说是不是新的信息
（如果是，通常还表达惊讶的心理）。例如，在拉萨话中，"我有钱"有两种说法。第一种
使用的情况是说话者知道自己带了钱，他和朋友一起想买样东西，说到钱的问题，说话者
会说（18）a。第二种情况是说话者不知道或忘了自己带了钱，与朋友说到钱的问题，在
不抱希望的情况下掏了掏口袋，发现自己原来带了钱，于是说（18）b。

（18）a. ngar   dngul   tog=tsam   yod

       第一人称单数：与格   钱   一些   存在

       "我有钱。"

     b. ngar   dngul   tog=tsam   'dug

       第一人称单数：与格   钱   一些   存在：新知

       "我有钱！"

换句话说，如果所描述的事实是早就存在于说话者的知识系统的，藏语就用存在动词yod；但
如果所描述的事实是说话者刚知道，尚未融入知识系统的，就用存在动词'dug。后者按此功能
被识别为表达"新知"（mirative）情态范畴的标记，通常暗示说话者对所叙述情况感觉惊讶。

第三节　构词法

语言会构造词，既能扩增词汇，也能依照不同的语法环境调整词的形态样貌。而且
这个过程是有规律、系统化的。语言构造词的方式有一套规律，我们称之为"构词法"

（word-formation process）。以下介绍几种以既有词汇为基础造出新词或依语法功能及环境调节形态的构词法。

一、加缀

加缀（affixation）就是在词干上加上词缀（可以是前缀、后缀、中缀、环缀）。在英语中，许多过去时动词的形成就是通过加上-ed这个后缀的手段构成的，如表4-16所示。

词干	现在分词	注释
cook	cooked	"烹煮"
kick	kicked	"踢"
walk	walked	"走路"

表4-16　英语动词过去式构词法

英语的过去时-ed是一个屈折后缀，其作用是将动词调整成适合过去时语法环境的形态，加缀后并没有改变词类和基本语义。

嘉戎语使用前缀来改变词类，例如，前缀kə-就会将动词名词化，用来指涉动词的施事者，因此是一种派生前缀，如表4-17所示。

词干	名词化
rama "干活"	kə-rama "干活的人"
za "吃"	kə-za "吃的人"
rjək "跑"	kə-rjək "跑的人"

表4-17　嘉戎语前缀构词示例

二、复合

复合（compounding）是将一个或多个词根（root）结合起来构成一个新词。在英语中，可以被复合的词根通常是名词、形容词、动词、介词等，复合出的词可以是名词、动词或形容词，例如（19）。

（19）　名词+名词　　　　→名词　　textbook　　　"教科书"

　　　形容词+名词　　　→名词　　greenhouse　　"温室"

　　　动词+名词　　　　→名词　　jumpsuit　　　"连身衣"

　　　名词+形容词　　　→形容词　rock-solid　　"如岩石般坚硬的"

　　　形容词+形容词　　→形容词　icy-cold　　　"冷冰冰"

　　　名词+动词　　　　→动词　　spoon-feed　　"用匙喂"

　　　形容词+动词　　　→动词　　dry-clean　　"干洗"

　　　介词+动词　　　　→动词　　out-rank　　　"居……上位"

　　　动词+动词　　　　→动词　　blow dry　　　"吹干"

构成复合词的成分也可以是通过加缀后形成的词，如（20）；通过复合手段构成的词也可以进一步与其他词构成复合词，如（21）。

（20）　rice cooker"饭锅"　　（cooker = cook + −er）

（21）　dog food box"狗食盒"　　（dog food= dog + food）

　　从上面的例子可以看出，英文书写复合词的方式并不统一，有时所有的成分都连在一起，中间没有空格；有时各个成分是分开的。不过，这并不妨碍复合词的判别，因为复合词的主要重音通常都落在第一个成分上。如果相同成分构成的是短语（而非复合词），则会在后面的成分带主要重音。试比较表4−18中相同成分所构成的复合词与短语。

复合词	释义	短语	释义
'greenhouse	"温室"	green'house	"绿色的房子"
'wet suit	"跳水服"	wet'suit	"湿的外衣"
'White House	"白宫"	white'house	"白色的房子"

表4−18　相同成分构成复合词与短语示例

除了重音的分布有别于短语，复合词的语义也不是组成成分语义的简单组合，这一点从上表的释义可以看得很清楚。

三、重叠

　　重叠（reduplication）是让一个自由语素形式重复叠加，构成新词。依照成分重复叠加的比例，可以分为"完全重叠"（total reduplication）和"部分重叠"（partial reduplication）。使用重叠作为构词手段的例子在英语中并不多，但是在世界上有些语言中，重叠是经常用的手段，例如，印尼语就可以用重叠来构成名词的复数形式，如表4-19所示。

单数	复数	注释
lalat	lalatlalat	"苍蝇"
rumah	rumahrumah	"房子"

表4-19　印尼语名词复数的重叠构成手段

从上面的例子可以看出，印尼语"苍蝇"和"房子"两个词的复数形式是通过"完全重叠"的手段构成的，表达单数的名词词干被完全复制。

　　他加禄语将来时的构成形式，则是通过"部分重叠"的手段，被重复的是词干的第一音节，如表4-20所示。

词干	将来时	注释
lakad	lalakad	"走"
kain	kakain	"吃"
bili	bibili	"买"

表4-20　他加禄语将来时构成手段

四、交替

　　要构成新词或调节形式表达词法上的区别，除了在外部添加成分（加缀和重叠）或从外部插入成分（中缀的使用），语言还可能在语素内部作形态的调节，这样的手段叫作"交替"（alternation）交替的手段就是以语音的改变来表示词的意义或功能的区别，英语中以交替手段调节形态的例子不少，名词单复数的对立有一些词会使用内部交替，如表4-21所示。例子中受调节的成分下面画了线，虽然英文的拼写无法反映出某些例子的变化（如"女人"一例），但从"交替方式"一栏，即可得知画线部分在读音上的变化。

单数	复数	注释	交替方式
m<u>a</u>n	m<u>e</u>n	"男人"	[æ] vs. [ε]
f<u>oo</u>t	f<u>ee</u>t	"脚"	[ʊ] vs. [i]
t<u>oo</u>th	t<u>ee</u>th	"牙"	[u] vs. [i]
w<u>o</u>man	w<u>o</u>men	"女人"	[ʊ] vs. [ɪ]

表4-21　英语名词复数的交替构成手段

英语的过去时及过去分词形式有些也是使用内部交替（元音）的方式来构成的，如表4-22所示。

词干	过去时	过去分词	注释
s<u>i</u>ng	s<u>a</u>ng	s<u>u</u>ng	"歌唱"
h<u>o</u>ld	h<u>e</u>ld	h<u>e</u>ld	"握，抱"
r<u>u</u>n	r<u>a</u>n	r<u>u</u>n	"跑"
dr<u>i</u>nk	dr<u>a</u>nk	dr<u>u</u>nk	"喝"

表4-22　英语过去时/分词的交替构成手段

英语中参与交替的不只有元音，辅音也可以有交替变化，辅音的变化可以造成名词-动词的交替，是一种派生手段，因为造成了词类的改变，如表4-23所示。

名词			动词		
advice	[əd'vaɪ<u>s</u>]	"建议、忠告"	advise	[əd've<u>z</u>]	"提出建议、忠告"
strife	[stɹaɪ<u>f</u>]	"争斗"	strive	[stɹaɪ<u>v</u>]	"努力奋斗"
bath	[bæ<u>θ</u>]	"沐浴；浴缸"	bathe	[be<u>ð</u>]	"给……洗澡"

表4-23　英语辅音交替与词类变化

五、异干（根）交替

异干交替（suppletion）是一种屈折形态手段。一般而言，屈折形态通常以相同或相似的语音形式为基础，通过外部（加缀、重叠）或内部（交替）的手段体现一个词在不同语法环境的变化形式。不过，语言中会有一些词在作屈折变化的时候，采用的是在语音上与词根毫无共同点的形式。这种完全的不规则变化我们称之为"异干（根）交替"。英语有少数的形容词用异干交替手段表达比较级和最高级，如表4-24所示。

形容词	比较级	最高级
good"好"	better"更好"	best"最好"
bad"坏"	worse"更坏"	worst"最坏"

表4-24 英语形容词比较级、最高级的交替构成手段

英语有少数动词也用异干交替的手段来区别现在时与过去时，如表4-25所示。

现在时（非过去）	过去时	注释
go	went	"去"
is	was	"是（第三人称单数）"
are	were	"是"

表4-25 英语动词时的交替构成手段

有趣的是，有不少语言的"去"这个动词都用异干（根）交替来区分时范畴，例如，嘉戎语的过去及非过去的词干区分，如表4-26所示。

非过去词干	过去词干	注释
tʃʰê	tʰel	"去"

表4-26 嘉戎语动词过去时与非过去时的交替手段

里汝语的"去"这个动词呈现了三种异干的交替，因为除了过去时与非过去时的分野，过去时的形式还有人称的区别，如表4-27所示。

非过去时	过去时第二、第三人称	过去时第一人称	注释
ji	da	pʰjæ	"去"

表4-27 里汝语过去时与非过去时的异干交替

西班牙语的"去"也有异干交替的不规则变化，以下限定动词以第一人称单数主语的变化为例，如表4-28所示。

不定式	现在时（第一人称单数）	简单过去时（第一人称单数）	注释
ir	voy	fue	"去"

表4-28　西班牙语动词 "去" 的异干交替形式

任何语言都有可能使用异干（根）交替的手段，不过一般来说这类例子数量都很小。

第四节　语言的形态类型

依形态划分的语言类型（morphological types of language），其分类基础是语言使用什么构词法、自由语素还是黏着语素为主以及语素结合的紧密程度，等等。按照语言在这些方面的表现差异，首先划出分析型（analytic）和综合型（synthetic）两大类，然后再将后者细化为三类：黏着型（agglutinating）、溶合型（fusional）以及多式综合型（polysynthetic）。

一、分析型

在分析型语言中，每一个词就是一个单一的语素。分析型语言的一个极端类型，就是"孤立语"（isolating languages），不使用加缀等手段构词，而且词与语素数量的比例几乎达到1：1。汉语可以说在形态上是分析型，黏着语素的使用整体来说比例不高，而且有许多词只内含一个语素。（22）是一个改编自新闻内容的小语段：

（22）在纽约，一年一度的独立日吃热狗大赛开始了，今年的冠军竟然能在10分钟内吃了62根热狗。

在这个例子中，除了表达完整体的"了"必须黏着于动词（在这个例子中是"开始"和"吃"），以及领属的"的"必须黏着于领属者名词，才能出现在语流中，其他的词都可以作自由语素单独出现在语流中，并没有带派生或屈折词缀。

分析型的语言比较集中分布在东南亚、非洲中部以及大洋洲，美洲和欧洲的分布相对稀少许多。各地的分析型语言包括了越南语、泰语、缅语、克伦语、马拉加西语、约鲁巴语、夏威夷语、大溪地语，等等。

二、综合型

在综合型语言中，黏着语素会接在其他语素上，所以一个词有可能是由多个有意义的成分组成。黏着语素有可能是在其宿主之上增加/赋予一个新的意义（派生功能），也可能是显示一个词干的功能变化（屈折功能）。

根据语素之间结合的紧密程度高低，以及词干词缀的数量和多样性，综合型的语言还可以细分为以下三种。

（一）黏着型

黏着型语言中，构成一个词的多个语素结合得比较宽松，因此比较容易确定语素和语素之间的界限。土耳其语就是高度黏着型的语言，一个词的每个语义单元都由一个语素负责表达，例如（23）。

（23）kiz-iniz　　　çok　　　iyi　　　piyano　　　çal-iyor-muş
　　　女儿-你的　　　非常　　　好　　　钢琴　　　弹-现在时-新知式
　　　"你的女儿钢琴弹得非常好。"

在这个例子中，"弹"这个动词是由一个词根（çal）和两个后缀（-iyor和-muş）组成的词根与后缀的边界相当清楚，而且每个语素各有一个语义，因此是黏着型的结构。-muş作为新知式语素，是一种情态范畴，表示句子的内容对说话的人来说是刚刚得知的新知识。

（二）溶合型

溶合型语言的特点是将多个语义单元"溶合"进一个语素形式，这与黏着型语言的特点不同，后者通常一个语素就带一个意义。嘉戎语可以说是一个溶合型的语言，请看（24），句中的数字2表示词干第二形式。

（24）　ta-scos　　　ko-　　　　　　　lât　　　　-ŋ
　　　名词-字　　　现在：非完整体：第一人称-写：词干2-第一人称单数
　　　"我 （现在） 正在写字。"

动词"写"所带的前缀ko-表达的意义包括：现在时、非完整体、第一人称。如果这些语义成分有哪一个不一样了，前缀的形式就要完全改变。例如，若将主语改成第三人称（"他"），动词就变成（25）中的样子，数字1表示词干第一形式。

（25）ta-scos   ŋe-   lêt

   名词-字   现在：非完整体：第三人称- 写：词干1

   "他（现在）正在写字。"

在这个例子的动词中，前缀ŋe-的意义是：现在时、非完整体、第三人称。两个例子的动词词干形式也不同，ko-黏着在第二词干上，ŋe-则加在第一词干前。

（三）多式综合型

在多式综合型语言中，一个词能由多个词干和词缀构成，通常是因为动词形式将名词（如主语、宾语）糅进其结构中。（26）这个例子来自爱斯基摩语的Yup'ik方言，整个词包含了两个动词"说"和"猎"、"猎"的宾语"麋鹿"、副词"再"、第三人称主语、将来时标记以及否定标记：

（26）tuntu － ssur － qatar － ni － ksaite － ngqiggte － uq

   麋鹿 － 猎 － 将来时 － 说 － 否定 － 再 － 第三人称单数：泛指

   "他还没有再说他将要猎麋鹿。"

第五节　词法分析：语素的辨识

在研究一个陌生语言时，可以用一些简单的办法将语素划分开并且找出其表达的语义。以嘉戎语为例，我们可以请母语老师先翻译一个以"走路"为词根的例子，例如"我走路"，得到的语料如（27）。

（27）ptʂêŋ

   "我走路。"

以（27）这个例子为基础，接下来我们一次只改变一个语义成分，然后观察哪个形式会随着语义成分的改变而改变，哪些成分维持不变。例如，可以将主语的"我"变成第三人称"他"，问母语老师"他走路"怎么说，得到的语料如（28）。

（28）ptʂê

   "他走路。"

两个例子对照之后，我们可以提出第一步分析，即ptşê是"走路"的词根，因为它是"我走路""他走路"两个例子中那个不变的成分（"走路"），而-ŋ是表示第一人称单数（我）的后缀，零标记（∅）则表示第三人称单数。以此为基础，我们可以继续将不同人称的变化形式收集起来，列表分析。

此外，以"我走路"和"他走路"的例子为基础，还可以改变时、体等范畴的语义，观察形态的变化。请记住，要把握"一次只改变一个语义单元"的原则。例如，以ptşê-ŋ"我走路"（现在已经可以将词干与后缀用连字符分开了）为出发点，可以先问"我在走路"（现在进行体），然后再问"我走了路"（完整体或过去时），得到语料如（29）。

（29）koptşe-ŋ

"我在走路。"

toptşe-ŋ

"我走了路。"

到这一步，可以先将ko-分析为"现在进行体"标记，将to-分析为"完整体或过去时"标记，同时声调从降调变成了平调（表示降调的标记没有了）。然后，根据我们目前的分析结果，可以将"他在走路"翻译成嘉戎语。就目前已有的材料分析，我们应该会构造出ko-ptşe，因为第三人称单数是零标记，现在进行体标记是ko-，而且声调不带降调。然而，请教了嘉戎语的老师之后，"他在走路"却是（30）那样的说法。

（30）ŋaptşê

"他在走路。"

于是从这个例子我们明白，ko-作现在进行体，是主语为第一人称单数的时候用的；如果主语换成了第三人称"他"，就不能用ko-，得用ŋa-。接下来一定要问的一个问题就是：以第三人称单数"他"作主语的完整体或过去时的标记还是to-吗？或者也会因为主语的人称而改变呢？为了厘清这些问题，我们请母语老师翻译"他走了路"，并得到（31）中的语料。

（31）toptşe

"他走了路。"

由此我们知道，嘉戎语的完整体或过去时前缀并不会因主语人称而使用不同的形式。以上的材料与分析，使我们可以初步整理出以下的嘉戎语语素及其意义与功能，请看（32）。

（32） ptşê   "走路" 词干， 用于第三人称、 现在进行体

ptşe   "走路" 词干， 用于完整体、 第一人称现在进行体

to-   完整体或过去时前缀

ko-   第一人称现在进行体前缀

ŋa-   第三人称现在进行体前缀

若能善用以上介绍的分析方式，就能够有效率地收集并分析陌生语言的词法。当然，这里所呈现的嘉戎语动词标记只是极小的一部分，而且分析也是较粗浅的，真正的嘉戎语词法远比这里所呈现的复杂，学术界已投入的研究时间比较可观，分析也更加深入仔细；不过，基本的调查分析手续与这里所介绍的相仿，只要细心设计，熟悉相关文献，就可以收集分析许多更复杂的词法现象与特点。

📑 原典选读

复合、去名词化、数与格

Thomas E. Payne. 1997. *Describing Morphsyntax*：*A Guide for Field Linguists*. Cambridge（UK）：Cambridge University Press.

【导　读】

这个原典材料选自上述文献，该书是一本旨在帮助语言学家从事形态句法田野调查的书。因为这是一本在田野调查方面使用的参考书及工具书，所以需要尽量囊括世界不同语族语言词法句法现象，同时行文必须简洁，分类要便于查找，因此也适合想了解世界语言词法现象的入门者阅读。

本材料选取的是名词及名词短语的相关词法功能及现象，包括复合（compounding）、去名词化（denominalization）、数（number）的系统及标记、格位（case），等等。此外，所选文献也用较小篇幅厘清冠词（articles）、限定词（determiners）和指示词（demonstrative）的区别。此外，作者还讨论了名词的领属结构（possessive constructions）以及给名词分类的类别标记及性别（gender）标记，最后简单地探讨了小称（diminution）及大称（augmentation）的形式与功能。

Many of the categories, structures, and operations mentioned briefly from a "form-first" perspective in the previous three chapters will receive more detailed treatment in the following seven. The present chapter describes tasks, or functions, that tend to be associated with noun phrases, and presents further details concerning how morphosyntactic operations are expressed in noun phrases.

5.1 Compounding

A **compound** is a word that is formed from two or more different words. For example the word *windshield* is composed of the words *wind* and *shield*. Of course, not every sequence of words is a compound. Hence there must be an explicit way of distinguishing compounds from simple sequences of words. The criteria for calling something a compound fall into two groups: (1) formal criteria, and (2) semantic criteria. Compounds may exhibit any of the following formal properties. (1) A stress pattern

92

93　*Compounding*

characteristic of a single word, as opposed to the pattern for two words, e.g., *bláckbird* (the species), has a different stress pattern than *black bírd* (any bird that happens to be black), cf. also *líghthouse keeper* vs. *light hóusekeeper*. (2) Unusual word order, e.g., *housekeeper* consists of a noun plus a verb where the noun represents the object rather than the subject of the verb. Normally objects come after the verb in English. (3) Morphophonemic processes characteristic of single words, e.g., the word *roommate* can be pronounced with a single *m*, whereas normally if two *m*'s come together accidentally in a sentence both are pronounced, e.g., *some mice* will be understood as *some ice* if both *m*'s are not pronounced. (4) Morphology specific to compounds, e.g., the *-er* of *can-opener*. *To can open* is not a verb, *"I can opened all evening*, but with the instrumental *-er* suffix the compound *can open* is treated exactly as though it were a verb stem, following the pattern of *slicer, grinder*, etc. In German, genitive case endings function as morphological "glue" in compounds when their use would be disallowed in the corresponding noun phrase:

(1) 　*German* (from Anderson 1985a)
　　Bischoff-s-konferenz
　　bishop-GEN-conference
　　"conference of bishops"

In this example the *-s* cannot be functioning as a genitive marker because it is a genitive *singular* marker, and the compound refers to a conference of many bishops. On the other hand, sometimes compounds are morphologically simpler than a corresponding noun phrase, e.g., English *spider web* as opposed to the phrase *spider's web*.

The dominant semantic property of compounds is that the meaning of a compound is either more specific or entirely different than the combined meanings of the words that make up the compound. For example, the term *windshield* cannot be used for any shield against wind, but only for those specific items made of transparent material used in vehicles of various sorts. So while a line of trees along a farmer's field could for the nonce be called a *wind shield* (though the technical term is *shelter belt*), it cannot be called a *windshield*. Similarly, *blackbird* (the compound) is only appropriately used to refer to particular species of bird, though members of other species, such as crows, vultures, etc., can legitimately be called *black birds*. Some compounds contain one part which is not a real word, e.g.,

94　*Noun and noun-phrase operations*

huckleberry, cranberry, etc. In fact, sometimes neither part is an independent word, at least not one that can be synchronically related to the meaning of the whole compound, e.g., *chipmunk, somersault, mushroom, blacksmith*.

5.2 Denominalization

A very common operation that applies to nouns is **denominalization**. The term **nominal** can be translated "noun-like;" so to **denominalize** something is to make it less noun-like, or turn it into a verb, adjective, or some other grammatical category. Sometimes operations that create verbs from nouns are called **verbalization** (Clark and Clark 1979). Perhaps the most common type of denominalization makes a possessive verb out of a noun. For example, the Yup'ik noun suffix *-ngqerr* means "to have N" where N is the noun to which the suffix is attached. The following examples

95　*Denominalization*

(from Reed *et al.* 1977) illustrate some common nouns with their denominalized counterparts:

(3) 　patu 　"lid" 　　　　　patungqerr 　"to have a lid"
　　qayar 　"kayak" 　　　　qayangqerr 　"to have a kayak"
　　irniar 　"child" 　　　　irniangqerr 　"to have children"
　　enr 　"bone" 　　　　　enengqerr 　"to have a bone"

Another common denominalization process takes a noun, N, and forms a verb that means "become N." These processes are called **inchoative** (we will distinguish inchoative as a nominal operation from **inceptive** as a verbal operation in the literature, though in the literature the term inchoative sometimes refers to a verbal aspect). For example in Panare the suffix *-ta* when applied to a noun usually means "to become N:" *i'yan* "healer," *i'yatan* "to become a healer."

The Eskimo languages are particularly rich in denominalization processes. The meanings of verbs formed by these suffixes include such concepts as the following (in these examples N refers to the noun to which the suffix attaches):

(4) 　to go toward N
　　to be N
　　to be at N
　　there is N/there lacks N
　　to have plenty of N
　　to be afflicted in one's N
　　to have cold Ns
　　to play with N
　　to hunt for N
　　to capture N
　　to eat N

Denominalization processes (other than possessives and inchoatives mentioned above) tend to express culturally "institutionalized" activities (Mithun 1984). This is illustrated in the Eskimo examples, e.g., hunting, capturing, eating, playing, being cold, and being afflicted are undoubtedly concepts that are very common in the Eskimo context.

Some denominalizers have a "generic" function: that is, when attached to a noun, they form a verb that refers to whatever activity is

96　*Noun and noun-phrase operations*

usually associated with that noun. The following examples are from Mapudugun (courtesy of María Catrileo):

(5) 　koſke 　"bread" 　　　koſke-tu 　"eat bread"
　　kaweyu 　"horse" 　　kaweyu-tu 　"ride horse"

Sometimes it is difficult to distinguish denominalization from noun-verb compounding (**noun incorporation**, see section 8.2.7). One criterion is that if the denominalizer is independently used as a verb in other contexts with substantially the same meaning, then it is incorporation. If the denominalizer is not attested as a verb (though it probably will be related to a verb), then it is "true" denominalization. Some of the Eskimo suffixes referred to above are clearly related to verbs, but they are distinct enough in form and meaning from their corresponding verbs to cause us to call them denominalizing suffixes.

5.3 Number

Nouns and noun phrases are often marked for **number**. The most common number distinction is between singular and plural. For example, the singular/plural distinction is obligatorily marked for all English nouns that refer to concepts that can be counted (those that consist of individually salient units), e.g., *dog* "singular" and *dogs* "plural." Other number distinctions are (1) singular vs. dual vs. plural, and (2) singular vs. dual vs. trial vs. plural. Dual refers to two items only, while trial refers to three items. The last type is very rare, and the singular, dual, plural type is fairly rare, at least in systems of noun-phrase marking; it is more common in participant reference marking on verbs (see section 9.5).

Many languages only mark number in noun phrases occasionally. An interesting question for such languages (probably the majority of the world's languages) is when to mark plurality and when not to mark it. Some languages only mark certain classes of nouns, e.g., animate nouns, for number, while other nouns are left unmarked, or are marked only "optionally" (see below). Other languages only indicate plurality of nouns that are highly "topical" (see section 10.0.3).

97 Number

For languages that have morphological case marking on nouns, it is common for number to be intertwined with the case-marking system. That is, there may be different forms for the case markers, depending on whether the item is singular, (dual, trial) or plural. This is the case, for example, in Latin and many other Indo-European languages:

(6) *Latin*

	Singular	Plural	Gloss
Nominative	porta	portae	"gate/s"
Genitive	portae	portārum	"of the gate/s"
Dative	portae	portīs	"to the gate/s"
Accusative	portam	portās	"gate/s"
Ablative	portā	portīs	"by/with the gate/s"

In most number-marking systems the singular is unmarked while the non-singulars are marked in some way. Some languages mark both singular and plural, e.g., Swahili (Bantu) *umu-ana* "child" vs. *aba-ana* "children." Another possibility is for the plural to be unmarked while the singular receives a mark of some kind, though this is rare. For example, in Desano, a Tucanoan language of Colombia, some nouns are unmarked in the plural but marked with a noun classifier when singular (see section 5.7 on noun classification):

(7)

suʔri	"clothes"	suʔri-ro	"one item of clothing"
gasi	"canoes"	gasi-ru	"canoe"
yukü	"trees"	yukü-gü	"tree"
nome	"women"	nome-o	"woman"

In some varieties of Arabic, the singular of most nouns is morphologically more complex than the plural:

(8) *Palestinian Arabic* (courtesy of Maher Awad)

tufax "apples"   tufaxa "apple"

Some languages only require plurality to be marked on certain kinds of nouns, e.g., animate nouns. For example, in Mandarin Chinese, plural pronouns are marked with the suffix *-men* (ex. 9). Nouns referring to people may be marked for plurality with the same suffix (ex. 10). Other nouns cannot be directly marked for plurality; rather, plurality is expressed via separate quantifiers (ex. 11) (Li and Thompson 1981):

98 Noun and noun-phrase operations

(9) *plurality obligatorily marked for pronouns*

tā	"he/she"	tā-men	"they"
nǐ	"you (sg.)"	nǐ-men	"you (pl.)"
wǒ	"I"	wǒ-men	"we"

(10) *Plurality optionally marked for human nouns*

háizi	"child"	háizi-men	"children"
kèren	"guest"	kèren-men	"guests"
péngyǒu	"friend"	péngyǒu-men	"friends"

(11) *Plurality optionally expressed periphrastically for other nouns*

shū	"book/books"	shū yīxiē	"some books"
yèzi	"leaf/leaves"	yèzi xǔduō	"many leaves"

Number can be expressed by any of the usual morphosyntactic processes, e.g., prefixation (see Swahili above), suffixation (English, Arabic), infixation (Ifugao, see below), stem change (Endo), reduplication (Ifugao), suprasegmental modification, suppletion (Endo), or distinct particles (Tagalog). So far no language has been found to use word order to express plurality, e.g., there are no languages in which the possessor precedes singular nouns but follows plural nouns. The following examples will illustrate some of the more unusual number-marking systems.

In Ifugao, a group of closely related Philippine languages, plurality is indicated by reduplication of the first syllable or by infixation:

(12) *Tuwali Ifugao* (courtesy of Lou Hohulin)

tagu	"person"	tatagu	"people" (reduplication of first syllable)
babai	"woman"	binabai	"women" (infixation of -in-)

In Ifugao reduplicative plural marking is "optional" when referring to plural entities. It is more common for an independent particle to occur in place of or in addition to the reduplication (see ex. 14 from Tagalog).

In Endo (Western Nilotic, Kenya), plurals are very complex. Most of them must be considered suppletive (13a, b), though there is regularity within certain classes of nouns (13c, d):

(13)

a.	aráan	"goat"	no	"goats"
b.	árááwa	"moon," "month"	áró	"months"
c.	chemur	"breastbone"	chemurtiin	"breastbones"
d.	eya	"mother," "maternal aunt"	eyaatíin	"mothers," "maternal aunts"

99 Number

Plurality in noun phrases is sometimes expressed by a special particle. This is especially common in Australian and Austronesian languages. The following are examples from Tagalog (Philippines):[1]

(14)   ang babae   "the woman"   ang *mga* babae   "the women"

In some languages there are noun markers that express the idea of "and company" or "*et al.*" This marker is often identical to the form that indicates accompaniment (the *with* of *I went with mother*). For example, Yagua employs a suffix *-ve* for this purpose:

(15) a. sa-súúy Manúngu
          3SG-sing M.
          "Manungu sings."

      b. ri-čúúy Manúngu-ve
          3PL-sing M. -AC
          "Manungu and company sing."

This suffix is not properly termed "plural" since it does not mean there were many "Manungus" (a man's name). Rather, it means that there was a group of people, including one salient person named Manungu.

A similar operation is found in Ifugao. In Ifugao, the accompaniment marker is a prefix, *hin-*. When occurring on a noun referring to a person, it refers to that person and relatives, or "the clan" (examples from Tuwali Ifugao, courtesy of Lou Hohulin):

(16)

ama	"father"	hin-ama	"father and child/children"
agi	"cousin"	hin-aagi	"a bunch of relatives"

When used with another noun, N, this prefix means "a quantity measured by N:"

(17)

basu	"cup"	him-basu	"a cup full" (e.g., a cup and its contents)
iduh	"spoon"	hin-iduh	"a spoon full"
kalton	"box"	hing-kalton	"a box full."

A more complex system is found in Dyirbal, an Australian language. In Dyirbal, animate nouns and pronouns can be marked as being members of a pair or a larger group (Dixon 1972: 51):

100 Noun and noun-phrase operations

(18) a. Bayi Burbula miyandaɲu.
          CL B.   laughed
          "Burbula laughed."   (singular)

      b. Bayi Burbula-*gara* miyandaɲu.
          "Burbula and one other person laughed."   (dual)

      c. Bayi Burbula-*maŋan* miyandaɲu.
          "Burbula and several other people laughed." (plural)

In this section, number marking on nouns and noun phrases has been described. Numeral systems are discussed in section 3.3.3; number as a verbal inflection is discussed in section 9.5.

5.4   Case

It is sometimes difficult to distinguish **case marking** from **adpositions** (the latter consist of **prepositions** and **postpositions**). This is undoubtedly because there is no necessary universal distinction between the two; like most structural distinctions, the two categories describe extremes of a continuum. The following is a rule that probably works 90 percent of the time. However, the distinction described by this rule is rather subtle, and so may not be obvious in early stages of language analysis. Furthermore, in any language there may be exceptions.

> *Rule of thumb.* Case marking is the morphosyntactic categorization of noun phrases that is imposed by the structure within which the noun phrase occurs. Adpositions are free of such configurational constraints.

So, for example, whether a noun phrase occurs in the dative or accusative case in some languages is determined by the grammatical requirements of the verb (or other case-**governing** element) with which that noun phrase is

101   Case

in some grammatical relationship. Whether a noun phrase occurs with a locative or benefactive adposition, however, probably depends purely on the communicative intent of the speaker – it is not imposed by some other grammatical element in the configuration.

In Latin, for example, verbs require that their objects occur in one of a few morphological cases. If the object occurs in some other case, either ungrammaticality or a different sense of the verb results. This is the sense in which Latin verbs **govern** the case of their objects (e.g., the verb *servire* governs the dative case, etc.). Prepositions in Latin also govern the case of their objects. So, e.g., *cum* governs the ablative case, while *contra* governs the accusative case. Prepositions in Latin are, however, not themselves governed by some other element in the configuration; so no verb requires that its object occur in a *cum* phrase, for example. Adpositional phrases are *usually* (though not always) "optional" sentence constituents. The following is an example from Yagua. In Yagua there is a pair of homophonous verb roots, *díiy*, meaning either "kill" or "see." The only grammatical difference between the two is that "kill" governs the accusative case (example 19a) while "see" governs the dative case (19b):[2]

(19) a. sa-díiy nurutú-0
          3SG-kill alligator-ACC
          "He killed an alligator."

      b. sa-díiy nurutí-fva
          3SG-see alligator-DAT
          "*He saw an alligator.*" (or "His vision rested on an alligator.")

Example 19b is evidence that -*fva* "dative" is in fact a case marker rather than a postposition. There are many postpositions in Yagua, such as -*imu* "locative" as in *nurutiimú* "to the alligator," but these are not governed by any verb. It is necessary to note that morphological binding does not distinguish case marking and adpositions. Case markers can be free or bound, prepositional or post-positional. The same is true for adpositions. It so happens that in the classical languages the case markers are phonologically as well as functionally distinct from the adpositions. In Yagua and many other languages, this is not the case. It is true that case markers (as defined above) tend to be more closely tied phonologically to their hosts than are adpositions, but this is not a defining property of case markers. Here we have given a definition based strictly on syntactic function.

102   Noun and noun-phrase operations

The following is a short list of semantic roles that typically are grammaticalized as morphological cases. Keep in mind, however, that there is never a direct, one-to-one mapping between semantics and morphosyntax. This list simply characterizes general tendencies:

Semantic role	*Morphological case*
AGENT	nominative, ergative (section 7.1)
PATIENT	accusative, absolutive
RECIPIENT	dative
POSSESSOR	genitive

Formatives that instantiate other semantic roles can usually be given the same label as the semantic role, e.g., locative, benefactive, instrumental. Insofar as possible, cases and adpositions should be labeled according to their prototypical, or basic, function.

5.5   Articles, determiners, and demonstratives

Operators, whether bound or free, which directly express something about the identifiability and/or referentiality of a noun phrase are often called **articles** (see section 10.0.1 for definitions of identifiability, referentiality, and other pragmatic statuses). Articles, such as the English *the* and *a(n)*, are relatively rare in the world's languages. More common are **demonstratives** (or **demonstrative adjectives**), such as *this*, *that*, *these*, and *those*. Some linguists use the term **determiner** to refer to formatives like *the* and *a(n)*. This term usually also includes quantifiers (*some*, *many*, *a few*, *each*, *every*), numerals, possessors, as well as demonstratives. This broad category does not very often exhibit consistent syntactic behavior, e.g., few languages consistently place them all in the same position in the noun phrase. Therefore, "determiner" is not very viable as a universal natural class.

However, probably all languages have a clear class of demonstratives. These are normally free forms, and may precede or follow the noun they function with. Demonstratives may also be anaphoric on their own, as in *What is that?*, in which case they may be termed **demonstrative**

103   Articles, determiners, demonstratives

pronouns. Demonstratives imply "pointing to," or "demonstrating," the object they refer to, e.g., ***that** house* (said while pointing to a house), or *I'll take three of **those*** (said while pointing at some group of objects).

In addition to exhibiting the features common to the pronoun system of the language (number, gender, etc.), demonstratives often express distance, or orientation with respect to the speaker/hearer. For example, the English system has two degrees of distance, represented by the forms *this* and *that* (*these* and *those* in the plural). Other languages have three degrees of distance. If there appear to be more than three degrees of distance, chances are there is some other parameter that the system is sensitive to in addition to the distance parameter. Some languages make a distinction between items close to the hearer, items close to the speaker, and items distant from both. Others code the difference between visible items and non-visible items. When two or more of these parameters interact within a single system, the results can be very complex.

Most operators that embody pragmatic or semantic information about a noun will tend to occur more often with nouns of particular grammatical relations (e.g., identifiers in English are more frequent in discourse on nouns that occur in the subject role). In many cases these tendencies have become grammaticalized. One common phenomenon is articles that mark identifiability only for direct objects. Farsi is one Indo-European language that does exhibit this property:

(20) *Farsi* (courtesy of Jalleh Banishadr)
      a. Man dombale kitob hæsdæm.
          I   look:for book AUX
          "I'm looking for a book."

      b. Man dombale kitob-ro hæsdæm.
          I   look:for book-DEF AUX
          "*I'm looking for the book.*"

This identifiability distinction in Farsi is not morphologically manifested for noun phrases in any other syntactic role.

In a few languages this grammaticalization has gone so far as to render it difficult to determine whether a given particle or affix is a noun-phrase or verb-phrase operator. For example, Panare (Carib, Venezuela) has a set of prenominal particles that function very much like articles in that they encode information about the identifiability/specificity as well as

104   Noun and noun-phrase operations

animacy and location of the noun that follows. However, they only occur before nouns that function as subject of the sentence, and then only subjects that come immediately after the verb, and then only in non-past tenses! Because these Panare particles have so many characteristics of verb-phrase operators (i.e., consistent position directly after the verb, occurring only in certain tenses) it is difficult to determine whether they should be regarded as functioning more closely with the verb to their left or with the subject nominal to their right.

5.6 Possessors

Languages typically express many semantic relationships with the same formal construction used to express ownership. We will call such formal constructions **possessive constructions**, even though the semantic relationship is not always one of possession, e.g., the phrase *my professor* does not refer to a professor that I "possess" in the same way that *my clothes* refers to clothes that I possess.

It is important to distinguish possessive noun phrases from **possessive clauses**, discussed in section 6.5. A possessive noun phrase contains two elements: a possessor and a possessed item. Sometimes the possessor is referred to as the **genitive** (regardless of whether the language has a morphological genitive case). The possessed item is referred to as the **possessum** or the **possessee**:

(21) Mary's   dog
      possessor possessee
      The love   of my life
      possessee possessor

Some languages make a formal distinction based on the semantic difference between **alienable** and **inalienable** possession. Semantically,

alienable possession is the kind of possession which can be terminated: e.g., I can transfer possession of my worldly goods to someone else, hence my relationship to my worldly goods is one of alienable possession. Inalienable possession is the kind of possession that cannot be terminated. Languages which distinguish inalienable possession always include kinship terms and body parts within the class of inalienably possessed items. My head will always be my head, and my brothers and sisters will always be my brothers and sisters. Apart from body parts and kinship terms, some languages include certain culturally important items within the class of inalienable possessions, such as cows, canoes, machetes, etc. Finally, there are usually a few items that semantically seem to go with one class, but which are grouped with the other class for no apparent reason: e.g., a language may treat rocks as inalienable and brothers as alienable.

The following sentence illustrates both inalienable and alienable possession in Ndjuká (Surinam Creole, example courtesy of George Huttar):

(22) [A wagi fu mi] de gi mi baala.
      the vehicle for 1SG COP give 1SG brother
      "My car is for my brother."

The bracketed portion of this example illustrates the standard way of expressing alienable possession: a preposition intervenes between the possessed item and a pronoun referring to the possessor. The last NP, *mi baala*, illustrates the standard way of expressing inalienable possession. As is common in alienable/inalienable possessive constructions, alienable possession requires more morphosyntactic material (in this case the preposition *fu*) than does inalienable possession. This fact may be seen as an **icon** of the closer conceptual link between possessor and possessed item in inalienable possession.

Similar but not identical to inalienable possession is **inherent** possession. Certain items are inherently possessed, e.g., body parts, kinship terms, and items of personal adornment. Other items are not normally possessed, such as trees, the sky, etc. Some languages require that references to inherently possessed items include reference to a possessor. So in such languages you cannot say simply *brother* or *hand*. You have to say whose brother or whose hand. There may be inherent possession in a language without an alienable/inalienable distinction. A language with inherent

possession may have just one kind of possessive construction, but simply require that some items be possessed, while imposing no such requirement on other items. In systems of alienable/inalienable possession there are two (or perhaps more) grammatically distinct kinds of possessor coding.

Mangga Buang, like many other Papuan languages, exhibits a combination alienable/inalienable and inherent/non-inherent distinction. When the possessed noun refers to one of the class of inalienably possessed items, it takes a possessive suffix (examples in 24). When the possessor of an inalienably possessed noun is third person singular, no pronoun or

suffix is used (examples in 25). Alienable possession is expressed by a pronoun with the genitive suffix *-te*, plus the head noun with no suffix (examples in 26). Thus there are three structures:

(23) a. PRN NP-POSS   inalienable, non-third person singular possessor
      b. NP   inalienable, third person singular possessor
      c. PRN-*te* NP   alienable possession

Examples of each of these structures are provided below (courtesy of Joan Healey):

(24) PRN N-POSS (*inalienable/inherent possession, non-third person singular possessor*)
      a. sa nama-ngg
          1SG hand-1
          "my hand"

      b. o   nama-m
          2SG hand-2
          "your hand(s)"

      c. ham nama-m
          2PL hand-2
          "your (pl.) hands"

      d. sa gaande-ngg
          1SG cousin-1
          "my cousin'

(25) N only (*inalienable/inherent possession, third person singular possessor*)
      a. nama   "his/her hand"
      b. gaande "his/her cousin"
      c. lava   "his/her speech/language"
      d. hali   "his brother/her sister"

(26) PRN-*te* N (*alienable possession*)
      a. sa-te   voow
          1SG-POSS dog
          "my dog"

      b. yi-te   bayêên
          3SG-POSS village/house
          "his/her village/house"

In this language inalienable nouns are inherently possessed insofar as they are always understood as possessed even though the most common possessive affix is 0 for third person possessors. Alienable nouns are not understood as possessed unless they are preceded by the genitive pronoun. Compare the following with 26 above:

(27) a. voow   "a dog" (*"his/her dog")
      b. bayêên "a village" (**"his/her village")

In some languages there is a class of "un-possessable" nouns. Some examples from Maasai are given in section 3.1.1.2.

5.7 Class (including gender)

A **noun class**, **gender**, or **grammatical gender** system is the grammatical classification of nouns, pronouns, and other referential devices. Often such a system correlates with some extralinguistic grouping, such as human vs. non-human or female vs. male. However, gender for a linguist is a *grammatical* classification, which may be quite independent of any natural classification (see examples below).

If there is to be a distinction between gender and noun class systems, it is that noun class systems typically involve the presence of **classifiers**, i.e., special operators that are used in some or all noun phrases to

directly express the class of the noun. For example, Yagua employs classifiers in noun phrases which involve numbers:

(28) a. tín-kïï vaturu
          1-CLS woman (married)
          "one married woman"

      b. tín-see vaada
          1-CLS egg
          "one egg"

Pure gender systems do not, generally, require classifiers; rather, the grammatical distinction is made via "agreement."

If the language has a noun class system, it will almost certainly be well installed in the number system. If nothing else in the language agrees with nouns in terms of class, numeral expressions will. Sometimes noun classes correspond (with varying degrees of directness) to semantic classes such as biological gender, physical shape, sociocultural function, etc. In many Indo-European languages, nouns are "masculine," "feminine," or sometimes "neuter." For example, Spanish expresses the difference between masculine and feminine by a suffix *-o/-a*: *niño* "boy," *abogado* "male lawyer," *maestro* "male teacher," *niña* "girl," *abogada* "female lawyer," *maestra* "female teacher," etc. Most adjectives must reflect the class of their head nouns, e.g., *abogado bueno* "good male lawyer" vs. *abogada buena* "good female lawyer." The class that a particular noun falls into is fairly clear for items that have a biological gender, namely animates. However, all nouns in the language are subject to the class system, and non-animates are classified apparently arbitrarily as masculine or feminine (rather than neuter). Romance languages even differ from one another as to the class that particular lexical items fall into, e.g., Italian *il tavolo* (m.), French *la table* (f.) "the table/board;" Italian *il mare* (m.), French *la mer* (f.) "the sea." There is even at least one word in Italian which is masculine in the singular and feminine in the plural: *il uovo* "the egg" and *le uova* "the eggs." This is simply to show that noun class systems, even those that seem to have a firm natural basis, often exhibit a certain degree of irregularity.

Other noun classification systems are based on other dimensions of reality than biological gender, e.g., shape (roundish objects, longish objects, stubby objects, etc.) or function (adornments, items associated with procuring food, items associated with fighting, foods, people, etc.). In every case, however, there are items that seem as though they should belong in one class, but for some apparently idiosyncratic reason, are placed in another class. For example, in Yagua rocks and pineapples are classed as animates.

The most famous noun class systems are those found in the Niger-Kordofanian languages of Africa. Noun class systems also occur in Australia, Asia, and in the Americas. The examples in table 5.1 are from Swahili, a Bantu (Niger-Kordofanian) language of East Africa. In the Bantu languages, singulars and plurals generally fall into separate classes.

5.8 Diminution/augmentation

Most languages employ operators in the noun or noun phrase that indicate unusual sizes. The term for operations that express unusual

110   Noun and noun-phrase operations

smallness is **diminutive** while operations that express unusual largeness are **augmentatives**. For example, Yagua employs the diminutive suffix *-déé*:

(29)   quivą́ą́   "fish"   quivąądéé   "little fish"

This suffix is also used on adjectives to express the idea of "a little bit ADJ:"

(30)   jį́ę́ę́mura   "big"   jį́ę́ę́muradéé   "a little bit big"

It can also occur on almost any other kind of word to express an idea similar to "just" as in English "just over there," "just a dog," or "just a minute," etc.

Typically, diminutives also carry an endearing sense, e.g.:

(31)   English: sweet-y   lamb-kins
                      DIM   DIM

Correspondingly, augmentatives often carry negative or undesirable connotations:

(32)   *Spanish*
         durmi-lon
         sleep-AUG
         "sleepyhead/lazybones"

There is an apparently universal iconic tendency in diminutives and augmentatives: diminutives tend to contain high front vowels, whereas augmentatives tend to contain high back vowels.

109   Diminution/augmentation

Table 5.1   Some Swahili noun classes

Class number	General content	Prefix	Example	Gloss
1	human, sg.	mu-	mwalimu	teacher
2	human, pl.	wa-	walimu	teachers
5	miscellaneous, sg.	ji-	jino	tooth
6	miscellaneous, pl.	ma-	meno	teeth
7	miscellaneous, sg.	ki-	kiazi	sweet potato
8	miscellaneous, pl.	vi-	viazi	sweet potatoes
10	everyday items, pl.	ny-	nyembe	razors
11	everyday items, sg.	u-/w-	wembe	razor

☯ 思考题

1. 嘉戎语表达名词的数的标记（嘉戎语主要分布于我国四川省阿坝藏羌自治州以及甘孜藏族自治州，是当地藏族所使用的一种语言。符号"^"表示降调。）

嘉戎语	汉语释义	嘉戎语	汉语释义
a. pakɲê	"一些猪"	e. təmindʒês	"两个女孩"
b. tɐpɐt kəmʃôrɲê	"一些美丽的花"	f. patsândʒês	"两只鸟"

续表

嘉戎语	汉语释义	嘉戎语	汉语释义
c．pak kətsʰondʒɐs	"两只胖猪"	g．təmi kəʃkrekɲɐ	"一些聪明的女孩"
d．tɕpetɲɐ	"一些花"	h．ȵelpoɲɐ	"几位国王"
中文注释	嘉戎语语素	中文注释	嘉戎语语素
"猪"		"女孩"	
"花"		"鸟"	
"国王"		"胖的"	
"美丽的"		"聪明的"	
双数标记		复数标记	

（1）仔细观察嘉戎语名词及名词短语表达数的形态，将与中文注释相应的嘉戎语语素填入空格中。

（2）嘉戎语的复数及双数标记是哪一种黏着词素？词缀还是依附词？请说明理由。

2. 里汝语助动词

（里汝语，又名"吕苏语"，分布于四川省西部藏区木里、冕宁、九龙、石棉等县的部分乡镇，是当地藏族日常交际所用语言。标示"ˋ"的词带高调；句子开头若带星号*表示该句子不合里汝语语法。）

里汝语有两个表达非完整体的助动词：/ˋbo/和/ˋgə/。审视下面两个助动词的分布与功能并回答问题：

a	ædi	tsʰipəˊ	tsʰu	ˋbo
	我们	花椒	舂	

"我们在舂花椒"

b	ˋtʰe	tsʰipəˊ	tsʰu	ˋgə
	他	花椒	舂	

"他在舂花椒"

c	*ˋtʰe	tsʰipəˊ	tsʰu	ˋbo
	他	花椒	舂	

"他在舂花椒？"

d	`æ	teɲimærɯ	tʰemʲama	dzi	`gə
	我	每天	多	吃	

"我每天吃很多"

（语境：食量超过了我应当摄取的量，但我还是吃。）

e	`æ	teɲimærɯ	tʰemʲama	dzi	`bo
	我	每天	多	吃	

"我每天吃很多"

（语境：我觉得自己太瘦了，所以注意增加自己的食量）

问题：助动词：/`bo/和/`gə/的区别是什么？先简单列出各自的功能，再提出你的分析。

📖 拓展阅读书目

- Timothy Shopen（ed.）. 2007. *Language Typology and Syntactic Description*. Second Edition. Volume Ⅲ：*Grammatical Categories and the Lexicon*. Cambridge：Cambridge University Press.

- Andrew Spencer（ed.）. 1998. *The Handbook of Morphology*. Oxford: Blackwell.

第五章

句 法

通过上一章的学习，我们知道了什么是形态学（morphology）或词法学，这是语法的一个方面。语法还包括另一个组成部分，也就是句法（syntax），这是本章要介绍的内容。句法关涉的对象很广，首先需要为句法研究的范围划界（第一节）。在此基础上，本章着重介绍如下内容：

几级句法单位（第二节）、两种类型的语类（第三节）、语法形式与语法意义（第四节）、论元结构与语类选择（第五节）、句法结构的性质（第六节）、短语类型及其规则（第七节）、变换及其准则（第八节）、短语结构的形式表征（第九节）。

第一节 句法界定及其研究范围

什么是句法呢？先来看几组句子（句子前面标有星号，表示该句子不好，下同）。

（1）a. 村子里来了一个陌生人。

    b. *一个陌生人来了村子。

（2）a. 倚天剑砍折了屠龙刀。

    b. *倚天剑砍屠龙刀折了。

（3）a. It is raining.

      "下雨了。"

    b. * is raining.（试图表达a的语义）

（4）a. John hit him.

      "约翰打他。"

    b. *John hit he.（语义同a）

（5）a. 张三跑步。

    b. *石头跑步。

（6）a. The man took the book.

      "那个男人拿了那本书。"

    b. * The book took the man.

      "那本书拿了那个男人。"

（7）a. The married man is happy.

      "那个已婚男人很开心。"

    b. *The married man is single.

      "那个已婚男人是单身。"

上述（1）-（7）几组句子中，有的句子好，有的句子不好。为什么？要回答这些问题，有些需要借助于句法知识。

"句法"一词，英文是"syntax"。一般认为，语言这个符号系统包括语音、词汇、语法、语义（一部分与语用相涉），相应地，就有语音学、词汇学、语法学、语义学、语用学。语法学包括形态学（汉语学界称为构词法）和句法学。可见，语言学界不把音系学包括在语法学之中，也将语义学排除在语法学之外。这种把音系学和语义学同语法学完全分开的语法学，是最狭义的语法学。如果再将语法学中的形态学剔除，就是句法学（syntax）。[1] 从研究对象上看，传统上一般认为句法以词与词之间的组配关系为着眼点，考察词与词之间在配列方面的规则与限制。根据国外语言学界的一般认识，句法学可定义为（8）（Carnie, 2011）。

（8）句法学是对句子结构的科学研究。

要理解（8）中的定义，需要理解"科学"与"结构"。读者可以参阅（Carnie, 2011）第一章第一单元的第2-3小节，这里做简单导引。

一般而言，人们倾向于将"科学"与自然科学连在一起，比如物理学、生物学、化学等。尤其是物理学，可以说，近代物理学基本上是建立在科学假说的基础上。不过，"科学"一词实际上也可以用来指研究方法，句法学当然也可以运用科学的方法。就句法而言，科学的研究方法的规程大致是：基于（一定的）语料观察→初步提出一个假设→重新回到（更多的）语料中验证→对原来的假设加以修正→对新的语料进行解释。下面透过两个实例来诠释句法学如何使用科学方法进行研究：一个是关于英语中是非问句的形成方式，一个是关于汉语中不同方言系词的差别。

（9）　a.　Tom is a handsome boy.

　　　　b.　Is Tom a handsome boy?

（10）　a.　Frodo will eat the magic beans.

　　　　b.　Will Frodo eat the magic beans?

（11）　a.　Frodo has eaten the magic beans.

　　　　b.　Has Frodo eaten the magic beans?

（12）　a.　John likes Mary.

　　　　b.　Does John like Mary?

通过观察（9）-（11）的a句和b句，初步可以得出（13）这样的结论：

---

1 徐烈炯（2009：35）指出，目前我国出版的实用语法书都把语法作狭义的理解。为了照顾这一习惯，有人主张把syntax译为"语法学"，但是这么一来grammar怎么译呢？不能译作"语言学"，因为语言学的范围比广义的语法学还要广。syntax译为"句法学"也有些缺点，容易使人以为它只研究句子。syntax的原意是排列组合，不论句子、词组还是词都有排列组合问题。比较恰当的译名似应是"语组学"或"语形学"。逻辑学家有把syntax译为"语形学"。不过在语言学领域中已经约定俗成，只好不改。请读者注意，生成语法学中一般没有分出独立的形态学（morphology），传统的形态学内容分别属于生成句法学和生成音系学。

（13）英语中的是非问句可以通过将陈述句中的第二个成分移至句首构成。

但是，将这个结论重新放到实际语言事实中，比如（12）中，会发现遇到难题，因为按照（13），从（12）a形成的疑问句并非（12）b，而应该是"*likes John Mary"，这在英语中显然不是一个合法的句子。于是，需要对（13）进行修正，初步修正为（14）。

（14）英语中的是非问句是通过将陈述句中的第一个助动词移至句首形成，或者借助助动词do-插入形成。

（14）较之（13）更为科学。不过，将（14）放到更多的语言事实中加以验证，会发现面临新的问题。

（15）a. The boy who is sleeping was dreaming.

b. Was the boy who is sleeping dreaming?

c. *Is the boy who sleeping was dreaming?

（16）a. The boy who can sleep will dream.

b. Will the boy who can sleep dream?

c. *Can the boy who sleep will dream?

面对（15）—（16）这样的事实，英语是非问句的形成规则可以概括为（17）。读者可以自行查验这一概括的科学性。

（17）将作主语的名词短语之后的助动词，即主句中的助动词提到句首，或者借助助动词do-插入形成。

下面再举一个汉语中不同方言系词的差异为例，进一步看看句法学是如何运用科学方法进行研究的。这里以普通话和粤语的系词差异为例，其中的a句与b句表达完全相同的意思。

（18）a. 狐狸是一个洞。

要表达的意思是：狐狸的屋子是一个洞。

b. *狐狸係一个窿。

（19）a. 这裤子是晴雯的针线。

要表达的意思：从针线方式看，这条裤子是晴雯做的。

b. *呢裤子係晴雯嘅针线。

（20）a. 那场大火是电线走了电。

　　　 b. *嗰场大火係电线漏电。

（21）a. 张三是父亲病了。

　　　　 要表达的意思：张三（没来上课）原因是父亲病了。

　　　 b. *张三係阿爸病咗。

（22）a. 张三没来上课是父亲病了。

　　　 b. *张三冇嚟上堂係父亲病咗。

普通话的系词"是"与粤语的系词"係"虽然"本是同根生"，但是从（18）—（22）的a、b两句对比来看，两者的句法表现很不相同。在与普通话相同的语境下，粤语的系词很难像"是"那样运用，除非将相应的成分补充完整。以（18）为例，通过将省略的与"屋子"对应的粤语成分（屋企）补出来，可以挽救原来不好的句子。基于上述事实，似乎可以得出（23）这样的初步观察：

（23）　普通话中的系词句允许省略某些成分造成语义特异的"是"字句，粤语中相应

　　　　　的系词句不允许进行普通话那样的省略。

假如（23）是一个合理的科学假设，那么将其放到语言事实中应该能经受住检验。事实果真如此吗？当看到（24）—（26）那样的句子时，是否要否定（23）所做的假设呢？

（24）嗰场大火，**梗**係电线漏电啦。

　　　　"那场大火，当然/肯定是电线漏电了。"

（25）张三冇嚟上堂，**梗**係佢阿爸病咗啦。

　　　　"张三没来上课，当然/肯定是他父亲病了。"

（26）佢整车，**梗**係自己畀钱啦。

　　　　"他修车，当然是自己出钱。"

仔细观察（24）—（26），发现这些句子跟（18）—（22）的b句颇为近似，然而都可以接受。那么，（23）的归纳是否错了呢？当然没有。比较之下，可以看到，（24）—（26）中系词前面都有一个表示说话人主观断定的副词"梗"。一旦去掉这个"梗"，这些句子同样不被粤语的母语者接受。可见，这个"梗"犹如汽车驾驶员的驾照（licensor），有了它，本来不好的句子获得允准（licensing），成为可以接受的句子。

　　可以看到，句法研究遵循科学的研究路子。"观察→假设→再观察→修正假设→……"

基本上是一切科学研究都要遵守的规程与方法。

那么，句法学一般关注哪些问题呢？我们仍以前面的（1）－（7）为例。这些句子中的b句都不好，不过，其中的原因有所不同。（1）－（4）的b句与句法有关，（5）－（7）的b句与句法无关，而跟语义相关，因为它们与相应的a句在构造上完全相同。（5）－（6）b句的主语不符合动词的语义选择（s-selection）的要求，（7）b的不好归因于"married"与"single"的语义矛盾。可见，不好的句子有的是句法造成的，有的是语义的荒诞造成的。为了说明这一点，不妨再举一个经典的例子，例如（27）。

(27) *Colorless green ideas sleep furiously.

"无色的绿色的梦想狂怒地睡觉。"

很明显，（27）完全符合句子的一般构造，句法上没有问题。问题在于这是一个毫无意义的句子，从语义着眼是一个不好的句子。句法研究应该将这类由语义造成的不好的句子排除在研究范围之外。

在学习句法学时，还需要区分一对重要的概念：合法性（grammaticality）和可接受性（acceptability）。大致说来，合法性是语法上的问题，也就是结构上是否是好的。可接受性是某种语言的母语者对某一形式的直觉判断，不仅跟语法有关，还跟语用、语义有关。合乎语法的句子不一定是可接受的，如上面的（27）。可接受的句子不一定是合乎语法的，如当下网络语言的某些形式，可以（28）为例。

(28) 习近平对话奥巴马。

"对话"在常规语法上是不能像（28）那样运用的，自然也是不可接受的。但在网络语言中，这种不合语法的形式却为某些人群所接受。

第二节 句法单位

句法研究需要确定相应的单位。句法规则犹如大楼的构架，而句法单位则是填入其中的一块块大小不等的砖。一般认为，句法的研究单位一般有四级：词、词组（短语）、从句、句子。

词（word）是最重要的一级句法单位。关于"词"的定义，有不同的说法，下面是几种常见的表述。

> （29）a. 造句的时候能够独立运用的最小单位。
>
> b. 最小的活动的语言片段。
>
> c. 句子中以前后两个可能的停顿为界的任何片段。
>
> d. 词是最小的自由形式。

综合上述几种说法，可以看出，作为语法单位，词具有两个特点：一是独立的自由形式，一是最小的形式。第一个特点将词与语素区分开来，因为语素是不独立运用的，那些能够独立运用的语素潜在具有词的身份，也就是成词语素。第二个特点将词与词组（短语）区分开来，因为词组是可以拆开的，而词不可以拆分。

对于"词"的界定中，"自由"和"最小"（不可拆分）是两个重要特征。"自由"（free）一般是指能够独立运用。"独立运用"通常就是指"能够单说"，而是否能够单说很多情况下就是指能不能单独回答问题。这样看来，"自由"基本上可以理解为能够单说，或者说，能够单独回答问题。请看（30）中的两组对比。a组中"好"能够单独回答问题，证明这个"好"是自由的；b组中的"好"不能单独回答问题，不是自由的。

> （30）a. 问：这种笔好不好？
>
> 答：好！
>
> b. 问：这种笔好使吗？
>
> 答：*好。（要说：好使。）

与"自由"相对的是"黏着"（bound）。所谓"黏着"就是不能单说，或者说不能独立回答问题，像上例中b组中的"好"。关于"自由"和"黏着"，可参阅本章原典选读一。

用"单说"或"单独回答问题"作为"词"的界定中的一个特征要素，可能存在如下问题：第一，某种特殊情况下单说的成分，是不是一个词？例如下面的（31）中un-显然只是词的一个组成部分，是前缀（参见第四章）。第二，那些不能单说的成分，是否就不是词？例如英语中的冠词和汉语中的助词（的、地、得）和连词（和、与、而且）显然都不能单说，可是没有人怀疑它们是词。

> （31）问：Did you say friendly or unfriendly?
>
> 答：un-.

　　对于"词"的第二个特征，也就是"最小"，是相较于"短语"而言的，这个特征将
词与短语区分开来。语法单位的大小是从级别上讲的，不是指构成形式的长短。在能够独
立运用的句法单位（词、短语、句子）之中，词是最小的。若从长度上看，短语不一定比
词长，词也不一定比短语短。例如，"白菜"和"白纸"相比，前者是词，后者是短语，
但是两者的长度是一样的。"devil-may-care"（满不在乎的）作为词反而比作为短语的
"may care"（可以在意）要长。关于词的分类以及与此相关的范畴问题，将在下一节详细
论述。这里专门介绍"最小"这一特征对于词和短语划分的作用，以及词作为最小的句法
单位的一些主要表现。

　　词和短语都是句法单位，都可以自由运用，两者的重要区分在于词比短语要小。这
一点可以从词的一些表现上看出，大致说来可以归结为如下几个方面：

　　第一，词的组成部分不能单独被修饰。比如，"马路"是一个复合词，如果在其前加
一个修饰语"小"，那么这个"小"只能修饰整个复合词，而不能仅修饰"马"。"小马路"
只能表示"小的马路"，而不能表示"小马的路"。"黑板"是一个复合词，"黑"是词内的
一个组成成分，不能被单独修饰，因而"很黑板"的说法不合法，"很"无法理解为整个
复合词的修饰语，因为整个复合词是名词性的，不能被副词修饰。可以说，所有的词都符
合这一标准，但符合这一标准的不一定都是词。黏合式偏正短语也符合这条标准，如"大
树"，一般被认为是短语而不是词（不过，也有人认为"大树"是句法上的复合词），但是
"很大树"不能说。

　　第二，复合词的中间不能插入其他成分。传统所说的离合词有些可以做有限扩展，例
如，"理发"可以扩展为"理一次发"，"游泳"可以扩展为"游了一小时泳"。不过，扩展
之后就成为短语，而不再是词。

　　第三，词的组成部分不能单独与其他成分组成并列结构。比如"汽车"是一个复合
词，我们不能说"汽和火车"，只能说"汽车和火车"。

　　第四，词内成分不能与词外成分相互照应，换句话说，词的组成成分不能作代词的先
行语（antecedent），请对比（32）中的两个句子：

　　（32）a. *我看到了一辆马$_i$车，它$_i$全身的毛都是白的。

　　　　　b. 我看到了一辆马车$_i$，它$_i$朝我直冲过来。

　　（32）a中复合词"马车"的组成成分"马"不能成为其后代词"它"的先行语，"马
车"只能作为一个词作为后面代词的先行语，如（32）b所示。

词的上述四个表现概括起来就是词是作为一个整体参与句法活动的，任何句法操作都不能渗透到词的内部，这个概括不妨称为"词汇完整性原则"（Lexical Integrity Hypothesis）。

短语（phrase）是比词高一级的句法单位。短语也称为词组，就是词与词组合在一起形成的结构。最简单的短语是两个词组成的，比如前面提到的"白纸"就是一个最简单的短语，像"很好""看书""我的""北京上海""孩子笑"等都是两个成分构成的短语。既然短语是由词构成的，一个短语至少包含两个词，那么，词与词之间不可避免发生结构关系，有关短语的内部结构问题，将在第七节详细论述。

从句（clause）从名称上看是一个句子，只不过是处于从属的（subordinate）地位，也就是句子之中的句子。有的语法书将从句称为小句，本书依照汉语学界传统，称之为从句。根据从句所处的句法位置，可以分为宾语从句、主语从句、定语从句、状语从句，分别如（33）-（36）所示。

（33）a. 张三认为语言学很有趣。

b. John thinks（that）linguistics is very interesting.

c. 张三想知道语言学是否有趣。

d. John wonders whether linguistics is interesting.

（34）a. 张三突然出国让大家很惊讶。

b. That John went aboard suddenly surprised everyone.

c. 张三是否出国尚不清楚。

d. Whether John will go aboard is not clear.

（35）a. 昨天失踪的孩子找到了。

b. The child who was missing yesterday was found.

（36）a. 当阿Q进来时，小D正在睡觉。

b. Xiao D was sleeping when A Qiu entered.

在生成句法学里，从句也称为内嵌句（embedded clause），它所在的整个句子被称为根句（root clause）。从句法地位上看，从句可以相当于一个同功能的短语（名词性成分或介词短语），充当主语、宾语、定语、状语。需要指出的是，宾语从句在生成句法学中被归入补足语从句（complement clause），并将补足语从句的引导词称为标补词或标句词（complementizer），像英语中的"that""whether"是两类典型的标补词。汉语在相同的条件下，宾语之前不需要这些额外的引导词。

句子（sentence）是用来交际的。根据第一节关于句法学的界定（参阅（8）），句子应该也是句法单位。如果说词、词组是句法的备用单位，那么，句子是句法的使用单位。对于句子的定义，向来分歧很大，下面是两个关于句子的经典界定。

> （37）句子是人所说的（相对）完整和独立的话语；完整性和独立性表现在它具有单独存在或可以单独存在的能力上，即它本身可以单独说出来。（《语法哲学》中译本：第442页）
>
> （38）句子是前后都有停顿并且带着一定的句调表示相对完整的意义的语言形式。如果一个语言形式的前头或后头没有停顿，那就不是一个句子。（《语法讲义》：第21页）

从（37）-（38）可以看出句子的几个特点：一是形式上相对独立，能单独说出来；二是具有相对完整的意义；三是带有一定的语调。前两个特点是潜在的，词或短语也具备；第三个特点为句子所独有。作为句子，必须有一定的语调。正是从这个意义上讲，词和短语是句法的备用单位，是静态的单位；句子是句法的使用单位，是动态的单位。从句由于处在从属的地位，不是相对独立的，所以，与句子的区别是明显的。在下面的句子中，"孩子们喜欢听故事"在（39）中前面没有停顿，在（40）中后面没有停顿，因而都不能成为独立的句子，只是一个包含于句子中的从句，在（41）中前后都有停顿，有一个陈述性的语调，是一个句子。

> （39）我知道孩子们喜欢听故事。
> （40）孩子们喜欢听故事是他们的天性。
> （41）孩子们喜欢听故事。

句子根据不同的标准有不同的分类，适用于不同的目的。从结构上看，可以将句子分成单句和复句。句法学研究句子一般以单句为对象，不涉及复句。单句可以通俗地理解为简单句（simple sentence），就是由短语或者一个单独的词构成的句子，单句不能再分析出更小的句子。单句可以再分为主谓句和非主谓句，分别如（42）-（43）所示。

> （42） 张三喜欢句法学。
> （43） 又是一个**雾霾**天。

综合来看，句法单位的四级分类大致可以表示为（44）。从词到词组是一种构（组）成关系，以箭头表示。从词组到小句或句子，是一种实现关系，以直线表示。

（44）　　句子
　　　　　　|
　　　　　　|
　　　　从句（小句）
　　　　　　|
　　　　　　|
　　　　词组（短语）
　　　　　　↑
　　　　　　|
　　　　　　词

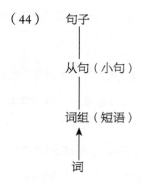

构成（constitution）和实现（realization）是两种不同的关系。构成关系一般是指对结构的微观描述，例如，分子由原子构成，原子由电子和质子构成。语言中较大的单位（词组）是由较小的单位（词）构成的。实现关系则是从一个层面到另一个层面的动态转换关系。词组是静态单位，从句、句子是实际使用的动态单位，词组与从句、句子属于不同层面，一个词组成为从句或句子（根句），是一种实现关系。

第三节　词汇语类与功能语类

依照传统的认识，词一般可以分为实词和虚词。名词、动词、形容词、数词、量词、代词等传统上归入实词，其他词归入虚词。

当代语言学理论将词分成词汇语类（lexical category）和功能语类（functional category）。先界定一下语类（category）。语类是句法上的一个重要概念，就是具有某种词汇属性和功能属性的成分。语类在外延上宽于传统语法的词类，不仅包括以往的词，还包括语素和短语，甚至将句子也纳入语类。

所谓词汇语类就是指具有实在语义内容的词或语素，大致相当于传统所说的"实词"，但与实词的外延又有不同。比如说，疑问代词作为代词的一个次类，在传统语法中属于实词，但在现代句法学中归入功能语类。功能语类是指那些语义内容比较空灵或者说语义较虚，只是具有某种语法功能的语类。词汇语类和功能语类的区分不是非此即彼的，从典型的词汇语类到典型的功能语类，是一个渐变的连续统（continuum）。以动词为例，如（45）所示（引自黄正德2006年6月在北京大学所做的报告），实义动词是词汇语类，居于最左端；有语义内容而没有语音形式的空成分（用小写斜体e表示）是典型的功能语类，居于最右端，在这两端之间，还有一些词或语素。

（45）实义动词＞轻动词（有语音）＞助动词＞附着词（clitic）＞词缀＞空语类e

对于（45），有几点需要说明：

第一，与传统的词类观相比，当代句法学不仅将一般意义上的词作为基本单位，还增加了一些并非自由运用的黏着语素，例如，屈折成分-ed的作用相当于助动词，但这类成分是一种黏着词缀，只能加于动词词根之上。同能够自由运用的词相比，附着词、词缀是一种不自由的或黏着的语类；空语类是在一定语境下没有语音形式的成分，也是一种不自由成分。有关"自由"与"黏着"的知识，可进一步参阅本章原典选读一。

第二，实义动词就是一般所说的词汇性动词，如"笑""哭""run""eat"之类。"e"是指有语义内容而无语音形式的成分，比如在（46）的问答中，答句的"喜欢"之前和之后都有一个空的成分e，分别指称"我"和"句法学"。这种空的成分在汉语中是广泛存在的，就是有些句子没有主语或宾语。这种空成分显然很难归入传统所说的实词与虚词，当代句法学引入词汇语类与功能语类，功能语类涵括这种空的成分。

（46）问：你喜欢句法学吗？

答：e 喜欢e 。

第三，在从实义动词到空语类"e"之间是一些从词汇向功能渐变的语类。轻动词（light verb）本来就是动词，指那些虽有语音形式，但意义比较空泛的动词，或称为虚义动词或泛义动词。比如，汉语的"进行打击""加以治理""打开水"中的"进行""加以""打"与英语的"take a walk""have a rest""make a movement"中"take""have""make"。当代句法学中，轻动词可以是一个没有语音形式的语类，其作用仅仅是为事件分类。比如，致使事件（causative event）表示一个事件导致另一个事件，"致使"就可以是一个轻动词，用大写的CAUSE表示。汉语的"使"、英语的"make"都是轻动词CAUSE的充当者，甚至英语的后缀-en，如lighten"使明亮"中的-en，也可以是致使轻动词的充当者。附着词是一个不能独立的黏着成分，按照语音的标准是词缀，按照句法的标准相当于词，它可以依附于单个的词之上，也可以附着于短语之上。例如，英语中表示所有关系的's，请比较：John's hat—the hat of John（约翰的帽子）；the king of England's hat—the hat of the King of England（英国国王的帽子）。（45）中的词缀不同于传统所说的构词词缀，而是一种屈折词缀。就动词而言，是指动词时体变化的标记，比如worked、working中的"-ed""-ing"之类。

　　第四，传统的词类观将词进行"实""虚"二分，一个词不是实词就是虚词。现代句法学将词纳入从词汇性到功能性构成的连续统之中。一个词（语义上）的实与虚是相对而言的，看它在连续统中处于哪个位置。显然（45）的连续统中，越是居于后面的语类，语义上越虚，其词汇性渐弱，功能性渐强。

第四节　语法形式与语法意义

　　我们知道，语言符号是由能指和所指两方面构成的。能指就是形式，所指就是意义。

　　关于形式，大致有以下几种理解：

　　第一，与概念相对，非概念的就是形式；

　　第二，与意义相对的语音；

　　第三，与语义相对的音韵、语法结构；

　　第四，音韵、语法、语义结构。

　　总起来讲，形式可以界定为：与概念（意义）相对的一种结构，或者是语音、语义、语法的结构表达形式。形式有两个特点：一是分布（distribution），一是变化（change）。当代形式语言学一派所说的"形式"就是指能够加以明确化表达，从结构上而非直觉上进行刻画。形式不一定都有意义或者表达意义，它可以只是区分意义。比如元音和辅音自身没有意义，只是区分意义。

　　语法形式（grammatical form）是指能表达一定语法意义的形式，是语法意义的依托。进一步说，不表达语法意义的形式不是语法形式。举例说，在"speaks"一词中，第二个"s"是语法形式，其语法意义为"第三人称、单数、一般现在时"。相比之下，第一个"s"不表达语法意义，只是一个辅音形式，而不是语法形式。汉语缺乏严格意义上的形态变化，在表达语法意义的形式方面有自己的特点，比如，无论是过去时、现在时还是将来时，无论是第几人称，动词"说"的外在形式都没有变。

　　语法形式的归纳概括，称为语法手段。在有形态变化的语言中，语法手段主要体现为形态手段或形态现象。常见的形态手段有内部屈折（internal inflection）、异干（suppletion）、附加（affix）、重叠（reduplication）、重音（stress）、零形式（zero）等。关于这些语法手段的详细介绍，请读者参阅第四章。在缺乏严格意义形态变化的语言中，语法手段主要涵括虚词和语序。

语法意义是语法形式所承载的意义，也就是一定的语法手段所呈现出来的关系意义、范畴意义或功能意义。在（47）中，a组所体现的是关系意义，b组是范畴意义，c组是功能意义。

（47）a. 红花：花红　　春天到来：春天的到来

　　　　b. works：worked　　book：books　　tall：taller：tallest

　　　　c. 鲁国小：登东山而小鲁　　light：lighten

以a组而论，"花红""春天到来"是被陈述与陈述的关系（主谓结构），"红花""春天的到来"是修饰与被修饰的关系（定中结构）。"被陈述-陈述"关系和"修饰-被修饰"关系等就是一种语法意义。b组动词之后所附的-s、-ed等是时范畴，名词之后所附的-s是数范畴，形容词之后所附的-er、-est是级范畴，这种范畴意义也是语法意义。关于范畴及其对应形式（形态）的介绍，可参阅第四章。至于功能意义，是语言中某些功能词或词缀所具有的意义。c组中从"鲁国小"与"小鲁"的比较可以看出，第二个"小"含有一个表示说话人主观上认为某物具有某性质的功能义，其意义就是"认为小"。"lighten"中的词缀"-en"具有"致使"这种功能义。像"小"以及"-en"所具有的功能义也是语法意义的一种。

同一个形式，可以表达不同的语法意义。英语中的's作为语法形式可以表达如下几种语法意义：第三人称单数现在时、名词所有格、is的减缩形式、has的减缩形式，这些形式之间是同音关系。相应地，同样的语法意义，可以用不同的语法形式来表达。比如，英语中表示领有意义的语法形式有：'s、of短语、关系小句、介词短语，如（48）所示。

（48）a. John's book（张三的书）

　　　　b. a book of John（张三的书）

　　　　c. a book that John has（张三所拥有的书）

　　　　d. a book on the desk（桌子上的书）

语法形式和语法意义一表一里，共同构成符号和符号序列。

第五节　论元结构与语类选择

"论元"（argument）一词是从逻辑学借鉴过来的概念，也有称为"主目"或者"主目语"的。由于语言学上大多将"argument"译作"论元"，所以，本书采取这个普遍接受的名称。

　　大家比较熟悉的初等函数式 $y=f(x)$，其中的"x"在数学上叫作变项，"f"是函项（function），"y"是"x"在"f"作用下的函数。在逻辑学上，可将这里的"x"看作"f"的主目。简单来讲，"主目"就是被函项作用的对象。语言学上，一般将动词或形容词关联或作用的对象称为这个动词或形容词的"论元"。或者说，谓词（包括动词、形容词）关联的对象对于谓词来说就是"论元"。论元大多是名词性短语，也可以是一个句子，如（49）c中"小明问爸爸火星上是否有生命"的"火星上是否有生命"就是句子充当论元。在（49）中，a组的动词"笑""来""跑"只关联一个论元（阿Q、小D、小明），b组的动词"打""吃""讲"都各自关联两个论元，c组的动词则各自关联三个论元。

　　（49）a. 阿Q笑　小D来　小明跑

　　　　　b. 小D打阿Q　小明吃苹果　张老师讲语言学

　　　　　c. 张三送李四一本书　妈妈告诉小明一个故事　小红问爸爸火星上是否有生命

　　根据关联论元数目，可以将谓词分为一元谓词（one-place predicate），如"笑""来""跑"，二元谓词（two-place predicate），如"打""吃""讲"等，三元谓词（three-place predicate），如"送""告诉""问"等。理论上，还应该存在零元谓词（zero-place predicate），也就是不与任何论元关联的谓词，如（50）中的"rain"和"下雨"。

　　（50）a. It rains.

　　　　　b. 下雨了。

　　　　　c. ？？天下雨了。

与"rain"关联的名词性成分是"it"，但是，这是一个无所指称的虚指代词，是形式主语。论元在语义上的一个重要特征就是要有所指称，无论是直接指称（张三、鲁迅、桌子、"十八大"），还是间接指称（我、你、他）。（50）a中的"it"不能算"rain"的论元，"rain"是一个零元谓词。类似地，"下雨"也是一个零元谓词。与"rain"不同的是，"下雨"不需要出现形式主语，（50）c是不好的说法。

　　为了说明论元结构，需要介绍一下"题元"（thematic）。这个术语语言学界也有称为"论旨"的，本书采用比较通行的术语"题元"。所谓"题元"，就是一个谓词的论元在该谓词所界定的事件中所扮演的角色，"题元"是一种语义关系。在（49）a中的"阿Q""小D""小明"在相应的谓词"笑""来""跑"所界定的事件中是动作的发出者，语言学上一般称为"施事"（agent）。（49）b中的"阿Q""苹果""语言学"在相应的谓词"打""吃""讲"所界定的事件中是动作的承受者，语言学上一般称为"受事"（patient）。（49）c中的"李四""小明"是"与事"（dative），"火星上是否有生命"是"命题"（proposition）。"施事""受事""与事""命题"等通常也被称为题元角色（θ-role）。每个谓词（主要是动词）都会有一定数量的题元角色要指派给其论元。一个谓词（动词）所拥有的题元角色的集合通常被称为该谓词（动词）的论元结构（argument structure）。论元结构的表达式一般是将论元所对应的题元角色放置于尖括号中。以（49）b中"小D打阿Q"为例，其论元结构可用（51）来表示。

（51）打 <施事 <受事>>

尖括号表示题元层级，外围的尖括号越少，表明这一题元角色在论元结构中所处的层级越高。有关论元结构更为详细的介绍，可参阅本章原典选读三。

从（49）中还可以看到，不同的动词不仅对于其论元数目有要求，而且对论元由什么样的成分来充当也有要求，这就是所谓的语类选择（category-selection，c-selection）。在（52）-（54）中，动词know、ask、wonder除了主语论元之外，各自对其补足语（这里指宾语）论元有不同的要求，呈现出不同的语类选择限制。

（52）a. John knows [NP the answer].

b. John knows [S that the world is full of love].

c. John knows [S what friendship is].

（53）a. John asks me [NP the answer].

b. John asks me [S what friendship is].

c. *John asks me [S that the world is full of love].

（54）a. *John wonders [NP the answer].

b. *John wonders [S that the world is full of friendship].

c. John wonders [S what friendship is].

know的补足语论元可以是NP（如（52）a），陈述性的句子S（如（52）b），或者疑问性的句子S（如（52）c）。ask的补足语论元除了一个名称性的表示来源的成分，如me之外，还要再带一个名词性的论元NP（如（53）a），或者带疑问性的句子论元S（如（53）b），但是句子论元不可以是陈述性的句子S，所以（53）c不合法。wonder的语类选择要求其补足语是一个疑问性的句子S（如（54）c），名称性的NP或者陈述性的句子S都不能作其补足语，所以，（54）a-b都是不可以接受的。

语类选择着眼于一个核心词（head），如动词要求带几个论元以及这些论元是由什么样的语类充当，论元结构则是指一个核心谓词将其所拥有的题元角色分派给一定的论元，这些题元按照一定的层级排列所形成的结构。

第六节　句法结构的性质

语言组织架构的过程就像是盖一座高楼大厦，其中离不开建筑材料，同样也离不开建筑图纸。对于语言系统来讲，各级单位就是建筑材料，而语言结构规则就是建筑图纸。语法规则是语言结构规则中最重要的一部分，它规定了语法单位以何种方式和怎样的形式组织在一起。语法结构规则体现在语言的各个层面，除了词法、句法外，有的甚至涵括语音、语义，本书所谈论的语法不包括语音和语义。语法结构规则的重要作用，在于它制约了语言结构组织搭配的过程，使得语言单位不是无组织、无规律地结合在一起。句法规则又是语法规则的重要组成部分，其最重要的性质是层次性和递归性。

一、层次性

任何事物的组织都是有层次的，而不是杂乱无章的。层次性是客观事物的普遍属性。就像我们在分析物质的组成时，必须一层一层离析出它的单位，其中分子可以由原子构成，原子可以由粒子构成，而粒子则可以由更小的单位夸克构成。生物个体的组织也是一样，细胞构成组织，组织形成各个器官，器官又构成不同的系统，系统最终组成一个生物个体。句法结构的组织也不例外。从表面来看，我们接触到的语言，不管是口语还是书面语，大多是一个个的句子或者更长的语言单位。这些句子好像是一个一个词线性地排列在一起，看起来没有什么规律。但实际上，这种排列是有规律的，句法学的任务就是要找出其中的规律。

应当看到，句子中各个成分的排列是有层级的（hierarchical），并非无组织地杂乱呈现。简单来讲，一个大的句法单位，例如句子，是由低一级的句法单位——短语组合而成的，而短语本身，也是由更小的句法单位——词组合而成。所有自然语言的语法构造都是有层次的，层次性是语言的本质属性之一。

　　一般来讲，语法结构的每一个层次直接包含比它小的两个语法单位，即由两部分直接组成。每部分（即较小的语法单位）又可以包含更小的语法单位，也就是由更小的两部分直接组成。句子的内在结构就是这样分层组合，只是由于时间维度的限制，表现出来的形式只能是链式排列。对句法结构进行分析，寻找层次的过程叫作层次分析法（Hierarchical Analysis）。

　　上面说过，句法结构的每一个层次一般直接包含比它小的两个语法单位，因此，层次分析法必须是二分的（binary）。每一层中直接组合起来构成一个更大的语法单位的两个组成成分叫作直接组成成分（immediate constituents），层次分析法也叫直接成分分析法（immediate constituent analysis，IC）。下面通过一个例子来看层次分析法的具体操作过程，如（55）所示。

　　（55）我们　都　喜欢　语言学

首先，可以将这句话切分成"我们"和"都喜欢语言学"两部分，这两部分构成主谓关系。其次，我们将"都喜欢语言学"切分成"都"和"喜欢语言学"两部分，这两部分构成状中关系。最后，我们可以进一步将"喜欢语言学"切分为"喜欢"和"语言学"两部分，这两者构成动宾关系。

　　需要说明的是，层次分析法一般分析到词为止。并且，层次分析法被借鉴过来运用于汉语，需要标明每个层次上两个直接成分之间的关系。通过层次分析法，我们可以看到，在上面的句子中，"我们"虽然在线性结构上紧邻"都"，但"我们都"并不构成一个直接成分；同样地，"都"和"喜欢"虽然紧邻，但两者也不是一个直接成分，而是"都"和"喜欢语言学"一起构成一个直接成分。于是，自然引发一个问题：如何判断两个或多个单位是否构成一个直接成分？换句话说，我们依据层次分析法，进行直接成分切分的时候，所依据的标准是什么？下面介绍几种常见的可以有效确定直接成分的方法。

（一）孤立法（stand-alone test）

　　所谓孤立法，就是如果一串语法单位可以用来单独回答问题，独立站得住，那么它就可以被认为是一个直接成分。"他正在读一本非常有趣的小说"这个句子，可以分别来看哪些成分可以用来单独回答问题。例如，可以设置（56）那样的对话场景。

（56）Q：他呢？

　　　A：正在读一本非常有趣的小说。

　　　Q：他正在做什么？

　　　A：读一本非常有趣的小说。

　　　Q：他在读什么？

　　　A：一本非常有趣的小说。

　　　Q：那本小说怎么样？

　　　A：非常有趣。

根据孤立法，"正在读一本非常有趣的小说""读一本非常有趣的小说""一本非常有趣的小说""非常有趣"都可以用来单独回答问题，因此，都可以看作直接成分。而"一本非常有趣"则不能单独用来回答问题，如例（57），因而不是一个直接成分。但是，在对举的语境如（58）中，"一本非常有趣"则可以用来回答问题，能通过"孤立法"测试，是一个成分。可见，某一个片段是否是一个成分还要看该片段所处的环境。

（57）Q：他在读什么？

　　　A：*一本非常有趣。

（58）Q：昨天你买的两本小说怎么样？

　　　A：哦，那两本小说一本非常有趣，一本没什么意思。

用孤立法确定的直接成分，可以是词和短语，这与前面第二节对词的界定时所说的"独用"或"单说"基本精神是一致的。差别在于，纯粹依靠独用或单说进行鉴定，有些比"词"低一级的成分，如语素，也能够被孤立出来。直接成分的确定只分析到词这一级就行了，无需进行过度孤立，将语素也作为直接成分提取出来。

（二）替代法（replacement test）

所谓替代法，即在不改变句子其他部分的情况下，如果一串语法单位可以被一个单独的词所代替，则可将这串语法单位看作一个直接成分。例如（59）-（60），我们要判断"The king of England opened Parliament"这句话的直接成分，可以采用替代法。

（59）<u>The king of England</u>　　　opened Parliament.

　　　<u>John</u>　　　　　　　　　　opened Parliament.

（60）The king of England　　　<u>opened Parliament.</u>

The king of England	worked.

首先，"John"可以用来代替"the king of England"，句子的剩余部分保持不变。因为"John"只有一个单词，自然是一个直接成分，据此可以认为"the king of England"也是一个直接成分。其次，我们可以用作为直接成分的"worked"来替代"opened Parliament"，前面的"the king of England"保持不变，据此可以认为"opened Parliament"也是一个直接成分。最后，可以用同样的方法对直接成分"the king of England"和"opened Parliament"做进一步切分，找出各自的直接成分。

与替代法在找出直接成分方面具有相同性质的另一种方法是扩展法（expansion）。所谓扩展法，就是将要分析的复杂形式看成同功能的某个简单形式的扩展结构；反过来说，某个简单形式通过同功能的扩展，得到复杂形式。建基于扩展法找寻简单结构，可以把原来的复杂结构还原成相应的简单结构。由于简单结构的层次容易看清并且没有分歧，通过复杂结构和简单结构的类比，就可以确定复杂形式的层次。就（59）-（60）的例子而言，"the king of England"显然比单独一个词"John"复杂，而"John"是一个成分，相应地，复杂片段"the king of England"自然也可以看作一个成分。

（三）移位法（displacement test）

如果一串语法单位可以作为一个整体进行移位，可以认为它是一个直接成分。例如，对于（61）a"他喜欢读老舍的小说"这句话，可以进行（61）b-d那样的移位测试。

（61）a. 他喜欢读老舍的小说。

　　　b. 老舍的小说，他喜欢读。

　　　c. 小说，他喜欢读老舍的。

　　　d. 读老舍的小说，他喜欢。

据此，可以认为"老舍的小说""小说""读老舍的小说"都是"他喜欢读老舍的小说"这个句子的直接成分。

需要说明的是，根据上述三种方法切分出的直接成分，有时候会出现不一致的情况，这就需要我们在进行层次切分，判断直接成分时，要结合多种方法，不能仅仅根据其中一条测试法来判断一串语法单位是不是直接成分。比如对于移位法来说，能否进行移位只是判断某一串语法单位是否为直接成分的一个参考，句法单位的移位还有很多其他限制因素，不能移位的不一定就不是直接成分。

这里只介绍了直接成分的三种判定方法，有关直接成分判断的方法还有很多，有兴趣的读者，可以参考拓展阅读书目中Bas（1997）的第十一章和第十二章。

关于层次分析法，还有几点需要说明：

首先，切分出来的各个成分都必须有意义，不能有任何一个成分没有意义。例如，"漂亮的姑娘"只能是"漂亮的 | 姑娘"，不能是"漂亮 | 的姑娘"，因为"的姑娘"没有意义。

其次，切分出来的各个成分在语义上的搭配必须跟整个组合的原意相符。例如，"大红花"里"大红"具有意义（一种红色），"花"也有意义，搭配起来的意思是"某种红色的花"。但是"大红花"的原意是"大的红花"，因此不能切分为"大红 | 花"，只能是"大 | 红花"。

最后，与上面第二点相应，就是要注意分解与还原参验，防止虚假切分。例如，"祖国壮丽的河山"中，"祖国壮丽"似乎是一个成分，但是"壮丽"其实与"河山"相关，第一层应该切分在"祖国"与"壮丽的河山"之间。

弄清结构的层次有时对正确理解语句的意义很重要。例如，我们经常遇到的歧义句"old men and women"以及"咬死猎人的狗"都有两种不同的切分（这里只给出第一层切分）。

（62）a. <u>old men</u> and <u>women</u>

     b. <u>old</u> <u>men and women</u>

（63）a. <u>咬死猎人的</u> <u>狗</u>

     b. <u>咬死</u> <u>猎人的狗</u>

（62）a的直接成分是"old men""and""women"（关于"and"的处理，新近的句法学理论有不同的策略，有的将其与后一个成分归在一起）。在这种切分下，"old"与"men"共同构成一个成分。（62）b的直接成分是"old"和"men and women"。在这种切分下，"old"是与"men and women"具有修饰关系的两个直接成分。（63）a的直接成分是"咬死猎人的"和"狗"，两者构成定中结构；（63）b的直接成分是"咬死"和"猎人的狗"，两者构成动宾结构。当然，这种结构层次引起的歧义一般只在书面语中存在。在口语中，语言结构层次的不同可以通过语音手段，比如停顿、重音等区分开来。

二、递归性

句法结构的另外一个重要特性是所谓的递归性（recursion）。我们知道，人可以说出自己从来没有说过的话，也可以理解从来没有听过的话。一个高产作家的每部作品，不可能使用完全相同的语句。我们在绪论里曾经提到，语言中的语素和词的数量尽管很大，但仍然是有限的。到了短语和句子层面，数量就是开放的了。从某种程度上来说，人能说出和理解的语句是无限的。换句话说，我们能够利用有限的规则和相对有限的词去造出数量上无限多、长度上不受限制的句子，语言的这种特性叫作递归性。对语言这一属性的首次发现，一般认为是德国的语言学家洪堡特。他认为语言具有创造性，人们能用少量规则说出无穷无尽的话语来。语言的这种创造性的本质，实际上就是递归性。

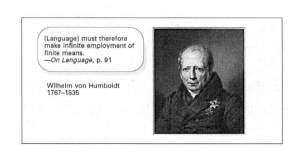

[Language] must therefore make infinite employment of finite means.
—On Language, p. 91

Wilhelm von Humboldt
1767–1835

一般认为，递归性是语言的本质属性之一，语法规则自然也具有递归性。从孩童学习语言开始，他们接触的是相对有限的语言现象，但当儿童真正掌握语言能力之时，他们完全可以说出从未听过的句子。可见，递归性也是语言习得的重要机制。

语言的递归性也是人类语言和动物"语言"的重要区别之一。关于动物是否存在语言这一问题，学术界一直存在争论。动物与人类一样，存在各种各样的交流手段，例如蜜蜂的舞蹈"语言"、长臂猿的叫喊、海豚独有的声波"语言"，以及大猩猩的"语言"，等等。以大猩猩为例，科学研究发现，大猩猩与人类DNA的98.7%都是相同的，因此部分学者坚信，通过一定的训练和学习，大猩猩也能获得与人类一样的语言能力。从20世纪60年代后期开始，美国的一些科学家陆续进行了一系列关于大猩猩学习人类语言的实验，但结果都以失败而告终。实验的结果发现大猩猩尽管可以学习一定数量的语词，但从来不曾真正学会人类的语言，其所谓的语言行为和条件反射没有什么区别，不像人类语言那样可以具有无限的生成性。人类语言的递归性决定了人类语言不像动物"语言"那样是一个封闭的交流系统，也是造成人与动物之间存在无法逾越的交际鸿沟的关键。

句法结构的递归性建立在层次性的基础之上。正因为语法的组合结构一层套一层，所以同样的结构才可以重复而不致造成结构上的混乱。也就是说，层次性是基础，递归性是在层次性的基础上的一种实现，没有层次性，递归性便失去存在的基础。人类语言可以通过以下几种手段来实现句法递归：

（一）附加（adjunction）

附加是一种重要的递归方式，即可以不加限制地重复增加修饰成分，如定语和状语等，请看下面的例子。

（64）a. He is an intelligent guy.

b. He is an intelligent, handsome guy.

c. He is an intelligent, handsome, romantic guy.

d. He is an intelligent, handsome, romantic, thoughtful guy.

e. He is an intelligent, handsome, romantic, thoughtful, adorable guy.

（65）a. 他悄悄地走进了房间。

b. 他悄悄地、不动声色地走进了房间。

c. 他悄悄地、不动声色地、神秘兮兮地走进了房间。

d. 他悄悄地、不动声色地、神秘兮兮地、蹑手蹑脚地走进了房间。

e. 他悄悄地、不动声色地、神秘兮兮地、蹑手蹑脚地从侧面走进了房间。

在（64）a-e中，中心语名词"guy"之前不断添加定语。在（65）a-e中，在动词短语"走进了房间"之前不断添加状语。定语和状语都是一种附加语，添加附加语是句法递归的一种手段。

（二）内嵌（embedding）

内嵌是指将一个句子嵌套于另外一个句子之中，充当另外一个句子的一个成分。例如，（66）a作为一个句子，经内嵌之后，在（66）b中充当宾语从句，在（66）c中充当主语从句，在（66）d中充当关系从句。

（66）a. 他一声不吭地离开了。

　　　b. 我知道他一声不吭地离开了。

　　　c. 他一声不吭地离开惹怒了大家。

　　　d. 他一声不吭离开的那个公司不久倒闭了。

句法的递归机制允许内嵌无限制地重复下去，比较常见的是宾语从句的反复嵌套，如（67）。

（67）a. 我知道他一声不吭地离开了。

　　　b. 她知道我知道他一声不吭地离开了。

　　　c. 他们都知道她知道我知道他一声不吭地离开了。

　　关系从句也可以无限递归。比较经典的例子可参看第二章（10）-（11）。这里举一个简单的例子（68）。在（68）a中，关系从句"that Jack built"修饰其前的名词"house"。这个关系从句在（68）b中又内嵌于关系从句"that lay in the house that Jack built"之中，修饰前面的名词"cheese"。后面这个关系从句在（68）c中又嵌套于关系从句"that nibbled the cheese that lay in the house that Jack built"之中，修饰其前的名词"mouse"。这样层层嵌套，不断递归，使句子越来越长，而基本结构不变。

（68）a. This is the house that Jack built.

　　　b. This is the cheese that lay in the house that Jack built.

　　　c. This is the mouse that nibbled the cheese that lay in the house that Jack built.

（三）并列（coordination）

　　第三种在人类语言中普遍存在的递归方式是并列。所谓并列，指的是使用连词，将两个或两个以上的句法单位组合在一起。例如在英语中，可以使用连词and、but、or等进行并列操作，从而增加句子的长度，实现递归，如（69）所示。

（69）John went to school, and Bill went to the store, but Nancy slept and Sally read a book.

　　汉语中的连词可以不出现，但同样可以进行相同的递归操作，如（70）所示。

（70）张华考上了北京大学，李萍进了中等技术学校，我在百货公司当售货员，我们
都有光明的前途。

对于上面所介绍的三种实现递归的方式来讲，前两种递归方式的相同点在于：结构中的某个单位可以不断地被一个功能相同、更长更复杂的词组所替代；差别在于：附加是修饰语成分的复杂化，内嵌是主语、宾语或者关系从句的复杂化。最后一种递归方式的特点在于将两个或几个本身可以成句的片段（词或短语）变成不独立成句而联合在一起构成一个具有完整语调的复句，可以看作句子本身的复杂化。递归操作的结果使得基本结构里面的简单形式扩展成更复杂的结构，但作用仍等于原来那个简单形式。

递归在理论上可以无限进行，但是，由于人的记忆限制，人们在日常的交流中，不需要也不可能说出太长的句子。实际上，用有限的句法手段生成无限的句子，这是语言的经济原则在起作用，反映了人类的求简天性，这与我国古代大道至简原则以及西方的奥卡姆剃刀定律的基本精神是一致的。

第七节　短语结构的类型与规则

汉语学界一般认为，短语从结构类型上看有五种类型：主谓短语、动宾短语、动补短语、并列（联合）短语、偏正短语。

主谓短语就是由一个被陈述的对象（主语）和相应的陈述内容（谓语）构成的结构，一般描述为"S–VP"（S为主语，VP为谓语），例如（71）－（73）（这里以短语为考量对象，所以不使用标点符号，下同）。

（71）　阿Q很迷茫

（72）　张老师讲授语言学

（73）　北京是中国首都

动宾短语是指支配和受支配这种关系构成的结构，也称为述宾结构，一般描述为"VO"（V是动词，O是宾语），例如（74）－（75）。

（74）　吃苹果　刺人　唱山歌　写文章……

（75）　吃食堂　刺红缨枪　唱高音　写宋体……

比较发现，（74）与（75）中虽然在结构上都是动宾短语，但是动词所表示的动作与其后名词所指之间的关系有所不同：前者是典型的动作与受事关系，后者在语义上并非典型的动作和受事，名词所指或是地点，或是工具，或是方式等。

与动宾短语相似的还有一种介宾短语，就是介词及其所带的宾语构成的结构，如（76）。介宾短语与动宾短语不同之处在于：前者不能独立作谓语，而是作附加语（定语、状语），后者可以独立作谓语。

（76）a.　在教室里　　关于这个问题　　为人民

　　　 b.　in the classroom　　about this issue　　for people

动补短语或述补结构可描述为"V（得/不）C"（C是补足成分），是指以动词或形容词为核心，后面的成分是对前面的核心成分的一种补充说明或描写摹状。形式上分为两种类型：一种是黏合式，就是V与C直接结合，中间没有插入"得/不"，如（77）所示。单音节的V和单音节的C构成的VC因为在功能上相当于一个词，句法学界有时也称为动（述）补复合词。另一类是组合式，即在V和C之间插入"得"（肯定形式）和"不"（否定形式），如（78）所示。

（77）写好　做完　吃饱　打开　想清楚　考虑周全

（78）a.　写得好　做得完　吃得饱　打得开　想得清楚　考虑得周全

　　　 b.　写不好　写不完　吃不饱　打不开　想不清楚　考虑不周全

值得注意的是，（78）b中的"考虑不周全"还可以看作主谓短语，语义上是"考虑是不周全的"。

并列（联合）短语是两个或多个语义上并列的词或短语一起构成的结构，这种结构形式上可以出现连接标记，如（79），也可以不使用连接标记，如（80）。

（79）　伟大而光荣　阿Q和小D　阿Q或者小D　你来还是我去　又唱歌又跳舞

（80）　伟大的光荣的　阿Q小D　你来我去　唱歌跳舞

需要指出的是，并列短语的几个构成成分不仅是语义上不分主次，形式上往往是可以验证的，也就是可以将并列成分的先后次序调换一下，比如（79）-（80）中的并列项目可以前后颠倒。

偏正短语是指由修饰与被修饰关系形成的结构，被修饰的成分可以是名词性的，如

（81），也可以是谓词性的，如（82）。

 （81）a. 红玫瑰 炎热的天气 聪明的男孩

    b. a red rose hot weather a clever boy

 （82）a. 很好 快跑 异常美丽 努力工作

    b. very good run quickly extraordinarily beautiful work hard

（81）中的修饰语是形容词，被修饰的是名词性成分；（82）中的修饰语是副词，被修饰的是谓词性的（形容词、动词）。

  上面所介绍的五种短语结构，是从语法意义上来讲的。有关语法意义的介绍，请参阅第四节。

  有意思的是，汉语在上述五种短语之外，还存在一些特殊的短语，为了区分，通常称之为"结构"，常见的有"的"字结构、连动结构、兼语结构等。

  "的"字结构顾名思义就是以"的"为煞尾标记的结构，也就是"的"用在某些成分（多为名词、动词、形容词或相应短语）之后所构成的结构，如（83）-（85）。

 （83）张三的 木头的 阿Q和小D的 木头桌子的（名词或名词短语+的）

 （84）吃的 卖的 吃苹果的 卖菜的 看电视的（动词或动词短语+的）

 （85）长的 短的 高大的 漂亮的 很美的 挺清楚的（形容词或形容词短语+的）

  连动结构（serial verb construction）就是由两个或两个以上的动词或动词短语连在一起构成的结构，语义上表达先后或者接续发生的动作。以简单的连动结构为例，两种动作之间或是一种前后承接关系，如（86）a，或是一种修饰关系，如（86）b。

 （86）a. 上街买菜 拿出钥匙开门 打一下就跑

    b. 开着窗户睡觉 穿着礼服迎接

  兼语结构传统语法认为就是结构中的名词性成分"一身二任"，相对于前面的动词而言是受支配者，相对于后面的动词而言是动作发出者，如（87）所示。

 （87）请阿Q吃面条 命令机械师打开机窗 称他打虎英雄 选小张当班长

    推荐张三入党 责备他不守信用

（87）中的兼语结构是举例性的，第一个动词的语义属性各有差别，但是，形式上都可以简单表示为：V_1+NP+V_2。单纯从形式上讲，兼语结构与连动结构有相似之处，有些连动结构也可以描述为"V_1+NP+V_2",比如（86）b。两者的差异在于：连动结构的两个动作是同一动作者发出的，"穿着礼服迎接"这一连动结构中，"穿"和"迎接"是同一动作者执行的；而兼语结构的两个动作分别由不同的动作者发出，"请阿Q吃面条"这一兼语结构中，"请"和"吃"是不同动作者发出的。兼语结构在汉语学界一直有不同的处理意见，本书不打算展开讨论。

上述短语的几种结构类型，是汉语语法研究者提出来的。有的语言，如英语，没有类似汉语"写得好""跑得快"这样的"V得C"式动补结构。

句法学界现在一般采取"中心语"（head）、"补足语"（complement）、"附加语"（adjunct）和"指示语"（specifier）来表示短语结构，分别形成"指示语–中心语""中心语–补足语""附加语–中心语"三种结构规则。可以看出，每种结构都有一个中心语（head），如（88）–（90）所示。这一观点在传统语言学那里已有论述，可参阅原典选读二。下面以前述几种短语为例，看看如何用这三种规则加以描述。

（88）a. 楼市走高 南海问题升温

　　　b. Stock prices rose. South China Sea is a focus.（指示语–中心语）

（89）a. 唱山歌 关于这个问题 写得好

　　　b. sing a song about this issue（中心语–补足语）

（90）a. 红玫瑰 异常美丽

　　　b. red rose very good extraordinarily beautiful（附加语–中心语）

关于上述三种结构规则与汉语学界所说的几种短语结构，需做如下几点说明：

第一，指示语在早期涵括不同成分，因短语类型而定，现在大致就是通常所说的主语。

第二，"补足语"大致就是传统语法所说的"宾语"，但外延上更为宽泛一些，除了一般意义上的宾语，还包括宾语从句、介词短语（名词和形容词的补足语）和表语（系词的补足语）。

第三，附加语包括定语（名词性成分之前）和状语（谓词性成分之前），从形式着眼是可以将其删除而不会影响结构的合法性；附加语的数目没有限制。

第四，中心语之外的指示语、补足语和附加语都有两个可选的位置，既可以位于相关联的成分之前，也可以位于该成分之后。

第五，并列结构通过连接成分构成，传统上认为存在两个或多个中心，若将连接成分视为功能成分（参阅第三节），可以将并列结构看作以连接成分为中心语的结构。

第六，连动结构内部存在差异，需要进一步区分。承接关系的连动结构可以仿照并列结构处理，修饰关系的连动结构可以按照偏正结构处理。

关于短语结构的形式表征，将在第九节详细介绍。

第八节　句法结构之间的关系与变换

表面上看，语言中的句子似乎各个不同，但最终可以归纳为有限的句子结构，这种撇开句子具体词汇构成及其内容的结构，也可以称为句法结构。尽管句子的数量是无限的，但是，句法结构的规则数量是有限的。

不同句法结构之间存在一定的依存关系，也就是它们含有一定数量的相同的实词，差异仅仅在于某些虚词（功能词）和语序的不同。这些具有依存关系的句法结构可以通过一定的句法手段关联起来，这种手段就是变换（transformation）。

变换并不属于严格意义上的美国描写语言学的范畴，而是一个介乎描写语言学和转换生成语言学之间的语法分析方法。以它为基础建立的变换语法（又作变形语法transforma-tional grammar），与描写语言学处于同一层面，拥有自己独立的地位。

需要说明的是，美国描写主义语言学家哈里斯等人所说的"transformation"与后来乔姆斯基所说的"transformation"含义不同。前者指的是同一层面上不同句法结构间的依存关系，后者最初指的是从核心句到非核心句的转化（20世纪50年代），后来指从深层结构到表层结构的转化（20世纪60年代以后）。这方面需要专门的知识，本书不作详细介绍。这里介绍的是美国描写主义关于转换的知识，区分起见，一般将哈里斯等人的"transfor-mation"译作"变换"。

变换可以定义为：在两个形式序列之间建立的一种关系，也就是在一个结构形式中出现的某些具体词（实词），可以同样出现在另一个结构形式中，这些具体词在两个结构形式中一同出现的频度（共现度）相同。例如，"weather"与"cold"在（91）a和b中的共现度相同，这两者之间具有变换关系。哈里斯将（91）a称为核心结构（kernel structure），而将（91）b称为非核心结构（non-kernel structure）。通俗地说，变换就是将一种结构变成与之包含部分相同词目（实词）的另一种结构。

（91）a. the weather is cold

　　　b. the cold weather

汉语学界很早就有人讨论变换的问题，比如刘复和吕叔湘等。下面是汉语中的变换实例，箭头表示变换操作。

（92）山高→高山　水流→流水（例子选自吕叔湘《中国文法要略》）

（93）a. 我在纸上写字→我写字在纸上

　　　b. 我在门口立→我立在门口

　　　c. 我装烟草在烟斗里→我把烟草装在烟斗里（比较：*我在烟斗里装烟草）

　　　（例子选自刘复《中国文法通论》）

可以看出，变换改变了原有结构的形式，但保留部分相同的实词。变换通常通过移位、添加、删除、替换等手段来进行。变换要遵循一定的准则，可以概括为如下两点：

第一，建立变换矩阵（matrix）。变换是句式之间的变换，必须在句式（结构）之间进行，而不是在某个具体句子（结构）之间进行。

（94）the N is A→ the A N

　　　a. the weather is cold→ the cold weather

　　　b. the sky is blue → the blue sky

　　　c. *the weather is leafy → *the leafy weather

（94）中的"the N is A→the A N"就可以建立一个变换矩阵。在这个变换矩阵里，箭头左边可以看作待变换结构，右边是变换之后的结构。N与A在变换前与变换后的结构中共现度是相同的：如果N与A在变换前的结构中能一起出现，那么，两者在变换后的结构中也能一起出现，如（94）a-b；如果N与A在变换前的结构中不能一起出现，则两者在变换后的结构中也不能一起出现，如（94）c。

第二，要考虑变换带来的意义上的变化。结构不同，意义自然有别。变换前后的意义有所不同，问题是：变换带来的意义改变应该满足什么样的条件？朱德熙提出的变换"平行性原则"给出了一个准则。请看（95）的变换实例。

（95）　　　A组　　　　　　　　B组

　　　NP +V$_r$着 +N　→　　N + V$_f$ +在 +NP

　　　a. 床上躺着病人　　　a' 病人躺在床上

　　　b. 台上坐着主席团　　b' 主席团坐在台上

　　　c. 墙上挂着月份牌　　c' 月份牌挂在墙上

d. 身上盖着毯子	d' 毯子盖在身上
e. 袖口上钉着纽扣	e' 纽扣钉在袖口上
f. 门上安着电铃	f' 电铃安在门上
g. 山上架着炮	g' 炮架在山上
h. 屋里摆着酒席	h' 酒席摆在屋里

根据变换的平行性原则，"NP+V$_f$着 +N→N+V$_f$+在+NP"（V$_f$是含有［附着］特征的动词）形成一个变换矩阵。在这个变换矩阵里，竖行的句子之间是同构关系，横行的句子之间是变换关系。从意义上讲，竖行的句子（A组或B组）的高层次上的语义关系相同，低层次上的语义关系不一定相同。横行的句子（如Aa与Ba'）低层次上的语义关系相同，高层次上的语义关系不同。变换矩阵里的句子在形式和语义上表现出一系列的平行性。简单来讲，高层次的语义关系，是指句式（结构）的意义；低层次的语义关系，是指句子（结构）中的动词与名词性成分之间的及物关系。

上述两个准则为确定变换能否成立提供了可靠的鉴别标准。根据这两个准则，可以断定在变换矩阵里，哪些是合法变换，哪些是虚假变换。

（96）有+ N +VP→有VP的+N

    a. 有理由不去→有不去的理由

    b. 有把握成功→有成功的把握

    c. 有条件上大学→有上大学的条件

    d. ?（也）有时候上当→（也）有上当的时候

    e. ? 有人在做报告→有在做报告的人

"有+ N +VP→有VP的+N"是一个变换格式。在这个变换所建立的变换矩阵中，只有（96）a–c的变换是合格的，d–e的变换是不好的，读者可对照上述准则自行验证。

变换在句法分析中有着其他分析方法不可替代的作用。大致说来，可以归纳为两方面：

第一，分化歧义结构。有些结构具有不止一种意义，也就是通常所说的歧义。当运用其他方法消除歧义不方便时，变换往往成为一种很好的消解歧义的分析法。例如（97）有歧义，直接成分分析法无法消除歧义，通过变换，可以很容易离析出（97）所包含的两种语义。

（97）小张谁都认识

    a. →谁小张都认识（意思是：小张认识每个人）

b.　→谁都认识小张（意思是：每个人都认识小张）

（97）的两种语义通过a、b两种变换，有效地加以区分。直接成分分析法不能进行歧义分解，读者很容易看出这一点。

第二，给某些结构定性。有些句法结构的性质归属不易确定，可以将其与性质容易确定的典型结构比对，看看两者在句法表现上的异同，进而确定其性质。具体做法是采取平行推导式，平行推导本质上就是一种变换。以（98）为例，其中的"今天（这儿）种树"的性质表面上看归入主谓结构和状中结构似乎都可以，但是，通过平行推导变换，发现它与"他们种树"的句法表现有一致性，而与"马上种树"不同。既然"他们种树"是主谓结构，那么，将"今天（这儿）种树"归入主谓结构也是合理的。

（98）他们种树（A）	今天（这儿）种树（B）	马上种树（C）
他们不种树	今天（这儿）不种树	*马上不种树
他们没种树	今天（这儿）没种树	*马上没种树
他们种不种树	今天（这儿）种不种树	*马上种不种树
他们种树没有	今天（这儿）种树没有	*马上种树没有
他们是不是种树	今天（这儿）是不是种树	*马上是不是种树
他们也许种树	今天（这儿）也许种树	*马上也许种树
他们要是种树	今天（这儿）要是种树	*马上要是种树
他们不但种树	今天（这儿）不但种树	*马上不但种树
他们所种的树	今天（这儿）所种的树	*马上所种的树

在一定范围内，变换作为一种句法分析手段有其用武之地，特别是对歧义结构的语义离析。变换需要遵循一定的准则，进行有效的形式转换。

第九节　句法树与框式图

在第七节的基础上，我们来看如何对句法结构进行形式化表征。从前面对各类短语的介绍可以看出，每个短语都有一个中心，称为中心语或核心词，短语结构规则可以简单表达为（99）。

（99）NP→…N…

VP→…V…

AP→…A…

PP→…P…

（99）中的N、V、A、P是几个主要的词类：名词、动词、形容词、介词，省略的部分是以这些主要词类为核心的其他成分。借用数学上变项的概念，可以将这些词类用一个变项X来表示，则（99）可以表达为（100）。

（100）XP→…X…

为了更为精准地描述短语的结构，句法学上还引入了一个中间短语，简单来讲，就是介于词和短语之间的一种成分，用X'表示，通常读作X-bar。这样，对于自然语言中的短语，就可以采取（101）这样的表达法。

（101） a. XP→Spec X'

b. X'→Adjunct X'

c. X→X Comp

从前面的介绍（参见第六节、第七节）可以看出，对于一个句法结构来讲，有两个表面上相反的操作。一个操作着眼于将较小的句法组成成分一步步组合，形成一个较大的句法结构，这种操作在句法上称作"合并"（merge）。另一个操作着眼于将一个较大的句法结构一步步顺次分解成较小的句法成分，这种操作在句法上叫作直接成分分析。合并是从小到大的操作过程，一般采取"两两归并"的做法。直接成分分析是从大到小的操作过程，一般分析到词这一级为止。以（102）为例，合并操作先将"喜欢"和"句法学"结合在一起，形成一个较大的单位"喜欢句法学"，然后再进一步将"喜欢句法学"和"张三"合并，形成一个更大的结构"张三喜欢句法学"。从直接成分分析操作来看，句法结构"张三喜欢句法学"第一步先切分为直接成分"张三"和"喜欢句法学"，第二步再将"喜欢句法学"切分为直接成分"喜欢"和"句法学"。通过这样一步步的切分，将一个像（102）这样的句法结构切分成一个个较小的成分，直至词一级单位。

（102）张三喜欢句法学。

对（102）的切分，离不开句法成分，与之相关的句法分析称为直接成分分析法，读者可参阅第六节。本节主要介绍句法分析中常见的两种形式表征：句法树（tree diagram）和框式图（bracket labeling）。

句法树是一个形象的比喻，或称为树形图，因其由一些线条彼此衔接，层层延伸，犹如树的枝条，最终形成一棵树，因此得名。通常情况下，以两条分支线最常见，所以，树形图又被不严格地称作"二叉树"（binary tree）。当然，树形图有时也呈现三叉或多叉的扁平结构（flat structure）。下面以（102）为例，其树形图如（103）所示。

（103）

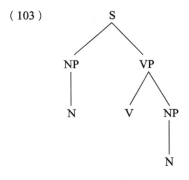

张三　　喜欢　句法学

在上图中，从成分合并的角度看，V（喜欢）及其宾语NP（句法学）合并为一个较大的成分VP（喜欢句法学），这个成分再与另外一个成分，也就是其谓述（predicated of）对象主语NP（张三）合并，最终形成一个更大的成分S（张三喜欢句法学）。从直接成分分析的角度看，刚好倒过来，将S逐层分析成为NP、VP、V、NP，这个分析过程可以用重写规则（rewriting rules）来表示，请看（104）。

（104）　a.　S→NP + VP

　　　　　b.　VP→V + NP

　　　　　c.　NP→…N…

　　　　　d.　V→喜欢……

　　　　　e.　N→张三、句法学……

在（104）中，"→"是改写符号，其意义也理解为"包含"。以（104）a为例，其含义是：句子"S"可改写为名词短语"NP"和动词短语"VP"，或者说，句子"S"包含"NP"和"VP"。

（105）是一个较为复杂的例子，其谓语部分跟（102）相比多出了"应该""非常"两个成分，若不严格遵循二叉树原则，可大略画成（106）那样的扁平结构。在严格二分的框架下，需要表示为（107）。其中，"Aux"是助动词符号，"AuxP"是助动词短语，"Adv"
是副词，"AdvP"是副词短语。

（105）张三应该非常喜欢句法学。

（106）

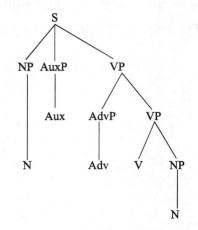

张三 应该 非常 喜欢 句法学

（107）

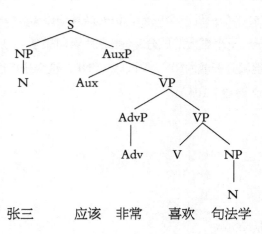

张三 应该 非常 喜欢 句法学

需要说明的是，根据（101）的表示法，（104）a以及上面的几个树形图需要修改，因
为其中的S并没有体现出哪个成分是其中心语，换句话说，S应该由一个体现其中心语的
短语来代替。句子S可以看作以屈折成分（inflectional element，INFL）为中心的短语，表
示为IP。屈折成分INFL是一个功能语类，用以表示动词的时（tense）、体（aspect）和一

致关系（agreement），例如，动词的过去时-*ed*、动词第三人称单数形式-*s*、完成体形式-*en*和进行体形式-*ing*等。（104）a可以表示为（108），其中的核心是屈折成分INFL（简缩为I），动词短语VP是I的补足语。（103）那样的树形图则表示为（109），由于汉语动词缺乏形态变化，所以，（109）中I位置上没有显性成分。

（108）IP ➡ Spec I'

    I' ➡ I VP

    VP ➡ V NP

（109）

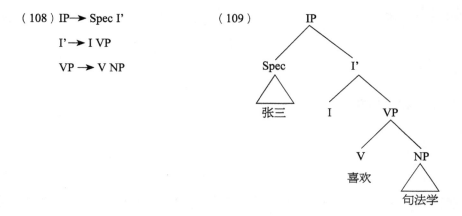

句法结构的另外一种形式表征是框式图。框式图是将结构中的所有成分置于方括号之中，由内而外层层加框，在左边框以下标方式标出每一成分的语类，犹如洋葱式的构造。仍以上面的（105）为例，用框式图表示如（110）。

（110）[ₛ [ₙₚ张三] [ₐᵤₓₚ [ₐᵤₓ应该] [ᵥₚ [ₐdᵥ非常] [ᵥₚ [ᵥ喜欢] [ₙₚ句法学]]]]]

在上述（110）中，"张三""应该""非常""喜欢""句法学"都是一个成分，有自己的语类，如下标所示。从合并的角度看，由小而大的成分依次是"句法学""喜欢句法学""非常喜欢句法学""应该非常喜欢句法学""张三应该非常喜欢句法学"，分别以下标表示。不过，这个框式图有点烦琐，可以将多余的框边去掉，简化为（111）。

（111）[ₛ张三 [ₐᵤₓₚ应该 [ᵥₚ非常 [ᵥₚ喜欢 [ₙₚ句法学]]]]]

如果考虑中间短语，并且将句子看作一个含有中心语的短语，则（111）需要修改为（112）。

（112）[ᵢₚ张三 [ᵢ' [ₐᵤₓₚ [ₐᵤₓ' 应该 [ᵥₚ非常 [ᵥₚ [ᵥ' 喜欢 [ₙₚ句法学]]]]]]]]

框式图和树形图各有用武之地，都是句法结构的形式表征。树形图比较直观，但占空间较大；框式图比较简洁，但看起来比较费力一些。

📖 原典选读

一、说"自由"和"黏着"

【导　读】

"自由"（free）与"黏着"（bound）是美国描写主义语言学在界定语言形式时所使用的术语，是语言学上的两个重要概念。这里的文献是吕叔湘（1962）发表在《中国语文》上的一篇文章。

文章首先检视了描写主义语言学关于"自由"与"不自由"（黏着）界定上存在的不足，比如，将"词"界定为"最小的自由形式"，而将"自由"界定为"能够单说"，就无法解释一些功能词（传统上所说的虚词）不能"单说"却仍然是"词"。这可以引发读者思考："词"是否必须是"自由"的？

文章将"自由"与"黏着"放到汉语中进行审视，结合大量事实，提出讨论这两个概念的时候应该充分考虑方言差异、语体、文体、风格、所处结构、意义等诸多因素，这些因素对于判定一个语素或词的"自由"或"黏着"都会产生影响。

作者认为将"词"界定为"最小的自由形式"在汉语里行不通。但是"自由"和"黏着"对于更好地理解很多语法现象有帮助，不主张将"自由"理解为"自由运用"。事实表明：不仅语素、词，就连词组、句子也存在"自由"和"黏着"的问题。"黏着"成分所黏附对象的性质也是值得关注的问题。

说"自由"和"黏着"

一

美国学派的语言学家很重视"自由形式"和"黏着形式"的区别，几乎一致主张用"最小的自由形式"来作为"词"的定义。一般认为首先提出这个理论的是 Leonard Bloomfield，其实早在 1876 年英国语言学家 Henry Sweet 就已经有过类似的议论：

> ……最后提出一些语音群，有独立的意义，不能再往小里划分。测验有没有独立意义用游离性，也就是能构成独立的句子的能力。因此我们不妨给词下一个定义，词是终极的，不能再分解的句子。①

Bloomfield 在 1926 年发表的《为语言科学用的一套公设》里说：

> 可以作为一句话来说的形式是自由形式。不是自由形式的形式是黏着形式。……一个最小的自由形式是一个词。这样，词就是一个可以单独说（并且有意义）但是不能分析成（全部）可以单独说（并且有意义）的几个部分的形式。②

在他的《语言论》里他又加以发挥：

> 一个全部由两个或更多的较小的自由形式组成的自由形式，例如 "poor John"（可怜的约翰）或是 "John ran away"（约翰跑了）或是 "yes, sir"（是，您哪）……（原来呢？）我们也可以想像一个人若否吐吐地说 "The…"（这个……）而为对方所了解。③

能不能用"最小的自由形式"作为词的定义，首先要看一个形式在正常的情况下是否自由。我们说某一个形式是自由的或是不自由的，应该是指它在正常的情况下能单独说或是不能单独说，正如

241

──二十世纪现代汉语语法"八大家"

同我们说一只手有五个指头的时候不去考虑那些六指儿一样。Bloomfield 的看法不是这样。他说：

> 我们可以设想一段对话："Is?—No; was."（现在是？——不；过去）。"Because?"（因为）这个词据说是女人们的回答。一个性子急的听话人奇嘴要说，"And?"（后来呢？）我们也可以想像一个人看否吐吐地说 "The…"（这个……）而为对方所了解。④

这是因为 is, because, and, the 这些虚词在一般情况下都不单独说，可是他也无法否认这些词作为词的资格，才不得不迁就这些希奇古怪的句子来。连他自己也说这是"想入非非"（farfetched）。

他的学生 Charles F. Hockett 也举过一个非常特殊的例子。他说他曾经实实在在听见过一段对话，可以证明 outside 不是一个词而是两个词⑤：

> A：Where're you going?（你哪儿去？）
> B：Out.（出）
> A：Out where?（出哪儿？）
> B：Side.（去）④

他这段话受到了应有的批评：

> 他好像没有想到，这种"只此一回"的用法，如果用它来做凭据，必然引导我们完全放弃自由和黏着的概念；我们都曾经听见过有人说 "Drive slow"（[把车]开慢点儿），旁边爱开玩笑的朋友给他加个 "-ly"（= 应该说 "Drive slowly"），或是有人问："Did you say friendly or unfriendly?"（你说的是友好还是非友好？）回答是 "un-"（非）。不必把实例看得那么神圣，以至于必须把偶发的和希奇的[实例]用来做一条规则或定义的根据。⑥

对于这些词，也就是一般所谓虚词，Sweet 倒是有一种比较通达的见解：

> ……在 [əmæn]（一个人）和 [ðəmæn]（这个人）的情形，则是一个词或两个词，在一定程度上是个可争论的问题。似乎是分别两个词，一种是全词，一种是半词，[mæn]（人）是全词，[ðə]（这）是半词。⑦

Sweet 还提出另外一条原则：类比。例如 goes 不能单独说，可

242

是可以跟命令式 go! 类比，后者是可以单独说的。Bloomfield 也说：the 这个词虽然难得单独说，可是作用跟 this, that 差不多，后者是可以单独说的，类比作用让我们把 the 也算做一个词。接受类比法，那就意味着不能严格遵守最小自由形式的原则。

另一方面，复合词常常可以分解成两个或更多的词，语法学家爱用重音型式来辨别复合词和短语，但是也常常遇到难以对付的情况，Bloomfield 就举了 devil-may-care（满不在乎的）、jack-in-the-pulpit（北美洲植物，学名 Arisaema atrorubens）做例子⑧。

比复合词更尴尬的是 the man I saw yesterday's [daughter]（我昨天看见的那个人的 [女儿]）之类的例子。Bloomfield 说，这里的 's 是一个黏着形式，所以整个这一串叫是一个词⑨。这是不容易令人接受的，Hockett 就不同意这种看法。Hockett 认为不能在"词"和"最小自由形式"之间划等号。他说，twenty-eighth（第二十八）是一个最小自由形式，可是是两个词⑩。

连 Bloomfield 自己，说了一大堆之后还是得承认：

> 这些标准没有一个能严格应用，许多形式处于黏着形式和词的边界上，或是处于词和短语的边界上，不可能在能够和不能够孤立地说出来的形式之间划下一道鸿沟⑪。

二

要把自由和黏着的概念应用到汉语的词和非词的问题上，首先遇到的也就是上面所说的怎样就算或才算自由的问题。汉语里的语素绝大多数是单音节。用一个单音节当做单独一句话来说，在汉语里比在例如英语里，似乎更受受限制。一个人主动说话的时候，只不大会只说一个字，除了发音字或是表示惊叹，像"来！""蛇！"之类。因此"能单独说"常常只是"能单独回答问话"的意思⑫。"这是什么？"——"笔。"证明"笔"能单独说。"这种笔好不好？"——"好。"证明"好"能单独说。可是回答问话也有个自然不自然，也就是是常例还是特例的问题。比如说，要试验"棋"字

243

──二十世纪现代汉语语法"八大家"

能不能单独说，你问"这是什么"，人家只会回答"象棋"或是"围棋"或是"跳棋"，决不会回答"棋"。要试验"错"能不能单独说，无论你问"对不对"或是"错不错"，回答都不会是"错"，只会是"错了"。再如"醒"，只能问"醒了没有"或"醒没醒"，不可能问"醒不醒"，回答自然也只会是"醒了"。有时候连发问都为难。比如张姓李的"姓"，怎么个问法？总不能说"让你姓张，你姓不姓"吧。

要是应用类比法，那就不但这些字，比这些更难游离的也不难证明是词⑬。

赢了球：赢了棋	坏不了：错不了
过了河：过了期	睡得早：醒得早
回个信：回个礼	搬过家：离过家
中了箭：中了暑	嫁了人了：姓了张了
新办法：老办法	一座山：一座楼
难回答：好回答	一桌饭：一桌席
说不完：说不尽	一个人：一个工
想对了：想左了	一门手艺：一门课

上面例子里加点的字都是不能单独说的，可是都能跟能单说的对比，算是自由形式呢，还是黏着形式呢？也许可以算是"半自由"吧。多数讲汉语语法的书里不说词可以"单说"，只说是可以"单用"（"独立运用"、"自由运用"），用意就在于要包括这些字（以及虚词）。

不管是单说还是单用，又都会遇到另一方面的问题，那就是：有些字在一种环境里能单说或单用，在另一种环境里不能单说或单用，那么作为一个语素，它是自由的还是黏着的呢？这跟一个自由语素也可以做构词成分（如笔可以出现在毛笔、水笔、笔锋、笔误里边）不一样，那是所有自由语素的共同特点，不牵涉某些特殊情况。这些情况是：

（1）方言不同。有些语素在某些方言里可以单说，在另一些方言里不能单说。例如：

244

鞋：鞋子　　　　　面：面条
梨：梨子　　　　　馍：馍馍

按说，一种方言自成一个系统，一个语素尽可以在不同的方言里具有不同的身分。问题在于这些并行的形式都在书面上出现，也都在一般应该算是说着普通话的人嘴里出现。也就是说，普通话的规范还没有确定到那么一个程度，可以让我们说：这是普通话，那不是普通话。

（2）书面语和口语不同。有些字书面上单用，可是口语里不单用。例如：

但：但是　　　　　云：云彩
或：或是　　　　　雁：大雁

最突出的是"儿化词"，书面上经常不把儿写出来。比方说的是花儿，写的是花，说的是一会儿，写的是一会。连剧本、小说里都常有这种情形，别的文章就更不用说了。底下是《骆驼祥子》里的一些例子：

他脸上有了点[儿]笑意。
拉包月就是凑合事[儿]，一年是一年的事[儿]，瞎知道！
我叫小马儿去，我的小孙子，在外面[儿]看着车呢？
老者一边[儿]走还一边[儿]说话。
老车夫的头慢慢[儿]地往下低。
把老车夫的脖领[儿]解开。
糖水刚放在老车夫的嘴边[儿]上。
儿子当兵去了，一去不回头；媳妇[儿]……

还有一种情形，书面上常用（没有文体的限制），口语里不说（另用别的字眼）。例如：

上午九时：上午九点
二月十二日：二月十二号

像这种情形，是以口语为准呢，还是以书面为准？研究语言嘛，自然该以口语为凭。可是书面语难道可以一笔抹杀？尤其像儿化词的情形，学普通话的人十个有九个是通过阅读，谁敢担保若干年之

245

后，随着普通话的推广，这些个儿字在多数人的嘴里还老是那么硬朗。

（3）文体不同。有些字专科文献里可以单用，但是一般不能单用。例如：

耳、鼻（医学）：耳朵、鼻子
金、氧（化学）：金子、氧气
虎、鲫（动物）：老虎、鲫鱼
叶、柳（植物）：叶子、柳树

此外像报纸上"新华社讯"的讯，画刊里照相附注"某某摄"的摄，也都是只有在这种特殊场合才能这样单用。

（4）风格不同。有些字一般不能单用，但是在成语、熟语里能单用。例如：

一问一答　　　　　前怕狼，后怕虎
不知不觉　　　　　你一言，我一语
就事论事　　　　　不分男、女、老、少
微乎其微　　　　　自编自导自演

（5）所处结构不同。有些字只在某种结构里可以单用，在别种结构里就得扩充成一个双音节的同义词。上面用来做类比的例子里就有这种情形，如期：期限、席：酒席。再举几个例子：

画面儿出了名：名声可大啦
夏秋两季：夏季、秋季
桌、椅、板凳：桌子、椅子
从左往右：左边、右边

这类例子里的单字是自由语素还是黏着语素，最难下结论了。这里既没有方言的分别，也没有书面语和口语的分别，也没有文体、风格的差异。

（6）意义不完全相同。比如下车的下，可以问："下车不下？"回答："下。"可是下班的下就不能这样问，这样答。下面的例子里，加圈的是能单说的，加点的是不能单说的：

下车：下班，下课　　推车：今天推明天

246

也许可以把同一个字看做两个同音的语素，一个能单说，一个不能单说？这就牵涉划分语素的原则问题：意义差别到多大才可以算是两个语素？像上面例子的下和撇各自分做两个语素是不是恰当？

以上这些情况，总起来说，出于一个根源。这些单字，不管古汉语里有没有这个字，有没有这个字义，按照古汉语法全能单用。汉语语法演变的趋势是越来越多的单字不能单用，可是并没有让一切单字在一切情况下都不用（也完全没有这种必要）。这样就形成了现在的局面。有些字是绝对自由，像来、去、手、脚；有些字是绝对黏着，像辉、煌、惺、惑；很多字是介乎二者之间，在这样那样的条件下，有较大或较小的自由。

三

显然，要用"最小的自由形式"来规定"词"，至少在汉语里是行不通的了。可是这不等于说自由和黏着的概念在语法分析里没有什么用处。不，通过自由和黏着的分别，我们可以更好地了解好些个语法问题。但是不能把"自由"扩大为"自由运用"，因为"自由运用"的界限不明确，也很不容易明确。必须守住"自由"的原来的意义，也就是能单说，并且必须是在正常的情况下能单说。

要谈的第一个问题是虚词。虚词是许多语言里都有的。虚词的取得词的资格，并不是因为它们像 Bloomfield 企图证明的那样，在特殊的情况下也能单说。也不是因为可以类比。The 可以跟 this, that 相比，of, for, as, than 这些词可以跟什么本身能单说的词相比呢？虚词的取得词的资格是因为它是另一个词的一部分。是用的剩余法，就是在一个语言片段里，把或为词的部分提开，剩下的东西既不能看做它前面的或后面的词的一个部分，就不得不承认它们本身是词[①]。

分别实字和虚字是我国语法学的传统理论。可是现代学者划分

247

实词和虚词，又多多少少跟传统的办法有些不同。一般是说：实词的意义比较具体，能够单独成句；虚词没有具体的意义，不能单独成句[②]。这表明语法学家虽然已经不再自由和黏着来区别词和非词，却仍然要用它来区别实词和虚词。这样划分，仔细推敲起来是有问题的。虚词不能单用，对的，除了极个别的例外（如不）。实词都能单说，不尽然。名词和谓词（动词和形容词）都有不能单说的例子，上文已经说过。不过就总的情况来说，这两类词的确多数都能单说。可是实词里边有整个的大类或小类是不能单说的，像黏着形式：量词、单音方位词、部分代词（它、大家、人家、自己、这、那、哪、几、多）。为什么把这些个放在实词里边呢？原来现代学者划分实词和虚词还有一个没有明白说出来的标准：能做句子成分（主、谓、宾、补、定、状）的是实词，其余的是虚词。按照这个标准，上面指出来的量词等等是可以归入实词的。可是副词就又不应该归入虚词了。总之这两个标准是不能得出一致的结果来的，现在的划分是依违两者的。我国古代学者所说的虚字，如《助字辨略》里的"助字"，《经传释词》里的"词"，范围都比较宽，代词、助动词、副词都包括在内[③]。这是用的什么标准呢？古人虽然不讲究下定义，倒也不是任意取舍。这些虚词类都有两个特征：（1）每一类词的数目都比较少，差不多可以列举；（2）在较短的时期内不容易有新的加入。如果我们愿意采用这个标准，就可以给虚词下一个定义：属于成员少而开放性小的那些类的词。跟虚词相反，实词的特征是类的成员多，并且随时有新的成员加入。在语义方面，这两类的区别是：实词的词汇意义和语法意义能分开，虚词的词汇意义和语法意义分不开，甚至没有多少词汇意义。从语法的角度看，实词只须研究每一类词的共性（包括大类和小类，总之是成类的），虚词则不仅要研究每一类词的共性，还得研究每一个词的个性。至于自由和黏着，虚词大都是黏着形式，实词则很多是自由形式，但是黏着形式也不少。

248

其次，除了单个的语素可以分别自由和黏着以外，我们还可以研究一下，是不是语素组合也有自由和黏着的分别。Bloomfield 只说"永远不单说的形式是黏着形式"[⑩]，没说黏着形式限于简单形式（语素）。可是他的书里讲到黏着形式总是讲的简单形式，这就很容易给人一种错觉，仿佛复杂形式（语素组合）总是自由形式似的。事实并不如此。不但是包含黏着语素在内的形式有的能单说，如自由，有的不能单说，如自动（步枪、控制），甚至原来都能单说的形式，组合在一起反而不能单说了，例如人和造都能单说，但是人造不能说，只出现在人造丝、人造石油、人造卫星这些更大的组合里。又如这一问（问得好），一天天（好起来），从这里（往南去），一跳（跳过去），你越说（他越恼），你既然知道（干吗不说），也都是不能单说的，是不是该算是黏着形式？这情形不限于汉语，英语里像 day in (day out)（一天天），the sooner, (the better)（越快越好），也都很难设想可以单说。

后面这一类例子，这一问等等，都是比词大的形式，是短语，甚至是句子（分句）。这些形式是自由的还是黏着的，还是一个只有理论意义的问题。不仅有理论意义的是前面那类自动、人造等例子；这些组合是词不是词？这种组合在现代汉语里多极了，像高射（炮、机关枪），野战（军、医院），国际（关系），星际（旅行），越野（赛跑），越冬（作物），无穷（大、小、远），无机（化学、肥料、盐），无名（英雄、作家、高地），多项（式），多边（形、协定），多幕（剧），多级（火箭），等等，等等，要几千有几千。不仅是数目大，而且正在不断地、大量地增加。因此承认还是不承认它们是词，关系不小。要是不承认它们是词，就只能说是构词成分，只有跟括号里的语素连在一起才是词，在拼音文字里就全得连写。这在实用上是极大的不便。有比这更长的，例如同分异构（体）、双轮双桦（犁）、字称守恒（定律）、可控制（热核反应）、特宽角多倍（测量仪）、脉冲频率远距离（测量）、线性可移算随机

249

（函数方程式）。要把这些个个全都连写，简直是不可想像。在理论上也大可商量。既然小于词的语素可以有自由有黏着，大于词的短语也可以有自由有黏着，为什么词这一级就必得是自由形式，不许有黏着形式呢？光从自由或黏着这个角度来考虑，没有肯定它们是词的理由，也没有否定它们是词的理由，门是敞开着的。要肯定，要否定，都得另有根据，也就是说，得给词另下定义。

另一个问题，除了一个语言形式本身是自由的还是黏着的之外，我们还可以检查一下，如果它是一个黏着形式，它所黏着的对象是什么？是一个黏着语素还是一个词？或者是一个短语，一个句子？还可以再检查一下由这个黏着形式跟它所黏着的对象组成的形式是自由的还是黏着的。

不同的词类在这方面也往往有所不同。比如量词，它总是跟数词组合，组成的短语如果数词限于"一"，就不能单说（溅了一身泥、笑了一笑），如果数词不限于"一"，就可以单说（一件、两件、一次、三次）。

介词的黏着对象是名词或名词性短语，连词的黏着对象是句子（句子形式）或谓词性短语（谓语形式），即使只是一个词，也代表一个句子或短语，这是这两类词不同之处。但是它们又有共同之点：黏着的对象是自由的（介词有例外），但是组合的结果是黏着的（把这件事、对于他）；要是能去、要是你要去）。连词里边，和、跟、同、与这一类跟其余的有所不同，黏着的对象是词或短语，不是短语或句子。这又有两种分析法。一种分析：和等黏着于一前一后的两个对象，组合的短语一般是自由的。另一种分析：和等只黏着于后面的词或短语，组成的短语是黏着的——这就非常接近介词了。（类似的还有或、或是、或者，但是、或是、或者也可以黏着于句子，那就跟一般连词相同。）

助词的情形最复杂。(1) 语气助词黏着于句子，这句子不论带不带语气助词都是自由的。这是语气助词跟别的助词不同之处，因此常常被划出来单独成为一个词类。(2) 另一极端是着和们，它们

250

的黏着对象一般只是一个词，组合的结果是一个自由形式（词?）。可是着也往往黏着于一个黏着语素，组合的结果更常常是一个黏着形式，如侧着（身子），背着（人）。想着（还给他），（一家子）指着（他）。(3) "笑得真不起腰来"的得，黏着的对象总是一个词，组合的结果却是一个黏着形式（笑不得不能单说），可是这是个词还是个短语好像还没有被作为问题提出来。(4) "数得清、数不清"的得和不，黏着于一个短语（动补结构），组合的结果是自由的短语。(5) 了和过黏着于一个词或短语（动补结构或并立结构），组合的结果是自由的短语。了、过、着的语法意义是同一类，都表示动态，因此好些语法学家认为是词尾（构形的）。但是在了和过上有困难："把腿都坐麻了"，"哪儿真有人哭断过肠子"，难于说坐麻和哭断是词。(6) 的和所的黏着对象都可以是一个词（说的、所说），一个短语（说了不止一次的、所已经说过），一个句子（我说的、我所说），但是的的组合结果是自由的（有例外），所的组合结果是黏着的。此外还有别种情形，暂时不能列举，因为助词的成员有哪些，到现在为止还没有人说过肯定的话。

汉语构词基本上只有一个方式：复合。一般的复合词，构词的成分可以都是自由，也可以都是黏着的，有的是自由的，有的是黏着的；这就是说，自由语素和黏着语素相互之间没有任何选择性，不论是相容还是不相容。组合的结果也是或者自由、或者黏着，不受构词成分的性质的约束。在底下的例子里，加点的字是黏着语素，加圈的是自由语素。

（自由）	（黏着）
国家：有心	国有（土地）：有线（电报）
国庆：有意	国际（关系）：有声（电影）
民兵：无心	民办（小学）：无线（电报）
民族：无意	民间（文艺）：无声（电影）

再拿那些用附加成分构成的词来看，词尾总是黏着的，可是所谓词

251

根就不一定都是黏着的。比较：

桌子、椅子	刀子、饼子
木头、石头	甜头、苦头
患者、著者	编者、读者

说词尾总是黏着的，指的是者、然、乎、子、儿、头这些个，至于那些只是有点像词尾的，就不一定，有完全自由的，如人，有半自由的，如家、界、员、度、量。所谓词头，情形也差不多，很多是自由或半自由的。这就是说，在汉语的构词法里很难区别复合和派生。

关于汉语里的"词头"和"词尾"，还有许多话可说，只是与本题无关，只能将来有机会时另写文章了。

附 注：

① "Word, Logic, Grammar", *Transactions of the Philological Society*, 1875—6。译文见《中国语文》1961 年 9 月号，引文见 37 页。
② "A Set of Postulates for the Science of Language", *Language*，第 2 卷 (1926)，155—6 页。
③ *Language* (1933)，178 页。
④ 同上，179 页。
⑤ *A Course in Modern Linguistics* (1958)，167 页。
⑥ "side" 不等于"去"，但是在这一段对话里 "outside" 只好译作"出去"。
⑦ R. Quirk: *Towards a Description of English Usage, Transactions of the Philological Society*, 1960，46—47 页。
⑧ 前引文，译文 37 页。
⑨ 前引书 180 页。
⑩ 前引书 178 页。
⑪ 前引书 168—9 页。
⑫ 前引书 181 页。
⑬ 人民教育出版社编：《汉语知识》(1960)，17—18 页。

252

⑭ 类比法很像转换法。转换法如果不加以限制，得出来的只是诉素，不是词。加以限制，指的是在类比的格式里没有把有关的语素看成跟它前面或后面的语素合成一个词的可能。这实际上等于剩余法，见下文第二节。

⑮ 这些例子都在《骆驼祥子》第十章，这里边的儿化都是根据作者老舍先生几年前在中央人民广播电台朗诵这一章（不全）的时候的实际发音加上去的。例子里包括了一些儿化的语素组合。

⑯ 参看 А. И. Смирницкий "词的分离性"，译文见陆志韦等著《汉语构词法》（1957）附录。

⑰ 例如北京大学汉语教研室编《现代汉语》上册152页；人民教育出版社编《汉语知识》17—18页。

⑱ 王了一先生在《中国现代语法》（21—24页）里把副词定为"半实词"，把代词定为"半虚词"，大概也是在意义标准和句子成分标准

的冲突之下想出来的办法，不过王先生仍然把它们都列在"语法成分"也就是广义的虚词之下，这是跟传统的虚字符合的。

⑲ 前引书160页。

（《中国语文》，1962年第1期）

二、三种词品（The Three Ranks）

Otto Jespersen. 1924. *The Philosophy of Grammar*. London：George Allen and Unwin Ltd.

中译本：[丹] 奥托·叶斯柏森. 语法哲学. 何勇，等，译. 北京：语文出版社，1988.

【导　读】

这个原典选自丹麦语言学家奥托·叶斯柏森《语法哲学》的第七章。由于原著出版较早（Jespersen, 1924），电子版不易获得，中译本在国内很有影响，所以这里选取中译本。

叶斯柏森的《语法哲学》对我国的语法研究产生过很大影响。老一代语言学家如王力、吕叔湘等都受到叶氏的影响。本书第七章提出的"三品说"是有关词类与词在结构中地位之关系的一种很有见地的论述。这种关系不仅存在于词组之中，也存在于句子之中。请比较：a furiously barking dog：the dog barks furiously，作者将前者称为组合式（junction），将后者称为连系式（nexus）。

所谓"三品"是指首品（primary）、次品（secondary）、末品或三品（tertiary），四品及以上的品级与三品属于同类，无须特别区分。以extremely hot weather为例，weather是首品，hot是次品，extremely是三品。这种分析反映了不同词在结构所处的地位（层次）不同，与美国结构主义的直接成分分析或者层次分析做法本质上是一致的，但叶氏的思想显然有开创性。叶氏指出，不仅单一的词有"三品"的区分，而且词组、从句也都可以有"三品"的分别。但无论是词、词组，还是从句，"三品"的区分是在结构中进行的。

第 七 章
三 种 词 品
(The Three Ranks)

主从关系. 名词. 形容词. 代词. 动词. 副词. 词组. 从句. 结束语.

主从关系
(Subordination)

关于一个词应该归于哪一类——名词,形容词,或是其他什么词——的问题,是一个关系到对这个词的看法问题。因此在词典里总能找到问题的答案①。我们现在就来考察词组,这里我们会发现虽然名词总归是名词,形容词总归是形容词,但在连贯的话语中却存在着主从关系的一定结构,同把词划分成"词类"一样,但又不完全依赖于它。

在任何一个表示事物或人的词组中(请比较我在 67 页上所举出的那些例子),我们总发现其中一个词最重要,而其他的词则结合在一起从属于该词。这个主词受另一个词的限定(后置修饰,前置修饰),而后者又会受到第三个词的限定(后置修饰,前置修饰),等等。因此我们就根据词与词之间限定与被限定的相互关

---

① 然而,值得注意的是任何词、词组或词的任何部分都可当作"引用语"(quotation word)而可看作名词,如 your *Late* was misheard as *Light* (你说的 *Late* 被错听成了 *Light*),his speech abounded in I think so's (他讲那番话时总是说他想是的) there should be two L's in his name (他名字里应有两个L)。

• 114 •

系确定词的"品级"(ranks)。在词组 extremely hot weather (极热的天气)中,最后一个词 weather 显然是主要的概念,可叫作首品(primary); hot 限定 weather, 可叫作次品(secondary); extremely 限定 hot, 可叫作三品(tertiary)。尽管三品词还会受另一个(四品)词的限定,而四品词又会受另一个(五品)词的限定,等等,但没有必要分出三种以上的词品,因为这些低品级词在形式和特点上与三品词没有什么区别。如在词组 a certainly not very cleverly worded remark (一句显然是措辞不清的话)中,certainly, not, very 虽然都是限定其后的词的,但它们在语法上同三品词毫无区别,如同在 certainly a clever remark (一句显然是机警的话),not a clever remark (并非一句机警的话),a very clever remark (一句很机警的话)中一样。

词组 a furiously barking dog (一条狂吠的狗)中,dog 是首品,barking 是次品,furiously 是三品。我们如果把该词组与 the dog barks furiously (这狗狂吠)相比较,就会清楚地发现后者也有与前者相同的主从关系,但这两种结构有着根本的区别,须用不同的术语加以表示:我们把前者叫作组合式(junction),把后者叫作连系式(nexus)。第 99 页提到过它们的区别,第八章中将会对它们进行更详细的讨论,我们会看到除了 the dog barks(狗吠)外,还有其他类型的连系式。应该注意 dog 不仅在作主语时是首品,如在 the dog barks 中,在作动词或介词的宾语时也是首品,如 I see the dog (我看见狗),he runs after the dog (他追狗)。

首品、次品、三品这些术语不仅适用于组合式,还适用于连系式,但仍有必要用专门的术语,把组合式中的次品叫作修品(adjunct),把连系式中的次品叫作述品(adnex)。三品可叫作次修品(subjunct),偶尔需用专门的术语称呼四品词时,可把它

• 115 •

叫作次次修品(sub-subjuncts)①。

可以有两个(或多个)并列的首品,如 the dog and the cat ran away (狗和猫跑走了)。同样,一个首品可带两个或多个并列的修品,如在 a nice young lady (一位可爱的年轻女士)中,a, nice, young 限定的都是 lady。再请比较 much(II) good (II) white(II) wine(I) (许多好的白葡萄酒),和 very(III) good (II) wine (I) (非常好的葡萄酒)。并列修品常常由连接词连接,如 a raining and stormy afternoon (一个风雨交加的下午),a brilliant, though lengthy novel (一本出色的,但篇幅颇长的小说)。如不用连接词,则说明最后一个修品与首品的关系特别密切,构成一个概念,可称为复合首品如 young lady (年轻女士),在某些固定结构中尤其如此;in high good humour (情绪特佳),by great good fortune (交上好运),extreme old age (老迈之年)。有时两个并列修品的前者似乎从属后者,接近于一个次修品,如 burning hot soup (滚热的汤),a shocking bad nurse (一个坏得怕人的护士)。这样,乔叟 a verrey parfit gentil knight (一位非常彬彬有礼的骑士)中的形容词 very (very 在今天的 the very day〔正是这一天〕中仍是形容词)先介于修品与次修品之间,后来又成为属副词类的次修品。在某种程度上类似的例子有 nice and warm (很暖和)中的 nice (and)。有趣的是意大利语中也有类似现象,bell'e; 贾科沙《落叶飘零》136,il concerto…On ci ho bell'e rinun-ziato(音乐会……啊! 我早就放弃了)|同上,117,Tu l'hai bell'e trovato (你已经找到它了)。其他该用次修品却用修品的例子

---

① 我现在认为首品(primary)这个词比我在《现代英语语法》第二卷中用的主词(principal)恰好。我们尽管可借助更新的术语,把组合式和连系式中的首品分别称为上修品(superjunct)和上述品(supernex),但这些最新的术语实在是多余的。

• 116 •

还有法语中的 elle est toute surprise (她感到很惊愕)| les fenêtres grandes ouvertes (窗户大开)。

并列次修品的例子有: a logically and grammatically un-justifiable construction (一个在逻辑上和语法上都不合理的结构),a seldom or never seen form (一种罕见或从未见过的形式)。

在上面所举的例句中,我们已看到了名词作首品,形容词作修品,副词作次修品的情况;这三种词类与这里所确立的三品词之间必然存在着某种程度的对应关系。我们甚至可以下定义说,名词是习惯上担任首品的词,形容词是习惯上担任修品的词,副词是习惯上担任次修品的词。但是这种对应关系并不是绝对的,下面的论述将会说明这一问题。词类和词品这两个体系的对应不是一成不变的。

名 词
(Substantives)

名词作首品 无需再引例子。

名词作修品 名词作修品的古老方式是把名词用于属格,如 Shelly's poems (雪莱的诗),the butcher's shop(肉店),St. Paul's Cathedral (圣保罗教堂)。但是应该注意,属格也可以用作首品(通过常说的省略法),如 I prefer Keat's poems to Shel-ley's (我喜欢济慈的诗而不喜欢雪莱的诗),I bought it at the butcher's (我在肉店购得此物),St. Paul's is a fine buil-ding(圣保罗教堂是一座精美建筑)。英语中,以前的复合词的第一部分现在常常作为一个独立的词,用作修品,如 stone wall (石墙),a silk dress and a cotton one (一件丝绸衣服和一件棉布衣服)。关于这些词经常用作形容词的问题,请参看前章。名词用作修品的例子还有:women writers (女作家),a queen bee (一

• 117 •

只蜂王），boy messengers（信童）。为什么 Captain Smith（史密斯船长），Doctor Johnson（约翰逊博士）不可看作这一类呢？请比较德语 Kaiser Wilhelms Erinnerungen（威廉的回忆）中无屈折变化的情况（但复合的爵位封号中的情况要复杂一些）。

有时，我们想联结两个名词概念，结果发现单凭简单的并列要使两个名词中的一个成为另一个的修品是不可能的，也是行不通的，这时语言常常要求助于"限定属格"(definitive genitive)或相应的介词词组，如拉丁语 urbs Romæ（罗马城，比较丹麦语中的相应词组 byen Rom〔罗马城〕以及 Captain Smith〔史密斯船长〕一类的组合，法语 la cité de Rome（罗马城），英语 the city of Rome（罗马城）等。还有一些颇有意思的表达法，如〔英〕a devil of a fellow（恶魔似的家伙）| that scoundrel of a servant（那个恶棍一般的仆人）| his ghost of a voice（他那鬼魂般的声音）|〔德〕ein alter schelm von lohnbedienter（魔鬼般的仆人，在 von 后用主格是例外现象）|〔丹〕den skurk av en tjener（那个恶魔一般的仆人）| et vidunder av barn（神童）| det fæ til Nielsen（野兽般的尼尔森）|〔法〕ce fripon de valet（那个奸刁仆人）| un amour d'enfant（一个可爱的孩子）| celui qui avait un si drôle denom（这个名字古怪的人）|〔意〕quel ciarlatano d'un dottore（那个假医生）| quel pover uomo di tuo pedre（你父亲那个可怜的人）等等。这种现象与斯塔的纳维亚语中使用所有格代词 dit fæ（你这个笨蛋）和西班牙语的 Pobrecitos de nosotros!（我们太可怜了!）| Desdichada de mí!（我真倒霉!）有着一定的联系。关于这个问题以及其他类似现象，请参见格里姆《人称变换》，舒哈特《雨果·舒哈特—布雷维尔》197，蒂格纳《论瑞典语中的性》，115ff.，桑菲尔德《丹尼亚》，VII。

名词作次修品（次述品） 这种用法除多用于一些固定词组外很少见（见125页）。名词作次修品的例子有 emotions, part religious…but part human（感情，一部分是宗教的…但是一部分是人性的—史蒂文森）| the sea went mountains high（大海掀起山一般的浪涛）。在 come home（来家）| I bought it cheap（我买得便宜）中，home, cheap 原先是名词，但现在一般看作副词；再请比较 go south（去南方）。

形 容 词
(Adjectives)

形容词作首品 You had better bow to the impossible〔单数〕（办不到的事你最好不要硬干），ye have the poor〔复数〕always with you（穷人总在你身旁）(《现代英语语法》II），但是 savages（野蛮人），regulars（正规军），Christians（基督徒），the moderns（现代人）等都完全是名词，因为它们有复数词尾；the child is a dear（这孩子是可爱的人）中的 dear 是名词，因为它前面有冠词 a。德语中的 beamter（官员）通常被看作名词，其实应该说成是形容词作首品，这一点可以从词尾变化上看出：der beamte, ein beamter。

形容词作修品 这里无须举例。

形容词作次修品 的观从历史点出发，应把 a fast moving engine（一台快速运转的发动机）| a long delayed punishment（一个拖延很久的惩罚）| a clean shaven face（一张刮得很光的脸）等例子中的斜体词看作是副词而不应看作是形容词次修品（现在，古老的副词词尾 -e 和其它类型弱音发音的 -e 一样，已不再发音）。关于 new-laid eggs（新下的鸡蛋），cheerful tempered men（天性快活的人们），等等，见《现代英语语法》II，15.3，关于 burning hot（火热），见第134页。

代 词
(Pronouns)

代词作首品 I am well（我身体健康）| this is mine（这是我的）| who said that?（那是谁说的?）| what happened?（出了什么事?）| nobody knows（没人知道）等。但 a mere nobody（区区小人物）中的 nobody 却是道地的名词，试比较其复数形式 nobodies。

代词作修品 this hat（这顶帽子）| my hat（我的帽子）| what hat?（什么帽子?）| no hat（没有帽子），等等。

在某些情况下，代词作首品和修品时在形式上没有区别。在另外一些情况下却有区别，试比较 mine（我的）：my（我的）| none（什么也没有），no（没有）；德语中的 mein hut（我的帽子），der meine（我的那个）亦如此。再请注意："Hier ist ein umstand（ein ding）richtig genannt, aber nur einer（eines）"（这是一种正确命名的状况〔一件东西〕，然而也只是一种〔一件〕。法语的代词在如下例子里有形式上的区别。mon chapeau（我的帽子）：le mien（我的东西）：ce chapeau（这顶帽子）：celui-ci（这顶）| quel chapeau（什么帽子?），lequel?（哪样东西?）| chaque（每个），chacun（各个），quelque（某个）：quelqu'un（某人，某物）。

代词作次修品 "代词性副词"(pronominal adverbs）无须举例说明。此外我们还会见到这样一些情况：I am that sleepy（我是这样想睡觉—粗俗语）| the more, the merrier（越多越快活）| none too able（没有一点能力）| I won't stay any longer（我一会儿也不多呆了）| nothing loth（没有丝毫不乐意）| somewhat paler than usual（比平常略有几分苍白）。①

动 词
(Verbs)

动词的限定形式只能作次品（述品），从不作首品或三品。但是分词同形容词一样，可作首品（the living are more valuable than the dead〔活着的人比死去的人更有价值〕）和修品（the living dog〔那条活狗〕）。然而，不定式根据具体情况可用作三品中的任何一品。不定式在某些情况下要求用 to（比较德语的 zu，丹麦语的 at）。严格地说，我也许应该把 to go（去）等词组归入"词组的品级"一节中。

不定式作首品 to see is to believe（百闻不如一见）（试比较 seeing is believing〔百闻不如一见〕）| she wants to rest（她想休息）（试比较 she wants more rest〔她想休息一会儿〕，这里的 rest 是相应的名词形式）。法语 espérer, c'est jouir（希望便是一种享受）| il est défendu de fumer ici（此处禁止吸烟）| sans courir（不跑）| au lieu de courir（不跑……而……）|〔德〕denken ist schwer（思考是困难的）| er verspricht zu kommen（他答应来）| ohne zu laufen（未跑）| anstatt zu laufen（未跑）等。

不定式作修品 in times to come（日后）| there isn't

① 有的代词性副词和数词性副词(numeral adverbs）与修品通用时很难进行语法分析，如 this once（就这一次）| We should have gone to Venice, or somewhere not half so nice（我们本应去威尼斯或不及威尼斯一半美好的某个地方去——奥斯菲尔德）| Are we going anywhere particular?（我们是不是去什么特别的地方?）从心理学上可作如下解释 once=one time（一次），somewhere 和 anywhere=(to)some, any place（到某处，到任何地方）；因此修品从属于位置的名词。

a girl to *touch* her（没有姑娘碰她）| the current thing to *do*（现在应该做的事）| in a way not *to be forgotten*（以一种不会被忘记的方式）| the never *to be forgotten* look（永远不会忘记的目光）《现代英语语法》II, 14, 4 和 15. 8）。〔法〕la chose *à faire*（要做的事）| du tabac *à fumer*（要吸的烟）。（德语从相应的不定式用法中产生了一种特殊的被动分词，das *zu lesende* buch（要读的书）。西班牙语中有 todas las academias existentes y *por existir*（所有现有的和有待建立的学术机构——加尔多斯）。不定式的这种用法部分地弥补了分词不够完全（将来，被动等）的欠缺。

不定式作次修品　　to see him, one would think（见到他，人们就会思索）| I shudder to *think* of it（想到此，我不禁瑟瑟发抖）| he came here to *see* you（他来这里见你）。

副　词
(Adverbs)

副词作首品　　这种用法很少见，例子有 "he did not stay for *long*（他没呆很久）| he's only just back from *abroad*（他刚从国外回来）"。代词性副词作首品比较普遍，from *here*（从这里）| till *now*（迄今为止），另一例子是 he left *there* at two o'clock（他两点钟离开那里），there 被看作 left 的宾语。在哲学语言里 here 和 there 也可用作真正的名词，Motion requires a *here* and a *there*（运动需要此处和彼处）| in the space-field lie innumerable other *theres*（空间还有无数其他的彼处）《新英语词典，见《现代英语语法》II, 8.12）。

·副词作修品　　这种用法也很少见，the *off* side（反面）| in *after* years（在以后的岁月里）| the few *nearby* trees（附

· 122 ·

近的几棵树——美语）| all the *well* passengers（所有身体健康的旅客——美语）| a *so-so* matron（一位平常的女管家——拜伦）。副词大多不必作修品用，因为有相应的形容词（或代词性副词）；the *then* government（当时的政府），the *hither* shore（邻近的海岸）《现代英语语法》II, 14. 9）。

副词作次品　　这是副词的普通用法，因此无须举例。

形容词或动词构成名词时，限定词好象离升了一级，成为次品而不是三品。只要有可能，这就表现在以形容词取代副词的用法上：

II + III	I + II
absolutely novel	absolute novelty
绝对新的	绝对的新
utterly dark	utter darkness
完全黑暗的	完全的黑暗
perfectly strange	perfect stranger
全然陌生的	全然的陌生人
describes accurately	accurate description
确切地描写	确切的描写
I firmly believe	my firm belief,
	a firm believer
我坚信	我的坚定信念，坚定的信仰者
judges severely	severe judges
严格地审判	严格的审判员
reads carefully	careful reader
细心地阅读	细心的阅读者

应该注意，表示大、小（great, small）的形容词可用作程度副词（much, little）的替代对等词，如，a great admirer o Tennyson（一个极崇拜丁尼森的人），〔法〕un grand admirate

ur de Tennyson（意义同前）。关于这类次修品向修品转化的情况，请比较《现代英语语法》II, 12.2 和本书第十章论连系式词的部分。寇姆（《德语语法》136）提到了德语中的 die geistig armen（精神穷者），etwas längst bekanntes（早已熟知的），其中 geistig 和 längst 虽然"修饰一个名词"，但却象副词一样，不发生屈折变化。对此的解释是，armen 和 bekanntes 不是名词，而仅是形容词作首品，这一点可从它们的屈折变化上看出。某些英语词可以有两种用法，these are full equivalents（for）（这些是……的完全对等词）或 fully equivalent（to）（与……完全对等），the direct opposites（of）（……的直接对立物）或 directly opposite（to）（与……直接对立）；麦考利写道，"The government of the Tudors was the *direct opposite* to the government of Augustus"（都铎政府与奥古斯都都政府针锋相对），其中 to 似乎属于形容词 opposite，而不属于名词，而 direct 则是名词的用法。在丹麦语中，人们在翻译 le malade imaginaire（假装的病人）时，拿不准应译作 den indbildt syge（假装的病人），还是 den indbildte syge（装假病的人）。

词　组
(Word Groups)

由两个或多个词构成的词组，其间的相互关系是多种多样的，但在多数情况下可作为一个词来看待。有时的确很难说它是一个词还是两个词。to-day（今天）原来是两个词，但现在愈来愈倾向于不用连词符，拼作 today。事实上，我们还可以说 from today（从今天起），这说明 to 已失去它的原义了。tomorrow（明天）现在也同样被看作是一个词，甚至可以说 I look forward

· 124 ·

to tomorrow（我期待着明天）。然而，就本章的目的而言，把这些及其他有争议的例子看作是一个词还是两个词无关紧要，因为我们知道一个词组（与一个单词相同）既可作首品，也可作修品或次品。

作首品的各类词组　　Sunday afternoon was fine（星期天下午天气晴朗）| I spent *Sunday afternoon* at home（我在家度过了星期天下午）| we met *the kind old Archbishop of york*（我们遇到了年迈、和蔼的约克大主教）| it had taken him *ever since* to get used to the idea（他花了其后的所有时间才习惯于这一概念）| You have *till ten tonight*（今晚十点以前的时间归你）| *From infancy to manhood* is rather a tedious period（婴儿到成人是一相当乏味的时期——考珀）。试比较法语 jusqu'au roi l'a cru（直到皇上相信他），nous avons assez pour jusqu' à samedi（星期六之前我们计钱够）；西班牙语 hasta los malvados creen en él（甚至坏人也相信他——加尔多斯）。

词组作修品　　a *Sunday afternoon* concert（星期日下午的一场音乐会）| the *Archbishop of york*（约克大主教）| the *party in power*（执政党）| the *kind old Archbishop of york's* daughter（年迈、和蔼的约克大主教的女儿）| a *Saturday to Monday* excursion（星期六至星期一的一次远足）| the *time between two and four*（两点至四点之间的时间）| his *after dinner* pipe（他的饭后烟）。

词组作次修品（三品）　　he slept *all Sunday afternoon*（星期天他睡了一下午）| he smokes *after dinner*（他饭后抽烟）| he went *to all the principal cities of Europe*（他去过欧洲的各主要城市）| he lives *next door to Captain Strong*（他住在斯特朗上尉的隔壁）| the canal ran *north and south*（运河贯

· 125 ·

穿南北）| he used to laugh *a great deal*（他过去常爱笑）| *five feet* high（五英尺高）| he wants things *his own way*（他希望一切都符合他的心愿）| things shall go *man-of-war fashion*（一切事情将用炮舰地解决）| he ran upstairs *three steps at a time*（他一步三蹬地跑上楼）。比较"连系式"一章（九）中的"独立结构"（absolute construction）。

正如上述例子所说明的，词组不论含首品、次品还是三品，其本身可以含有这三种词品所表明的各种相互的从属关系。词组的品级是一回事，词组内部的品级则又是一回事。其结果必然会出现相当复杂的关系，然而根据本章所阐明的观点，这些复杂的关系是不难分析的。举几个例子就可以说明这个问题，We met the kind old Archbishop of York（我们遇到了年迈、和蔼的约克大主教）中，后六个词构成一个词组首品，作 met 的宾语。但这个词组本身是由一个首品词 Archbishop 和四个修品词 the, kind, old, of York 构成的。或者说，Archbishop of York 是由首品词 Archbishop 和修品 of York 所构成的，它们构成一个词组首品，再由三个修品词 the, kind, old 修饰。但修品 of York 又是由小品词（介词）of 和它的宾语，首品词 York 构成的。如果把整个词组用作所有格就会使其变成词组首品，We met the *kind old Archbishop of york's* daughter（我们遇到了年迈、和蔼的约克大主教的女儿）。

He lives *on this side the river*（他住在河这边），句中由五个词构成的整个词组作 lives 的三品；on this side 由小品词（介词）on 及其宾语 this（修品）side（首品）构成，形成一个介词词组，以词组 the（修品）river（首品）为宾语。但是在 the buildings *on this side river* are ancient（河这边的建筑物年代颇久）一句中，由 on this side the river 五个词构成的词组作 buildings 的修品。用这种方法我们就可以对实际语言中所存

在的哪怕是最复杂的组合进行自然的和一致的分析。①

从 句
(Clauses)

通常被叫作从句的那些词组具有特别重要的意义。我们可以给从句下这样的定义：从句是句子的某一成分，但本身也具有句子的形式（通常含有一个限定动词）。根据不同的情况，从句既可作首品、次品，也可作三品。

I. 从句作首品（首品从句） *That he will come* is certain. 他要来是毫无疑问的。（试比较：His coming is certain.〔他的来是毫无疑问的〕）

Who steals my purse steals trash. 谁偷我钱包就是偷废物（试比较：He steals trash.〔他偷废物〕）。

What you say is quite true. 你讲的千真万确（试比较：Your assertion is…〔你的话…〕）。

I believe *whatever he says*. 他说的无论什么话我都相信（试比较：…all his words…〔他说的一切〕）。

I do not know *where I was born*. 我不知道自己是在哪里出生的（试比较：my own birthplace〔我自己出生的地方〕）。

I expect *(that) he will arrive at six*. 我想他将在六点到达（试比较：his arrival〔他的到达〕）。

We talked of *what he would do*. 我们谈到了他将干的事情（试比较：…of his plans〔……他的计划〕）。

① 有个期友曾对我说过一个 7 岁男孩的故事。那个孩子问他爸爸：婴儿出世前会不会说话。"不会！"爸爸说。孩子说："那么这就怪了，《圣经》里的约伯故事是说他出生那天就说了。"这孩子把词组（短语）误认为是词组三品。Job cursed the day that he was born 中的 that he was born 修饰 the day，全句的意思是：约伯咒骂他出生的那一天。

Our ignorance of *who the murderer was*. 我们不知道凶手是谁（试比较：…of the name of the murderer〔……凶手的名字〕）。

在前三句中，从句作主语，在其余的句子中，作动词或介词 of 的宾语。但是我必须提醒读者提防一种不妥的语法分析，即认为在类似第 2 句的句子中，steals trash（偷废物）的主语是一个 he（他），he暗含于 who 之中，关系从句和 he 的关系与 the man who steals（偷东西的人）中的he的关系和 man 的关系相同——这是一种多此一举的假设，诸如此类的假设还有许多，它把语法搞得混乱复杂，无助于对语言事实的真正理解。①

① 斯威特（《新英语语法》§112 及 120）说，在 what you say is true（你说的是实话）中有综合现象，what 同时起两个词的作用，它在关系从句里作 say 的宾语，同时在主句里作防词 is 的主语；在 what I say I mean（我的话是算数的）中，what 在两个从句里都作宾语。在 what is done cannot be undone（木已成舟）中，What 在两个从句里都作主语。但还须说，由一缩合关系代词（a condensed relative）引导的从句位于主句之前而不落之后，我们如果想改变成这种句子的结构，那常要恢复没有出现的先行词（antecedent）：it is quite true what you say（你讲的千真万确）；if I say a thing, I mean it（我讲什么都是真的）。但是上面最后一句话主语在句子上并不等于 what I say I mean（我的话是算数的），其中既没有先行词也没有关系代词，这样一来我们不可有先行词，而我们不愿把 it 说成是 what 的先行词，因为不能说 it what you say；至于这种结构的真正的特点，请参看本书第 14 页。what 不可有先行词，当然同从句在句子之前而不落之后并非是含有"缩合"代词从句的转点。在斯威特的某些句子中，我们看到主语在前的正常语序，在 what I say I mean 中，为了强调宾语，将其前，I mean what I say 则是完全正常的句子。但是 what 与关系代词，虽然斯威特不承认 what 是"综合代词"。（在接纳其别的假设中，他没有看到关系从句与疑问从句的区别，从而制造了不必要的困难。

然而，对于斯威特的观点所持的主要不同意见是：把 what 说成是同时起两个词的作用很难令服。what 本身不是 is true（的名谓），同样只可能是 what you say（你说的），而不会是 what,其他可子都知此。what 只能是 say 的宾语，其他什么也不是，这与 the words which you say are true（你讲的话是真实的）中的 which 毫无二致，但是我这个 true 在后句中，are 的主语是 the words which you say，而不只是 the words，只有这样，语法分析才能符合常识。奥托耶斯《高级英语句法》§84 所讨论的话中有力个省略现象"To help who want, to forward who excel"（择贤拔能），即 those who，但他没有看到这并不能有助于他分析 I heard what you said（我听到了你

II. 从句作修品（修品从句） I like a boy *who speaks the truth*. 我喜欢说实话的孩子。（试比较：…a truthful boy〔……说实话的孩子〕）

This is the land *where I was born*. 这是我出生的地方。（试比较：my native land〔我的故乡〕）

有必要指出，常常有两个关系从句似乎都在修饰同一个先行词（即首品），其实第二个从句修饰的是已为第一个从句修饰了的先行词。因此，第二个从句是作一个词组首品的修品，这个词组首品是由先行词及其第一个修品从句构成的。下面例子中的斜体部分是词组首品：they murdered *all they met* whom they thought gentlemen（他们谋害了所有他们遇到的，并认为是正人君子的人）| there is *no one who knows him* that does not like him（认识他的人无不喜欢他）| it is not *the hen who cackles the most* that lays the largets eggs（叫得最响的母鸡下的蛋并非最大）。

说的），因为 what 之前不能据进任何东西。奥托耶斯并不把 what 看作关系代词，这进行证据许多仙的休系。在这一点上，他和斯威姆德就了海到"不完全关系代词"（indefinite relatives）whoever（无论谁），whatever（无论什么），虽然它们与"综合关系代词"的区别当然只是多了 ever。对于"Whoever steals my purse steals trash"（谁偷了我的钱包，谁就偷了废物），"Whatever you say is true"（你说的不管是什么，都是实话的），"I mean whatever I say"（我不管说什么都是算数的）这类句子的分析有各方面都能反映对合 who、what 以及句子部分的分析倾向，致更早期的"Peggotty always volunteered this information to whomsoever would receive it（佩戈蒂总是把这资料告诉别人——《大卫·科波菲尔》45），中的 whom 使用得不妥，因为 whosoever 是句子的主语，虽然整个从句作 to 的宾语；但具句如果是（to）whomsoever it concerned（不论与谁有关），whomsoever 就不错了。同类比较："he was angry with whoever crossed his path"（谁挡他的道路，他就给他的气），以及金斯利的"Be good, sweet maid, and let who can be clever"（请你多做好事而自己，拉斯金曾写道，"I had been writing of *what I knew nothing about*"（我一直在写我一无所知的东西），这里的 what 受介词 about 的支配，而 of 支配的是由 what I knew nothing about 构成的整个从句。

Ⅲ. 从句作次修品或三品（**次修品从句**）　*Whoever said this*, it is true. 这话不管是谁说的，这都是实话。（试比较：anyhow〔不论〕）

It is a custom where I was born. 在我出生的地方，这是一种习俗。（试比较：there〔那里〕）

When he comes, I must go. 他一来，我就得走。（试比较：then〔然后〕）

If he comes, I must go. 他如果来，我就得走。（试比较：in that case〔在那样的情况下〕）

As this is so, there is no harm done. 情况就这样，没什么危害。（比较 accordingly〔因此〕）

Lend me your knife, *that I may cut this string.* 把你的刀子借给我，我就能割断这根绳子。（试比较 cut it with〔用它割〕）

这里请特别注意第一个例子，其中由 Whoever 引导的从句不同于上述例句，它既不是主语也不是宾语，与 it is true 的关系不紧密。

对"从句"这个术语所下的定义促使我们要讨论一番流行的术语。根据这些术语，这里所讨论的从句被叫作与"主句"(the principal clause) 或"主题"(principal proposition)相对而言的"从属"句 (dependent 或 subordinate clauses)；其他语言里也有与之相应的术语，如德语的"nebensatz, hauptsatz"(副句)。但根本没有必要再用一个专门的术语来表示通常所说的主句。首先应当指出，主要的思想并不总是由"主句"表达的，如 *This was* because he was ill（这是因为他病了）。*It is true* that he is very learned（这一点不假，他很有学问），这个句子中主句表达的思想可用一个简单的副词来表达，*Certainly* he is very learned（的确他很有学问）——把从属的思想变为

• 130 •

主要思想难道会改变此人有无学问这一事实吗？再请比较 I tell you that he is mad（我告诉你，他是个疯子）和 He is mad, as I tell you（他是个疯子，正如我告诉你的）两个句子。此外，如果"主句"的定义是：去掉从句后的剩余部分，那么我们常常会得到十分有趣的结果。必须承认，在一些情况下，从句去掉后并不影响句子的意义，因为句子的意义在某种程度上是完整的，如 I shall go to London (if I can)（要是我能）我将到伦敦去或 (when he got back) he dined with his brother（他回来后）他同弟弟一道用餐。但即使在这里，似乎也没有必要再用一个专门的术语来称呼去掉括号中的内容的剩余部分。句中省略了另一种形式的其他同义说法而结果相同，就没有必要用专门术语来称剩余的部分，如 I shall go to London (in that case)（在那样的情况下）我将去伦敦），(After his return) he dined with his brother（他回来后）他同弟弟一道用餐）。我们如果从前面引用的三个句子中拿掉从句 where I was born（我出生的地方），剩余部分就是 (1) I do not know, (2) This is the land, (3) It is a custom；但是没有理由把它们当作一个独立的语法范畴，因为它们的产生不是通过对下面句子中斜体部分的省略来实现的：(1) I do not know my *birth-place*（我不知道我的出生地），(2) This is my *native land*（这是我的故乡），(3) It is a custom *at home*（这是家乡的一种习俗）。更糟糕的是，去掉从句后的剩余部分常常毫无意义，如（Who steals my purse) *steals trash*（谁偷我钱包就是偷废物，下句更为荒唐，(What surprises me) is (that he should get angry)（使我吃惊的是〔他竟然动起肝火来了〕）。难道真能说 is 这个小词包括了主要思想？这里的语法单位是整个句子，它包括说话人或作者集中起来表达他思想的所有内容，所以应作为一个整体看待，因此其主语或其他成分是否以句子形式出现，能否被称作从句，

是否还一个单词还是一个其他形式的词组就无关重要了。

结 束 语
(Final Remarks)

采用本章所用的语法术语，就可以说明三种词品之间的区别不同于名词、形容词、副词之间的区别。比起许多语法著作中那些常常是混乱不清、自相矛盾的术语，这些术语就更为可取。常常与我的三种词品相对应的术语还有：名词的 (substantival)，形容词的 (adjectival)，副词的 (adverbial)，或是说，一个词"作副词用" (used adverbially)，《新英语词典》在说到怎样表示 *a sight too clever*（非常聪明）时就采用了这样一种说法。有人（冯特）干脆有时把 what 或 several 叫作名词，有时把它们叫作形容词，但又把这两种词都置于代词项下。福尔克和托波把挪威语中的 sig 叫作名词性反身代词 (substantival reflexive pronoun)，把 sin 叫作形容词性反身代词 (adjectival reflexive pronoun)，但后者在 hver tog sin, så tog jeg min（各人拿了自己的，于是我就拿了我的）中却是名词。许多学者提出与"副词性属格"(adverbial genitive) 相对而言的"名词性属格"(adnominal genitive, 相当于修品)，但有些人，并不是所有的人，把前面一种说法只限用于动词。在《标准英语》里，"状语"(adverbials) 这一术语用来表示次修品词组和从句，但我没有见过有人把"形容词"(adjectivals) 或"名词"(substantivals) 这些术语用来表示相应的修品和首品。类似我的"形容词首品"(adjective primary) 的术语有：名词性形容词 (substantival adjective)、名词化形容词 (substantivized adjective)、绝对形容词 (absolute adjective)、独立使用的形容词 (adjective used absolutely，但是"绝对"还用于完全不同的其他场合，如:"绝

• 132 •

对离格"〔absolute ablative〕)、准名词 (quasi-substantive，如《新英语词典》中的 the great〔伟大者〕)、自由形容词 (a free adjective，斯威特在《新英语语法》§178 中论及了德语中的 die gute〔好的（东西）〕)、部分名词化的形容词(an adjective partially converted into a noun，斯威特在上书 §179 中论及了英语中的 the good〔利益〕)、名词对等词 (a substantive-equivalent 或 nounequivalent)。奥尼恩斯（《高级英语句法》§9）采用了最后一种说法；他还把"形容词对等词"(adjective-equivalent) 这一术语运用于"同位名词"(a noun in apposition，如 Simon Lee, the old *huntsman*〔西蒙•李，那个老猎人〕) 以及"构成复合名词的一部分名词或动名词"(a noun or verb-noun forming part of compound noun，如 cannon ball〔炮弹〕)。他认为 a lunatic asylum（疯人院）中的 lunatic 是名词（这话不错，因为有复数 lunatics 的形式），但这个名词应叫作形容词对等词，如果这样认为，他就必须承认 sick room（病房）中的 sick 是形容词，应叫作名词对等词（§9. 3），但这个名词对等词根据他的 §10. 6 又必须是形容词对等词！这是用于索хра夏丛书中"简化了的"统一术语的一个例子。比较《现代英语语法》Ⅱ, 12.41。the London papers（伦敦报纸）中的 London 叫作形容词对等词，the poor（穷人）单独使用时是一名词对等词，因此 the London poor（伦敦的穷人）中的名词一定是形容词对等词，形容词一定是名词对等词。有人说 the top one（头等者）中的名词先是形容词化，后来又名词化，这两种转变都是由 one 实现的。比较《现代英语语法》Ⅱ.10. 86；top 在我的语法体系里既是一名词，但在这里作 one 的修品。我用的术语比普兹玛在《语法》里用的简单得多，在他那本书里，我用的"介词（词组）修品" (prepositional〔group〕adjunct) 被说成是"由一个介词接名词（代词）构成的定语名词性修品"。普兹玛的 adjunct 比我

• 133 •

的含义要广。

现在我们就能够正确地评价斯威特在 1876 年所说的话（《论文集》24）："语法学家和逻辑学家至今一直忽视了这样一件奇特的事实：名词的定义，严格地说，只能使用于名词主格（nominative case）。间接格（oblique cases）实际上是修饰语，其屈折变化不过是把一个名词转为一个形容词或副词的一种手段。这在属格中十分清楚……同样清楚的是，flet noctem（夜哭）中的noctem 是一个纯粹的时间副词（adverb of time）。"然而，斯威特在他自己的《盎格鲁—撒克逊语法》中没有把属格名词置于形容词项下，他这样做是对的，他说的只对了一半，间接格只是将名词（名词用于主格作首品）转变为次品词（修品）或三品词的手段，但是名词仍然始终是名词。名词、形容词、副词的三分法和三种词品之间存在一定的对应关系，最终我们常常发现名词的修品形式转变为真正的形容词，次修品形式转变为副词（或介词，等等），但这种对应只是部分的，并不完全如此。"词类"的划分以及"词品"的划分是从不同的角度观察同一个词。"词类"研究的是词的本身，"词品"研究的是词与其它词的结合。

· 134 ·

三、论元结构（Argument Structure）

C.-T. James Huang, Y.-H. Audrey Li, Yafei Li. 2009. *The Syntax of Chinese*. Cambridge: Cambridge University Press. 中译本：黄正德，李艳慧，李亚非. 汉语句法学. 张和友，译. 北京：世界图书出版公司，2013.

【导 读】

这个原典选自上述著作第二章。文章着重讨论论元结构的本质。汉语中动词及其主语和宾语之间的语义关系受到的限制远不及英语。基于这一久为人知而使人迷惑的事实，借鉴其他人的近期研究，作者提出一种动词的词汇-语义（lexicon-semantic）分解理论。这一理论使规约的机制及其组成成分的数量减到最少，因而使理论的解释力达到最大。文章特别论证，一个含有事件类成分的小集合与词根相互作用，可以产出类似英语动词较"严格的"论元结构。在缺少事件类成分时，可以运用光杆词根作为动词，再加上有关的世界知识（百科知识），构成论元结构。这种论元结构的形成方式解释了汉语动词语义上的自由度。作者关于汉语和英语的动词与宾语之间语义联系紧密度差别的论证，进而提出汉英动词差别的观点是值得关注的。

2

Argument structure

Each category affects the grammaticality of a sentence differently. For verbs, the most conspicuous property is transitivity, which we investigate in this chapter. Following the convention in theoretical syntax, the subject and object(s) of a verb are called its *arguments*, and the semantic relation between a verb and any of its arguments called a *thematic* relation. The first section introduces the basic properties of thematic relations and demonstrates how they can help explain certain linguistic phenomena. A few recent attempts to understand the nature of thematic relations are critically reviewed in Section 2.2. An alternative theory is proposed in Section 2.3.

2.1 Arguments and theta-roles

It is obvious to any linguistically minded observer that in a typical[1] active sentence built around a transitive action verb, such as *ta chang minge* 'she sing folk.song' or *ni xie shi* 'you write poem,' the subject argument is always the one initiating and performing the action while the object argument is always what is acted upon. This simple fact suggests the possibility that not every detail in the thematic relation between an argument and a verb matters in syntactic computation. For instance, *ta* 'she' and *ni* 'you' are subjects only because these NPs represent the "doers" of the actions; whether an action is done through singing or writing has no effect on qualifying an NP as the subject argument.

Based on this fact, thematic relations are classified into types. *Agent* is the relation where the argument is the doer/initiator, *Patient* labels the "do-ee" argument, *Theme* is for the argument that undergoes change, and a few others like *Beneficiary*, *Goal*, and *Source* all represent self-explanatory relations. The guiding principle

---

[1] By "typical," we hope to leave room for certain uses of transitive verbs where no Agent or Patient/Theme argument is required; cf. Sections 2.2 and 2.3.

38

---

here is that such relations are identified because of their relevance to syntax. A metaphor is typically adopted to talk about this aspect of language: Agent, Patient, etc. are called *thematic roles*[2] (theta-roles); a lexical word W, usually a verb, is said to have a certain number of theta-roles to *assign* to arguments; the set of theta-roles that W has for assignment is referred to, somewhat confusingly for historical reasons, as W's *argument structure*.

2.1.1 Basic properties of theta-roles

Recall that in a typical active sentence, Agent is always assigned to the subject and Patient to the object. One way to look at this correlation is that theta-roles are intrinsically ranked, with Agent being the highest in the hierarchy, Patient being lower, and so on. It is already well established that arguments are structurally ranked in the syntactic structure in the sense that the subject is more prominent than the object(s). The precise nature of this structural prominence will become clear later. For now, it will suffice to hypothesize a linking operation in the human language faculty that aligns the thematic hierarchy among theta-roles with the structural hierarchy among syntactic arguments.

Another property of theta-roles is shown with the examples in (1):

(1) a. tamen gei-le   jingli   *(yi-fen baogao).
        they give-LE manager   a-CL report
        'They gave the manager *(a report).'

     b. ta zou-le   (*women).
        he walk-LE   us
        'He walked (*us).'

Out of context, (1a) is unacceptable without the second object *yi-fen baogao* 'a report.'[3] It is intuitively clear why this is so: the verb *gei* 'give' has three theta-roles to assign, namely Agent, Goal, and Theme, but in the bad sentence, there are only two arguments to receive them – *tamen* 'they' as Agent and *jingli* 'manager' as Goal. There is no other argument available for assignment to the Theme role.

---

[2] See Gruber (1965) and Jackendoff (1972) for initial works on this concept.
[3] Unlike its English counterpart, a sentence like (1a) might be allowed if a report is mentioned earlier in the discourse. This doesn't pose a problem for our analysis because there is independent evidence that languages like Chinese but not English use a phonetically empty constituent as the "missing" object in the presence of a discourse topic. See Chapter 6 for relevant discussions. Also see Sections 2.2 and 2.3 for another property of Chinese verbs: that the thematic relations a verb holds with its arguments are not as restricted as in many other languages.

In another words, (1a), as well as its direct translation in English, justify the cross-linguistic generalization in (2a):

(2) a. Every theta-role must be assigned to an argument.

(1b) proves the inverse of (2a) to be true as well. The postverbal NP *women* 'us' makes the sentence bad because semantically it cannot be integrated with the rest of the meaning of 'walk.' Again, the explanation is simple: with the meaning of 'walk,' *zou* has only one theta-role to assign, the Agent role, but there are two NPs in the sentence. Hence we arrive at the statement in (2b):

(2) b. Every argument must receive a theta-role.

Together, (2a–b) constitute the *theta-criterion*.

2.1.2 Chinese resultative compounds: a case study

That theta-roles do more to language than classifying the semantic types of arguments is best illustrated by resultative compounds in Chinese. A couple of examples are given below, with the compounds marked out in bold face:[4]

(3) a. tamen **za-sui-le**   yi-kuai boli.
        they pound-broken-LE a-CL   glass
        'They smashed a piece of glass.'

     b. wo **zhui-lei-le**   ta le.
        I   chase-tired-LE   him SFP
     i.   'I chased him, which made him tired.'
     ii. 'I chased him, which made me tired.'

The two verbal morphemes[5] in each compound are in a causal relation, with the one on the left (hereafter referred to as V1) indicating a causing event and the one on the right (V2) indicating the resulting event. The most common form of the compound is found in (3a), in which V1 is a transitive verb, V2 is an intransitive, and the object NP *yi-kuai boli* 'a piece of glass' is understood as having been pounded on and consequently broken. The semantics of this interpretation can be easily captured if certain theta-roles from V1 and V2 merge into a composite theta-role as the verbal morphemes merge into the compound. Example (4) below illustrates this thematic composition, called *theta-identification* in Higginbotham

---

[4] Much of this section is based on Y. Li (1990).
[5] For the purpose of this discussion, we will not distinguish A from V, given the fact that both categories can directly function as the predicate in a clause (cf. Chapter 1, Section 1.1.3) and a resultative compound essentially puts two [F0, +V] words into a bigger [F0, +V] word.

(1985), by giving the argument structures of V1, V2, and the compound:

(4) *za* 'pound': <Agent <Patient>>[6]
     sui 'broken': <Theme>
     za-sui 'pound-broken': <Agent <Patient-Theme>>

The theta-identification of the Patient role from V1 and the Theme role from V2 is indicated with a hyphen. Once theta-identified, the two theta-roles are assigned together to the object NP, yielding the reading in (3a).

From the point of view of linguistic computation, theta-identification is a random process. Under certain conditions, one of which may be pragmatics, a resultative compound can be ambiguous, as shown in (3b). In terms of thematic composition, therefore, the single theta-role of V2 may be optionally identified with either the Agent role or the Patient role of V1:

(5) *zhui* 'chase': <Agent <Patient>>
     lei 'tired': <Experiencer>
     zhui-lei 'chase-tired': <Agent <Patient-Experiencer>> or
                                <Agent-Experiencer <Patient>>

It is this option that allows either the subject or the object of the compound in (3b) to be understood as the one becoming tired from chasing. In fact, even theta-identification itself is optional in the context of resultative compounding. Consider the examples in (6), with the corresponding argument structures in (7). Given the general nature of this analysis, we use $\theta 1$, $\theta 2$, etc. to represent theta-roles in our discussion in place of specific labels:

(6) a. ta xiao-feng-le.
        he laugh-insane-LE
        'He laughed to the extent that he became insane.'

     b. ni ku-zou-le   henduo keren.
        you cry-leave-LE many   guest
        'Your crying made many guests leave.'

(7) V1: <θ1>
     V2: <θ2>
     V1-V2: <θ1-θ2> (for (6a))   or
             <θ1 <θ2>> (for (6b))

We leave it to the reader to verify that the argument structures of the V1-V2 compound in (7) indeed corresponds to the semantics of the examples in (6).

---

[6] Pairs of angled brackets are used to reflect the thematic hierarchy. The fewer pairs a theta-role is surrounded with, the higher it is ranked in the argument structure. This notation is from Y. Li (1995). Grimshaw (1990) uses parentheses for the same purpose.

At this point, one naturally wonders whether the creation of the composite argument structure for the compound out of those of V1 and V2 is subject to any restrictions. It is. First, though theta-identification is an optional process in itself, its actual application is partially driven by the Case Filter (as introduced in Chapter 1). Consider (5) again. When the two verbal morphemes collectively have three theta-roles, each of them expected to be assigned under the theta-criterion in (2a–b), three NP arguments would be needed. However, the Case Filter requires that every NP receive a Case. In the context of a typical clause which contains a verb, in this case the compound, and no other Case-assigners, there are maximally two Cases, one for the subject and one for the object. This limit on the number of available Cases effectively forces two of the three theta-roles to be merged into one so as to be assigned to a single NP. Provided that this merging can satisfy the Case Filter, it is up to the speaker to decide how exactly to implement theta-identification. This is the source of the ambiguity in (3b)/(5).

Support for this analysis comes from the correct prediction it makes: that no theta-identification is needed precisely when the total number of Cases available matches that of the theta-roles from V1 and V2. The example in (6b) already illustrates one possible scenario where this may happen: when V1 and V2 together have two theta-roles, the compound may assign them separately to the subject and object, each receiving a Case in a typical clause. Note that theta-identification may still take place so that the compound has one composite theta-role, as shown in (6a). In terms of theta-role and Case assignment, the compound with such an argument structure is no different from a monomorphemic intransitive verb. Chinese also has ways to provide extra Cases in a clause, one of which is the use of the morpheme *ba*. Certain semantic and syntactic details of *ba* will be investigated in Chapter 5. It suffices for now to simply recognize the fact that *ba* can license a third NP in a clause:

(8)   ta **ba** naxie tudou qu-le   pi.
        he BA those potato remove-LE skin
        'He peeled those potatoes.'

As is typical of transitive verbs, *qu* 'remove' provides Cases only to the subject *ta* 'he' and the postverbal object *pi* 'skin.' So *ba* must be the provider for the Case needed by *naxie tudou* 'those potatoes.' With this in mind, consider the following example:

(9)   a. (?)ta ba wo chang-wang-le yi-tian-de fannao.
           he BA me sing-forget-LE a-day-DE worry
           'His singing made me forget the whole day's worry.'
        b. chang 'sing': <Agent>
           wang 'forget' <Experiencer <Patient>>
           chang-wang 'sing-forget': <Agent <Experiencer <Patient>>>

The three theta-roles from V1 and V2 are assigned individually to three NP arguments in (9), one of which receives a Case from *ba*. No theta-identification is necessary.

The second restriction on composite argument structure formation can be appreciated, again, by considering (6b), where the two theta-roles are not identified. Taking for granted that the event in question is one party's crying leading to the other party's leaving, why can't (6b) mean that many guests' crying made you leave? To obtain this reading, the same compound *ku-zou* 'cry-leave' would need the impossible argument structure in (10):

(10)   cry: <θ1>
        leave: <θ2>
        cry-leave: *<θ2 <θ1>>

In Y. Li (1990) and (1993a), it is suggested that, of the two verbal components in the compound, V1 serves as the morphological *head*.[7] It is a well-established fact that certain key properties of the head H are always maintained in the word containing H (cf. Lieber 1983, Di Sciullo and Williams 1987). For instance, in *xiao-hai* 'little-child,' *xiao* is A in category and *hai* is N; the whole compound is N, inheriting the category from *hai*, the head of the word. Extending the list of inheritable properties to thematic information, it is proposed in Y. Li (1990) that the prominences of the theta-roles of the head, i.e., V1, must not be altered in the resultative compound. Since θ1 is, trivially, the most prominent theta-role in the argument structure of V1, it must stay as the most prominent in the composite argument structure of the compound. This explains why (10) is ungrammatical, where θ1 is placed lower than θ2 from V2, the non-head. Meanwhile, since no similar restriction applies to V2, θ2 may be either treated as a less prominent theta-role in the argument structure of the compound, or it may be merged with θ1, as seen in (6).

2.1.3   Compounds vs. phrases

We start with a brief introduction of the basic theory for phrase structure. There is no doubt that language employs some combinatorial algorithm so as to construct a potentially infinite number of phrases and clauses from words. A major task of syntax is to figure out what this algorithm is. The most widely adopted

---

[7] The most direct support for this claim lies in comparing resultative compounds in Chinese and in Japanese, the latter being a well-known head-final language. Y. Li (1993a) shows that the different locations of the head lead to differences in the two languages both in the semantic behavior of the compound and the transitivity options of its components. The reader is referred to the original work for details.

hypothesis at the moment is the X′-theory (read as X-bar), initially proposed in Chomsky (1970) and revised into the current form via the works of many subsequent researchers:

(11)
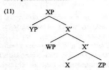

X is a word/morpheme and serves as the head of its own phrase, XP. ZP is the *complement* of X. When X is a lexical item such as a verb (cf. Chapter 1, Section 1.2), ZP would be called the object of X in traditional terminology. The head and its complement combine, as indicated by the linking branches, to form a "sub-phrase" inside XP, labeled as X′. WP is the *adjunct*, performing the typical function of a modifier. Merging WP with X′ yields another X′. X′-theory itself imposes no intrinsic limit to the number of adjuncts inside any given phrase, i.e., XP may contain any number of X′ nodes. YP is the *specifier* (Spec) which corresponds to, among other things, the subject if X is a verb and the possessor if X is a noun.

In (11), X, Y, W, and Z are variables ranging over all lexical and functional categories. In other words, this theory claims that the way a phrase is constructed is cross-categorial. Example (11) is also held to be cross-linguistic with respect to the hierarchical relations among the constituents in it. The most important hierarchical relation for syntax is *c-command*, defined as follows:

(12)   Let A, B, and C be any symbols in a tree, then
        A c-commands B iff
        a. neither A nor B contains the other, and
        b. every C containing A contains B.

For instance, the specifier YP in (11) c-commands the complement, ZP, because neither of them is a component of the other (i.e., (12a)) and YP is part of XP which also contains ZP (= (12b)). The same logic prevents ZP from c-commanding YP, as the reader can verify. While this asymmetric c-command relation between the specifier and the complement of the same phrase is taken to hold for all phrases in all languages, linear relations among constituents vary from language to language and sometimes perhaps from category to category. If the head precedes the complement, as in Chinese VP, the phrase structure is *head-initial*; if the head follows the complement, found in Japanese and Korean, then the phrase is *head-final*.

Now consider the examples below:

(13)   a. ta sheng-chi-guo henduo shucai.
           he raw-eat-GUO many vegetable
           'He has eaten many (kinds of) vegetables raw.'
        b. ?/*ta sheng-zhe chi-guo henduo shucai.
           he raw-ZHE eat-GUO many vegetable
           Intended reading: same as above.
        c. henduo shucai, ta sheng-zhe chi-guo.
           many vegetable he raw-ZHE eat-GUO
           Same as (13a).

Upon first hearing it, native speakers' judgments of (13b) vary somewhat, from marginal to downright bad, but everyone we consulted agrees that it sounds worse than the other two sentences. That (13a) is good is no surprise. The two morphemes, *sheng* 'raw' and *chi* 'eat,' have the argument structures <θ1> and <θa <θb>>, respectively. (The numbers and letters after θ are used to help distinguish the theta-roles from the two verbs.) In (13a), they form a compound with the argument structure <θa <θb-θ1>>. These theta-roles are assigned to the subject and object of the compound in syntax, yielding the reading that the object of the verb *chi* also refers to the material which is raw. As we would expect from the previous section, this is legitimate given that *chi* is the head of the compound.

In contrast with (13a), *sheng* and *chi* in (13b–c) are in separate phrases, as indicated by the presence of the aspectual suffix *zhe*. Omitting many irrelevant details (via triangles, as is the convention), the VP structure of (13b) is given in (14):

(14)
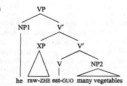

Whatever is the category of the phrase containing *sheng* 'raw' and the aspect marker *zhe*, the single theta-role of *sheng* needs to be assigned under the theta-criterion. Anticipating more substantial justification in later chapters, we assume that this theta-role is assigned to a phonetically empty pronoun, call it Pro, in the Spec of XP in (14). Cross-linguistically, a basic property of Pro is that its antecedent, if there is one, must c-command it (Chomsky 1981, Y. Li 1985, Huang 1989). In (14), NP2 doesn't c-command the Pro inside XP, so it is not a good antecedent, and the poor acceptability of (13b) is explained.

This analysis receives support from its predictive power. First, it predicts that putting NP2 at the beginning of the sentence improves its acceptability. As (14) suggests, constituents occuring earlier in the utterance generally c-command those occuring later (cf. Kayne 1994). It follows that if the object *henduo shucai* 'many vegetables' is placed at the beginning of the sentence, it will c-command every other constituent, including the Pro inside XP. As a result, it becomes a legitimate antecedent for Pro. This is corroborated by (13c). Second, we also expect a good sentence if Pro can take the subject as antecedent, for the simple reason that the subject NP c-commands Pro, among other things. The examples below confirm this prediction:

(15) a. ta ku-su-le   qinluezhe-de baoxing.
         he cry-tell-LE   invader-DE   atrocity
         'He complained about the invaders' atrocities tearfully.'

      b. ta ku-zhe   sushuo-le qinluezhe-de baoxing.
         he cry-ZHE   tell-LE   invader-DE   atrocity
         Same as (15a).

(15a) contains the compound *ku-su* 'cry-tell'. If *ku*'s argument structure is <θ1> and *su*'s is <θa <θb>>, the compound has the structure <θ1-θa <θb>>. In (15b), *ku* heads a separate phrase and is suffixed with the aspectual marker *zhe*. The VP structure of this example is identical to the one in (14). But the subject of the whole sentence, *ta* 'he,' is a semantically felicitous antecedent for the Pro inside XP. Since the subject also c-commands Pro, (15b) is 100 percent acceptable.

2.2   On the nature of theta-roles

Given the fact that theta-roles and thematic operations participate significantly in linguistic computation, as illustrated in the previous section, it is inevitable to wonder why theta-roles have the particular properties that they do. In this section, we review three works, Hale and Keyser (1993), T.-H. Lin (2001), and Borer (2005), which attempt to answer this question.

2.2.1   Theta-roles produced by the syntax

Hale and Keyser (1993) (hereafter referred to as H&K) are the first authors to attempt an explicit theory on the origin of theta-roles. Specifically, they hope

to explain why there are so few theta-roles and why language links theta-roles to syntactic arguments in this particular manner (cf. 2.1.1).[8] In their view, both of these properties of theta-roles result from a particular form of syntax in the lexicon.

2.2.1.1   Hale and Keyser's theory

The key assumption in H&K is given in (16):

(16)   At the lexical level, a verb can be represented as a *lexical relational structure* (LRS) which is constructed only with the four lexical categories, V, N, A, P, associated with four elementary notional types: event, entity, state, and interrelation, respectively.

Given the X'-template in (11) minus the irrelevant adjunct, (16) produces four possible LRSs for verbs, in which the relation between V and its complement phrase translates to semantic "implication." The LRSs based on A and P are given below:

(17)   a.   VP   b.   VP
              NP   V'   NP   V'
                       V   AP   V   PP

Example (17a) is the LRS for intransitive verbs like *clear* as in *The sky cleared*, with the adjectival root √*clear* heading the AP. (We use √ to mark a root, borrowing from Pesetsky's (1995) notation.) Semantically, it represents an event implicating a state. For H&K, this is interpreted as a "change resulting in a state" (p. 73). The subject of AP (= NP in the tree) is therefore understood as the Theme of the whole verb because it refers to an entity undergoing a change of state. In other words, the Theme role is nothing more than the semantic interpretation of the NP being in the Spec of VP in this particular LRS. The semantics associated with (17b) is

---

[8] Actually, H&K's second question is about the Uniformity of Theta Assignment Hypothesis (UTAH), as defined by Baker (1988):

(i)   Identical thematic relations are represented by identical syntactic relations.

The UTAH is a stronger condition on theta-role assignment than simply aligning the thematic hierarchy with the syntactic hierarchy of arguments, as we introduced in 2.1 above. Since the content of this book doesn't hinge on the UTAH, we will not bring it into the text. See Y. Li (2005) for a critical evaluation of its status in the human language faculty.

Also worth noting is that the theory in H&K differs in many ways from Hale and Keyser (2002). However, the essence of H&K remains intact in their later work, and the essence of our discussion in this section applies accordingly.

an event implicating an interrelation, or in plainer words, the situation in which an entity, referred to by the NP, "comes to be involved in an interrelation" (p. 71) expressed through the PP. This LRS again expresses the meaning of change, so the NP also carries the Theme reading.

A verb also may be formed out of a nominal or verbal category. Rather than directly substituting NP and VP for AP and PP in (17), however, H&K propose two extra conditions for LRS:

(18)   a. The Spec position of VP in the LRS representation of a lexical verb is filled only when forced by predication (p. 76).
       b. NP and VP are not predicates in the LRS (pp. 76, 80).

The direct consequence of (18) is the following LRSs:

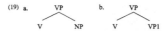

(19)   a.   VP   b.   VP
              V   NP   V   VP1

Given (18b), neither the NP in (19a) nor the VP1 in (19b) is a predicate; namely, neither supports an external subject. In the absence of an external subject, then, no constituent will fill the Spec position of the (upper) VP according to (18a). The LRSs in (19) illustrate the "Specless" LRSs. In contrast, since AP and PP are predicates, each has a subject. This forces the Spec position of the VP to be filled, as shown in (17) above.

The LRS in (19a) is for denominal verbs such as *sneeze* in *The colt sneezed*. This LRS explicitly codes the verb's relation with the corresponding noun in *the colt had a sneeze*, translated as an event implicating an entity (e.g., a sneeze). H&K paraphrase (19a) as "the implicating event is completed, or perfected, by virtue of the 'creation,' 'production,' or 'realization' of the relevant entity" (p. 74). Example (19b) describes an event implicating another event, the typical causal relation. This LRS also provides the basis for *recursion*. With VP being a possible complement of V, any basic LRS in (17) and (19) may occur as a complement, giving rise to new and more complex LRSs and hence more verb types. For instance, the LRS for the verb *put* is analyzed as substituting (17b) for VP1 in (19b), roughly paraphrased as someone "causing X to be in an interrelation with whatever is the object of P." For reasons to become clear shortly, H&K also adopts (20) (cf. pp. 78, 82), which is based on Marantz' (1984) study of syntactic idioms (also see Kratzer 1996):

(20)   The subject of the verb types in (19) are external to the LRSs and occur only in a clausal context. The relation between this subject and the VP is interpreted as Agent.

In summary, H&K propose that the two most fundamental theta-roles, Agent and Theme, are nothing more than relations between an NP and the rest of a given LRS, which is composed of some generic type of V and other lexical categories. In the literature, the generic verb type is often called a *light verb*[9] and attributed with more graspable semantic content in the given context. In this tradition, a light verb is conventionally, though not necessarily accurately, expressed with a capital lettered verb – CAUSE for (19b), DO or HAVE for (19a), and BE or BECOME for (17a–b). This tradition is adopted in this section merely to facilitate discussion.

In support of this syntactic representation of a verb's LRS, H&K offer arguments most of which are based on denominal verbs in English. Due to limited space, only two of their arguments are presented below for illustration. One of these concerns English denominal verbs, which show the following pattern:

(21)   a. A cow calved.
       b. *It cowed a calf.

Assuming both of them to correspond to *a cow had a calf*, the generalization is then that a denominal verb can be formed only when the nominal root is understood as the object of the light verb HAVE, but not as the subject. This follows directly from (19a), repeated below with details:

(22)   VP
              V   NP
                            N'
                            N
         HAVE   √calf

By hypothesis, the nominal root, say √*calf*, must be merged with the light verb in order to appear as a verb. In the current theory, this merger of two lexical categories is done through movement, as was systematically used first by generative semanticists in the late 1960s and early 1970s and later popularized by Baker (1988).

---

[9] The term "light verb" was originally used to refer to verbs like *take* and *give* in expressions such as *take a walk* and *give him a kick*, which are lexical verbs that are semantically "light" because the action is actually described by the nominal object. In current syntactic literature, a light verb is typically a structural or semantic component of a lexical verb and hence often has no independent phonetic form of its own. This is the sense used in the text.

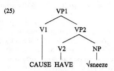

Critically, √*calf* as the head of the object NP can move to HAVE because movement is known to obey the *Proper Binding Condition* (cf. Fiengo 1977, Lasnik and Saito 1993):

(23)   Movement must target a c-commanding position.

In (22), V c-commands N, so the nominal root may move to the light verb as desired. On the other hand, the subject of the whole VP (= √*cow* in (21b)) is not even part of the LRS in (22) because of (20). It follows that the head of the subject NP cannot be c-commanded by V at all. This is sufficient to block the merging of √*cow* with HAVE, and the contrast in (21) is thus explained.

The conditions in (18) and (20) are also used by H&K to account for the impossible examples in (24):

(24)   a.   *The clown laughed the child.
              (cf. The clown made the child laugh.)
        b.   *The alfalfa sneezed the colt.
              (cf. The alfalfa made the colt sneeze.)

As intransitive denominal verbs such as *sneeze* have the LRS in (19a), substituting this LRS for the VP complement in (19b) would generate (25), with √*sneeze* moving to V2 and V1 to produce the hypothetical causative variant of *sneeze* in (24b):

(25)

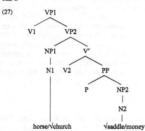

This LRS determines, however, that *the alfalfa* in (24b) is the Agent subject of CAUSE and *the colt* is the Agent subject of HAVE, and that both are necessarily outside the LRS and represented only via a clause. This variant of *sneeze* would be a "double-subject" verb. If each clause can only license one subject, there is no legitimate way in syntax to license both *the alfalfa* and *colt*, and the impossibility of (24) is expected.

Denominal locatum verbs such as *saddle* and *blindfold* provide another argument for H&K when compared with impossible verbs like *church* in the pair below:

(26)   a.   She saddled the horse.
        b.   *She churched her money.

Taking the verbs in these examples to have the same LRS in (27) below,[10] the question is why the noun root √*saddle* can become a verb whereas √*church* can't.

(27)

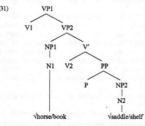

horse/√church   √saddle/money

The answer lies with another UG principle that has the following effect:

(28)   No constituent can move out of a non-complement phrase.

That is, non-complements (adjuncts and subjects) are "islands" (in the sense of Ross 1967) that block extractions, but complements are not.[11] This straightforwardly prohibits N1 from merging with V1 (or V2), explaining the impossibility of (26b). On the other hand, N2 can move to P, V2, and finally V1, at each step moving out of a complement phrase and to the closest c-commanding position, in satisfaction of (28) and the Proper Binding Condition in (23). This explains the grammaticality of (26a).

---

[10] H&K paraphrased *church her money* in two different ways: *give a church her money* and *provide a church with her money*, but paraphrased *saddle the horse* only as *provide the horse with a saddle*. Meanwhile, the LRS they provide for both verbs seem to follow the *provide . . . with* pattern. This illustrates an intrinsic weakness in semantic decomposition: how do we know for sure that a verb's LRS takes one form but not another? We leave this question open.

[11] This falls under Huang's (1982b) Condition on Extraction Domain (CED). H&K actually used a version of the Empty Category Principle (ECP) in Chomsky (1981, 1986b) to account for the data. Also see Y. Li (1997c) for a Minimalist derivation of part of the ECP. Some principles mentioned in this book, as well as in the general literature, overlap in the range of data they deal with. For thoughts on the redundancy of the UG theory, see Y. Li (1997d).

2.2.1.2 The critique

H&K's theory of theta-roles and syntactic LRSs for lexical verbs (which they call l-syntax in order to distinguish it from the conventional sense of syntax, referred to as s-syntax) is influential among scholars working on the interactions between the lexicon and the syntax. In this subsection, we evaluate some technical claims in their theory, hoping to arrive at a better understanding of the issues involved.

To begin with, we note that the essence of H&K's proposal, that the general types of semantic roles of a lexical verb (i.e., theta-roles) are associated with the small number of lexical categories available in the lexical-relational decomposition of the verb, is independent of their particular utilization of the l-syntactic LRS. Suppose that a lexical verb may indeed be decomposed into various "atoms" (root and light verb(s)) but the relation between these atoms are not syntactic, with "syntactic" meaning conforming to the X'-structure and subject to various constraints at the sentential level (cf. (23) and (27)). Dubbed as *lexicalist*, this alternative view on word-formation was first explicitly articulated in Chomsky (1970) to counter the attempt at the time to unify both word-formation and sentence-formation with syntactic tools. In a typical lexicalist theory, the components of a word are directly concatenated and interpreted accordingly, without the help of a syntax-like structure. For a representative of this approach, see Di Sciullo and Williams (1987). In such a theory, one may still treat a theta-role as the semantic relation resulting from combining a light verb with the lexical root of a particular category, simply minus the syntactic structures shown in the previous subsection. With this in mind, one way to evaluate H&K's l-syntactic theory is to see how it compares with a lexicalist alternative in accounting for various theta-role-related facts.

Suppose that we agree with H&K and adopt (20). Then the data in (21), which provides one of the arguments for H&K's l-syntax, have an alternative explanation. In particular, H&K's decomposition of the denominal verbs *calve* and **cow* in (22) can be directly translated into two lexicalist representations in (29), which we call lexico-semantic structures (LSS) (with linear order between components for facilitating discussions only):

(29)   a.   [HAVE-√calf] → calve (cf. (21a))
        b.   [√cow-HAVE] → *cow (cf. (21b))

That (29a) is allowed is straightforward: the light verb HAVE requires an object in its basic semantics, and the noun √*calf* fills the spot. The result is the intransitive verb *calve* meaning 'to have a calf.' Example (29b), on the other hand, is in violation of the principle of Full Interpretation (FI; cf. Chomsky 1995: 151), which is also adopted by H&K:

(30)   An element can appear in a representation only if it is properly interpreted.

According to (20), HAVE is incapable of supporting a subject until a VP is constructed from it in syntax. Because there is no VP (or any phrase) at the word-formation level under the lexicalist theory, √*cow* in (29b) cannot bear the intended semantic relation with the light verb HAVE and thus has no interpretation. It follows from (30) that *cow* cannot be used as a verb this way. Note that both the lexicalist theory and H&K's allow *cow* to mean 'to have a cow.' Whether this reading is indeed available depends on factors outside the current concern. In sum, with assumptions such as (20), the contrast in (21) can be explained with the Proper Binding Condition in (23) through H&K's l-syntactic LRS, but can also be naturally accounted for in a lexicalist theory which critically employs no syntactic LRS. In other words, this argument for their theory is weak in the sense that the data *can* be handled by the theory, not that the data *must* be handled by it.

Next consider H&K's argument based on (26). Given their LRS of locatum verbs such as *saddle*, the generalization from (26) is that the head of the nominal complement may merge with a light verb to form a denominal verb, whereas the head of an NP in the Spec position may not undergo this process even when the NP is understood as an object of the whole denominal verb. For H&K, this fact follows directly from a general UG principle (i.e., our (28)). However, this theory also wrongly rules out well-formed compounds such as *horse-saddling* and *book-shelving*. The LRS of these verbs is given below, adapted from (27):

(31)

√horse/book   √saddle/shelf

N2 moves up via P, V2, and V1 to form the verbs *saddle* and *shelve*, but N1 is prohibited from merging with any of these heads because of the CED violation it would incur, for the same reason that **church the money* is not possible (cf. (26b)). But this predicts *horse-saddling* to be bad, contrary to fact. It is also worth noting that this conclusion stays unchanged whether such compounds are formed in l-syntax or s-syntax, because for H&K, the l-syntactic LRS of a lexical

54　The Syntax of Chinese

verb is "inserted into an s-syntactic structure as a phrasal category, and its insertion will be grammatical if the point of insertion sanctions a verb phrase" (p. 95). Minimally, this means that both l-syntax and s-syntax refer to the same structure, (31) in our case.

In comparison, a lexicalist theory of word-formation, without utilizing X′-structures and syntactic principles such as the CED, can handle the relevant data without a hitch. Let the LSS of *saddle* be something like [CAUSE [BE [P √saddle]]]. Since there is no known reason against associating such a structure with the argument via the Theme relation, *horse-saddling* is permitted in a trivial manner. We return with a more specific account in a later section. Overall, the data H&K use to argue for an l-syntactic theory of word-internal structure and theta-roles all have a straightforward lexicalist explanation, whereas certain compounds prove to be problems for them but not for a lexicalist theory. See Y. Li (in progress) for details in this regard.

2.2.2　What's in a verb?

T.-H. Lin (2001) observes that the thematic relations between a Chinese verb and its arguments are more miscellaneous than those found in English. First consider the thematic interpretations of the subject:[12]

(32)　ta kai-guo zhe-sou[13] motuoting.
　　　he drive-GUO this-CL motorboat
　　　'He drove this motorboat before.'

(33)　a. zhe-sou motuoting yijing kai-le xuduo nian le.
　　　　this-CL motorboat already drive-LE many year LE
　　　　'This motorboat has already been driven for many years.'
　　　b. zhe-tiao he bu neng kai motuoting.
　　　　this-CL river not can drive motorboat
　　　　'A motorboat can't be driven on this river.'

In (32), *kai* 'drive' is used as a transitive verb, as in any other language. Unlike English, however, the subject of the verb is not limited to being an Agent. Example (33a) shows a Theme subject and (33b) a Location, and in both examples, the verb form remains intact, in contrast to the required passive form in English when the Agent subject is absent (cf. the English glosses). To this observation, we also add the following fact:

[12] All the examples in this section are ours, but where it matters, they confirm Lin's original observation on the freer theta-relations between the verb and the subject/object in Chinese.
[13] According to the *Ci Hai* dictionary, this classifier may also be read as *sao*.

Argument structure　55

(34)　a. zhe-sou motuoting yijing bei xiaoxinyiyi de kai-le xuduo nian le.
　　　　this-CL motorboat already BEI cautious DE drive-LE many year SFP
　　　　'This motorboat has already been cautiously driven for many years.'
　　　b. ??zhe-sou motuoting yijing xiaoxinyiyi de kai-le xuduo nian le.
　　　　this-CL motorboat already cautious DE drive-LE many year SFP
　　　　Intended reading: same as (34a).

The adverb *xiaoxinyiyi de* implies an Agent. Example (34a) is perfectly acceptable, where this adverb is coupled with *bei*, a "passive" morpheme to be carefully examined in Chapter 4. This is compatible with the general understanding that passives have an implied Agent.[14] In contrast, though native speakers' judgment varies somewhat, (34b) without *bei* is generally perceived to be less acceptable. The contrast can be explained if *kai* 'drive' in (33a) and (34b) are truly Agentless for the purpose of syntax. The reason that (34b) is not totally ruled out can be attributed to a separate fact mentioned earlier: that Chinese allows a phonetically empty Pro subject. Those who find (34b) marginally acceptable perhaps try to treat an otherwise ungrammatical sentence as if it had an Agent subject in the form of Pro.

Chinese also differs from English in allowing non-Theme objects more freely:

(35)　a. ta kai-guo weixian shuiyu.
　　　　he drive-GUO dangerous waters
　　　　'He drove in dangerous waters.'
　　　b. ta xihuan kai shangwu.
　　　　he like drive morning
　　　　'He likes to drive in the mornings.'
　　　c. ta neng kai yibiao.
　　　　he can drive instrument
　　　　'He can drive only by instruments.'

As reflected through the English translations, the object in (35a) is actually a Location, the one in (35b) a Time, and the one in (35c) an Instrument. Before turning to Lin's specific proposal, it should be pointed out that the situation is not as clear-cut as it appears. Even though Chinese allows *he da bei* 'drink big cup,' presumably another case of an Instrument serving as an object, it is nonetheless very odd to say *he ci shao* 'drink porcelain spoon' with the same Instrumental reading, at least when out of context. Also, there are actually various expressions in English where a verb typically taking a Theme object can take an Instrument instead. *Drive the stick* is an idiomatic expression for driving a car with a manual transmission, which sports a gear shift control in the vague shape of a stick. Less idiomatically, one can either *slash someone with a sword* or *slash a sword at*

[14] For proposals that implement this idea syntactically, see Baker, Johnson, and Roberts (1989), Feng (1995), Ting (1995, 1998), and Chapter 4.

56　The Syntax of Chinese

someone. Still, we agree with Lin that Chinese is far less restrictive in this respect than English. The examples below make the point:

(36)　a. xie maobi
　　　　'write calligraphy.brush = write with a calligraphy brush'
　　　b. za da chui
　　　　'pound big mallet = pound with a big mallet'
　　　c. chang yangsangzi
　　　　'sing Western.style.of.singing = sing in Western style'
　　　d. ci hongyingqiang
　　　　'stab red.tasseled.spear = stab with a red tasseled spear'
　　　e. ......

In sum, Chinese verbs are demonstrably less rigid than their English counterparts in terms of thematic relations, a fact deserving an explanation.

Along the lines of H&K's l-syntactic decomposition of lexical verbs, T.-H. Lin (2001) proposes a theory that consists of two assumptions:

(37)　a. A verb contains both the lexical root and the light verb(s) in English but only the lexical root and no light verb in Chinese (p. 109).[15]
　　　b. The combination of lexical roots and light verbs can be "quite liberal" in s-syntax (p. 106).

The l-syntactic LRS of *drive* in English is given below (Lin deviates from H&K in various technical details, one of which is to ignore (20) by placing every argument, including the subject, in the Spec of a VP headed by a light verb):

(38)
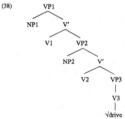

[15] This is only part of Lin's theory, which is actually based on a three-way contrast among Chinese, Japanese, and English. We focus on the Chinese–English contrast here due to the nature of this book. Also see Y. Li (in progress) for a critical review of Lin's three-way contrast.

Argument structure　57

Moving √*drive* to the light verbs V2 and V1 derives the transitive verb *drive*, with NP1 the Agent subject and NP2 the Theme object. Crucially, the lexical entry of *drive* contains no more and no less than (38), and the thematic relations encoded in the structure are not subject to change. *Kai* 'drive' in Chinese differs from English *drive* in having only VP3 as the lexical entry (cf. (37a)). It may merge with the same light verbs as *drive* does, but only in s-syntax. The result would be non-distinguishable from *drive*, as shown in (32). But given (37b), other light verbs are also available in s-syntax that may be "quite liberally" merged with √*kai*. Depending on the selection of these light verbs, some licensing an Instrument relation and some a Location, all the examples in (33) and (35) are generated. Lin's theory interprets theta-role in the same way as H&K's, i.e., that a theta-role is simply the relation between a light verb V and the argument in the Spec of the VP headed by V. However, given the difference between Chinese and English, as stated in (37b), the theta-roles of an English verb are all determined in l-syntax, whereas those of a Chinese verb come into existence only in s-syntax.

Lin's theory offers a way to account for the Chinese–English contrast in a verb's permitted argument structure(s) which we find insightful. In effect, (37b) also recognizes that the lexicon, with its mechanism for generating lexical entries, needs to be somewhat autonomous from syntax despite all the efforts, as exemplified in H&K, to assimilate it into syntax – in order to explain certain critical facts, we need lexical operations to behave differently from those in syntax. This is a point we made in the previous section while reviewing H&K's third argument for an l-syntactic LRS; it is restated via (37b). Lin's theory also raises questions. First, by adopting H&K's l-syntax to represent the compositional structure of a verb and by placing all arguments in the Spec positions, Lin inherits H&K's problem with compounds such as *horse-saddling* (cf. 2.2.1.2). Second, the assumption in (37b) inevitably makes one wonder why the combination of light verbs and roots is not as liberal in the lexicon when, by hypothesis, the same X′-structure is used as the combinatorial mechanism. The question is actually weightier than it first appears. If Chinese employs all those light verbs in s-syntax to provide arguments of Instrument, Location, and several more (cf. Lin, Chapters 3 and 4), are these light verbs part of UG? If they are, why doesn't English (or Japanese) use them in l-syntax or even s-syntax? If they are not part of UG, then something more needs to be said in order to properly constrain the utilization of light verbs in the cross-linguistic context.

2.2.3　Squeezing a lexical foot into a functional shoe

Whereas H&K and Lin have attributed the origin of theta-roles to relations between arguments and particular light verbs in some syntactic structure, Borer (2005) goes further by claiming that a theta-role, to the extent we can still refer to it as such, only reflects the interpretation that a phrase acquires in the Spec position of a certain functional category in syntax. Given the voluminousness of Borer's theory, only what we consider to be directly relevant to the content of this section is addressed. To avoid sophistications unnecessary for this book, not all terminology in Borer's work is adopted here.

Briefly, Borer proposes that the linguistically critical properties of the event described by a clause are largely determined not by the lexical root √ of the verb, contra intuitions and common beliefs, but by the syntactic environment that √ is placed in, with the syntactic environment being the phrases headed by the event-related functional categories. The sentence *Anna read the book*, for instance, is given the following (somewhat simplified) structure (cf. p. 85):

(39)

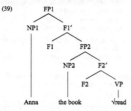

F1 and F2 are the event-related functional heads. Together with the constituents that fill the Spec positions of their phrases, these functional heads define a particular type of event labeled with the root. Roughly, (39) is interpreted as "there is an event *e* such that Anna is the originator of *e*, the book measures *e*,[16] and *e* is an event of reading." In this theory, the small number of event-related functional categories determines that there can be only a few interpretations (e.g., originator, . . .) for the phrases in their Spec positions. The √ doesn't participate in semantic role-assignment at all (e.g., see p. 227); it functions in the sentence merely as a modifier to the event type defined by FP1 and FP2 (p. 30). It doesn't change the event type thus defined but is instead affected by it.

One of the motivations for this theory is the class of "variable-behavior" verbs, the intransitive verbs whose single argument functions like either an Agent or

---

[16] That the object of a verb provides a way to measure the event is generally accepted in the field; see Dowty (1991) for an explicit proposal on this. We return to this issue in Chapter 3.

Theme, depending on the context. Borer drew data from Dutch, Italian, and Hebrew. We use Chinese to illustrate the same point. In Chinese, as in any other language, there are adverbs that specifically require the subject of the sentence to be an Agent. The examples in (34) were such, and more are given in (40):[17]

(40) a. ta (guyi) han/chang/tiao.
          he intentionally yell/sing/jump
          'He intentionally yelled/sang/jumped.'
      b. yi-kuai boli (*guyi) sui/diao-le.
          a-CL glass intentionally break/fall-LE
          'A piece of glass (*intentionally) broke/fell.'

Given this fact, the examples below show that in a resultative compound, the second verb (V2) must not be one with an Agent:

(41) a. tamen za-sui/peng-diao-le yi-kuai boli.
          they smash-break/knock-fall-LE a-CL glass
          'They smashed/knocked to the ground a piece of glass.'
      b. *tamen qi-han/da-tiao/dou-chang-le na-ge moshengren.
          they infuriate-yell/hit-jump/cheer-sing-LE that-CL stranger

Compare the examples in (41b) with another resultative form, call it V-*de*, in (42):

(42) a. tamen qi-de na-ge moshengren dasheng han.
          they infuriate-DE that-CL stranger loudly yell
          'They made that stranger so angry he yelled loudly.'
      b. tamen da-de na-ge moshengren luan tiao.
          they hit-DE that-CL stranger aimless jump
          'They hit that stranger and made him jump around.'
      c. tamen dou-de na-ge moshengren chang-le qilai.
          they cheer-DE that-CL moshengren sing-LE up
          'They cheered that stranger into singing.'

We return to more properties of this V-*de* construction in Chapter 3. For now, (42) indicates that there is nothing semantically or pragmatically wrong with (41b) because both groups use the same V1 and V2 sets and are meant to have the same interpretations.

Given the contrast in (40a–b), it is interesting to note that certain Agentive verbs are nonetheless permitted as V2 in a resultative compound:

(43) a. ta guiyi xiao/ku/pao/zou-LE.
          he intentionally laugh/cry/run.away/leave-LE
          'He intentionally laughed/cried/ran away/left.'

---

[17] For using *guyi* 'intentionally' to force the Agent reading, see Cheng and Huang (1994).

      b. ta ba haizi dou-xiao/ku-le.
          he BA child play.with-laugh/cry-LE
          'He treated the child playfully and made him laugh/cry.'
      c. ni ba huaidan da-pao/zou-le.
          you BA bad.guy hit-run.away/leave-LE
          'You hit the bad guy and made him run off.'

One must conclude from (40), (41), and (43), then, that certain verbs have variable behaviors. In the literature, intransitive verbs with an Agent argument are called *unergative* verbs and those with a Theme argument, *unaccusative* verbs. Variable-behavior verbs alternate between the two classes.

For Borer, the existence of such verbs suggests that the lexical root does not determine the argument structure, the decisive factor being the environment in which the root occurs. But if the lexical root is ruled out, it must be functional categories that perform the task of introducing arguments, hence the theory shown in (39). Compared with miscellaneous proposals, including Lin's, which quite freely use light verbs with lexical meanings (e.g., CAUSE, USE, AT) in syntax to introduce thematic arguments, Borer's theory is more restrictive: no matter what the lexical root is, the number and the semantic content of the arguments in a clause are already determined by the couple of event-related FPs. If such FP structures are part of UG, then it automatically follows that languages in general have only a tiny number of "theta-roles" with cross-linguistically identical behavior. What is not addressed sufficiently in her theory is the lexical root. This is where Lin's study of Chinese becomes significant.

As we saw in (33)–(35), Chinese allows more thematic relations to be associated with the subject and object of a clause. Later on, we will examine another fact in Chinese where even the basic thematic hierarchy appears to be violated. The question is how such "anomalies" are to be accounted for. Chomsky (1995) proposes that the syntax consists of a set of simple structure-building and structure-altering operations that function identically in all languages, with linguistic variations solely due to parametric differences among languages at the lexical level. From this perspective, the reason for the Chinese–English contrast can be sought only in the lexicon, and Lin's theory points at a viable solution: in comparison with English, a verb in Chinese is underspecified in thematically relevant ways, which in turn gives syntax more freedom in choosing what arguments to represent.

2.3   Sketching an alternative theory of theta-roles

The theories reviewed in Section 2.2, and indeed all the theories regarding theta-roles and arguments, have tried to answer one central question: How much information does a lexical verb contain that bears on syntactic computation? For

H&K, each lexical verb contains a fully developed syntactic structure (l-syntax) and much of what is coded in l-syntax is also available to clause-formation (their s-syntax). Borer (2005) denies any direct involvement of lexical roots in argument-related syntactic computation, exploring the possibility that what participates in syntactic computation is purely syntactic, with the lexical root contributing only as a modifier with semantic details that enrich but don't fundamentally determine the representation of arguments. Lin (2001) leans on H&K's view while arguing that languages may vary in how much syntactically coded information is in a lexical verb. In this section, we articulate a theory that combines some important ideas from these authors. To keep the task more manageable, we focus only on verbs that describe dynamic events.

2.3.1   How a lexical entry contributes to the argument structure

To begin with, it must be noted that the very fact that Borer can talk about the class of variable-behavior verbs entails that there are verbs that behave differently. For instance, though *xiao* 'laugh' and *ku* 'cry' may alternate between having an Agent argument or a non-Agent (cf. (43)), there are also many verbs that either intrinsically reject an Agent, as in (40b), or cannot acquire a non-Agent interpretation even in the context that converts *xiao* and *ku* (41b). At least on the surface, this rigidity suggests that a lexical entry affects argument-representation in non-trivial ways, irrespective of the syntactic context in which it occurs. Borer's theory attempts to address this problem by saying that lexical entries determine the functional structure only "insofar as some denote concepts which are 'odd' in certain grammatical contexts, in the sense that such grammatical contexts return an interpretation that conflicts with world knowledge" (p. 1). Logically, this is a plausible way out of the problem. Whether it is how language works, however, can only be determined empirically.

Both resultative constructions in Chinese, the compound (in 44) and the V-*de* construction in (45), exhibit a phenomenon that has been known for a long time due to its apparent thematic oddity:

(44) a. na-ping jiu he-zui-le quan zhuo de ren.
          that-CL wine drink-drunk-LE whole table de person
          'Drinking that bottle of wine made everyone at the table drunk.'
      b. zhe-pi ma qi-lei-le wo le.
          this-CL horse ride-tired-LE me SFP
          'Riding this horse made me tired.'

(45) a. na-ping jiu he de ta zui-le san-tian.
          that-CL wine drink DE he drunk-LE three-day
          'Drinking that bottle of wine made him drunk for three days.'

   b. zaochen de xinwen ting   de dajia   feichang zhenfen.
      morning DE news   listen DE everyone very   excited
      'Listening to the morning news made everyone excited.'

All these examples share the same three traits: the first verb (V1) is a typical transitive verb, the subject of the whole sentence is interpreted as the Theme argument of V1, and the NP after V1 carries the reading of V1's Agent. In other words, with respect to the argument structure of V1, the thematic hierarchy seems to be associated with the two NP arguments in the sentence in reverse order.

    Various analyses have been proposed within the theoretical framework we adopt here (Cheng and Huang 1994, Y. Li 1995, 1997b, 1999, Sybesma 1992). Regardless of the technicalities used to account for this phenomenon, however, it is clear that the fundamental factor cannot be syntactic in Borer's sense. English also has a resultative construction, but no thematic inversion is allowed:

(46) a. Bill drank himself into a stupor.
      b. *This bottle of whisky drank Bill into a stupor.

If the argument structure of a predicate were solely determined by the event-related functional structure of a clause and the effect of the lexical verb were merely found at the level of naturalness with respect to world knowledge, then the fact that *he* 'drink' in Chinese can be used as in (44a) should be enough to prove that this particular way of utilizing Borer's universal functional structure (cf. (39)) is not at odds with world knowledge. The ungrammaticality of (46b), then, must have an explanation outside Borer's system. An obvious possibility is to attribute the Chinese—English contrast to intrinsically lexical differences. In fact, it is quite straightforward to link the apparent thematic anomalies in (44)−(45) to the facts behind Lin's theory: that Chinese transitive verbs like *he* 'drink,' *qi* 'ride,' and *kai* 'drive' may easily drop their Agent argument (cf. 2.2.2).

2.3.2   The theory

    The essence of the theory is simple: a lexical root $\sqrt{}$ conceptualizes a set of events *e* and contains the information on all the participants of *e*; a lexical verb V is composed of $\sqrt{}$ and a small number of light verbs (Lv) which indicate the event type(s) of *e*; only the information on those participants of *e* which bear directly on the nature of the event type sifts through Lv and remains accessible to syntax – this is the origin of stereotypical theta-roles; Chinese differs from English in allowing the option of not having any Lv in V, exposing all participant information encoded in $\sqrt{}$ to syntax and thereby creating the effect of thematic liberality. The theory is more explicitly defined as follows:

(47) V∈ {($\sqrt{}$), [Lv1 $\sqrt{}$], [Lv2 $\sqrt{}$], [Lv2 [Lv1 $\sqrt{}$]]}, where the option of V = $\sqrt{}$ is available only in Chinese.

(48) Let E stand for a dynamic event, S for a state, and R for a relation, then:

    a. Lv1 manifests the type of event which happens without an external cause and may be approximately described as "enter S" or "enter R." The participant that enters the state or relation is interpreted as Theme.

    b. Lv2 manifests the type of event with an external cause which may be approximately described as "bring about E" or "bring about R."[18] The external cause, interpreted as Agent (or perhaps more accurately, Originator; cf. van Voorst 1988 and Borer 2005), is implicated by Lv2 but is not an argument of V because, as an external factor, it is *not* conceptualized as part of the event described by V.

    c. Other intrinsic participants of E, S, and R are manifested as optional or obligatory theta-roles, as determined by $\sqrt{}$.

    d. The choice of an Lv must not conflict with the type of event already coded in $\sqrt{}$.

(49) Participant-information resulting from (48) must satisfy the theta-criterion.

Other than the language-specific option of V = $\sqrt{}$, to which we return shortly, (47) is a lexicalist adaptation of H&K's theory of l-syntactic LRSs. With these authors, we assume that there must be intrinsic reasons for why, when both Lv1 and Lv2 are in V, the former combines with $\sqrt{}$ first – somehow, the fact that Lv2 is associated with an external cause determines its peripheral position, but we will not speculate any further at this point. Another insight from H&K (also see Hale and Keyser 2002) finds its place in (48a–b), namely the theta-roles Theme and Agent/Originator are the results of Lv1 and Lv2 combined with $\sqrt{}$. Where we differ from H&K, and indeed from every other author working with light verbs, is that for us, an Lv does not add meaning to $\sqrt{}$; rather, it only spells out the event type already included, albeit "mixed" with other information, in the meaning of $\sqrt{}$. Likewise, a theta-role such as Theme is not provided by Lv1. The root already contains information about participants and other relevant factors for the event; Theme is simply the one that is "selected" by Lv1 because it is the participant in the Lv1-type of event.

    Condition (48c) is best illustrated with an example. Consider V = [Lv2 $\sqrt{}$] with Lv2 marking an event of "bring about R." It is the intrinsic property of a relation to involve two parties. According to (48c), then, both participants can be manifested via the theta-roles of V; that is, this particular type of event may maximally have three theta-roles, two due to the nature of R and one implicated as Agent/Originator. Whether or not a given verb actually has the two R-related theta-roles depends on the event conceptualized in $\sqrt{}$. $\sqrt{give}$ describes the bringing about of the transactional relation between an entity and goal of the transaction (cf. Bowers 1993 and H&K), with both parties viewed as necessary participants of the event. This results in *give* with two object theta-roles, as in *give X to Y*. Aside

from semantic details irrelevant at the thematic level, $\sqrt{donate}$ conceptualizes the same type of event as $\sqrt{give}$, but differs from the latter in not treating the goal of transaction as a necessary participant. Hence we have *donate X (to Y)*.

    That the theta-roles a given V may or must have are fundamentally determined by the type of event already coded in the root is stated in (48d), contra Borer. With this information carried in the root, an Lv, by default, is only a linguistic "spell-out" of that information, not something totally independent of the semantics of the root. It is for this reason that $\sqrt{sneeze}$ in English and $\sqrt{han}$ 'yell' in Chinese are compatible only with Lv2, which implicates an external Agent role, whereas the intransitive use of verbs such as *melt* and *hua* 'melt' must consist of the root plus Lv1 and thus necessitates a Theme role. Presumably, in human conceptualization, events of sneezing and yelling necessarily have an originator but the melting of snow is identified as an event that simply comes about, with snow being an intrinsic part of melting. The event of snow-melting may also be viewed as being caused by an external factor, resulting in both Lv1 and Lv2 inside the verb. In this view, variable-behavior verbs exist precisely because certain events are perceived to be ambiguous between the two types. In this respect, one language may opt to define the set somewhat differently from another. English simply treats laughing and crying on a par with sneezing, but Chinese regards such events as either ones with an originator or involuntary outbursts of emotions that just happen in the right context.[19] Below are the LSSs of these Chinese verbs:

(50) a. han 'yell':   [Lv2 $\sqrt{han}$]
      b. hua 'melt': [Lv1 $\sqrt{hua}$]   or   [Lv2 [Lv1 $\sqrt{hua}$]]
      c. ku 'cry':   [Lv2 $\sqrt{ku}$]   or   [Lv1 $\sqrt{ku}$]

Example (50a) represents the unergative; (50b) shows the alternation between the unaccusative and the causative. Verbs with these two options are also referred to as being *ergative*. Example (50c) characterizes Borer's variable-behavior verbs.

    As it is, (48d) also leaves room for denominal verbs like *calve*. In (48d), the nominal root $\sqrt{calf}$ doesn't describe any event. Combining it with Lv2, then, would have no interpretation unless a calf is the intrinsic participant of some presumed event which is compatible in type with Lv2. In the case of *calve*, the presumed event is to give birth to a calf. In other words, $\sqrt{calf}$ functions as a cue to help "fill up" the missing information about the exact nature of the event. Similarly, we find the following data in certain subdialects of northern Chinese:

(51) a. ta caoji-le.
      he hen-LE
      'He chickened out.'

---

[18] For lack of space, we leave aside the discussion on whether Lv2 has the interpretation of "bring about S."

[19] A similar idea was independently expressed in Gu (1992).

    b. *ta zhengzai caoji.
      he PROG hen
      'He is chickening out.'
    c. *ta guyi caoji-le.
      he on.purpose hen-LE
      Intended reading: 'He chickened out on purpose.'

The unacceptable (51b–c) suggest that *caoji* 'grass.chicken = hen' in this use is perhaps not an action verb or does not have an Agent subject. If this is correct, then *caoji* should be decomposed into [Lv1 $\sqrt{caoji}$], with the interpretation of, roughly, 'entering a hen-like state,' i.e., being cowardly like a chicken. As in the case of *calve*, $\sqrt{caoji}$ does not describe any event in itself, only helping to furnish the missing information of the Lv-type event.

    Two points are worth making at this moment. First, it should be noted that in neither Chinese nor English are these brute-force conversions from a nominal root to a verb fully productive. It is impossible to say *ta laohu-le* 'he tiger-LE' to mean he was fierce or fearless like a tiger, nor is it considered acceptable to replace *This hen just laid an egg* with *This hen just egged*. This fact has a natural explanation in our theory. The function of Lv is to spell out the event type of a root. Once the UG mechanisms in (47–48) are in place, a language may choose to allow non-event-describing roots to merge with an Lv provided that the critical information can be recovered from the root on the basis of world knowledge, but doing so is a stretch of the Lv-system, not the norm. The second point, closely related to the first, is that when the root is non-event-describing, the interpretation of the relation between the root and the light verb is essentially out of the control of the deterministic mechanisms of UG and into the hands of pragmatics, idiomaticity, and language-specific choices.[20] So even though English allows a cow to calve and a mare to foal, Chinese has no denominal verbs of this kind, nor should English be expected to apply this form of denominalization to all offspring-denoting nouns.

    Lin's proposal on the Chinese—English distinction is incorporated in (47). We directly adopt from Lin the notion that a Chinese verb may consist of the bare root regardless of its event type and thereby differs from its Lv-containing counterpart in English. Departing from his theory in (37), however, ours does not reallocate these Lvs to syntax. Conceptually, (47) retains the logical minimum of (37) by discarding two stipulations. First, if an Lv is not present in a lexical entry, we see no logical necessity that it must be found another home. By default, a verb with a missing Lv in the lexicon remains that way in all other components of language and thus exhibits whatever behavior the lack of Lv causes during subsequent linguistic

---

[20] This is the same idea as Borer's (cf. Section 2.2.3) but applied inside a lexical verb.

computation. As the direct consequence of this minimalist approach to Lv, (47) also avoids another and arguably more problematic stipulation in Lin's theory: that light verbs are used "liberally" in syntax. As we note in Section 2.2.2, this liberality is a powerful mechanism with unclear theoretical and empirical repercussions.

Last, to the extent that Lv1 and Lv2 give rise to what are called theta-roles, it is self-evident in the UG framework that such theta-roles obey the theta-criterion, as specified in (49). Especially worth clarification is the Agent role. According to (48b), the external cause of an event is "implicated" by Lv2 but not considered part of the event described by the lexical verb containing Lv2. What this means is best illustrated by an analogy. Consider a university in which a faculty committee is designated to provide advice to the president. The committee has its own composition (chair and a set number of members), and its existence necessarily implicates the existence of the president who is, nonetheless, not part of the committee. Comparably, when Lv2 implicates Agent, the latter must satisfy the theta-criterion even though it is not regarded as part of the event described by the lexical verb containing Lv2. Now we proceed to demonstrate how the theory formulated in (47) through (49) works toward accounting for various English and Chinese data, taking for granted that a function of syntax is to license NPs, via the Case filter, etc., so as for the NPs and the verb to satisfy the principle of Full Interpretation defined in (30).

2.3.3   Facts explained

The basic subject–object asymmetry in denominal verb formation, demonstrated in (21), follows straightforwardly from our theory. That *calve* means 'to give birth to a calf' is just accounted for. The impossible *cow*, meaning 'a cow gives birth to,' is the outcome of (48b). Since Lv2 implicates an Agent role but does not "have" it, merging $\sqrt{cow}$ with Lv2 at the lexical level leaves the root semantically unconnected from Lv2, in direct violation of Full Interpretation. This is the same analysis we gave in Section 2.2.1.2 while evaluating H&K's work. The ungrammatical *The alfalfa sneezed the colt* in (24b) also has a simple account. Adopting the essence of H&K's LRS of the transitive *sneeze* in (25) yields (52):

(52)   *sneeze:*   [Lv2 [Lv2 $\sqrt{sneeze}$]]

This LSS is not legitimate according to (47), which in turn is based on the assumption that in human conceptualization a single event may have no more than one external cause (cf. Borer 2005 for the same effect achieved via syntax).

The same logic also explains why the second verbal morpheme of a resultative compound must be non-Agentive (cf. (41)). To the extent that such a compound

behaves like a regular verb (cf. Y. Li 1997b, 2005), what it encodes must be regarded as one (albeit internally complex) event, with (53) being the maximum composition it may have ($\sqrt{1}$ and $\sqrt{2}$ standing for the two lexical roots[21]):

(53)   [Lv2 [Lv1 $\sqrt{1}-\sqrt{2}$]]

Given the fact that $\sqrt{1}$ is the head of the root-cluster and determines the fundamental properties of the whole word (Y. Li 1990, 1993a, Cheng and Huang 1994; also see note 8 of this chapter), whether the event they together describe has an external cause hinges on $\sqrt{1}$. Put differently, if the compound verb has Lv2 in its composition, the light verb must spell out the event type of $\sqrt{1}$, the head. As there is no more than one Lv per verb, $\sqrt{2}$ is effectively prevented from having its own Lv2, resulting in the data in (41). In contrast, the resultative V-*de* construction in (42) consists of two separate verbs, each heading its own clause (Huang 1989, Y. Li 1999) and thus describing a separate event. It is only expected that each event may have its own external cause.

Proceeding to the locatum verbs in (26), suppose the LSS of the denominal verb *saddle* is as follows, a lexicalist conversion of H&K's (27):

(54)   *saddle:*   [Lv2 [Lv1 $\sqrt{saddle}$]]

As in the case of *calve*, the root in (54) doesn't describe any event, making it necessary to provide the missing information on the event in question, with $\sqrt{saddle}$ being the only overt cue. If H&K are correct (cf. (27)), [Lv1 $\sqrt{saddle}$] is to be interpreted as entering a relation R with a saddle. The precise nature of R is again determined by factors outside the theory of (47–49).[22] Next consider the impossible *church the money (cf. (26b)). Given H&K's decomposition of *church* in (27), where the nominal root $\sqrt{church}$ is interpreted as a Theme, it is straightforward that the hypothetical verb violates the principle of Full Interpretation in (30). Recall that in our theory (and in H&K but not in Lin), Lv1 does not create the Theme theta-role by itself; rather, the Theme is that participant of the event, described by the root, which enters the specific state or relation and is thus "picked out" by Lv1. Since there is no Theme from Lv1 alone, merging $\sqrt{church}$ with a bare Lv1, with the intended Theme reading, would only leave the root semantically unrelated with the light verb, making it impossible for

---

[21] See Borer (2005) for a comparable analysis of the resultative cluster, out of partially overlapping considerations.

[22] Again, Borer's world-knowledge factor may be at work, with $\sqrt{saddle}$ restricting the plausible nature of R. It has also been suggested that spatial relations are among the most basic notions in human conceptualization of the world. For recent works on this fairly old idea, see Svorou (1994) and Haspelmath (1997). In this view, it is natural for R to be understood as a spatial relation when $\sqrt{}$ fails to provide relevant information.

church to have the hypothetical use in (26b). This theory can also explain why, though *church the money* and *horse the saddle* are bad, *horse-saddling* is acceptable, a problem intrinsic to H&K's l-syntactic theory of denominal verb formation (cf. 2.2.1.2). Since *saddle* has a legitimate derivation in (54), in which Lv1 and $\sqrt{saddle}$ are properly combined, the resulting denominal verb does have a Theme role, which *horse* receives in *horse-saddling* to satisfy Full Interpretation.

It is worth noting that locative and locatum denominal verbs also require filling the missing information on events by means of world knowledge and/or language-internal choices. This explains why such verbs, though quite popular in Modern English (*can the beans, cradle the child,*...) as well as in Old Chinese (*sheng zhi yi fa* 'rope him with law,' *yi zhi* 'clothe him,'...), are hard to find in Modern Chinese.

Now we move to the differences between Chinese and English, a significant fact being that the thematic relations between a transitive verb in Chinese and its NP arguments are generally more flexible (cf. (33), (35), (36)). Two possibilities arise from (47). If the event type intrinsically coded in the root is spelled out with an Lv, the resulting verb in Chinese is thematically the same as its counterpart in English. Apparently, this is the cross-linguistic norm. Alternatively, a Chinese verb may choose to contain the lexical root only. When such a verb, call it V_{root}, appears in syntax, two factors come into play:

(55)   a. V_{root} has no theta-roles in the sense defined in (48) and therefore, according to (49), whatever semantic relations the lexical root encodes between the event and its participants are not subject to the theta-criterion.

b.   Syntax provides ways, through such mechanisms as the X'-structure (cf. (11)) and the Case Filter (cf. (52) of Chapter 1), to license NPs that are independently expected to satisfy the principle of Full Interpretation.

From (55a–b) one deduces that an NP may function legitimately as the subject or object of V_{root} provided that it bears some compatible participant-relation with V_{root}. This, we suggest, is the reason for the "liberal thematic relations" found with the Chinese NP subject and object.

As a specific example, when *kai* 'drive' takes the Lv-less option, the NPs in the subject and object positions of the clause may still satisfy Full Interpretation, as long as they are understood as, say, the location where the driving event takes place and the vehicle that is involved in the driving event. Hence the example in (56):

(56)   zhe-tiao he   bu   neng   kai   ni-de na-sou po   motuoting.
        this-CL river not can   drive your that-CL shabby motorboat
        'That shabby motorboat of yours can't be driven on this river.'

In fact, at least given the way our theory is formulated at the moment, it imposes no restriction on how these semantic relations are represented in syntax. Therefore,

unless there are other independent principles preventing it, the semantic relations, which we still call Location and Theme just for the purpose of easy discussion, may be reversely represented as well:[23]

(57)   ni-de na-sou po   motuoting bu neng kai   zhe-tiao he.
        your that-CL shabby motorboat not can   drive this-CL river
        Intendend meaning: same as (56).

The examples below illustrate other "thematic" relations represented in this flip-flopped manner:

(58)   a.   xiao bei   he   lücha.   (subj = Instrument, obj = Theme)
             small cup drink green.tea
             'Use the small cup to drink the green tea.'

        b.   lücha   he   xiao bei.   (subj = Theme, obj = Instrument)
             green.tea drink small cup

(59)   a.   ni-de keren shui na-zhang chuang ba.   (subj = Experiencer?, obj = Location)
             your guest sleep that-CL bed   SFP
             'Let your guest sleep on that bed.'

        b.   na-zhang chuang shui ni-de keren ba.   (subj = Location, obj = Experiencer?)
             that-CL bed   sleep your guest SFP

(60)   a.   jieri   liwu dou gei-le   pengyou-men le.   (subj = Theme, obj = Goal)
             holiday gift all give-LE friend-PL   SFP
             'Holiday gifts were all given to the friends.'

        b.   pengyou-men dou gei-le   jieri   liwu le.   (subj = Goal,[24] obj = Theme)
             friend-PL   all give-LE holiday gift SFP
             'Friends were all given gifts.'

---

[23] This may also be the reason why temporal and locative adjuncts don't display intrinsic hierarchy even in English, where other classes of adverbs are known to be hierarchically arranged:

(i)   Sam chased the coyote noisily deliberately.
(ii)   *Sam chased the coyote deliberately noisily. (only good if *deliberately* modifies *noisily*)
(iii)   Sam chased the coyote yesterday in the woods.
(iv)   Sam chased the coyote in the woods yesterday.

Assuming that manner and subject-oriented adverbs are parts of corresponding functional phrases (Cinque 1999), then their linear order is determined by the intrinsic hierarchy in which their functional phrases are arranged in a clause. On the other hand, if time and location are two of the relations already coded in the lexical root as part of the event, the fact that they are not "picked up" by Lv1 and Lv2 exempts them from the θ-criterion. Then whatever reason allows the flip-flop in (57–58) in Chinese allows these adjuncts to do the same in English.

[24] The subject NP of this sentence may also take the Agent reading, which is irrelevant to our discussion at this point.

We hasten to note that it is not our intention to claim that such "thematic liberality" is a fully productive process in Chinese. In fact, it is easy to find action verbs in the language that do not permit such swaps. This alone, however, does not falsify the theory because there may well be other principles/factors at work. The question we hope to address with the proposed theory is why the examples above and in Section 2.2.2 are not observed in English or many other languages, though they are so easily produced in Chinese. Also, quite independently of the thematic flip-flop, Lin's original observation is still valid: the subject and object in Chinese are not limited to Agent and Theme even with an action verb in a non-passive context. At a dinner party not long ago, a university professor of Chinese linguistics passed a pair of chopsticks to one of the authors and said:

(61) ni   chi zhe-shuang kuaizi   ba.
      you   eat this-CL   chopstick SFP
      'Use this pair of chopsticks for the dinner.'

Such sentences, perhaps deemed unacceptable in formal texts, are nonetheless produced by native speakers in everyday conversations quite freely. This is a fundamental difference between Chinese and many other languages; our theory, built on Lin's initial proposal, aims to address it.

Another issue worth bringing up is the Agent interpretation. In the presence of Lv2, a verb necessarily implicates an Agent/Originator. Given (49), this theta-role must be borne out by an argument in syntax. We side with the various authors (Marantz 1984, Hale and Keyser 1993, Kratzer 1996, Borer 2005, among others) that syntax provides a particular way to manifest this Agent argument in a clause, which will be elaborated on in Chapter 3. The question for now is what happens when Lv2 is not present. The most straightforward answer is that without Lv2, no Agent theta-role is implicated, the theta-criterion doesn't apply, and therefore a verb that would have an obligatory Agent subject in English can occur without one in Chinese. This explains the fact in (33).[25] Interestingly, though such data from Chinese argue against Borer's indiscriminate claim that the Agent/Originator and Theme (Subject-of-quantity for her) roles are purely from syntax (cf. 2.2.3), our treatment of Chinese V_{root} is conceptually very close to

[25] Another question is whether in the absence of Lv2, the NP bearing the interpretation of the external cause, which we conveniently call Agent, is also subject to the kind of flip-flop shown in (56) through (60). The logic of the theory suggests that it is not, because the external cause is not part of the event and therefore depends on a syntactic structure outside VP to be introduced. This seems to be consistent with the facts: typical action verbs reject an Agent reading on the object.

her theory: the verb without any Lv in it has no theta-role, the NPs structurally licensed in syntax are "thematically" interpreted based on their semantic relations with the root, and as we saw through the examples above, such miscellaneous "thematic" readings are characterized with a certain degree of context-dependent flexibility. Meanwhile, we disagree with Borer by recognizing that given the contrast between Chinese and English, if Chinese verbs are best analyzed this way, then English verbs, at least typical ones, must not be. The solution lies in keeping syntax universally identical and accounting for the thematic "anomalies" in Chinese at the lexical level. In this respect, we echo with Chomsky (1995; also see Chomsky 1970) that linguistic variations should be attributed to the lexicon.

The last phenomenon to be addressed is the apparently reversed theta-role assignment in Chinese resultative constructions, shown in (44)−(45). The compound form of the data is schematically illustrated below, with a simple explanation:

(62) wine drink-drunk me

Since Chinese has the option of not including Lvs in a verb, the whole compound as a verb may be composed of just the two roots √drink and √drunk.[26] Specifically, in the absence of Lv2, no Agent reading is required under the theta-criterion. When this V_{root} compound is placed in syntax, the NP wine is interpreted in connection with √drink as the passive participant of drinking, and the NP me is interpreted in connection with √drunk. Both NPs satisfy Full Interpretation semantically and are licensed syntactically by receiving the subject and object Cases, respectively. That me is also understood as the drinker can be attributed to "world knowledge" without any structurally established relation between me and √drink (cf. Hoekstra 1988): in a normal state, if wine-drinking caused me to get drunk, then I must have done the drinking. In brief, the problematic thematic reversal is only apparent, due to the unique property of Chinese in (47).[27] The V-de construction receives the same account:

(63) wine drink-DE-I drunk

The only difference is that with two separate verbs, only the first verb needs to be a V_{root} to generate (63). In this analysis, English (or any other language we know

[26] Unlike in English, these two roots are not derivationally related in Chinese.
[27] This account, arrived at from a different perspective, resembles in spirit the analysis in Her (2007), which proposed accounting for Y. Li's (1995) data by suppressing the subject theta-role of V1. Her's theory is constructed in Lexical Functional Grammar.

of) doesn't have the comparable phenomenon precisely because the Agent subject is obligatory for such verbs, which in turn is attributed to (47).

Direct support for this analysis comes from the examples below:

(64) a. na-shou ge   chang-ku-le   wo le.
         that-CL song sing-cry-LE   me SFP
         'Singing that song made me cry.'

      b. na-shou ge   chang-de wo luo-le lei.
         that-CL song sing-DE I shed-LE tear
         'Singing that song made me shed tears.'

Pertinent to the current discussion is that the singer in these sentences can be either me or some unidentified person. At least with the second reading, chang 'sing' must be used as an Agentless verb, necessarily excluding wo 'me' as the thematic subject of the first verb morpheme. Further substantiating the V_{root} analysis are the examples in (65):

(65) a. ?na-zhi da wan he-zui-le   wo le.
         that-CL big bowl drink-drunk-LE me SFP
         'Drinking with that big bowl made me drunk.'

      b. xin kai de na-jia fanguan chi de tamen zhang-le haoji bang.
         newly open DE that-CL restaurant eat DE they gain-LE several pound
         'Eating in that newly opened restaurant made them gain several pounds.'

In (65a), the subject of the sentence is understood as the instrument of eating; in (65b), the subject of the matrix clause is the location of eating. Similar examples may be easily constructed, indicating that the Theme reading on the subject is not required. Given the option of treating the compound or the matrix verb in the V-de construction as V_{root}, this thematic flexibility is expected.[28]

[28] Jen Ting pointed out the following contrast (personal communication):

(i) *wo he-zui-le   jiu.
    I   drink-drunk-LE wine
    'Drinking wine made me drunk.'

(ii) *wo he-zui-le   da wan.
     I   drink-drunk-LE big bowl
     Intended reading: 'Drinking in a big bowl made me drunk.'

To this data, we add (iii):

(iii) *wo he-zui-le   xiangbin/na-ping jiu/henduo jiu.
      I   drink-drunk-LE champagne/that-bottle wine/much wine

Apparently, there are restrictions even on the Patient/Theme PN object of he 'drink' when the verb is used in the context of the compound, indicating factors at work independently of thematic flexibility.

Also pertinent is the next set of examples, starting with (66):

(66) a. gangcai de bisai pao de tamen manshendahan.
         just.now DE race run DE they sweat.all.over
         'Running the race a moment ago made them sweat profusely.'

      b. *gang lai de jiaolian pao de tamen manshendahan.
         just arrive de coach   run DE they sweat.all.over
         Intended reading: 'The new coach made them run to the extent of sweating profusely.'

Example (66a) is a perfect sentence because the verb pao 'run' may independently take bisai 'race' as the object (cf. pao yi chang bisai 'run a race'). As long as the verb takes the form of V_{root}, the Agent argument is "dropped," with tamen 'they' understood as the runners on the basis of world knowledge. That is, the sentence receives the same analysis as a typical "thematically anomalous" case. Example (66b) is unacceptable because, under the intended interpretation, there is no plausible semantic relation between the subject xin lai de jiaolian 'new coach' and the verb pao 'run,' whether the latter is V_{root} or has corresponding Lv(s) in it.[29]

In comparison, (67) below look like similar examples but display a milder contrast:

(67) a. (?)na-chang dianying ku de wo xin dou sui le.
         that-CL   movie   cry DE I heart even broken SFP
         'I cried so much during that movie that my heart broke.'

      b. ?(?)na-ge dianying ku de wo xin dou sui le.
         that-CL movie   cry DE I heart even broken SFP
         'That movie made me cry so much that even my heart broke.'

[29] This NP, of course, may serve as the Agent of the verb, creating a totally different reading. The problem then would be lack of real world plausibility: Why would the coach's running make THEM sweat? If a different predicate is used, then the sentence becomes acceptable:

(i) xin lai de jiaolian pao de tamen dou buhaoyisi le.
    new arrive DE coach run DE they all embarrassed SFP
    'The new coach's running made them feel not at ease.'

The scenario may be, for instance, that the coach ran so fast or practiced so hard that the athletes felt embarrassed because they should have done better.
Worth stressing is that the unacceptability of (66b) suggests that thematic interpretations, whether via theta-roles resulting from Lvs or through more liberal participant interpretations between an NP and a verb root, don't just come out of the blue. Logically, it is imaginable that the coach functions solely as the "causer" for making the athletes run and sweat. But √pao 'run' does not encode such a causer participant (nor does √manshendahan 'sweat profusely'), so what's logically possible in the real world is not allowed in a linguistic construction such as (66b).

74   The Syntax of Chinese

The native speakers we consulted vary in how readily they accept (67b), but there is a consensus that (67b) is not as good as (67a). Especially interesting is that the two examples differ only in the choice of the classifier inside the subject NP. The explanation, we believe, lies in the fact that the classifier *chang*, meaning a ground for a special purpose in its original nominal interpretation, allows the NP to mean either a movie or the space/time in which a movie is shown. Example (67a) is acceptable, then, because the matrix verb *ku* 'cry' can be used as V_root and the subject NP is interpreted as holding a space/time relationship with the event of crying. In (67b), however, the classifier *ge* limits the interpretation of the subject NP to the movie itself, which has no natural semantic relation with the verb *ku*.[30] That the example isn't as bad as (66b) is the result of a separate fact in Chinese, i.e., under marked contexts, *ku* may indeed be used as a transitive action verb:

(68) a. Zhuge Liang ku   Zhou Yu.
          Zhuge Liang cry.for Zhou Yu
          'Zhuge Liang cried for (= mourned weepingly for) Zhou Yu.'
      b. ni zai ku   shenme? wo zai ku   shidao de bu gongping!
          you ASP cry.about what   I ASP cry.about world DE not fair
          'What are you crying about? I'm crying about the lack of fairness in the world!'

This use of *ku* is not fully productive in Modern Chinese, but it helps salvage (67b). That is, *na ge dianying* in the sentence may be marginally understood as what the crying is about, making it more interpretable than (66b).

Comparing (67) with two other pairs of examples lends support to this analysis. First, substituting *ku* with *kan* 'watch' eliminates the contrast caused by the two different classifiers:

(69) a. na-chang dianying kan de wo feichang bushufu.
          that-CL movie   watch DE I very uncomfortable
          'Watching that movie made me very uncomfortable.'

---

[30] The contrast in (67) is likely to be connected with the following contrast:

(i)   ?ta ku-le zhengzheng yi-chang dianying.
       he cry-LE whole   a-CL   movie
      'He cried throughout the whole time of the movie.'

(ii) *ta ku-le zhengzheng yi-ge dianying.
       he cry-LE whole   a-CL movie

Only the NP with *chang* as the classifier and thus meaning the time of the movie is acceptable in the postverbal position. So (i) may be the base for the example in (67a). For sure, the subject NP in (67a) doesn't just have the space/time/process reading; it is also understood as the cause for my broken heart. But there is evidence that this is the result of a separate semantic factor at work; see Y. Li (1995, 1999).

Argument structure   75

      b. na-ge dianying kan de wo feichang bushufu.
          that-CL movie   watch DE I very   uncomfortable
          Intended meaning: same as (69b).

This is because the normal use of *kan* allows both *na chang dianying* and *na ge dianying* as the semantic object. As a result, the subject NP in (69) is consistently associated with the V_root *kan* as the "Theme," unlike in (68b) where the semantic relation between the two components can be established only through a stretch. Second, compare (67) with (70):

(70) a. na-chang xiangsheng xiao de wo duzi   dou teng-le.
          that-CL cross.talk laugh DE I stomach even ache-LE
          'I laughed during that talk show so much that even my stomach ached.'
      b. na-ge xiangsheng xiao de wo duzi   dou teng-le.
          that-CL cross.talk laugh DE I stomach even ache-LE
          'That piece of talk show made me laugh so much that even my stomach ached.'

The two examples both use *xiao* 'laugh' as the matrix verb, differing again in choosing between the classifiers *chang* and *ge*. Remarkably, both examples are perfect, in contrast to (67). At first sight, it may seem unexpected that *ku* and *xiao* should differ in this way. But the difference correlates with another one between these otherwise similar verbs:

(71) zui xiao-ren   de shi vs. *zui ku-ren de   shi
      most laugh-person DE thing most cry-person DE thing
      'the most amusing thing'   'the most saddening thing'

Independently, *xiao* has a causative use, shown in (71), whereas *ku* doesn't. No matter why this happens (recall from 2.2.3 that both *ku* and *xiao* may be used as Agentless verbs in certain contexts, suggesting that the contrast in (71) is language-specific in nature), (71) is sufficient to help understand (70) vs. (67). That is, if *xiao* already has a causative use, (70b) doesn't even need to involve V_root. *na ge xiangsheng* 'that piece of talk show' is already the thematic subject of the verb with *wo* 'I/me' being the object. Each NP has the standard thematic interpretation, fundamentally different from the stretched semantics involved in interpreting (67b).

2.4   In place of a conclusion

We finish this chapter with a question and an observation. The question is why Chinese differs from English in the manner of (47) in the first place. A possible direction in which to look is whether the existence of V_root is correlated with its

76   The Syntax of Chinese

high degree of analyticity. For example, compared to Old Chinese, where words were primarily monosyllabic, Modern Chinese has clearly shifted to a disyllabic- or multi-syllabic-word language. Logically, if a monosyllabic word is deprived of its "wordhood" and reused as a component of the new disyllabic word, then its original lexical boundary might be removed, exposing the inside. Possibly, this process involves separating the Lvs from the lexical root.[31]

The observation is with respect to the status of theta-roles and the various analyses based on them. If Chinese allows V_root which, by definition, has no theta-roles and provides semantic interpretations for NPs in the syntactic structure only on the basis of world knowledge more or less in the sense of Borer (2005), then are those theta-role-based accounts of Chinese compounds in 2.1 still valid? The answer is yes, for the following reasons. First, there is no evidence that Chinese verbs *always* take the V_root form. At least when verbs do contain Lvs, everything we have said remains valid. Second, whether a compound always consists of two bare roots or not, the fact remains that a given NP may still be interpreted as the participant of the subevents described by both morphemes in the compound. At some level of description, multiple semantic relations can still be said to converge on a single NP argument. In other words, we still need the identification, in Higginbotham's (1985) sense, of semantic relations, thematic or not. Third, regardless of the nature of these semantic relations, the number of NPs available in a given clause is still restricted by such principles as the Case Filter – Chinese may allow thematic liberality as Lin calls it, but it doesn't mean a Chinese verb could take five or eight NP arguments. Fourth, even in the cases where the compound can be shown to be a V_root, the first root ($\sqrt{1}$) still determines the basic properties of the compound. For instance, there is no proper use of the compound where the subject of the sentence is semantically related only with $\sqrt{2}$. In short, all the basic principles introduced in 2.1.2 are intact. It is for this reason that in subsequent chapters, unless necessary, we will simply use the term theta-role to describe all the semantic relations between a verb and its arguments.

---

[31] For works that explore the extensions of this possibility, see Huang (2005, 2006, to appear) and Y. Li (in progress).

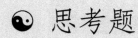 思考题

1. 什么是句法？句法关注哪些现象？请举例说明。

2. 举例说明什么是语法形式和语法意义。

3. 请分析下列结构中动词的论元结构。

 （1）阿 Q 愿意参加革命党

 （2）武松打死了老虎

 （3）天边飞来一朵云彩

4. 下面的结构有多个意思，请指出有哪些意思，再尝试分析歧义产生的原因。

 （1）倚天剑砍折了屠龙刀

 （2）山上架着炮

 （3）Flying planes are dangerous

5. 本章中的（45）只给出了动词从"实"（词汇语类）到"虚"（功能语类）的变化连续统，请结合汉语实例谈谈名词从实到虚的变化情况。

📖 拓展阅读书目

- Bas Aarts. 1997/2001. *English Syntax and Argumentation*. New York：Palgrave.

- Andrew Carnie. 2011. *Modern Syntax：A Course Book*. Cambridge: Cambridge University Press.（constituent, head/complement）

- Ralph W. Fasold, Jeff Connor-Linton（eds）. 2014. *An Introduction to Language and Linguistics*. Second edition. Cambridge: Cambridge University Press.

- W. Grady, M. Dobrovolsky, F. Katamba. 1997. *Contemporary Linguistics：an introduction*. London: Longman Limited.

- 朱德熙. 句法结构. 中国语文，8-9月号. 此文收入《现代汉语语法研究》. 北京：商务印书馆，1980.

- 朱德熙. 语法讲义. 北京：商务印书馆，1982/1997.

- Otto Jespersen. 1924. *The Philosophy of Grammar*. 中译本：［丹］奥托·叶斯柏森. 语法哲学. 何勇，等，译，北京：语文出版社，1988.

第六章

语 义

　　语言是人类最重要的交际工具，这一功能的完成最终是靠语义。我们能判断一个词是否有意思、有几个意思，也能判断一个句子是否有意义、是否有歧义、是否有语义矛盾，这都说明我们有语义知识。意义是个很复杂的问题，对于究竟什么是意义，说法不一，有指称说、意念说、行为反应说、用法说、验证说、真值条件说，等等。词义涉及理性意义、附加意义（如感情色彩、语体色彩）等不同层面的意义，还具有概括性和模糊性。

　　词义之间具有各种聚合关系，包括同义、反义、上下位义、整体-部分义、多义等。意义上有联系又有区别的词组成语义场。词义可以分解成一束更小的语义成分。语义成分分析离不开语义场，又可以很好地反映出语义场内不同词之间的异同，而且可以描写语义场的变化和不同语言语义场的差异。

　　句义并不是词义的简单相加，句法结构和关系、词语的语义指向等都会影响句子的意思。不同句子的真值之间可以存在逻辑推导关系，比如，蕴涵和预设。此外，句子还有表达说话人态度或观点等的主观语义信息。

第一节 概 述

一、语义合适与语义异常

语言之所以能够作为交际的工具，是因为它有意义。语言是一个符号系统，符号是形式和意义的结合体。语言的主要功能是传递信息，一个句子要传递信息光合语法是不够的，还必须合语义。（1）是乔姆斯基所造的句子，虽然合语法，但是却不合语义：第一，colorless（无色的）与green（绿色的）在语义上是矛盾的；第二，sleep（睡觉）要求主语是有生命的，idea（思想）显然不符合要求；第三，sleep furiously（愤怒地睡觉）违反常理。这个例子证明了语义层面是存在的。（2）中a与b的对比进一步说明，语义影响句子的可接受性。

（1）*Colorless green ideas sleep furiously.

　　"无色的绿色想法愤怒地睡觉。"

（2）a. 猴子吃香蕉。

　　 b. *香蕉吃猴子。

我们将合语法而不合语义的现象称为语义异常（semantic anomaly）。

词没有意义也会导致语义异常。比如刘易斯·卡罗尔（Lewis Carroll）的荒诞诗Jabberwocky中大部分词都是作者编的，没有实际意义。Jabberwocky本身就是个自造词，不过现在已经进入了英语词汇，意思是"无意义的话"。在下面节选的这一小节里，除了and、the、did、in、were、gyre、gimble，其他的词都是杜撰的。

Twas Brillig, and the slithy toves

Did gyre and gimble in the wabe：

All mimsy were the vorogoves，

And the mome raths outgrabe.

还有一类语义异常是违背逻辑的，例如（3）-（5）。

（3）*他生孩子了。

（4）*他杀了自己的遗孀。

（5）*The orphan's mother lives in New York.

有些句子表面看上去违反常识，但却是可以接受的，例如（6）。

（6）他是一个变色龙。

从字面义来理解，这个句子存在语义异常，他是人，不可能是一只变色龙。这个句子之所以能接受，是因为可以理解为比喻，实际上的意思是"他像变色龙一样善于变化"。英语中也有"He is a fox"（他是一只老狐狸）这样的说法。诗歌、广告语等艺术语体中往往充满了超常搭配，通过隐喻、拟人等修辞获得解释。超常的搭配会造成陌生感，在看似荒诞的表达中充满着想象。下面是席慕容的诗《成熟》，其中"童年的梦幻褪色了""一页页深蓝浅蓝的泪痕"等都是超常搭配。

> 童年的梦幻褪色了
> 不再是一只
> 长了翅膀的小精灵
> ……
> 不再写流水账似的日记
> 换成了密密的
> 模糊了的字迹
> 在一页页深蓝浅蓝的泪痕里
> 有着谁都不知道的语句

下面是臧克家的《有的人》中的一段，从字面上看，这段话是矛盾的，不合乎逻辑。在看似矛盾的表达中，精神和肉体的"死""活"形成了鲜明的对比，两种人的本质以及作者对他们的评价在这种对比中得以显示。

> 有的人活着，
> 他已经死了；
> 有的人死了，
> 他还活着。

有意思的是，生活中，我们通常默认自己听到的话是对的，在传达某种意思。因此，总是试图给一些表面上异常的搭配以合理的解释。只要开动脑筋，上文中的一些语义异常好像都能获得解释。比如"*香蕉吃猴子"在童话故事中可能是有意义的。"他生孩子了"只是说"他有孩子了"。"他杀了自己的遗孀"，可能是说他的死间接导致了"遗孀"的死亡，比如他的死让妻子悲伤过度而死，或者让妻子陷入了经济或者其他方面的困境，导致其自杀，等等。The orphan's mother可能指的是孤儿的继母或者养母。对于乔姆斯基的那个著名谬句，不少学者也曾试图以戏谑的方式来编写小故事，以使这个句子有意义。下面这则小故事就是著名语言学家赵元任先生编的：

Making Sense out of Nonsense: the Story of My Friend, Whose Colorless Green Ideas Sleep Furiously

I have a friend who is always full of ideas, good ideas and bad ideas, fine ideas and crude ideas, old ideas and new ideas. Before putting his new ideas into practice, he usually sleeps over them, to let them mature and ripen. However, when he is in a hurry, he sometimes puts his ideas into practice before they are quite ripe, in other words, while they are still green. Some of his green ideas are quite lively and colorful, but not always, some being quite plain and colorless. When he remembers that some of his colorless ideas are still too green to use, he will sleep over them, or let them sleep, as he puts it. But some of those ideas may be mutually conflicting and contradictory, and when they sleep together in the same night they get into furious fights and turn the sleep into a nightmare. Thus my friend often complains that "his colorless green ideas sleep furiously".[1]

最有意思的是汉语中的"是"，生活中经常产生一些超常的搭配，比如"我是中国太太，他是日本太太""他是炒饭，我是面条（餐馆点餐）"，仔细一想，这些话的表面意思都很奇怪，让人不禁哑然失笑。说话人可以通过设置一定的语境使不合语义的句子获得解释，透过形式寻找其中的意义，这也说明了语义层面的存在。同时，这些现象还说明有无意义、是否合语义是有一定弹性的，没有明显的界限。

能识别语义异常，并揭示其反常的原因，说明我们拥有系统的语义知识。那么，究竟什么是意义呢？

二、什么是意义

关于什么是意义，历来众说纷纭，比较常见的有指称说（the referential theory）、意念说（the ideational theory）、行为反应说（the behaviorist theory）、用法说（the theory of

1 引自：M. Yagullo. 1998. *Language through the Looking Glass*. Oxford: Oxford University Press, p.128.

usage）、验证说（the verificationist theory）和真值条件说（the truth-conditional theory）。这里只讨论指称说，其他的说法和关于意义的进一步阐释详见原典选读一。

指称说认为词语是代表某事物的符号，词语的意义就是它所指的事物或者它与所指事物之间的联系。指称说把词语的意义与其所指称的对象等同起来了。意义（sense）和指称（reference）能否画等号呢？答案是否定的。这一观点存在很多问题。其一，所指相同，意义未必相同，例如（7）-（8）。

(7) The Morning Star is the Evening Star.

（晨星就是昏星）

(8)（上一任美国的）总统是奥巴马。

（7）中的Morning Star 和Evening Star都指金星，（8）中"总统"与"奥巴马"都指奥巴马这个人。它们的所指相同，但意义不一样，不然就成了同义反复（tautology）。比如"奥巴马是奥巴马"就是同义反复。《诗经》中也有"东有启明，西有长庚"这样的说法。可见，不论是西方还是东方，都曾把早晨出现的金星和晚上出现的金星误认为两个东西。再比如，"月亮"和"月球"所指一样，但意思不完全相同，表现在"弯弯的月亮小小的船""十五的月亮十六圆"说成"弯弯的月球小小的船""十五的月球十六圆"会觉得很别扭，"人类探测月球"也不能说成"人类探测月亮"。同样地，"盼望着，盼望着，春天的脚步近了"中的"春天"不能换成"春季"，"春季招生已经结束"中的"春季"也不能换成"春天"。这说明，除了指称，词还有其他方面的意义，就是第二节要讲的附加意义。指称是就词和它所代表的事物（包括动作、性状等）之间的关系而言的，而词义指的是一个词在和其他词的对立关系中所处的地位。例如，"月亮"与"太阳""星星"等属于一类，是日常用语，而"月球"与"地球""卫星""行星"等属于一类，是科学术语。"春天"与"夏天""秋天""冬天"一类，"春季"与"夏季""秋季""冬季"一类。

其二，同一个词在不同的场合可以指称不同的对象，但意义却一样。比如"总统"可能指林肯、肯尼迪、布什等，但不管指谁，"总统"都有一国首领的意思，与其具体的所指无关。

其三，有些词语并不指称事物，比如"Nobody can stop the wheel of history"里的"nobody"并不指称某个或某些具体的人，但是这个句子是有意义的。另一方面，专名有指称却没有太大意义，比如人名。有些词语有意义，但并不指称客观世界中的对象，比如"孙悟空、玉皇大帝、哈利波特、龙"。

其四，有些词（尤其是虚词）很难说明其指称对象是什么，比如"了、着、过、的、of、by、can"。指称说明词与指称物之间的联系，意义是要完成这种联系，说明指称物的性质特点。关于指称与意义的关系可进一步阅读原典选读二。

　　古希腊的哲学家曾经提出词的意义是反映在人们大脑里的心理映像（mental image），这能帮助我们理解"孙悟空"这样的词，因为虽然在真实世界中没有指称，我们却能够想象出它所指的形象。但是，对于无色无味的"空气"、肉眼看不到的"细菌"并不能唤起某种心理映像，更别说像"但是""的""吧"这样的虚词了。

　　还有语言学家认为词的意义就是对词所指的事物所下的科学定义，只有了解相关的科学知识，才能准确地理解意义。比如"盐"的意义是"氯化钠"。可是，不知道"盐"的主要化学成分是"氯化钠"，并不影响人们用"盐"这个词。而且，语言的意义与科学的知识并不总是一致。比如生物学的知识告诉我们，鲸鱼是哺乳动物，而古人以为鲸鱼是一种鱼。从德语词walfisch（字面意思是"巨大的鱼"）看，德国人也曾经把鲸鱼看成一种鱼。从"想"的字形看，古人认为是用心想，而实际上我们是用脑子想。可是，这些不科学的看法并不会影响人们的交际，甚至我们今天也会说"你好好用心想一想"。另外，"爱""恨""美""好"等词很难给出科学定义。

　　总之，意义是个很复杂的问题，不只是涉及指称，而且分为不同层面。

三、从词义到句义

　　句子是最小的言语交际单位，我们平时所说的话都是由句子构成的。句子通常是由词组成的，只有一个词的句子叫独词句，比较少见。

　　那么，我们是如何实现对句子的解码，获得句子所表达的意义的呢？想一想，我们在学习外语的时候，是如何理解句子的意思的呢？首先，我们要知道每个词的意思，如果有不认识的词，就会影响句子的理解。俗话说，"隔行如隔山"，很多时候听不懂专家的话是因为不知道专业术语的意思。比如美国电视剧《生活大爆炸》中充满了物理学术语，即使英语母语者也很难明白。词义对句义的影响从多义词造成的歧义中也可以看出，比如，下面的句子是有歧义的，"杜鹃"可能指一种鸟，也可能指一种花。

　　（9）杜鹃很好看。

　　只知道词的意思还不行，还要知道这些词义之间是如何互相组合在一起的，这就涉及句子的结构。"红太阳"与"太阳红"包含的词一样，意思却不同，一个指称一种事物，一个陈述一种性质。原因就是它们的语序不同，句法结构也不同，一个是定中结构，一个是主谓结构。下面这个句子是有歧义的，原因是"我和哥哥的朋友"有两种结构层次，可能是"我（和哥哥的朋友）"，也可能是"（我和哥哥的）朋友"。这说明，结构层次不同，意思也不同。

（10）照片上是我和哥哥的朋友。

此外，结构关系不同，句子的意思可能也不同。（11）是有歧义的，因为其中的"烤红薯"可能是偏正结构，也可能是动宾结构。

（11）我喜欢烤红薯。

即使结构层次和结构关系相同，句子仍然可能会有歧义。（12）只有一种句法结构层次，一种结构关系（主谓结构），却有"鸡不吃东西了"和"不吃鸡了"两种意思，这是因为"鸡"可能是"吃"这个动作的执行者，也可能是受这个动作影响的对象。也就是说，名词与动词之间的语义关系不同，也会影响句子的理解。这是第五节中要讲的语义角色。

（12）鸡不吃了。

句子中的一个词究竟与哪个词有语义关系，也会影响句子的理解。（13）有两种意思，一种意思是"盘子里的菜他们全部吃光了"，另一种意思是"盘子里的菜他们每个人都吃了"。这种歧义是因为"都"可能与"盘子里的菜"产生语义关系，也可能与"他们"产生语义关系。这是第五节要讲的语义指向。

（13）盘子里的菜他们都吃了。

至此，我们知道，一个句子的意思取决于词的意思，以及这些词义如何组合。换句话说，一个句子或短语的意义是由其组成部分的意义及其各部分组合方式决定的，这就是语义的组合性原则（principle of compositionality）。组合方式主要涉及结构层次、结构关系、语义结构以及语义指向。组合性原则同样适用于词，只是与句义相比，词的意思具有很强的约定俗成性和不可预测性，词的意思并不一定是语素义的相加之和。比如"黑板"并不等于"黑色的板"，"白菜"也不等于"白色的菜"。我们可以说"绿色的黑板""绿色大白菜"。"hamburger"（汉堡）中不一定有"ham"（火腿），"pineapple"（菠萝）中既没有"pine"（松球）也没有"apple"（苹果）。"sweetmeat"是"糖果"，而"sweetbread"是"杂碎肉"。

当然，有些短语和句子的意思也并非词义的相加之和。习语就不符合组合性原则，比如"上天堂""翘辫子""见阎王""kick the bucket"（死）并不能从字面来理解。"what's this fly doing in my soup"这样的句子并不是问"苍蝇在做什么"，而是在抱怨。这些意思无法从词义预测的习语和句子通常被称为构式（construction）。还有些句子的意思大于词义相加之和，例如（14）的意思不是"John开始了这本书"，而是"John开始写这本书了"或"John开始读这本书了"，等等，其中隐含着一个谓词。

（14）John began the book.

句子的意思还受时、体、语气和情态的影响，比如"乌鸦喝了水"与"乌鸦正在喝水"意思不同。"他来了。"与"他来了？"意思不一样。词表达概念，句子可以表达判断，判断所表达的语义是命题，命题有真假之分，取决于句子表达的判断是否真实地反映了现实世界中的现象或事件。除了命题表达的客观意义，句子常常还附加了说话人的主观看法和态度，因此具有主观性，语言中的情态词大多就是表达说话者的主观性。此外，句子的意义还会受语境的影响，例如（15），在不同的语境中可能指"天亮了"或"天晴了"。说话人说这句话的意思可能是觉得太晚了，该起床了；也可能是天晴了，可以出去玩了。语境义与语用有关，将在语用学一章详细介绍。

（15）出太阳了！

语义学（semantics）研究语素、词、词组和句子的意义，其分支是词汇语义学（lexical semantics）和词组、句子语义学（phrasal or sentential semantics）。前者涉及词义，以及词之间的语义关系；后者关注词以上句法单位的意义。

第二节　词义的不同层面与性质

一、词汇的构成

在介绍词汇意义之前，我们先看看词汇的构成。词汇是集合概念，词是个体概念。可以说"这个词"，不能说"这个词汇"。词汇包括语言中的词和固定词组，固定词组包括成语、惯用语、谚语、歇后语、专名等。（16）是部分例子。

（16）词：天　地　我　你　吃　走　大　小　很　也

　　　成语：杞人忧天　唇亡齿寒　飞扬跋扈　千娇百媚　车水马龙　汗牛充栋

画蛇添足

惯用语：炒鱿鱼　拍马屁　走后门　碰钉子　戴高帽　抱佛脚　穿小鞋

不管三七二十一　侃大山　换汤不换药　挤牙膏　卷铺盖卷儿

谚语：擒贼先擒王　伤筋动骨一百天　芝麻开花节节高　世上无难事，

只怕有心人

歇后语：八仙过海——各显神通　泥菩萨过江——自身难保　箭在弦上——

不得不发

专名：北京大学　捷克斯洛伐克　中央电视台　《红楼梦》《人民日报》

英语的习语大致对应汉语中的成语、惯用语、谚语等，如（17）。

（17）No pain, no gain. 不劳无获

Practice makes perfect. 熟能生巧

Seeing is believing. 百闻不如一见

Easy come, easy go. 来得容易，去得容易

Look before you leap. 三思而后行

Live and learn. 活到老，学到老

　　固定词组之所以属于词汇，是因为它们更像词而不是自由词组。一方面，固定词组与词一样，都需要记忆，都存储在心理词库中，作为一个造句的单位直接调用。其成分是固定的，不能自由拆卸重新组装，如"千娇百媚"不能改成"万娇千媚"。自由词组是临时组合而成的，可自由拆卸重组，不需要记忆和存储。另一方面，固定词组和复合词一样，其实际意义与表面意义不一致，并不像自由词组那样由其组成部分的意义加和而成。比如，"杞人忧天"形容不必要的无根据的忧虑；"炒鱿鱼"指解雇；"擒贼先擒王"比喻在解决事情上抓住关键，解决主要矛盾，其他的细节便可以迎刃而解；"八仙过海——各显神通"比喻各自拿出本领或办法，把事情做好；"北京大学"并不指在北京的所有大学，而是专指一所大学。

　　词汇有基本词汇和一般词汇之分。基本词汇是一种语言的词汇中最常用的那部分词，具有稳固性，这些词构成一种语言词汇的核心部分。核心词常常是单音节的，而且构词能力强，常常作为语素构成复合词。（18）是现代汉语中的部分基本词汇。

（18）自然物：天、地、人、太阳、月亮、星星、风、雨、雷、电

身体部件：眼睛、鼻子、耳朵、嘴、手、脚

方位：前、后、上、下、左、右

数字：一、二、三、千、万

日常行为：吃、走、看、听、打

常见性质：大、小、多、少、红、白、长、高

这些词所表达的事物、动作和性质都与人们的日常生活关系非常密切。美国语言学家斯瓦迪士（Swadesh）曾从统计学的角度分析了不同的语言（以印欧语系语言为主），得出了一个核心词表，包含207个词，后来又从中选出了最核心的100个词（参见表6-1）。这些词几乎在所有语言中都有，包括一些常见的名词、动词、形容词、数词、人称代词、指示代词、否定副词等。

1. I	26. root	51. breast	76. rain
2. you	27. bark	52. heart	77. stone
3. we	28. skin	53. liver	78. sand
4. this	29. flesh	54. drink	79. earth
5. that	30. blood	55. eat	80. cloud
6. who	31. bone	56. bite	81. smoke
7. what	32. grease	57. see	82. fire
8. not	33. egg	58. hear	83. ash
9. all	34. horn	59. know	84. burn
10. many	35. tail	60. sleep	85. path
11. one	36. feather	61. die	86. mountain
12. two	37. hair	62. kill	87. red
13. big	38. head	63. swim	88. green
14. long	39. ear	64. fly	89. yellow
15. small	40. eye	65. walk	90. white
16. woman	41. nose	66. come	91. black
17. man	42. mouth	67. lie	92. night
18. person	43. tooth	68. sit	93. hot
19. fish	44. tongue	69. stand	94. cold
20. bird	45. claw	70. give	95. full
21. dog	46. foot	71. say	96. new
22. louse	47. knee	72. sun	97. good
23. tree	48. hand	73. moon	98. round
24. seed	49. belly	74. star	99. dry
25. leaf	50. neck	75. water	100. name

表6-1　Swadesh的核心100词

除了基本词汇以外的词构成语言的一般词汇。一般词汇的主要特点是不常用，不稳固，容易发生变化，构词能力弱。一般词汇主要包括新词、古词、方言词、专业术语和外来词，请看（19）中的例子。

（19）新词：菜鸟、高富帅、屌丝、逆袭

古词：若干、摒弃、令尊、如厕

方言词：孬、嬲、嗲、给力

专业术语：原子、位移、语法、音位

外来词：酷、的士、拷贝、粉丝

一般词汇也很重要，正是因为易变，社会的发展变化首先在一般词汇中得到反映，我们可以从一般词汇的更新中把握社会发展的脉搏。

二、词义的不同层面

词的意义可以分成两类。一类是表示语法关系的语法意义。比如语法范畴"性""数""格"等，以及"陈述""支配""修饰"等。这是某一类词所共同具有的抽象意义，不与具体的概念、事物相联系。另一类是词汇意义，即我们通常所说的"词义"，是某个具体的个体词的意义，与某一个或某一类具体的事物、事件、性质等相联系。词汇意义是语义研究的基础，包括理性意义和附加意义两个部分。理性意义是词义的基本部分，附加意义是附加在理性意义上的。

（一）理性意义

理性意义又叫"概念意义"（conceptual meaning），是人们在对现实世界的认知过程中形成的共同的主观映像，是对现实世界中各种现象分类、概括的反映。人们在对现实世界的认知中，通过切分、分类包装，把特定的映像与特定的语音形式结合在一起，就形成了词。对于说同一种语言的人来说，一个词的理性意义是共同的。比如世界上有各种各样的"鸟"，大小、颜色、叫声、生长区域等都不相同，但它们一般是会飞的，身上长着毛，这是"鸟"区别于其他动物的比较显著的特征，讲汉语的人就用niǎo这个语音形式来表示具有这些特征的一类事物，形成了其理性意义。词的理性意义不等于科学知识，反映的是人对现实世界的认知，即使这种认知是不科学的。比如鲸鱼并不是鱼，汉语却叫"鲸鱼"，德语叫walfisch，说明语言的分类并非科学的分类。熊猫是一种熊科动物，大陆称之为"熊猫"，在台湾被称为"猫熊"，反映了认知分类的不同。

现实现象不仅包括具体事物，还包括抽象的事物、动作、性质等，比如"想法""坐""红"。词的概念意义还可以反映精神世界中的对象，如"神仙""妖怪""阎王""魔鬼""龙"等。反映的不是客观现实，而是心理现实。心理现实好比是镜子中的事物，发生了一定的变化，二者不完全一致。

（二）附加意义

附加意义依附在理性意义上，不能脱离理性意义而存在，常见的有感情色彩、语体色彩等。

[1] 感情色彩

对于同样的现实现象，人们的主观态度可以不同，因此会使词义带有感情色彩。比如"帮手"和"帮凶"都指帮助别人的人，但一个是"帮助工作"，一个是"帮助行凶或作恶"，分别带有褒义和贬义。褒义表现的是对现实现象持有赞扬、肯定和喜爱等态度。贬义表现的是对现实现象持贬斥、否定和厌恶等态度。"聪明、坚强、勇敢、卓越、珍视、渴望、百折不挠、永垂不朽、任劳任怨"等都是褒义词，"愚蠢、顽固、自大、阴险、充斥、恭维、煽动、企图、嘴脸、张牙舞爪、搔首弄姿"等都是贬义词。（20）中的几组词都是前褒后贬。

（20）英雄-奸雄、理想-妄想、鼓励-怂恿、团结-勾结、宣传-炒作、揭发-告密、捐躯-毙命、聪明-狡猾

还有一类词不带任何主观感情倾向，如"大""桌子""吃"，我们称之为中性词。理性意义相同的一组词可以带有不同的感情色彩，"成果-结果-后果"分别是褒义词、中性词和贬义词。同样形容瘦，英语中的thin（瘦）是中性词，slender（苗条）是褒义词，skinny（皮包骨头、枯瘦如柴）则是贬义词。同样是"领导"，"领袖"是褒义的，"头目"是贬义的。不只是名词、动词、形容词有感情色彩，量词也有，比如"个"是中性的，"位"是褒义的。可以说"一个小偷""一个英雄""一位英雄"，但不能说"一位小偷"。不同语言中的词在感情色彩上也可能不同，比如英语的ambition是中性的，分别对应汉语的褒义词"雄心"和贬义词"野心"。形容词ambitious（有雄心的、有抱负的）也是中性的，greedy（有野心的、贪婪的）则带有贬义。

有时候褒义词会贬用，贬义词会褒用。（21）-（24）中的"狡猾""偷偷"就含有喜爱的意思，而"聪明""标致"都是反语，含有讥讽的意味。

（21）我用儿童狡猾的眼光察觉，她爱我们，并没有存心要打的意思。

（22）小草偷偷地从土里钻出来，嫩嫩的，绿绿的。

（23）而且我这样大年纪的人，难道还不能料理自己吗？唉，我现在想想，那时真是太聪明了！

（24）也有解散辫子，盘得平的，除下帽来，油光可鉴，宛如小姑娘的发髻一般，还要将脖子扭几扭。实在标致极了。

[2] 语体色彩

语体色彩指词义中所反映的词的语体倾向和特征，是为适应言语交际的场合、文体或其他交际因素而产生的附加意义或色彩。语体色彩通常可以分为口语语体和书面语语体。带有口语语体色彩的词通常出现在日常会话中，也常出现在文学作品（如小说）中，比如"老婆""哥们儿""玩儿""溜达"。带有书面语色彩的词通常用于比较正式、严肃的非私人交际场合和书面语写作中（如学术性、政治性的演讲词），比如"夫人""造诣""苍穹""嗜好""凯旋""徜徉"。在（25）中，"及其""已"具有书面语色彩，"下榻"和"入住"都具有书面语色彩，相比之下，"下榻"的书面语色彩更浓。

（25）总统及其随行人员已下榻北京饭店。

　　　总统和他的随行人员已经入住北京饭店。

（26）是更多的例子。在每一组中，前一个都具有口语色彩，后一个都具有书面语色彩。

（26）爸爸-父亲　事儿-事物　今儿-今日　家-家园　　书-图书　　问问-咨询

　　　写-书写　　吓唬-恐吓　读-阅读　动身-启程　商量-商榷　聊天-闲谈

　　　叫-令　　　渐渐-日益　小气-吝啬　高兴-喜悦　要是-倘若　还-仍

既用于口语也用于书面语的词是通用词，大部分词都是通用词，比如"逐渐""今天"。书面语词多是文言词汇在现代汉语中的留存。书面语体可以进一步分为文艺语体、科技语体、政论语体、公文语体等。"旖旎""摇曳""翱翔""涟漪""荡漾""沸腾""澎湃"带有文艺语体色彩；"井喷""同理""恒星""化合物"带有科技语体色彩；"法人""体制""改革"带有政论语体色彩；"兹""贵校""特此""予以"带有公文色彩。同样指马，horse是一般用语，steed是诗歌用语，nag是俚语，gee-gee是儿语。同样是住宅，home是一般用语，domicile用于很正式的公文，residence用于正式场合，abode

则用于诗歌。[1]

　　比较而言，汉语的固定短语里，成语、专名、术语多具有较明显的书面色彩，歇后语、惯用语、谚语等则具有较明显的口语色彩。此外，外交辞令多是书面词。口语词通俗易懂，平易朴素，生动活泼；书面语词庄重典雅，讲究分寸。如果不注意词语的语体色彩，用得不合适，就会使人感到很不协调。

三、词义的概括性与模糊性

　　词义具有概括性，这种概括性表现在词是对现实事物和现象的分类和归类。现实事物和现象千差万别，错综复杂。一定的言语社团会从中抽取共性的东西，而舍弃那些个性化的东西，从而把具有共同特点的事物和现象归并为一类，并赋予其特定的名称，经过这种化繁为简的过程，实现分类和归类。比如当我们说"你坐到桌子边"时，"桌子"指的是某一张具体的桌子。而当我们说"我今天要去买桌子"时，"桌子"指的可能是任何一张桌子，可能是白色的，也可能是黑色的、棕色的；可能是方的，也可能是圆的、三角形的；可能是折叠的，也可能是非折叠的；可能是木质的，也可能是塑料的、石头的；可能是用来吃饭的，也可能是用来看书的，或者是用来放电脑的。总之，"桌子"所指的事物可能大小、形状、颜色、材料、用途等各不相同，但其共同点是"属于家具，上有平面，下有支柱，可以在上面放东西或做事情"，与"椅子"这种"有腿有靠背的坐具"不同。再比如，汉语中的"做"和英语中的do，概括了"吃饭、睡觉、走路、打"等各式各样的动作。人们在对世界的认知加工中形成了概念，这些概念会包装成一个词。不同的语言会有不同的包装，因此，词义的概括性也就不同。汉语用"笔"来概括钢笔、铅笔等各种各样的笔；而英语中只有pen、pencil等指具体种类笔的词，没有一个与"笔"对应的词。英语中的borrow（借入）和lend（借出）在汉语中只用一个词"借"来概括。另一方面，汉语中的"抬""拿"都对应英语的carry，"穿""戴"都对应英语的put on。这都反映了不同语言对意义切分的颗粒度不同，分类的大小不同，概括性不同。

　　经过分类归类而来的词有些意义是精确的，如"二""米""长江"。而有些意义是模糊的，所指的事物没有明确的界限。词义的模糊性主要是由词的离散性与意义的连续性之间的矛盾造成的。（27）是《现代汉语词典》（第7版）对"少年、青年、中年、老年"这

---

1 英语例子引自：利奇. 1974. 语义学. 李瑞华，等，译（据1981年修订版）. 上海：外语教育出版社，1987：20.

几个词的释义。

> （27）少年：①人十岁左右到十五六岁的阶段。
>
> 青年：①人十五六岁到三十岁左右的阶段。
>
> 壮年：①三四十岁的年纪。
>
> 中年：①四五十岁的年纪。
>
> 老年：①六七十岁以上的年纪。

它们的词义涵盖的都是年龄段，核心区域是确定的，比如十三岁属于少年阶段是不会有争议的。同时它们的词义又是有交叉的，在边界上就比较有争议，比如十五岁到底属于少年还是青年？三十岁到底属于青年还是壮年？五十五岁属于中年还是老年？正是因为这些词的词义具有模糊性，所以才会有"青少年""青壮年""中老年"这样的说法。同样地，"早晨、上午、中午、下午、晚上"等词的意思也都是模糊的，到底一天中几点到几点是早晨，几点到几点是上午，并没有明确的标准。虽然我国习惯称立春到立夏的三个月时间为"春天"，但实际上"立春"之后是不是就是"春天"了，人们的看法并不相同，"春天"与"夏天、秋天、冬天"的区分到底以哪一天为界不好说。光谱是连续的，各种颜色之间没有明确的界限，而颜色词是有限的，一个颜色词往往表示光谱上很长一段距离的光，标示颜色的词自然也就有很大的模糊性。"红""黄""绿""蓝"等颜色词所指的中心区是清楚的，边界却是模糊的。其实，指具体事物的名词意义也是模糊的，比如"鸟"所指的对象有典型与非典型之分。如果让你画一只鸟，你可能会画燕子、麻雀，一般不会画一只企鹅。燕子、麻雀属于典型的"鸟"，企鹅却不是。形容词的词义也不明确，具有相对性，比如多大算"大"，多小算"小"，很难给出明确的界限。

语言中有些模糊限制词（hedges），会使语义更加模糊，如"很、非常、比较、大概、可能、大约、左右"等。不只是词义具有模糊性，词组的意义也具有模糊性。比如"请三十岁以下的老师于10月30日之前到办公室报名参加比赛"，这句话中的"三十岁以下"到底包不包括三十岁？报名截止日期到底包不包括30日？每个人的理解不一样。有时候为了表义的明确性，会说"三十岁以下（含三十岁）"或者"三十岁以下（不含三十岁）"。

表义的精确性和模糊性都是言语交际的需要。该精确的时候就要精确，该模糊的时候就要模糊，并不是越精确越好。比如法律条文、科技文章、合同、通知、说明文中的用词要准确，药品说明书会写"一次10毫升，一日一次"，而不会写"一次少许"。菜谱里则常常用"盐少许，糖一勺"这样模糊的表达。该模糊的地方追求精确会让人觉得比较奇怪，用模糊限制词反而会使表达更准确，比如有人问你电影院怎么走，你可以回答"从这儿直行，走大概200米就到了"；若回答"从这儿直行，走205米就到了"就很奇怪。再比如介绍一个人，我们一般会用"个子一米七左右，稍微有点儿胖"这样的表达方式，如果说"个子1.68米，体重75.2公斤"反而令人费解。

第三节　词义的各种关系

一个词的意义不是孤立的，与其他词存在各种各样的关系，最常见的是同义、反义、上下位义、整体与部分和多义关系。

一、同义关系

同一种语言或方言中意义相同或相近的一组词是同义词（synonyms）。比如"美丽""漂亮""好看"就是同义词。同样，"死"，英语可以说die、kick the bucket、pass away；汉语可以说"死、逝世、辞世、去世、离世、亡故、呜呼、蹬腿儿、翘辫子、升天、驾崩、离开"等。同义词通常可以分为等义词和近义词两类。等义词是理性意义完全相同的词，近义词是理性意义相近的词。前者如"星期日-礼拜天"，"水泥-洋灰"，后者如"成果-后果"，"尊敬-尊重"。因为同义词意义相同或相近，又略有差异，所以会造成口误。下面句子中的说话人一开始用的是"关怀"，后来意识到不够准确，所以又改口用"关心"。"模型"和"模式"也是近义词。这种口误充分证明了同义词的存在是有心理现实性的。

（28）我们也应该多加关怀，多加关心他们。
（29）我们的广告很多还是照搬西方的很多广告的模型，模式。

有些同义词是借用方言词的结果，如"知道"和"晓得"，"西红柿"和"番茄"，"欢喜"和"喜欢"。有些同义词是对外语词进行意译和音译的结果，如"扩音器"和"麦克风"，"公尺"和"米"，"出租车"和"的士"。有些同义词的编码理据不同，如"扩音器"和"话筒"指称的事物一样，"扩音器"的表面意思是"具有扩音功能的机器"，"话筒"的意思是"可以用来说话的筒状物"。再如"电脑-微机-计算机""套袖-袖套"。

同义词的理性意义基本相同，但在语体、感情色彩等方面存在差别，可以从以下几个方面辨析同义词。

A. 感情色彩不同

（30）a. 教导-教唆　赞美-奉承　果断-武断　节俭-抠门

statesman–politician thrifty–stingy bravery–foolhardiness shrewd–sly

b. 把握-把持　尖锐-尖刻　严厉-刻薄

c. 结果-成果-后果　保护-爱护-庇护　famous（著名的）-noted（著名的）-notorious（臭名昭著的）

（30）a组中横线前面的词都是褒义词，后面的词都是贬义词。b组中横线前面的词都是中性词，后面的词都是贬义词。c组中分别是中性词、褒义词和贬义词。

B. 语体色彩不同

（31）a. 老婆-妻子　大夫-医生　肚子-腹部　吹牛-吹嘘　编造-杜撰　小气-吝啬　大方-慷慨

b. 死者-死人　擅自-私自　准予-可以　给予-给　部署-安排

c. 飞-飞翔　好-美好　静-寂静　犟-倔犟

（31）a组中横线前面的词都是口语词，后面的词都是书面语词。b组中横线前面的词常用在比较正式的公文中，横线后面的词一般是通用的。c组中后一个词常用在文艺作品中。"夫人"用于外交场合和书面用语以表示庄重；"妻子"用于书面和比较庄重的场合；"老婆"用于口语和表现口语风格的文艺作品。同样指警察，policeman 是正式用语，cop是口语，nab是俚语。

C. 适用的对象不同

"逝世"用于有一定地位的人，带有敬意；"去世"通用，可以用于平常百姓。"关怀"是上级对下级，长辈对晚辈；"关心"多是平级、平辈之间。学生要"尊敬"老师，老师要"尊重"学生，学生和学生之间也要互相"尊重"。"爱护"既可用于人，也可用于物，既可用于上，也可用于下；而"爱戴"只用于人，并且不能用于上对下。古代汉语中的"唯"和"诺"都是表示应答的词，但"唯"用于应答地位或者辈分比自己高的人，"诺"用于应答地位或者辈分与自己相同或比自己低的人。所以，《礼记》中有"父命呼，唯而不诺"的说法。high和tall都有"高"的意思，high指无生命的事物，tall指有生命的事物。可以说tall tree、tall man，不能说high tree、high man；可以说high mountain，却不能说tall mountain。many和much都表示"多"，many只能修饰可数名词，much只能修饰不可数名词。few和little也有类似的差别。

D．程度不同

"失望"还有希望，"绝望"就几乎没有希望了。新东方的名言"从绝望中寻找希望，人生终究辉煌"中的"绝望"换成"失望"程度就太轻了。上课迟到被老师"批评"很正常，被老师"批判"就太严重了。英语中的surprise、astonish、amaze和astound都表"惊奇"，程度依次增加：surprise是一般用语，表示"出乎意料地惊讶或惊喜"；astonish较surprise程度加强，表示"令人惊异到无法相信的程度，多指无法解释的事情；amaze程度更强，表示"惊讶到使人惶惑不解的程度"；astound表示"令人震惊或惊愕"，程度最高。anger、rage、fury分别表示"发怒""大怒""狂怒"，程度也依次增强。

E．所指范围不同

"事情"指一切活动和所发生的现象，意义范围最大；"事件"指已经发生的不平常的事情，范围比较小；"事故"指由于某种原因而发生的不幸的事情，范围最小。有些名词可以指集体也可以指个体，有些名词只能指集体不能指个体。这也是一种意义范围大小的区别。"树"可以指集体，也可以指个体，"树木"只能指集体，不能说"院子里有一棵树木"。类似的还有"车－车辆""信－信件""人－人口""马－马匹"。"我有一个小奥秘，就不告诉你"不是很好，其中的"奥秘"应当改成"秘密"。"奥秘"侧重指尚未被认识的秘密，范围更小；"秘密"侧重指不愿公开、不愿让外界知道的事情。

同义词之间还有其他很多方面的差别，不易辨析，可以通过搭配来区分。比如"交流"和"交换"都有互换的意思，但"交流"一般跟"思想、经验、文化"搭配，"交换"一般跟"意见、资料、产品、礼物"搭配。"发挥"和"发扬"都有"发展扩大"的意思，"发挥"经常同"作用、威力、智能、力量、干劲、创造性、积极性"等搭配；"发扬"则经常同"作风、精神、传统、民主、风格"等搭配。再比如，"采取"通常与"措施、方法、政策"等搭配，"采用"则通常与"技术、药物、稿件"等搭配，"采纳"通常与"建议、意见"等搭配。

"语言""城郭""疾病""朋友""镂刻""切磋""琢磨""哭泣"都是古代汉语中的一些单音节同义词组合、凝固而成的。其中的单音节词意思不完全相同，各有侧重，如表

6-2所示。

语：回答别人的问话，或和人谈论事情（论难曰语）	言：自动地跟人说话（直言曰言）
城：内城	郭：外城
疾：一般的病	病：重病（疾甚曰病）
朋：同师曰朋	友：同志曰友
镂：金谓之镂	刻：木谓之刻
切：骨谓之切	磋：象谓之磋
琢：玉谓之琢	磨：石谓之磨
哭：有声为哭	泣：无声为泣

表6-2　古代汉语单音节同义词的差别

　　需要注意的是，同义并不是简单的一对一的关系。多义词的各个意义会与不同的词义构成同义关系。一个多义词，由于有多个意思，就可能有多个不同的同义词，比如"深"的同义词有："久"（年深日久）、"厚"（情深义厚）、"浓"（深红）等。"骄傲"的同义词有："自大"（骄傲使人落后）、"自豪"（中国，我为你骄傲）。

　　同义词用得好，可以增强表达效果，表现在以下几个方面。

　　A. 使内容表达更加精确、严密

　　（32）铁道部增开临时列车，缓解春运压力。

　　（33）解决灾区群众的饮水问题是刻不容缓的。

"缓解"不是"解决"，两个词有程度不同的区别，不能互相替换。

　　B. 同义词的细微差异使表达更细致，表现力更强

　　（34）窃书不能算偷……窃书！读书人的事，能算偷么？（鲁迅《孔乙己》）

"窃"与"偷"本是同义词，只是一个是书面语词，一个是口语词。在孔乙己看来，自己是读书人，高人一等，"书"也不是一般的东西，叫"偷书"辱没了身份。两个同义词的对比，将他的强词夺理、迂腐刻画得淋漓尽致。

　　C. 同义词的前后换用，生动灵活，富于变化，避免重复单调

　　（35）它是站在海岸遥望海中已经看得见桅杆尖头了的一只航船，它是立于高山之巅

远看东方已见光芒四射喷薄欲出的一轮朝日……（毛泽东《星星之火，可以燎原》）

（36）惜秦皇汉武，略输文采，唐宗宋祖，稍逊风骚。（毛泽东《沁园春·雪》）

"站"和"立"，"遥望"和"远看"，意思相同，分别使用，增加了语言的生动性。"略"与"稍"也是同义词。对偶句中经常通过同义词的换用来避免重复，比如下面的"逢"和"遇"，"与"和"共"。

（37）棋逢对手，将遇良才。

（38）落霞与孤鹜齐飞，秋水共长天一色

再看《过秦论》中的一段话：

（39）秦孝公据崤函之固，拥雍州之地，君臣固守以窥周室，有席卷天下，包举宇内，囊括四海之意，并吞八荒之心。

其中的"据""拥"，"席卷""包举""囊括"和"并吞"意思相近，可以看作两组同义词。同义词灵活运用的现象成语里面也非常多，例如"呼风唤雨""招风引蝶""如花似玉""提纲挈领""提心吊胆""捕风捉影"各成语中的前后两个动词。

D．几个同义词连用，可增强表达力

（40）你们的这样许多言论行动，既然和敌人汉奸的所有这些言论行动一模一样，毫无二致，毫无区别，怎么能够不使人们疑心？（毛泽东《质问国民党》）

"一模一样""毫无二致""毫无区别"意思相同。在这里三个词连用，使意思表达更加明确，还加重了语气，态度鲜明。（41）是圣地亚哥野生动物园里一个告示牌上的话，多个同义动词的连用是要强调严禁做有害动物的事。

（41）Please do not annoy, torment, pester, plague, molest, worry, badger, harry, harass, heckle, persecute, irk, bullyrag, vex, disquiet, grate, beset, bother, tease, nettle, tantalize, or ruffle the animals.

二、反义关系

意义相反的词被称为反义词（antonym），它们之间的关系被称为反义关系（antonymy）。常见的反义词有"真-假、男-女、上-下、左-右、生-死、聚-散、白天-黑夜、胜利-失败、前进-后退、支持-反对"等。

反义词一般可以分为两大类。一类是级差反义词（gradable antonyms）或叫相对反义词，对立的反义词意义之间存在中间状态，肯定A就否定B，否定A不一定就肯定B，反之亦然。例如，"不多"不一定是"少"，"不少"不一定就是"多"，因为还有不多不少。"多"和"少"是相对反义词。"冷"和"热"也是相对反义词，因为不热不一定是冷，还可能是"温""凉"。（42）是更多的例子。

（42）a. 大-小　高-矮　胖-瘦　长-短　快-慢　美-丑　黑-白　甘-苦
　　　　轻-重　输-赢　爱-恨　升-降　进攻-撤退　朋友-敌人　多-少
　　　　哭-笑　反对-拥护

　　　b. big-small　long-short　rich-poor　old-young　hot-cold　happy-sad
　　　　rich-poor

相对反义词多是形容词，可以以比较级和最高级的形式出现，如"He is taller than me.""Yangtze is the longest river in Asia."值得注意的是，级差反义词的地位有时候并不完全相等，在实际使用中呈现不对称性，例如（43）-（44）。

（43）问：How old are you?
　　　　　*How young are you?
　　　答：Ten years old.

（44）问：他多高?
　　　　　*他多矮?
　　　答：一米八。

无论是在汉语还是英语中，我们询问一个人的年龄时都会用"how old（多大）"而不会用how young（多年轻）。同样地，询问身高用"高"（tall）而不是"矮"（short），都是表量大的一方。"他多矮"也可以说，但并非询问身高，而是在知道"他"矮的情况下想知道他到底有多矮。级差反义词还可以进一步分类，详见原典选读三。

另一类是互补反义词（complementary pairs），又叫绝对反义词，即两个对立的反义词的意义之间没有中间状态，肯定A就是否定B，否定A就是肯定B，反之亦然。也就是说，A和B之间是非此即彼的关系。例如，一个人的性别不是男就是女；一个人不是死了就是活着，没有模棱两可的状态。互补反义词一般不用于比较级或最高级。例如，不能说*This man is deader than that one。（45）列举了汉语和英语中常见的绝对反义词。

（45）a. 正-反　死-活　有-无　对-错　雌-雄　是-非　真-假　内-外

　　　　　昼-夜　寤-寐　干-湿　曲-直

　　　b. male-female alive-dead pass-fail married-single awake-asleep

此外，还有一类关系反义词（relational opposites），两个词在意义上互相对立，又互相依存，存在对称性。关系反义词之间以对方的存在为前提，比如"买"一定意味着"卖"的存在，"我买了一本书"一定意味着某人或某书店卖了一本书。"张三是王芳的丈夫"一定意味着"王芳是张三的妻子"。（46）是汉语和英语中一些关系反义词的例子。

（46）a. 南-北　东-西　前-后　左-右　上-下

　　　　　老师-学生　丈夫-妻子　父母-孩子　领导-下属　医生-病人

　　　　　父-子　主-客　主-仆　聚-散

　　　　　买-卖　问-答　借-还　开-关　教-学　收-发　来-去　穿-脱

　　　　　取-予　收-放

　　　b. borrow-lend speak-listen write-read employer-employee

有关关系反义词的详细介绍参见原典选读三。

多义词在不同的意义上与不同的词构成反义关系，所以一个词可能会有多个反义词。例如"失败"的反义词可以是"成功"（失败是成功之母），也可以是"胜利"（非正义的战争注定是要失败的，不可能胜利）。"正"的反义词有"反""误""歪""负""副"等。"生"的反义词可以是"死"（生死相许），也可以是"熟"（半生不熟）。"老"的反义词可能是"新"（新老朋友），也可能是"嫩"（这些四季豆老了）、"少"（男女老少）。英语clever在"聪明"、"机灵"和"灵活"三个意思上分别与stupid（愚蠢）、dull（迟钝）和clumsy（笨拙）构成反义词。

屈折语中常常用否定词缀来构成反义词，如英语中的否定前缀有un-、im-、in-、dis-、ir-、il-等，否定后缀有-less。例如，happy-unhappy、possible-impossible、ability-inability、agree-disagree、regular-irregular、legal-illegal、hopeful-hopeless。

上文中的反义词都是约定俗成的，不以上下文或语境为转移。有些反义词则是临时的，只出现在特定的语境中，如（47）。

（47）旧社会把人变成鬼，新社会把鬼变成人。

（47）中的"鬼"指过着非人生活的人，与"人"临时构成了一对反义词，离开了具体句子，不是反义词。

反义词的对举往往会带来鲜明对比的表达效果，因此经常出现在名言警句、广告语和警示语中，比如（48）-（53）。

（48）虚心使人进步，骄傲使人落后。

（49）让梦想接入现实。（中国电信宽带）

（50）小钱让你拥有一个大家。（某楼盘）

（51）聪明人选傻瓜。（某傻瓜相机广告）

（52）Impossible made possible.使不可能变为可能。（佳能打印机）

（53）No business too small, no problem too big. 没有不做的小生意，没有解决不了的大问题。（IBM公司）

很多成语和四字格是由反义词构成的，如"深入浅出""口是心非""头重脚轻""南辕北辙""左顾右盼""积少成多""进退两难""貌合神离""弱肉强食""取长补短""大惊小怪""不男不女""非此即彼"。

同和异是对立统一的。同义词是"同中有异"，反义词所概括反映的是同类现象中的两个方面，是"反中有同"，必须以共同的意义领域为前提，没有"同"就无所谓"反"。比如"大"和"小"都是就尺寸而言的，"大小"这个词就有尺寸的意思，可以说"试试大小是否合适"。"高"与"矮"是就身高而言的，"大"和"矮"不能构成反义关系，因为它们没有共同的意义领域，无所谓反义。汉语中的联合式双音复合词常常是由同义或反义语素构成，"简单、困苦、美丽、丰富"是同义语素并列，"本末、因果、阴阳、恩怨、利弊、纵横、反正、死活、作息、动静、褒贬、盈亏、兴亡、问答、出入、往来、是非、异同、好歹、横竖、彼此"都是反义语素并列。

三、上下位义关系

当一个词A所表达的意义被另一个词B的意义所包含时，B与A存在上下位义关系（hyponymy）。通常可以用"A是一种B"来判断，B是上位词（hypernym），A是下位词（hyponym）。比如"菠菜是一种菜""杨树是一种树""狗是一种动物""啤酒是一种酒"，

"菠菜""杨树""狗""啤酒"分别是"菜""树""动物""酒"的下位词，"菜""树""动物""酒"分别是"菠菜""杨树""狗""啤酒"的上位词。一个上位词可以有多个下位词，比如"蔬菜"包括"菠菜、白菜、芹菜、胡萝卜、茄子"，等等。

如图6-1所示，上下位义关系是有层次的，比如"轿车""卡车""客车"的上位词是"汽车"，"汽车""自行车""火车"的上位词是"车"，而"车"的上位概念是"交通工具"，"交通工具"的下位词除了"车"还有"飞机""船"等。再如，"水果"的下位词有"苹果、梨、桃、橙子、西瓜"等，而"苹果"又有下位词"国光""红富士""黄香蕉"等。再如，"家具-桌子-书桌、武器-枪-手枪"依次是上下位义关系。英语中的vehicle-automobile-car也构成上下位义关系。动词也存在上下位义关系，如march是walk的下位词，"感冒"是"生病"的下位词。

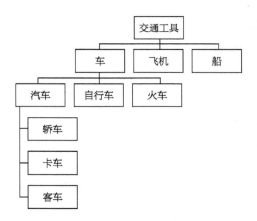

图6-1 "车"的上下位关系

值得注意的是，汉语中的上位词常常作为中心语素出现在下位词中。如果用XY来标记下位词的话，XY是偏正关系，Y常常是XY的上位词。这是汉语中很常见、高能产的构词模式。比如"铅笔"是一种"笔"，"白菜"是一种"菜"。正是因为这种构词模式很能产，beer会译成"啤酒"，tank也可以译成"坦克车"。词的上下位义关系在不同语言中可能不一样。比如汉语中的"长裤、短裤、内裤"等有一个上位词"裤子"，英语中有对应的trousers（长裤）、shorts（短裤）、underpants（内裤），却没有一个上位词与"裤子"对应。英语中有pen（钢笔）、pencil（铅笔），却没有与汉语"笔"对应的词。同样地，英语中有turnip（白萝卜）、carrot（胡萝卜），却没有一个上位词与"萝卜"对应。汉语中的"车"可以统称各种各样的车，不同的车的构词模式是"X车"。英语中缺乏这样一个表示统称的词，而且有些车名称中没有共同的语素，请看表6-3汉英车名比较：

车							
汽车	火车	自行车	货车	马车	出租车	越野车	救护车
automobile	train	bike	lorry	carriage	taxi	road vehicle	ambulance

表6-3　汉语和英语中指"车"的词

　　另一方面，汉语中有"叔叔、伯伯、姨夫、舅舅、姑父"等，却没有一个相当于英语中uncle的词。每种语言的词汇系统中都会存在一些空缺。"走"大致对应英语中的walk，但它们的下位词数量差别比较大，英语中还有30多个动词分别表达不同方式的"走"，如（54）。

（54）limp：一瘸一拐地走

　　　　shuffle：拖拖拉拉地走

　　　　dodder：摇摇晃晃地走

　　　　falter：瑟瑟缩缩地走

　　　　swagger：大摇大摆地走

　　　　pad：蹑手蹑脚地走

　　　　……

　　有些词可以同时占据上位词和下位词的位置，如图6-2所示：[1]

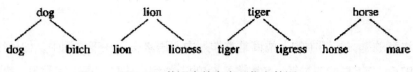

图6-2　英语中兼有上下位义的词

dog、lion、tiger、horse既可以指雄性动物，也可以泛指雄性和雌性动物。例如，dog既可以指"公狗"，也可以泛指"狗"。同样的情形也见于汉语，古代汉语中的"口"专指人的嘴，也泛指人、鸟和兽的嘴，如图6-3所示。

---

1 引自：D. Alan Cruse. 1986. *Lexical semantics*. Cambridge: Cambridge University Press, p.256.

图6-3　口、喙和嘴的上下位关系

四、整体与部分关系

如果可以说"A是B的一部分",那么词B与词A就构成整体与部分关系(meronymy),这种关系在客观世界中普遍存在。如图6-4所示,头是人体的一部分,"人体"与"头"构成整体与部分关系。一个物体相对于另一个物体来说是部分,但这个物体本身可能又能分出不同的部分,整体与部分关系具有层级性。例如,"上肢"与"手"、"手"与"手掌"、"手掌"与"手心"也构成整体与部分关系。

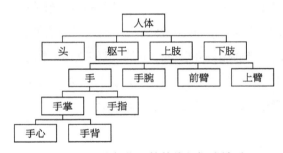

图6-4　人体部位词的整体与部分关系

整体与部分关系具有传递性,比如,树叶是树枝的一部分,树枝是树的一部分,所以树叶也是树的一部分。但是,这种传递性可能会被阻断。部分具有自主性,相对于整体有固定的功能,其发挥作用的范围就是其功能域(functional domain)。(55)中的c句有点别扭,就是因为"把手"的功能域是"门"而不是"房子",其作用是使门打开或关闭,而"房子"作为整体已超出了"把手"的功能域,所以可以说"门把手",而不能说"房把手"。

　　(55) a. 房子有门。

　　　　 b. 门有把手。

　　　　 c. ? 房子有把手。

部分依赖于整体,因此,对于表示部分的名词的理解离不开表示整体的名词。比如要理解"腰"的意思，需要知道它是人体的一部分，在身体的中部，只有这样才能理解"山腰"的意思。要理解footnote（脚注），需要知道脚在人体的最下面。"耳朵聋了"只有确定了是谁的耳朵，才能知道是谁聋了。指整体的名词在具体的上下文中可能指整体的某个部分，如"这把刀很锋利"中的"刀"指的并不是整体的"刀"，也不是"刀柄"，而是"刀刃"。

现代汉语中，很多偏正式复合词是以整体部分关系为基础构成的，其中表示整体的语素充当修饰成分，而表示部分的语素充当中心成分，词义是指称整体中的某个部分。例如上面的手掌（palm）、手指（finger）、树根（root）、树干（trunk）、树枝（branch）、树叶（leaf）、树皮（bark）、树冠（crown）。相比之下，括号里对应的英语词则不能显示这种关系。finger本身就指手指，hand finger在英语中不能说。不过，"手心""手背"倒可以说palm of the hand、back of the hand。"整体+部分"式的定中复合词在汉语中普遍存在，又如，衣领、房门、眼皮、嘴唇、表链、瓶盖、鞋跟、鸡腿、楼顶。

在汉语构词中，表示部分的构词成分可以与不同的表示整体的构词成分结合，如手腕（wrist）-脚腕（ankle）、手掌（palm）-脚掌（sole），对应的英语词从词面上则看不出这种关系。汉语中表示同一整体的不同部分的词可以相互结合构成并列式复合词，如"手足、手脚、股肱、枝叶、耳目、血肉、筋骨、眉目、领袖、爪牙"。这些词往往不只是字面义，而引申为其他意思，比如"手足"指兄弟。

五、多义关系

多义关系（polysemy）是指一个词有多个意义，而且这些意义之间互有联系。单义词只有一个意义。科学术语一般是单义词，如"千克""元音""纳米"。多义词由单义词发展而来。本义是多义词中最初产生的那项意义，引申义是在本义的基础上衍生出来的意义。中心意义（又叫基本义）指使用比较多，在一个词中占中心地位的意义。比如"兵"的本义是"兵器"，后来引申为"士兵"，后一种意思现在用得最多，是中心意义。词典中绝大部分词都是多义词。比如，"花"在《现代汉语词典》（第7版）列了18个义项，常见的如：

① 种子植物的有性繁殖器官，由花瓣、花萼、花托、花蕊组成，有各种颜色，有的很艳丽，有香味。

② 可供观赏的植物：花盆、花匠。

③ 形状像花朵的东西：雪花、浪花。

④ 烟火的一种：花炮、礼花。

⑤ 花纹：白底蓝花。

⑥ 颜色或种类错杂的：花白、花猫。

⑦（眼睛）模糊迷乱：眼花、昏花。

⑧ 用来迷惑人的；不真实的或不真诚的：花招儿、花言巧语。

⑨ 比喻事业的精华：文艺之花。

⑩ 比喻年轻漂亮的女子：校花。

⑪ 指妓女：寻花问柳。

⑫ 指棉花：弹花。

⑬ 指某些小的像花的东西：泪花、葱花。

词义的引申途径主要有两种，隐喻（metaphor）和转喻（metonymy）。隐喻建立在两个意义所反映的现实现象、事物具有某种相似性的基础上，比如上面"花"的引申义大多是隐喻的结果，如"火花""雪花""泪花"中的"花"指形状像花的东西，这一意义基于形状的相似性。"烟花""文艺之花""校花"中的"花"也是从本义隐喻引申出来的。"脚"的本义是"人和动物的腿的下端，接触地面支持身体的部分"，通过隐喻引申为"物体的最下部"，如"山脚""墙脚"中的"脚"。英语中的foot也有类似的引申义，可以说the foot of the mountain。汉语中的"头"和英语中的head都隐喻引申出了"首领"的意思。转喻则是因为两个意义所反映的两类现实现象、事物之间存在着某种联系。比如pen的本义是"羽毛"，后来引申出"钢笔"的意思，因为古代西方用羽毛蘸墨水写字。glass由"玻璃"引申出"玻璃杯"的意思，是因为玻璃杯的材料是玻璃。"兵"由"兵器"发展出"士兵（拿兵器的人）"的意思，也是转喻的结果。"丹青"原来指绘画的材料，后来引申为"绘画"。"白宫"可以转喻指"美国政府"。有些多义是呈系统性的，比如"玫瑰""茉莉""牡丹"等都兼指一种植物和这种植物的花，请比较："我在院子里种了几株玫瑰"（一种植物）、"这朵玫瑰开得最好"（玫瑰花）。

与多义词不同，同音词指的是两个或多个词的音相同而意义没有联系。同音词又分为同音同形（homonymy）和同音异形（homophony）。比如，"花钱"的"花"与"鲜花"的"花"同音，但意思截然不同，属于同音同形词。另如bank既可以指"银行"，也可以指"河岸"；bear既指"熊"，也指"出生"；nail既指"指甲"，也指"钉子"。同音不同形的词，如"话、画、化、划"，英语中的to、too和two，for与four，bear与bare。一些双音节同音词常常有一个音节是相同的，例如"权利－权力、退化－蜕化、治病－致病、专辑－专集、盈利－营利－赢利、圆形－原型－原形。"赵元任编的（56）这首有名的绕口令就包含了大量的同音词。

> （56）石室诗士施氏，嗜狮，誓食十狮。氏时时适市视狮。十时，适十狮适市。是时，
>   适施氏适市。氏视是十狮，恃矢势，使是十狮逝世。氏拾是十狮尸，适石室。
>   石室湿，氏使侍拭石室。石室拭，氏始试食是十狮尸。食时，始识是十狮尸，
>   实十石狮尸。试释是事。

同音词在口语交际中有时候能造成歧义，比如"这种草可以zhìbìng"，可能是"治病"，也可能是"致病"，意思截然不同。（57）是《爱丽丝历险记》（*Alice's Adventures in Wonderland*）中的一段有趣的文字。

> （57）"Mine is a long and sad *tale*" said the Mouse, turning to Alice, and sighing.
>   "It is a long *tail*, certainly," said Alice, looking down with wonder at the mouse's
>   tail: "but why do you call it sad？"

Alice和the Mouse说的完全是两种不同的东西，一个是tale（故事），一个是是tail（尾巴）。

生活中有些忌讳就是因为同音词造成的，比如送人礼物不能"送钟"，有"送终"之嫌。广告语则经常利用同音词来制造广告效应，例如，（58）是海水浴场的英文广告。

> （58）We have more *sun* and *air* for your *son* and *heir*.（度假村广告语）
>   我们这里为您的儿子——继承人提供更多的阳光和空气。

这则简短的广告语里出现了两对同音词：sun和son，air和heir。汉语中的双关语利用的也是同音词（字），如"外甥打灯笼——照旧（舅）"。

第四节 语义场与语义成分分析

一、语义场

"场"原来是物理学术语，是物质存在的一种基本状态。事物之间的相互作用依靠有关的场来实现，如磁场、电场。"场"理论研究的是事物或现象之间的相互关系，有某种关系的事物或现象必然或可能聚集在同一个"场"内。类似的，意义上相互有联系又有区别的词也形成一个场，即语义场（semantic field）。语义场实际上是以一个共同的意义成分为核心聚集起来的词义的聚合。比如"红""黄""蓝""绿"等构成颜色语义场，"颜色"是它们共同的意义成分。"父亲""母亲""叔叔""伯伯""舅舅""姑姑""姨"等构成亲属语义场，"亲属"是它们的共同意义成分。"煎""炸""炒""煮""炖"等构成烹饪语义场，它们都属于烹饪方式。

语义场是分等级的。比如"水果""肉""蔬菜""粮食"等构成食物语义场，"苹果""梨""香蕉""橘子"等构成水果语义场。

语义场可以分为不同的类别，常见的有同义语义场、反义语义场和类属语义场，分别对应同义关系、反义关系和上下位义关系。另外，还有整体部分语义场、顺序语义场、循环语义场等。例如，"人体-头、躯干、上肢、下肢-上臂、前臂、腕、手"构成整体部分语义场。表示军阶、职称、职务、年龄等的词构成顺序语义场，如"军长-师长-团长-营长-连长-排长-班长""教授-副教授-讲师-助教""老年-中年-壮年-青年-少年-儿童""优秀-优良-良好-合格""金牌-银牌-铜牌"都属于顺序语义场。"春天-夏天-秋天-冬天""星期一、星期二……星期日"属于循环语义场。

同一语言的语义场会发生变化。比如，古代汉语中表示"马"的语义场有"骊""骓""骛""骁""骉""骦"等几十个指马的词；现代汉语中常见的大概只有"马""驹"。古代汉语中表示行走的语义场是"走""趋""行"，现代汉语中则是"走""跑"，成员数目不同，意思也发生了变化。"走"在古代汉语中是"跑"的意思，"行"才表示"走"的意思。表示温度的语义场在古代汉语中有"热""温""凉""寒"，到了现代汉语中，变成了"热""温""凉""冷"，虽然语义场中的成员数目没变，却发生了词语替换；而且"凉"的意思有所变化，古代汉语中"凉"表示的温度在现代汉语中可能要用"冷"来表示，如"秋风萧瑟天气凉，草木摇落露为霜"。可见，不能孤立地研究一个词的意义变化，需要考虑这个词所在的语义场。

不同语言的语义场大体是相同的，但语义场中的词汇成员可能不同。比如表示行走的语义场英语和汉语中都有，但是语义场中的成员数量差别比较大，英语中有30多个动词分别表达不同方式的"走"，而汉语只有几个（参见第三节）。

同一场内的词义相互有一定的制约关系，体现了词义的系统性。词义是一个相互关联、相互制约的整体系统。由于语义场的存在，我们只有通过分析和比较词与词之间的关系，才能理解一个词的真正意义。比如，要知道Sunday的意思，必须知道它与week这个语义场中的Monday、Tuesday、Wednesday、Thursday、Friday、Saturday之间的关系；要知道"春"的意思，需要知道它与"夏""秋""冬"之间的关系。只有这样，才能真正理解"冬天已经来了，春天还会远吗？""一年之计在于春"这些句子的意思。要确定一个词的真正意义，还需要深入到词义内部，看看词义是否能分解为更小的单位。不仅要找出同一语义场中各个词共同的意义成分，还要找出能区别它们的意义成分，也就是对同一语义场内的各个词进行语义成分分析。

二、语义成分分析

（一）什么是语义成分分析

词的每一个意义称为一个义位（sememe），粗略地说，义位大致相当于词典中的义项。义位不是最小的语义单位，就像化学中的分子可以分解为原子，音位学中可以把音位分解为一束区别特征，义位也可以分解为一束更小的语义成分，语义成分又叫义素。把义位分析为语义成分的方法叫语义成分分析法（semantic componential analysis），又叫义素分析法。下面是一个典型的例子。大括号中的是义位，方括号中大写的HUMAN、ADULT和MALE是语义成分，用大写的形式是强调这些语义成分具有超越具体语言中的词汇的一般性，在不同的语言中具有普遍性。+表示具有这一语义成分，−表示没有这一语义成分。对于"man""woman""boy""girl"的语义成分分析可用（59）来表示。

（59）{man}：［+HUMAN］［+ADULT］［+MALE］

{woman}：［+HUMAN］［+ADULT］［−MALE］

{boy}：［+HUMAN］［−ADULT］［+MALE］

{girl}：［+HUMAN］［−ADULT］［−MALE］

从（59）可以看出，HUMAN是man、woman、boy和girl这四个词共享的语义成分；

ADULT是man和woman共享的语义成分，却是boy和girl所不具有的语义成分；MALE是man和boy共享的语义成分，却是woman和girl所不具有的语义成分。这四个词彼此之间至少有一个语义成分是不同的，保证了每个词词义的独特性。比如man和woman，boy和girl的语义差别是平行的，都是在性别上有差异；man和boy，woman和girl的语义差别也是平行的，在语义成分ADULT上对立。由此也可以看出，语义成分分析法能够清晰地揭示出词义之间的共性、差异以及对称性。也就是说，用两个语义成分就可以区别这四个词的意思。表6-4这个语义矩阵能更清晰地显示出这四个词的共性和差异。

语义成分	man	woman	boy	girl
HUMAN	+	+	+	+
ADULT	+	+	−	−
MALE	+	−	+	−

表6-4　man、woman、boy和girl的语义成分分析

　　进行语义成分分析首先要确定分析的对象，也就是要从语义场中找出对比的词群，然后从中找出共同的语义成分和区别性语义成分，这样既可以清晰地看到这组词之间的联系，也可以看到它们之间的区别。最后，简化语义成分，通过横排列式（如（59）所示）或矩阵式（如表6-4所示）来呈现分析的结果。

　　动词和形容词也可以进行语义成分分析。动词的语义成分分析中区别性语素常常涉及动作的对象、方式、主体等的不同。比如古代汉语中洗浴类动词有"洗""沐""浴""盥""涤""浣"；所洗部位不同，"洗"是洗脚，"沐"是洗头，"浴"是洗身，"盥"是洗手，"涤"是洗物，"浣"是洗衣。再比如"仰望""俯视"、"张望""眺望""回眸""凝视""端详""窥视""瞟""瞧"都有共同的语义成分"看"，但看的方向、方式不同，"仰望"是向上看，"俯视"是向下看，"张望"是向四周或远处看，"眺望"是从高处向远处看，"回眸"是向后看，"凝视"是聚精会神、不眨眼睛地看，"端详"是仔细地看，"窥视"是偷偷地看，"瞟"是斜着看，"瞧"是随意地看。"鸣""吠""咩""哞"都是动物的呼叫声，但主体不同，分别是"鸟""狗""羊""牛"。形容词的语义分析中区别性语素常常涉及程度、主体等的不同，如"热"和"温"程度不同，"冷"和"凉"程度也不同。"肥""胖"都指含脂肪多，但"肥"通常用于动物，"胖"通常用于人；"瘦"

指含脂肪少，既可以用于人也可以用于动物。

（二）语义成分分析与语义场的关系

语义成分的提取离不开语义场。语义成分分析首先要确定语义场，然后再进行对比分析。反过来，语义分析又可以很好地反映出语义场的变化和不同语言语义场的差异。语义成分分析主要用于分析语义场、词典编纂等，服务于词汇语义研究。词义之间有各种联系，各种词义关系是通过共同的语义成分联系在一起的。在词义上下位关系中，下位词一定具有上位词的全部语义成分，同时又具有上位词所没有的一些语义成分。比如"火车""汽车"和"飞机"都具有语义成分［运输］。即使是反义词也有共同的语义成分，比如"大"和"小"是反义词，具有共同的语义成分［尺寸］；"大"和"低"不构成反义关系，就是因为它们没有共同的语义成分。

从人类的认知结构（cognitive structure）中分解出来的语义成分是属于语言共性的东西，适用于分析任何语言，只不过在不同的语言中语义成分会有不同的结合。通过分析和比较不同语言中的语义场，可以发现语言之间的文化共性和差异。莱雷尔（Lehrer）考察了法语、德语、波斯语、日语、汉语等许多语言中的烹饪词汇，发现所有语言都有［cooking with water］这一语义成分，之下又有［boiling］与［non-boiling］的区别。[1]再如，汉语中的同胞亲属场中包括"哥哥""弟弟""姐姐""妹妹"这四个词，彼此之间可以通过性别和长幼来区分；而英语中，表示同胞亲属的只有brother和sister这两个词，二者只在性别上有差异，不存在长幼之分。这可能反映了两种语言乃至两种文化上的深层差异：汉语文化更注重长幼之序，见表6-5。

		同胞	男性	年长
汉语	哥哥	+	+	+
	弟弟	+	+	－
	姐姐	+	－	+
	妹妹	+	－	
英语	brother	+	+	
	sister	+	－	

表6-5　汉语和英语的同胞亲属语义场比较

1 引自：Adrienne Lehrer. 1974. *Semantic Fields and Lexical Structure*. Amesterdam: North-Holland.

语义场的变化、意义的变化也可以用语义成分变化来解释，比如古代汉语中洗浴语义场有"洗""沐""浴""盥""浣"等动词，"洗"专指洗脚。到了现代汉语，这一语义场严重萎缩，常用词就剩"洗"了，原来的对立消失了，"洗"的语义成分［洗脚］就消失了，"洗"泛指洗各种东西，意义扩大了。

（三）语义成分的心理现实性

语义成分不是语言学家造出来的，而是客观存在的，具有心理现实性，但不易观察到。语义成分的存在可以从口误现象中窥见一斑，见表6-6。

实际说的	想要说的
这位老人满脸白发。	这位老人满头白发。
咱们干了这杯茶，一醉方休。	咱们干了这杯酒，一醉方休。
你该交水费了，电用完了。	你该交电费了，电用完了。
你手套不穿了吗？	你手套不戴了吗？
我今天早上起早了，没赶上火车。	我今天早上起晚了，没赶上火车。

表6-6　从口误看语义成分的心理现实性

仔细观察会发现，说话人实际说出来的词和脑子里想的存在某种意义联系，实际上是共享某一个语义成分："脸"和"头"都是"身体部位"；"茶"和"酒"都属于"饮品"；"水费"和"电费"都与"钱"有关；"穿"和"戴"都与"打扮"有关；"早"和"晚"都与"时间"有关。语义成分从儿童语言习得早期的语言中也可以看出，比如，有的孩子会说："妈妈，走大一点"，他实际上想说的是"妈妈，走快一点"，"大"和"快"都有表示"量大"的意思。

不同语言中语义成分的重要性也不同，有些语义成分在语言中有标记。在斯瓦希里（Swahili）语中，含"人"这一语义成分的名词有独立的前缀，单数是m-，复数是wa-，如mtoto（孩子）、watoto（孩子们）。含"人造物"这一语义成分的名词也有独立的前缀，单数是ki-，复数是vi-，如kiti（chair）、viti（chairs）。西班牙语中有明确表示性别的后缀，-o表示男性，-a表示女性，[1] 见表6-7。

---

1 引自：F. G. Lounsbury. 1956. A Semantic Analysis of Pawnee Kinship Usage. *Language*, 32（1）.

西班牙语	英语	西班牙语	英语
tio	uncle	tia	aunt
hijo	son	hija	daughter
abuelo	grandfather	abuela	grandmother
hermano	brother	hermana	sister

表6-7　西班牙语中表示性别的后缀

英语中的"女性"这一语义成分常常以-ess为标记，如actor-actress。前缀"tri-"有表示"三"的意思，如tricycle、triangle（三角形）。词缀en-、-en、-fy往往含致使义，如enable、brighten、beautify。英语中表示动物性别的语义成分虽然有时候不出现在词层面，但也广泛存在，是隐性的。从表6-8可以看出，第一列中的词都含有语义成分［公］，第三列中的词都含有语义成分［母］，这种性别差异在汉语词中是显性的。第一列中的词也可以表示统称。

英语	汉语	英语	汉语
bull	公牛	cow	母牛
ram	公羊	ewe	母羊
rooster	公鸡	hen	母鸡
horse	公马	mare	母马
dog	公狗	bitch	母狗
lion	公狮	lioness	母狮
gander	公鹅	goose	母鹅
stag	公鹿	doe	母鹿

表6-8　英语动物词汇中表性别的语义成分

（四）语义特征

分解词义能更好地说明词之间的关系，证明语义成分是概念成分，是词义的一部分。不仅如此，词语的语义成分在很大程度上制约了其组合分布情况，比如，带有语义成分［互相］的动词不能带宾语，如"结婚、吵架、竞赛"等。也就是说，有些语义成分会影响句子的可接受性，这类语义成分通常被称为语义特征（semantic feature）。[1]

1 参见：邵敬敏，周芍. 语义特征的界定与提取方法. 外语教学与研究，2005，37（1）：21-28.

　　语义特征是从属于"词"的。语义特征只是语义成分中的一部分，特指影响某种句法组合可接受性的那些语义成分。例如，（60）中的每个句子在语法上都没有任何问题，都是主谓宾结构。但a、b句能说，而c、d句一般不能说，除非是在拟人化的童话故事里。a-b与c-d唯一的不同是主语位置上的名词。"吃"要求其主语所指的事物能够吃东西，是动物。"大树""盘子"显然不能满足这一语义要求。

　　（60）a. 孩子们在吃香蕉。

　　　　　b. 猴子在吃香蕉。

　　　　　c. *大树在吃香蕉。

　　　　　d. *盘子在吃香蕉。

　　名词具有的语义特征同样也可能会影响句子的可接受性。比如，（61）中A组的句子都可以说，而B组的句子都不能说，是因为A组的名词都具有顺序义，军衔、季节等都是可变的，而B组的名词没有顺序义，所指内容没有可变性。

（61）　　　A组	B组
都将军了！	*都学生了！
都春天了！	*都中国了！
都婆婆了！	*都女性了！
都星期五了！	*都气球了！

　　有些歧义的产生可能与语义特征的不同有关，例如（62）a-b的对比。

　　（62）a. 小王没找到。

　　　　　b. 书没找到。

（62）a-b句子形式看上去是一样的，结构也一样，可是a句有歧义，b句没有。因为"小王"具有语义特征［+人］，既可以是执行"找"这个动作的人，也可以是被找的对象。而"书"只能是被找的对象。

　　语义特征体现了词义与句法语义的接口。名词常见的语义特征有［±抽象］、［±生命］、［±动物］、［±人］等，动词常见的语义特征有［±活动］、［±可控］、［±自主］。

第五节　句法层面的意义

一、词义的组合与词语的搭配

词是人们将特殊复杂的现象化繁为简概括而成的，是分类包装的结果，词义具有概括性和模糊性。词义的组合则是一个相反的过程。词进入组合后，概括和模糊的词义变得具体清晰，因为词的意义在组合中要互相协调，适应彼此的语义要求，尤其是谓词的语义要求，从而根据上下文凸显自己某一方面的意思。"窗户"在《现代汉语词典》（第7版）中的解释是"墙壁等物体上通气透光的装置"，主要说明其功能和安装的位置，并没有说明其具体的构造。但（63）—（67）中的"窗户"意思更具体，凸显了窗户的不同部分。

（63）装修工人正在装窗户。（整个窗户）

（64）他从窗户爬出去了。（窗洞）

（65）请打开窗户。（窗户可以活动的部分）

（66）装修工人正在给窗户刷漆。（窗框）

（67）窗户打破了。（窗玻璃）

（68）中烧的是书的物质载体，（69）中相信的是书里包含的信息。

（68）The police burned the book.

（69）Mary believed the book.

由于同一词语可以指称事物的不同部分，所以，同一词语有时候有不同的理解，出现歧义。比如，red pencil可能指表面是红色的铅笔，也可能指笔芯是红色的笔，因为red既可以激活pencil的表面颜色，也可以凸显笔芯的颜色。

词义的组合通过词语的搭配来实现，而词语的搭配是有限制条件的。词语搭配的限制条件除了语法规则的限制之外，主要包括语义条件的限制、附加色彩、惯用法等。

语义条件的限制分为两类，一类是现实现象可能性的制约。比如"猴子吃香蕉"可以说，而"香蕉吃猴子"就不能说，因为后者所指现象是现实世界中不会发生的。词义可以分解成一束语义成分，词与词组合时在语义成分上要互相匹配。比如"猴子吃香蕉"可以说，而"香蕉吃猴子"就不能说，是因为"吃"通常要求其主语具有［+动物］这一语义特征，否则，句子就不成立。"那个男人生孩子了"一般不能说，因为"生孩子"要求其

主语含有 [+雌性] 这一特征，而"男人"含有 [-雌性] 这一语义特征，二者是矛盾的。相声《假行家》中的很多句子从语义上说都是讲不通的，平时是不说的，用在相声中只是为了造成某种艺术效果。

假行家（单口相声）

南北大道东西走，

十字街前人咬狗，

捡起狗来砍砖头，

倒叫砖头咬了手。

有个老头才十九，

嘴里喝藕就着酒，

从小没见过这宗事儿，

三轮儿拉着火车走。

另一类是附加意义的制约。词的意义还包括感情色彩、语体色彩等附加意义，因此语义的组合也要受这两方面的限制。首先，词语的搭配受感情色彩的制约。比如"警察抓了一位小偷"很别扭，因为"位"多与褒义名词连用，"小偷"是贬义词，两者不能搭配。祈使句"X一点儿"要求进入其中的形容词具有 [+可控] 这一语义特征，同时是非贬义的。"谦虚/大方/细致"等符合这两个要求，所以，可以进入这一结构。"漂亮/出色"不具有可控性，"骄傲/小气/粗心"是贬义词，所以都不能出现在X的位置。

（70）a. 谦虚/大方/细致一点儿

     b. *漂亮/*出色一点儿

     c. *骄傲/*小气/*粗心一点儿

其次，词语的搭配还要保证语体色彩匹配。比如"何时签署合同，请尽早告诉我方"中的"告诉"应该换成"告知"，因为"何时""我方"等都是书面语用词。"总统及其孩子们"应该改成"总统和他的孩子们"或者"总统及其子女"，因为"及其"比较书面化，"孩子们"比较口语化。"她是我老婆，我是她先生"很别扭，因为"老婆"是口语用词，"先生"是书面用词。"弯弯的月球小小的船"不能说，也是因为语体不协调，"月球"是科技用语。语义特征不匹配会导致语义错误，附加意义不匹配会导致结构不好或不得体，都属于语义异常。

此外，词语的搭配还受社会习惯的制约，即"惯用法"。比如，"帅"只能形容男性，

"漂亮""美"既可以形容女性也可以形容男性，还可以形容物。可以说"帅小伙"、"漂亮的姑娘"和"漂亮的小伙"，却不能说"帅姑娘"。"美男子""美女""美酒"都可以说。不同的语言和方言搭配习惯不同。汉语的"昨天下午、昨天夜里、昨天晚上"分别对应英语的yesterday afternoon、last night和yesterday/last evening。普通话中说"戴手套"，而粤语中说"穿手套"。普通话中的"胖"只用来与指人的名词搭配，"肥"通常只与指动物的名词搭配；粤语中"肥"既可以修饰人，也可以修饰动物。再比如，普通话中的"吃"只能与含有［+固体］这一语义特征的词搭配，"喝水、喝酒""吸烟"中的"喝""吸"不能换成"吃"，上海话则可以说"吃水""吃酒"和"吃烟"。傣语中的kin（吃）也可以与含［+液体］这一语义特征的词搭配，如kinhao（吃饭）、kinlan（喝水）、kinlau（喝酒）。

二、语义角色

句子中词与词之间除了语法结构关系还有语义结构关系。语义结构关系体现的是词语之间在语义上的联系，是一种深层的关系。语义结构关系中最重要的是动词与名词之间的关系。（71）-（73）中的a句没问题，而颠倒主语和宾语形成的b句不成立，不是因为不合语法，而是因为不合语义。具体来说，不同的名词与动词之间语义关系不一样，或者说在事件中扮演的角色不同，即语义角色不同。比如"乌鸦"是动作的发出者，而"水"是动作"喝"的承受者。相应地，不同的动词对同一语义角色的要求不同，限制其语义特征。比如"喝"会要求动作的发出者是动物，"买""receive"会要求动作的发出者是人。此外，不同的语义角色通常与句子的语法成分有不同的关联。（71）-（73）的a句中，动作的发出者都是主语，动作的承受者都是宾语。

（71）a. 乌鸦喝到了水。

b. *水喝到了乌鸦。

（72）a. 张三买了苹果。

b. *苹果买了张三。

（73）a. Bill received the package.

b. *The package received Bill.

在有"格"的语言中，有些"格"能显示动词与名词之间的语义关系。在（74）这个拉丁语的例子中，canis（狗）是主格形式，是动作的发出者；hominem是宾格形式，是动作的承受者。所以a-b两个句子虽然语序不一样，但意思是一样的，都是"狗咬人"。

（74）a. Canis　　　hominem　　　mordet.

　　　狗　　　　人　　　　咬

　　　"狗咬人。"

　　　b. Hominem　　　canis　　　mordet.

　　　　人　　　　狗　　　咬

　　　　"狗咬人"。

　　　语义角色到底有多少种？观察的视角不同，分类的粗细不同，结果也不同。常见的有如下几种。[1]

　　　施事（agent）： 自主性动作、行为的发出者。比如上面的"张三"和"Bill"，以及（75）-（77）中的"小王""妹妹"和"the boy"。

（75）小王吃了一个馒头。

（76）妹妹笑了。

（77）The boy rolled a red ball.

　　　受事（patient）： 因施事的行为而受到影响的事物，是跟施事相对的。例如（78）-（79）中的"茶杯"和"小刚"。

（78）弟弟打了一个茶杯。

（79）韩老师批评了小刚。

　　　与事（dative）： 动作、行为的非主动参与者，最常见的是因施事的行为而受益或受损者，例如（80）-（82）中的"李四""王五"和"当事人"。

（80）张三给了李四一本词典。

（81）张三偷了王五一支笔。

（82）你向当事人打听一下。

施事、受事和与事是双宾动词的三个必有成分。

　　　主事（theme）： 性质、状态或发生非自主变化的主体，如（83）-（85）中的"树

---

1 关于语义角色的更多分类和说明，参见：袁毓林. 论元角色的层级和语义特征. 世界汉语教学, 2002（3）：11-22.

叶""脸"和"雪"。

（83）树叶很绿。

（84）脸圆圆的。

（85）雪融化了。

致事（causer）：某种致使性事件的引起因素，如（86）-（87）中的"城市"和"老师的夸奖"。

（86）城市，让生活更美好。

（87）老师的夸奖使孩子很兴奋。

结果（result）：由施事的动作、行为造成的产物，如（88）-（89）中的"一本小说"和"一件毛衣"。

（88）他写了一本小说。

（89）妈妈给我织了一件毛衣。

对象（target）：感知行为的对象，如（90）中的"刘校长"和（91）中的"芭蕾舞"。

（90）爸爸认识刘校长。

（91）妹妹喜欢芭蕾舞。

上述这些语义角色属于基本语义角色，是动词关联的核心成分。除此之外，还有一些外围语义角色，包括工具、材料、时间、处所等。

工具（instrument）：动作、行为所凭借的器具，如（92）-（94）中的"铅笔""一把钥匙"和"枪"。

（92）他用铅笔写字。

（93）一把钥匙开一把锁。

（94）枪打出头鸟。

材料（material）：动作、行为所凭借的材料，如（95）-（96）中的"木头"和"油漆"。

（95）小王用木头做了个木偶。

（96）装修工人正在刷油漆。

　　如果某一成分兼有一种以上的语义角色，就会造成歧义。"鸡不吃了"有歧义就是因为"鸡"可能是"吃"的施事，也可能是受事。在一个句子中，不是所有的角色都必须出现。有些非核心的角色可以省略，如"John broke the window"就省略了工具角色。

　　语义角色与语法成分有一定的对应关系，不同的语义角色有相对固定的句法位置。比如施事通常会作主语，受事通常会作宾语。但二者又不完全一致，相互独立。受事也可以出现在主语位置，如"衣服洗了"中的"衣服"。主语位置还可以是其他语义角色，例如（97）中的a hammer是工具。

　　（97）A hammer broke the window.

　　语义结构与语法结构既互有联系又相对独立。语义结构是比语法结构更深层、更基本的结构。一方面，语法结构相同，语义结构可能不同，最典型的是汉语中的述宾结构，宾语可能是受事、结果、对象、施事、工具、材料、处所等多种语义角色，如（98）所示。

　　（98）喝豆浆（动作–受事）　　挖地窖（动作–结果）　　喜欢音乐（动作–对象）

　　　　　捆绳子（动作–工具）　　来了一个客人（动作–施事）

　　　　　刷油漆（动作–材料）　　睡客厅（动作–处所）

即使是同一个动词构成的动宾结构也可能有不同的语义结构。比如"吃苹果"中的"苹果"是受事，而"吃食堂"中的"食堂"则是方式。不同的语义结构与不同的"问–答"关联，前者是"吃什么？—吃苹果。"后者是"中午怎么吃（饭）？—吃食堂。"（99）的两个句子表面上看起来一样，实际上在a句中John是please的受事，b句中John则是施事。这种区别分别对应于（100）的a和b。

　　（99）a. John is easy to please.（约翰很容易被取悦）[1]

　　　　 b. John is eager to please.（约翰急于取悦别人）

　（100）a. That people please John is easy.

　　　　 b. John is eager to please people.

　　另一方面，语法结构不同，语义结构可能相同。比如，"老头看大门"与"看大门的老头"，一个是主谓结构，一个是偏正结构，但语义结构相同，都是"施事（老头）–动

---

[1] 引自：Noam Chomsky. 1965. *Aspects of the Theory of Syntax*. Cambridge, MA: MIT Press.

作（看）-受事（大门）"。（101）的a-b中"John""Mary"和"a book"与动词之间的语义关系是相同的，但是语法结构显然不同：a句是"动词-指人宾语-指物宾语"的双宾结构，b句是"动词-指物宾语-指人宾语"的与格结构。

（101） a. John gave Mary a book.（约翰给玛丽一本书）

b. John gave a book to Mary.（约翰一本书给玛丽）

句法结构关系存在于直接组成成分之间，而语义结构关系则可以跨越直接成分，出现在非直接成分之间。比如在上述两个短语中，"老头"与"看"都不是直接成分，但却都是"施事-动作"关系。

三、语义指向

什么是语义指向？不妨先看两个实例。

（102） 我重重地摔了一跤。

（103） 我狼狈地摔了一跤。

从句法结构上看，上面句子的结构层次和结构关系一模一样，"重重地""狼狈地"都是状语，与"摔了一跤"是直接成分。但是从语义上看，"重重地"与"摔"语义相关，即描写"摔"的情况；而"狼狈地"则与"我"语义相关，描写"我"的状态。这种区别就是语义指向的不同，我们说"重重地"语义上指向"摔"，"狼狈地"语义上指向"我"。语义指向是指句中某一成分在语义上跟哪个成分直接相关。句法结构相同，语义指向可能不同。不是所有的句法成分都有必要去考察它的语义指向，如"吃苹果"，我们就没有必要去考察"苹果"的语义指向。语义指向主要指非连续直接成分之间的语义依存关系，最受关注的是状语和补语的语义指向。下面的短语都是"动+形+了"述补结构，但作补语的形容词语义指向各不相同。

（104） 砍光了。[补语"光"在语义上指向"砍"的受事，如"树砍光了"。]

砍累了。[补语"累"在语义上指向"砍"的施事，如"我砍累了"。]

砍钝了。[补语"钝"在语义上指向"砍"的工具，如"这把刀砍钝了"。]

砍快了。[补语"快"在语义上指向"砍"这一动作本身，如"你砍快了，得慢点儿砍"。]

砍疼了。[补语"疼"在语义上有时可指向"砍"的受事，如"把他的脚砍疼了"；有时可指向"砍"的施事的隶属部分，如"砍了一下午柴，我的胳膊都砍疼了"。]

砍坏了。［补语"坏"在语义上有时可指向"砍"的受事，如"别把桌子砍坏
了"；有时可指向"砍"的工具，如"他那把刀砍坏了"。］

从（104）的例子也可以看出，语义指向可以指向句子中没有出现的成分，即句外成分。
语义指向如果是多向的，会造成歧义，如"砍疼了""砍坏了"。

四、蕴涵与预设

句义是词义根据一定方式组合的产物。从语言和思维的关系来看，词表达概念，句子
表达命题，即说话者对客观世界中事件或状态的判断。句子的命题有真值（truth value）：
一个陈述句如果真实地反映了外部世界的某个现象，则其真值为"真"（true）；如果对某
现象做出了不正确的、虚假的描述，则为"假"（false）。比如"中国的首都是北京"这个
句子的真值为"真"；"2014年APEC峰会在英国伦敦举行"这个句子的真值为"假"，因为
2014年APEC峰会是在北京举行的。有些句子是恒真的，即重言式（tautologies），如"所
有的三角形都有三个边""他要么去了，要么没去"。有些句子的真值永远为假，是矛盾式
（contradictions），如"所有的单身汉都是已婚的"，这类句子在语义上是自相矛盾的。

我们可以进一步研究句子的真值条件，即研究一个句子在什么场合下为真，什么场合
下为假。真值条件语义是形式语义学研究的核心内容。语义学关心句子的真值，但并非到
真实世界中去检验，而是要找出不同句子真值之间的逻辑推导关系。蕴涵和预设就是其中
两种重要的推导关系。

（一）蕴涵（Entailment）

如果：

① 句子S_1为真，句子S_2就一定为真；

② 句子S_2为假，句子S_1就一定为假；

③ 句子S_1为假，句子S_2可以为真也可以为假；

那么：S_1句义蕴涵S_2句义。

简单地说，就是从一个句子的语义一定能推导出另一个句子的语义，反向推导则不成立。
例如，在（105）中，如果a为真，那么b-d都是真的，我们说a蕴涵b-d。但是，b不蕴涵a，

因为张三买的可能不是桌子，而是柜子；c不蕴涵a，因为买桌子的可能是别人而不是张三；很显然，d也不蕴涵a，"有人"不一定是"张三"，"家具"可能不是"桌子"。

（105） a. 张三买了一张桌子。

→ b. 张三买了一件家具。

→ c. 有人买了一张桌子。

→ d. 有人买了一件家具。

仔细观察会发现，蕴涵关系与词义的上下位关系有关。比如，"桌子"是"家具"的下位词，"买了桌子"一定意味着"买了家具"，而"买了家具"不一定意味着"买了桌子"。"张三"和"有人"也可以看作一种上下位义关系。也就是说，如果两个句子中相同语义角色的词有下位和上位关系，则这两个句子一定有蕴含关系。（106）中的每个句子都蕴涵后面所有的句子，因为BMW（宝马）-car-automobile-vehicle有上下位关系，前面的词都是后面的词的下位词。

（106） a. John bought a BMW yesterday.

→ b. John bought a new car yesterday.

→ c. John bought an automobile yesterday.

→ d. John bought a vehicle yesterday.

如果句子是否定句，这种蕴涵关系就要颠倒过来。比如"他从来没出过国"蕴涵"他没有去过美国"，"美国"是"国家"的下位词。

如果两个句子互相蕴涵，那么它们就是同义句，如（107）-（109）。

（107） 有人买了桌子。↔ 有人卖了桌子。

（108） 张三是李四的老师。↔ 李四是张三的学生。

（109） 张三在李四左边。↔ 李四在张三右边。

这类同义句与关系反义词有直接关系，如买-卖、老师-学生、左边-右边都是关系反义词。

（二）预设（Presupposition）

如果：

① 句子S_1为真，句子S_2就一定为真；

② 句子S₂为假，句子S₁就一定为假；

③ 句子S₁为假，句子S₂仍然为真；

那么：S₁句义预设S₂句义。

例如，（110）中a句"英格兰的女王年迈"预设b句"英格兰有女王"；（111）中a句"未名湖边的柳树绿了"预设b句"未名湖边有柳树"。

（110）　a.　The queen of England is old. (英格兰的女王年迈。)

　　　　　b.　England has a queen. (英格兰有女王。)

（111）　a.　未名湖边的柳树绿了。

　　　　　b.　未名湖边有柳树。

有些动词与预设密切相关，要求所带的宾语句子必须为真，如"后悔"一词表达的是对已经存在状态的一种心理，所以，要求其宾语句子所指是真的，（112）a预设（112）b。读者可根据上面的定义自行验证其中的预设关系。

（112）　a.　他后悔打了儿子。

　　　　　b.　他打了儿子。

蕴涵是句子的基本信息；预设则是交谈双方共享的知识，是句子的附带信息。蕴涵和预设的主要区别在第三个假设条件上，所以，可以用否定法来区分二者。比如（113）中a句"他哥哥买了一张桌子"如果是假的，即"他哥哥没买桌子"，则b句"他哥哥买了一件家具"可真可假，但c句"他有哥哥"还是真的。所以a句"他哥哥买了一张桌子"蕴涵b句"他哥哥买了一件家具"，预设c句"他有哥哥"。

（113）　a.　他哥哥买了一张桌子。

　　　　　b.　他哥哥买了一件家具。

　　　　　c.　他有哥哥。

预设与蕴涵在生活中很常见。下面是一个关于预设在审讯中使用的案例：公交车上，犯罪嫌疑人王某刚偷了一个钱包，还未及转手，就被反扒公安人员发现，于是公安人员上前暂扣了钱包并进行盘问。下面是一段询问记录。

　　　　民警：这是你的钱包吗？

　　　　王某：是。

民警：买了多长时间了，我看有点儿旧。

王某：两年了。

民警：是你一直在用吗？

王某：是。

民警：钱包里有张照片，是你女儿吗？挺可爱的。

王某：（犹豫了一下）是。

民警：看来照片放了好长时间了，都有点儿发黄了。

王某：是，一直在里面放着。

民警出示钱包，钱包里根本没有照片。

通过这段审讯，王某的谎言不攻自破。在这个案例中，公安人员设置了一个虚假的预设——"钱包里有照片"，如果王某真熟悉这个钱包，就应该否定这个预设。

五、命题与主观性

命题（proposition）只是表达句子客观的基本的语义信息。在命题之外，句子还有表达说话人态度或观点等的主观语义信息，这些语义信息就是命题的情态表达成分。命题是说话人所要传递的信息，情态（modality）是说话人对所传递的信息的主观看法和态度。命题是客观的，而情态是主观的。情态常常通过"可能""一定"等情态词，以及"我以为""我看""我相信"等小句引导成分来体现。请看下面的例子：

（114） a. 明天下雨。

　　　 b. 明天一定会下雨。

　　　 c. 明天可能会下雨。

　　　 d. 我认为明天会下雨。

（114）中四个句子表达的基本信息"明天下雨"是一样的，但说话人对这一信息真实性的确定性不同。a是最客观的陈述，主观性最弱，说话人之所以这样说可能是有依据的，比如看了天气预报。b-d的主观性比较强，主要是表达说话人的主观看法，至于"明天下雨"这件事的确信度则依次降低。

原典选读

一、Theories of meaning and kinds of meaning

John Lyons. 1995. *Linguistic Semantics: An Introduction.* Cambridge: Cambridge University Press.

【导　读】

这里的原典选自上述著作40-45页，主要讨论意义的理论和各种意义。Lyons首先对指称说（the referential theory）、意念说（the ideational theory）、行为反应说（the behaviorist theory）、用法说（the meaning-is-use theory）、验证说（the verificationist theory）和真值条件说（the truth-conditional theory）的含义做了简单说明。然后指出了意义的复杂性，提到了各种意义，比如说话者的意义、词汇意义、句子意义、语法意义和话语意义等。Lyons对意义持一种比较宽泛的看法，认为意义与言语交际之间存在内在联系。他主要区分了两种意义：描述性意义（descriptive meaning）和非描述性意义（non-descriptive meaning）。前者大致相当于命题意义、认知意义和指称意义，有真假之分。后者具有异质（heterogeneous）性，包括多种意义。Lyons特别提到的是表情意义（expressive meaning），这一意义主要表达说话人的信仰、态度和感情。

There are several distinguishable, and more or less well-known philosophical, theories of meaning: theories which seek to provide an answer to the question *What is meaning?* Among them, one might mention the following:

(i) the **referential** (or **denotational**) theory ("the meaning of an expression is what it refers to (or denotes), or stands for"; e.g., 'Fido' means Fido, 'dog' means either the general class of dogs or the essential property which they all share);

(ii) the **ideational**, or **mentalistic**, theory ("the meaning of an expression is the idea, or concept, associated with it in the mind of anyone who knows and understands the expression");

(iii) the **behaviourist** theory ("the meaning of an expression is either the stimulus that evokes it or the response that it evokes, or a combination of both, on particular occasions of utterance");

(iv) the **meaning-is-use** theory ("the meaning of an expression is determined by, if not identical with, its use in the language");

(v) the **verificationist** theory ("the meaning of an expression, if it has one, is determined by the verifiability of the sentences, or propositions, containing it");

(vi) the **truth-conditional** theory ("the meaning of an expression is its contribution to the truth-conditions of the sentences containing it").

None of these, in my view, will serve alone as the basis for a comprehensive and empirically well-motivated theory of linguistic semantics. But each of them has contributed in one way or another to the background assumptions of those who are currently working towards the construction of such a theory. I will not go into the details of any of those theories of meaning listed above. However, I will make reference to some of the key-concepts which distinguish them in the course of the chapters that follow, and I will explain these concepts in the context in which they are invoked and applied. Limitations of space will prevent me from discussing the historical connexions among the several theories or the philosophical issues associated with them. I should add that the list I have given is by no means complete and that the definitions in brackets have in certain cases been deliberately simplified.

It is now worth noting that one philosophically defensible response to the question *What is meaning?* is *There is no such thing as meaning.* This was the response, for example, of the later Wittgenstein (1953); and it has to be taken seriously. It clearly makes sense to enquire about the meaning of words, sentences and utterances, just as it makes sense to ask what they mean. In doing so, we are using the English words 'meaning' and 'mean' in one of their everyday metalinguistic functions. As we saw earlier, there are also other everyday meanings, or uses, of the noun 'meaning' and the verb 'mean'; and some philosophers at least have held these to be intimately connected with and perhaps more basic than the one that has just been exemplified. Interestingly enough they cannot always be matched one-to-one with the meanings or uses of otherwise comparable expressions in such familiar European languages as French, German,

Italian, Russian or Spanish. For example, the following two English sentences,

(30) 'What is the meaning of 'concept'?'

and

(31) 'What do you mean by the word 'concept'?',

might be translated into French as

42   *Metalinguistic preliminaries*

(30a) 'Quel est le sens de 'concept' [en anglais]?'

and

(31a) 'Qu'est-ce que tu veux dire par le mot [anglais] 'concept'?'

(and comparably into Italian and Spanish), respectively; into German as

(30b) 'Was ist die Bedeutung von 'concept' [auf Englisch]?'

and

(31b) 'Was meinst du mit dem [englischen] Wort 'concept'?';

into Russian as

(30c) 'Čto znacit [anglijskije slovo] 'concept'?'

and

(31c) 'Čto vy podrazumyvaete pod [anglijskym] slovom 'concept'?';

and so on.

In supplying these translations I have not translated the English word 'concept', because I have assumed that French, German and Russian are being used metalinguistically with reference to English. There are, of course, other possibilities, especially in the case of (31a–c). In fact, there is a whole range of possibilities, as anyone who has any practical experience of translation will be aware. But we need not go into these in the present context. What these examples show, on the basis of translation into just a few other languages, is that, in each case, the second of the two translated examples, (31a–c), uses an expression which reveals, at least etymologically, a sense of the English verb 'to mean' - **utterer's meaning**, as it is sometimes called – which relates it either to communicative intention (French 'vouloir dire', German 'meinen') or to understanding and interpretation (Russian 'podrazumevatj'). There are those who have seen utterer's meaning as being, ultimately, the basis for linguistic meaning.

For the present, however, I am concerned to make the simple point that we cannot infer the existence of meaning or meanings from the existence and meaningfulness of the everyday English word 'meaning'. Moreover, even if there is such a thing as

1.7 Theories of meaning and kinds of meaning 43

meaning (whatever 'thing' means in this context), its ontological and psychological status is surely more questionable than that of form. We shall come back to this point.

It was part of the later Wittgenstein's purpose to emphasize the diversity of the communicative functions fulfilled by language. His slogan "Don't look for the meaning, look for the use" (which does not necessarily lead to the meaning-is-use theory, though it is commonly so interpreted) must be understood with reference to this purpose. Like the so-called ordinary-language Oxford philosophers, such as J. L. Austin (whose theory of **speech acts** we shall be looking at in Part 4), he pointed out that the question *What is meaning?* tends to attract answers which are either so general as to be almost vacuous or so narrow in their definition of meaning as to leave out of account much of what ordinary users of a language think is relevant when one puts to them more specific questions about the meaning of this or that expression in their language.

In this book we are taking a fairly broad view of meaning. We are also assuming that there is an intrinsic connexion between meaning and communication. As was noted earlier, this assumption is not uncontroversial. It has been strongly challenged, for example, by Chomsky, but it is one that is commonly made by philosophers, psychologists and linguists. It enables us to give a better account of the relation between form and meaning in natural languages than does any currently available alternative.

And I would emphasize that, although I have referred here to various philosophical theories of meaning and shall draw freely upon them throughout, I am not concerned with philosophical issues as such but with the theoretical and practical problems that arise in the description of natural languages.

So far we have been talking, in a preliminary way, about the meaning of words, sentences and utterances. We have also seen that there are distinguishable senses of the English word 'meaning' which may well correspond to different, but related, kinds of meaning. But how many kinds of meaning are there? Are they all of concern to the linguist? And how do they correlate with the distinction we have drawn between lexical meaning and sentence-meaning (including, as we shall see, grammatical

44   *Metalinguistic preliminaries*

meaning), on the one hand, and between sentence-meaning and utterance-meaning, on the other?

In this book, I will make no attempt to provide a comprehensive classification of the different kinds of meaning that a linguistic theory of semantics (and pragmatics) should cover. However, it might be helpful to draw even now one very broad distinction which can be developed in more detail later. This is the distinction between **descriptive** (or **propositional**) and **non-descriptive** (or **non-propositional**) **meaning**. (Alternative terms, more or less equivalent with 'descriptive' and 'propositional', are 'cognitive' and 'referential'.) With regard to descriptive meaning, it is a universally acknowledged fact that languages can be used to make descriptive statements which are true or false according to whether the **propositions** that they express are true or false. This fact is given particular prominence in the truth-conditional theory of semantics, which has been extremely important in recent years.

Non-descriptive meaning is more heterogeneous and, in the view of many philosophers and linguists, less central. It includes what I will refer to as an **expressive** component. (Alternative more or less equivalent terms are 'affective', 'attitudinal' and 'emotive'.) Expressive meaning – i.e., the kind of meaning by virtue of which speakers express, rather than describe, their beliefs, attitudes and feelings - is often held to fall within the scope of stylistics or pragmatics. It will be demonstrated in Part 3, however, that some kinds of expressive meaning are unquestionably a part of sentence-meaning. It follows from this fact that for anyone who draws the distinction between semantics and pragmatics in terms of the distinction between sentences and utterances, expressive meaning falls, at least in part, within semantics. It also follows, as we shall see in due course, that sentence-meaning is not wholly truth-conditional.

Natural languages vary considerably in the degree to which they grammaticalize expressive meaning. English does so to a relatively low degree. For example, it does not have a rich system of grammatical moods (subjunctive, optative, dubitative, etc.) as many languages do. Like all natural languages, however, it encodes expressive meaning in much of its vocabulary and in

1.7 Theories of meaning and kinds of meaning 45

the prosodic structure of spoken utterances. We are, of course, taking the view (which, as I have noted, is not widely shared) that the meaning of sentences (in contrast with the meaning of utterances) is independent of the prosodic contour with which they are uttered: i.e., that the same sentence can be uttered with various, significantly different, prosodic contours. It can also be argued that exclamatory and contextualizing particles of the kind that one finds in many languages, are not constituents of the sentence, but of utterances which result from the use of the sentence. But expressive meaning is also lexicalized in combination with descriptive meaning, as we shall see, in many ordinary nouns, verbs and adjectives.

Other kinds of non-propositional meaning may be left until later. It is worth emphasizing, however, that the expressive functions of language cannot be sharply differentiated from their social and instrumental functions. Human beings are social beings with socially prescribed and socially sanctioned purposes. They may not always be consciously projecting one kind of self-image rather than another; they may not be deliberately expressing the feelings and attitudes that they do express in order to manipulate the hearer and achieve one goal rather than another. Nevertheless, it is impossible for them to express their feelings and attitudes in language, however personal and spontaneous these attitudes and feelings might be, otherwise than in terms of the distinctions that are encoded in particular language-systems. As we shall see throughout this book, but more especially in Part 4, expressive meaning necessarily merges with what many authors have referred to as **interpersonal**, **instrumental**, **social** or **conative**, **meaning**. In other words, as far as the structure and function of natural languages are concerned, the expressive is necessarily **socio-expressive** and the personal is necessarily **interpersonal**. Unless this fact is appreciated, it would seem to be impossible to give a proper semantic account of even such common, though not universal, grammatical categories as tense, pronouns or mood.

二、Denotation and sense

John Lyons. 1995. *Linguistic Semantics: An Introduction.* Cambridge: Cambridge University Press.

【导　读】

　　这里的原典选自上述著作77-82页，讨论指称与意义。Lyons主要讨论指称与意义之间的区别与联系。denotation和reference都表示"指称"，Lyons首先对二者进行了区分：denotation是不变的，不依赖于话语，是语言系统中某个表达形式意义的一部分；reference则会随着话语环境而变化，属于话语意义（utterance-meaning）。比如dog这个词指称一个动物类或者说定义这个类的特征，而the dog、my dog等则会随着语境的变化而指这个类中不同的个体成员。因此，他选择采用denotation这一术语。"指称"反映的是表达形式（expression）与外部世界中事物类之间的对应关系，而"意义"反映的是同一语言内部不同表达形式之间的意义关系（sense relation），如dog与animal（动物）、hound（猎犬）等词之间的关系。二者都既可以用于词这种简单的表达形式，也可以用于词的组合表达形式。二者互相依存，成逆相关关系：指称范围越大，意义就越小，反之亦然。比如animal的指称范围比dog大，但意思却没有dog具体，被包含在dog的词义中。二者之间的关系跟外延（extension）与内涵（intension）之间的关系类似。不过Lyons认为外延与内涵是指称的两个部分，成互补关系。从外延的角度讲，一个表达形式指称一个事物类；从内涵的角度讲，则是定义这个类的特征。

3.1 DENOTATION AND SENSE

Standard monolingual dictionaries of a language explain the meaning of words by providing them with metalinguistic definitions in which the object language is used as its own metalanguage (see 1.2). The format of these definitions will vary somewhat from dictionary to dictionary. It will also vary from one class of words to another, especially in the case of so-called function words, or lexically empty word-forms, such as prepositions (*of*, *in*, etc.) or the definite and indefinite articles (*the*, *a*): it is notoriously difficult to devise satisfactory dictionary definitions for such forms, whose meaning is primarily grammatical, rather than lexical (see 2.4). In this chapter we are concerned with lexically full words: lexemes that belong to the major parts of speech (nouns, verbs and adjectives, and some subclasses of adverbs).

In the definition of such words, bilingual dictionaries rely heavily on the notion of interlingual synonymy: e.g., by saying, in an English–French dictionary, that (the English word) 'dog' has (more or less) the same meaning as (the French word) 'chien'. Monolingual dictionaries also make use of the notion of synonymy (intralingual, rather than interlingual). But monolingual-dictionary definitions will usually combine paraphrase, in terms of partial intralingual synonymy, with analysis and description. For example, in defining the word 'dog' (in one of its meanings) a dictionary entry might tell us that dogs are animals belonging to a particular genus and species and that they are carnivorous, have been domesticated, and so on. We shall look at two examples of such definitions in the following section. Here I want to point out that traditional dictionary definitions can be seen as defining (in the case of words such as 'dog') two different, but complementary, aspects of lexical meaning: denotation and sense.

To say what the word 'dog' **denotes** is to identify all (and only) those entities in the world that are correctly called dogs. How one goes about identifying, in practice, everything and anything that is denoted by 'dog' is a question that we will take up presently. The important point for the moment is that some (though not all) words may be put into correspondence with classes of entities in the external world by means of the relation of **denotation**.

Denotation, as we shall see later, is intrinsically connected with **reference**. Indeed, many authors (especially those who subscribe to a referential theory of meaning: see section 1.7) draw no distinction between them, subsuming both under a broader notion of reference than the one which we shall be adopting. However, it is intuitively obvious that 'dog' does not stand for the class of dogs (or, alternatively, for some defining

property of this class) in quite the same way that 'Fido' can be used to **stand for**, or **refer to**, some particular dog.

The crudest version of the referential theory of meaning, which has been aptly dubbed the 'Fido'-Fido theory, will not work for anything other than proper names; and, as we shall see later, it does not work all that well even for proper names. There are more sophisticated and philosophical versions of the referential theory of meaning, which would justify the adoption of a broader notion of reference than the one we shall be employing in this book. But whatever terms are used and whatever theory of meaning is adopted, it is important to take account of the difference in the two ways in which language hooks on to the world. This difference, which I am associating with a terminological distinction between 'reference' and 'denotation', is all too often obscured by a loose use of the term 'reference'.

The crucial difference between reference and denotation is that the denotation of an expression is invariant and **utterance-independent**: it is part of the meaning which the expression has in the language-system, independently of its use on particular occasions of utterance. Reference, in contrast, is variable and **utterance-dependent**. For example, the word 'dog' always denotes the same class of animals (or, alternatively, the defining property of the class), whereas the phrases 'the dog' or 'my dog' or 'the dog that bit the postman' will refer to different members of the class on different occasions of utterance. Reference, as distinct from denotation, will be dealt with (as part of utterance-meaning) in a later chapter. The important point to note, for the present, is that lexemes, as such, do not have reference, but may be used as referring expressions or, more commonly, as components of referring expressions in particular contexts of utterance.

The lexeme 'dog', then, denotes a class of entities in the external world. But it is also related, in various ways, to other lexemes

ance-independent: it is part of the meaning which the expression has in the language-system, independently of its use on particular occasions of utterance. Reference, in contrast, is variable and **utterance-dependent**. For example, the word 'dog' always denotes the same class of animals (or, alternatively, the defining property of the class), whereas the phrases 'the dog' or 'my dog' or 'the dog that bit the postman' will refer to different members of the class on different occasions of utterance. Reference, as distinct from denotation, will be dealt with (as part of utterance-meaning) in a later chapter. The important point to note, for the present, is that lexemes, as such, do not have reference, but may be used as referring expressions or, more commonly, as components of referring expressions in particular contexts of utterance.

The lexeme 'dog', then, denotes a class of entities in the external world. But it is also related, in various ways, to other lexemes and expressions of English, including 'animal', 'hound', 'terrier', 'spaniel', etc. Each such relation that holds between 'dog' and other expressions of the same language-system, may be identified as one of its **sense-relations**. Descriptive synonymy, which we discussed in the last chapter, is one kind of sense-

relation. We shall look briefly at some of the other sense-relations exemplified above for 'dog' in Chapter 4. Meanwhile, the examples themselves will suffice for the purpose of explaining both the distinction between denotation and sense and, no less important, their interdependence.

The **sense** of an expression may be defined as the set, or network, of sense-relations that hold between it and other expressions of the same language. Several points may now be made in respect of this definition.

First, sense is a matter of **interlexical** and **intralingual** relations; that is to say, of relations which hold between a lexical expression and one or more other lexical expressions in the same language. Sense, as I have defined it here, is wholly internal to the language-system. This distinguishes it clearly from denotation, which relates expressions to classes of entities in the world.

What has just been said is not invalidated by the existence, in all natural languages, of various kinds of metalinguistic expressions; and this point must be emphasized (see 1.2). The distinction between sense and denotation applies to metalinguistic expressions such as 'lexeme', 'word' or 'linguistic expression' in exactly the same way as it applies to other expressions. Admittedly, it is much harder to keep one's thinking straight in the case of metalinguistic expressions than it is in respect of expressions that denote dogs and cats (or shoes, ships, sealing wax, cabbages and kings) and other such denizens of the external world. Nevertheless, it should be clear that linguistic expressions such as 'linguistic expression' and 'lexeme' are related to one another in terms of sense exactly as 'animal' and 'dog' are, whereas 'linguistic expression' and 'lexeme' are related to one another in terms of denotation in the same way as 'animal' is related to some particular dog or other animal. For example, just as 'animal' denotes a class of entities whose members are the dogs Fido, Rover, etc., as well as other subclasses of the class of animals (cows, tigers, camels, etc.), so the English-language expression 'linguistic expression' denotes a class of entities whose members are the linguistic expressions 'linguistic expression', 'lexeme', 'word', etc., as well as, say, 'dog', 'animal', etc.

Denotation, as we have seen, is a relation which holds primarily, or basically, between expressions and physical entities in the external world. But many, if not all, natural languages also contain expressions which denote various kinds of non-physical entities. Although metalinguistic expressions are not the only such expressions, they are of particular interest to the semanticist.

The second point that needs to be made explicit about sense and denotation is that both notions apply equally to lexically simple and lexically composite expressions. For example, 'domesticated canine mammal' is a lexically composite expression, whose sense and denotation is determined by the sense and denotation of its component lexemes. To make the point more technically: the sense and denotation of the composite expression is a **compositional function** of the sense and denotation of its component parts. What is meant by this will be explained in Chapter 4.

A third point, which is perhaps obvious but, like the preceding one, will be important later and needs to be clearly stated, is that sense and denotation are, in general, interdependent in that (in the case of expressions that have both sense and denotation) one would not normally know the one without having at least some knowledge of the other. This raises the possibility that either sense or denotation should be taken to be logically or psychologically more basic than the other. I will take up this question in the following section.

Sense and denotation are not only interdependent: they are inversely related to one another. The nature of this inverse relation can be explained informally as follows: the larger the denotation, the smaller the sense, and conversely. For example, the denotation of 'animal' is larger than, and includes, that of 'dog' (all dogs are animals, but not all animals are dogs), but the sense of 'animal' is less specific than, and is included in, that of 'dog'.

A comparable inverse relation is well recognized in traditional logic in terms of the difference between extension and intension. Roughly speaking, the **extension** of a term, or expression, is the class of entities that it defines, and the **intension** is the defining property of the class. Modern formal

82   *Defining the meaning of words*

semantics, as we shall see later, has exploited and developed the distinction between extension and intension in various ways. And some scholars have actually identified the sense of an expression with its intension. For reasons which become clearer later, I prefer to treat extension and intension as complementary aspects of denotation. Regardless of the view that one takes of the ontological status, or reality, of properties, it is convenient to be able to say that an expression denotes (extensionally) a class of entities and (intensionally) its defining property (i.e. the property which all members of the class share and by virtue of which they are members of the class in question). For example, it is convenient to be able to say that the word 'red' denotes, not only the class of red things, but also the property of redness. This is intended to be a philosophically neutral way of talking: neutral with respect to the long-standing philosophical controversy between nominalists and realists and neutral with respect to the typically empiricist thesis of extensionality, which has been so influential in twentieth-century logic and philosophical semantics.

Finally, as far as this section is concerned, it must be emphasized that nothing said here about sense and denotation is to be taken as implying that either the one or the other is fully determinate in the case of all, or even most, lexemes in the vocabularies of natural languages. On the contrary, the sense of most lexemes, and therefore of most lexically composite expressions, would seem to be somewhat fuzzy at the edges. Similarly, it is very often unclear whether a particular entity falls within the denotation of an expression or not. What then does it mean to say that someone knows the descriptive meaning of particular expressions in his or her native language? Indeed, how do we manage to communicate with one another, more or less successfully, by means of language, if the descriptive meaning of most lexemes – their sense and denotation – is inherently fuzzy or indeterminate? This question will be taken up in section 3.4.

三、Sub–classes of antonyms

D. Alan Cruse. 1986. *Lexical semantics*. Cambridge: Cambridge University Press.

【导 读】

这里的原典选自上述著作206－214页，重点介绍级差反义词的子类。文中的antonyms特指级差反义词。Cruse将级差反义词分成了三小类：两极反义词（polar antonym），如long－short、heavy－light、fast－slow；重叠反义词（overlapping antonym），如good－bad、kind－cruel、polite－rude；等值性反义词（equipollent antonym），如hot－cold、happy－sad。其中重叠反义词还可以分出一个否定反义词（privative antonyms），如clean－dirty、safe－dangerous，表现得像互补反义词。heavier是heavy的假比较级（pseudo－comparative），因为heavier并不预设参与比较的东西都是重的；hotter是hot的真比较级（true comparative），因为hotter的前提是两个比较项都是热的。这三类反义词可以通过假比较级和真比较级来区分：两极反义词中的两个形容词只有假比较级；重叠反义词中的两个形容词一个有假比较级，另一个有真比较级；等值性反义词中的两个形容词都有真比较级。这三类反义词描述的性质不同：两极反义词往往是中性、客观地描述，大部分词的级差属性可以用英寸、克等单位来度量；重叠反义词都带有极端评价义，往往一个描述人们期望的性质，另一个描述人们不期望的性质；等值性反义词比较少，通常表达主观的感觉、情感或评价。形容词进入How X is it? 格式有两种意思，How heavy is it? 只是问重量，并没有说明东西重还是轻；How hot is it? 则是在热的前提下问热到什么程度。前一种问句是不偏不倚型的（impartial），后一种问句则是定向型的（committed）。这三类反义词在进入这一问句时的表现不一样：两极反义词中只有一个可以形成how问句，而且这个问句是不偏不倚型的，如How long is it? 可以说，How short is it? 不太好；重叠反义词都可以形成how问句，一个是不偏不倚型的，如How good is it? ，另一个则是定向型的，如How bad is it? ；等值性反义词都可以形成how问句，而且两个都是定向型的，如How hot is it? 和How cold is it? 此外，三类反义词还存在一系列语义差异，为了说明这些细微的差异，作者采用了图示的方法。阅读时，需要注意汉语中对应的反义词是否也有类似的差异。

9.4 Sub-classes of antonyms

Antonyms can be divided into three (possibly four) sub-types. I shall delimit the types initially on the basis of the relationship between the semantic properties of those lexical units of the adjective lexemes which appear in sentences of the form *It's X*, and the semantic properties of the lexical units which appear in corresponding comparative forms (although, as we shall see, there are other correlated differences). There are basically two possible relationships, one involving what we shall call †**pseudo-comparatives**, and the other †**true comparatives**. Consider, first, the relation between the occurrences of *heavy* in 5 and 6:

5. This box is heavy.
6. This box is heavier than that one.

Notice that a preceding assertion that the box is *light* yields oddness in the case of 5, but not with 6:

206

7. ? This box is light, but it's heavy.
8. This box is light, but it's heavier than that one.

In other words, *heavier* does not mean "heavy to a greater degree", but "of greater weight". We shall therefore describe *heavier* as the pseudo-comparative of *heavy* (in, e.g., *It's heavy*). (Evidence will be offered below that two distinct, but related, senses of *heavy* are involved here – *heavier* is the true comparative of one, and the pseudo-comparative of the other.) Consider, now, the relation between the occurrences of *hot* in 9 and 10:

9. It's hot today.
10. It's hotter today than yesterday.

A preceding assertion that the weather is *cold* produces oddness in both cases:

11. ? It's cold today, but it's hot.
12. ? It's cold today, but it's hotter than yesterday.

It seems that *hotter* DOES mean "hot to a greater degree". We shall therefore describe *hotter* as the true comparative of *hot*, and it will be argued that 11 and 12 contain the SAME sense of *hot*.

We are now in a position to define the three groups of antonyms:

Group I: there is a pseudo-comparative corresponding to each member of a pair.

It's short, but it's longer than the other one.
It's long, but it's shorter than the other one.
e.g. *heavy : light, fast : slow, high : low, deep : shallow, wide : narrow, thick : thin, difficult : easy*

Group II: there is a pseudo-comparative corresponding to one member of a pair, but the other member has a true comparative.

John's a dull lad, but he's cleverer than Bill.
? Bill's a clever lad, but he's duller than John.
e.g. *good : bad, pretty : plain, kind : cruel, polite : rude*

Group III: both members of a pair have true comparatives.

? It's hot, but it's colder than yesterday.
? It's cold, but it's hotter than yesterday.
e.g. *nice : nasty, sweet : sour, proud of : ashamed of, happy : sad*

Group II has a sub-group consisting of those hybrid opposites like *clean :*

207

dirty and *safe : dangerous*, which in the positive degree behave like complementaries. In respect of their graded uses, however, there is no doubt that they belong to Group II:

? It's still clean, but it's dirtier than before.
It's still dirty, but it's cleaner than before.

Accordingly, two sub-groups will be distinguished. It would be useful to have names for these antonym types. We shall therefore call those in Group I †**polar antonyms**, those in Group II †**overlapping antonyms**, and those in Group III †**equipollent antonyms**. Group II(b), a sub-class of overlapping antonyms, will be termed †**privative antonyms**.[10]

The three groups that have been established also display differences with respect to certain other properties. First, members of the three groups differ in respect of the sort of properties they typically refer to. Polar (Group I) antonyms (e.g. *long : short*) are typically evaluatively neutral, and objectively descriptive. In the majority of cases, the underlying scaled property can be measured in conventional units, such as inches, grams, or miles per hour. Overlapping (Group II) antonyms all have an evaluative polarity as part of their meaning: one term is commendatory (e.g. *good, pretty, polite, kind, clean, safe, honest*) and the other is deprecatory (e.g. *bad, plain, rude, cruel, dirty, dangerous, dishonest*). What distinguishes privative antonyms in this respect is not entirely clear: it may be that they characteristically refer to situations where the desirable state is less the presence of some valued property than the absence of an undesirable one, such as dirt or danger. All equipollent (Group III) antonyms – there are not many of them – refer to distinctly subjective sensations or emotions (e.g. *hot* : *cold*, *happy* : *sad*), or evaluations based on subjective reactions, rather than on 'objective' standards (e.g. *nice* : *nasty*, *pleasant* : *unpleasant*).

Second, the three groups differ in respect of the possibility of forming questions on the pattern of *How X is it?*, with the main (nuclear) stress of the sentence on *X* (all antonyms occur normally in *how*-questions with the stress on *how* or *is*); and they differ too, with regard to the semantic nature of the questions thus formed. Consider the question *How heavy is it?* Just as *X is heavier than Y* tells us nothing about the actual weight of X or Y, the questioner here expresses no presumption or expectation concerning the weight of the questioned item. Such expressions will be described as **'impartial** (in this case, impartial with respect to the contrast between *It's heavy* and *It's light*). On the other hand, *How hot is it?* and *It's hotter than before* both carry a presupposition that *hot*, rather than

208

cold, would be an appropriate description of the questioned item.[11] These expressions will be described as **'committed**. (Notice that although *How heavy is it?* is impartial, *How heavy is it?* is committed.) The characterisation of the three groups in respect of *How X is it?* questions (which will henceforth simply be referred to as *how*-questions) is as follows:

Polar: Only one member of a pair yields a normal *how*-question (cf. *How long is it?* but *? How short is it?*), and this question is impartial.[12]

Overlapping: Both terms of a pair yield normal *how*-questions, but one term yields an impartial question (e.g. *How good is it?*), and the other term yields a committed question (e.g. *How bad is it?*).

Equipollent: Both terms of a pair yield normal *how*-questions, and both questions are committed (*How hot is it?*, *How cold is it?*).

It is worth noting that quantified comparatives of the form *twice as*/*half as X* show the same patterning as *how*-questions in respect of normality and impartiality.[13]

This is a convenient point to raise the matter of distinctions of lexical units within lexemes. Consider the occurrences of the form *long* in 13, 14 and 15:

13. It's long.
14. This one is longer than that one.
15. How long is it?

How many different lexical units *long* occur in these sentences? The following evidence is relevant. First of all, 16 is zeugmatic. This suggests that the sense of *long* which appears in 15 is different from that which appears in *It isn't long* (and presumably also in 13):

16. A: How long is it?
    B: ? It isn't.

On the other hand, if B's answer in 17 can be taken as equivalent to a comparative, it is not odd in the way that would be expected if 15 and 14 contained different senses:

17. A: How long is this one?
    B: More so than the last one, but still a bit short.

(cf. also:

A: What is the length of this one?
B: Greater than that of the last one, but still short.)

209

On this evidence, then, it would seem that 14 and 15 contain one and the same sense of *long*, and 13 a different one. This is confirmed by the suggestion of zeugma in 18, which indicates a distinction between 13 and 14:

18. A: Is this one long?
    B: ? No – more so than the last one, though.

The *long* in *twice as long* is harder to test, but it seems reasonable to assume that it is the same as that in 14 and 15. Similar considerations lead to the conclusion that *short* in *It's short* and *It's shorter* represent distinct senses; likewise *clean* in *It's clean* is different from *clean* in *It's cleaner* and *How clean is it?* The two senses of *long* (likewise those of *heavy*, *wide*, *fast*, *clean*, etc.) are, of course, systematically related and their respective units are to be assigned to the same lexeme. Notice that in 19, 20 and 21 there is no need to postulate different lexical units *hot*:

19. It's hot.
20. It's hotter than yesterday.
21. How hot is it?

Many of the differences between the groups can be given an intuitively satisfying explanation if we assume that for overlapping and equipollent antonym pairs (but not polars) the properties denoted by each of the members of a pair are conceived as being quasi-autonomous. That is to say, whereas SHORTNESS, for example, is no more and no less than the absence of LENGTH, GOODNESS and BADNESS, CLEVERNESS and DULLNESS, and HOTNESS and COLDNESS are to some extent independent properties. At a more abstract level, of course, there is a common underlying gradable property for both members of a pair (otherwise they would not be opposites): MERIT for *good* : *bad*, TEMPERATURE for *hot* : *cold*, etc. But at a more superficial level, the properties have a certain independence. We can thus say that whereas a single scale underlies a pair of polar antonyms, there are two scales underlying a pair of overlapping or equipollent antonyms. This already offers a natural explanation for certain of the differences between polar antonyms, on the one hand, and overlapping and equipollent antonyms on the other. It is reasonable to assume that the normality of *twice*/*half as X* and *How X is it?* depends on the existence of a scale of X-NESS. *Short*, *slow* and *shallow*, for example, are odd in these frames because there is no scale of X-NESS. *Short*, *slow* or SHALLOWNESS. (A speaker is, of course, free to create an ad hoc scale: *How slow is it?*, although not fully normal, is by no means uninterpretable.)

210

The relationship between the senses associated with a pair of polar antonyms can be portrayed diagrammatically as shown in fig. 9.2. We need now to be able to picture overlapping and equipollent antonyms in a way

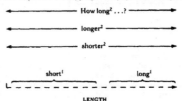

Figure 9.2

which will account naturally for their differences. Consider, first, the equipollent type, represented by *hot* : *cold*. Since nothing that is *colder* can be *hot*, and nothing *hotter* can be *cold*, then if we assume that each term is restricted to its own scale it appears that nothing can fall simultaneously on the two scales; or, to put it another way, there is no overlap between the scales of COLDNESS and HOTNESS. The relationship between the scales can therefore be represented as shown in fig. 9.3.

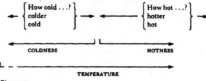

Figure 9.3

There is an important difference between the *hot* : *cold* contrast and the *long* : *short* contrast: the difference between *hot* and *cold* is in a sense absolute, rather than relative. The distinction is based neither on an average nor on a norm, but ultimately on a difference of sensation quality. However, although the distinction between *hot* and *cold* is absolute, once we are on one or other of the scales a principle of relativity applies. The temperature required for a day to qualify as *hot* is much lower than that required of an oven, which in turn is lower than that required of a furnace.

211

Let us now consider how *warm* and *cool* fit into the picture. The facts are somewhat complex. First, the normality of all the following sentences suggests that each of the terms operates on its own scale:

How hot is it?	X is twice as hot as Y.
How warm is it?	X is twice as warm as Y.
How cool is it?	Z is twice as cool as Y.
How cold is it?	X is twice as cold as Y.

How cool is it? and *twice as cool* are the least normal of these expressions, but even here the oddness is not of the same order as that of *? twice as short*. (It is interesting to note that hotness, warmness and coldness – but not coolness – are physiologically distinct sensations.) If we accept the linguistic evidence for the existence of separate scales, then the picture is as shown in fig. 9.4.

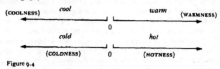

Figure 9.4

This arrangement, however, fails to account for the peculiar distribution of *cooler* and *warmer*. The problem is that *cooler* can be used of any temperature provided that it does not fall within the range of *cold*, and *warmer* can be used of any temperature that does not fall within the range of *hot*. Thus we can speak of one *hot* furnace being *cooler* than another, and of the temperature at the North Pole as being *warmer* than that of the surface of the moon. It is almost as if there were two different lexical terms *cool*: *cool*¹, which had its own scale, and denoted a moderate degree of coldness, and *cool*², which acted as a polar antonym of *hot*; similarly, there might be a *warm*¹ with its own scale, and a *warm*², which was a polar antonym of *cold*. This would yield a picture like that shown in fig. 9.5. In this way the observed range of *cooler* could be explained as the

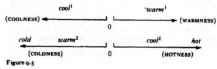

Figure 9.5

212

combined ranges of *cooler*¹ and *cooler*² and, similarly, *mutatis mutandis* with *warmer*. An obvious difficulty with this proposal is that there do not, at first sight, appear to be any normal uses of *cool*² and *warm*² to denote, respectively, 'relatively *cool* on the *hot* scale' and 'relatively *warm* on the *cold* scale'. A day on which the temperature is 'mildly hot' is a *warm* day, and by no stretch of the imagination a *cool* day. There do occur, however, in special circumstances, uses of *cool* and *warm* which correspond closely to what one would expect from *cool*² and *warm*²:

> Place the mixture in a cool oven.
> This substance burns with a cool flame.
> Put it in the warm part of the refrigerator.

An *oven* and a *flame* can perhaps be regarded as inherently *hot*, and a *refrigerator* as inherently *cold*: under these circumstances, *warm* and *cool* behave like polar antonyms of *cold* and *hot*. If the above analysis is correct, then we have four opposite pairs: *hot* : *cold*, *warm*¹ : *cool*¹, *hot* : *cool*², and *cold* : *warm*². This account sheds some light on the properties of, and relations between, *cold*, *cool*, *warm* and *hot*, but it cannot be denied that many problems remain, and it could be that a rather different sort of model is required from the one we have been using.

In the case of overlapping antonyms, exemplified by *good* : *bad*, things that are *bad* may nonetheless be *better*; whatever is *good*, however (for the majority of speakers), cannot be normally qualified as *worse*. Thus the scale of BADNESS must overlap the scale of MERIT (over which *good*²

)erates), but not extend into the region on the MERIT scale covered by *good*¹. The relationships between the terms associated with the scale of MERIT can therefore be pictured as shown in fig. 9.6.

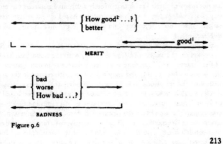

Figure 9.6

213

There is a theoretical third possibility for the relation between two sub-scales, which, if realised, would yield a fourth group of antonyms. There could be two completely overlapping scales, as shown in fig. 9.7. The predicted properties of such a group would be:

a. both terms of a pair would have pseudo-comparatives
b. both terms would yield impartial questions
c. both terms would be normal and impartial in quantified comparatives

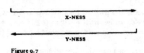

Figure 9.7

There are no fully convincing examples of this type of opposition in English, although the pair *hard* : *soft* (as applied, for instance, to cheese or butter) is difficult to classify, and might be a candidate.

9.5 Inherentness

It has been argued that the scale of MERIT on which *good* and *better* operate overlaps with that of BADNESS, a consequence of this being that something *bad* can be described as being *better* than something which is even worse. However, this general statement needs qualification and refinement, in view of cases like 22:

22a. Bill's accident was worse than John's.
b. ? John's accident was better than Bill's.

It appears that, after all, not every *bad* thing can be normally described as *better* than something else, even when that something else is qualifiable as *worse*. The following is a selection of lexical items which do not collocate normally with better: *headache, depression, failure, debt, famine, drought, storm, earthquake, flood*. They are all nouns whose referents may be said to be 'inherently bad'. Apparently *better* will collocate normally only with nouns which can collocate normally with *good*. A related peculiarity of inherently bad nouns is that they cannot be questioned with *How good is . . .?*:

23. ? How good was the drought last year?

214

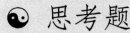

思考题

1. 根据下列材料回答问题。

瓜							
冬瓜	南瓜	西瓜	苦瓜	丝瓜	黄瓜	木瓜	哈密瓜
wax gourd	pump-kin	watermel-on	bitter gourd	towel gourd	cucum-ber	papaya	hami mel-on

（1）"瓜"与"冬瓜""南瓜"等是什么词义关系？

（2）从材料看，汉语和英语有什么不同？

2. 下列词具有什么共同的语义成分？

（1）tigress hen aunt maiden

（2）doe mare debutante widow

（3）ewe vixen girl woman

3. 请从现代汉语烹饪语义场找出至少六个动词，并用语义成分分析法分析。

4. 分析下列句子中状语的语义指向。

（1）他早早地炸了盘花生米。

（2）他喜滋滋地炸了盘花生米。

（3）他脆脆地炸了盘花生米。

5. 说说下列句子的蕴涵和预设。

（1）连爱因斯坦都不会解这个方程式。

（2）她比以前更漂亮了。

6. 分析下列句子的歧义及其产生原因。

（1）我今天碰到了一个同学。

（2）He sold the car to his brother in New York.

（3）我想起来了。

（4）放弃美丽的女人让人心碎。

（5）父母让我找好房子。

（6）They are visiting firemen.

（7）被控谋杀两岁亲生女 美妇获判无罪震惊全美（新闻标题）

（8）Call me a taxi.

📖 拓展阅读书目

📄 D. Alan Cruse. 1986. *Lexical semantics*. Cambridge: Cambridge University Press.

📄 John Lyons. 1977. *Semantics* (Vol. 1). Cambridge: Cambridge University Press.

📄 利奇. 1974. 语义学. 李瑞华, 等, 译（据1981年的修订版）. 上海：外语教育出版社, 1987.

第七章

语用与语篇

　　本章介绍语用和语篇。言语交际中信息的表达和理解是最为重要的，因此需要弄清楚与信息结构相关的一些概念，比如新信息和旧信息、话题和说明、预设和焦点。语言的使用不仅局限于言语的表达和对信息意义的理解，还涉及语言与行为之间的关系，所以本章还着重介绍了言语行为和会话含义理论。在言语交际过程中，要使交际顺利进行，言谈双方就要共同遵守合作原则及相关准则等。

　　第二节则从三个方面介绍语篇：语篇类型、语篇的切分（涉及语篇韵律）以及语篇语法的分析原则。

第一节 语 用

语用，用通俗的话来说，是指语言的使用。这可以从"语用学"的英语术语pragmatics看出来，该词中的拉丁语词根pragma-的意思是"行动，做"。所以，语用一般理解为语言的实用或使用。

语言的使用，简言之，就是指说话人运用语言符号进行言语交际的活动。若从信息论的角度来看，整个言语交际的活动大致可以概括为：在一定的交际场景下，说话人将自己要说的话语信息通过选用恰当准确的语言形式进行编码，然后表达出来；输出后的言语信息传递到听话人一方；当受话人接收到言语信息后，会根据说话人话语信息的字面意义并结合当时的环境来对所听到的信息进行解码和理解，并及时做出反馈，从而继续进行下一轮交际。言谈双方的交际过程如图7-1所示。

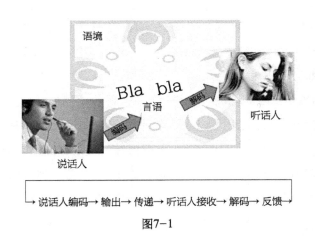

图7-1

语言学的语用研究是要考察在不同语境中话语意义是如何被恰当地表达和准确地理解的，并且要寻找和确立使话语意义得以恰当表达和准确理解的基本原则和准则。具体来说，语用就是要研究在语言的使用过程中，说话人针对特定的语境如何把自己的意图通过恰当的语言形式表达出来，听话人依据说话人话语信息的字面意义和特定的环境又是如何推导出说话人所说话语的准确含义的。

可以看出，语言的使用涉及与语用交际相关的概念和知识。比如，与信息结构相关的新信息和旧信息、话题和说明、预设和焦点。另外，语言的使用不仅仅是局限于对言语信息意义的理解，还涉及语言与行为之间的关系。因此，还要了解言语行为这一重要的语用学理论。在言语交际过程中，要使得交际顺利地进行，交际双方就要共同遵守一些规则，这就涉及合作原则及相关准则等基本的语用原则。这一节将对上述与语用相关的基本内容进行介绍。

一、旧信息与新信息

在言语交际中，人们会常说"某某说的话信息量很大"，这不光是指信息数量之大，也指信息内容对听话人来说是新的，是有价值含量的。所以，新信息（new information）是说话人认为听话人未知的信息；相对地，旧信息（given information）是说话人认为听话人已知的信息。

  （1）<u>公务员基本工资标准</u>将每年或每两年调整一次。

    <u>旧信息（已知的）</u> + <u>新信息（未知的）</u>

当说话人告诉听话人（1）这则信息时，首先认为"公务员都有一个基本工资标准"是听话人已经知道的信息，是旧信息；但后面说这个标准"将每年或每两年调整一次"则被认为是听话人不知道的，是新信息。所以，一般而言，信息结构是按照由已知信息到未知信息，也就是从旧信息到新信息来编排的。

  如果从概念在大脑中的认知状态的角度来看，在当前言谈交际中已经处于激活（active）状态的概念，是听话人已知的信息，即旧信息。而有些在当前言谈交际中暂时未被激活的概念，但是听话人可以通过背景知识来推知它的所指，这种概念信息处于半激活（semi-active）状态，这类信息是易推信息（accessible information）。完全不能被激活的概念，亦即对听话人来说是全新的，这类就是不可被激活（non-active）的新信息。易推信息的理解，或者被完全激活，需要依靠听话人的知识系统，这主要包括如下三方面：人类的共有知识、涉及言谈场景的知识、说话人和听话人共享的知识。

  （2）a. 北京是中华人民共和国的首都。

    b. 去建国门，坐1号线和2号线都可以。

    c. 2014年年末，北京市常住人口2151.6万人。

上面a句"北京是中华人民共和国的首都"若在中国人的言谈交际中出现，它一定是已经处于激活状态的旧信息，这是每个中国人都应知道的常识。b句可以认为是易推信息，假设交际双方都是北京人，或者对北京地铁交通比较熟悉，那么听话人可以根据"共享知识"来推知"1号线和2号线"是指北京地铁的线路。c句是不可被激活的全新的信息，一般人，即使是地道北京人，也未必知道北京市常住人口的具体数字，所以该信息对普通交际者来说完全不能被激活。

相对而言，"旧信息—易推信息—新信息"的三分要比"旧信息—新信息"的二分更符合人们日常交际的实际情况。信息的新与旧不是截然二分的，还有介于二者之间的信息状态。对介于两者之间信息状态的理解需要听话人借助相关的背景知识和当前的交际环境来进行。

二、话题和说明

人们在交际时，说一句话也好，说一段话也好，都应该围绕着一个关涉的对象进行交谈，从而使得交际的内容明确。一个句子中信息内容所关涉的那个对象就是"话题（topic）"，准确地说是句话题（sentence topic），它是句子表达信息的基点；而句子中针对话题展开的其他部分是"说明"（comment），是对话题所关涉对象的陈述。

就一段语篇（无论是口语还是书面语）而言，则有个语篇话题（discourse topic）。语篇话题可以理解为语篇的语义中心，这是从语篇的语义结构着眼的。一个实体对象被认定为语篇话题，当且仅当：说话人说出这段话和听话人在听到并处理这段话时，说话人能够预测听话人可以理解他所说的这段话的意图，是要向听话人进一步提供或要求其反馈有关这个实体对象的信息。

（3）a 它的干呢，通常是丈把高，像是加以人工似的，一丈以内，绝无旁枝；b 它所有的丫枝呢，一律向上，而且紧紧靠拢，也像是加以人工似的，成为一束，绝无横逸斜出；c 它的宽大的叶子也是片片向上，几乎没有斜生的，更不用说倒垂了；d 它的皮，光滑而有银色的晕圈，微微泛出淡青色。（选自茅盾《白杨礼赞》）

（3）中的这段文字是以"白杨树"为话题的语篇。先单看由分号隔开的四个句子：a句的句话题就是"它的干"，其中语气词"呢"的作用在于标明其前成分是话题，而后面的几个小句"通常是丈把高，像是加以人工似的，一丈以内，绝无旁枝"是对句话题"白杨树的干"的说明。同理，后面b、c和d三句的句话题分别是："它的丫枝""它的叶子"和"它的皮"。

从整体上来看这段话，显然"白杨树"是语篇的话题。其中四个分句分别从树干、树枝、树叶和树皮四方面作为陈述内容来说明话题。图7-2清晰地反映了"白杨树"作为话题在语篇中的统领作用。树干、树枝、树叶和树皮这四个说明项分别从不同角度，如树干的高度、树枝的密度、树叶的生长方向和树皮的质感、颜色等对白杨树的特征做了陈述。图7-3展示了在这个语篇中，语篇话题和句话题之间的关系。

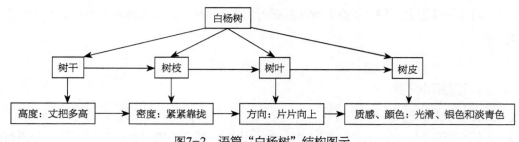

图7-2　语篇"白杨树"结构图示

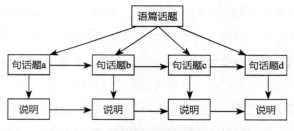

图7-3　语篇话题与句话题的关系图示

　　上文说到，句话题是说话者选择的传递信息的基点，而这一选择跟说话者如何组织整个语篇信息结构有关。整篇话语中各个句子的话题往往有内在的联系，组成"话题链（topic chain）"。比如，在（3）中，树干、树枝、树叶和树皮这四个句话题是从不同角度来描写整个语篇的话题"白杨树"。可见，话题链是一段由一个或数个句子所组成并由各句所共有的话题所统领的话语。每个句话题都是围绕语篇话题展开的，一个语篇有一个共同的语篇话题，使得语篇中的各个语段凝聚为整体；各个段落和段落中的句话题，使得语篇的组织有了层次和结构。

　　在一个话题链中，当语篇话题首次引入之后，后面相继出现的各个句子中涉及语篇话题时，说话人会选用各种指代形式，比如代词指代，或者省略，或重复原话题形式等来回指语篇话题。这种回指语篇话题所采用的不同形式手段直接影响话题的延续性。就零形回指、代词、完整的名词形式这三种回指话题的手段而言，形式越轻，延续同一话题的可能性越大，即零形回指＞代词＞完整的名词形式。采用越轻的形式手段，说明被代替的成分可及性（该成分所指对象在大脑中的激活程度）就越高，表明它与之前的话题成分延续性越大；采用较重的形式手段，则说明所替代的成分可及性低，表明指代成分与之前话题成分的延续性越小。

从句子信息结构的角度来看，一个句子所传达的信息，分为旧信息和新信息两部分。旧信息是已知的，它是被陈述说明的部分，也就是句话题。由此可见，句话题所关涉的对象一般是已知的、有定的。也就是说，说话者所选择的话题，是说话者所认为的听说双方都可以确定所指的对象。

从句法上看，不同语言话题的句法表现可以不同。比如汉语中，如果使用正常语调和一般句式，则句首的第一个担任语义角色的成分是话题。所以，汉语的句话题一般都位于句首，是句子的主语，可以由语气词"啊、呐、噻、吧"来标记其前成分为话题，比如（4）-（7）。

（4）这个人啊，一定是个好人。

（5）他自己的小孩呐，也不大听他的话。

（6）他辞职的意思噻，已经打消了。

（7）丈夫吧，找不着事儿；孩子们吧，又不肯念书。

上面各句中"啊、呐、噻、吧"之前的成分都是句话题，都在句首，都是句子的主语。在有些语言中，比如日语，有专门标记话题的助词は（wa），比如（8）。

（8）象は　　　　鼻が　　　　長い。

大象-话题　　鼻子-主语　　很长

"大象鼻子长。"

（8）中，"象"是说话者要谈论的对象，即话题。说话人以此为基点，要说明的是和大象相关涉的信息，即后一部分"鼻子长"。其中，"鼻子"是句子的主语，"长"是句子的谓语。

虽然汉语的主语一般就是话题，但是话题和主语还是有区别的：主语与谓语动词有直接的密切关系，由施事、受事等中心语义角色的成分充当。而话题则可以由担任外围语义角色的成分（时间、方所、工具等）充当，还可以与谓语动词完全没有关系，比如（9）-（10）。

（9）他是个日本女人。（意思是：他的佣人是个日本女人。）

（10）你也破了。（意思是：你的鞋也破了。）

（9）-（10）两个例子中，"他"和"你"与各自句中的谓语没有语义角色关系。真正和谓语有语义角色关系的是主语"他的佣人"和"你的鞋"。但是，从语用的角度看，这两句话所传达的信息是关于"他"和"你"的。

三、预设和焦点

"预设"（presupposition）有狭义和广义两种理解。从狭义上研究预设，认为一个句子一经形成，预设就已寓于句义之中，即语义预设，这是完全抛弃了语境的概念。从广义上研究预设，是将预设看成交际双方预先设定的已知共享信息，即语用预设。语用预设是以句子意义和结构为基础，结合语境推导出来的。

当我们说X预设Y时，是说Y是X成立的先决条件。换句话说，如果对X的肯定和否定都不影响Y为真这一事实，那么Y是X的预设。在（11）中，无论是肯定形式X（约翰的自行车需要修理），还是对X的否定（约翰的自行车不需要修理），都不影响Y（约翰有一辆自行车）为真。

（11）X：John's bike needs repairing.（约翰的自行车需要修理。）

　　　Y：John has a bike.（约翰有一辆自行车。）

从真值条件的角度来分析上面的预设关系，可以总结如下：① 如果X为真，Y一定为真。例如，如果约翰的自行车需要修理，他一定拥有一辆自行车。② 如果X为假，Y仍然为真。例如，如果约翰的自行车不需要修理，他还是拥有一辆自行车。③ 如果Y为真，X有可能为真，也有可能为假。例如，如果约翰确实有一辆自行车，他的自行车既可以是需要修理，也可以是不需要修理，两种情况皆可。④ 如果Y为假，X一定为假。例如，如果约翰没有自行车，那么说他的自行车需要修理则为假。

在交际过程中，听话人可以通过说话人所说语句中的一些语言成分来判断这句话预设了什么，我们把这些能产生预设的语言成分叫作预设触发语（presupposition-triggers）。从句法特征角度看，预设触发语的类型很多，（12）和（13）分别以定指名词组和时间从句的时间词作为预设触发语。

（12）John saw/didn't see **the man with two heads**.

　　　→There exists a man with two heads.

　　　（约翰看见/没看见**有两个头的人**。→存在一个有两个头的人。）

（13）**Before** Strawson was even born, Freg noticed/didn't notice presupposition.

　　→Strawson was born.

　　（甚至在施特劳森出生**之前**，弗雷格就注意到/没有注意到预设。→施特劳森出生了。）

（12）中"the man with two heads"是一个定指名词成分，尤其是其中的定冠词，预设了存在一个交际双方共知的定指对象，所以不管约翰看没看见有两个头的人，它都预设了有这么一个长有两个头的人的存在。（13）中时间从句中的"before"，是说在它引导的从句所述事件之前，即施特劳森出生之前，这预设了从句所描述的事件已经发生存在了，即施特劳森出生了。可见，预设触发语有助于交际双方理解话语中的共享知识背景，它在言语交际中有重要的作用。

在言语交际中，说话人总是会将一些重要的、有价值的信息，即新信息传递给对方。而句子的新信息一般是说话人想要表达的意义重点，是希望听话人能多加关注的部分，这就是句子的"焦点（focus）"之所在。

焦点的类型很多，它的表现手段也不尽相同。从信息结构的角度来讲，在汉语中，焦点对应着新信息，也对应着话题结构中的说明部分，这是信息焦点（information focus），如"张三考了第一名"，其中"第一名"是焦点，在表现形式上焦点成分承载语调重音。有些句子的焦点成分可以通过焦点敏感算子（focus-sensitive operator）来标明，这类叫作语义焦点（semantic focus），如"李四明天只上数学课"，其中"只"是焦点敏感算子，表明其后成分"数学课"是语义焦点。再比如对比焦点（contrastive focus），它可以通过"是"来标明对比焦点之所在，如"是王二打碎了鱼缸"，其中"是"是焦点标记，标明其后是对比焦点成分，同时排除了其他人打碎鱼缸的可能。还有像话题焦点（topical focus），它一般是两个对举的"话题-说明"结构，构成对比性话题（contrastive topic），两个话题本身就是焦点之所在，如"猪肉赵五不吃，牛肉他吃"，其中"猪肉"和"牛肉"是两个对比性话题，是两个话题焦点。

在有些语言中，焦点成分会由专门的句法形态标记来标示，如索马里语中，表示焦点的虚词baa放在名词后面，那么这个名词就是句子传递的信息焦点，例如（14）。

（14）Amina　　　baa　　　wargeyskii　　keentay.
阿米娜　　　焦点标记　　报纸　　　买
（是阿米娜买了报纸。）

英语中的"It is...that..."句式也是标示焦点的，is后的成分为焦点，例如，在It is Bill who writes poetry（是比尔写的诗）这句话中，Bill 就是焦点。

四、言语行为

言语行为理论（Speech Act Theory），是语用学研究中的一个重要理论。它最初是由英国哲学家约翰·奥斯汀（John Austin）在20世纪50年代提出的。根据言语行为理论，我们说话的同时是在实施某种行为。奥斯汀将言语行为分为如下三类，这就是他著名的"言语行为三分说"。

第一，言内行为（也叫叙事行为、说话行为）（the locutionary act）：是指使用发音器官，发出语音，并按照规则将它们排成合格的词或句子。这种发出语音、说出带有意义的词和句子的行为，就是言内行为。

第二，言外行为（也叫施事行为、行事行为）（the illocutionary act）：是表达说话者的意图的行为，它是在说某些话时所实施的行为。

第三，言后行为（也叫成事行为、取效行为）（the perlocutionary act）：是通过某些话所实施的行为，或是讲某些话所导致的行为，它是话语所产生的后果或所引起的变化，是通过讲某些话所完成的行为。

言内行为、言外行为和言后行为这三种言语行为实际上是整个言语过程的三个不同阶段，是统一于同一话语之中的。这从下面奥斯汀所举的一个例子中可以看出：

A. 言内行为（也叫叙事行为、说话行为）

他对我说："你不能做这件事！"

B. 言外行为（也叫施事行为、行事行为）

他抗议我做这件事。

C. 言后行为（也叫成事行为、取效行为）

他使我恢复了理智，把我劝阻了。

或者：他使我烦恼。

美国的哲学语言学家约翰·塞尔（John Searle）把言外行为分为五类，每一类行为都有一个共同的、普遍的目的。这五大类分别是：① 断言类（Assertives），是说话人对某种事情的状况、被表达命题的真实性承担义务，如（15）；② 指令类（Directives），是说话人试图要听话者做某事情，如（16）；③ 承诺类（Commissives），是说话人自己承诺他将要做某事情，如（17）；④ 表达类（Expressives），是说话人要表达对某一事情、事态的感情和态度等，如（18）；⑤ 宣告类（Declarations），是说话人通过说话来改变所提及的事情或实体的现状，如（19）。

（15）We concluded to go out/that we would go out. 我们决定出去。（断言类）

（16）Open the window! 打开窗户！（指令类）

（17）I will bring you the book tomorrow without fail. 我保证我明天把书带来。（承诺类）

（18）It's really kind of you to have thought of me. 你能为我们着想真是太好了。（表达类）

（19）I now declare the meeting open. 我宣布大会开幕。（宣告类）

根据交际意图的实现方式的不同，可以把言语行为分为直接言语行为（direct speech act）和间接言语行为（indirect speech act）。说话人采用某种言外行为（行事行为）的表达方式来实现其自身预期所能实现的意图，这是直接言语行为，如用祈使句来表示请求，用疑问句来表示询问。直接言语行为句中往往含有"告诉、请求、保证、感谢、宣布"之类具体指明言外行为的施为动词。有时候，人们出于某种考虑，采用某一种言外行为的表达方式来完成另一种言外行为，这是间接言语行为。间接言语行为理论是美国哲学语言家塞尔提出来的。塞尔指出，要理解间接言语行为这个概念，先得接受"字面用意"的概念，间接言语行为就是从"字面用意"推断出来的间接用意。

间接言语行为又可以分为两种：规约性间接言语行为（conventional indirect speech act）和非规约性间接言语行为（non-conventional indirect speech act）。规约性间接言语行为是指依据习惯由句子的"字面用意"推断出来的间接言语行为。使用规约性间接言语行为往往是出于礼貌的需要，或是为了求得表达上的委婉。当然，习惯上用作规约性间接言语行为的句子有时在一定的语境中只是表达的字面用意。例如，"吃了没有"如果是对出差刚进门的丈夫说出，那就不是招呼或问候了，而是真正的询问。又如，如果是在操场上问"Can you play football?"那很可能是向对方发出"邀请"，是一种间接言语行为；但如果是在旅行的火车上说这句话，那显然是表达的字面用意询问对方是否会踢足球，是一种直接言语行为。

相对于规约性间接言语行为，非规约性间接言语行为要相对复杂一些，是指依据交际双方共知的信息和所处的语境推断出来的间接言语行为，例如（20）。

（20）甲：傍晚能一起打篮球吗？

乙：我明天要考试。

在上面的对话中，乙的回答就字面用意而言，是一种"断言"行为，但实际上是间接地"拒绝"甲的"请求"和"邀请"。这一间接行为的会话含义就是依据双方共知的信息通过推断来实现的：因为乙明天要考试，今天晚上应该需要复习功课，因此也就没时间接受甲的邀请打篮球。所以，其中包含了上述这样一个推理过程。从这一例子的分析可以看出，塞尔的间接言语行为理论实际上是引进了格赖斯的"会话含义"理论（详见下一节介绍）。

由此可见，非规约性间接言语行为由于需要依据双方的共知信息和所处语境进行推断，所以，在使用时要注意共知信息充足，语境限制明确；否则，就有可能造成歧解，影响听话人对说话人间接言语行为含义的正确理解和把握。

五、语用原则和会话含义

美国语言哲学家格莱斯（Herbert Paul Grice）于1967年在哈佛大学所作的题为 *Logic and Conversation*（《逻辑与会话》）的演讲（该讲座全文发表在 *Syntax and Semantics*，Vol. 3：Speech Acts（《句法学和语义学：言语行为》第3卷上））中提出了"合作原则"和"会话含义"理论，着重论述了"合作原则"的具体内容及其如何制约"会话含义"产生的过程。本小节要介绍的语用原则主要就是合作原则。

格莱斯在上述讲座中提出，为了保证会话的顺利进行，谈话双方必须共同遵守"合作原则（cooperative principle）"。合作原则包括四个范畴，即"量""质""方式""关系"，这是效仿哲学家康德的"范畴表"划分出来的。其中每个范畴又包括一条准则和一些次准则：

（A）量的准则（The Maxim of Quantity）：说话的量要适当。

（a）所说的话应该满足交际所需的信息量（Make your contribution as informative as is required for the current purpose of the exchange）；

（b）所说的话不应超出交际所需的信息量（Do not make your contribution more informative than is required）。

（B）质的准则（The Maxim of Quality）：说话要真实可信。

（a）不要说自知是虚假的话（Do not say what you believe to be false）；

（b）不要说缺乏足够证据的话（Do not say that for which you lack adequate evidence）。

（C）关系准则（The Maxim of Relation）：说话要有关联。

（D）方式准则（The Maxim of Manner）：说话要清楚、明了。

（a）避免晦涩（Avoid obscurity）；

（b）避免歧义（Avoid ambiguity）;

（c）简练（Be brief, avoid unnecessary prolixity）;

（d）有条理（Be orderly）。

　　下面我们举一个例子来做简要的说明。1972年，美国总统尼克松访华期间的一次酒会上，周恩来总理说："由于大家都知道的原因，中美两国隔绝了20多年。"如果在这里总理明确说出"大家都知道的原因"具体是什么，很可能就会令场面变得尴尬。但是周总理没有说，而是让听话人自己体会，这里似乎违背了合作原则中量的准则，但却达到了双重效果：既让人体会到造成这一事实的原因是美国侵略和干涉的结果，又照顾到了美国客人的面子，在场的人都会发出会心的微笑。可见，在这个例子中，周总理表面上违背合作原则中量的准则是有意为之，但实际上是为了保证交际能够有效而顺利地进行。

　　在言语交际过程中，说话人出于各种原因并不是都能严格遵守会话原则及其准则的。当听话人意识到说话人的话语违背了某一会话原则或准则时，就会去寻找原因，就会设法让自己跨越说话人的话语表面意思去领悟其中的言外之意，这种言外之意就是"会话含义（conversational implicature）"。格莱斯的会话含义理论是关于人们如何使用语言的理论，它不是从语言系统内部来研究语言本身的言外之意，而是根据语境来研究深层的话语含义，尤其是言外之意。简言之，会话含义关注的不是说话人说了什么，而是他说这话意味着什么。

　　格莱斯的会话含义有两类：一类是一般性会话含义（generalized conversational impli-cature），它不需要利用特殊的语境就能推导出来；另一类是需要依靠特殊的语境才能推导出来的含义，称为特殊性会话含义（particularized conversational implicature）。这里举例说明后一类，如（21）。

　　　（21）A：What on earth has happened to the roast beef?

　　　　　　（烤牛肉究竟怎样了？）

　　　　　B：The dog is looking very happy.

　　　　　　（那只狗看上去挺得意的。）

　　　　　　→ Perhaps the dog has eaten the roast beef.

　　　　　　（也许那只狗把烤牛肉吃掉了。）

从A和B的对话中可以看到，B对于A问题的回答，从表面上看似乎违反了会话原则中的关系准则，因为"狗"与"烤肉"之间没有必然的联系，似不相关。但是结合会话的场景：A和B正在烤肉，而烤牛肉不翼而飞，并且在旁边有只得意而满足的狗。于是，将烤肉的不见、那只狗的得意与当时的场景联系起来就可以推导出，在B对A问题的回答中所暗含的会话含义就是："也许那只狗把烤牛肉吃掉了"。

自格莱斯提出合作原则和会话含义理论之后，很多学者又提出了其他相关的但又不尽相同的语用原则。1978年牛津大学的布朗和莱文森（Brown&Levinson）教授提出了礼貌原则（politeness principle）。他们认为，每个人都有面子（face），包括积极面子（positive face）和消极面子（negative face）。积极面子是指被别人认同的，消极面子是自身利益不被别人侵犯。为维护面子而产生的话语行为就是礼貌行为。另一位语用学家利奇（Leech）也提出礼貌准则，主要包括得体准则（tact maxim）、慷慨准则（generosity maxim）、赞扬准则（approbation maxim）、谦逊准则（modesty maxim）、一致准则（agreement maxim）、同情准则（sympathy maxim）。

第二节　语　篇

语篇（discourse）的定义有多种，其中一个相当简约的定义是：多于一个句子的连续语言就可以算是语篇。不过，近年来兴起的"语篇分析"（discourse analysis）所着重的是语篇的功能定义。从这个角度来说，语篇呈现出（22）中的几个特点。

（22）a. 语言在使用中的样貌；

　　　 b. 思想的沟通；

　　　 c. 各种社会情况中人与人的互动方式。

因为语篇具有以上几个特点，所以，除了语言学家观察语篇，分析其形式、功能与使用情况之外，心理学以及社会学等学科的研究也关注语篇。心理学分析语篇以研究人的思想及沟通这些思想的方式和过程为目的，而社会学则通过语篇材料深入了解分析不同社会情况中的互动关系。

可见，语篇的研究带有交叉学科的性质，知识范围非常广，本节的讨论无法面面俱到。下面以语言学的视角为主，选取语篇类型、语篇的切分以及语篇语法的分析原则三个方面来简单介绍。

一、语篇类型

语篇可以是撰写的，也可以是口说的。在语言研究中，口语一直有特殊而重要的地位，而口语的类型也因不同分类条件，有不同的划分方式。以下介绍针对口语语篇材料分类的几个常见的条件：

（一）语篇参与者

语篇参与者可能只有一人，也可能是多人。如果只有单一的说话者，其构建的语篇材料称为"独白"（monologue）。多位说话者共同构建的语篇称为"对话"（dialogue）。两者的区别并不在于事前准备程度的差异，独白的准备程度不一定高于对话。一份独白的语篇有可能是没经过事先演练的；而一个政客面对采访者随机提出问题时，虽然进行着对话，但双方可能早就针对可能发生的状况反复推演，因此一来一往的互动都是演练过的反应。对话因为牵涉到参与者之间的互动，因此分析对话的时候能观察到许多独白所没有的语言信息，包括表达同意或反对的语言标记、争取或保留或让出话语权的手段，等等。

（二）自发即兴的还是朗诵

口语语篇也可以是自发的（spontaneous）或朗诵的（read）。前者没有书面材料，后者有，而且要读出来。这两者的关键差异仍然不是准备程度的问题，朗诵一份从来没看过的稿子和朗诵一篇事前已重复研读的文章，两者有准备程度的差别，但都是朗诵。许多有文字的语言都发展了自己的朗诵规范，所使用的部分语调、语气、语句组织断句的方式，都有别于自发即兴的口语。

（三）交流场合

语篇还可以区分为是在公开场合进行还是私下交流。两者使用的互动策略会有所不同。例如，在公开场合中，接受访问的人可能会有意识地减少自己话语中的"嗯""啊"等词的使用，以留给人口齿清晰表达清楚的印象。针对同一个议题，课堂中的交流与较轻松的交流相比，所使用的句式、回应对方的方式也可能会不同。

（四）有无特殊目的

说话带着目的与否也会产生不同的语篇类型。例如，在同一个屋子里澄清一个误会相对于漫无目地闲聊，无论韵律、词汇的选择还是互动的模式等，都会体现出差异。

二、语篇的切分：语调单元

若是以撰写方式构成的语篇，大抵能够以小句为单位作切分，例如本书的内容也是语篇的一种，大抵上以句号和逗号分开的都是完整的语法单元（主要是小句，另外一些状语和连词也能用逗号分开）。而自然口语，特别是自发性高的口语，就不见得是这样组织语篇的。当我们聆听口语语篇的材料，特别是陌生语言的语篇时，听到的是一段又一段气流喷发带动声带的发声，中间往往夹着或长或短的停顿（有时候没有停顿）。从语言形式来看，自然说话和撰写的语篇呈现着不同的样貌，比如，自然口语常会有犹豫、停顿、重复，甚至说到一半放弃，重新开始一个新语句等现象，而这些都是书面撰写的材料中较少见到的。下面的例子（23）是一个北京大学中文系的同学收录并转写的一段自然语篇，在此以两点（..）表示较短的停顿、连字号（－）表示字没有说完全（例如说到一半中断了）、等号（＝）表示音节拉长，每一个气流喷发段占用一行。

（23）你还记得小时候去那种公园里面有拿那－

　　..有拿那种就是

　　..糖＝然后画成动物的十二生肖有

　　..你们有吗

上面这个例子显示，在自然口语中，信息不一定会按照语法的原则来组织呈现，第三行的"糖"按语法应该位于第二行最后；而第三行的"有"从结构上看纯粹是多余的。事实上，第一行在"有拿那"停止，内容并不完整，说话者在第二行以重复一次"有拿那"重新开启语句并加入更多信息。不过第二行的信息和语法结构也不完整，必须加入第三行的"糖"才得到完善。而第三行最后的"有"开启了语句却没有继续，说话者在第四行放弃了以"有"开头的语句，改以"你们有吗？"来表达。

由以上的例子我们知道，自然口语语篇体现出人类语言行为的真实面貌，值得科学地研究细察；然而，要切分自然口语语篇，以语法甚至语义为基础都是无法胜任的（如（23）中第三行末尾的"有"，因为后来被抛弃不用，所以无法按照语义连贯的原则和其他的成分结合成一个单元）。从事语篇分析的语言学家已经观察到，口语语篇可以以停顿、音高调节、语速等属韵律（prosody）层面的信号来划分基本单元，这个基本单元一般称为"语调单元"（intonation unit, IU）。语调单元被认为是在说话中反映认知输出（cognitive output）的单元。如果一段话语是事前预备过的，可能在一个语调单元中包入不少语法结构，呈现非常丰富的信息；但在自发、即兴，甚至必须处理陌生信息的说话中，一个语调单元可能只涵盖一个名词，多则一个名词加一个动词，甚至可能只有一个"嗯"。换句话说，语调单元是一种韵律的单位，呈现认知的信息，在划分的时候不需考虑语法的结构或语义的完整与否。

语调单元是用韵律信号来界定的，要将语篇切分为不同的语调单元，最常使用的韵律信号如下：

第一，一致连贯的语调调型：一个语调单元是以一个一致连贯的语调调型体现的。

第二，音高重置：一个语调单元开头的音高有可能比前一个语调单元的末尾高。换句话说，一个语调单元结束后，说话者可能会在一个比较高的音域开启下一个语调单元。

第三，停顿：不同的语调单元之间经常以停顿分隔。停顿可以长达一分钟以上，也可能只有零点几秒。

第四，语速加快：语调单元开头可能会有加快的语速。使语速加快的手段可能是每个音节的时长缩短，也可能是词的形式缩减等。

第五，音节拉长：语调单元的末尾可能会将最后的音节拉长。

三、语篇语法的分析原则

语法可以从许多方面探讨和研究，在这里所介绍的是语篇功能（discourse-functional）的视角。语篇功能的基本主张是：语言的语法无论是形成、运用或演变，都发生在人类使用语言沟通的自然环境——语篇中。语篇不只是语法可以体现的地方，更是其形成并涌现的发源地，而这一切是通过语流中重复出现的语言样式（一般是指用不同成分组合而成的固定形式）慢慢形成的。因为这些样式在语言的使用中不停地被提取使用，所以还在继续改变样貌。因此，从语篇的角度来说，如果一个人能清晰有效地判断某个例子的语法是正确的，那是因为这个例子符合说话者最常接触或使用的语言样式。

因为视角不同，所以语篇功能所关切的语法问题也可能不同于其他语言学理论所关切的问题。例如，谈到名词和代词用来指涉相同的对象（如用"小武"和"他"来指涉同一个人）时，语篇分析（discourse analysis）所关切的就可能是：什么条件下使用名词，什么时候使用代词。另外，在英语中，I like to eat ice-cream.以及I like eating ice-cream.两句话都可以说，字面意思也一样，但语篇分析会研究是什么支配人使用其中一句而非另一句。

此外，就语法范畴来说语篇分析也会探究如下问题：

第一，为什么许多语言都有某个语法范畴，如名词、动词或者传信标记？

第二，这个语法范畴在语言中主要担负什么沟通作用？例如许多语言会将主语的位置安排在动词之前，从语篇功能的角度来说，主语所指涉的对象通常是语篇的话题，而话题都是在句子中比较早出现的。

语篇功能的视角在分析解释语法现象时，通常会从以下三个方面分析理解：

［1］认知的处理

也就是说话者如何处理信息、如何理解对方的话语并决定跟对方说什么。虽然语言学家可能同意语法是语言在认知层面的组织，然而以语言使用为分析基础的理论研究会更明确地提出，语法是人与语言接触的经验在认知层面被整理归纳后组织而成的。这里的主张是：人凭着一般的认知能力，能够按照同质性、类似性和差异性为事物作归纳分类，而这样的一般认知能力也会被应用在人所经历的各种语言事件上，将其归纳分类并储存于记忆中，这么做所产生的结果就是一种认知概念的体现——语法。语法虽然像所有的认知范畴一样可以很抽象，却也紧紧联系着一个人使用语言的经验。

［2］社会互动

这个方面关涉到对话参与者如何受社会互动的常规以及沟通目的的支配，调整语言的选取和使用。

［3］历时的演变

观察上面的两种因素如何影响语言形式的每一次使用，并导致演变。这三者彼此息息相关，因为沟通的种种目的和重复发生的情况会迫使说话者选择相同或不同的语言成分；而在重复的使用中，一些非常普遍的语言样式就渐渐形成，并且往固化的方向发展，说话者可以辨认哪些语言结构是固化、习惯成自然的，哪些不是。

在语篇语法的研究中，重复（repetition）是研究得比较多的语法形成机制。一个词或多个词组成的序列（sequence）会因为重复的频率（frequency）不同而造成不同的语法演变效应。以下介绍三种常见的效应：

［1］缩减效应

重复出现频率高的词及短语跟低频的序列相比，前者语音缩减的速度较快。缩减效应（reducing effect）会发生在出现频率极高的短语上，例如I will、I do not会分别缩减成I'll和I don't（don't已经进一步脱落了末尾的t）。此外，美国英语在非正式场合打招呼时常用的What's up其实已经成了tsup，what's的起始辅音和元音已经脱落，只剩下t's与后面的up结合发音了。

要解释这种效应的产生，语篇功能的视角会诉诸神经运动的例行程序（routine）。也就是说，词和词的连续排列组合在生理发音层面的体现是借由神经运动的例行程序实现的。当一个神经运动的程序被重复激发，其执行就会越来越流畅；在这个过程中，一个新的例行程序被建立起来，反映在语言上则是有一个词的序列开始被当作一个整体来处理了，因为内部成分彼此的分野已经没有先前重要，所以当例行程序被重复激活的时候，序列成分的生理发音动作便会发生弱化、彼此重叠。

[2] 保守效应

第二个频率所造成的效应是保守效应（conserving effect），牵涉到词对新语法规律的接受情形。一个重复频率高的词或序列会在其原有的形态句法结构中深深扎根，即使后来新兴了一种能产性高的语法规律使许多词发生结构重组，高频的词和序列也能不为所动，坚决抵制新规律带来的形态改变与重组。例如，英语的动词曾经在时范畴的形态上经历新规律所导致的改变，即过去时动词的形成是词干加上－ed这个后缀。像weep "哭泣"就是一个使用频率并不是太高的词，其过去时形式按照字典记载是wept，但在实际说话时，weeped已经渐渐兴起代替wept。不过，一个语音结构相仿，但使用频率高很多的词keep "保持"，则抵制新兴的语法规律，继续以其原有的形态体现过去时，即keep vs. kept，没有随着大部分动词进入新形态变化的轨道里，所以现在keep vs. kept被视为 "不规则" 动词变化。

以上所描述的变化趋势之所以会发生，是因为高的重复频率加强了词或短语的记忆体现，使它们更容易带着环境要求的语法标记和形式被整体提取，也不大容易因为类推（analogy）而发生形态的重塑。这个频率效应也发生在句法层次的序列上，例如英语的助动词出现的频率高于一般动词，因此形成问句的时候，就保留了比较古老的 "动词与主语" 互换的语序。在（24）中，第一个句子是直述句，第二个是问句，两者形式的不同仅在于主语和助动词的位置互换。这与古英语将主语与（一般）动词位置互换构成问句是一致的，如（25）。

（24）a. <u>John</u>   will be in town tomorrow.（约翰明天会到镇上来。）
       主语   助动词

    b. <u>Will</u>   John be in town tomorrow?（约翰明天会到镇上来吗？）
       助动词 主语

（25）<u>Lovest</u>   <u>thou</u>   me?（你爱我吗？）
     动词（爱）   主语（你）   宾语（我）

但是现代英语中一般动词在形成问句时，遵守的是新规律，也就是借由助动词do来构成，主语与（一般）动词互换的规则不复存在，如（26）（请与（25）比较）。

（26）<u>Do</u>　　<u>you</u>　　love　me？（你爱我吗？）
　　　助动词　　主语

[3] 自主性

自主性（autonomy）的意思是在形态上复杂的形式（或一串词）如果使用频率高，其内部构造的成分渐渐失去独立性，整个序列被当成一个整体，以致与其他本有相同构造原理的形式脱钩。因高频重复而产生自主性的典型例子可举英语的复杂结构短语be going to。原来这个形式可以与许多动态动词作构造上的类比，例如（27）中的几个短语都具有"be V-ing to"形式。

（27）be going to

be coming to

be running to

be walking to

be talking to

然而，随着be going to重复的频率增高，语法化发生，它成了将来时的标记，而且也发生形式上的改变，读成了be gonna，自此失去了句法构造的透明度，不再能类比于其他带有be、go和to的结构了。

以上关于语言使用的重复现象及其效应，都指出一个事实，那就是语法其实是语言使用经验在认知层面的组织、汇整与归纳。语言的使用促成语法的构成，而语法也决定了语言体现的形貌。在语法的研究中，对语言实际使用的观察不能缺席。

原典选读

一、论言有何为？

J. L. Austin. 1962. *How to Do Things with Words*. Oxford: Clarendon Press.

【导 读】

这份原典选自上述著作第8讲（Lecture Ⅷ）（原书94-107页），主要讨论有关言语行为的三分说。奥斯汀将言语行为分为如下三类：①言内行为（the locutionary act）：是指使用发音器官，发出语音，并按照规则将它们排成合格的词或句子。这种发出语音、说出带有意义的词和句子的行为，就是言内行为。②言外行为（the illocutionary act）：是表达说话者的意图的行为，它是在说某些话时所实施的行为。③言后行为（the perlocutionary act）：是通过某些话所实施的行为，或是讲某些话所导致的行为，它是话语所产生的后果或所引起的变化，是通过讲某些话所完成的行为。

言内行为、言外行为和言后行为这三种言语行为实际上是整个言语过程的三个不同阶段，是统一于同一话语之中的。

IN embarking on a programme of finding a list of explicit performative verbs, it seemed that we were going to find it not always easy to distinguish performative utterances from constative, and it therefore seemed expedient to go farther back for a while to fundamentals—to consider from the ground up how many senses there are in which to say something *is* to do something, or *in* saying something we do something, and even *by* saying something we do something. And we began by distinguishing a whole group of senses of 'doing something' which are all included together when we say, what is obvious, that to say something is in the full normal sense to do something—which includes the utterance of certain noises, the utterance of certain words in a certain construction, and the utterance of them with a certain 'meaning' in the favourite philosophical sense of that word, i.e. with a certain sense and with a certain reference.

The act of 'saying something' in this full normal sense I call, i.e. dub, the performance of a locutionary act, and the study of utterances thus far and in these respects the study of locutions, or of the full units of speech. Our interest in the locutionary act is, of course, principally to make quite plain what it is, in order to distinguish it from other acts with which we are going to be primarily concerned. Let me add merely that, of course, a great many further refinements would be possible and necessary if we were to discuss it for its own sake—refinements of very great importance not merely to philosophers but to, say, grammarians and phoneticians.

We had made three rough distinctions between the phonetic act, the phatic act, and the rhetic act. The phonetic act is merely the act of uttering certain noises. The phatic act is the uttering of certain vocables or words, i.e. noises of certain types, belonging to and as belonging to, a certain vocabulary, conforming to and as conforming to a certain grammar. The rhetic act is the performance of an act of using those vocables with a certain more-or-less definite sense and reference. Thus 'He said "The cat is on the mat"', reports a phatic act, whereas 'He said that the cat was on the mat' reports a rhetic act. A similar contrast is illustrated by the pairs:

'He said "I shall be there"', 'He said he would be there';

'He said "Get out"', 'He told me to get out';

'He said "Is it in Oxford or Cambridge?"'; 'He asked whether it was in Oxford or Cambridge'.

To pursue this for its own sake beyond our immediate requirements, I shall mention some general points worth remembering:

(1) Obviously, to perform a phatic I must perform a phonetic act, or, if you like, in performing one I am performing the other (not, however, that phatic acts are

a sub-class of phonetic acts—as belonging to): but the converse is not true, for if a monkey makes a noise indistinguishable from 'go' it is still not a phatic act.

(2) Obviously in the definition of the phatic act two things were lumped together: vocabulary and grammar. So we have not assigned a special name to the person who utters, for example, 'cat thoroughly the if' or 'the slithy toves did gyre'. Yet a further point arising is the intonation as well as grammar and vocabulary.

(3) The phatic act, however, like the phonetic, is essentially mimicable, reproducible (including intonation, winks, gestures, &c.). One can mimic not merely the statement in quotation marks 'She has lovely hair', but also the more complex fact that he said it like this: 'She has lovely *hair*' (shrugs).

This is the 'inverted commas' use of 'said' as we get it in novels: every utterance can be just reproduced in inverted commas, or in inverted commas with 'said he' or, more often, 'said she', &c., after it.

But the rhetic act is the one we report, in the case of assertions, by saying 'He said that the cat was on the mat', 'He said he would go', 'He said I was to go' (his words were 'You are to go'). This is the so-called 'indirect speech'. If the sense or reference is *not* being taken as clear, then the whole or part is to be in quotation marks. Thus I might say: 'He said I was to go to the "minister", but he did not say which minister' or 'I said that he was behaving badly and he replied that "the higher you get the fewer" '. We cannot, however, always use 'said that' easily: we would say 'told to', 'advise to', &c., if he used the imperative mood, or such equivalent phrases as 'said I was to', 'said I should', &c. Compare such phrases as 'bade me welcome' and 'extended his apologies'.

I add one further point about the rhetic act: of course sense and reference (naming and referring) themselves are here ancillary acts performed in performing the rhetic act. Thus we may say 'I meant by "bank" . . .' and we say 'by "he" I was referring to . . .'. Can we perform a rhetic act without referring or without naming? In general it would seem that the answer is that we cannot, but there are puzzling cases. What is the reference in 'all triangles have three sides'? Correspondingly, it is clear that we can perform a phatic act which is not a rhetic act, though not conversely. Thus we may repeat someone else's remark or mumble over some sentence, or we may read a Latin sentence without knowing the meaning of the words.

The question when one pheme or one rheme is the *same* as another, whether in the 'type' or 'token' sense, and the question what is one single pheme or rheme, do not so much matter here. But, of course, it is important to remember that the same pheme (token of the same type) may be used on different occasions of utterance with a different sense or reference, and so be a different rheme. When different phemes are used with the same sense and reference, we might speak of rhetically equivalent acts ('the same statement' in one sense) but not of the same rheme or rhetic acts (which are the same

statement in another sense which involves using the same words).

The pheme is a unit of *language*: its typical fault is to be nonsense—meaningless. But the rheme is a unit of *speech*; its typical fault is to be vague or void or obscure, &c.

But though these matters are of much interest, they do not so far throw any light at all on our problem of the constative as opposed to the performative utterance. For example, it might be perfectly possible, with regard to an utterance, say 'It is going to charge', to make entirely plain 'what we were saying' in issuing the utterance, in all the senses so far distinguished, and yet not at all to have cleared up whether or not in issuing the utterance I was performing the act of *warning* or not. It may be perfectly clear what I mean by 'It is going to charge' or 'Shut the door', but not clear whether it is meant as a statement or warning, &c.

To perform a locutionary act is in general, we may say, also and *eo ipso* to perform an *illocutionary* act, as I propose to call it. To determine what illocutionary act is so performed we must determine in what way we are using the locution:

asking or answering a question,

giving some information or an assurance or a warning,

announcing a verdict or an intention,

pronouncing sentence,

making an appointment or an appeal or a criticism,

making an identification or giving a description,

and the numerous like. (I am not suggesting that this is a clearly defined class by any means.) There is nothing mysterious about our *eo ipso* here. The trouble rather is the number of different senses of so vague an expression as 'in what way are we using it'—this may refer even to a locutionary act, and further to perlocutionary acts to which we shall come in a minute. When we perform a locutionary act, we use speech: but in what way precisely are we using it on this occasion? For there are very numerous functions of or ways in which we use speech, and it makes a great difference to our act in some sense—sense (B)[1]—in which way and which *sense* we were on this occasion 'using' it. It makes a great difference whether we were advising, or merely suggesting, or actually ordering, whether we were strictly promising or only announcing a vague intention, and so forth. These issues penetrate a little but not without confusion into grammar (see above), but we constantly do debate them, in such terms as whether certain words (a certain locution) *had the force of* a question, or *ought to have been taken as* an estimate and so on.

I explained the performance of an act in this new and second sense as the performance of an 'illocutionary' act, i.e. performance of an act *in* saying something as opposed to performance of an act *of* saying something; and I shall refer to the doctrine of the different types of function of language here in question as the doctrine of 'illocutionary forces'.

It may be said that for too long philosophers have neglected this study, treating all problems as problems of 'locutionary usage', and indeed that the 'descriptive fallacy' mentioned in Lecture I commonly arises through mistaking a problem of the former kind for a problem of the latter kind. True, we are now getting out of this; for some years we have been realizing more and more clearly that the occasion of an utterance matters seriously, and that the words used are to some extent to be 'explained' by the 'context' in which they are designed to be or have actually been spoken in a linguistic interchange. Yet still perhaps we are too prone to give these explanations in terms of 'the meanings of words'. Admittedly we can use 'meaning' also with reference to illocutionary force—'He meant it as an order', &c. But I want to distinguish *force* and meaning in the sense in which meaning is equivalent to sense and reference, just as it has become essential to distinguish sense and reference within meaning.

Moreover, we have here an illustration of the different uses of the expression, 'uses of language', or 'use of a sentence', &c.—'use' is a hopelessly ambiguous or wide word, just as is the word 'meaning', which it has become customary to deride. But 'use', its supplanter, is not in much better case. We may entirely clear up the 'use of a sentence' on a particular occasion, in the sense of the locutionary act, without yet touching upon its use in the sense of an *illocutionary* act.

Before refining any further on this notion of the illocutionary act, let us contrast both the locutionary *and* the illocutionary act with yet a third kind of act.

There is yet a further sense (C) in which to perform a locutionary act, and therein an illocutionary act, may also be to perform an act of another kind. Saying something will often, or even normally, produce certain consequential effects upon the feelings, thoughts, or actions of the audience, or of the speaker, or of other persons: and it may be done with the design, intention, or purpose of producing them; and we may then say, thinking of this, that the speaker has performed an act in the nomenclature of which reference is made either (C. *a*), only obliquely, or even (C. *b*), not at all, to the performance of the locutionary or illocutionary act. We shall call the performance of an act of this kind the performance of a *perlocutionary* act or *perlocution*. Let us not yet define this idea any more carefully—of course it needs it—but simply give examples:

(E. 1)

Act (A)   or Locution

He said to me 'Shoot her!' meaning by 'shoot' shoot and referring by 'her' to *her*.

Act (B)   or Illocution

He urged (or advised, ordered, &c.) me to shoot her.

Act (C. *a*)   or Perlocution

He persuaded me to shoot her.

Act (C. *b*)

He got me to (or made me, &c.) shoot her.

(E. 2)

Act (A)   or Locution

He said to me, 'You can't do that'.

Act (B)   or Illocution

He protested against my doing it.

Act (C. *a*)   or Perlocution

He pulled me up, checked me.

Act (C. *b*)

He stopped me, he brought me to my senses, &c. He annoyed me.

We can similarly distinguish the locutionary act 'he said that...' from the illocutionary act 'he argued that...' and the perlocutionary act 'he convinced me that...'.

It will be seen that the consequential effects of perlocutions are really consequences, which do not include such conventional effects as, for example, the speaker's being committed by his promise (which comes into the illocutionary act). Perhaps distinctions need drawing, as there is clearly a difference between what we feel to be the real production of real effects and what we regard as mere conventional consequences; we shall in any case return later to this.

We have here then roughly distinguished three kinds of acts—the locutionary, the illocutionary, and the perlocutionary.[1] Let us make some general comments on these three classes, leaving them still fairly rough. The first three points will be about 'the use of language' again.

(1) Our interest in these lectures is essentially to fasten on the second, illocutionary act and contrast it with the other two. There is a constant tendency in philosophy to elide this in favour of one or other of the other two. Yet it is distinct from both. We have already seen how the expressions 'meaning' and 'use of sentence' can blur the distinction between locutionary and illocutionary acts. We now notice that to speak of the 'use' of language can likewise blur the distinction between the illocutionary and perlocutionary act—so we will distinguish them more carefully in a minute. Speaking of the 'use of "language" for arguing or warning' looks just like speaking of 'the use of "language" for persuading, rousing, alarming'; yet the former may, for rough contrast, be said to be *conventional*, in the sense that at least it could be made explicit by the performative formula; but the latter could not. Thus we can say 'I argue that' or 'I warn you that' but we cannot say 'I convince you that' or 'I alarm you that'. Further, we may entirely clear up whether someone was arguing or not without touching on the question whether he was convincing anyone or not.

[1] [Here occurs in the manuscript a note made in 1958 which says: '(1) All this is not clear (2) and in all senses relevant ((A) and (B) as distinct from (C)) won't all utterances be performative?']

(2) To take this farther, let us be quite clear that the expression 'use of language' can cover other matters even more diverse than the illocutionary and perlocutionary acts. For example, we may speak of the 'use of language' *for* something, e.g. for joking; and we may use 'in' in a way different from the illocutionary 'in', as when we say 'in saying "p" I was joking' or 'acting a part' or 'writing poetry'; or again we may speak of 'a poetical use of language' as distinct from 'the use of language in poetry'. These references to 'use of language' have nothing to do with the illocutionary act. For example, if I say 'Go and catch a falling star', it may be quite clear what both the meaning and the force of my utterance is, but still wholly unresolved which of these other kinds of things I may be doing. There are parasitic uses of language, which are 'not serious', not the 'full normal use'. The normal conditions of reference may be suspended, or no attempt made at a standard perlocutionary act, no attempt to make you do anything, as Walt Whitman does not seriously incite the eagle of liberty to soar.

(3) Furthermore, there may be some things we 'do' in some connexion with saying something which do not seem to fall, intuitively at least, exactly into any of these roughly defined classes, or else seem to fall vaguely into more than one; but any way we do not at the outset feel so clear that they are as remote from our three acts as would be joking or writing poetry. For example, *insinuating*, as when we insinuate something in or by issuing some utterance, seems to involve some convention, as in the illocutionary act; but we cannot *say* 'I insinuate . . .', and it seems like implying to be a clever effect rather than a mere act. A further example is evincing emotion. We may evince emotion in or by issuing an utterance, as when we swear; but once again we have no use here for performative formulas and the other devices of illocutionary acts. We might say that we use swearing[1] *for* relieving our feelings. We must notice that the illocutionary act is a conventional act: an act done as conforming to a convention.

(4) Acts of all our three kinds necessitate, since they are the performing of actions, allowance being made for the ills that all action is heir to. We must systematically be prepared to distinguish between 'the act of doing *x*', i.e. achieving *x*, and 'the act of attempting to do *x*': for example, we must distinguish between warning and attempting to warn. We must expect infelicities here.

The next three points that arise do so importantly because our acts are *acts*.

(5) Since our acts are acts, we must always remember the distinction between producing effects or consequences which are intended or unintended; and (i) when the speaker intends to produce an effect it may nevertheless not occur, and (ii) when he does not intend to produce it or intends not to produce it it may nevertheless occur. To cope with complication (i) we invoke as before the distinction between attempt and achievement; to cope

with complication (ii) we invoke the normal linguistic devices of disclaiming (adverbs like 'unintentionally' and 'so on') which we hold ready for personal use in all cases of doing actions.

(6) Furthermore, we must, of course, allow that as acts they may be things that we do not exactly *do*, in the sense that we did them, say, under duress or in any other such way. Other ways besides in which we may not fully do the action are given in (2) above.

(7) Finally we must meet the objection about our illocutionary and perlocutionary acts—namely that the notion of an act is unclear—by a general doctrine about action. We have the idea of an 'act' as a fixed physical thing that we do, as distinguished from conventions and as distinguished from consequences. But

(*a*) the illocutionary act and even the locutionary act too may involve conventions: consider the example of doing obeisance. It is obeisance only because it is conventional and it is done only because it is conventional. Compare the distinction between kicking a wall and kicking a goal;

(*b*) the perlocutionary act may include what in a way are consequences, as when we say 'By doing *x* I was doing *y*': we do bring in a greater or less stretch of 'consequences' always, some of which may be 'unintentional'. There is no restriction to the minimum physical act at all. That we can import an indefinitely long stretch of what might also be called the 'consequences' of our act into the act itself is, or should be, a fundamental commonplace of the theory of our language about all 'action' in general. Thus if asked 'What did he do?', we may reply either 'He shot the donkey' or 'He fired a gun' or 'He pulled the trigger' or 'He moved his trigger finger', and all may be correct. So, to shorten the nursery story of the endeavours of the old woman to drive her pig home in time to get her old man's supper, we may in the last resort say that the cat drove or got the pig, or made the pig get, over the stile. If in such cases we *mention* both a B act (illocution) and a C act (perlocution) we shall say '*by* B-ing he C-ed' rather than '*in* B-ing . . .'. This is the reason for calling C a *per*locutionary act as distinct from an illocutionary act.

Next time we shall revert to the distinction between our three kinds of act, and to the expressions 'in' and 'by doing *x* I am doing *y*', with a view to getting the three classes and their members and non-members somewhat clearer. We shall see that just as the locutionary act embraces doing many things at once to be complete, so may the illocutionary and perlocutionary acts.

[1] 'Swearing' is ambiguous: 'I swear by Our Lady' *is* to swear by Our Lady: but 'Bloody' is not to swear by Our Lady.

二、语篇与语法（节选）

Susanna Cumming, Tsuhoshi Oho. 1998. Discourse and Grammar. In van Dijk (ed.) *Discourse Studies: A Multidisciplinary Introduction, Vol. 1: Discourse as Structure and Process.* London: Sage.

【导　读】

　　这份原典阅读材料是将语篇与语法的研究介绍且铺陈得相当好的一篇。它先介绍语言的使用如何导致语法的产生，汇整语篇语法在分析时所使用的三种主要视角，梳理了语篇语法研究的相关文献（这里没有选录），借着观察语篇研究语法时采用的基本方法论及概念工具，然后是一些实际语料分析与方法操作（这里没有选录）。虽然都是纯叙述的文字，但是短短的篇幅将语篇语法的中心主旨介绍得相当清楚，适合想了解语篇语法研究理论原则的入门者阅读。

This chapter deals with the relation of discourse to grammar, setting forth what we will call a 'discourse-functional approach' to grammatical phenomena. Discourse-functional grammarians view discourse – that is, spoken, signed or written language used by people to communicate in natural settings – as the primary locus for the grammars of the world's languages, not only as the place where grammar is manifested in use, but also as the source from which grammar is formed or 'emerges' (Hopper, 1988). In this view, grammar originates in recurrent patterns in discourse, and these patterns continually shape it. This approach to grammar is distinct from what might be called the 'autonomist' approach, which views grammar as having an existence entirely independent of its communicative uses.

Discourse-functional approaches to grammar have two goals. The first goal is a descriptive one: given the richness of the grammatical resources languages typically have for expressing the 'same' content, how do speakers choose among them? That is, what are the functions of the grammatical and lexical alternations of a language? We can ask, for instance, how speakers choose between a full noun phrase and a pronoun, or between two alternative orders for subject and verb. The second goal is explanatory: why do languages have the resources they have? That is, why are particular grammatical resources, such as pronouns, available in many or all languages, and why are certain functions typically realized by certain kinds of forms? This second concern has consequences for language universals and typology: for instance, the universal tendency for subjects to precede objects can be explained in terms of the fact that subjects typically have referents which are related to the discourse topic, and that topical information tends cross-linguistically to occur early in the clause.

Discourse linguists interested in grammar have tended to focus on three general kinds of explanations. Cognitive explanations appeal to the cognitive resources and processes used by interactants in producing and understanding language. Social or interactional explanations appeal to the dynamics of the interactional situations in which language (especially spoken language) is produced and consumed, and with the social and/or cultural norms, resources, and goals of interactants. Finally, diachronic explanations focus on the relationship between discourse-functional pressures on grammars and grammatical change; this type of explanation is often called 'grammaticalization', a topic which is beyond the scope of the present chapter.

These three sources of explanation are not, of course, mutually exclusive; they are interrelated in many complex ways. Discourse linguists believe that the great variety of formal repertoires among the world's languages comes about through the interaction of different functional pressures, which sometimes compete – forcing speech communities to 'choose' between two or more well-motivated outcomes – and sometimes converge, leading to very general or even universal patterns of language structure (see Du Bois, 1985).

Methodology and Data

As suggested above, a discourse-functional linguist believes that the use of language to communicate in natural settings is fundamental to the organization of languages. The primacy of grammar in discourse both as an object of description and as a source of explanations has had important methodological consequences for discourse grammarians.

Most importantly, unlike 'autonomist' grammarians, discourse grammarians have over the last three decades increasingly restricted their attention to naturally occurring data, as opposed to invented examples. Increasingly, too, discourse-functional linguists have attempted to include in their database as much as possible of the context within which the discourse occurs – not just the linguistic context, but also the ethnographic and extralinguistic context, including both its social and its physical aspects. This is because context can often provide clues to locally relevant functional pressures not detectable from the linguistic signal alone. Awareness of the importance of context in grammatical choice has led to increasing interest in the nature of 'context' as an object of study in itself. Many discourse linguists have come to the realization that we have to understand discourse and its context as mutually creating and constraining, rather than seeing this simply as a unidirectional process.

Another concomitant of the discourse-functional perspective has to do with the issue of text frequency. Many discourse grammarians feel that text frequency is vital to understanding the discourse motivations for particular grammatical constructions. This is because they have come to realize that those functional pressures that have the most opportunity to affect communicators are those most likely to affect language form: in the words of Du Bois (1985), 'grammars code best what speakers do most.' This observation has had two significant consequences for the methodology of discourse approaches to grammar. First, many discourse grammarians have adopted a quantitative methodology, and have been very concerned with statistical correlations between particular grammatical forms and aspects of the linguistic and non-linguistic context. Second, many discourse grammarians have recently begun to focus increasingly on the form of language which occupies most of the time and attention of most language users everywhere in the world: everyday 'talk in interaction'. While other discourse genres and styles, produced under different kinds of functional constraints and pressures, are still considered relevant, interactive talk is seen as having a privileged position as a source of explanation for language structure and change. For this reason, the examples given in this chapter in so far as possible are taken from interactional data.

These factors are responsible for the distinctive methodological characteristics associated with studies in the discourse-functional mold: an insistence on carefully recorded natural data and an interest in quantitative and distributional information about grammatical patterns.

☯ 思考题

1. 请举例说明"旧信息-新信息""话题-说明""预设-焦点"之间的关系。

2. 阅读下面一段文字，请指出这段文字的语篇话题是什么，是如何确定的，并标明其中的话题链，分析话题的延续性。

祥子已经跑出二三十步去，可又不肯跑了，他舍不得那几匹骆驼。他在世界上的财产，现在，只剩下了自己的一条命。就是地上的一根麻绳，他也乐意拾起来，即使没用，还能稍微安慰他一下，至少他手中有条麻绳，不完全是空的。逃命是要紧的，可是赤裸裸的一条命有什么用呢？他得带走这几匹牲口，虽然还没想起骆驼能有什么用处，可是总得算是几件东西，而且是块儿不小的东西。

（选自老舍《骆驼祥子》）

3. 请使用奥斯汀言语行为三分说的理论分别分析下面三句话语所呈现的言语过程的三个不同阶段，并指明下面各句表达的是直接言语行为还是间接言语行为。

（1）"把垃圾扔掉！"

（2）"我明天一定来拜访你。"

（3）"能把那本书递给我吗？"

4. 列举言语交际中违反合作原则的实例，并以它们为例分析其中的会话含义。

📖 拓展阅读书目

➤ 有关"语用学"领域研究的书目

📖 S. C. Levinson. 1983. *Pragmatics*. Cambridge: Cambridge University Press.

➤ 有关"信息结构""话题""话题延续性"和"焦点"研究的书目

📖 Wallace Chafe. 1987. Cognitive Constraints on Information Flow. In R. Tomlin, (ed.) *Coherence and Grounding in Discourse*. Amsterdam: John Benjamins, pp.21-52.

📖 Talmy Givón. 1983. Topic Continuity in Discourse: An Introduction. In Talmy Givón. (ed.) *Topic Continuity in Discourse: A Quantitative Cross-language Study*. Amsterdam and Philadelphia: John Benjamins Publishing Company, pp.1-41.

📖 Knud Lambrecht. 1994. *Information Structure and Sentence Form: Topic, Focus, and the Mental Representation of Discourse Referents*. Cambridge: Cambridge University Press.

📖 Charles N. Li., Sandra A. Thompson. 1976. Subject and Topic: A New Typology of Language. In Charles N. Li. (ed.) *Subject and Topic*, Academic Press Inc. 中译本：［美］查尔斯·李，桑德拉·汤普森. 主语与主题：一种新的语言类型学. 李谷城，摘译. 当代国外语言学，1984（2）：38-44.

📖 Feng-Fu Tsao（曹逢甫）. 1977. *A Functional Study of Topic in Chinese: The First Step Toward Discourse Analysis*. Taipei: Student Book Co.

➤ 有关"言语行为理论"和"语用原则与会话含义"研究的书目

📖 J. L. Austin. 1962. *How to Do Things with Words*. Oxford: Clarendon Press.

📖 H. P. Grice. 1975. Logic and Conversation. In Cole and Morgan (eds.), *Syntax and Semantics 3: Speech Acts*. New York: Academic Press, pp.41-58.

📖 G. N. Leech. 1983. *Principles of Pragmatics*. London and New York: Longman.

➤ 有关语篇转写的文献

📖 John W. Du Bois, Susanna Cumming, Stephan Schuetze-Coburn, Danae Paolino. 1992. *Discourse Transcription: Santa Barbara Papers in Linguistics*, Vol. 4.

📖 John W. Du Bois, Stephan Schuetze-Coburn, Susanna Cumming, Danae Paolino. 1993. Outline of Discourse Transcription. In Jane A. Edwards, Martin D. Lampert. (eds.) *Talking Data: Transcription and Coding in Discourse Research*. Hillsdale, NJ: Lawrence Erlbaum, pp.45-89.

⊓ John W. Du Bois, Stephan Schuetze-Coburn.1993. Representing hierarchy: Constituent structure for discourse databases. In Jane A. Edwards, Martin D. Lampert. (eds.) *Talking Data: Transcription and Coding in Discourse Research.* Hillsdale, NJ: Lawrence Erlbaum, pp.221-260.

第八章

文 字

  本章介绍文字的性质、作用、类型、与语言的关系以及文字的源起、发展和形成条件。文字是音、形、义三要素结合的书写语言的视觉符号系统。文字的出现对语言、对人类文化乃至对人类社会成员的生存发展都有着重要的作用。文字和语言在产生的时间、表现功能和所处的地位等方面都表现出差异。文字和语言之间是相互影响和制约的关系。文字是语言最重要的辅助性交际工具,而语言是文字产生的基础,语言的特点决定文字的特点。从文字发生学的角度来说,文字分为自源文字和借源文字两大类。从文字符号的功能角度来看,文字体系有表音文字和意音文字两种。文字的起源和发展可以从实物记事、图画记事和刻画记事三种非文字的形体记事方式来看。文字系统形成的重要条件是,它的形体所表达的信息一定是与某种语言的音义结合体及其排列相对应的信息,而不是直接描画现实。

第一节 文字的性质

一、什么是文字

我们通常所说的"文字"一词有三个意思：一是指书写语言的视觉符号系统，如"文字学""文字改革"等；二是指用文字符号书写的书面语言形式，如"文字优美""文字流畅"等；三是指单个的字符。本章所讲的文字，指的是第一个意思。

有关文字的性质，我们可以从如下三方面去理解：

第一，文字是记录人类语言的书写符号。也就是说，不是用来记录人类语言的符号不是文字。文字在语言的基础上产生。语言是音义结合的符号系统，其中的语素、词这些单位包括音和义两个方面，文字是对语言中这些小的音义结合体的再编码。这样，作为书写语言的视觉符号系统，文字除了具有语言的音、义之外，还有自己可视的形体。所以，文字是音、形、义三要素结合的书写符号系统。文字记录语言，有的是一个字代表一个词，比如英文的bird，字母串"bird"是字形，[bə:d]是字音，"鸟"是字义。有的是一个字代表一个音节，汉字就是这样。古代汉语中单音节词占绝对优势，一般是一个字记录一个词。但现代汉语中有不少双音或多音节词，那么就需要两个或两个以上的字来记录一个词，这样，一个方块字一般就记录一个语素了，比如"电脑""手机""自行车"等。有些情况较为特殊，像联绵词是两个音节构成的一个语素，其中单个的字只有字形和字音而没有独立的字义，它们必须与其他字结合起来才能表义，而每个字都为表义做了贡献，比如"伶俐""徘徊"等。可见，不同的文字其形体不同，所对应的语言单位的大小也不同，但文字系统中的某一级文字单位都与语言系统的某一级单位（如语素或词）相对应，这一点则是相同的。

第二，文字是成系统的书写符号。它是由一套特定的形体符号和书写规则组成的。比如，汉字是记录汉语的书写符号系统，它是由偏旁、笔画、笔顺等组成的符号体系；而英文是记录英语的书写符号系统，它是由二十六个字母、书写规则等（如大小写规则、以音节为单位换行的规则、自左向右的书写规则）等组成的符号系统。另外，文字的系统性还体现在它跟所记录的语言形式之间保持着特定的关系。语言是一种系统，文字也是一种系统。语言有大小不同的、音义结合的各级单位，有单位的聚合类和组合规则；文字也有大小不同的形体符号单位，有文字单位的聚合类和组合规则。同时，由于文字是对语言的再编码，所以文字单位与语言单位、文字的组合规则与语言的组合规则有着系统的对应关系。关于这一点，下文谈到"文字与语言的关系"时会详论。

　　第三，文字是作用于视觉的书写符号。所谓"作用于视觉"，是说可视的字形是文字的存在方式。任何一种文字都是用各种不同的形体来记录语言的。文字不同于语言之处，在于它具有可视的形体特征，也就是字形。字形是把语言的听觉符号转换为视觉符号的主要手段，因而它是文字三要素中最基本的要素。人们在日常生活中用于表情达意、传递信息的符号各种各样，比如交通灯、旗语、盲文、手语、电报代码、生物学符号等。这些符号虽然作用于人的视觉，但都不是记录语言的书写符号，所以不能算是文字。录音机等一些录音设备可以把人的自然语言记录保存下来，但是它作用于人的听觉而不是视觉，所以也不是文字。

　　总之，文字是书写语言的视觉符号系统。文字具有视觉性、系统性，并且与所记录的语言系统有密切的关系。文字在记录语言时，它的字形、字音和字义的关系是稳固统一的。这是文字用于书写记录语言的重要前提和基础。

二、文字的作用

　　文字的发明是人类文明的重要标志。恩格斯在《家庭、私有制和国家的起源》一书中指出："人类从铁矿的冶炼开始，并由于文字的发明及其应用于文献记录而过渡到文明时代。"美国的路易斯·亨利·摩尔根（Lewis Henry Morgan）在其《古代社会》中曾说过："没有文字记载，就没有历史，也就没有文明。"可见，文字的出现对整个人类的发展有着重要的作用。我们可以从文字对语言的影响、文字对人类文化的功能以及文字对人类社会成员的生存发展的意义诸方面来认识文字的重要作用。

　　第一，文字克服了所记录的语言在信息传达上的局限。"言者意之声，书者言之记。"（《〈书·序〉正义》）"声不能传于异地，留于异时，于是乎书之为文字。文字者，所以为意与声之迹也。"（陈澧《东塾读书记》卷十一）这两句话既说明了语言和文字的关系，也说明了文字和语言的基本性质：文字是书写语言的视觉符号系统；而语言是通过口、耳交际的，本质上是通过声音来实现交际过程。因为声音是一发即逝的，所以人们说话要受到时间和空间的限制。所谓空间限制，是说交际的双方距离太远，不在交谈现场就听不见；所谓时间限制，是指过去说的话现在听不见。为了克服有声语言在时间和空间上的限制，人们发明了文字，使语言除了说和听的形式以外，又增加了一种写和看的形式。所以说，文字的发明克服了语言传达信息在时间和空间上的局限，使一发即逝的语言能够"传于异地，留于异时"，从而提高了语言的交际功能。

　　第二，文字使人类文化得以积累，使人类社会得以发展。文化是人类在社会历史发展过程中所创造的物质财富和精神财富的总和，也是整个社会价值系统的总和。一般认为，语言文字、传统习俗、思维方式、价值观念等都属于文化范畴。由此可见，文字本身就体现了人类文化，是文化所涵盖的重要内容之一。文字是记录和传播文化的有力工具。文字产生以前，人们通过口耳相传的方式来传承历史文化遗产、劳动技能经验等。比如许多重要的文化活动过程主要是通过专门的人来传诵史诗和传说来记录，各种文化知识、生产经验只是靠父子或师徒间的口耳相传得以继承，一旦传诵者或传承者不在了，那么文化活动的记录和文化知识以及生产经验的继承也就随之消失了。除此之外，人的记忆力有一定的限度，不可能把自己或他人说过的话记忆得准确无误，即便暂时记住了，也会随着时间的流逝而遗忘。可见，通过听和说的形式，凭借记忆力来传承人类文化是具有很大的局限性的。文字产生以后，人类就有了文字记载的历史。文字通过书面形式能更好地记录人类的文化活动，使得前人的创造性成果能够流传和继承下来，成为人类社会发展的基石。可以说，如果没有文字，人类就没有先进的科学文化，也就不会进入高度发达的文明社会。

第三，文字对社会成员的自我发展具有重要的意义。在日常生活中，我们常把一个人识不识字看成有没有文化，比如把不识字的人叫作"没文化的人"。可见，人们常把文字视为文化的标志。不识字的人自身体验到的经验和获得的知识比识字的人要少得多，这也会制约他文化素质的发展。因此，在高度发达的文明社会，识字是每一个成员适应社会的基本技能。由于文字是书写语言的视觉符号系统，所以，它能使人的思维有了在二维空间中分布的形体表象，于是可以通过文字来进行思维，从而促进了大脑的思维能力。总之，社会成员可以通过文字了解古今中外的各种文化知识和技能经验，从而有助于自己认识和改造世界，对自身的发展有着重要的意义。

文字是人们为记录语言而创制的一种书写的视觉符号系统。文字不只是被动地记录语言，它对人类文化的积累和传承，对人类社会及其成员的良性发展都有着积极的作用。因此，文字的出现是人类进入文明社会的重要标志之一。

三、文字和语言的关系

认识文字和语言的关系可以从它们之间的差异入手。文字和语言的差异主要在于：首先，它们产生的时间不同。语言产生的时间远远早于文字，世界上最早的文字也只有几千年的历史。文字是为了记录语言而产生的，先有语言才有文字。其次，它们的功能也不同。语言是社会现象，是社会交际的工具，同时也是心理现象，是人类思维的工具。文字是辅助语言进行交际和思维的工具，它帮助语言打破时空的限制，使得语言更好地发挥其功能。再次，它们的地位也不同。一个社会可以没有文字，但决不能没有语言。世界上很多语言都没有文字，在某些国家和地区，有些社会成员至今还不识字，但他们能够通过语言进行思维和交流。可见，语言是第一性的，文字是第二性的。总之，在人类文化的演进过程中，语言的出现是第一个里程碑，它使得人类脱颖于动物；文字是第二个里程碑，它使人类由原始社会进入文明社会，或者说从史前时期进入有史时期。

由此，可以认为文字和语言之间是相互影响的关系。一方面，文字并非消极被动地记录语言，它对语言有着积极的影响。上文在谈到文字的作用时，已经说到文字能够克服语言在传达信息时在时空上的局限。文字的出现使语言由听觉符号转化成视觉符号，使得语言能够"传于异地，留于异时"。虽然现在人们可以利用像录音机、电话等设备作为语言存储和交际的载体，但是这些远不如书面的文字用于记录语言方便。所以，文字是语言最重要的辅助性交际工具。

另一方面，语言对文字也有影响和制约。语言是文字产生的基础，语言的特点决定文字的特点。文字要更好地记录语言，就必须符合所记录语言的特点。具体来说，语言中的语法单位都是音和义的结合体，文字是对语言中这些小的音义结合体（比如语素和词）的再编码。因此，在文字系统中，有一级较小的形体单位对应于语言的某一级音义结合的语法单位。比如，汉语的书写符号一般以占据一个方块空间的形体单位"字"来对应汉语里的最小语法单位语素，它是最小的音义结合体，这样就大致构成了汉语"一字一音节一义"的对应关系；而英语这种拼音文字是以文字系统中的次小单位文字词（或叫形体词）来对应语言中的次小语法单位"词（word）"，它在文字形式上表现为前后由空格隔开的一串字母（letters）。可见，语言系统对文字系统有重要的制约作用。尽管不同的文字形体各异，它所对应的语言单位的大小也不同，但相同的是，文字必有一级较小的单位是可以用语言中音义结合体的音读出来并表达意义的。

第二节　文字的类型

一、文字发生学的角度分类

从文字发生学的角度来说，文字分为自源和借源（他源）两大类。所谓自源文字，是指从文字产生开始，就独立发展的文字，在文字的形状和体系上是自己独创的，历史也比较悠久。世界上四大自源文字包括古中国的汉字、古埃及的圣书字、居住在古美索不达米亚的苏美尔人的楔形字和中美洲的玛雅文字。这些自源文字中，只有汉字至今存在，其余的都已死亡，或者只是后裔留存。

中国的"甲骨文"（又称"契文"、"甲骨卜辞"或"龟甲兽骨文"，如图8-1），主要指中国商朝晚期王室用于占卜记事而在龟甲或兽骨上契刻的文字，是中国已知最早的成体系的文字形式。它上承原始刻绘符号，下启青铜铭文，是汉字发展的关键形态。现代汉字即由甲骨文演变而来，图8-2就是几个简体汉字和甲骨文的对照。

图8-1

汉字 简化字	日	雨	水	四	北
甲骨文	☉	☲	氺	亖	北

图8-2

美索不达米亚平原一路向西就是埃及，这里出现了最古老的四大文字系统之一的圣书字。大约5500年前，生活在北非尼罗河流域的古埃及人创造了璀璨的文化和优美的圣书字，也叫埃及象形文字。之所以有这样的名字，是因为古埃及人把文字看成神圣的，称为"圣书"，如图8-3。狭义的圣书字仅指主要用于写在祭礼器物，或者雕刻在神庙墙壁和坟墓石碑上的碑铭体，出现的时间最早。图8-4是古埃及记功碑上的圣书字。

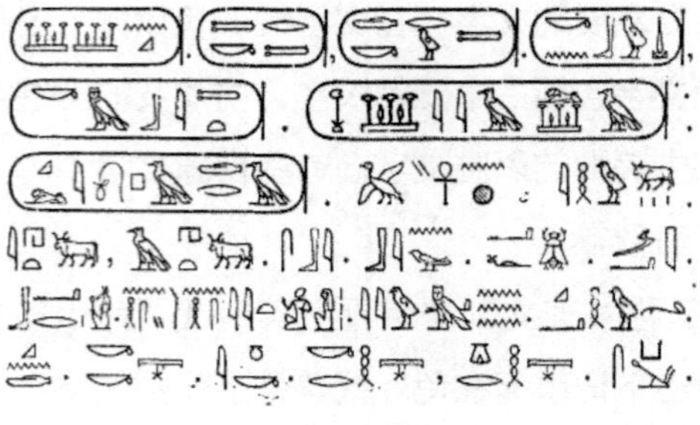

图8-3

图8-4

　　楔形文字（也叫钉头字、丁头字）是发源于底格里斯河和幼发拉底河流域的古老文字。这种文字是由公元前3200年左右苏美尔人所发明，是世界上最早的文字之一。在其大约3000年的历史中，楔形文字由最初的象形文字系统，经过字形结构逐渐简化和抽象化，文字数目从青铜时代早期的约1000个，减至青铜时代后期的约400个。已被发现的楔形文字多写于泥板上，少数写于石头、金属或蜡板上。书吏使用削尖的芦苇杆或木棒在软泥板上刻写，软泥板经过晒或烤后变得坚硬，不易变形，如图8-5和图8-6。

图8-5

图8-6

　　玛雅文字是唯一发展到成熟水平的美洲自源文字。最早的玛雅象形文字记载可追溯至公元前3世纪，而之后玛雅象形文字被持续使用，直到16世纪西班牙的征服者入侵中美洲后不久为止。玛雅象形文字多刻在石碑和庙宇、墓室的墙壁上，或是雕在玉器和贝壳上，如图8-7。玛雅古抄本（也叫玛雅刻本）是将玛雅文字写在脱毛榕木的内树皮制成的纸上，它是记载玛雅文明的重要文献，它有马德里刻本、巴黎刻本、格罗里刻本等类型，图8-8是玛雅文马德里古抄本。

图8-7

图8-8

下面简单介绍一下借源文字。借源文字是指借用或参照其他文字形体或系统而建立的文字，如日文是借源于汉字，英文、法文等都借源于拉丁字母和希腊字母，而希腊字母又借源于古埃及文。亚洲一些国家像日本、朝鲜、韩国、越南等国的文字都是借源文字，它们不仅引进汉字，并且同时引进大量的汉语借词。这些国家引进的汉字既用来书写汉语借词，也用来作为书写自己语言的文字符号。多年之后，由于各种原因，这些民族国家又都创制了另外一套字符或文字系统，其中日本创制的假名和朝鲜、韩国创制的谚文是表音字符体系，越南创制的喃字则是与汉字造字法相同的、方块形的意音文字体系。这些新创制的字符或文字体系与汉字曾长期共用。

二、文字符号的功能分类

语言是音义结合的符号系统，其中的语素、词这些单位包括音和义两个方面。文字是对语言中这些小的音义结合体的再编码。按照构成文字的符号所记录语言的不同功能，可以给文字分出不同的类型。这里构成文字的符号是指，每种语言的文字还可以拆成更小的形体单元，即"字符"。比如，英文的词可拆分为字母：glass（玻璃）→g+l+a+s+s；汉语的方块字可拆分为不同的字符：灯→火+丁。从字符的层级上看它们所对应的语言项，不同文字的差异十分明显。英文的字符只与英语的音有关系，而与英语语词的意义无关。比如glass可拆为g、l、a、s、s五个字符（或字母），单独的字母都没有意义，但分别表示/g/、/l/、/a:/、/s/四个音位，这五个字母要排列在一起再加上前后的空格才能表示"玻璃"的意义。而汉字的字符则有的与语素的意义有关，有的与语素的音有关。比如"灯"的左边字符"火"，其意义与"灯"的意义有关（火有光亮），所以称为"义符"；右边字符"丁"与"灯"在语音上有十分相近的关系，所以称为"声符"。

从理论上说，造字方式只有表意和表音两种，意音文字是这两种方式的结合。但实际上，完整记录语言的文字体系只有两种：表音文字（又叫拼音文字）和意音文字。能够完整记录语言的纯表意文字是不存在的，因为从字符层面上看，表意文字就意味着这种文字所有的字符都是不表音只表意的，而这是不可能的。

首先来看表音文字，又叫作"拼音文字"或"字母文字"。其性质在于，最小文字单位，即字符，只表示语言符号的音，而不表示语言符号的意义。表音文字还可以根据所表示的语音单位的性质分为更小的类，包括音位文字、辅音文字、音节文字，下面简要介绍这几种文字。

音位文字是指字符可以记录语言中所有的音位，有的字符表示元音，有的字符表示辅音，如拉丁字母。英文就是使用拉丁字母作为字符的音位文字。

辅音文字是指字符只表示语言中的辅音，元音没有专门的字符表示，如阿拉伯文。

音节文字是指字符表示语言中的音节，如日语的假名。

再来看意音文字。意音文字的性质在于，有的字符提示语言符号的音，有的字符只提示语言符号的义。提示音的字符叫作声符，与音无关只与意义有关的字符叫作义符。汉字是典型的意音文字。

总的来说，意音文字和拼音文字的本质区别在于记录语言的方式有差异。拼音文字只通过字母记录一个语言的音节或音位。不同的语素或词，只要读音相同，字形也可以相同。比如英语的book，代表了"书"和"预定"两个词，由于这两个词的语音形式相同，都写成相同的字。

这里要强调的是，意音文字也必须记录语言的语音。不过意音文字除了记录语音，还要通过表意方式把不同的语素或词区别开来，也就是说，即使两个语素或词的语音形式一样，只要是不同的语素或词，通常都必须通过形体区别开来。比如"长、常、场、尝、肠、偿"等不同的语素或词，尽管语音形式相同，但不把它们写成相同的字，而是要保留它们在字形上的区别，以便说明它们是不同的语素或词，所以意音文字的字数很多。

另外，有人把汉字说成是象形文字或表意文字，这只是一种比喻或形象的说法。严格地说，这种说法是不准确的，它使人误以为汉字只和表形或表意有关系，而和语音没有关系。这种说法的产生大概是因为汉字最早形成时，普遍使用了象形和会意的方法。前面谈到，文字是音、形、义三要素结合的书写符号系统。汉字和所有完整记录语言的文字一样，除了形和义之外，也必须完整地记录汉语的读音。一个汉字往往就是一个音节，所以汉字是通过字形记录汉语音节的文字。汉字的这种性质可以概括成两点：一个汉字一个音节一个意义；不同的语素往往用不同的字表示。

第三节　文字的起源和发展

文字是对语言的再编码，是语言的书写、视觉符号系统，它的产生经历了一个漫长的过程。在文字产生以前，以及那些至今还没有文字的民族，人们是如何记事的呢？解答这一问题对我们了解文字的起源和发展很有帮助。这一节主要从实物记事、图画记事和刻画记事三种非文字的形体记事方式来看文字的起源。

一、实物记事

实物记事就是人们用具体的实物记录事情，表达思想，传递信息。在众多的实物记事方式中，结绳记事比较普遍。结绳记事是文字发明前，人们在一条绳子上打结，用以记事。上古时期的中国及秘鲁印地安人皆有此习惯。一直到近代，一些没有文字的民族，仍然采用结绳记事来记载信息，如图8-9所示。

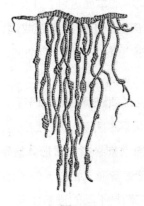

图8-9

据史书记载，我国古代就曾使用过这种方法。《易经》说："上古结绳而治，后世圣人易之以书契。"有关结绳的具体方法，据古书记载为："事大，大结其绳；事小，小结其绳，之多少，随物众寡"（《易九家言》），即根据事件的性质、规模或所涉数量的不同结系出不同的绳结。民族学资料表明，近现代有些少数民族仍在采用结绳的方式来记事，如过去的云南省的怒族、佤族用大小不同的绳结表示不同的事情和数目。

再比如，古代印加人（Inca，又称印卡人，是南美洲古代印第安人）使用一种叫作奇普（Quipu或Khipu）的结绳记事方法用来计数或者记录历史，如图8-10。它是由许多颜色的绳结编成的。这种结绳记事方法已经失传，目前还没有人能够了解其全部含义。

图8-10

实物记事的实物，除了使用绳结外，还可以用其他的实物来记事。比如有的部落用一块牛排表示友好和希望联合，用一根砍断了的牛肋骨表示断交，苦果表示同甘共苦，藤叶表示永不分离等。再比如，我国境内的瑶族曾经用禾秆记录一年的收成，用木板刻点和玉米来记工分。云南陇川县的景颇族有一种以实物代替信息的习惯。假如小伙子爱上了一个姑娘，他就用树叶包上树根、大蒜、辣椒、火柴梗，再用线精巧地包扎好送给女方。树根表示想念，大蒜表示要姑娘考虑两人的事，辣椒代表炽烈的爱，火柴梗表示男方态度坚决，等等。这些都是今天还在使用的实物记事、传递信息的具体例子。但是，实物记事有很大的局限性，能够表达的信息很少，它与文字的产生没有直接的关系。

二、图画记事

和实物记事相比，图画记事表达的信息更加丰富。实物记事多只是表达静态的事物或事件整体的大小或数量。而图画记事不仅可以记录事物，还可以记录有发展过程的事件，事件内部的各个要素及其空间关系，可以表达心里的意愿和要求。比如，人类在岩壁上画出一些图形，用于记录生存的经验或事件，如狩猎等，图8-11就是图画记事的复原。

图8-11

图8-12是印第安人奥基布娃（Ojibwa）部落的一个女子的情书。这幅图画就是该女子在赤杨树的树皮上写给自己情人的信。左上角的"熊"是女子的图腾，左下角的泥鳅是男子的图腾，曲线表示应走的道路，帐篷表示聚会的地方。帐篷里画一个人，表示她在那里等候。旁边的三个"十"字，表示周围住的是天主教徒。帐篷后面画大小三个湖泊，用于指示帐篷的位置。

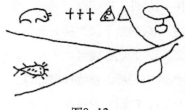

图8-12

上面这种图画把男女约会事情作为一个整体来具体描绘，比如约会的人、人所在的具体位置、位置的参照物等。收到信件的人，是否看得懂这幅画，取决于看画的人和画画的人生活经历上的关联性，这跟他们是不是说同一种语言并没有关系。换一个熟悉当地人文地理环境的、说不同语言的人去看这一封情书，大致也应该可以看得懂；而如果对当地的人文地理一无所知，恐怕只能望图兴叹，不知所云了。另外，即使是能够看懂这幅图画的人，描述这幅图画的意思也可以用完全不同的语言或同一种语言不同的句子。

三、刻画记事

最后介绍一下刻画记事。由于刻画记事可以创造出许多符号，刻画在不同的物件上，所以这种记事方法有广阔的发展余地。唐兰在《中国文字学》中指出："文字本于图画，最初的文字是可以读出来的图画。"其中他所指的图画其实就是由刻画符号演变而来的。在我国的大汶口、良渚、西安半坡、临潼姜寨等文化遗址出土的不少陶器、玉器上，有一些刻画有族徽、图绘、文饰、陶符、图案、记号等形体，其中不少与甲骨文的形体近似，如图8-13至图8-16。

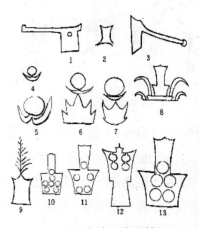

图8-13　大汶口陶器符号

图8-14　良渚玉器符

图8-15　西安半坡陶器符号

图8-16　临潼姜寨陶器符号

　　刻画记事中有一种刻木记事，它是通过在木片、竹片或骨片上刻痕的方法来记录数字、事件或传递信息，是一种原始记事的方法，如图8-17所示。在中国古代文献中，称木刻为"券契""契"。像《列子·说符》中说："宋人有于道得人造契者，密数其齿……"，这里的"齿"就是指木刻上的缺口或刻痕。

　　中国少数民族曾经使用木刻记事的，有独龙、傈僳、佤、景颇、哈尼、拉祜、苗、瑶、鄂伦春、鄂温克、珞巴等族。像苗族用木刻记录歌词，叫作刻道，是由五言体组诗的形式构成。它叙述了苗族古老的婚姻婚俗，刻木符号不复杂。它产生的年代大约是苗族母系氏族向父系氏族过渡的年代。有人称它为苗族婚姻的史诗或苗族婚姻发展的活化石。它用酒歌这种形式记载苗族婚姻的起源、演绎及它的发展和进步，如图8-18所示。除了中国少数民族地区，世界其他地区也存在刻木记事的情况，较著名的有澳大利亚土著居民的通信木刻及阿尔衮琴（Algonquins）印第安人记录神话的木刻等。

图8-17

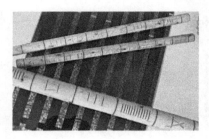

图8-18

　　总的来说，刻画符号的数量是相对有限的，并且它所表达的意义要么与符号有相似性联系，要么仅仅局限在很少的几个领域，这与数学符号、象征性图形符号的性质更加近似。也就是说，并不能确定这些刻画符号已经比较完备地对应于语言符号，也不能确定这些符号已经有固定的排列次序来与语言中音义结合体的排列次序相对应，因此还不能说当时已经产生了文字系统。

四、文字系统形成的基本条件

　　原始的图画文字是早期的文字。原始图画文字看上去与记事图画十分相像，但是两者已有很大差别。我国纳西族用一种与记事图画十分相像的形体系统记录他们民族的古老传说，这些记录叫作"东巴经"。经专家研究，记录东巴经的形体系统已经属于文字，与记事图画有着本质性的差别。图8-19是用东巴文书写的《白蝙蝠取经记》中的一小段（参见傅懋勣1981年《纳西族图画文字〈白蝙蝠取经记〉研究》（上册））。

图8-19

当东巴文经师看到这段很像图画的经文时，总是会用相同的语音诵读出来，它对应着三个有固定的词和词序的句子。这三句大致的意思是：人类搬迁，（是）从灵山顶上搬下来；鸟类飞，（是）从山凹处飞出来；水类流，（是）从高高的高山牧场上流下来。

由上图可以看出，虽然从形体和图画相似的程度来看，东巴的图画文字与图8-12印地安少女记事图画的情书差不多，但实际上两者已有本质的区别：首先，东巴经中的图形与语言有直接关系，经文中的各个小图形都有其固定的语音形式，是通过形体去表达语言中的音义结合体从而再表达意义，而不是像图8-12那样用直接描画现实的方式去表达意义。其次，通过象形、形声、假借、指事等手段，东巴文已经可以表示语言中绝大多数的音义结合体，这些图形都可以重复使用而表达相同的意义，从而可以比较完善地记录语言；而印地安少女情书中只有部落图腾、宗教标记等少数符号。最后，东巴文各个小图形的排列次序已经大致反映语言中音义结合体的排列次序，而不是现实中各个物体的空间关系。

由此可以总结出判定文字系统形成的三个基本条件：第一，具有数量足够多的与某种语言里的语素或词相对应的小图形符号，这些小图形符号可以按这种语言的音读出来；第二，这些小图形符号可以重复使用而所表达的音义不变；第三，这些小图形符号的排列规则足以反映这种语言说话时语素或词的排列次序，小图形符号排列的顺序不同，所反映的语言单位的排列次序也就不同，表达的意思也因此不同。也就是说，文字形体所表达的信息一定是与某种语言的音义结合体及其排列相对应的信息，而不是直接描画现实。

需要进一步说明的是，原始文字的形体没有完全定型，字形和语词的对应关系也没有完全固定，而且有些语词（特别是虚词）还没有造出字来。这样的文字工具当然只能粗略地记录语句。这种文字经过漫长的发展过程才成为能够完整地记录语言的成熟的文字体系。和原始文字比较，成熟的文字系统应该更加严格地符合文字系统形成的三个基本条件。

原典选读

一、语言和文字

【导 读】

这里的原典选自吕叔湘《语文常谈》（第7-14页），北京：生活·读书·新知三联书店，1980。我们所选的三个小节："文字不能超脱语言""语言和文字不完全一致"和"语言和文字要两条腿走路"，都是吕叔湘先生在论述语言和文字的关系。其中谈到文字的产生要远远晚于语言；谈到了文字的起源、文字形成所具备的特点、文字的发展阶段；论述了文字（书面语）和语言（口语）的特点，以及在人们的生活中，语言和文字的作用和适用范围等问题。

文字不能超脱语言

自从有了人类，就有了语言。世界上还没有发现过任何一个民族或者部落是没有语言的。至于文字，那就不同了。文字是在人类的文化发展到一定阶段的时候才出现的，一般是在具有国家的雏形的时候，直到现在，世界上还有很多语言是没有文字的，也可以说，没有文字的语言比有文字的语言还要多些。最早的文字也只有几千年的历史，而且就是在有文字的地方，直到不久以前，使用文字的也还是限于少数人。

文字起源于图画。最初是整幅的画，这种画虽然可以有表意的作用，可是往往意思含胡不清，应该怎么理解取决于具体环境，例如画在什么地方，是谁画的，画给谁看的，等等。这种图画一般都比较复杂，这里设想一个简单的例子来说明。比如画一个井，里边画三只兔子。如果是一个猎人画在一棵树上的，就可能是表示附近的陷阱里有三只兔子，等后边来的伙伴处理。如果是画在居住的洞壁上的，就可能表示猎人们的愿望，这种画有法术的作用，那里边的三只兔子就不是确实数目而只是许多兔子的意思。

图画发展成为文字，就必须具备这样一些特点：（1）把整幅的画拆散成个别的图形，一个图形跟语言里的一个词相当。（2）这些图形必须作线性排列，按照语言里的词序。比如先画一个井，再画三个直道儿或横道儿，再画一个兔子，代表"阱三兔"这样一句话。如果把三个道儿画在井的前边，就变成三个陷阱里都有兔子的意思了。（3）有些抽象的意思，语言里有字眼，不能直接画出来，得用转弯抹角的办法来表示。比如画一只有手代表"有"，把它画在井的后边，就成为"阱三兔"。这种文字是基本上象形的文字，但是可以念，也就是说，已经跟语言挂上钩，成为语言的视觉形式了。

到了这个阶段以后，为了便于书写，图形可以大大简化（图案化，线条化，笔划化），丝毫不损害原来的意思。从汉字形体变化的历史来看，甲骨文最富于象形的味道，小篆已经不太像，隶书、楷书就更不用说了。从形状上看，第二阶段的零碎图形和第一阶段的整幅画很相似，第三阶段的笔划化图形和第二阶段的象形图形可以差别很大。但是从本质上看，象形文字和表意画有原则上的区别，而象形文字和后来的笔划化的文字则纯粹是字形上的变化，实质完全相等。

图画一旦变成文字，就和语言结上不解之缘。一个字，甚至是最象形的字，也必然要跟一定的字音相联系；表示抽象意思的字，笔划化了的字，就更加离不开字音了。这样，语言不同的人看不懂彼此的文字，哪怕是象形成分最多的文字。假如一个人的语言里"有"和"右"不同音，他就不懂一只手夹在一个井和三只兔子中间是什么意思。

文字发展到了这种"词的文字"之后，仍然有可能进一步发展成纯粹表音的文字，这等来再谈。这里所要强调的是：尽管文字起源于图画，图画是与语言不相干的独立的表意系统，只有在图画向语言靠拢，被语言吸收，成为语言的一种形式（用图形或笔划代替声音）之后，才成为真正的文字。

对于文字和语言的关系没有好好思考过的人，很容易产生一些不正确的理解。很常见的是把文字和语言割裂开来，认为文字和语言是并行的两种表达意思的工具。这种意见在我国知识分子中间相当普遍，因为我们用的是汉字，不是拼音字。有人说，文字用它自己的形体来表达人的思维活动、认识活动。当人们写文字的时候，目的在写它的思想而不仅为的是写语言；当人们看文字的时候，也只是看它所包含的内容，不一定把它当作语言；只有把它读出来的时候，才由文字转化为语言。这个话显然是不对的。文字必须通过语言才能表达意义；一个形体必须同一定的语音有联系，能读出来，才成为文字。如果一个形体能够不通过语音的联系，直接表达意义，那就还是图画，不是文字。代表语音，也就是能读出来，这是文字的本质，至于写的时候和看的时候读出或者不读出声音来，那是不关乎文字的本质的。事实上，教儿童认字总是要首先教给他读音；不通过语言而能够学会文字的方法是没有的。粗通文字的人看书的时候总是要"念念有词"，那怕声音很小，小到你听不见，你仍然可以看见他的嘴唇在那儿一动一动。完全不念，只用眼睛看（所谓"默读"），是要受过相当训练才能做到的。

有人拿阿拉伯数字和科学上各种符号作为文字可以超脱语言的例子。这也是只看见表面现象，没有进一步观察。数字和符号也都是通过语言起作用的，不过这些符号是各种语言里通用，因此各人可以按照各自的语言去读罢了。例如"1，2，3"可以读成"一，二，三"，可以读成"one，two，three"，可以读成"один，два，три"，等等，但是不把它读成任何语言的字音是不可能的。而况在任何语言的语汇里这种符号都只是极少数呢？

语言和文字也不完全一致

文字（书写符号）和字音不可分割，因而文字（书面语）和语言（口语）也就不可能不相符合，但是事实上文字和语言只是基本上一致，不是完全一致。这是因为文字和语言的使用情况不同。说话是随想随说，甚至是不假思索，脱口而出；写东西的时候可以从容点儿，琢磨琢磨。说话的时候，除了一个一个字音之外，还有整句话的高低快慢的变化，各种特殊语调，以及脸上的表情，甚至浑身的姿态，用来表示是肯定还是疑问，是劝告还是命令，是心平气和还是愤愤不平，是兴高采烈还是悲伤抑郁，是衷心赞许还是嘲讽讥刺，等等不一；写东西的时候没有这一切便利，标点符号的帮助也极其有限。因此，说话总是语汇不大，句子比较短，结构比较简单甚至不完整，有重复，有脱节，有补充，有插说，有填空的"呃、呢"，"这个、这个"；而写文章就不然，语汇常常广泛得多，句子常常比较复杂，前后比较连贯，层次比较清楚，废话比较少。这都是由不同的使用条件决定的。另一方面，语言和文字又互相作用，互相接近。语言里出现一个新字眼或者新说法，慢慢地会见于文字，例如"棒"、"搞"、"注点儿意"；文字里出现一个新字眼或者新说法，慢慢地也会见于语言，例如"问题"、"精简"、"特别是"、"在什么什么情况下"。剧作家和小说作者得尽可能把人物对话写得流利自然，生动活泼，虽然不能完全像实际说话。而一个讲故事或者作报告的人，却又决不能像日常说话那样支离破碎，即使不写稿子，也会更像一篇文章。所以一个受过文字训练的人，说起话来应该能够更细致，更有条理，如果有这种需要。一个原来善于说话也就是有"口才"的人，也应该更容易学会写文章。

一般说来，文字比语言更加保守。这是因为人们只听到同时代的人说话，听不到早一时期的人说话，可是不仅能看到同时代的文字，也能看到早一时期的文字，能摹仿早一时期的文字，因而已经从口语里消失了的词语和句法却往往留存在书面语里。再还有一些特殊的著作，例如宗教经典、法律条文，它们的权威性叫人们轻易不敢改动其中的古老的字句；优秀的文学作品也起着类似的作用。在文字的保守力量特别强烈的场合，往往会形成文字和语言脱节的现象。中国，印度，阿拉伯国家，古代罗马，都曾经出现过这种情况。这时候，书面语和口语的差别就不仅是风格或者文体的差别，而是语言的差别了。但是只有在文字的使用限于少数人，也就是多数人是文盲的条件下，这种情况才能维持。一旦要普及文化，这种情况就必定要被打破，与口语相适应的新书面语就必定要取古老的书面语而代之。

语言文字要两条腿走路

在人们的生活中，语言和文字都有很大的用处，也各有使用的范围。面对面的时候，当然说话最方便；除非方言不通，才不得不"笔谈"。如果对方不在面前，就非写信不可；如果要把话说给广大地区的人听，甚至说给未来的人听，更非写成文章不可。（有了录音技术之后，情况稍有不同，也还没有根本改变。）人们既不得不学会说话，也不得不学会写文章，也就是说，在语言文字问题上，不得不用两条腿走路。可是自从有了文字，一直就有重文轻语的倾向。为了学习写文章，人们不吝惜十年窗下的工夫，而说话则除了小时候自然学会的以外，就很少人再有意去讲究。这也难怪。在古时候，语言只用来料理衣、食、住、行，也就是只派低级用场；一切高级任务都得让文字来担任。可是时代变了。三天两天要开会，开会就得发言。工业农业的生产技术以及其他行业的业务活动都越来越复杂，交流经验、互相联系的范围越来越大，以前三言两语可了的事情，现在非长篇大论不成。语言不提高行吗？再还有传播语言的新技术。有了扩音器，一个人说话能让几千人听见；有了无线电广播，一个人说话能让几千里外面的人听见。很多从前非用文字不可的场合，现在都能用语言来代替，省钱，省事，更重要的是快，比文字不知快多少倍。语言文字两条腿走路的道理应该更受到重视了。可是人们的认识常常落后于客观形势。学校的"语文"课实际上仍然是只教"文"，不教"语"。是应该有所改变的时候了，不是吗？

① 《礼记·曲礼》：鹦鹉能言，不离飞鸟；猩猩能言，不离禽兽。

二、文字形成的过程

【导 读】

原典选自裘锡圭《文字学概要》第一章：第1—9页，北京：商务印书馆，1988。这一章首先给文字进行定义，狭义派认为文字是记录语言的符号；广义派认为人们用来传递信息、表示一定意义的图画和符号，都可以称为文字。"文字"可以指一个个的字，也可以指文字系统。这一章着重讨论了文字的形成过程。在原始文字阶段，文字和图画是长期混在一起使用的。首先产生的是跟图画有明显界限的文字，而表示具体事物的象形符号随后产生，这二者称为表意字。然后使用跟所表示的对象没有内在联系的硬性规定符号的记号字产生。随后为了克服表意字和记号字局限性造成的困难，表音的假借字应运而生。表意字和假借字的出现，是文字形成过程正式开始的标志。最后，为了克服假借引起的字迹混淆现象，又造了形声字。

一　文字形成的过程

讨论文字的形成，需要先给文字下个定义。在文字定义问题上，语言文字学者分狭义和广义两派。狭义派认为文字是记录语言的符号。广义派大致认为，人们用来传递信息的、表示一定意义的图画和符号，都可以称为文字。我们觉得这种分歧只是使用术语的不同，很难说谁是谁非。我们是狭义派，因为在传统的汉语文献里，历来是用"文字"这个词称呼记录语言的符号的。采取狭义派的立场，讲起话来比较方便。

在汉语里，"文字"一语可以用来指一个字，也可以用来指记录某种语言的文字符号的整个体系。在有必要的时候，我们把后者称为文字体系。

事物都有一个发展过程，文字也不例外。以别的语言的文字为依傍，有时能为一种语言很快地制定出一套完整的文字来。但是对完全就基本上独立创造的文字来说，从第一批文字的出现到能够完整地记录语言的文字体系的最后形成，要经过一段很长的时间的。我们把还不能完整地记录语言的文字称为原始文字。

在文字产生之前，人们曾经用画图图画和作图解的办法来记事或传递信息。通常把这种图画和图解称为文字画或图画文字。按照"文字"的狭义用法来看，图画文字这个名称是不恰当的，文字画这个名称则可以采用。文字画是作用近似文字的图画，而不是图画形式的文字。

从表面上看，似乎从人类会画图的时候起，就有了产生文字的可能。有些旧石器时代的原始人已经会画人和野兽等事物了。他们为什么不能画一个人为作个字，画一头鹿为作鹿字呢？难道原始人没有可能指着画出来的一头鹿说出"鹿"这个词吗？这种可能当然存在。但是这跟有意地用鹿的图形来记"鹿"这个词，完全是两回事。文字的产生是需要一定的社会条件的。在社会生产和社会关系还没有发展到使人们感到必须用记录语言的办法来记事或传递信息之前，他们只可能直接用图画来代表事物，而不会想到用它们来记录事物的名称——语言里的词。通常要到阶级社会形成前夕，文字才有可能开始出现。

也许有人会问，原始社会里用来表本数量的符号，难道跟我们的数字有什么本质区别吗？文字产生之初，文字的确已经在使用划道道、立立子等办法记数了。但是同样是四道线或四个立，可能在某一场合代表四天时间，在某一场合代表四个人，在某一场合代表四头鹿，在另一些场合还可以代表四个别的什么东西。所以这种记数符号还不是语言里的数词的符号，还不是文字。从画四头鹿或四道线来表本四头鹿的意思，进步到用"三鹿"这两个符号来记本"四鹿"这个词（在古汉语里，"四"本来就写作三），是经历了很长的时间的。

当一个社会发展到需要记录语言的时候，如果有关条件都已具备，文字就会出现。前面已经讲过，独立创造的文字体系的形成需要一个很长的过程。目前我们还不可能精确地描绘这个过程，因为大家比较熟悉的几种独立形成的古老文字，如古埃及的圣书字、古代两河流域的楔形字和我们的汉字，都缺乏能够充分说明它们的形成过程的资料。但是根据关于这些文字的已有的知识，并参考某些时代较晚的原始文字的情况，还是有可能为文字形成的过程划出一个粗线条的轮廓来的。在原始文字方面，我们准备引用我国云南纳西族使用过的一种文字，即所谓"纳西图图文字"（以下简称纳西文）的资料。

按照一般的想法，最先造出来的字应该是最典型的象形字，如象人形的"人"字、象鹿形的"鹿"字等，因为这一类字似最易得。但是实际情况恐怕并不是这样的。跟这类字相比，图画的表达能力不见得有多大逊色。唐兰先生在《中国文字学》里曾经引原始岩画里象人射鹿的图画，跟古汉字里的"人射鹿"三个字对比。谁都能明白看出来，如果我们为了表本人射鹿这一类意思，并没有必要撇开图画去发造文字。从后面要谈到的纳西文的情况来看，在原始文字阶段，文字和图画大概是长期混在一起使用的。对人、鹿等物本那这类具有动作的象形字来说，文字和图画的界线是不明显的。

人们最先需要为它们配备正式的文字的词，其意义大概都难于用一般的象形方法来表示的，如数词、虚词、表本事物属性的词，以及其它一些表本抽象意义的词。此外，有些具体事物也很难用简单的图画表示出来，例如各种外形相近的鸟、兽、虫、鱼、草、木等，各有不同的名称，但是要用简单

的图画把它们的细微差别表现出来，往往是不可能的。这些事物的名称在语言里经常出现，也不能没有文字来记录它们。

在文字画阶段，已经开始用抽象的图形，或者同象征符等比较晚近的手法来表意了。这些办法可以用来为一部分上面提到的那些词造字。有些词的意义可以用抽象的图形表示。例如为较小的数目造字的时候，可以继承文字画阶段划道道或立立子的表意办法，古汉字的"一"、"二"、"三"、"亖"（四）就是例子。又如古汉字以"囗"、"〇"表示〔方〕、〔圆〕，圣书字以"X"表示〔划分〕等等。还有一些词可以用象征等手法来表示。例如古汉字用戉牟身于的图形来表示〔大〕，因为戉牟人比孩子"大"（也有人认为"大"字以镀有两臂的人形来本"大"的意思，这也是一种曲折的表意方法）。圣书字用王芴的图形去表示〔统治〕，因为王芴是统治权的象征。用这些方法造出来的字，虽然仍形体酷似图画，本身上都跟图画截然有别。例如用"介耸"表示〔大鹿〕，跟画一头很大的鹿来表示这个意思，是根本不同的两种表意方法。不知道介耸代表〔大〕，就无法理解"介耸"说的是什么。鹿这一类具体事物的象形符号，大概要在"亖"、"大"等表限图画有明确界线的文字开始产生之后，才在它们的影响之下逐渐摆脱图画区分开形来，成为真正的文字符形的。

凡是字形本身跟所代表的词的意义有联系、跟词的语音没有联系的字，也叫前面讲过的"鹿"、"射"、"大"等表意字。很显然，语言里有很多词是根本就完全不可能给它们造表意字的。上面指出过的那些难以用一组的象形方法来表示其意义的词，其中的大多数，即使采用象征等等比较曲折的表意方法，也仍然无法为它们造出合适的文字来。

在文字产生之初，除了一般的表意字之外，人们还使用过跟所表本的对象没有内在联系的理性规定的符号，把这种符号用作指称的标记，或是用来表本数量或某种意义。例如，云南红河地区哈尼族女使用过的刻木，以•代表一元，I代表十元，X代表五十元，∜代表百元。∜代表一元的小点，跟"一"、"二"、"三"、"亖"（四）所用的线条一样，可以用看作抽象的符号。代表十元、五十元、百元的符号，显然是后来才发明的。跟上面所说的那种理性规定的符号一样。这种符号根本不命名，我们如且借用一个现成的词——记号，作为它们的名称。那些难以为它们造表意字的词，是不是可以分别为它们规定某种记号作为文字的呢？

在文字形成过程刚开始的时候，通常是会有少量流行的记号被吸收成为文字符号的。古汉字里"X"（五）、"∧"（六）、"十"（七）、"∥"（八）这几个数字的前身，很可能就是原始社会阶段用来记数的记号（参看三(-)1）。但是最新造很多记号字，跟它们所代表的词没有内在联系，比较难记难记，不容易被人接受。事实上，一种独立创造的文字体系，在形成过程中都极少造记号字。记号字的局限性比表意字还要大得多。

要先服表意字和记号字的局限性所造成的困扰，只有一条出路：采用表音的方法。这就是借用某个字或某种事物的图形作为表音符号（以下简称音标），来记录跟这个字或表达种事物的名称同音或音近的词的。这样，那些难以为它们造表意字的词，就也可以用文字记录下来了。这种记录语言的方法，在我国传统文字学上称为假借。用这种方法为词配备的字，就是假借字。

由于传统文字学的影响，不少人觉得假借的道理很深奥。其实这是一种错觉，我国民间歌谣和谚语中所用的谐音原则，就是借假借是文本义上同样的原则，例如"外甥打灯笼——照旧（舅）"这个歇后语，就是由于"舅"、"旧"同音而错当为"旧"的。从民族学资料来看，有不少还没有文字的民族，在利用事物表意的方法中也已经用上了谐音原则。例如：西非的约鲁巴人曾经习惯于用海贝来传递信息。在他们的语言里，为"六"讲和书"被取引"讲的那两个词是同音的，为"八"讲和书"同意"讲的那两个词也是同音的。所以，如果一个年轻男子把事起来的六个贝送给一个姑娘，这就是为"我为你所吸引，我爱你"。姑娘的答复可能是事起来的八个贝，这就是说："同意，我跟你一样想。"我国云南的景颇族过去通行"树叶信"。他们把一些不同种类的树叶和草叶本西分别用来表本某种固定的意思。在最近这某笔义来用来该诗道里本的树叶信中，"蒲如'树叶所表本的意思是'我来到你们那里来'，'豆门'树叶所表本的意思是'你收好抬起来吧'。因为在他们的语言里，书'来'讲的那个词跟树名"蒲如'同音，书'抬'讲的那个词跟树名"豆门'同音。看来，语音原则早在文字产生之前就已经普通为内的人们所熟悉了。

前面已经说过，最先需要为它们配备文字的那些词，有很是难以用表意的造字方法来对付的。人们无疑很快就会发现，可以利用自己本来就熟悉的语音原则来解决面临的问题。所以，跟图画有明确界线的表意字的开始出现和假借方法的开始应用应该是两件事，在时间上不会相距很远，很可能基本上是

同时发生的。

在古汉字、圣书字、模形文字等古老文字体系和一些原始文字里，都有大量假借字，而且有不少极为常用的词就是用假借字记录的。例如：在古汉字里，常用的语气词"其"是用音近词"箕"的象形字"囗"来记录的。在圣书字里，"大如"这个词是用同音词"燕子"的象形字来记录的。在古西文里，"有"这个词是用音近词"羌羊"的象形字来记录的。这种现象也说明假借字的历史一定非常悠久。在文字形成的过程中，表意的造字方法和假借字方法应该是同时发展起来的，不过不是像有些人想象的那样，只是在表意字大量产生之后，假借字方法才开始应用。

前面曾经指出，限图画有明确界线的表意字的产生，有助于使那些本来跟图画分不出明确界线的象形字符，逐渐跟图画区分开来，成为真正的文字符。假借方法也能起这样作用。那些性质还不明确的象形符号，如果经常跟假借字放在一起使用，或是被假借来记录跟它们所表示的事物的名称同音或音近的词，就会较快地成为真正的文字符。可以说，限图画有明确界线的表意字和假借字的出现，是文字形成过程正式开始的标志。

假借方法的适应性是很强的。对找不到合适的单个假借字的双音节或多音节词，可以假借两个以上的字组合起来记录它。例如在纳西文里，对双音节词"化育"〔pʰɯ² pa²〕，就是把"篇"〔pʰɯ²〕和"娃"〔pa²〕这两个词的象形字组合起来记录的。在圣书字和模形文字里，这种现象更为常见。

假借方法的应用，大大提高了文字记录语言的能力。但是假借字多起来以后，又出现了新的问题。被假借的字本身有自己所代表的词，同时又被假借来记录同音或音近的词，因此假借字的词可以有好几个，因此阅读文字的人往往难以断定某一个字在某一具体场合究竟代表哪一个词。

此外，早期表意字的原始性也给阅读文字的人带来了麻烦。在早期的文字里，存在着表意的字形—形多用的现象。同一个字形可以用单来代表两个以上意义却有不同的联系，但是彼此也不完全没有联系的词。例如：在古汉字里，象杯子形的"出"，既代表"答"这个词，又代表"饮"这个词（二词完全不同音）。在古汉字里，象成年男子的"大"最初既是"夫"字又是"文"字（"夫"的本义就是成年男子），象月亮的"〕"最初既是"月"字又是"夕"字。在圣书字和模形文字里，这是例子也很常见。这种表意字的存在，当然也会影响到表意字表达语言的明确性。

为了克服假借所引起的字义混淆现象，人们把有些表意字或表意符号（以下简称意符）同作指事字的用，加注在假借字上。例如：在古汉字里，〔翼〕的象形字"羽"（象鸟或虫的翼），在假借来表示分明不讲的〔竖〕的时候，有时加注"日"字形作"翼"。在纳西文里，〔薇菜〕的象形字，在假借来表示同音的〔小宫〕的时候，有时加注端坐人形的形符。在圣书字里，这类现象有相当是多的例子。例如由三个符组成的"子"这个表音组，可以用来表示〔纸草〕、〔蜡〕、〔青年〕这三个不同的语音词。为了加以区别，在用来表示〔纸草〕时就在后面加上表示植物的区别性意符"凵"，表〔蜡〕形就在后面加上表意粗笨的区别符号"凸"，表〔青年〕的时候就在后面加上表意粗男的区别性意符"囗"。这种由意符和音符混在一起组成的字，在我国传统文字学上称为形声字，表音部分称为声符，表意部分称为意符。形声在普通文字学上称之为意符或音符。

人们一方面在一些被假借的字上加注定符来区别它们的不同用途，另一方面还在一些表音字上加注音符，使它们跟所代表音的联系更为明确。例如：在古汉字里，"凤"字本作"象高冠美羽的凤鸟，后来加注音符"凡"（凡）而成为（"凤"、"凡"古音相近。更后，凤鸟形简化为"鸟"字，"凡"字又移到上方，就成了"凤"的繁体"鳳"）。在纳西文里，〔山崖〕写作纳西语言"山崖"讲和音"鸣"讲的那两个词同音，所以在山崖的象形符号上加注一个鸣头尖作为声符，传统文字学把这种形声字上加注音符加以称的的一种特殊类型，即所谓"象形声"。其实还不如把它们看作为一种特殊的形声字来得合理。

在表意字上加注音符，有时旦就是为了区别由一形多用或其他原因而有两种以上读音的字形的不同用法。例如，在纳西文里，象太阳的"田"，读〔bit〕时当"太阳"讲，读〔mit〕时当"天"讲，如果要当"天"讲，有时加注当"科"的象形字作符号，因为当"科"讲的那个词也读〔ʂɔ²〕。在圣书字里，象耳朵的"囗"既可以表示〔耳〕，也可以表示〔听〕。表示〔听〕的时候，后面要加注一个表示这个词的末一个辅音的符号；表示〔耳〕的时候，则往往在前面加上一组表示这个词的全部辅音符（圣书字只表辅音，不表元音）。

在古汉字里，为了区别一形多用的表意字形的不同用法，往往采用字形分化的办法。例如：前面讲过的"大"本来也可以写作"夫"。这两种字形都

既可以用来表示〔大〕，也可以用来表示〔夫〕。后来专用前一形表示〔大〕，后一形表示〔夫〕，把它们分化成了两个字。"大"和"夫"本来也都是既可以用来表示〔月〕，也可以用来表示〔夕〕的。不过，加注音符以区别不同用法的情况，大概也是存在的。古汉字里有少数形声字，字义与形声完全相同。例如"鼻"字以"自""畀"声，"自"字本作"囗"，本义就是鼻子。这就是说，"可能本用"自"、"鼻"二音（《说文·王部》"皇"字下说"自读若鼻"），代表两个同义词。后来才在表示〔鼻〕的"囗"字上加注"畀"声，分化出了"鼻"字。

形声字起初都是通过在已有的文字上加注定符或音符而产生的，后来人们还直接用意符和音符组成新的形声字。不过就汉字的情况来看，在已有的文字上加注意符或音符，始终是形声字产生的主要途径。

形声字的应用大大提高了文字表达语言的明确性，是文字体系形成过程中的一个极为重要的步骤。但是形声字的应用似乎并没有使具有较高导数的文字体系的最后形成。已经使用形声字的纳西原始文字就是一个例证。

下面是引自丽江纳西经典《古事记》的一段原始文字：

象表示食粮。下本是〔解开〕的表意字，右纳西语言"解开""讲和音"白"讲的两个同音词，所以这假借字来表示〔白〕。●·是〔黑〕的表意字。◎是风。○是星。〇是湖，〓是土。是上月之林着是〔山崖〕的形声字。据纳西族经师的解释，这段原始文字的全部意思是：把这名抛在湖里头，右边次复风凰海港着湖水，湖水荡滚着黑，着撞在山崖上，便生出一个光辉灿烂的东西来。在这段原始文字里，虽然已经使用了假借字和形声字，但是很多意思仍然是用文字画直接画出来的。

古汉字、圣书字、模形文字等独立形成的古老文字体系，一定也经历过跟纳西文相类似的、把文字跟图画混合在一起使用的原始阶段。

在已知规模的时代较早的古汉字——商代后期的甲骨文里，可以看到还接近图画的表意字的一些残迹余笔迹。其中比较突出的一点，就是某些表意字往往随语言环境而改变字形。例如：甲骨卜辞里常常提到用手把光带打进献食品的"羞"答。"羞"在典籍里多作"登"（《仪礼·夏官·羊人》，"祭礼，割羊牲，登其首"，郑言注："登，升之。"）卜辞"羞"字本作"囗"，象两手持着手做"羞"的象食器形。"羞"字往往改写作"羞"，两手所持的"玄"换成"世"，文里有"羞电"之文，后来"羞"仅似是"羞"字所规定用途的一个异体。但是在汉字发展的较早阶段，情况恐怕并不如此简单。纳西文在这方面可以给我们一些启示。例如纳西语言环境的变化的现象很常见。例如"叫"字通常作写作"囗"，象牛嘴咬步骂，如果误到"马叫"，通常就把这个字里的牛头换作头，并不需要另外加一个"马"字，在汉字发展的较早阶段，"羞"也应该是用来表示〔羞电〕的。到商代后期，这种比较原始的用字习惯基本上已经被抑弃，"羞"字列作"羞"的特殊异体的一样子以下来。类似的例子在甲骨文里还可以找到一些。此外，文字排列方式跟语言中的词序不完全相对应的现象，在甲骨卜辞里偶而也出现着，这些都可以用作古汉字曾经历过把文字跟图画混合在一起使用的原始文字阶段的证据。

在形声字出现之后，原始文字大概还要经过多方面的改进，才能发展成为能够真切地记录语言的文字体系。估计在不断增加新字的同时，至少需要进行这样一些改进：通过将表意字画或表意字，简化字形并使之越于比较固定，使文字的排列逐渐变得与语序完全一致。

凡是被自形成的文字体系，都是像古汉字、圣书字、模形文字那样兼用意符和音符的文字，串续使用音符的拼音文字，最初是在这种文字的影响下形成的。

注 释

① 本章所用纳西文资料，语引自傅懋勣《丽江么些象形文〈古事记〉研究》（武昌华中大学1948年出版，"么些"是"纳西"的旧译名）。傅先生在近作《纳西族图画文字和象形文字的区别》一文中说，"过去所举的象形文之字，实际上己经两种文字。其中一种是似连环画的文字，我认为应该称为图画文字，绝大多数东巴文经也是用这种文字写的。第二种是一个字表示一个音节，但绝大多数字形结构来源于象形表意的成分，应为仍称象形文字。"（《民族语文》1982年1期1页）我们所说的纳西原始文字相当于傅先生所说的图画文字。

② 本章所用古汉字的例子，皆转引自甲骨文或商代金文。关于这两种资料，参看〔四（一）〕。

③ 本章所用的各书名字的例子，皆转引自《大英百科全书》"圣书字"条（1973年版）和苏联伊思特林《文字的发展》等书。由于所据的第二手资料，很可能有错误，故析出待正。

④ 唐兰先生在《中国文字学》里说"真正的文字，要到表意文字发生才算成功的"（30页），已经点出了我们上面这段话的主要意思。唐先生所说的表意文字不包括那些最典型的象形字如"人"、"鹿"之类。

⑤ 汪宁生《从原始记事到文字发明》，《考古学报》1981年1期12页。她见人用五个小横表"五元"，符号不记录语言，这是原始记事将不是文字的一个明证。

⑥ 转引自美国 I. J. Gelb《A Study of Writing》（芝加哥大学出版社 1963年版3页）。

⑦ 上引汪宁生文五—6页。

⑧ 参看上引汪宁生文42页。他认为"真正的文字从表音（引者按：指假借）开始"。

⑨ 沈兼士对汉字早期表意字的这种特土曾作过研究。他指出这种一形多用的现象"在形非字书所无重义、或体之谓，在文非训诂萃所云引中假借之谓，在音非古音萃所云声韵通转之谓，为其形其音其义之津谊后世认为别谊于不相干者"。（《初期意符字之特性》，收入《段观斋录文》）参看拙作《汉字形成问题的初步探索》，《中国语文》1978年3期160—165页。

⑩ 关于拼音文字的形成，可用有光《字母的故事》（上海教育出版社1958年修订版）。

三、Representation of a Language by Writing

F. de Saussure. 1972. *A Course in General Linguistics*. London: Gerald Duckworth and Co. Ltd.

【导　读】

这份原典选自瑞士语言学家索绪尔《普通语言学教程》中"绪论"部分的第六章"文字表现语言"（第22-31页）。这一章主要讨论了如下五方面的内容：

第一，为什么要研究文字。我们研究的具体对象是储存在每个人脑子里的社会产物，一般通过文字来认识不同的语言。

第二，文字的威望。语言和文字是两种不同的符号系统，后者唯一存在的理由在于表现前者。即使没有文字，也不会损害语言保存，因此语言是可以离开文字独立的。文字的威望来自于：①词的书写形象使人突出地感到它是永恒的和稳固的，比语音更适宜于经久地构成语言的统一性；②在大多数人的脑子里，视觉印象比音响印象更为明晰和持久，因此他们更重视前者；③文学语言更增强了文字的重要性（但文字的重要性多少被夸大了）；④当语言和正字法发生龃龉时，除语言学家外，任何人都难以解决争端。

第三，文字的体系。谈到了两种：①表音体系；②表意体系。

第四，写法和发音发生龃龉的原因。语言是不断发展的，而文字却有停滞不前的倾向，后来写法终于变成了不符合于它所应该表现的东西。另外，当一个民族向另一个民族借字母时，这一书写体系的资源往往不能适应新任务，于是不得不随机应变，例如用两个字母表示一个声音。此外还有词源上的偏见。

第五，写法和发音发生龃龉的后果。许多符号表示同一个音，同一符号表示几个音，有时文字还没固定，正在探索规则，因此有反映过去时代为了表示声音所尝试做出的举棋不定的拼写法。这样文字就遮掩了语音的面貌。当文字越不能表示它所该表现的语音时，人们把它当作基础的倾向反而越强。实际上，决定一个词发音的，不是正字法，而是历史，是它的词源。

Representation of a Language by Writing

§1.　Why it is necessary to study this topic

The actual object we are concerned to study, then, is the social product stored in the brain, the language itself. But this product differs from one linguistic community to another. What we find are languages. The linguist must endeavour to become acquainted with as many languages as possible, in order to be able to discover their universal features by studying and comparing them.

Languages are mostly known to us only through writing. Even in the case of our native language, the written form constantly intrudes. In the case of languages spoken in remote parts, it is even more necessary to have recourse to written evidence. The same is true for obvious reasons in the case of languages now dead. In order to have direct evidence available, it would have been necessary to have compiled throughout history collections of the kind currently being compiled in Vienna and in Paris, comprising recordings of spoken samples of all languages. Even then writing is necessary when it comes to publishing the texts thus recorded.

Thus although writing is in itself not part of the internal system of the language, it is impossible to ignore this way in which the language is constantly represented. We must be aware of its utility, its defects and its dangers.

§2.　The prestige of writing: reasons for its ascendancy over the spoken word

A language and its written form constitute two separate systems of signs. The sole reason for the existence of the latter is to represent the former. The object of study in linguistics is not a combination of the written word and the spoken word. The spoken word alone constitutes that object. But the written word is so intimately connected with the spoken word it represents that it manages to usurp the principal role. As much or even more importance is given to this representation of the vocal sign as to the vocal sign itself. It is rather as if people believed that in order to find out what a person looks like it is better to study his photograph than his face.

This misconception has a long history, and current views about languages are tainted with it. For instance, it is commonly held that a language alters more rapidly when it has no written form. This is quite false. In certain circumstances, writing may well retard changes in a language. But, on the other hand, linguistic stability is in no way undermined by the absence of a written form. The Lithuanian which is still spoken today in Eastern Prussia and part of Russia is attested in written documents only since 1540; but at that late period it presents on the whole as accurate a picture of Proto-Indo-European as Latin of the third century B.C. That in itself suffices to show the extent to which a language is independent of writing.

Certain very subtle linguistic features can long survive without the assistance of written notation. Throughout the Old High German period, we find the written forms *tōten*, *fuolen* and *stōzen*, but at the end of the twelfth century appear the spellings *töten*, *füelen*, whereas *stōzen* persists. What is the origin of this difference? Wherever it occurred, there had been a *y* in the following syllable: Proto-Germanic had **daupyan*, **fōlyan*, but **stautan*. On the eve of the literary period, about 800, this *y* weakened and vanished from writing for three hundred years. However, it had left a slight trace in pronunciation, with the result that about 1180, as noted above, it reappears miraculously in the form of an 'umlaut'! This nuance of pronunciation had been faithfully transmitted without any support in writing.

A language, then, has an oral tradition independent of writing, and much more stable; but the prestige of the written form prevents us from seeing this. The first linguists were misled in this way, as the humanists had been before them. Even Bopp does not distinguish clearly between letters and sounds. Reading Bopp, we might think that a language is inseparable from its alphabet. His immediate successors fell into the same trap. The spelling *th* for the fricative *þ* misled Grimm into believing not only that this was a double consonant, but also that it was an aspirate stop. Hence the place he assigns to it in his Law of Consonantal Mutation or 'Lautverschiebung' (see p. [199]). Even nowadays educated people confuse the language with its spelling: Gaston Deschamps said of Berthelot 'that he had saved the French language from ruin' because he had opposed spelling reforms.[1]

[1] The reforms in question were proposed just a few years before Saussure's lectures were given. The issue was a topical one. (Translator's note)

But what explains the prestige of writing?

1. The written form of a word strikes us as a permanent, solid object and hence more fitting than its sound to act as a linguistic unit persisting through time. Although the connexion between word and written form is superficial and establishes a purely artificial unit, it is none the less much easier to grasp than the natural and only authentic connexion, which links word and sound.

2. For most people, visual impressions are clearer and more lasting than auditory impressions. So for preference people cling to the former. The written image in the end takes over from the sound.

3. A literary language enhances even more the unwarranted importance accorded to writing. A literary language has its dictionaries and its grammars. It is taught at school from books and through books. It is a language which appears to be governed by a code, and this code is itself a written rule, itself conforming to strict norms – those of orthography. That is what confers on writing its primordial importance. In the end, the fact that we learn to speak before learning to write is forgotten, and the natural relation between the two is reversed.

4. Finally, when there is any discrepancy between a language and its spelling, the conflict is always difficult to resolve for anyone other than a linguist. Since the linguist's voice often goes unheeded, the written form almost inevitably emerges victorious, because any solution based on writing is an easier solution. In this way, writing assumes an authority to which it has no right.

§3.　Systems of writing

There are only two systems of writing:

1. The ideographic system, in which a word is represented by some uniquely distinctive sign which has nothing to do with the sounds involved. This sign represents the entire word as a whole, and hence represents indirectly the idea expressed. The classic example of this system is Chinese.

2. The system often called 'phonetic', intended to represent the sequence of sounds as they occur in the word. Some phonetic writing systems are syllabic. Others are alphabetic, that is to say based upon the irreducible elements of speech.

Ideographic writing systems easily develop into mixed systems. Certain ideograms lose their original significance, and eventually come to represent isolated sounds.

The written word, as mentioned above, tends to become a substitute in our mind for the spoken word. That applies to both systems of writing, but the tendency is stronger in the case of ideographic writing. For a Chinese, the ideogram and the spoken word are of equal validity as signs for an idea. He treats writing as a second language, and when in conversation two words are identically pronounced, he sometimes refers to the written form in order to explain which he means. But this substitution, because it is a total substitution, does not give rise to the same objectionable consequences as in our Western systems of writing. Chinese words from different dialects which correspond to the same idea are represented by the same written sign.

Our survey here will be restricted to the phonetic system of writing, and in particular to the system in use today, of which the prototype is the Greek alphabet.

At the time when an alphabet of this kind becomes established, it will represent the contemporary language in a more or less rational fashion, unless it is an alphabet which has been borrowed from elsewhere and is already marred by inconsistencies. As regards its logic, the Greek alphabet is particularly remarkable, as will be seen on p. [64]. But harmony between spelling and pronunciation does not last. Why not is what we must now examine.

§4.　Causes of inconsistency between spelling and pronunciation

There are many causes of inconsistency; we shall be concerned here only with the most important ones.

In the first place, a language is in a constant process of evolution, whereas writing tends to remain fixed. It follows that eventually spelling no longer corresponds to the sounds it should represent. A spelling which is appropriate at one time may be absurd a century later. For a while spelling is altered in order to reflect changes in pronunciation; but then the attempt is abandoned. This is what happened in French to *oi*.[1]

	period	pronounced	written
1	11th c.	*rei, lei*	*rei, lei*
2	13th c.	*roi, loi*	*roi, loi*
3	14th c.	*roè, loè*	*roi, loi*
4	19th c.	*rwa, lwa*	*roi, loi*

In this case, spelling followed pronunciation as far as stage 2, the

[1] The examples in the table are the French words for 'king' (*roi*) and 'law' (*loi*). (Translator's note)

history of orthography keeping in step with the history of the language. But from the fourteenth century onwards, the written form remained stationary while the language continued its evolution. From that point, there has been an increasingly serious disparity between the language and its spelling. Eventually, the association of incompatible written and spoken forms had repercussions on the written system itself: the digraph *oi* acquired a phonetic value ([wa]) unrelated to those of its constituent letters.

Such examples could be cited *ad infinitum*. Why is it that in French we write *mais* and *fait*, but pronounce these words *mè* and *fè*? Why does the letter *c* in French often have the value of *s*? In both cases, French has kept spellings which no longer have any rationale.

Similar changes are going on all the time. At present our palatal *l* is changing to *y*: although we still go on writing *éveiller* and *mouiller*, we pronounce these words *éveyer* and *mouyer* (just like *essuyer* and *nettoyer*).

Another cause of discrepancy between spelling and pronunciation is the borrowing of an alphabet by one people from another. It often happens that the resources of the graphic system are poorly adapted to its new function, and it is necessary to have recourse to various expedients. Two letters, for example, will be used to designate a single sound. This is what happened in the case of *þ* (a voiceless dental fricative) in the Germanic languages. The Latin alphabet having no character to represent it, it was rendered by *th*. The Merovingian king Chilperic tried to add a special letter to the Latin alphabet to denote this sound, but the attempt did not succeed, and *th* became accepted. English in the Middle Ages had both a close *e* (for example, in *sed* 'seed') and an open *e* (for example, in *led* 'to lead'): but since the alphabet did not have distinct signs for these two sounds, recourse was had to writing *seed* and *lead*. In French, to represent the consonant *š*, the digraph *ch* was used. And so on.

Etymological preoccupations also intrude. They were particularly noticeable at certain periods, such as the Renaissance. It is not infrequently the case that a spelling is introduced through mistaken etymologising: *d* was thus introduced in the French word *poids* ('weight'), as if it came from Latin *pondus*, when in fact it comes from *pensum*. But it makes little difference whether the etymology is correct or not. It is the principal of etymological spelling itself which is mistaken.

In other cases, the reason for a discrepancy is obscure. Some bizarre spellings have not even an etymological pretext. Why in German did they write *thun* instead of *tun*? It is said that the *h* represents the aspiration following the consonant: but in that case an *h* should have been written wherever the same aspiration occurred, and yet there are very many words (*Tugend*, *Tisch*, etc.) which have never been spelt this way.

§5. Consequences of this inconsistency

An exhaustive list of the inconsistencies found in writing systems cannot be given here. One of the most unfortunate is having a variety of characters for the same sound. In French, for *ž* we have: *j*, *g*, *ge* (*joli*, *geler*, *geai*). For *z* we have both *z* and *s*. For *s* we have *c*, *ç* and *t* (*nation*), *ss* (*chasser*), *sc* (*acquiescer*), *sç* (*acquiesçant*), and *x* (*dix*). For *k* we have *c*, *qu*, *k*, *ch*, *cc*, *cqu* (*acquérir*). On the other hand, different sounds are sometimes represented by the same sign: we have *t* representing *t* or *s*, *g* representing *g* or *ž*, and so on.

Then there are 'indirect' spellings. In German, although there are no double consonants in *Zettel*, *Teller*, etc., the words are spelt with *tt*, *ll*, in order to indicate that the preceding vowel is short and open. An aberration of the same kind is seen in English, which adds a silent final *e* in order to lengthen the preceding vowel, as in *made* (pronounced *mēd*) as distinct from *mad* (*mǎd*). This *e* gives the misleading appearance of indicating a second syllable in monosyllabic words.

Irrational spellings such as these do indeed correspond to something in the language itself: but others reflect nothing at all. French at present has no double consonants except in the future tense forms *mourrai*, *courrai*: none the less, French orthography abounds in illegitimate double consonants (*bourru*, *sottise*, *souffrir*, etc.).

It also happens sometimes that spelling fluctuates before becoming fixed, and different spellings appear, representing attempts made at earlier periods to spell certain sounds. Thus in forms like *ertha*, *erdha*, *erda*, or *thri*, *dhri*, *dri*, which appear in Old High German, *th*, *dh*, and *d* evidently represent the same sound; but from the spelling it is impossible to tell what that sound is. Hence we have the additional complication that when a certain form has more than one spelling, it is not always possible to tell whether in fact there were two pronunciations. Documents in neighbouring dialects spell the same word *asca* and *ascha*: if the pronunciation was identical, this is a case of fluctuating orthography; but if not, the difference is phonetic and dialectal, as in the Greek forms *paizō*, *paizdō*, *paíddō*. In other cases the problem arises with a chronological succession of spellings. In English, we find at first *hwat*, *hweel*, etc., but later *what*, *wheel*, etc., and it is unclear whether this is merely a change in spelling or a change in pronunciation.

The obvious result of all this is that writing obscures our view of the language. Writing is not a garment, but a disguise. This is demonstrated by the spelling of the French word *oiseau*, where not one of the sounds of the spoken word (*wazo*) is represented by its appropriate sign and the spelling completely obscures the linguistic facts.

Another result is that the more inadequately writing represents

what it ought to represent, the stronger is the tendency to give it priority over the spoken language. Grammarians are desperately eager to draw our attention to the written form. Psychologically, this is quite understandable, but the consequences are unfortunate. The use acquired by the words 'pronounce' and 'pronunciation' confirms this abuse and reverses the true relationship obtaining between writing and the language. Thus when people say that a certain letter should be pronounced in this way or that, it is the visual image which is mistaken for the model. If *oi* can be pronounced *wa*, then it seems that *oi* must exist in its own right. Whereas the fact of the matter is that it is *wa* which is written *oi*. To explain this strange case, our attention is drawn to the fact that this is an exception to the usual pronunciation of *o* and *i*. But this explanation merely compounds the mistake, implying as it does that the language itself is subordinate to its spelling. The case is presented as contravening the spelling system, as if the orthographic sign were basic.

These misconceptions extend even to rules of grammar: for example, the rule concerning *h* in French. French has words with an unaspirated initial vowel, but which are nevertheless spelt with an initial *h*, because of the corresponding Latin form, e.g. *homme* 'man' (in former times *ome*), corresponding to Latin *homo*. But there are also French words of Germanic origin, in which the *h* was actually pronounced: *hache* ('axe'), *hareng* ('herring'), *honte* ('shame'), etc. As long as the *h* was pronounced, these words conformed to the laws governing initial consonants. You said *deu haches* ('two axes'), *le hareng* ('the herring'), whereas in accordance with the law for words beginning with a vowel you said *deu-z-hommes* ('two men'), *l'omme* ('the man'). At that period, the rule which said 'no liaison or elision before aspirate *h*' was correct. But nowadays this formulation is meaningless. For aspirate *h* no longer exists, unless we apply the term to something which is not a sound at all, but before which there is neither liaison nor elision. It is a vicious circle: the aspirate *h* in question is an orthographic ghost.

The pronunciation of a word is determined not by its spelling but by its history. Its spoken form at any given time represents one stage in a phonetic evolution from which it cannot escape. This evolution is governed by strict laws. Each stage may be ascertained by referring back to the preceding stage. The only factor to consider, although it is most frequently forgotten, is the etymological derivation of the word.

The name of the town of Auch is *oš* in phonetic transcription. It is the only case in French orthography where *ch* represents *š* at the end of a word. It is no explanation to say: *ch* in final position is pronounced *š* only in this word. The only relevant question is how the Latin *Auscii* developed into *oš*: the spelling is of no importance.

Should the second vowel of the French noun *gageure* ('wager') be pronounced *ö* or *ü*? Some say *gažör*, since *heure* ('hour') is pronounced *ör*. Others say it should be pronounced *gažür*, since *ge* stands for *ž*, as in *geôle* ('jail'). The dispute is vacuous. The real question is etymological. For the noun *gageure* was formed from the verb *gager* ('to bet'), just like the noun *tournure* ('turn') from the verb *tourner* ('to turn'). Both are examples of the same type of derivation. The only defensible pronunciation is *gažür*. The pronunciation *gažör* is simply the result of ambiguous spelling.

But the tyranny of the written form extends further yet. Its influence on the linguistic community may be strong enough to affect and modify the language itself. That happens only in highly literate communities, where written documents are of considerable importance. In these cases, the written form may give rise to erroneous pronunciations. The phenomenon is strictly pathological. It occurs frequently in French. The family name *Lefèvre* (from Latin *faber*) had two spellings: the popular, straightforward spelling was *Lefèvre*, while the learned etymological spelling was *Lefèbure*. Owing to the confusion of *v* and *u* in medieval writing, *Lefèbure* was read as *Lefèbure*, thus introducing a *b* which never really existed in the word, as well as a *u* coming from an ambiguous letter. But now this form of the name is actually pronounced.

Probably such misunderstandings will become more and more frequent. More and more dead letters will be resuscitated in pronunciation. In Paris, one already hears *sept femmes* ('seven women') with the *t* pronounced. Darmesteter foresees the day when even the two final letters of *vingt* ('twenty') will be pronounced: a genuine orthographic monstrosity.

These phonetic distortions do indeed belong to the language but they are not the result of its natural evolution. They are due to an external factor. Linguistics should keep them under observation in a special compartment: they are cases of abnormal development.

四、Constituency of Writing

M. A. K. Halliday. 1994. *An Introduction to Functional Grammar.* London: Edward
Arnold.

【导 读】

韩礼德的《功能语法导论》主要分析英语小句语法的结构（structure），因此，首先要
分析英语语法层的成分结构（constituency）。"成分结构"的观念，是语法能够得以讨论
而必需的基础观念之一。而语法单位看不见、摸不着，所以本章从可视的文字单位入手来
说明"成分结构"这一关键概念。成分结构是线性流小单位组成大单位的多分层的组织体
系（hierarchy）。而结构成分（constituent）是成分结构中的一个成分。就文字的成分结构
（constituency of writing）而言，以英文为例，在一般文体中，可以粗分为段（前有空行，
后有断行）——句（有更大的空格隔开，并有句号等标记）——词（有相当于一个字母长
度的较大空格隔开）——字母。语流中同级单位是接续出现的：一个字母接着一个字母，
一个词接着一个词，一个句子接着一个句子。这就构成了文字的成分结构。

1

Constituency

1.1 Constituency in writing

If we look at a passage of writing in English, we can see clearly that it consists
of larger units made up out of smaller units. These smaller units, in their turn, are
made up of units that are smaller still.

These units are what we call sentences, words and letters. A passage of written
English consists of sentences, which consist of words, which consist of letters. This
relationship can be diagrammed as in Figure 1-1.

Fig. 1-1 The units of written English

We are able to diagram it in this way because each unit begins where the previous
one ends. Sentences follow sentences, words follow words, and letters follow letters
in a simple sequence; they do not overlap, nor does anything else occur in between.
The spaces that separate them — narrow spaces between letters (at least in print),
wider spaces between words, and still wider spaces, with accompanying full stop,
between sentences — serve to mark the units off one from another. These spaces
and stops are not part of the substance of writing; they are signals showing how
it is organized. We can refer to them as STRUCTURE SIGNALS.

This kind of layered part-whole relationship which occurs among the units of a
written text is referred to as CONSTITUENCY. Each unit consists of one or more of
the next smaller — each sentence of one or more words, each word of one or more
letters. It is important to point out that the number may be one or more; in other
words, in any given instance there may be one constituent only. Thus in Figure 1-2
the word *a* has a single constituent; it consists of only one letter:

Fig. 1-2 An example of single constituency

It is possible to have single constituents on successive layers, as in Figure 1-3, where
I is a sentence consisting of one word consisting of one letter.

Fig. 1-3 Single constituents on successive layers

Not a very common sentence, in modern English; but recognizable as the answer
to "Who killed Cock Robin?"

There are other structure signals in written English besides spaces, namely the
punctuation marks such as ! ? ' ' ( ) , ; : and —. The first six of these signal the
meaning of a unit, or its status in the text; they are not primarily boundary signals,
although they may tend to go at particular places in the structure — for example
! and ? usually occur at the end of sentences. The last four mark off some kind
of sub-sentence, some unit that is intermediate between the sentence and the word.
We might in fact want to build these in to our constituent hierarchy by introducing
the notion of sub-sentence as shown in Figure 1-4.

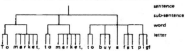

Fig. 1-4 Introduction of a unit between sentence and word

There are likely to be some uncertainties at this point. We might want to recognize
not just one but two layers of sub-sentence, one for units separated by a colon or
semicolon and another one for units separated by a comma. We might want to insist
that all sentences consist of sub-sentences, even if in any given text the majority
may contain only one; or we might allow that some sentences consist of sub-
sentences while others consist directly of words. We might want to build in another
unit above the sentence, and say that written English consists of paragraphs and
the paragraphs consist of sentences. The decisions on such matters would depend
partly on the kind of writing we were interested in and partly on the kind of analysis

we wanted to make, which in turn would depend on the purpose for which we were making it. There are various ways of describing orthographic constituents in English, ranging from that of sentence – word – letter, which is perhaps the simplest one that will work at all, to that of paragraph – sentence – colon unit – comma unit – word – letter, which is more complex but also accounts for more of the facts. All these would be possible representations of the CONSTITUENT STRUCTURE of a written text.

This type of analysis into constituents is often known as BRACKETING; and the constituent structure can be shown equally well by the use of brackets:

[[(To)(market)] {(to)(market)} {(to)(buy)(a)(fat)(pig)}]

Fig. 1-5 Constituency shown by brackets

Whichever device we use, brackets or trees, the notation shows what goes together with what; and in what order, beginning with the units that are most closely bonded (letters bonded into words) and working up through the hierarchy of graphic units until we reach whatever is the highest one to be identified.

Note that in the discussion so far we have been concerned only with the nature of writing, without reference to the grammatical structure that lies behind it. Any stretch of written text could be analysed in this way provided it was written in alphabetic characters, with spacing and punctuation; for example, Figure 1-6. We do not need to know what it means in order to be able to analyse it in this way, since what we are describing here is its organization as a system of orthography. We can see how writing is organized into constituents just by looking at the letters and any structure signals that may be present; we do not even need to be able to recognize the letters, as might be the case in Figure 1-7.

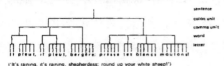

('It's raining, it's raining, shepherdess; round up your white sheep!')

Fig. 1-6 Constituency in French orthography

Even a writing system that is not alphabetic will still display a definite constituent structure, although the units will be different from those of English or Russian. In Figure 1-8 there are characters, but no words or letters.

When writing first evolved, through the gradual mapping of pictograms on to words, it took the form of simple strings of symbols. But in their early stages all writing systems developed some kind of constituent structure; and this tells us something about the nature of language itself. If discourse can be adequately represented by sequences of written symbols arranged like this in constituent hierarchies, it is

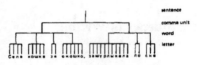

('The cat sat by the window, purring in its sleep!')

Fig. 1-7 Constituency in Russian orthography

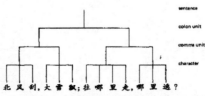

北风刮，大雪飘；往哪里走，哪里逃？

('The North Wind is blowing, snow fills the sky; where can I go, where can I fly?')

Fig. 1-8 Constituency in Chinese orthography

reasonable to assume that language is inherently organized along something like these lines. It does not mean, of course, that this is the only form of organization in language, or even necessarily the most fundamental one; it might be merely the mode of organization that is most readily observable, or the one that is most easily adapted to another symbolic system. But it is likely that the idea of constituency will play some part in any general interpretation of the patterns of language.

In this book we are concerned with grammar, so when we use the notion of constituent structure it will be mainly grammatical constituency that we are talking about. We shall begin to explore this when we get to Chapter 2. Meanwhile we need to raise the question of constituency in spoken language. Seeing that writing systems display such regular patterns, if these do reflect some inherent property of language that property should also appear in speech — in language in its spoken form. Language evolved first as speaking and listening, and languages were spoken for many thousands of generations before any of them came to be written down; so the general principles on which language is organized are bound to be manifested in speech. Where then do we find the principle of constituency embodied in the spoken language?

☯ 思考题

1. 数学公式符号、化学元素符号和文字符号有何差别？请简要说明文字的性质。

2. 结合教材所述和本章原典选读一，谈谈语言和文字之间的关系。

3. 有人说，汉字是象形文字或表意文字。这种说法是否正确？请简要说明原因。

4. 为什么原始的图画文字是早期的文字？请简要谈谈文字系统形成的基本条件。

📖 拓展阅读书目

裘锡圭. 文字学概要（修订本）. 北京：商务印书馆，2014.

唐兰. 中国文字学. 上海：上海古籍出版社，2005.

周有光. 世界文字发展史（第3版）. 上海：上海教育出版社，2011.

Steven Roger Fischer. 2004. *A History of Writing*. London: Reaktion Books. 中译本：[新西兰] 史蒂文·罗杰·费希尔. 书写的历史. 李华田，等，译. 北京：中央编译出版社，2012.

第九章

语言演变

　　本章介绍语言的变化事实及其中的规律。语言在使用中会随着时间的变化而变化，语言的各个方面都会发生变化，有的方面变化得快一些，比如词汇；有的方面变化得慢一些，比如语法。在语言的演变中，存在很多跨语言的共性。

　　首先概括介绍了语言演变的事实（第一节），并简要讨论了其背后的原因（第二节），然后从语音演变（第三节）、原始词汇形式的构拟（第四节）、语法演变（第五节）、词汇和词义的演变（第六节）几个方面进行了具体论述，通过具体的例证阐明了常见的演变类型，并探讨了演变的机制。

第一节　语言演变的事实

语言会随着时间的变化而发生变化。只要是使用中的语言就会发生变化，一种语言只有在死亡之后才不再出现变化。在一个较短的时期内，语言的变化可能不明显，但是在一个较长的时期内，当人们对比当下的语言与书面语记录的更早期的语言时，就会发现变化。人们的交往越是密切，变化越容易出现。在当代社会，随着通信手段的改进，互联网的普及，人们之间的交际更为迅速和便捷，语言的变化比以前显得更快了。个人的言语创新在网络环境下可以得到更为快速的传播，网络用语中出现的新的表达可以很快被广大的网络使用者所知晓和模仿。应该指出的是，言语中的创新是经常发生的，但是，个人或一部分语言使用者的言语创新最终不一定能够被全民语言所接受并成为语言中稳定的部分。比如，在当代社会中我们可以观察到，不少网络语言中的创新是昙花一现式的，最终消失了，并没有能够进入全民语言。然而也有一些创新会被逐渐接受而成为语言中稳定的部分，这正是我们所要重点关注的。

语言变化可以体现在语音、词汇、语法等各个方面，也就是说语言系统的方方面面都可能发生变化。因此，对语言变化的研究，即对语言的历时研究也涉及语言的各个方面，可以分出历史语音学、历史句法学和历史语义学等分支。

正因为语言会变化，因此如果不经过专门的学习，阅读古代的文献时，人们就会遇到障碍，可能会不理解有些词的意思，在词与词的组合顺序与规则等方面也会看到与当代语言的不同之处，用现代的语音朗读古代的诗词时，也会发现有的应该押韵的地方不押韵了。凡此种种，都是语言变化的结果。比对不同时期的历史文献，可以发现语言变化的轨迹。在当今社会，人们对语言变化的感受变得更为直接和真切。由于网络时代语言变化的速度加快，我们有可能在较短的时间内见证语言变化的发生，更全面地追踪记录语言变化的具体过程，更好地探讨语言变化的原因。

同一种语言在不同地域可能出现不尽相同的演变，从而造成了各种地域方言或者亲属语言。地域方言和亲属语言的存在本身就是语言演变的证据。地域方言和亲属语言表面上体现的是语言在不同空间的差异，但实际反映的是语言在不同时间内的流变。

语言演变不是突然的，而是渐变的。个人的创新可以是突现的，但是，一个新的发音特征、一个新词或一条新的语法规则，要被全体语言使用者所接受，需要一个过程。语言的渐变性是由语言作为交际工具的性质所决定的。为了保证交际的顺利进行，语言就必须具有相当的稳定性，而不能朝令夕改。

第二节　语言演变的原因

语言的演变是普遍存在的。那么，语言为什么会发生演变呢？

从语言自身而言，语言符号的任意性为语言的变化提供了可能。单个语言符号的意义和形式之间不存在必然的联系，因此，形式和意义中任何一个方面都有发生改变的可能，形式和意义的对应关系也就相应地发生了变化。如果语言的形式和意义之间有必然的联系，语言的变化就不太可能了。

不过，另一方面，语言符号的任意性又使语言使用者缺乏主动改变语言的愿望。人一生下来就落入了一个语言的"大网"中，并在不知不觉中轻松地掌握了自己的母语。因此，从主观上讲，个人并不具有改变自己语言的主观要求和动力。所以语言的演变往往并不是语言使用者有意为之，而很多都是在语言使用者的意识之外客观地发生的，有意识的语言创新只占语言变化的少数。

由于语言的变化是在语言的传承和使用中自然而然地发生的，语言的使用具有规律性，因此，语言的变化也会呈现出规律性。这种规律性在语音变化、语法变化和词汇变化中都有体现。研究语言的变化就要着力于揭示语言在这三方面变化的规律。

语言发生变化的一个可能原因在于孩子对语言的习得。他们的语法是从听到的语言输入中总结构建出来的，与父母一代不会完全相同，因为每个孩子听到的语言输入是随机的、有差别的。在习得语言的过程中，一些语言规则可能被简化，也可能被过度使用而泛化。这些差异在累积几代之后就会变得逐渐明显起来。

语言变化的另一个原因在于语言的使用。语言的交际是言者和听者的合作与互动。言者希望尽量说得简单，而听者需要听得明白，就希望减少模糊和歧义。因此语言中有两股力量，一股是尽量倾向于简单的力量，这是从言者的需要出发的；另一股是要求明确的力量，要减少和限制潜在的歧义，这是从听者的需要出发的。正是这两股力量制约着语言的变化，很多语言变化就是这两股力量之间平衡的结果。这是对语言变化的宏观制约。从微观的角度看，为了交际的成功，言者要尽量地提供信息，而听者也需要付出努力，从言者所说的有限话语中推理出言者的真实意图。言者与听者的这种合作决定着语言形式的使用和理解模式。在交际中，言者和听者逐渐达成某种规约，使一定的语言形式获得某种特定的含义，从而导致语言发生变化。

语言接触也是导致语言变化的一个重要原因，这是来自语言系统之外的影响。语言使用者可以从其他语言中借来词汇或其他表达方式，语言之间接触时间长了，不仅带来词汇的变化，也会影响到语音和语法，甚至导致一个语言社团原来所用语言的整体替换。

　　语言为什么变化是一个很复杂的问题，语言演变的原因还有哪些？这还需要进一步的探索。

第三节　语音演变

　　语音演变（sound change）可以简称为"音变"。与共时性的语音变异不同，音变是一种语言的语音系统在一个时间段里的发展变化。在历史语言学的发展中，语音演变是研究范围最广、研究历史也最长的领域。它之所以如此受关注，一方面是因为语音研究的发展历史长，人们对其了解较深；另一方面，它是了解其他层面演变的基础，音变所牵涉的往往不只是语音层次的变化，更进一步关联到词法，甚至扩及语义和句法；更重要的是，音变是推定语言谱系关系、构拟原始语言的基础。因此，在研究音变的时候掌握好音变类型、确定音变的成因，是研究历史语言学要做的基本功。

一、语音演变是规律的

　　如果演变的时间足够长，音变都会变成完全规律的；也就是说，如果某一个音的音变成立了，那么所有带那个音位的词语都会呈现这个变化。所以，我们可以说古英语的[u:]变成[aʊ]是有规律的，因为每一个中古英语词的[u:]都变成[aʊ]了，例如，（中古英语）hus [hu:s] >（现代英语）house [haʊs] "房子"、（中古英语）mus [mu:s] >（现代英语）mouse [maʊs] "老鼠"、（中古英语）ut [u:] >（现代英语）out [aʊt] "外面"、（中古英语）ku [ku:] >（现代英语）cow [kaʊ] "母牛"。这个变化可以用一个"大于"符号（>）来表示：[u:] > [aʊ]，其中，左边是较早的音，右边是演变之后的音。

　　当然，这样的音变并不是瞬间就发生在所有符合条件的词上面，语言的使用群体也不是片刻就能完全采纳一种音变。一个群体对一种音变的接受是渐进的，从一个词到另一个词、一个词类到另一个词类，从一个语言使用者到另一个语言使用者，一直到符合条件的所有词汇和所有的语言使用者都受到影响，才能达到完全规律的局面。在一个音变还没有彻底完成的时候，一个词在不同的人那里就可能有不同的读音，其差异可能源于不同的地区、社会地位、年龄，等等。

二、无条件音变与有条件音变

音变可以是有条件的，也就是在特定语音环境下发生；也可以是无条件的，也就是在任何语音环境下都发生。例如刚才提到的 [u:] > [aʊ] 就是无条件音变（unconditioned sound change），因为无论这个元音的两边有什么音，都一律从 [u:] 变成 [aʊ]。当然，也有许多音变是受到相邻的语音影响所致，因此是有条件音变（conditioned sound change）。上面提过的古英语 [k] 的腭化就是有条件的音变，因为它是后接前元音的时候才变成舌面前音 [tʃ]，例如，cinn [kinn] > chin [tʃɪn] "下巴"、cēse [kɛsi] > cheese [tʃiz] "奶酪"。为什么这是有条件音变呢？因为只有在适当的条件得到满足的时候（后接前元音），[k] 才会腭化成 [tʃ]。如果这个条件没有被满足，古英语的 [k] 就还是 [k]，例如 ku [ku:] > cow [kaʊ] "母牛"，在这个词中的 [k] 位于后高元音 [u:] 前，没有满足腭化这个音变的条件，所以音变没有发生。

三、语音演变的类型

所有的语言都会随时间的推移而改变。有意思的是，不管各种语言在类型上如何不同，语音演变的轨迹却是类似的。以下介绍几种非常普遍的语音演变类型。

（一）同化

同化（assimilation）是一个音变得像另一个音，是最常见的一种音变。例如意大利文的 "夜晚" 写成 nocte，所反映的读音是 [nokte]，但是到现代意大利语已经读成了 [notte]。较早的读音 [k] 经历了与后面的 [t] 同化的过程，变成了 [t]。

前面提及的腭化也是一种同化。在这个过程中，非腭音（在硬腭部分成阻的音是 "腭音"，包括腭龈音，如 [ʧ、ʤ、ʃ、ʒ] 和 "硬腭音"），例如齿音 [t]，软腭音 [k] 等，会因为后接 [i] 或 [e] 等前元音而腭化。这是因为前元音带有腭音的部位特征（发音的时候舌的前部是比后元音更靠近硬腭的），所以与腭音发音部位邻近但不是腭音的辅音就有可能因部位与元音趋同而发生腭化。

（二）异化

异化（dissimilation）是两个类似的音变得彼此相异。以南非荷兰语（Afrikaans）（从欧洲语言发展来的，主体是荷兰语）为例，如（1）所示。

（1）*sxo:n   >   sko:n   "干净的"

     *sxoudər   >   skoudər   "肩膀"

     *sxœlt   >   skœlt   "债"

从例子可以看出，在原始语中（每个形式以星号标示），这些词都以 [sx] 的组合开头，[s] 和 [x] 都是擦音；而到了现代南非荷兰语，擦音 [x] 变成了同部位的塞音 [k]，因此，我们可以说 [x] 发生了发音方式的异化，通过异化，它和擦音 [s] 的差异就加大了。

（三）脱落

如果一个本来存在于词中的音经过变化再也不被念出来，那么，脱落（deletion）这个音变就发生了。在中古英语中，nose "鼻子" 这个词最后的央元音 [ə] 是要读出来的（读成 [nɔ:zə]），但是后来不带重音的词尾央元音ə脱落了，所以现在nose "鼻子" 读成 [noz]。

以上央元音 [ə] 的脱落是一种有条件的音变（不带重音），另外还有一种条件可能导致语音脱落，那就是复辅音的简化。例如拼写成bomb "炸弹" 和long "长的" 的词现在分别读成 [bɔm] 和 [lɒŋ]，但其拼写形式末尾的b和g早先是要发音的。

在语言演变过程中，脱落的不只是单个的音位，也有可能是整个音节。例如England "英格" 这个词本来是Anglaland（盎格鲁人（Angles）之地），但后来两个la的音节只剩一个，等于整个音节脱落，加上后来拼写改变，因此成了England。

（四）插入

插入（insertion）是一种与脱落相反的音变机制，就是在一个词既有的发音中加入某个音位。巴布亚新几内亚莫土语（Motu）语的演变历程中，原来是元音 [a] 开头的词演变到现代莫土语后，都在开头插入了一个 [1]，如（2）所示。

（2）*api   >   lahi   "火"

     *asan   >   lada   "鱼鳃"

     *au   >   lau   "我"

（五）单元音化

单元音化（monophthongization）是将复元音（由两个元音组成的复杂元音）变成简

单元音，也就是单元音（monophthong）。现代英语曾经发生过无条件单元音化，也就是中古英语的 [ɪʊ] 简化成单元音 [u]，例如rude"粗鲁的"以前读成 [rɪʊdə]，在现代英语的某些方言已经无条件单元音化，读成 [rud]。new"新的"本来读 [nɪʊə]，现在是 [nu]。due"应有的权利"以前是 [dɪʊə]，现在是 [du]。

（六）复元音化

复元音化（diphthongization）与单元音化相反，就是一个单元音分裂成复元音（diph-thong），这是一种相当常见的音变。在巴布亚新几内亚的卡瑞鲁语（Kairiru）中，单元音 [a] 分裂成 [ia]，请看（3）。

（3）*pale	>	pial	"房子"
*manu	>	mian	"鸟"
*ndanu	>	rian	"水"
*lako	>	liak	"去"
*namu	>	nian	"蚊子"

以上例子的原始语形式都有两个元音，而且第一个都是 [a]；到了现代卡瑞鲁语，我们可以看见原始语的词尾元音脱落了，而第一个元音a分裂成复元音。

英语也经历过几种复元音化。15世纪到17世纪英语的元音大转移（Great Vowel Shift）发生时，中古英语的长单元音 [iː] 演变成现代英语的复元音 [aɪ]，而长单元音 [uː] 演变成 [aʊ] 之类的例子，在本节的开头已经提及，这里不再举例。

（七）换位

换位（metathesis）是一种比较不常见的音变。它涉及的不是语音的脱落或增加，或改变某个语音的模样与性质；换位发生的时候，语音成分不变，只是排列顺序改变。在菲律宾的伊洛卡诺语（Ilokano）中就发生过换位的音变。在下面的例子中，我们将伊洛卡诺语的词汇与他加禄语（Tagalog）相对照，可以看出：他加禄语反映的是没有经过音变的情况，而在伊洛卡诺语中，原来在他加禄语中每个词开头的 [t] 和末尾的 [s] 发生了换位，如（4）所示。

（4）**Tagalog**	**Ilokano**	
taŋis	saːŋit	"哭"

tubus	subut	"赎回"
tigis	si:git	"倒出"
tamis	samqit	"甜的"

在英语中，现代英语的horse"马"、first"第一"、third"第三"、bird"鸟"等词以前在古英语中分别是hros、frist、thridde、bridd。在这些例子中，"辅音–r–元音–辅音"的序列经过换位变成"辅音–元音–r–辅音"的序列，也就是r从元音前调换到元音后。需要注意的是，这是一种有条件的换位，不是所有的r都可以从元音前换到元音后；在r前后都有辅音存在，r才可以换位。以rude这个词为例，r就没有换位到u后面，这是因为虽然r后面有一个辅音d，但是它前面没有其他辅音。另外一个例子是brew这个词，虽然r的前面有一个辅音b，但是因为其后没有另一个辅音，所以换位也没有发生。

（八）舌位的升高与降低

牵涉到舌位升高（raising）与降低（lowering）的音变体现在元音上。在15世纪的英语中east"东方"这个词的元音是［ɛ:］，到18世纪的时候发生了舌位升高的音变［ɛ:］>［i:］，在现代英语east就读成［i:st］了。元音的降低则反过来，例如，非洲裔美国人经常把sing读成［sɛ］。

这里所举的英语例子属无条件音变，但舌位的升高和降低更多是有条件音变。例如在我国境内的藏语迭部方言中，古藏语的/o/出现在/g/前时升高为/u/，同时/g/这个软腭塞音成了喉塞音/ʔ/，因此古藏语的/kʰog/"阻挡（祈使）"这个动词在现代迭部方言便读成了/kʰuʔ/。在迭部方言中我们也可以观察到元音舌位降低的情况，那就是古藏语的/u/在/b/和/g/前舌位会降低并略靠中央成为［ʊ］，例如古藏语的/tʰub/"能够"和/dug/"毒"在现代迭部方言发音分别为/tʰʊʔ/和/tʊʔ/。

（九）舌位的前移与后退

牵涉到舌位前移与后退的音变也是体现在元音上。在现代英语发展的初期有一个无条件的音变，就是后元音［ɑ］前移变成［æ］，例如ask［æsk］"问"，path［pæθ］"途径"，glass［glæs］"玻璃"，等等。

（十）融合

在融合（fusion）的过程中，两个原来独立的音合并为一个音，而且合并之后的音会带有原来两个音的部分特征。藏语迭部方言的鼻化元音就是在历史上元音与鼻音尾融合之后的结果。如果用音系特征来表现（细节参见第二章），鼻音和元音各自的特征可简单呈现为：

鼻音：[+辅音性]、[+鼻音性]

元音：[+音节性]

而融合之后的鼻化元音带了两者的（部分）特征：

鼻元音：[+音节性]、[鼻音性]

迭部方言元音与鼻音尾融合的例子如（5）所示。

（5）古藏语　　　　　　　迭部方言

/ⁿtʰim/　　　>　　　/tʰĩ/　　　　　"渗透"

/ⁿbroŋ/　　　>　　　/ⁿdʐõ/　　　"野牦牛"

/rluŋ/　　　>　　　/lũ/　　　　　"风"

四、语音演变与音系变化过程的不同

以上第三小节所介绍的音变种类，有一些（例如"同化""异化"等）与音系变化（phonological process，参见第三章第二节）一样。那么，历时的语音演变与共时的音系变化有什么不同呢？

音变的开端是一个音经历了一种音系变化过程。如果一种音系变化过程本来没有出现在某种语言中，但是后来发生了（或者是从其他语言引进的），就有可能导致音变。例如在英语早期的历史中，清软腭塞音 [k] 出现在前长元音 [i:] 前面，例如chide"责备"以前的形式是cidan，读成 [ki:dan]，并不会腭化；在英语后来的发展中，前长元音 [i:] 前的 [k] 就要读成 [tʃ]，这是 [k] 经历腭化的音系变化。但是，音系变化的发生并不等同于历史音变的实现，只是有可能导致音变。在初期，音系变化只在特定的语言使用环境中改变一个词的语音结构；当这个变化不受限于语言使用环境，才能被认定为音变。

我们可以从interesting"有趣的"这个词的使用情形来理解"语言使用环境"。这个词的读音现在有两个：一个是 [ɪntɹəstɪn]，另一个是 [ɪntɹəstɪŋ]，前者大多用在正式的语言环境中，后者则用于非正式的场合，比如，跟亲近的人交谈。换句话说，英语母语者的确会允许一个音系变化发挥作用，删除流音 [ɹ] 之前的央元音 [ə]，将 [ɪntəɹɛstɪn] 读成 [ɪntɹɛstɪn]。然而，我们不能据此就主张英语已经发生了"央元音在流音前脱落"这样的音变，因为这个变化只出现在非正式场合的语境中。如果要主张"央元音在流音前脱落"是一种音变，这个变化必须永久地在所有的语境中都发生。拿interesting这个例子来说，必须在所有的言谈中都是 [ɪntɹɛstɪn] 顶替了 [ɪntəɹɛstɪn]，音变才算真正发生。就像本节开头提到的古英语"房子"是hus（读音 [huːs]），到现代英语演变成house [haʊs]，已经没有视社会语言环境而有两读的情况。至此，就可以说英语里经历了/uː/> /aʊ/的音变。

五、语音层次的音变和音位层次的音变

音变可以区分为语音层次（phonetic）的音变和音位层次（phonemic）的音变。语音层次的音变只牵涉到音位变体的发音，不会导致一种语言的音位系统发生增减。例如，在中古英语中，清塞音在词首的位置并不送气，都只有一个音位变体，请看（6）。

（6）/p/　　　/t/　　　/k/
　│　　　　│　　　　│
　[p]　　　[t]　　　[k]

后来这些音开始变化，若处于词首带重音的元音之前，就会送气。这个音变给每个清塞音音位增加了一个音位变体，如（7）所示。

（7）　/p/　　　　/t/　　　　/k/
　　　∧　　　　∧　　　　∧
　[p][pʰ]　　[t][tʰ]　　[k][kʰ]

这个音变只对音位的实际体现产生影响，音位还是只有/p/、/t/、/k/三个，并没有因送气与否造成语义的不同，因此送气与不送气的清塞音并不是对立的音位。据此可以认定，清塞音的送气是一种语音层面的音变，为同一个音位增加了一个新的音位变体。

相比之下，音位层面的音变则会改变一种语言的音位格局，例如增加或减少音位。在古英语中，本来是没有/ʒ/这个音位的，但是后来/z/在某些环境里会被读成 [ʒ]，然后 [ʒ] 慢慢从/z/的音位变体变成了一个独立的音位。在法语的词汇大量借入英语之后，/ʒ/

的音位地位就更稳固了，因为像pleasure［ˈplɛʒə］"喜悦"、azure［ˈeɪʒə］"蔚蓝"都是大家熟悉的词汇，而最小对立对seizure［ˈsiʒə］"癫痫"和Caesar［ˈsizə］"凯撒"也证实了/ʒ/具有区别语义的功能。所以，z>ʒ原来是语音层面的音变，但是后来演变成了音位层面的音变，因为该音变为英语增加了一个新的音位/ʒ/。到了现代美国英语（初步观察是美国东部口音），甚至连Beijing"北京"这个地名都会使用/ʒ/来读拼写里的j这个字母，读成［beɪˈ ʒɪŋ］，而不是［beɪˈ dʒɪŋ］或者更接近普通话发音的［beɪˈ tʃɪŋ］。

第四节　历史比较法与构拟

在了解语音演变的基础上，这里打算专门介绍一下历史语言学上的一个重要概念：构拟（reconstruction）。

历史语言学探究语言如何随时间而改变面貌，而要知道这样的演变，语言学家不仅必须掌握语言当前的面貌，也要掌握其之前的面貌。要做到后者，时空穿越是一个很吸引人但目前不可能实现的理想途径，因此，我们需要在现有的条件下发展出一种可行的办法。

文字记录是我们最先寻求的解决办法，但是全世界七千多种语言中，有文字记录的语言不到十分之一，因此这个方法对大部分的语言都不适用。当然，语言如果能有古老的、反映早期语音的文字记录，对历史语言学的研究将大有裨益。但若是语言没有文字记录，构拟就成为推定语言演变轨迹的比较可行的手段。

历史语言学的构拟方法，根据研究对象是不同语言还是单一语言，可分为历史比较法（comparative method）和内部构拟法（internal reconstruction）。历史比较法系统性地比较多个有亲缘关系的语言，并推定这些语言共有的原始语言可能是什么面貌。内部构拟法则只分析单一语言的材料，从系统的内部寻找线索，并借此推导出这个语言可能经历的历史演变。

一、历史比较法

通过历史比较法的分析，不仅可以确定某些语言之间是否有亲缘关系以及亲缘关系的远近，而且还可以重构原始语（protolanguage）（即这些亲属语言的共同来源）的样貌。

要确认亲缘关系，必须观察语音对应（correspondence），这是非常关键的一环。

（一）语音对应

初步认定语言有亲缘关系后（认定的方式详下），可以从这些语言中选取语义相同或相近的基本词，排列在一起。若这些语言的确有亲缘关系，我们会发现它们彼此间会在词汇的语音形式上呈现一些有规律的对应。下面观察一下"脚"和"蜂蜜"这两个语义在西班牙语、葡萄牙语、加泰隆尼亚语和法语中的词汇形式，如表9-1所示。

西班牙语	葡萄牙语	加泰隆尼亚语	法语	释义
pie	pɛ	pɛw	piɛ	"脚"
miel	mɛl	mɛl	miɛl	"蜂蜜"

表9-1 "脚""蜂蜜"在西班牙等语言中的词汇形式

如果我们比对上面表9-1所有语言的元音，我们会发现"脚"这个词呈现出以下的对应：西班牙语的ie对应葡萄牙语和加泰隆尼亚语的ɛ，以及法语的iɛ。在历史比较法中，语言学家提出的对应应该是系统化且规律的，在表9-1的这个例子中，"脚"这个词西班牙语、葡萄牙语、加泰隆尼亚语以及法语之间的对应关系可以表述为：ie-ɛ-ɛ-iɛ。进一步地，在这些语言中，当我们排列出其他呈现语义相同或相近的词汇组时，也应该能观察到这个对应规律。因此，在上面的例子中，我们从表示"脚"的词中所得出的对应规律在表示"蜂蜜"的词汇组里也出现了。在这四种语言中，表达"蜂蜜"这个语义的形式是相仿的，而且其元音同样呈现出ie-ɛ-ɛ-iɛ这种对应。这样的有规律的对应我们称之为系统性对应（systematic correspondence），这对识别语言的亲缘关系起关键的作用。系统性对应有两个特点：一是它们不会只出现在一两个词汇组里，而是可以在为数不少的词汇组中观察到，因此，它们的语义-形式配对并不是因偶然因素才看起来相似的，这跟无亲缘关系的语言间因巧合而出现一些音义接近词汇完全不同；二是ie-ɛ-ɛ-iɛ并不是唯一能将这四种语言联系在一起的语音对应，应该还有许多辅音及其他元音的对应模式在这些语言的不同词汇组上重复出现。

在分析过语言间的语音对应、确认其是否有亲缘关系之后，历史语言学的比较工作还必须进一步探究有亲缘关系的语言是如何从原始语言（proto-language）演化成当前这个模样的，而要达到这个目的，就要进行原始语构拟。

有些语言有古老的文献资料，可以供我们核对所构建的系统是否与早期文献反映的面貌一致。但是更多的时候，这样的书面材料是不存在的，不过这并不表示人们就完全无法得知语言先前的面貌了。通过观察当前有亲缘关系的语言，比较其语音形式和语法，我们可以依据收集到的事实推定原始语的结构和系统。例如，原始印欧语的一些词可以以其子语（daughter languages）的词汇为基础进行重构。表9-2的词在四种印欧语言中都有一样的语义，星号（*）所标示的是该词的构拟形式（reconstructed form）或原始形式（proto-form）。要注意的是，这些形式是我们根据其子语所带的遗传特征推断出来的，并不是谁听过或看过的形式，这也就是为什么历史比较法所做的工作是"构拟"而不是"还原"。

释义	英语	希腊语	拉丁	梵语	原始印欧语
父亲	faðə	pate:r	pater	pɪtər-	*pəte:r
母亲	mʌðə	me:te:r	ma:ter	ma:tər-	*ma:te:r
兄弟	bɹʌðə	pʰra:te:r	fra:ter	bʰra:tər-	*bʰra:te:r

表9-2　三组亲属词汇的原始印欧语构拟形式及其子语间的对应

以上对原始语形式的推论，建基于我们假设某几种语言有亲缘关系，进而找出语音形式和语义的匹配方式相仿、可能反映出亲缘关系的词，然后根据语音对应模式确认语言间亲缘关系的远近。之所以能如此，是因为语言的演变是有规律的。如果有两种以上的语言，其词汇在语义和语音形式的匹配上呈现有规律的对应，就表示这些词来自同一个源头。亲缘关系确立后，语言学家会进一步构拟其原始语的形式。这样的研究方法就是历史比较法。

（二）历史比较法的构拟程序

历史比较法的构拟程序大致如下：

第一，通过审慎查验，初步认定哪几种语言有亲属关系，也就是共有一个祖先。执行这一步的方法有很多种，可以查考文献历史的记载，也可以采访母语者，请他们分享与母语相关的知识，还可以直接从（田野调查）收集到的语料中观察可能的规律。这些方法都可以得到对构拟有用的线索。

第二，收集编制同源词群，并且排除借词。如果不同语言中的几个语义对应的词是从同一个源头发展而来的，这几个词就是同源词（cognates）。同源词在语音形式上彼此相仿，而且表达的语义是相同或者相似的。先将要研究的语言中有相同或相似语义的词排列在一起，然后审视其语音形式。下面的三种语言是虚拟的语言，这个同源词群形式相近，表达的意思都是"黄瓜"。

甲	乙	丙	释义
tisa	stiha	tiza	黄瓜

表9-3 虚拟语言的同源对应形式

由于在语义及语音的层面相似，这三个词形成一个同源词群。在汇整同源词群的时候要注意观察，把一些看起来突兀的形式排除。具体来讲，有时在整理一群语言的同源词群时，可能会看到一个突兀的形式，这个形式在语音上与同源词群其他成员差异很大。这样的形式不大可能是从同一个源头发展来的，而有可能是从一个没有亲缘关系的语言借入的。有可能在过去某一段时间里原来的同源词被当前这个借词取代了。借词不可用作历史比较法的分析材料，所以遇到借词的时候，应直接剔除。

第三，确认语音对应。在这一步，我们要确认语音是否呈系统性的对应。在一个同源词群中比对每一个词同一个位置的语音。上面所列举的"黄瓜"这个例子，在三种语言中呈现出四个位置的语音对应，如表9-4所示。

位置	甲	乙	丙
1	t	st	t
2	i	i	i
3	s	h	z
4	a	a	a

表9-4 同一位置上的语音对应例示

第四，为每一个对应的位置构拟一个原始音。我们为每一组对应推定一个可能的原始形式（proto-form），在推定每一个音时，都必须能对它的演变轨迹提供合理的解释，说明它是如何演变成当前众子语中的语音形式。要做到这一点，就要熟悉历史音变的特性，并按照以下原则操作：

A. 完全对应

如果在同源词群中，所有的语言在同一个位置上都用同一个音，原始形式就以那个音构拟。在表9-4的例子中，每个语言在位置2和4上的语音都一样，所以位置2上的原始形式就构拟为i，位置4上的原始形式构拟为a。因为位置1和3上的原始形式目前还没确定，所以到这一步我们对这个词的构拟可以用*__i__a来标记，把已经构拟好的位置填上音，尚未构拟的位置预留空格"__"。

B. 最自然的演变

如果没有完全对应，就需要（不一定是必须，也可以构拟一个在后代子语中都不存在的原始形式）从出现在同源词同一位置上的几个音里面挑选一个，这种情况下哪一个音经历的音变最自然，就最能够被选中作为原始形式。但我们怎么知道哪些音变是自然的，哪些不自然呢？语音学及历史语言学长期积累下来的研究已经证实，有一些音变非常普遍，而有些则几乎不可能出现，这样的知识使我们得以将构拟的基础建立在自然的语音演变的基础上。以下列出一些最普遍的音变，如果演变的方向与这里呈现的相反，就非常罕见，或者说"不自然"。

[1]在元音之间，塞音变擦音；

[2]在元音之间以及在浊辅音之前，清音变浊音；

[3]在前元音之前，辅音腭化；

[4]复杂的复辅音简化；

[5]发音难度高的辅音降低难度（例如，内爆浊塞音可能变成一般浊塞音）；

[6]复元音被插入辅音断开；

[7]在鼻音前，元音鼻化；

[8][h]以外的擦音变成[h]（失去原来的发音部位差别）；

[9]在元音之间的[h]脱落。

按照以上的语音演变原则，我们就可以为"黄瓜"这个词的位置1推定出st这个复辅音作为其原始形式，理由是甲语言和丙语言经历了复辅音简化（*st>t），所以得到了当前的形式。将位置3上的音构拟成*s，*s从原始语到当前的三种子语，经历了哪些变化？甲语言没有经历变化，乙语言则是由s变成了h，丙语言的z则是清辅音在元音之间变浊音的结果。

C. 最简原则筛选

如果有两种以上的分析方式都很合理，也符合自然的语音演变发展趋势轨迹，那么就采用步骤最少最简单就能涵盖全部事实的分析。

第五，整词构拟。分析出每个位置的语音变化轨迹后，我们就来看整个词，使用第四步的分析结果，将整个词的语音形式构建出来。到这一步，以甲乙丙三种语言的"黄瓜"一词的同源对应已经可以构拟出原始形式：*stisa。

第六，查验音变规律在整个系统中的适用性。上面介绍的步骤可以构拟一个一个的同源词原始形式，但在这之后还必须通盘考虑已经提出的音变规律能否应用在所有同源词群上。之所以需要如此，是因为语音演变是有规律的，所以每一个子语都应该有一套统一的演变规律可以为所有的同源词群推定原始语形式。万一发现已经提出的音变规律无法做到这一点，就要在最小的幅度内调整音变规律的项目、内容或排序，以使最终的结果呈现出系统整体的一致性。

　　有一种检验的方式是特别观察一对在甲语言中是同音词（语音的组合一模一样），但在乙语言中却是有差异的词。遇到这样的情况，原则上要以乙语言的差异当作构拟的依据，请看下面表9-5所呈现的例子。

甲	乙	释义
ase	ase	"牛"
ase	ose	"蝇卵"

表9-5　同音词与近音词

建基于甲乙两种语言的比较，在原始语的构拟中，"牛"这个词因为在两种语言中每个位置完全对应，所以直接构拟为*ase。至于"蝇卵"则构拟为*ose，因为要是构拟为*ase的话，无法解释为何在乙语言a变成了o，而且"牛"这个词并没有经历由a到o的演变；但是构拟为*ose的话，就可以假定在甲语言中，"蝇卵"这个词在位置1上经历了o变a的音变。

　　第七，将原始语的音系构建出来。同源词群的构拟能使我们构拟原始语中一个个音位，这些音位按照音质、发音部位与方法加以分类归纳，原始语的音位系统就构建起来了。

　　上面是历史比较法构拟程序的简单介绍，读者可以阅读本章的原典选读一，详细了解构拟的操作规程。

（三）历史比较法的时间限制

　　历史比较法的时间估测是有限制的。大部分的学者都认为十万年前现代人出现在地球上时就开始使用语言，有一些学者甚至会把时间估测得更长远。若是历史语言学的理论和技术都能有所突破，大部分的语言学家可能都愿意相信、也会试图去证明所有人类的语言最终都能追溯到同一个起源——一个在我们这个物种兴起的时候就开始涌现的语言。不过，很遗憾的是，在目前遗传学对人类起源的探索有长足发展与挺进的时刻，语言的历史比较法却无法与之并驾齐驱。毕竟，历史比较法很大程度上必须依赖现存的子语所保留的原始语遗迹，但语言在时间的长河中发展演化，终究会在某一个阶段，由于音系演变、词汇替换和语法重塑等长期变化的累积，以至于连最后一点能指示我们通往共同始祖的淡淡轨迹也覆灭了，或者被各种因巧合而出现的表面相似性给遮盖了。

那么，这样的阶段一般要经历多长时间才会来到呢？也就是说，两个语言从共同的始祖分化后要经过多少时间的演变，才会让人找不到一丝确切的证据，证明它们来自同一个源头呢？这个问题并没有确切的答案，但是一般语言学家估计是6000~8000年，乐观一点的看法是到一万年。之所以划出一个范围，是因为有些语言可能会演变得比其他语言慢，因此其祖语的残存特征也保留得比较多、比较久。不过，即使是最有优势的语系（有许多语言存留下来，也有古老的历史文献可以佐证）也同样有时限问题。如果要严谨地施行历史比较法，就要知道它的时间估测是有上限的。

二、内部构拟

语言学家也可以只检视一个语言的材料，并借由材料的比对推敲，对该语言的发展演变做出假设，这样的分析方法称为内部构拟法。使用内部构拟法，语言学家可以了解一种语言发展历史中的许多细节。此外，世界上有不少语言与任何语言都没有亲缘关系，因此无法采用历史比较法来探究其祖语的面貌，对这些"独立语"（isolates，也就是没有亲属语的语言）而言，内部构拟法也是一个能够帮助人们了解其历史演变轨迹的选择。

英语有历代文字的材料，在呈现内部构拟的时候比较一目了然，可以帮助人们了解如何从形态交替的变化中取得材料，推定较早阶段发生的音变。以下表9-6的例子，我们从英文拼写的实际发音中，可以看出一种有条件的音变：

英文拼写	现代读音	释义
sign	[saɪn]	签名（动词）
paradigm	['pærəˌdaɪm]	词形变化（名词）
signature	['sɪgnətʃə]	签名（名词）
paradigmatic	[ˌpærədɪg'mætɪk]	词形变化的（形容词）

表9-6　英文字母g在现代英语中的发音情况例示

这些例子中的变化显示，有一些词的拼写形式里的g是不发音的（sign、paradigm），但是以它们为词根的派生形式（signature、paradigmatic）中，g又是发音的。据此我们可以说，sign和paradigm这两个语素在不同的语法环境有不同的读音，呈现出一种形态交替（morphological alternation）。当音变造成形态交替的时候，我们可以先检视这些不同读音的语音环境，并且确定是什么音变造成了这样的交替。从表9-6的材料，我们得到的规律如下：如果出现在词尾的鼻音前，浊舌根塞音g是不发音的，例如sign就读成 [saɪn]；但是如果该鼻音不是出现在词尾，g就发音，例如signature ['sɪɡnətʃə]。这样的规律还发生在其他符合上述环境的词中。根据这些形态交替变化，我们可以对英语的演变历史作一些推断。我们可以假设英文在刚开始拼写这些词的时候，这个有条件的音变并不存在，也就是说，拥有 [gn]、[gm] 这样组合的语素只有一种读音，其中的g发音。但是，后来音变发生了，使得g不再发音，条件是出现在词尾鼻音前。经历了这样的语音变化，就造成了现在的形态交替现象。

下面谈谈内部构拟法的操作规程，大致说来，施行内部构拟的步骤如下：

[1] 在一个语言里观察语法（通常是词法）的规律；

[2] 锁定一种规律，细察是否有些形式会成为这条规律的例外；

[3] 若有例外，我们假设这些例外的形式本来是符合规律的，也就是说，假设在更早的时期，这条规律是没有例外的；

[4] 从例外的例子中推测出可能的音变，这样的音变扰乱了原来具有完美规律的系统，导致了例外的出现。

当进行到第4步的时候，我们尽力确保所推测的音变是自然并且合理的。

我们来看看在拉丁文的材料中，如何实践以上的步骤。拉丁语有一类动词，其第一人称单数现在时的形式是在动词词干上接后缀-o，动词不定式是词干加后缀-ere，第一人称完成体是加后缀-si，而动名词则是加上后缀-tum。表9-7中的动词呈现完美的规律变化，其中x读成 [ks]，c读成 [k]（同样的读音规律也适用于表9-8）。

	第一人称单数现在时	不定式	第一人称完成体	动名词	注释
a	carpo	carpere	carpsi	carptum	采摘
b	dico	dicere	dixi	dictum	说
c	duco	ducere	duxi	ductum	带领
d	repo	repere	repsi	reptum	爬行
e	scalpo	scalpere	scalpsi	scalptum	雕刻

表9-7 拉丁文动词规则变化例示

根据表9-7的动词词形变化，识别动词词干是很轻松的工作，因为无论是哪个动词形式，词干的形态都不变：carp-"采摘"、dic-"说"、duc-"带领"、rep-"爬行"、scalp-"雕刻"。

不过，有些动词在这几类变化中出现异常行为，如表9-8所示。

x	第一人称单数现在时	不定式	第一人称完成体	动名词	注释
a.	figo	figere	fixi	fictum	修理
b.	scribo	scribere	scripsi	scriptum	书写
c.	nubo	nubere	nupsi	nuptum	结婚
d.	sugo	sugere	suxi	suctum	吸吮

表9-8　拉丁文动词不规则变化举例

这些词干在第一人称单数现在时以及不定式这两栏，词干是浊塞音结尾，但是到了第一人称完成体和动名词，就成了清塞音，因此每个动词都有两种词干形式，呈现出异干的交替变化：fig-~fic-"修理"、scrib-~scrip-"书写"、nub-~nup-"结婚"、sug-~suc-"吸吮"。若我们假设在早期拉丁语中并没有这样的词干变异，那就要推定原来的词干是浊塞音结尾还是清塞音结尾，以及是什么音变造成了现在所看见的异干格局。如果只看表9-8中的材料，我们认为将原来的词干假设为浊塞音结尾或清塞音结尾都是可能的，例如，将"结婚"的原词干推定为nub，我们可以说b后面接清辅音时，会清化成p，因此nub第一人称完成体由于后面接了-si，b清化，词干变成了nup，同样的原则也适用于动名词的情形。另一方面，我们也可以将原词干推定为nup，然后说p后面接元音的话，就浊化成了b，毕竟清辅音在两个元音之间浊化也是很自然的音变，因此在不定式中，nup后面接-ere，p浊化，词干就变成了nub。不过，如果我们将表9-7中的动词形态也纳入考量（这是应该做的，必须达到整个系统一致），就会发现塞音浊化的分析站不住了，特别是表9-7中"爬行"这个动词，就显示词尾的清塞音并不会因为后面接-o或-ere等元音开头的后缀就浊化。因此，通盘考量之下，我们应选择第一种分析，也就是表9-8中的词原来的词干都是以浊塞音结尾，将原词干推定为：*fig-"修理"、*scrib-"书写"、*nub-"结婚"、*sug-"吸吮"。

第五节　语法演变

语法规则具有高度的抽象性，因此也具有巨大的稳固性。尽管如此，语法规则还是在表达的要求、语音的演变、语法的类推等各种因素的作用下，处在逐渐的演变之中。

一、常见的语法变化

（一）语序变化

很多语言的语序都在历史发展过程中发生过变化。比如，一些印欧语的语序从"宾-动"语序（宾语位于动词之前）变为了"动-宾"语序（动词位于宾语之前），修饰语（包括关系从句）从中心语前变到中心语后。以英语为例，原来的"领属性修饰语+中心语"的语序逐渐向"中心语+领属性修饰语"的语序演变，也就是说，the student's book 式的语序逐渐变为the book of the student 式的语序。据统计，10世纪时，of 结构只占领属结构的1%；而到14世纪时，of结构占领属结构的85%。不过，这种演变并没有彻底完成，直到现代英语，这两种语序依旧并存。

汉语历史上也发生了一些语序变化，比如上古汉语中代词宾语在否定句和疑问句中位于动词前，分别如（8）（9）所示。

（8）不患人之不己知，患不知人也。（《论语·学而》）

（9）吾谁欺？欺天乎？（《论语·子罕》）

但是到东汉以后，代词宾语就逐渐转移到了动词之后，与名词性宾语的位置变得相同了，例如（10）-（11）。

（10）比三代，莫敢发之。（《史记·周本纪》）

（11）愿闻其校此者，皆当使谁乎？（《太平经》卷五十一）

上古汉语中有所谓的"大名冠小名"现象，即在名词性复合词中名词性中心语位于名词性修饰语之前，请看（12）-（14）。

（12）公会齐侯于城濮。（《左传·庄公二十七年》）

（13）孟夏行春令，则蝗虫为灾；仲冬行春令，则蝗虫为败。（《礼记·月令篇》）

（14）郢人垩漫其鼻端若蝇翼，使匠石斫之……（《庄子·徐无鬼》）

（12）中的"城濮"就属于"大名冠小名"，按照后代的语序应说成"濮城"。（13）中的"蝗虫"根据清代学者王念孙的考证在当时应该说成"虫蝗"。（14）中的"匠石"照今天的说法应该是"石匠"。这种"大名冠小名"现象在后代消失了，只在部分方言中还有所保留，比如在江淮官话与西南官话的某些地方，还有"鸡公""鸡婆"的说法，在大部分汉语方言中则要说成"公鸡""母鸡"。

汉语中发生的另一个比较显著的语序变化是，大部分介词短语都经历了从位于动词后到位于动词前的演变。（15）-（16）显示，上古汉语中，介词短语可以位于动词之后。

（15）杀人以梃与刃，有以异乎？（《孟子·梁惠王上》）

（16）冬，齐、郑盟于石门。（《左传·隐公三年》）

（15）中"以梃与刃"是表示工具的介词短语，（16）中"于石门"是表示处所的介词短语，都位于动词之后。

演进到现代汉语中，除了引进目标（goal）的介词短语之外，大部分介词短语都位于动词之前了，如（17）-（19）。

（17）他用左手写字。（表示工具的介词短语位于动词之前）

（18）他在北京工作。（表示处所的介词短语位于动词之前）

（19）他给张三讲故事。（表示对象的介词短语位于动词之前）

（二）新的语法形式的出现

语法形式指没有词汇意义而仅仅表示语法意义的成分，包括虚词、屈折词缀等。这类形式在语言的历史上是后起的。

比如，汉语里的体标记"了""着""过"都是在唐宋之后才产生的，本来这些形式都是动词，是由动词变为体标记的。

汉语中具有特色的个体量词，如"一本书"的"本"，"一个人"的"个"等，也是后起的。在上古汉语中，数词可以直接出现在名词之前，如（20）中的"一鸡"与（21）中的"三鼎""二鼎"。

（20）今有人日攘其邻之鸡者，或告之曰："是非君子之道。"曰："请损之，月攘一鸡；

以待来年，然后已。"(《孟子·滕文公下》)

（21）奠定，雍人陈鼎五，三鼎在羊镬之西，二鼎在豕镬之西。(《仪礼·少牢馈食礼》)

到了东汉以后，量词开始出现在数词之后，南北朝时期就大量使用了，如（22）-（24）。

（22）即使人多设罗，得鹊数十枚。(《论衡·书虚》)

（23）斋前种一株松，恒自手壅治之。(《世说新语·德行》)

（24）以麻子二七颗，赤小豆七枚，置井中，辟疫病，甚神验。(《齐民要术·小豆》)

量词这个词类出现之后，汉语的数词就不再直接出现在名词之前了。

英语中的助动词或称情态动词，如can、may、must等原本是动词，它们是在历时发展中从普通的动词中分离出来，逐步变成了一个新的语法形式类。

（三）旧的语法形式的消失

一些原本存在的语法形式有可能在后代消失。比如，上古汉语常见的虚词"而""於""者""之"在后代都趋于消失或衰落了。下面以"而"和"之"的变化为例。

"而"在上古汉语中是一个用得十分广泛的虚词，可以连接两个动词性结构，这种连词用法一直延续到现代汉语中。但是，现代汉语中"而"的使用有很大程度的萎缩，很多原来要用"而"连接的结构现在不用了。在现代汉语中，"而"主要表示并列和转折。在上古汉语中，"而"的使用范围要比现代汉语宽得多，不但可以表示并列和转折，也可以作为承接连词，其前后的两个动词性成分可以表示相继发生的动作行为，译成现代汉语时无法找到对应成分，如（25）-（30）。

（25）校人出，曰："孰谓子产智？予既烹而食之，曰：'得其所哉！得其所哉！'"
（《孟子·万章上》)

（26）匠人斫而小之。(《孟子·梁惠王下》)

（27）孔子登东山而小鲁，登泰山而小天下。(《孟子·尽心上》)

（28）见兔而顾犬，未为晚也；亡羊而补牢，未为迟也。(《战国策·楚策四》)

（29）天地设而民生之。(《商君书·开塞》)

（30）通人扬子云亦以为肉刑宜复也，但废之来久矣，坐而论道者，未以为急耳。
（《抱朴子·用刑》)

以上结构中的"而"在后代都不再使用了。

　　古代汉语中处于主谓之间取消句子独立性的"之"在后代也消失了。这种"之"的功能基本上是使一个句子变为名词性短语或从句，如（31）－（34）所示。

　　（31）桑之未落，其叶沃若。（《诗经·卫风·氓》）

　　（32）岁寒，然后知松柏之后凋也。（《论语·子罕》）

　　（33）仁之胜不仁也，犹水胜火。（《孟子·离娄下》）

　　（34）天之弃商久矣。（《左传·僖公二十二年》）

这种取消句子独立性的"之"到中古时期就消亡了。

（四）原有形式的语法功能发生改变

　　实词和虚词的语法功能都可能在发展过程中出现变化。比如，上古汉语中形容词和名词有使动用法和意动用法，能比较自由地用作动词，如（35）－（39）中加粗体的词都发生了功能变化，请参考其后的释义。

　　（35）尔欲**吴王**我乎？（《左传·定公十年》）[吴王：使……成为吴王]

　　（36）晋侯围曹，**门**焉，多死。（《左传·僖公二十八年》）[门：攻打城门]

　　（37）齐威王欲**将**孙膑。（《史记·孙子吴起列传》）[将：使……做将（军）]

　　（38）孔子登东山而**小**鲁，登泰山而小天下。（《孟子·尽心上》）[小：认为……小]

　　（39）吾妻之**美**我者，私我也。（《战国策·齐一》）[美：认为……美]

名词和形容词的很多使动用法和意动用法后来都消失了，在现代汉语中名词和形容词不再能较为自由地用为动词了。

　　名词在上古汉语可以直接作状语，如（40）－（43）中的粗体词。

　　（40）豕**人**立而啼。（《左传·庄公八年》）[人：像人一样]

　　（41）嫂**蛇**行匍伏。（《战国策·秦策》）[蛇：像蛇一样]

　　（42）项庄拔剑起舞，项伯亦拔剑起舞，常以身**翼**蔽沛公。（《史记·项羽本纪》）[翼：像翅膀一样]

　　（43）夫匈奴之性，**兽**聚而**鸟**散，从之如搏影。（《史记·主父偃列传》）[兽：像野兽一样；鸟：像鸟一样]

后来名词作状语的功能衰落了。

　　总起来看，汉语实词的发展趋势是：句法功能越来越固定，词类的界限越来越清楚。

　　不仅是实词，有些虚词的功能也发生了变化，比如，"与"在上古汉语中可以作选择连词，相当于"或"，请看（44）－（47）。

　　（44）杀人以梃与刃，有以异乎？（《孟子·梁惠王上》）

　　（45）我所以知命之有与亡者，以众人耳目之情，知有与亡。（《墨子·非命中》）

　　（46）桓公不知臣欺主与不欺主已明矣。（《韩非子·难二》）

　　（47）正行而遗民乎？与持民而遗道乎？（《晏子春秋·内篇杂下》）

"与"表示选择的功能在后代衰落了，"或"成了表示选择的连词，"与"作为并列连词，表示"和"的用法则保留了下来，一直沿用到现代汉语。

　　再如，"了"作为体标记，最初只能出现在动词之后，后来也可以出现在形容词和名词之后了。

　　对语法变化的研究一直滞后于对语音变化的研究，但是从20世纪70年代之后，对于语法变化的研究有了较大的突破，语法变化的规律逐渐被认识。其中，对语法化的研究取得的成果较为突出。

二、语法化

（一）语法化的定义及具体表现

　　语法化是一种常见的语法变化，指的是语法形式或语法范畴的形成。通俗地讲，语法化是指词汇项变为语法项，或者语法化程度较低的形式变为语法化程度较高的形式。

　　语言中的词可以分为实词和虚词。虚词也叫语法词（grammatical word）、功能词（functional word）或语法项（grammatical item），没有词汇意义，只有语法意义。实词存在的理据比较明显，可以说，实词的存在是出于对外部世界的指称需要，对实词的语义解释比较容易。虚词由于比较虚灵，在现实世界中找不到其所指的对象，因此其存在理据比较模糊，语义解释比较困难。没有受过专门的语言学训练的人，往往很难向外国人解释清楚其母语中虚词的含义和用法。从历时演进的角度看，相对于实词来讲，虚词是后起的，很多是由实词变化而来的。也就是说，虚词最初也是实词，只是在发展过程中其较为实在的意义变得抽象化了，不再指示外部世界中的某个对象（包括物体、动作行为、属性等），而专门用来表示某种概括的或抽象的意义，或指示语言形式间的结构关系。这样原来的实词就虚化了，也就是发生了语法化。虚词在产生之后还可以进一步演化，意义上变得更虚，也就是说，语法化的过程可以连续不断地进行。语法化过程的连续进行可以形成一个演变的链条，可用（48）来表示。

（48）实词>语法词>附着形式>屈折词缀

其中，附着形式（clitics）是介于词和词缀之间的一种形式，具有句法独立而语音依附的性质，即从句法的角度看是词，但从语音的角度看又像是词缀。也可以说，附着形式是一种语音上依附的词。比如英语的助动词have有一个缩略形式的变体've，这个've从句法的角度看是词，但在语音上是黏着的，像个词缀，因此，这个've就是附着形式。附着形式的语法化程度介于虚词和屈折词缀之间，如以上（48）演变链条中的位置所示。

在现代汉语中，我们会发现一些形式既有实词用法，又有虚词用法，如"把""在""加上"等，分别如（49）（50）（51）所示。

（49）a. 妈妈手把手教儿子写字。（动词）

b. 我把他的名字忘了。（介词）

（50）a. 我在厨房。（动词）

b. 我在做菜。（持续体标记，副词）

（51）a. 在咖啡里加上牛奶。（动词）

b. 金华县境内溪流纵横，水库、湖塘密布，加上全年雨量适中，气候温和，适宜养殖高档优质珍珠。（连词）

以上这些词的实词用法和虚词用法之间不是偶然同形，而是有历史演变关系，其中，虚词用法正是由实词用法语法化而来的。可见，一个形式发生语法化之后，旧有的用法和新的用法可以并存，从而形成共时的多义关系。这种共时的多义关系可以为语法化的发生提供证据与线索。

有时语法化之前的形式（词汇项）和语法化之后的形式（语法项）可以在一个句子中共现。比如现代汉语的体标记"了"从历时的角度看，是从"完了，了结"义的动词语法化而来的，在其成为完成体标记之后，"了"原来的动词用法还保留着，并可以与体标记用法出现在一个句子中，如（52）。

（52）了了一桩心愿。

有的情况下，原有的用法消失了。比如，"的""们"原来的实词用法都彻底消失了，学者们对它们的来源还没有完全达成共识。

　　汉语是孤立语，在语法化链条上也体现出一些特点。比如汉语的实词可以虚化为副词、介词、助词、语气词、连词等，没有虚化为屈折成分的。汉语的虚词进一步虚化的方向不是变成屈折词缀，而是变成了不贡献意义的词内成分。比如，"但是""可是""总是""若是""按着""随着""为了"等词中包含的"是""着""了"都是从独立的虚词变成了无法分析的词内成分。

　　语法化不仅关注语法形式的来源，也关注一些语法范畴的来源。比如，主语是很多语言中都存在的语法范畴，在不少语言中都有一些形式上的要求，像在英语中，主语是不能省略的，在找不到语义上的主语时，要使用it或there充当形式上的主语；而且，主语要与谓语动词保持一致关系。但是，主语这个语法范畴不是语言中自古以来就存在的。直到现在，在一些语言中，比如在汉语中，主语还不是一个高度语法化的范畴，汉语是话题凸显的语言，汉语中所谓的主语实际上是话题。话题是语用的概念，是话语的起点。对话题的叙述部分可以称为"述题"。话题没有严格的形式上的要求，话题与述题之间的结构和联系是很松散的。从历时的角度看，主语和话题这两个概念是有联系的。主语这个语法范畴是话题这个语用范畴逐渐经历语法化的过程而形成的。

（二）多重语法化及语法化中的规律

　　同一个源头形式可以沿着不同的语法化路径而发展成为多个具有不同功能的语法形式，这种情况被称为"多重语法化"（polygrammaticalization）（Craig 1991）。比如，"就"原本是一个动词，意思是"接近"，"迁就""避难就易"中的"就"就是这个意思。"就"发生语法化之后获得了多种语法功能，可以作介词，表示"趁着、借着"，如"就着灯光看书"，也可以表示动作的对象或话题的范围，如"他们就这个问题进行了讨论"。"就"也可以作副词，有多种用法，比如可以表示在很短的时间以内，相当于"马上"，如"我就来"。还可表示前后事情紧接着，如"他一提起这件事就伤心"。还有其他副词用法，这里不一一列举。"就"还可以作连词，表示假设的让步，如"你就送来，我也不要"。除了"就"之外，其他的虚词也往往是有多种用法的。可见，同一形式的语法化路径可以是多样的。

　　语法化的路径看起来纷繁复杂，但语法化的发生并不是随机的，而是有规律可循的。词汇意义相近的词往往发生相似的语法化。比如，表示意愿的动词经常可以发生语法化，变为表示将来的助动词，如"要""欲""想"等，请看（53）（54）（55）的a与b句。

（53）a. 我要一杯牛奶。（意愿动词）

　　　b. 火车要开了。（表示将来的助动词）

（54）a. 姜氏欲之。（意愿动词）

　　　b. 山雨欲来风满楼。（表示将来的助动词）

（55）a. 我想回家。（意愿动词）

　　　b. 这个天想下雨。（表示将来的助动词，山东方言）

英语的will也是从意愿动词发展为表示将来时的助动词的。由此可以概括出一条语法化路径，如（56）所示。

（56）意愿>将来

意愿是未实现的，在这一点上与将来是相通的，这是其发生语法化的语义基础。

语法化现象在不同语言的历史上普遍存在，语法化研究指出了一些语法和语义演变的方向，因此成为近年来历史语法学研究的热点。

（三）语法化的机制：重新分析和类推

语法化的发生主要是通过重新分析和类推这两个机制。

[1] 重新分析

所谓重新分析，是指语法结构在外部形式不变的情况下被赋予与原先不同的新的理解。一般认可的重新分析的定义是兰盖克（1977）给出的：在一个结构或一类结构中不涉及表层形式的直接的或本质的改变的变化。[1]换句话说，重新分析改变了一个语言形式的底层结构，但不改变其表层显示（surface manifestation）。底层结构主要包括以下方面：

A．成分组构（constituency）与层级结构（hierarchy）

所谓成分组构，是指句中词与词组成的有意义的片断，是大小介于词与句子之间的形式与意义的对应体。在一个句子中仅仅线性顺序相连的形式组合不一定是成分组构，比如在"我很喜欢学语言学"这个句子中，虽然"我"和"很"在线性顺序上相连，但二者并不构成一个成分组构，因为"很"与其后的动词性成分的关系更为紧密。"学语言学"是一个成分组构，"喜欢学语言学"和"很喜欢学语言学"也都是成分组构。哪些词之间构

---

1 Langacker（1977:58）："change in the structure of an expression or class of expressions that does not involve any immediate or intrinsic modification of its surface manifestation."

成成分组构不是从表面一眼就可看出的，因而属于底层结构。成分组构的存在，表明了句子中形式之间的结合状况，构成一个成分组构的两个或几个形式是组合密切的形式。层级结构指的是句法结构是有层次的，而不是线性的。

在重新分析发生时，成分组构的状态和层级结构都可能发生变化，而且二者的变化经常是相互关联的。比如，在一个线性顺序为ABC的句法结构中，原来是B与C组成一个成分组构，可能在重新分析后，A与B组成一个成分组构了。相应地，层级结构也可能发生改变。

比如，英语的"be going to"原来并不形成一个成分组构，比如在I am going to the market这个句子中，to the market形成一个成分组构，但是当be going to变成将来时标记后，比如在I am going to think about it这个句子中，be going to变成了一个成分组构，并可进一步在语音上融合为be gonna。

汉语中副词"极其"的形成也是一个合适的例子。最初，"极"和"其"是两个独立的词，二者并不形成一个成分组构，处于不同的层次上，如（57）–（60）。

（57）**极其**数，遂定天下之象。（《易·系辞上》）

（58）袭王庭，穷**极其**地，追奔逐北，封狼居胥山，禅於姑衍，以临翰海，虏名王贵人以百数。（《汉书·匈奴传》）

（59）永平二年，遂杀主，被诛，父母当坐，皆自杀，国除。帝以舅氏故，不**极其**刑。（《后汉书·阴识传》）

（60）诸如此类，自非至精不能**极其**理也。（《晋书·刑法志》）

以上诸例中，"极"和"其"不在同一个句法层次上。"极"是一个动词，义为"穷尽、竭尽"，"其"是一个限定词（包括定指标记和代词所有格两种用法），与其后的名词性成分组成一个成分作"极"的宾语。

在五代时期以后，"极其"变为一个副词（志村良治，1984），义为"非常、十分"，如（61）–（62）。

（61）专欲振起儒教，后生谒见者，率以经学讽之。而周其所急，理家理身，**极其**俭薄。（《旧唐书·郑余庆传》）

（62）峻于枢密院起厅事，**极其**华侈，邀太祖临幸，赐予甚厚。（《新五代史·王峻传》）

在这个重新分析的过程中，"极"和"其"从两个分立的词变成了一个词，相关的结构层次也发生了变化。

B. 语类标示（category label）

语类标示包括动词、名词等不同的词类标示及动词性短语、名词性短语等对短语的类属标示。

语类标示可以在重新分析中发生变化，比如英语中的助动词may、must、can等是由动词经重新分析而产生的。

汉语中一个典型的例子是"把"从动词变为处置标记。请比较（63）-（65）：

（63）无把铫推耨之劳，而有积粟之实。（《战国策·秦策》

（64）莫愁寒族无人荐，但愿春官把卷看。（唐·杜荀鹤《入关因别舍弟》）

（65）莫言鲁国书生懦，莫把杭州刺史欺。（唐·白居易《戏醉客》）

在（63）中，"把"是一个动词，表示握持，与下一分句中的动词"有"处于相同的句法位置，其后的名词"铫"是其宾语；（64）中，"把"所处的小句中还有另一个动词"看"，"把"的宾语"卷"也是动词"看"的宾语，可以理解为"把卷"的目的是"看"，这是一种目的结构。在这种结构里，"把"有了重新分析的可能，既可以理解为动词，在这一理解下，"把"是句子的主要动词，也可以理解为处置标记，在这种理解下，"把"发生了语法化，词汇语义弱化，句子的主要动词是"看"，"把"的作用是使宾语提前。（65）是发生了重新分析之后的结构，"把"不可能再分析为实义动词，因为其后名词性成分的所指不是能够被握持的东西，"把"虚化了，只能理解为处置标记，句子中的主要动词是"欺"。重新分析前和重新分析后"把"所在句法结构的表层结构没有变化，都是"把+NP+VP"，但是重新分析之后，语类范畴发生了变化，"把"从动词变成了虚词。处置标记的"把"，传统分析认为是介词。句子的结构核心也从"把"转移到了"把NP"后的动词上。"把+NP+VP"结构从连动结构变成了状中结构。

C. 语法关系

语法关系是指句法成分之间的结构关系，比如，动宾关系、偏正关系、并列关系等。在重新分析的过程中，语法关系有可能发生改变，如从动宾关系变为偏正关系。比如以上提到的"极其X"就从动宾关系变为了偏正关系。再比如，"加上"在发展过程中与其后成分由动宾关系变为连词与小句的关系，分别如（66）（67）所示。

（66）二加上二等于四。

（67）全日制学生的MBA学制为二年，一年后便转入夏季实习阶段，加上第二年找工作，实际花在书本上的时间并不多。

"不免"在重新分析过程中也涉及语法关系的变化。"不免"原来是动词性短语，如（68）。

（68）夫阳子行廉直於晋国，不免其身，其知不足称也。（《国语·晋语八》）

（68）中"不免"是"不能免除，不能幸免"的意思，是一个状中式短语，其后可以带宾语。后来，"不免"在连动结构中发生了重新分析，请看（69）。

（69）余本心欲送和上直到汾州，在路作主人，今到此间勾当事未了，不免停住十数
　　　日间。（《入唐求法巡礼行记》卷三）

在（69）中，"不免"与其后成分由动宾关系变为修饰关系。"不免"也语法化为一个副词，义为"免不了"。

　　D. 紧密性（cohesion）

　　紧密性指的是整个语言形式是独立的词还是附着形式、词缀、不可分析的词内成分等不同的情况，因为不同的性质决定了与其他成分结合紧密度的大小。如果是词，就受句法操纵；如果是词缀，就受词法操纵；如果是不可分析的词内成分，就只受音系规则的操纵。在变化中，词、附着形式、词缀或不可分析的词内成分构成一个连续统，它们在句法上和韵律上的独立性依次减弱。在重新分析的过程中，词有可能变为附着形式、词缀或不可分析的词内成分。紧密性可看作与边界（boundary）种类有关，有的形式有词边界，有的形式有语素边界，有的形式中无边界。比如，"按着"中的"着"原来是一个独立的虚词，但在"按着"中已失去了原来的语法功能，变成一个不贡献语义的词内成分。"按"与"着"之间原有的词边界消失了。再如，"但是""可是""总是"中的"是"从独立的词变为了不可分析的词内成分。这些变化导致了紧密性的增强。

　　表层显示包括音系形式、形态标记（如形态格、一致标记、时、体、态等）以及语序。表层显示有外部可见的标记，能够被直观地确认。

　　重新分析并不是永远不影响表层结构，只是不会立刻影响表层结构。在重新分析发生之后，变化了的底层结构会要求表层结构与之一致。如果说重新分析是一种"旧瓶装新酒"的现象，即让旧有的表层显示继续表达新的变化了的底层结构，那么新酒迟早也会要求换新瓶，即变化了的底层结构会要求表层显示进行调整。比如，当实词被重新分析为虚词之后，往往会逐渐发生语音的弱化，弱化的语音正对应于变得空灵的意义。语音形式的变化就属于表层显示方面的变化。再比如，当英语的情态词从动词经重新分析而产生之后，原有的现在分词形式就失去了，即不能再带-ing后缀了，这种形态上的变化也属于表层显示的变化。

重新分析是建立在表层歧义的基础之上的。新义可以是语言系统中全新的，也可以只是该结构以前不具备的。关于重新分析，读者可以进一步阅读后面的原典选读。

[2] 类推

所谓类推（analogy），是规则适用范围的扩大。在语法化研究出现之前，类推现象在语言学中早就被提及。

类推所涉及的对象在语言系统中往往比较孤立，没有相关现象给予模式上的支持，因而不稳定，容易向大量同类现象支持的规则模式靠拢。

类推作用可以使一些不规则的形式规则化。英语swell（膨胀）的过去分词原先是swollen。由于绝大多数过去分词的形式是在词干后加-ed，这就形成了一股力量，把不规则的swollen也拉到规则的行列里来。类推作用已经使得英语中很多动词的不规则形式规则化了。

但是，仍有一些英语动词保留不规则变化，如go、be。一个动词越是常用，就越容易保持其不规则的变化形式，而抗拒类推作用的发生。

语法化研究中也提到类推的作用。在一个形式发生语法化后往往会出现类推现象。通过类推，这个语法形式可以扩展应用到以前不能出现的句法环境中去。类推的机制实际就是放松规则使用的条件限制。一般情况下，规则的扩展需要一步一步地进行，不可能跳跃式地进行，只能从环境A扩展到与之仅有一个因素差别的环境B，而不能一下子从环境A扩展到与之差别巨大的环境C。由此看来，类推扩展在本质上是与渐变相联系的。正是由于类推扩展的存在，语法演变才在整体上给人以渐变进行的印象。

第六节　词汇和词义的演变

词汇比起语法和语音来，是语言系统中变化比较快的部分。在词汇内部，变化也是不平衡的，一般词汇变化得较快，而基本词汇是比较稳定的。

从演变的结果状态来看，词汇的演变表现在新词的产生、旧词的消亡以及词义的演变上。

一、新词的产生

新词的产生分为两种情况。

第一种情况是由于出现了新的事物或现象，这种情况跟外部世界的变动有关。比如，"手机""课件""微信"这些当代词语都是在相应的事物产生以后才应运而生的。有一些新词是由外语借入的，借入的原因也是为了表达某种语言中原来没有的事物或观念，如"咖啡""伏特加"等。可以说，这都是由于客观表达需要而产生的新词。

第二种情况是一个新产生的词所指称的事物现象其实早就存在，只是语言中原来没有一个专门的词来表达，而是需要用短语表达。比如，"何不"原来是一个短语，"何"表示疑问，"何不"义为"为什么不"。在长期的连用中，"何不"变成一个表示建议的副词，用来向别人委婉地提建议。向别人提建议在以前的语言系统中当然也可以表达，只是不是用"何不"这样一个专门的词，而是用了短语形式。一些由外语借入的新词，所表达的概念其实在本族语中已经有词语可以表达，借用只是由于该外语有较高的声望。比如，"粉丝"一词是由英语借入的，但是这个词所表达的概念在汉语中其实可以由"崇拜者"来表达。

二、旧词的消亡

一个原来存在的词后来在语言系统中消失了，也可以分为两种情况。

第一种情况是，随着社会的变化，一个词所指称的事物或现象消失了，因而这个词在后代口语中一般就用不到了，但是在叙述历史时还会用到，比如"辇""太监"等。这是由于外部世界的变化而引起的词语的变化。由于新词不断出现，而旧词往往又不会完全消失，因此语言系统中的词汇总量会随着时间的推移而有所增加。

第二种情况是，一个词所指称的现象还存在，但是语言系统后来不用词来表达了，而是改用短语来表达了，因而这个词就消失了。比如，"沐"在古代汉语中表示"洗头"，但后来这个词消失了，同样的意义必须用短语来表达。

三、词语的替换

词语替换是一个新的词语形式替代了原来存在的一个词语形式，但二者的所指是相同的。词语的替换同时包含了新词的产生和旧词的消亡。比如，表示进食的"吃"这个词是后出现的，原来进食这一意义是由动词"食"表达的。词语替换的原因包括三种情况，一是语言系统内部原因导致的词语替换。在汉语词汇发展史中，由于语音的简化而出现了词汇的双音化趋势，即词汇系统从以单音词为主发展为以双音词为主，在这一发展大潮中，古汉语中的一些单音词不再作为词单独使用了，其所表达的概念要由双音词来表达。比如，"看见"替换了"见"，"见"只能作为黏着语素使用了；古代汉语的动词"眠"现在也不能作为词单独使用了，只能作为黏着语素使用，"眠"所表达的概念由"睡觉"来表达，等等。二是由于社会文化的变化而引起的词语替换，比如新中国成立后，汉语中好多词语由于被认为观念上不适合而被替换，如车夫—司机，洋火—火柴，信差—邮递员等。三是由于受到另外的语言系统或方言系统的影响而引起的词语替换。比如，外来的借词有可能替代语言中原来的词。比如"站"就是一个借自蒙古语的词，替代了汉语中原有的表达相同概念的"驿"，现在"驿"只能作为黏着语素而存在了。再如，历史上随着朝代的更替而导致的权威方言的变化也可能引起标准语中词语的替换。权威方言会在很大程度上影响标准语，因此权威方言的兴替就会导致标准语的变化。比如唐代的都城在长安（今陕西西安），因此长安话是权威方言，而到了北宋，都城在汴梁（今河南开封），汴梁话成了权威方言，因此标准语就会发生一些相应的变化。在当代，我们可以观察到方言中固有的词被标准语中的词所替换的现象，这也是因为系统外的原因而引起的词语替换。

新词产生以后，旧词往往不是马上消失，这样新产生的词与旧有的表达同一概念的词会在语言中并存一段时间，不过二者不能长期并存，最终的结果往往是新词胜出，旧词消亡，比如汉语中很多双音词产生之后，原来的单音词就逐渐丧失了词的地位，降格成为黏着语素。例如，在现代汉语中，"后悔"是词，而"悔"已变为黏着语素。另一种情况是新词和旧词间产生一些细微的差别，从而不再表达完全相同的概念，这样二者就可以相安无事地在同一个系统中长期并存下去。比如英语的shirt和skirt，在原始日耳曼语中是一个词，其词首辅音原为sk-，在英语中演变为sh-，在北欧语中保持原样，后来北欧人入侵英国，英语从古代挪威方言引进了skirt这个词，但后来两个词在意义上有了新的分工，所以都保留了下来。

四、词义的演变

词义的演变是指词的形式不变，而意义发生了变化。

传统上对词义的演变，一般分为词义扩大、词义缩小和词义转移三种情况。所谓词义扩大，是指词义的所指范围变得比原来大了，比如，"江""河"从特指长江和黄河变为泛指河流。所谓词义缩小，是指词义的所指范围变得比原来小了，比如"禽"原来指所有的动物，后来只指鸟类。所谓词义转移，是指不属于以上两类词义演变的其他演变

351 ◀

第九章 语言演变

类型，即词义变得和原来所指的类别有了不同。比如，"信"原指信使，即送信的人，后来指书信。

词义扩大、词义缩小和词义转移实际上是从词义演变结果的角度概括了词义演变的几种逻辑可能性，并没有太多有价值的内容，即没有揭示出词义演变的内在规律。而且，从这种分类来看，词义演变似乎是随机的，因为词义既可以扩大，也可以缩小，这样看来，词义可以向着完全相反的方向发展，因而显得词义的演变好像是没有规律、没有制约的。

实际上，词义演变虽然表面上呈现出纷繁多样的图景，但是深入观察就可以发现，词义演变内部隐藏着深刻的规律性。对词义演变的研究，重要目标之一就是揭示词义演变的规律。

在探讨词义演变的规律之前，我们先对词义演变作一个界定。这里以名词词义演变为例。名词所指称的事物的具体样貌可能随着时代的变化而变化。举例来说，"笔""房屋"的具体所指古今不同，比如，中国古人使用毛笔，而现在一般使用钢笔或圆珠笔、铅笔等，毛笔的使用很有限了。古代人的房屋可能是茅草的，到后来变成木制的，而现在则是以钢筋混凝土的为主了。这些方面的变化都属于概念外延性的变化，而不是内涵性的变化。不论笔的样貌如何变化，笔作为书写工具的内涵始终未变，因此，我们可以认为"笔"的词义没有发生变化。同理，房屋的具体形制虽然有很多变化，但是房屋作为人居住的建筑物的内涵却没有变化，因此也可以说词义没有变化。外延性的变化与社会文化的演进有关，很难从语言学上加以概括，因而一般被排除在词义演变研究之外。词义演变研究一般针对的是词义内涵上的变化。

词义在内涵方面的演变确实有规律可循，存在一定的方向性。特劳戈特和达舍（Traughott & Dasher）（2002）提出了语义演变的单向性倾向这一重要命题，这种单向性表现为在甲义和乙义之间，从甲义演变到乙义是可能的或普遍的，但相反的演变不可能或非常罕见。某一特定语言中意义相近的词往往经历相同的语义演变，即沿着相同的演变路径发生变化，而且还存在着一些跨语言的语义演变模式，即不同语言中语义类似的词可能发生类似的语义演变。比如，原本表示空间的词经常发展出表示时间的意义，"前""后"本指空间方位，后来也可以指时间界限，如"三天前""一个月后"。"来""去"本来是指示空间中的位移趋向的，但也可以指示时间，如"来年""去年"。表示感知的动词经常发展为表示认知或心理状态的动词，比如，"看"本是表示视觉的动词，但可以引申为认知动词，"看出"可以表示"知道"（英语中的I see也是"我明白了"的意思），"我看"可以表达"我认为"的意思；"听"本是表示听觉的动词，但也可以表示"听从"这种心理行为，如"听老师的话"。这些类型的语义演变广泛发生在很多不同的语言中，表明这些类型的语义变化是具有规律性的，带有一定普遍性。

汉语研究者们实际早已观察到了语义演变的系统性和规律性，如孙雍长（1985）所提到的"词义渗透"、许嘉璐（1987）谈到的"同步引申"、蒋绍愚（1989）谈到的"相因生义"、江蓝生（1993、2000）谈到的"词义的类同引申"，实际上都是注意到了在意义相近或相反的词中反复出现的类似的语义演变模式，并对其进行了一定程度的归纳。这些研究认为，词的意义之间是相互联系的，因而一个词的意义变化可以引起和它有联系的词的意义发生变化，特别是处于同义聚合或反义聚合中的词语，在词义发展过程中更容易互相影响。比如，"叫"和"喊"是同义词，这两个词在一系列义项上都构成了同义关系，二者都可以表示发出大的声音，可以说"大叫"，也可以说"大喊"；二者都可以表示对人的称呼，如妈妈可以让自己的孩子"叫妈妈"，也可以说"喊妈妈"；二者都可以表示"招呼，呼唤"，比如可以说"有人叫你"，也可以说"有人喊你"。"叫"在普通话中还可以表示使役，相当于"让"，比如"这件事叫他做"；"喊"在普通话中还没有发展出使役用法，但在四川方言中，"喊"也发展出了使役用法，相当于"让"，可以说"这件事喊他做"。由此可见，"叫"和"喊"作为初始语义相近的词，在以后的语义演变道路上经历了类似的引申，在其后来获得的义项上也形成了近义关系。再比如，具有反义关系的"深"和"浅"，最初指的是水的深浅，后来泛指从上到下或由外及内的距离大或小。再后来二者都引申到时间领域，形容时间的长短，比如可以说"年深日久"，"浅"指时间短的例子如："寡人年少，莅国之日浅。"（《战国策·赵策》）。"深"和"浅"还引申到抽象的性质领域，"深"可以指"深奥、深刻"，"浅"可以指"浅显，肤浅"；二者也都可以用来形容颜色，可以说"深红""浅红"，指的是颜色的浓或淡。由此可见，"深"和"浅"在其最初的义项上形成反义关系，后来二者的引申方向具有平行性，其后产生的一系列义项也形成了反义关系。同义词和反义词的这些平行引申或者说同步引申现象表明处在同一意义领域内意义相关的词往往具有相似的语义演变路径，这也从一个侧面反映出了语言的系统性。

不过，汉语的研究者们没有将这种概括提升为一种普遍的语言规律，没有揭示同义词或反义词平行引申现象背后的认知基础，也没有强调语义演变的单向性。

当代的语言演变理论比较强调语义演变的单向性。以下我们举例说明一些在汉语史中可以证明的语义演变模式，从中可以看出语义演变的确具有一定的方向性。比如，表示心理感觉的动词经常转变为表示对客观事物或情况的判断推测的副词，但没有发现反向演变的情况。（70）－（75）分别以"爱""好""喜""怕""恐""惧"为例，来说明心理感知类动词的语义演变方向。可以看到，意义相近的"爱""好""喜"的演变路径是相同的：从"喜爱"义动词演变为"经常"义副词，意义相近的"怕""恐""惧"的演变路径也是相同的：从"畏惧"义动词演变为"大概"义副词。

（70）爱

　　a. 爱人者，人恒爱之；敬人者，人恒敬之。（《孟子·离娄下》）（动词：喜爱）

　　b. 时时爱被翁婆怪，往往频遭伯叔嗔。（《敦煌变文集·父母恩重讲经文》）（副词：相当于"容易"或"经常"，表示事物具有出现某种情况的倾向性）

（71）好

　　a. 吾未见好德如好色者也。（《论语·子罕》）（动词：喜爱）

　　b. 人事好乖，便当语离。（陶渊明《答庞参军诗·序》）（副词：相当于"容易"或"经常"，表示事物具有出现某种情况的倾向性）

（72）喜

　　a. 我有嘉宾，中心喜之。（《诗·小雅·彤弓》）（动词：喜爱）

　　b. 夏喜暴雨，冬则积雪。（《洛阳伽蓝记》卷五）（副词：相当于"容易"或"经常"，表示事物具有出现某种情况的倾向性）

（73）怕

　　a. 不畏官军十万众，只怕荣公第六郎。（《北史·来整传》）（动词：畏惧）

　　b. 如太史公说古诗三千篇，孔子删定三百，怕不曾删得如此多。（《朱子语类》卷二十三）（副词：大概，可能）

（74）恐

　　a. 虽杀戮而奸人不恐。（《韩非子·用人》）（动词：害怕）

　　b. 赵员外道："此处恐不稳便，可请提辖到弊庄住几时。"（《水浒传》第四回）（副词：可能，大概）

（75）惧

　　a. 将恐将惧，维予与女。（《诗·小雅·谷风》）（动词：害怕）

　　b. 当谓使君与国同规，而舍是弗恤，完然有自取之志，惧非海内企望之意也。（《后汉书·袁术传》）（副词：大概，恐怕）

　　心理动词表示的是人的主观感受，由此引申出人对事物或命题的主观判断，这种语义演变是比较自然的。

推断和推测是命题意义之外的，是基于说话人的认识得出的，因此带有主观性。从心理动词到表示推测或判断的副词，这种语义变化属于主观化（subjectification），指的是语义变得越来越倾向于表达说话人的立场、态度和感情，即越来越具有主观性。主观化在语义演变中是很普遍的一种现象。

语义演变的规律性是客观存在的，这决定于人们的认知规律与语用规律。人们对世界的认识方式有相似之处，对于事物之间的联系有相近的理解，而且人们使用语言的原则也有相通之处，因此相似的语义演变路径可能出现在不同的语言中。

但是，不同的语言社团由于所处环境的差异，对世界的认识也可能有一些差别，而且事物之间的联系是多种多样的，体现在语义联系中就可能表现出多样性，因此不同的语言中又可能存在不尽相同的语义演变路径。语义演变规律值得深入探究。语义演变模式中的语言共性与差异可以成为语言类型学研究的一个课题。

📃 原典选读

一、怎样进行历史比较与构拟

R. L. Trask. 1996. *Historical Linguistics*. New York: Oxford University Press.

【导　读】

这份原典选自R. L. Trask 的经典历史语言学教科书。首先介绍历史比较法的操作步骤，然后选取四种语言（葡萄牙语、西班牙语、加泰隆尼亚语以及法语）中的同源词群作为样品，进行构拟的示范操作。这里介绍的构拟程序比本章第四节描述的更为详尽复杂一些，第四节所考察的元音现象相对简单，而这份原典材料则展示了辅音的构拟程序。作者以一种口语化的表达方式，站在读者的角度进行讲解，给人一种"手把手教你做历史构拟"的感觉。

8.2 *Comparative reconstruction*

We have already seen that the existence of systematic correspondences allows us to make at least educated guesses about the sounds that must have been present in particular words in ancestral proto-languages. But we can often go much further than this, in several respects. First, we may be able to work out, not just individual ancestral sounds, but *all* the ancestral sounds in individual words. Second, as an immediate consequence, we may be able to work out roughly what whole words must have sounded like in the ancestral language. Third, as a further consequence, we may be able to work out what the entire phonological system of the ancestral language must have been like: what phonemes it had, and what the rules were for combining those phonemes. This process is **comparative reconstruction**, and the procedure we use for doing it is the **comparative method**. The comparative method is the single most important tool in the historical linguist's toolkit, and we have in many cases enjoyed great success in *reconstructing* important aspects of unrecorded proto-languages.

Informally, the comparative method works like this:

1. We first decide by inspection that certain languages are probably genetically related and hence descended from a common ancestor.
2. We place side by side a number of words with similar meanings from the languages we have decided to compare.
3. We examine these for what appear to be systematic correspondences.
4. We draw up tables of the systematic correspondences we find.
5. For each correspondence we find, we posit a plausible-looking sound in the ancestral language, one which could reasonably have developed into the sounds that are found in the several daughter languages, bearing in mind what we know about phonological change.
6. For each word surviving in the various daughters, we look at the results of (5) and thus determine what the form of that word must have been in the ancestral language.
7. Finally, we look at the results of (5) and (6) to find out what system of sounds the ancestral language apparently had and what the rules were for combining these sounds.

This, of course, is a vastly oversimplified picture of what happens in practice, but it gives you the general idea of what's going on. Let's look at a typical example, but first a warning. In practice, the successful use of the comparative method requires the use of large amounts of vocabulary from all the languages being compared. But, in a textbook, I just don't have the space to provide such

huge numbers of data. I am therefore obliged to present, somewhat artificially, small sets of data by way of illustration: no more than fifty words, often no more than ten. This is not realistic, but it's the best that can be done in a textbook. But do not think that comparative reconstruction is normally done on tiny sets of data: it is not.

Table 8.4 lists, in phonemic transcription, a number of words from four western Romance languages: Portuguese, Spanish, Catalan, and French. Unless otherwise marked with an acute accent, stress falls upon the next-to-last syllable of a word of more than one syllable. We are interested in reconstructing Proto-Western-Romance as far as possible. We will therefore work through the data in an orderly way. I suggest you keep a copy of Table 8.4 handy to consult as we go; you might like to photocopy it. Read the next few pages *very* slowly and carefully, and check against the data in the table at every opportunity. This exercise will require a great deal of time and thought, but there is no other way to do comparative reconstruction.

We now begin setting up systematic correspondences. This may require some trial and error. Let's begin with the correspondences involving voiceless plosives, shown in Table 8.5.

For correspondences (1) and (3) we can clearly reconstruct *p. But (2) is a slight problem. We would also like to reconstruct *p here, but Portuguese is a problem, since it doesn't show the expected /p/. Before trying to reconstruct something different, though, let's look for a conditioning factor. Note that, in item [25], all the languages except Portuguese have an /l/ following the initial /p/, while Portuguese has no /l/ either. Hence the correspondence is more accurately stated as P /š-/ : S /pl-/ : C /pl-/ : F /pl-/, and we can therefore reconstruct initial *pl in this word, with *pl developing into /š-/ in Portuguese.

For sets (4) and (5), we reconstruct *t. Set (6) is a problem, but observe that Catalan and French regularly fail to show the final vowels visible in Portuguese and Spanish. Hence the expected /t/ in Catalan and French would have been word-final, and we may reasonably suppose that these two languages have simply lost word-final /t/. We therefore reconstruct *t for this case too.

Sets (7) and (8) are even messier, but note that they look just like sets (5) and (6) apart from Portuguese. As a matter of economy, let us therefore reconstruct *t here too, and assume that there is some conditioning factor for the development of /t/ to /č/ in Portuguese – a rather natural change, after all, in some environments, and we do have a following /i/ here.

For sets (9) and (11) we reconstruct *k. Set (13) looks very much like set (6), and so we draw the same conclusion: we reconstruct *k, and assume that final /k/ has been lost in Catalan and French. Set (12) is awkward: it seems as though French this time failed to lose final /k/, as expected. Let us provisionally reconstruct *k here too, and merely note the problem for later attention. That leaves set (10), in which French has /š/ in place of the expected /k/. Can we find a conditioning factor? Before reading further, compare the cases in set (10) carefully with those in set (9), and see if you can spot a conditioning factor.

Table 8.4 Western Romance

		Portuguese	Spanish	Catalan	French
1.	'against'	kõtra	kontra	kontrə	kɔ̃tr
2.	'bag'	saku	sako	sak	sak
3.	'bald'	kalvu	kalbo	kalp	šov
4.	'beard'	barba	barba	barbə	barb
5.	'believes'	kre	kree	krew	krwa
6.	'big'	grãdi	grande	gran	grã
7.	'blood'	sãgi	sangre	saŋ	sã
8.	'bright'	klaru	klaro	kla	klɛr
9.	'country'	pajíš	país	pəis	pei
10.	'court'	korti	korte	kor	kur
11.	'cup'	kopa	kopa	kop	kup
12.	'daughter'	fiʎa	ixa	fiʎə	fij
13.	'dear'	karu	karo	kar	šɛr
14.	'fire'	fogu	fwego	fɔk	fø
15.	'five'	síku	θinko	siŋ	sɛ̃k
16.	'foot'	pɛ	pje	pɛw	pje
17.	'game'	žogu	xwego	žɔk	žø
18.	'green'	verdi	berde	bert	vɛr
19.	'hard'	duru	duro	du	dyr
20.	'high'	altu	alto	al	o
21.	'honey'	mɛl	mjel	mɛl	mjɛl
22.	'iron'	fɛrru	jerro	fɛrru	fɛr
23.	'lady'	dama	dama	dam	dam
24.	'late'		tardo	tar	tar
25.	'lead' (metal)	šũbu	plomo	plom	plõ
26.	'low'	bajšu	baxo	baš	ba
27.	'moon'	lua	luna	ʎunə	lyn
28.	'new'	nɔvu	nwebo	nɔw	nøf
29.	'says'	diš	diθe	diw	di
30.	'sea'	mar	mar	mar	mɛr
31.	'seal'	selu	seʎo	sažeʎ	so
32.	'seven'	sɛči	sjete	sɛt	sɛt
33.	'sky'	sɛu	θjelo	sɛl	sjɛl
34.	'so much'	tãtu	tanto	tən	tã
35.	'strong'	fɔrti	fwerte	fɔrt	fɔr
36.	'ten'	dež	djeθ	dɛw	dis
37.	'thousand'	mil	mil	mil	mil
38.	'tooth'	deči	djente	den	dã
39.	'tower'	torri	torre	torrə	tur
40.	'well' (adv)	bej	bjen	be	bjɛ̃
41.	'wine'	víɲu	bino	bi	vɛ̃
42.	'weight'	pezu	peso	pɛs	pwa
43.	'what'	ke	ke	kɛ	kwa
44.	'white'	brãku	blanko	blaŋ	blã
45.	'you (sg)'	tu	tu	tu	ty

Table 8.5 Correspondences involving voiceless plosives

	Portuguese	Spanish	Catalan	French	
(1)	p-	p-	p-	p-	[9, 16, 42]
(2)	š-	p-	p-	p-	[25]
(3)	-p-	-p-	-p	-p	[11]
(4)	t-	t-	t-	t-	[24, 34, 39, 45]
(5)	-t-	-t-	-t-	-t-	[1]
(6)	-t-	-t-	Ø	Ø	[10, 20, 34, 35?]
(7)	-č-	-t-	Ø	Ø	[38]
(8)	-č-	-t-	-t	-t	[32]
(9)	k-	k-	k-	k-	[1, 5, 8, 10, 43]
(10)	k-	k-	k-	š-	[3, 13]
(11)	-k-	-k-	-k	-k	[2]
(12)	-k-	-k-	Ø	-k	[15]
(13)	-k-	-k-	Ø	Ø	[44]

There is one, but it's subtle. Items [3] and [13] are the only ones in which the /k-/ of the other three languages is followed by /a/. So let's assume that original /k-/ developed to /š-/ in French always and only before /a/. That works, but is it phonologically plausible? Well, we might expect a /k/ to be palatalized before a front vowel, so, if we can assume that /a/ in French has (or once had) a very front realization, it's just about plausible – and note that French now has /e/ in these words. Let's therefore reconstruct *k here too, on grounds of economy. (The alternative would be to reconstruct an additional phoneme, say a palatalized velar *k′, but, since we have a conditioning factor available, that hardly seems to be necessary.)

So far, then, we have reconstructed three voiceless plosives *p *t *k for our proto-language, with palatalization or loss in mostly identifiable circumstances in all the languages except Spanish. Now let's look at the correspondences involving voiced plosives, shown in Table 8.6.

These are altogether messier than the voiceless plosives, particularly the labials. In sets (14) and (16), all four languages have /b/, while in (15) and (17), only Spanish and Catalan have /b/ (or /p/), while Portuguese and French have /v/. Can we find a conditioning factor? Have a look and see if you can find one.

Not much leaps to the eye. If you make a list of the environments for all the cases in these four sets, they look pretty miscellaneous. With more data, perhaps we could spot something, but, as it stands, if we try to reconstruct *b for all four sets, we're going to have to posit a change from /b/ to /v/ in some rather mysterious circumstances. This time, then, it looks as though we have to reconstruct two different segments. The obvious guesses are *b for sets (14) and (16) and *v for sets (15) and (17), with a merger of these two in Spanish and Catalan, and a devoicing of final [b] in Catalan. So let's do that.

212   *The comparative method*

Table 8.6 Correspondences involving voiced plosives

	Portuguese	Spanish	Catalan	French	
(14)	b-	b-	b-	b-	[4, 26, 40, 44]
(15)	v-	b-	b-	v-	[18, 41]
(16)	-b-	-b-	-b-	-b-	[4]
(17)	-v-	-b-	-b-	-p	[3]
(18)	-v-	-b-	-w	-f	[28]
(19)	-b-	-m-	-m	Ø	[25]
(20)	d-	d-	d-	d-	[19, 23, 29, 36, 38]
(21)	-d-	-d-	Ø	Ø	[6]
(22)	-d-	-d-	-t	Ø	[18]
(23)	?	-d-	Ø	Ø	[24]
(24)	g-	g-	g-	g-	[6]
(25)	-g-	-g-	Ø	Ø	[7]
(26)	-g-	-g-	-k	Ø	[14, 17]

While set (18) is seemingly more complicated, it should remind you of what we decided above. There, it appeared, final consonants were lost in Catalan and French – except for the labial /p/. This time we have another final labial, so let's reconstruct *v here, on the basis of the Portuguese and Spanish evidence, and assume that final /v/ develops as shown in Catalan and French. (Note that final /b/ is not lost in French in set (16).)

Finally, set (19) is so messy that it might be a good idea to leave it for later.

But we have a clear pattern emerging here. Catalan and French tend to lose final vowels, and the resulting final consonants are usually lost if they are coronal or velar – though once in a while they survive, in circumstances we haven't identified. This pattern is repeated in the next two groups, and we can therefore reconstruct *d and *g with some confidence.

Let us turn our attention to the nasals, shown in Table 8.7; here the notation Ṽ means a nasalized vowel. For set (27) we at once reconstruct *n. For sets (28) to (32) we would like to do the same, but we have some work to do to explain the variable behaviour in all the languages but Spanish. We can see that nasal vowels generally result in Portuguese and French when the nasal is syllable-final in the other languages. Set (30) differs in that the nasal is not syllable-final, and this time we take Ø in Portuguese and -n in French. In set (29), Catalan shows an unexpected velar nasal, but here Portuguese and Spanish show a following velar plosive, so we can take this as a reasonable conditioning factor, even though the velar plosive has disappeared in Catalan itself (we already know that Catalan loses final consonants). In set (32), and perhaps also in set (33), Catalan has apparently also lost a final *n. That leaves only the Portuguese palatal nasal in set (32) to account for. Here we might have expected zero, by analogy with set (30), but note that in item [41], the only one in set (32), the nasal is preceded by the vowel /i/, so let's assume this is the conditioning factor.

Comparative reconstruction   213

Table 8.7 Correspondences involving nasals

	Portuguese	Spanish	Catalan	French	
(27)	n-	n-	n-	n(-)	[28]
(28)	-Ṽ-	-n-	-n-	-Ṽ-	[1, 6, 15, 34, 38]
(29)	-Ṽ-	-n-	-ŋ	-Ṽ	[7, 44]
(30)	-Ø-	-n-	-n	-n	[27]
(31)	-Ṽ	-n	-Ø	-Ṽ	[40]
(32)	-ñ-	-n-	-Ø	-Ṽ	[41]
(33)	m-	m-	m-	m-	[21, 30, 37]
(34)	-m-	-m-	-m-	-m	[23]
(35)	-Ṽ-	-m-	-m	-Ṽ	[25]

For sets (33) and (34), of course, we reconstruct *m. Set (35) is a puzzle, but recall that Portuguese and French get nasal vowels from a syllable-final *n, so let's assume that the same happens with syllable-final *m.

Hence we have two nasals, *n and *m. Of these, *n remains in all positions in Spanish and initially in all four languages; French converts *n to nasalization in syllable-final position but otherwise retains it; Portuguese also converts *n to nasalization syllable-finally, but loses it intervocalically except after i, where it becomes ñ; Catalan loses *n finally, converts it to a velar nasal before an original velar plosive, and otherwise retains it. With *m, Portuguese and French convert to nasalization syllable-finally, but *m is otherwise unchanged everywhere.

Next, the fricatives, shown in Table 8.8. For set (36), it seems we should reconstruct *s. But now what do we do with set (37)? Comparison of items [32] and [33] reveals no conditioning factor for the s/θ contrast in Spanish. It really looks as if we need to reconstruct *two* sibilants. We might call them *s and *θ, but here I will cautiously call them *s₁ and *s₂; these remain distinct in Spanish as /s/ and /θ/, respectively, but fall together in the other languages. Naturally, we would like to reconstruct *s₂ also for sets (38) and (39), but French and Portuguese are a problem. (Catalan /w/ is surprising, too, but let's assume that this has something to do with the usual Catalan loss of final consonants.) Rather than multiply sibilants, though, let's assume that there must be some conditioning factors at work: note that the segment in question is word-final in Spanish in set (39) but word-medial in set (38). Now it looks as if we need to reconstruct *s₁ for sets (40) and (41), with the familiar loss in final position in French (but not in Catalan this time), and different results in Portuguese depending on position. Finally, for sets (42) and (43), we can easily reconstruct a single segment, with different positions in the word accounting for the variable outcomes, but what should that segment be? If we choose *ž, we have a curious devoicing in intervocalic position in Portuguese. Let us therefore reconstruct *š, which undergoes initial voicing in all but Spanish and becomes /x/ everywhere in Spanish.

214   *The comparative method*

Table 8.8 Correspondences involving fricatives

	Portuguese	Spanish	Catalan	French	
(36)	s-	s-	s-	s-	[2, 7, 31, 32]
(37)	s-	θ-	s-	s-	[15, 33]
(38)	-š	-θ-	-w	Ø	[29]
(39)	-ž	-θ	-w	-s	[36]
(40)	-z-	-s-	-s	Ø	[42]
(41)	-š	-s	-s	Ø	[9]
(42)	ž-	x-	ž-	ž-	[17]
(43)	-š-	-x-	-š	Ø	[26]
(44)	f-	Ø-	f-	f-	[12, 22]
(45)	f-	f-	f-	f-	[14, 35]

Hence we reconstruct three sibilants, *s₁, *s₂, and *š, with the developments outlined.

For set (45), we obviously reconstruct *f. Set (44) is at first puzzling, but observe that, in set (45), Spanish /f-/ is always followed by /w/, but never so in set (44). We may therefore reconstruct *f for both sets, with initial *f- retained in Spanish before /w/ but lost otherwise.

Next, we examine the liquids, shown in Table 8.9. For sets (46) and (47) we reconstruct *r. For sets (48) to (50), we'd like to do the same, but we need some conditioning factors to explain the losses. We already know that Catalan tends to lose final consonants, and for the unique set (49) we can appeal to the presence of the awkward cluster *ngr to account for the additional losses in Portuguese and French. For set (51), however, we must apparently reconstruct *rr, which we might view either as a distinct consonant or as a gemination of *r; since we have reconstructed no other geminates, let's treat it as a separate consonant.

For sets (52) and (53) we reconstruct *l. Set (54) is more difficult, but note that the items in this set all have /alC/ in the other languages, where C is a consonant, while French has /o/. Let's therefore reconstruct *l for this set too, and posit that *al has developed to /o/ in French before a consonant – a very common type of change, as it happens. For set (55), only Portuguese is a problem, but note that we have already explained the loss of *l in item [25], while item [33] is the only one in the data with an intervocalic l, so let's assume that *l, like *n, was simply lost intervocalicaly in Portuguese. Set (56) presents a different problem, but observe that this is the only set with word-initial l, so let's reconstruct *l here, too, and posit a change of initial *l to ʎ in Catalan. Set (57) is a much bigger puzzle. Since we have already decided that intervocalic *l is lost in Portuguese, we can't reconstruct *l here, because Portuguese shows intervocalic /l/ in this set. We must therefore reconstruct something different. We could try *ʎ, but then we have a problem with set (58), which is different from (57) but which also looks like a good bet for *ʎ.

Comparative reconstruction   215

Table 8.9 Correspondences involving liquids

	Port	Sp	Cat	Fr	
(46)	-r-	-r-	-r-	-r(-)	[1, 4, 5, 6, 10, 13, 18, 24, 35]
(47)	-r	-r	-r	-r	[30]
(48)	-r-	-r-	Ø	Ø	[8]
(49)	Ø	-r-	Ø	Ø	[7]
(50)	-r-	-r-	Ø	-r	[19]
(51)	-rr-	-rr-	-rr-	-r	[22, 39]
(52)	-l-	-l-	-l-	-l-	[8]
(53)	-l	-l	-l	-l	[21, 37]
(54)	-l-	-l-	-l(-)	Ø	[3, 20]
(55)	Ø	-l-	-l(-)	-l(-)	[25, 33]
(56)	l-	l-	ʎ-	l-	[27]
(57)	-l-	-ʎ-	-ʎ	Ø	[31]
(58)	-ʎ-	-x-	-ʎ-	-l	[12]
(59)	-r-	-l-	-l-	-l-	[44]

Without further data, we appear to be at an impasse, and so I shall somewhat helplessly reconstruct *ʎ₁ for (57) and *ʎ₂ for (58), while recognizing that this is phonetically very implausible. Finally, set (59) is a mystery, since Portuguese differs here from every other set, and particularly from set (52), which is otherwise identical. We might decide to set up yet another liquid here, but we've already reconstructed five liquids, and not many languages have six contrasting liquids, so let's just reconstruct the obvious *l and assume that there is an invisible conditioning factor for the odd Portuguese development.

So far, then, we have reconstructed the following phonemes for Proto-Western-Romance: *p, *t, *k, *b, *d, *g, *v, *m, *n, *s₁, *s₂, *š, *f, *r, *rr, *l, *ʎ₁, and *ʎ₂. These apparently suffice to account for all the data, apart from one or two puzzling forms which we have placed aside as problems.

We now need to reconstruct the vowels. For lack of space, I won't attempt that here; instead, I suggest that you continue the reconstruction by yourself, drawing up correspondence sets for the vowels and reconstructing an appropriate vowel system for the proto-language. It would be a *very* good idea to attempt this before reading further.

As it happens, these data require seven different proto-vowels, and only seven. (In fact, it is only in stressed syllables that we require seven vowels; elsewhere, five suffices.) These I shall represent as *i, *e, *ɛ, *a, *ɔ, *o, and *u. When we have finished, we can then display the reconstructed PWR forms of all forty-five items; this is done in Table 8.10. With just a couple of outstanding puzzles, the forms in this table appear to represent the best available reconstructions. You can see that Spanish appears to be the most conservative of the four languages and French the least conservative.

216 *The comparative method*

Table 8.10 Proto-Western-Romance

Gloss	Reconstruction	Gloss	Reconstruction
1. 'against'	*kontra	24. late	*tardo
2. 'bag'	*s₁ako	25. lead	*plombo
3. 'bald'	*kalvo	26. low	*bašo
4. 'beard'	*barba	27. moon	*luna
5. 'believes'	*kree	28. new	*nɔvo
6. 'big'	*grande	29. says	*dis₂e
7. 'blood'	*s₁angre	30. sea	*mar
8. 'bright'	*klaro	31. seal	*s₁eʎ₁o
9. 'country'	*país₁	32. seven	*s₁ɛte
10. 'court'	*korte	33. sky	*s₂ɛlo
11. 'cup'	*kopa	34. so much	*tanto
12. 'daughter'	*fiʎ₂a	35. strong	*fɔrte
13. 'dear'	*karo	36. ten	*dɛs₂
14. 'fire'	*fɔgo	37. thousand	*mil
15. 'five'	*s₂inko	38. tooth	*dɛnte
16. 'foot'	*pɛ	39. tower	*torre
17. 'game'	*šɔgo	40. well	*bɛn
18. 'green'	*verde	41. wine	*vino
19. 'hard'	*duro	42. weight	*peso
20. 'high'	*alto	43. what	*ke
21. 'honey'	*mɛl	44. white	*blanko
22. 'iron'	*fɛrro	45. you	*tu
23. 'lady'	*dama		

And is this reconstruction the definitive last word on Proto-Western-Romance? No, it is not. Examination of a much wider set of data has shown that we have oversimplified in a few places, and specialists in fact reconstruct a couple more consonants in addition to the ones we have identified here, and they make different reconstructions in several cases.

二、重新分析（Reanalysis）

P. J. Hopper, E. C. Traugott. 2003. *Grammaticalization* (Second edition). Cambridge: Cambridge Unviersity Press.

【导　读】

　　这份原典选自上述著作第3.3节。这是关于重新分析的一个简要介绍。作者指出，在重新分析这种情况下，听话人的理解和说话人的意思不一样。当一个结构存在被歧解的可能时，重新分析就可能发生。重新分析是隐性的（covert），直到形式上的某些变化将其结果明确显示出来。对于重新分析，不同的学者其实有不同的理解。在语法化研究领域，比较广泛引用的重新分析的定义是兰盖克（1977）的定义。在阅读其他文献时需要注意重新分析的其他定义。下述引文举例解释了在重新分析中底层结构的哪些方面会发生改变。作者还举例说明了如何通过句法、语音和语义上的对比来判断一个形式是否发生了重新分析。

3.3 Reanalysis

In reanalysis, the hearer understands a form to have a structure and a meaning that are different from those of the speaker, as when [*Hamburg*] + [*er*] 'item (of food) from Hamburg' is heard as [*ham*] + [*burger*]. Sooner or later someone substitutes the word *cheese* or *beef* for *ham*; but this substitution is merely the symptom of a change that has already occurred silently. The reanalysis itself is covert until some recognizable modification in the forms reveals it. The *hamburger* example illustrates reanalysis in a single lexical item; but syntactic sequences may also be reanalyzed. In current English, for example, the sequence *try and VERB* has under some circumstances been reanalyzed as Auxiliary + Verb, as *I'll try and contact her*. 'Try' in this use is distinct from 'try' in *They have tried and failed to contact her*, as well as from *I'll try to contact her*. In *I'll try and contact her*, there is evidence that *try and* is stored as a single word:

(i)   The *and* is intonationally and phonetically bound to *try* ('try-ən').

(ii)   Only *try*, not *tried, trying, tries*, is possible (e.g., not *He tries and contacts her*).

(iii)   Adverbs may not intervene between *try* and *and* (e.g., *I'll try hard to contact her*, but not *I'll try hard and contact her*).

Moreover, the meaning of *try and* is more modal-like than *try to*. It signals the agent's inability to achieve the complement verb and the speaker's lack of confidence in the agent's success (Hopper 2002).

In a major paper on syntactic change, Langacker defined reanalysis as: "change in the structure of an expression or class of expressions that does not involve any immediate or intrinsic modification of its surface manifestation" (1977: 58). From this perspective, reanalysis involves a change in constituency, hierarchical structure, category labels, grammatical relations, and cohesion (type of boundary)

(A. Harris and Campbell 1995: 61). Very often a single instance of reanalysis will show several of these characteristics correlated with one another, as is the case with *try and* in the preceding paragraph. The examples of grammaticalization in Chapter 1 are all examples of reanalysis that involve changes in constituency (rebracketing of elements in certain constructions), and reassignment of morphemes to different semantic-syntactic category labels: *be going to* from *be* + main verb + progressive aspect + purposive preposition to tense marker; *let us* from main verb + object to modal particle; and Ewe *bé* from main verb to complementizer.[3] Another example of several types of change is the reanalysis of a construction consisting of a head noun and a dependent noun (3a) as a (complex) preposition and head noun (3b):

(3)　　　a. [[back] of the barn] >
　　　　　b. [back of [the barn]]

The change from (3a) to (3b) probably did not happen in one step, but rather is the outcome of a set of smaller changes. The point here is that the change illustrates the first three of the five characteristics mentioned above. The rebracketing is an instance of constituency change (what goes with what). The change in head noun status is an instance of hierarchical structure change (what is dependent on what). The reinterpretation of the noun *back* as an adposition in a complex prepositional construction is an instance of category label change. Changes in grammatical relations are illustrated by the development of subject out of topic mentioned in Section 2.3 and by the requirement in English that clauses have grammatical subjects. An example of the latter is the change from (4a) to (4b) (multiple negation was the norm in Old English; the many intermediate steps between (4a) and (4b) are omitted):

(4)　　　a. Đonne ðam menn ne lyst nan god don
　　　　　　　when　that-DAT　man-DAT　not　wishes　no　good　do-INF
　　　　　　　　　　　　　(c. 1000, ÆLS (Memory of Saints) 297; cited in Allen 1995: 86)
　　　　　b. when the man doesn't wish to do any good

Changes in degree of cohesiveness have been illustrated by *be going to* > *be gonna*, *let us* > *let's* > *lets*. In both cases, a formerly separable morpheme has become fused with the one that preceded it. Such changes always involve rebracketing (i.e., change in constituency), but not all changes in rebracketing involve changes in cohesiveness. The type most often associated with grammaticalization is fusion.

In every instance of reanalysis we can posit that it is the result of abduction. In some contexts two interpretations were possible, that is, there was at least the potential for ambiguity (also called "opacity") that allowed for the structure to continue to be analyzed as before, and for a new analysis to be innovated, and then to coexist with the earlier analysis.[4] For example, given a reanalysis such as was illustrated in (3), the abduction account of what has happened here is as follows. A hearer has heard the "output" (3a) (the "result"), but assigns to it a different structure (3b) (the "case") after matching it with possible nominal structures (specified by the "laws"). The conclusion is not identical with the original structure of which (3a) is a manifestation, but is nonetheless compatible with (3a) in that the surface string is the same. The structural differences provide the potential for different subsequent developments. Both analyses continue to exist, but with different meanings. The abduction account of the reanalysis illustrated in (4) is considerably more complex because it requires intermediary stages involving a variety of factors, among them word-order change and case loss, and will not concern us here (for detailed accounts of word-order changes from Old to Middle English, see, e.g., Fischer 1992; Allen 1995).

☯ 思考题

1. 以汉语浊音清化为例说一说语音演变具有怎样的特点。

2. 请将以下古汉语中的句子与相应的现代汉语的句子相比较，指出这些材料所反映的汉语在语法方面的变化：

（1）九月及宋人盟于宿。（《左传·隐公元年》）

（2）哀公问社於宰我。（《论语·八佾》）

（3）不如食以糠糟。（《庄子·达生》）

（4）青，取之於蓝而青於蓝。（《荀子·劝学篇》）

（5）冬，王归自虢。（《左传·庄公二十一年》）

（6）三公咸有功於民。（《史记·殷本纪》）

3. 请考察自己方言中相当于普通话完成体标记"了"的成分的历史来源。

4. 请考察汉语史中表示"等待"义的动词的语义演变，并总结其中的演变规律。

5. 考察网络语言中"各种"的用法，并分析"各种"的新用法的产生机制。

📖 拓展阅读书目

- A. C. Harris, L. Campbell. 1995. *Historical Syntax in Cross-Linguistic Perspective*. Cambridge: Cambridge University Press.

- P. J. Hopper, E. C. Traugott. 2003. *Grammaticalization*（Second edition）. Cambridge: Cambridge University Press.

- E. C. Traugott, R. B. Dasher. 2002. *Regularity in Semantic Change*. Cambridge: Cambridge University Press.

- 董秀芳. 词汇化：汉语双音词的衍生和发展（修订本）. 北京：商务印书馆，2011.

- 江蓝生. 近代汉语探源. 北京：商务印书馆，2000.

- 蒋绍愚. 汉语词汇语法史论文集. 北京：商务印书馆，2000.

- 沈家煊. 复句三域"行、知、言". 中国语文，2003（3）.

- 沈家煊. 语用原则、语用推理和语义演变. 外语教学与研究，2004（4）.

- 孙雍长. 古汉语的词义渗透. 中国语文，1985（3）.

- 吴福祥. 语法化与汉语历史语法研究. 合肥：安徽教育出版社，2006.

- 徐通锵. 历史语言学. 北京：商务印书馆，1991.

- 许嘉璐. 论同步引申. 中国语文，1987（1）.

第十章

语言与社会

本章主要介绍语言与社会的关系。语言的变化与社会的变化息息相关。社会内部的成员因年龄、性别、职业、阶级等差异而在语言使用上表现出一些变异，从而会形成不同种类的社会方言。随着社会的发展，民族间的贸易往来、文化交流、移民杂居，甚至战争等都会引发不同类型的语言接触，像不同语言之间词语的借用、语言的替换、"洋泾浜"和"混合语"的产生等。这些都是语言随着社会的发展而产生的一些重要现象。另外，语言规划是语言与社会关系的重要议题，因此，本章还将介绍语言规划的内容以及影响语言规划的各种因素。

第一节　社会方言

一、什么是社会方言

语言随着社会的变化而变化。社会的发展造成社会内部进一步的分工或社团居民在地域上的向外扩展。这样，原来内部交际密度均匀的单一社会就分化为若干个社团，社团内成员的交际比较密切，而不同社团的成员交际则较为稀疏。于是，在某一个社团内出现的语言变化往往能在本社团内很快地推广开来，但却不能同样快地扩展到其他社团中去，从而形成不同的社会方言或地域方言。地域方言上一章已经介绍过，本节主要介绍社会方言。

社会方言（sociolect）是由于社会群体的不同性质而形成的语言变体。社会方言和地域方言没有直接的渊源，它是由不同的职业属性、社会地位、政治信仰、受教育程度等因素或由这些因素构成的社团的交际习惯所形成的语言变体。主要差别是在语言风格和表达方式，以及一些特殊词汇的使用上。从语言学角度来讲，社会方言指的是在某一社会团体、社会阶层或次文化群中被使用的语言。在此意义上，它区别于个人方言，即个人使用的特殊形式的语言。

社会方言和地域方言是有显著差异的。但是，地域方言通常有其特殊的社会地位，所以一种特定的语言变体可以同时被视为地域方言和社会方言。例如，标准意大利语相对于托斯卡纳语来说是一种地域方言。但作为意大利民族的语言，它也是社会方言，因为它作为通用语在全国的广播、新闻媒体和上流社会中被使用。

二、社会方言的种类

社会方言的类型很多，日常生活中人们说的"官腔""干部腔""学生腔""娃娃腔"，等等的"腔"，就是对某一言语社团在语言表达上的一些共同特点的概括和分类，表明这种"腔"就是一种社会方言。既然社会方言是社会内部不同年龄、性别、职业、阶级、阶层的人们在语言使用上表现出来的一些变异，那么就可以据此来给社会方言进行分类。下面对社会方言的种类一一举例介绍。需要说明的是，根据分类标准的不同，所分出的类别也不尽相同，因此，社会方言的种类并不局限于以下几类。

（一）阶层变体

人们由于生活环境、文化程度、社会地位的不同形成不同的阶层和集团，也就有了各自的语言习惯，形成阶层变体。阶层变体这一提法早先是指阶级习惯语，即指不同阶级的人在语词运用中的差异。比如，我国古代按照阶级等级的不同，有些语词的使用就不同，例如对"妻子"的称呼就有"后""夫人""孺人""妇人""妻"等。随着社会语言学的兴起，对阶层变体的认识已有了改变。美国社会语言学家拉波夫对纽约市居民的发音调查提出了阶层变体现象。他按照不同社会阶层对英语中"r"的发音是否卷舌的情况做了调查，发现低层阶级较少发卷舌音，中层阶级则较多。

（二）领域语言变体

领域语言变体也叫作领域用语，是指不同的职业、专业、爱好、政治集团、宗教信仰等有各自的领域术语或一些特殊的用语。也就是俗话说的行话和术语。比如在科学专业领域中，物理学术语"光速"、生物学术语"细胞"等。宗教集团领域的一些用语，如佛教有"涅槃""五戒"等；道教有"道士""八卦"等；基督教有"耶稣""上帝"等；伊斯兰教有"真主""阿訇"等。再比如，随着互联网络兴起和电脑与手机的普及，人们使用种种方便键盘打字的，特别是用阿拉伯数字、英文或汉语拼音字母、同音不同义汉字的谐音、合音来表示的网络新语词，如"再见"用88（bye-bye 的谐音），"一生一世"用1314，"哥哥"用"GG"，"大侠"用"大虾"，"喜欢"用"稀饭"，"这样子"用"酱子"，等等。另外，黑话是一种特殊的社会方言，它也属于领域语言变体的社会方言。其他的社会方言没有排他性，不拒绝其他言语社团的人们了解、运用，因而其中的有些词语也可以被全民语言所吸收而成为日常的交际用语。但是黑话具有强烈的排他性，对本集团以外的人绝对保密，所以一般不会进入日常交际。

（三）语言的性别变体

性别差异不仅反映在生理上，而且在社会属性上也有区别。在语言的运用中，我们总能体会到男女差异，这就形成了语言的性别变体。像在日语中，不同的性别可以组成不同的言语社团，语言上各有特色。日语里有些词是只有成年男性才说的，另外一些词则是只有妇女和孩子才说的，因此在教材里往往提醒学习日语的人要特别注意这种区别。这些都是某一言语社团的社会方言的具体表现。再比如，在北京有一种表现在性别差异的社会方言团体，年轻的姑娘在发"j、q、x"的时候往往舌位偏前，带有明显舌尖色彩，学界称为"女国音"，中、老年妇女以及各个年龄的男性却没有这种现象，这说明该社会方言的差异也表现在年龄变体上。

（四）年龄变体

年龄的级差也会反映在语言里，成为一种变体。不同年龄的言语团体在社会中担任的角色不同，形成了一些不同年龄段有特色的语言使用差异。年龄变体中一种是"代差"，即指一代人与另一代人之间的差别。在讲汉语的老一代人中，还保留了一些旧时代的词语，如有的老人还会把"日光灯"叫"电棒"，把外企公司叫"洋行"等。另外，在儿童语言中，尤其是学龄前儿童多使用重叠词"球球""果果""坐凳凳"等。正因为儿童这个语言群体有因年龄变体而形成的"社会方言"，所以，成年人在跟两三岁的儿童说话时，也会使用儿童的"社会方言"，比如"乖宝宝，快吃饭饭，然后睡觉觉，起床后，妈妈带你玩球球，买糖糖给小乖乖吃……"。

第二节　语言接触

语言接触（language contact）是语言学研究的一个现象，发生在不同的语言系统相互接触或影响之时，这种研究又称接触语言学（contact linguistics）。当不同语言的说话者密切地接触时，它会影响至少一种语言，并带来语音、句法、语义等语言方面的变化。民族之间的贸易往来、文化交流、移民杂居、战争征服等各种形态的接触，都会引起语言的接触。语言的接触有不同的类型，其中最常见的是词的借用。只要社会之间有接触，就会有词语的借用。每一种语言都有一定数量的借词。如果两个民族由于集体迁徙或军事征服而共同生活在一个社会共同体里面，这两个民族就有融合成一个民族的可能，它们的语言就有可能发生替换。语言的接触也会产生"洋泾浜""混合语"等特殊的语言现象，甚至使人们提出人造的国际辅助语的要求。这些都是语言随着社会的发展而产生的一些重要现象。

一、借词

借词（loanword），也叫外来词，是指音义都借自外语的词。借词不仅引入了新的外来概念，而且还引入了外语的音义结合关系。例如"沙发"借自英语的sofa，它不仅引入了汉语社会原来不曾有的"装有弹簧或厚泡沫塑料等的两边有扶手的坐具"这一新概念，而且还引入了以两音节"shāfā"（对应于英语中的双音节"sofa"）与"某种坐具"的意义组成的音义结合的关系，这是汉语中原来没有的。

意译词是指，只引入新的外来概念，但用本族语的构词材料和构词规则构成新词来表达它，所以我们不把它们看作借词。有的意译词构词所用的本族语的构词材料和构词规则与意译词所源自的外语完全没有关系，如汉语词"水泥"的构词材料是词根语素"水"和"泥"，是以"修饰语+中心语"次序的定中关系组织起来，而它所源自的外语词是英语的cement，是个单纯词，既不含有英语中"水"（water）的音和义，也不含有英语中"泥"（mud）的音和义。有意思的是，汉语中有很多借词后来都被意译词所代替，例如表10-1中的例子。

语种	原语	借词	意译词
英	telephone	德律风	电话
英	microphone	麦克风	扩音器
英	cement	士敏土、水门汀	水泥、洋灰
英	piano	披亚诺	钢琴
英	ink	因克	墨水
俄	хлеб	裂巴	面包

表10-1　汉语部分借词和意译词对照

意译词中有一类叫作仿译词，它的特点是构词所使用的本族语的构词材料和构词规则分别与所源自的外语词有对应关系。比如汉语词"黑板"的构词材料是"黑"（形容词性，表颜色）和"板"（名词性，表厚度小而面积大的较硬的事物），以"修饰语+中心语"次序的定中关系组织起来，而它所源自的外语词是英语的blackboard，含有的构词材料也是两个：black（形容词性，表颜色）和board（名词性，表厚度小而面积大的较硬的事物），两成分的关系也是"修饰语+中心语"次序的定中关系。也就是说，仿译词是分别将外语中的构词材料按外语中的次序依次译成本族语，使构词成分的选择和构词结构的选择与外语词一一对应。类似的例子还有很多，例如："足球"（英：football），"鸡尾（酒）"（英：cocktail），"机关枪"（英：machine gun），"铁路"（英：railway），"超人"（德：Ubermensch），"洗钱"（英：money laundering）。成语的借用也往往采用仿造的方式，例如"鳄鱼眼泪"（crocodile tears）、"泥足巨人"（feet of clay）、"走钢丝"（walk a tightrope）、"鸵鸟政策"（ostrich policy）、"特洛伊木马"（Trojan horse）、"烫手山芋"（hot potato）、"尘埃落定"（the dust settles）等外来成语在汉语里已广为使用。

由此，我们可以将构词成分的选择和构词结构的选择也叫作"词的内部形式"，词的具体读音也叫作"词的外部形式"。所以，仿译词是借入词的内部形式而不借入词的外部形式的外来概念词，它是意译词的一个特类。另外，在吸收外来成分的时候，为了便于理解，有时采用音译加意译的办法。音译兼意译是指借词在语音和意义上都与外语原词相近，但完全用本族语的材料和规则，并且不要求内部形式相同。汉语中有相当一部分这种类型的借词。例如，"啤酒"（英：beer）、"卡片"（英：card）、"卡车"（英：car）、"法兰绒"（英：flannel）、"拖拉机"（俄：трактор）、"哈巴狗"（蒙：хапа），这些词里的"酒""片""车""绒""机"和"狗"等成分，其实是有关事物所属的类名，给前面的成分作了注解。

汉语用多音节、多语素来意译外语语词其实是一个重新创造命名的造词过程。创造出的汉语语词的内部形式义与外语原词的词义的关系有的看上去比较直接，有些则一看就比较远。但实际上，意译词都是重新创造的命名，与外语词义一般都没有直接的关系。比如，意译词"基因"的内部词义"基本的（遗传）因子"与英语gene的整体词义的关系似乎比较直接，不少汉语者认为这本来就是gene的词义，其实gene的词源是"出生于""有亲缘关系"的意思，与"基因"一词字面上没有出现的"遗传"才有直接的意义关系。另外，音译兼意译词与所借外语词义的关系则一看就是间接的，是对外语的词义经过各种不同角度的联想而创造的。比如，德国的Daimler-Benz集团生产的Benz汽车在20世纪三四十年代刚进入中国市场时译作"本茨"，这是一个音译词。到20世纪80年代又改译为"奔驰"，这是音译兼意译词。

下面简要谈一下借词与社会的关系。首先，借词在语言上的结构规则与两个社会接触程度的深浅有密切关系。借词虽然音义都借自外语，但如果两个社会的接触程度不深，即地域上不相邻且只有一般性的物质交换或文化交流，比如像我国汉代的通西域或现代与西方的英、法、德、荷兰各国的接触这一类的情况，则借词在语音、语法上还得服从本族语言的结构规则。如果碰到本族语言中没有的音，就用相近的音去代替，而不产生新的音位。例如汉语借自俄语的"喀秋莎"（指苏联传说中一个美丽的女人，也指火箭炮）中的"莎"，是俄语катюша的ша的对音，"ш"的音值是[ʃ]，汉语中没有这个音，于是就用相近的"sh"去代替，而并未因为词语的借用而在汉语中产生新的音位。语言接触的这种结果属于"不成系统的词汇借用"这一类型。

其次，语言中借用词语的方向取决于两社会接触时文化传播的方向。如果文化传播是单向性输出或输入，则词语的借用也是单向的；如果文化交流是双向的，则词语的借用也双向的。汉族自古和其他民族交往，从外族语借入词语。有些词一直流传下来，使用年代久远，人们已经觉察不到它们是借词了。例如，"葡萄""石榴""苜蓿""菠萝""狮子""玻璃"等是汉代从西域借入的词；"佛""菩萨""罗汉""阎罗""魔""僧""尼""和尚""塔"等是汉代以后从印度借入的佛教用词；"胡同""站""蘑菇"等是元代时借入的蒙古语词。

再次，在词的借用过程中还可能有借出去的词再借回来的现象，一出一进之间，音、义等方面都会有一些变化。汉语的"百姓"借入蒙古语后意思是"土房子"，之后又变成

"店铺"的意义。汉语后来又把这个词从蒙古语中借回来，叫作"板生"（[paicing]），简称"板"（[paii]）。现在呼和浩特市的一些地名如"麻花板""库库板"等之中的"板"，就是汉语的"百姓"借入蒙古语后再借回来的一个词。

另外，借词如果适合使用的需要，有时甚至能在长期的竞争中战胜本族词，取而代之。"站"就是这方面的一个有趣的例子。表示车站意思的"站"，汉语中原来叫作"驿"，这个词后来借入日本，今天在日本仍叫驿，例如"东京驿"（"东京站"的意思）。南宋时汉语从蒙语中借用"站"，"驿""站"两词并用，后来随着元蒙政权的建立，在各地设立"站"，"站"就代替了"驿"。元朝灭亡后，明朝皇帝曾通令从洪武元年起改"站"为"驿"，但是在老百姓的口语里一直用"站"。清代时"驿""站"并用，"九一八"事变后日本帝国主义在东北建立"满洲国"，也改"站"为"驿"，但这些行政措施始终行不通。可见借词只要符合社会的需要就会在语言中扎根。

总之，语言之间接触程度的深浅与社会之间接触程度的深浅密切相关。语言浅程度接触的结果是语言中出现不成系统的、文化层面的借词。词语借出借入的方向与文化输出输入的方向相一致，因此借词是研究民族史、社会史的重要材料。

二、洋泾浜与克里奥耳语

操不同语言的人聚集在一起时，相互间的交流会受到种种限制，彼此都不能掌握对方的语言。如果接触时间短，交流也不多，那么，双方就会设法简化自己或对方的语言，彼此借用一些词汇就应付过去了；但在经常打交道（如长时间的商业往来）的情况下，人们就必须设法建立一个用于交际的"共同语言"符号系统，于是洋泾浜语和混合语就这样应运而生了。

洋泾浜，原是上海的一条河浜，位于从前的公共租界和法租界之间，后来被填成一条马路，图10-1为洋泾浜的旧貌。所谓"洋泾浜英语"，是指那些没有受过正规英语教育的上

图10-1 洋泾浜旧貌

海人说的蹩脚英语。它的特点一是不讲语法，二是按中国话"字对字"地转成英语。它最初是19世纪中外商人使用的混杂语言，只有口头形式，没有统一的书面形式，而且变体很多。该语言流行于当时的上海洋泾浜周边地区，故由此得名。由于该语言已经退出历史舞台，"洋泾浜英语"（Pidgin English or Pidgin）一般被认为与中式英语具有相同的含义，但事实上它只是中式英语的一个代表，且在一定程度上具有更为特殊的历史意义。这里需要说明的是，"洋泾浜"是出现在世界很多通商口岸的一种常见的语言现象，不是中国所特有。可是国外语言学界对中国的"洋泾浜"发生了兴趣，根据中国人发英语business这个词的讹音，给这种语言现象起了一个学名，叫"皮钦语"（pidgin）。

在洋泾浜英语中，它在语音表现上有其独特之处。比如，汉语的音节一般不用辅音结尾，而洋泾浜英语常常将以辅音结尾的词加上一个元音，如make [meik] 读成 [meiki:]，将make变成了makee，同样将much变成了muchee。语音上受上海话影响，把辅音"r"说成"l"，如"all-light（all right）""loom（room）"；把辅音"t"读成"chee"，如"My-no-wanchee（I don't want it）"。

在词汇的使用上，个别英语单词以错误方式被频繁使用。中国的洋泾浜英语只有大约700个单词，所以一个词不得不兼有原先几个甚至十几个英文单词的意思。例如，belong（属于）这个英语单词在洋泾浜英语中用得很频繁。例如，"You belong ploper?"（你好吗），其中ploper就是proper；"How muchee belong?"（多少钱），muchee就是much。真正造成belong一词使用频率特别高的原因是，在洋泾浜英语中，系动词be以及它的各种形式都不存在，一律用belong代替，如I am、you are、he is统统说成I belong、you belong、he belongs。如果要说"对不起"，并不说"I am sorry"，而是说"My belong sorry"。如果要说"他现在在中国"不说"He is in China now"，而是说"He belongs China-side now"。在洋泾浜英语中似无give一词，要表示"给"这个意思时，常用"pay"。例如，外国女主人在接待客人时，让中国仆人上茶，就得说："Pay the missy tea"，甚至连外国人跟中国舞女告别时都会说："Pay my kissy"。受汉语量词的影响，piecee（piece）这个词的使用很广，洋泾浜英语说two piecee book，而不说two books；用side和time表示空间和时间，如用top-side表示"above（上边，上面）"。

洋泾浜英语未形成独立的语法体系，无法依一定的规则、句型和词法来复制和扩充它。另外，洋泾浜英语虽被冠以"英语"之名，但它受汉语的影响较受英语的影响要深。它似乎宁可服从于汉语表达习惯和词序，而不肯遵从英语的基本语法，置英语的数、格、人称、时、体、态等基本造句结构于不顾。在人称代词的使用上，这一特点表现得尤为明显。例如，在洋泾浜英语中my就是I、we、mine、ours等人称代词的同义语。因此，"我不能"被说成"My no can","我们什么也不要"说成"my no wants"。

世界上现存最有活力的"洋泾浜"是广泛使用于新几内亚的Tok Pisin。它经过长期发展，已经成型，有自己的文字、文学、报纸、广播，并且曾经在联合国的大会上被用于发言。它的主体是英语，在大约1500个词汇项目中，80%来自英语，有简单而明确的音位和语法规则。Tok Pisin的音位数目比较少，每一音位可有很多变体发音。实词的形态变化已大大简化，因而词序严格。和一般的洋泾浜一样，Tok Pisin的词汇量比较小，不便于表达细微的意义差别，许多词的意义负担很重，要靠上下文来排除歧义。使用拐弯抹角的比喻说法的场合比较多，比方胡子叫"grass belong face"（脸上的草），口渴叫"him belly alla time burn"（肚子里直发烧）。

"洋泾浜"这种语言现象的产生与17世纪以后帝国主义的殖民扩张有联系，是语言接触中的一种畸形现象。它要么随着社会制度的改变而消亡，像我国的"洋泾浜"在解放后便停止通行；要么会发展为混合语（克里奥耳语），成为某一地区人们通用的交际工具。

克里奥耳语（créole，也叫混合语）最初的语言形态与洋泾浜完全相同（基本取自殖民者语言的数量很小的词汇和经大幅改造的音系、极简单的语法），两者的区别在于克里奥耳作为母语传递给下一代，已成为某个语言社团唯一的交际语。也就是说，克里奥耳语（是混血儿的意思），是作为某个社会群体的母语来使用的、由两种或多种语言混合而成的语言。这种语言实际上就是母语化的洋泾浜语，是一种语言混合形式，区别于洋泾浜语。

克里奥耳语的产生也与17世纪后的殖民主义有关。它主要出现在非洲、美洲某些地区殖民统治者的种植园里。但与洋泾浜产生的社会条件不同的是，种植园的劳工来自彼此不能通话的不同部落，不仅他们与殖民统治者之间没有共同的语言，而且就是他们之间也无法用自己的语言通话。因此，洋泾浜化的殖民者语言就成了当地唯一共同交际的工具。这样，随着来自不同部落的劳工相互通婚，这种语言就作为母语传递给后代，洋泾浜就发展成了克里奥耳语。

尽管克里奥耳语最初的语言形态与洋泾浜相同，但日后的发展完全不同。一旦作为母语传递，成为一个社会唯一的交际语，它就开始逐步扩大词汇，严密语法，迅速发展丰富起来。可以看出，洋泾浜和克里奥耳是一种特殊类型的语言接触。殖民统治者语言的一方只有极少数的成员远渡重洋涉足异域，其他绝大多数成员与异域人民在地域上并不连续，不发生接触。也就是说，双方社会的接触不是全方位的，不会发生两个社会融合为一体的情况。因此，少数殖民者尽管有强大的经济、文化、政治的优势，深入异域后也不能以自己完整的语言系统完全替代异域语言，只可能产生一种走了形的语言混合形式。

另外，我国语言学家在多民族交界地区发现了个别混合语。这些混合语的特点是两种语言的词汇、语法、语音特点都占有相当的比例，既有些像A语言又有些像B语言，也可以说既不像A语言又不像B语言，如青海黄南自治州同仁县五屯镇有2000多人使用的一种汉藏混合语。

三、语言替换

不同民族之间进行深度而不平衡接触的结果是导致语言的替换。语言替换（language replacement）并不是指产生"混合语"，而是指相互接触中的一种语言排挤代替了其他语言，即其中某一种语言成为胜利者，保留自己的语法构造和基本词汇，并且按自己发展的内在规律继续发展，成为趋向于融合的各民族人民的共同交际工具，而其他语言则由于无人使用而消亡。由于"语言融合"很容易被误解为两种语言的成分有机地混合起来并产生出一种新的语言，所以这一术语已被学术界废除，而改称"语言替换"或"语言替代"。

语言替换首先是民族间要深度接触，也就是说不同的民族要在同一片区域内交错居住，属于同一个国家共同体或经济文化圈。不在同一地区生活的民族，或虽然生活在同一地区但保持独立聚居的民族，一般不会发生语言替换。比如南北朝以来前后入主中原的鲜卑（北魏）、契丹（西夏）、女真（金）、满族（清）诸族，入主中原后逐渐与汉族杂居，因而他们的语言也逐渐融入汉语而消亡。而蒙古族则在漠北地区一直保有民族独居的大本营，进入汉族地区也基本保持相对独立聚居，所以除少数后来没有北归而与汉族杂居的蒙古人换用了汉语外，蒙古语没有融入汉语。其次是接触的不平衡性，这里所谓的不平衡是指进行接触的诸民族中有一个民族在人口和文化上具有十分显著的优势，这一优势民族一直保持有聚居的人口而其他民族的聚居人口逐渐减少以至消失。语言深度但不平衡接触的一般结果是优势语言排挤和替换其他语言而成为不同民族的共同交际工具，弱势语言则因被替换而停止使用。

究竟哪一种语言能够代替其他语言而成为全社会的交际工具，这是由社会历史条件决定的。在语言替代过程中并不是政治上处于统治地位的民族语言一定会成为胜利者，语言替换的结果是经济文化地位高的一方排挤替代经济文化地位低的一方。比如汉民族在几千年的历史发展过程中曾数度被一些经济、文化上比较落后的民族所统治，但由于它在经济上、文化上处于先进的地位，汉语在语言接触中总是被其他民族所采用而成为胜利者。恩格斯在谈到这种规律的时候说："在长时期的征服中，比较野蛮的征服者，在绝大多数情况下，都不得不适应征服后存在的比较高的'经济情况'；他们为被征服者所同化，而且大部分甚至还不得不采用被征服者的语言。"[1]

---

[1] 马克思恩格斯选集：第2卷. 北京：人民出版社，1995：222.

在汉语和其他语言的接触过程中有些民族顺乎历史发展的规律，自觉放弃使用自己的语言，选用汉语作为共同交接语，这是语言的自愿替换。但是，有些民族为保持本民族的语言进行了艰苦的斗争，但迫于经济、文化发展的需要，也不得不放弃自己的语言，学会汉语，实现语言的替换，这是语言的被迫替换。在我国的历史中，自愿替换和被迫替换都有不少的例子。就总的趋势看，隋唐以前，以自愿替换占优势，而在隋唐以后，被迫替换的比重大一些。

从秦汉到隋唐，和汉民族发生融合关系的主要是所谓"五胡"，即匈奴、鲜卑、羯、氐、羌民族。这些民族在取得政权以前，多数已与汉族杂居，受汉民族的文化影响比较深。由于交际的需要，这些民族的人民大多已学会汉语，如氐族"语不与中国同"，但"多知中国语，由与中国错居故也"（《魏略·西戎传》）。所以，这些民族在建立政权以后，把汉语作为相互间共同的交际工具，并没有多大的障碍。鲜卑族的拓跋氏在建立北魏王朝以前虽然没有与汉族杂居，但在中原地区建立政权之后，由于经济、文化发展的需要，也学会说汉语。为了加速语言的替换过程，魏孝文帝还制订了一系列政策，禁止讲本民族的鲜卑语，提倡说汉语。唐以后与汉族融合，在语言上替换为使用汉语的主要是契丹、女真（包括后来的满族）等民族。这些民族和魏晋南北朝时期的各个少数民族有所不同：一是在建立王朝以前没有与汉族杂居，二是在建立王朝以后反对学习汉语，总想采取一些相应的措施阻止语言的替换，最后的语言替换是被迫的。例如，金世宗屡次告诫群臣，或发出诏谕，要求使用女真语，保持女真旧风。

上述的所谓"自愿替换"和"被迫替换"，只是就统治者所采取的政策而言，而不是说"被迫"中没有客观经济、文化发展的基础，"自愿"中没有斗争。北魏孝文帝的汉化政策是民族自愿融合的典型，但也曾遭到以太子为代表的贵族保守集团的强烈反对，最后不得不废弃太子，甚至处以极刑。在这些语言换用中，汉族在政治上处于被统治地位，因而不可能给其他民族的语言施加任何特权。这种不以特权而进行语言替换的方式，是符合历史的发展规律的。

从语言替换的过程来看，语言替换大体上是先出现双重语言现象，最后导致一种语言排挤、替代另一种语言而完成语言的统一。双语现象是指被融合民族的成员一般会讲两种语言：一是本族语，一是在替换过程中占优势的那种语言。双语现象的出现是两种或几种语言统一为一种语言的必经的过渡阶段，语言替换必定经过较长时期的双语阶段。当不同民族长期生活在同一地区，交际的需要必然会使他们各自学习对方的语言，许多人成为双语者。长期并存的双语，各自的使用范围会逐渐此长彼消，经济、文化发达一方的语言使用场合逐渐增多，而经济、文化较为落后的一方的使用场合逐渐萎缩，慢慢发展到只在家庭中使用，再到无人使用而消亡。双语现象发展的结果有两种，一是如果两个民族向融合的方向发展，相互间的关系越来越密切，其中一个民族就会放弃自己民族的语言而使用经济文化水平较发达一方的语言，最后完成语言的替换；二是如果两个民族向分离的方向发展，那么，他们就会继续说自己的语言，语言各自发展，最后也不会发生语言的替换。

四、语言规划

语言规划（language planning）是国家或社会团体为了对语言进行管理而进行的各种工作的统称。所以，语言规划是某种语言政策的体现。语言政策表现国家或社会团体对语言问题的根本态度。例如在殖民主义时代，殖民地政府通常推行语言同化政策，把宗主国的语言强加给被压迫民族，在正式场合禁止使用被压迫民族的语言。在实现民族平等的国家，少数民族地区实行双语政策，例如在我国内蒙古自治区，汉语和蒙古语都是官方语言。

语言规划的内容涉及很多方面，包括：贯彻执行国家语言文字工作的方针政策；确定和制订语言文字应用的规范、标准、法规规章；实现语言文字的规范化、标准化；民族共同语的确立和推广，民族共同语的规范和完善；语言选择、语言协调、语言调查；科技术语的统一和标准化，文字创制和改革等。就语言选择而言，在多民族杂居的地方（如印度的许多邦），往往只能选择一两个或两三个民族的语言作为官方语言。许多殖民地获得独立之后，都不再以宗主国的语言为官方语言（或至少不以它为唯一的官方语言），而以当地的民族语言为官方语言。在民族复兴的目标下，有时甚至采用某种古代语言；这种古代语言于是得以复活（当然还要使之现代化）。在巴布亚新几内亚，政府已经赋予当地的克里奥耳英语以正式语言的地位，从而为这个语言的进一步发展开辟了道路。在非洲，不少国家采用斯瓦希里语为通用语言。在联合国，选择了英语、法语、俄语、西班牙语、汉语和阿拉伯语为工作语言。

采取语言的协调措施也是语言规划的主要内容之一。为了对抗英语的过大影响，法国和意大利就采取过保卫本国语言的协调行动。1954年，荷兰和比利时两国开始共同使用新的荷兰语正词法；1980年，两国又签订条约成立荷兰语联盟；比利时的弗拉芒语本是荷兰语的一种方言，这个联盟实际上使弗拉芒语进一步向标准荷兰语接近。马来西亚使用的马来西亚语和印度尼西亚使用的印度尼西亚语，是马来语的两种方言。1972年，印度尼西亚语采用了和马来西亚语一致的正词法，从而促进了两国的语言合作和文化交流。在苏联和中国，那些新创文字的民族语言通例分别采用俄文字母和拉丁（汉语拼音）字母，也是为了方便少数民族和主体民族之间的语言合作和文化交流。

另外，语言规划的主要内容还包括民族共同语的确立和推广以及民族共同语的规范和完善。我国在1923年由"国音字典增修委员会"提出以北京语音为我国"国语"的语音标准并得到当时教育部的批准和支持。1956年，中国人民共和国正式发布文件，确定"普通话"为现代汉民族民族共同语的口语形式，"普通话以北京语音为标准音，以北方话为基础方言，以典范的现代白话文著作为语法规范"。这里也涉及语言的选择问题，一个民族或一个国家的共同语是在某一种方言的基础上形成的。究竟选哪一种方言作为基础方言，这并不取决于人们的主观愿望，而取决于客观的社会经济、政治、文化等各方面的条件。现代汉民族共同语，即普通话，确定以北方话为基础方言、以北京语音为标准音，这主要是政治的原因。我国北方的黄河流域的中段，即所谓"中原地区"是汉民族的发源地，是夏商周以至秦汉的中心地区，汉民族从这一中心地区逐渐扩展到了南方，而"中原"一直是汉民族心目中国家的中心。伦敦方言成为英吉利共同语的基础方言是由于经济的原因。英国产业革命之后，首都伦敦成为工业的中心，需要大量的劳动力，各地居民纷纷迁入伦敦。操各种方言的人杂居在一个城市之中，使英吉利民族共同语在伦敦方言的基础上吸收其他方言的一些成分而发展起来。多斯岗方言成为意大利共同语的基础方言主要是由于文化的原因。意大利在统一以前，著名的文豪，如但丁、彼特拉克、薄伽丘等人已用这种方言写了许多脍炙人口的作品，人们要欣赏这些作品，就得依照多斯岗方言去阅读，因而就得学习这种方言。因此，文化的力量使多斯岗方言在全国的方言中取得了特殊的地位，成为共同语的基础方言，而该方言区的首府佛罗伦萨的语音就成为意大利民族共同语的标准音。

语言规划与人们的语文生活息息相关。到底有哪些因素影响着语言规划呢？推究起来，以下几个方面似乎值得注意[1]。

第一，政府的力量。在以往的研究中，政府的力量一直很受重视。语言规划具有政府性，它是政府授权的、长期进行的、有意识的努力，旨在改变某语言在社会中的功能，从而解决交际中出现的问题。虽然个人或一些社团的努力可有助于语言规划，但若无政府授权，很难成功。

第二，语言观念。语言规划实际上是要改变一种语言的功能，这是一个复杂的过程。在这个过程中，不同的语言观念、对语言性质的不同角度的认识对规划的影响可能会是巨大的。例如，把语言看成"问题"，那么，规划的目标就是"解决问题"；如果把语言看成"文化"，那么规划中就会考虑如何保护这种文化；如果把语言看成一种资源，规划中就会考虑如何开发和利用这种资源。

第三，语言主体使用者的实力。语言的主体使用者的经济、文化或政治实力和该语言或方言的推广与传播有密切关系。当今英语之所以成为"国际语言"，许多国家的语言规

---

1 郭熙. 论华语视角下的中国语言规划. 语文研究，2006（1）.

划中开始重视汉语的学习，都与此不无关系。

第四，对一种语言的定位。语言地位规划中常常要选择一种或多种语言作为官方语言，并打造成为标准语加以推广。比如在中国的语言规划中，普通话具有国家通用语言的地位，从20世纪50年代开始，它在中国大陆获得了非其他语言或方言所能企及的地位。

第五，语言使用者的认同和接受。对一种语言的认同有助于对该语言的学习，也有助于对该语言的相关规划的接受。

上述五个方面实际上涉及了语言规划的不同内容，都不可忽视。只强调其中的任何一个方面都是不完整的。总的来说，语言观念影响到规划的制定，政府和规划者的权威则影响到规划的落实，语言主体使用者的实力以及他们的认同和接受度则影响到入选语言的社会支持力，进而影响到规划的结果。

📖 原典选读

一、当代中国的语言规划

陈章太. 当代中国的语言规划. 语言文字应用，2005（1）：2-12.

【导　读】

这篇论文讨论了当代中国的语言规划显现出传承性和阶段性的特点，认为其主要内容大多传承自清末以来中国语文革新运动的内容，并明显地分为以语言地位规划为主的前一阶段和以语言本体规划为主的后一阶段。论文对两个阶段的汉语规划和少数民族语言规划的内容、活动、做法、效应等进行具体论述，并对当代中国语言规划进行评价。

文章还强调，当代中国的语言规划还有许多事情要做，这些工作主要包括：进一步处理好语言关系，保障人民群众的语言权利，加强社会语言生活监测与社会语言问题调查研究，加速推广和普及普通话，加强语言文字规范化、标准化，认真实行双语政策，保护弱势、濒危语言与方言，正确对待汉语的对外影响和英语对我国的影响，保持语言生活的统一性与多样性等。文章认为这些工作应该给予更多的关注，从而促进我国的社会语言生活继续朝着丰富、健康、有序的方向发展。

一 概 说

当代中国的语言规划,是指20世纪50年代初以来的中国语言规划,实际由中华人民共和国建立至现在中国大陆的语言规划。中国的台湾、香港、澳门三地,因其语言生活与大陆有所不同,其语言规划与大陆的语言规划也有差别,本文对台港澳三地的语言规划未加论述。

这个时期的中国语言规划显现出两个主要特点。(1)具有相当强的传承性。当代中国语言规划的主要内容,大多传承自20世纪上半叶乃至更早的中国语文运动、语文改革的内容,是此前语文运动、语文改革等的延续与发展。(2)表现出明显的阶段性。当代中国的语言规划,明显地分为前后两个阶段,即从20世纪50年代初至70年代末的立国建设阶段,以语言地位规划为主,也就是实行语言平等,保障民族语权利,选择、推广全民共同语,实行文字改革为主要任务的前一阶段;从80年代初至现在的改革发展阶段,以语言本体规划为主,也就是以加强语言文字规范化标准化和普及普通话,以及语言文字信息处理管理为主要任务的后一阶段。在立国建设阶段的后半期,因为"文化大革命"的破坏与影响,中国的语言规划也陷于停滞,造成重大的损失,直到"文革"结束后,语言规划才开始恢复,并为改革发展阶段进行语言规划创造了条件。

二 立国建设阶段的语言规划

(一)社会背景。这个阶段的中国,是建立新中国、建设新国家,全社会一切工作都要围绕国家这个总任务来进行。语言规划也不能例外,其主要目的是为国家统一、民族团结、社会进步、事业发展与社会交际服务,并有利于建设经济、普及教育、提高文化、科技水平。

(二)立国建设阶段语言规划的主要内容。依据这个阶段语言规划的目的,确定语言规划的内容,主要有以下几项。(1)贯彻、推行国家制定的各民族语言平等和推广全民共同语等各项语言政策。(2)进行文字改革。(3)推广普通话。(4)加强现代汉语规范化。(5)彻底完成文体改革。

(三)立国建设阶段语言规划工作的方针、任务。总方针是:文字必须改革,现代汉语需要规范化,文字改革和现代汉语规范化要积极稳妥地进行。(1)文字改革方面。方针是:文字必须改革,汉字改革要走世界文字共同的拼音方向,而在实现拼音化以前,必须简化汉字,以利目前的应用,同时积极进行拼音化的各项准备工作。具体任务有2项:整理并简化汉字,制定并推行汉语拼音方案。(2)推广普通话方面。方针是大力提倡,重点推行,逐步普及。具体任务有3项:确定普通话的规范标准,大力宣传、推广普通话,在全国范围内以县市为单位进行汉语方言普查。(3)现代汉语书范化方面。没有确定具体方针,按总方针积极而稳妥地开展工作。具体任务主要有4项:大力宣传、提倡汉语规范化,开展标准语和汉语规范问题的讨论与研究,对汉语语音、词汇、语法进行规范,制定规范标准,编写规范性语言辞书、教材、读物。(4)文体改革方面。在以前文体改革的基础上,彻底完成文体改革,白话文完全替代文言文。具体任务有5项:书面语口语统一,新闻、公文、布告等用白话文写作,汉字排版、书写横排、竖写,采用新式标点符号,采用阿拉伯数字,进行文风改革。

(四)立国建设阶段语言规划的措施、方法。(1)发挥立法、行政的权威作用。如国务院成立语言规划主管部门中国文字改革委员会和中央推广普通话工作委员会,地方成立相应的机构,负责语言规划工作。1955年由教育部和中国文字改革委员会联合召开"全国文字改革工作会议",会议明确了文字改革和推广普通话的具体工作。1956年1月28日国务院公布汉字简化方案,1956年2月6日发出"关于推广普通话的指示";1957年11月1日作出"关于公布汉语拼音方案草案的决议;1958年1月10日周恩来总理在政协全国委员会会议上作"当前文字改革的任务的报告;1958年2月11日全国人大第一届第五次会议作出"关于汉语拼音方案的决议",以及国务院各部委及地方政府就上述内容发出一系列指示、通知,认真贯彻、落实上述语言规划内容。(2)发挥新闻、出版的作用。大力宣传语言规范化的意义、作用、内容、做法和规定,号召、动员社会大众广泛参与,如1951年6月8日《人民日报》发表重要社论《正确地使用祖国的语言,为语言的纯洁和健康而斗争》,并同时开始连载吕叔湘、朱德熙合写的《语法修辞讲话》,这对当时以及后的语言规范化影响很大。1955年10月26日《人民日报》拟为促进汉字改革、推广普通话、实现汉语规范化而努力的社论,对当时中国语言规划的几个重要问题作了全面、深刻的阐述,号召全国人民积极参与语言规划活动,为实现这些语言规划目标而努力。其他大部分报刊也都发表许多关于文字改革、推广汉语拼音和汉语规范化方面的文件、报道、社论、报道、文章,收到显著效果。出版部门出版了大批语言规划方面的书籍、读物,扩大了社会影响。广播、电视除播发大量语言规划方面的新闻、报道、专文等,还举办文字改革、普通话语音知识等专题讲座,广泛传授语言规划知识。(3)发挥学术界的作用。如1955年10月中国科学院在北京召开"现代汉语规范问题学术会议",对普通话和规范化的涵义作了说明,指出"普通话以北方话为基础方言,以北京语音为标准音","规范化在于以北京音,北方话为基础方言的内部规律,把语言在其发展过程中所产生的一些分歧适当地加以整理,引导它向更加完善的方向加速发展"。会议还作出重要决议,提出6点意见建议,为现代汉语规范化提供了重要的学术促证。会议的前后,学术界研制了多项语言审读审查表,如普通话异读词审音表、地名审音表,常用词表,中学汉语教学语法体系,新式《标点符号用法》,编纂规范性的《新华字典》和《现代汉语词典》等,对社会语言应用和语言规范产生重要影响。(4)发挥社会团体的作用。这一阶段中,各级工会、妇联、共青团、青联、文联,都积极参与语言规划活动,如共青团组织、参与各种有关会议、活动,发表倡议书、文章,宣传、落实语言规划工作,动员社会各界广泛参与语言规划活动,对语言规划的制定与实施作出重要贡献。(5)发挥政治家、社会活动家、科学家、教育家、文学艺术家的作用。许多政治家、社会活动家和社会名人等的个人作用,如毛泽东、周恩来、陈毅、吴玉章、胡乔木关于文字改革、汉字简化、汉语拼音、推广普通话、语言规范化等问题的言论、讲话、报告、文章,对这一阶段的中国语言规划起到极大的推动和促进作用,郭沫若、马叙伦、胡愈之、叶圣陶、老舍、巴金、罗常培、王力、吕叔湘、周有光等积极参与语言规划活动,充分发挥社会名人这方面的重要作用与影响。(6)加强干部队伍建设,大力培养专业人才。新中国成立后,即在高等学校设立语言专业,开设语言规划方面的课程,并成立语言专修班、研究班、短收、培养了大批语言专业干部,如许多中外多人从事语言规划工作。教育部和中国文字改革研究所从1956年开始,合办普通话语音研究班,1959年8月开始中国文字改革委员会参加会议,该研究班共举办9期,培养语言规划专业干部1666名。全国各地也举办各种形式的语言培训班、研究班,培养了大批语言规划地方干部,这一大批专业干部,在这一阶段及以后的语言规划工作中发挥了极其重要的作用。

三 改革发展阶段的语言规划

(一)社会背景。这个阶段的中国,给国家造成巨大损失的"文化大革命"彻底结束,国家实行改革开放政策,社会由动乱而治,开始向现代化建设,各项事业蒸蒸日上,社会生活和语言生活发生重大而深刻的变化。整个中国呈现一派欣欣向荣的景象,语言规划进入新的发展时期。为适合国家、社会和人民大众的需要,这个阶段的语言规划,主要目的是为改革开放和现代化建设服务。

(二)改革发展阶段语言规划的主要内容。根据这个阶段语言规划的主要目的,确定语言规划的内容,主要有这样几项:(1)贯彻、执行国家新时期语言政策和法令。(2)巩固、消化前一阶段语言规划的成果,延续前一阶段语言规划的主要内容和主要方法。(3)确定推广普通话和加强语言规范化为核心内容。(4)加强语言文字信息处理的研究与管理。(5)加强语法规范说,依法管理语言文字工作。

(三)改革发展阶段语言规划工作的方针、任务。1986年1月,国家教育委员会和国家语言文字工作委员会在北京召开"全国语言文字工作会议",会议总结了前一阶段的语言文字工作,制定了新时期语言文字工作方针任务,标志着中国语言规划进入以规范化、标准化、信息化为主要内容的新时期。会议确定这一时期语言文字工作的方针:贯彻执行国家关于语言文字工作的政策和法令,促进语言文字规范化、标准化,继续推动文字改革工作,使语言文字工作在社会主义现代化建设中更好地发挥作用。规定的主要任务是:做好现代汉语规范化工作,大力推广和积极普及普通话,研究和整理现行汉字,制定各项有关标准,进一步推行汉语拼音方案,研究并解决实际使用中的有关问题,研究汉语汉字信息处理问题,参与鉴定有关成果;加强语言文字的基础研究和应用研究。做好社会调查和社会咨询、服务工作。1997年12月教育部和国家语委召开第二次全国语言文字工作大会,重申继续贯彻国家新时期语言文字工作方针、政策,并根据跨世纪国家、社会发展的需要和新时期语言文字工作的具体任务作了适当调整,使其更加全面、具体、完善。

这一阶段确定了语言规划各项工作的具体方针、目标,推广普通话的方针为:大力推行,积极普及、逐步提高。目标是2010年前全面初步普及普通话,2050年前全国普及普通话。在汉字方面,指出对汉字简化应持较为谨慎的态度,使汉字形体保持相对的稳定,对现行汉字进行四定,即定量、定形、定音、定序,加强社会用字管理,改变社会用字混乱现象。到2010年汉字的社会应用基本达到实现规范化。在汉语拼音方面,强调汉语拼音的实际作用,强调进一步扩大汉语拼音文字的使用范围。在语言文字信息处理方面,强调加强宏观管理,逐步实现中文信息技术产品的优化、统一。还有,加强汉语和少数民族语言文字规范标准研制,开展中国语言文字使用情况调查等。

(四)改革发展阶段语言规划的措施、方法。(1)进一步发挥立法、行政的作用。在语言立法方面,最重要的是1982年颁布、实施的《中华人民共和国宪法》中规定:"各民族都有使用和发展自己的语言文字的自由"。2000年10月31日由第九届全国人民代表大会常务委员会第十八次会议审议通过,并于2001年1月1日起施行的《中华人民共和国国家通用语言文字法》,是有史以来第一部语言文字工作的专项法律,它体现了国家的语言文字工作方针政策,科学地总结了新中国成立50多年乃至近百年语言规划的成功经验。第一次以法律的形式规定普通话和规范汉字作为国家通用语言文字的地位,并对国家通用语言文字的使用作出具体规定,这部专项法律的颁布与实行,对规范、规范社会用字,促进语言文字规范化和标准化,提高汉语水平,发展经济文化教育科技,便利各民族交流和社会交际,增加中华民族凝聚力,都具有极为重要的意义。《中华人民共和国民族区域自治法》和《中华人民共和国教育法》等多部国家法律中,也有关于语言文字及其使用的有关规定,充分发挥了语言立法在语言规划中的作用。在行政方面,主要是建立、健全各级语言规划机构和工作网络,协调、发挥政府各相关部门的作用;1986年教育部和国家语言文字工作委员会联合召开全国语言文字工作会议,制定新时期语言文字规划,确定新的工作方针任务,1997年两部委又联合开第二次全国语言文字工作会议,采取更有力的行政措施,进一步实施新时期国家语言文字规划,加强语言规划队伍培训与建设,提高社会语言文字问题的行政管理水平。1997年国务院第134次总理办公会议决定,自1998年起,每年9月的第三周在全国开展"推广普通话宣传周"活动,对普通话的推广与普及,以及社会语言观念的改变有重要作用。(2)继续加大媒体的宣传力度,形成正确的舆论导向。这个阶段的新闻出版、广播电视等,在宣传、贯彻国家新时期的语言文字政策和语言文字工作中进一步发挥作用。特别是对国家通用语言文字法、推广普通话宣传周、全国普通话大赛、社会用字管理、城市语言文字工作评估和语言文字信息处理等的宣传,更加集中、有力,让社会各界对这些重要工作和活动有更多的了解,并积极参与,收到更大的实效。(3)制定、推行各项语言文字规范标准。为切实加强语言文字规范化标准化,这个阶段中制定了多项语言文字规范标准。如1985年12月27日,由国家语委、国家教委和广电部联合发布普通话异读词审音表;1988年1月26日,由国家语委和国家教委联合发布《现代汉语常用字表》;1988年3月25日,由国家语委和新闻出版署发布现代汉语通用字表;1988年7月1日,由国家教委和国家语委公布《汉语拼音正词法基本规则》;1990年3月22日,由国家语委和新闻出版署联合发布《标点符号用法》;1997年4月,由国家语委和新闻出版署发布《现代汉语通用字笔顺规范》;2001年12月19日,由教育部和国家语委发布《第一批异形词整理表》(草案)。还有电脑、媒体、地名、商标广告、出版物、公共场所等用字的规范,科学技术名词的规范、科技术语等方面的语言文字规范标准。(4)加速推广、普及普通话,广泛开展普通话培训与测试。在推广普通话方面,从前一阶段重视南方方言区的推广,转而加强西部地区的推广,并把这项工作与国家西部地区的开发及发展事业结合起来,如对西部地区乃至全国的普通话与民族语言培训,强调在推进中更发挥教育部门的基础作用,国家机关工作人员的带头作用,新闻出版、广播影视等媒体的示范作用,交通、邮电、电子技术、商业、旅游、工商等社会服务行业的先行作用,以及各部门、行业的有关人员等社会各界的积极作用。国家语音规划主持者还制定普通话水平测试等级标准》和普通话水平测试大纲》,编制普通话水平测试实施细则》,对中小学教师、播音员、节目主持人和国家机关工作人员等进行普通话水平测试。这些措施与做法,有效促进普通话的普及。(5)加强语言文字的应用研究。比较重要的如,①由语言规划主管部门国家语委编制语言文字应用研究"十五"科研规划,拨出专项经费,立项近下个课题,组织力量集中攻关,限期做出成果,为语言规划的科学制定和有效实施创造条件。②经国务院总理办公会第134次会议批准,"中国语言文字使用情况调查"立项,由国家语委组织实施,由国务院出专项经费,地方财政给予支持。该项目从1998年正式启动,历时6年基本完成,比较全面地调查了解了全国语言文字使用的基本情况。具体内容包括被调查者的自然情况、普通话、汉语方言、少数民族语言文字、简化汉字、繁体汉字、汉语拼音、外国语文、信息处理用语文的使用及掌握程度,还有语言态度等。调查方式分入户调查和专项调查；专项调查包括公务员、商业工作人员、医务工作人员、中学生、大学生、教师的语言文字使用情况。问卷分家庭问卷和个人问卷，这是中国有史以来第一次全国性语言文字使用情况调查，是国情调查的一部分，对全国及地方制定、实施语言规划和教育文化、科技与劳动、人事部门的有关决策，促进精神文明和物质文明建设，以及语言学和应用语言的研究、发展，都有重要意义。③加强语言规划重要问题研究，如语言规划理论研究，推广普通话方略研究，现代汉语通用词表研究，规范汉字表研究，推广普通话与西部开发研究，双语问题研究，对外汉语教学与国际交流研究，（6）培养语言规划高层次专业人才。这一阶段中，有些高等院校设置了应用语言学专业，开设语言规划课程，招收、培养语言应用与语言规划的硕士生、博士生，为中国语言规划的持续发展提供重要条件。

四 少数民族语言规划

（一）少数民族语言及民族语言政策。中国是一个统一的多民族多语言的国家，少数民族有55个。中国少数民族语言有多少种，目前还没有公认的说法。《中国少数民族语言使用情况》一书（1994）认为有80种以上，戴庆厦等《中国少数民族语言文字应用研究》（2000）一书认为有92种，新近还有120多种之说。各民族都有自己的语言，有的民族转用其他民族的语言，如回族、满族、畲族、土家族大多转用汉语，乌孜别克族、俄罗斯族许多人转用哈萨克语。有的民族使用1种以上的语言，如景颇族使用5种语言，瑶族、怒族使用3种语言，裕固族使用2种语言；不少民族的语言是跨境语言，如拉祜语在中国、缅甸、泰国、越南、老挝5国跨祜族共同使用的语言，蒙古语是中国和蒙古国的蒙古族共同使用的语言。中国55个少数民族中，共有33种少数民族文字（戴庆厦等，2000），有的民族没有自己的文字，有的民族使用其他民族的文字，有的民族有1种以上的文字，如傣族、景颇族使用4种文字。

中国是保护、发展少数民族语言文字、保障少数民族语言权利、制定了一系列民族语言政策，其核心是实行语言平等，禁止语言歧视，保障少数民族语言权利，鼓励各民族互相学习语言文字，并用法律的形式对民族语言政策加以肯定。国家大法《宪法》规定："各民族都有使用和发展自己的语言文字的自由，都有保持或者改革自己的风俗习惯的自由。""民族自治地方的自治机关在执行职务的时候，依照本民族自治地方自治条例的规定，使用当地通用的一种或者几种语言文字。""各民族公民都有用本民族语言文字进行诉讼的权利。人民法院和人民检察院对于不通晓当地通用的语言文字的诉讼参与人，应当为他们翻译。在少数民族聚居或者多民族共同居住的地区，应用当地通用的语言进行审判；起诉书、判决书、布告和其他文书应当根据实际需要使用当地通用的一种或者几种文字。"《国家通用语言文字法》《民族区域自治法》等，对民族语言权利、地位及使用等有更详细的规定，并且采取许多措施，保证少数民族语言文字在司法、行政、教育、文化、传媒、翻译、宗教等领域及政治生活、社会生活中的有效使用。

中国语言规划具体贯彻了中国民族语言政策，并坚持实事求是、分类指导、分类规划，积极、慎重、稳妥地开展民族语言工作，为增进民族团结和社会进步，促进民族地区政治、经济、文化事业全面发展而服务的工作方针，取得了显著的成绩。具体规划大致分为两个阶段，即立国建设阶段的民族语言规划和改革发展阶段的民族语言规划。

（二）立国建设阶段的少数民族语言规划。在立国阶段时，特别是"文革"前的15年，中国少数民族语言规划处于大发展时期，取得很大的成绩。这个阶段的少数民族语言规划偏重于语言地位规划，主要是贯彻、体现国家语言平等与各民族都有使用和发展自己语言文字的自由的政策，在确定民族语言地位、维护民族语言权利、加强语言接触与交流、调查、识别民族语言，创制与改革民族文字等方面做了大量工作。（1）成立民族语言规划职能部门和研究、教学、翻译、出版机构。为做好民族语言规划工作，国家主要是设立少数民族语言规划部门和研究会，后又在民族事务委员会内设立民族语文工作组。具体主持民族语言规划工作，中国文字改革委员会也负责少数民族语言规划的部分工作。1956年在中国科学院内成立少数民族语言研究所（1962年与民族研究所合并），负责民族语言规划并配合做好民族语言规划工作；创办民族院校，设置民族语文教学、翻译、出版机构，培养民族语言专门人才，做好民族语文翻译、出版工作；各有关省、区也建立民族语文工作机构，主持并指导地方民族语言规划工作。（2）加强民族语言立法，确定民族语言地位，保障民族语言权利。在《宪法》《民族区域自治法》《国家通用语言文字法》以及《教育法》《义务教育法》《刑事诉讼法》《居民身份证条例》《人民法院组织法》《全国人民代表大会和地方各级人民代表大会选举法》《全国人民代表大会组织法》等法律中，都有这方面内容的规定。（3）开展民族语言大调查，1950年至1954年，中国科学院组织少数民族语言专家对广西、云南、贵州、四川等南方各少数民族语言进行初步调查，1955年又对甘肃、青海、内蒙古等北方各少数民族语言进行初步调查，1956年中国科学院组织7个工作队、近200名少数民族语言工作者对各少数民族语言进行全面调查，调查点总数在1500个以上。基本了解了各民族语言情况，取得了大批珍贵资料，编写、出版了一批少数民族语言调查报告和少数民族语言概况，还出版了一套中国少数民族语言简志，为语言规划的制定与实施创造了极为重要的条件。（4）少数民族创制、改革文字。为做好这项工作，民族语言规划部门采取积极慎重的方针，认真细致地做好充分准备。1955年12月在北京召开全国民族语言科学讨论会，制定了创制和改革民族文字的全面规划。1955年制定了壮文方案，改革了西双版纳傣文和德宏傣文。1956年至1979年，为布依、彝、傈僳、苗、哈尼、侗、纳西、佤、载瓦、黎、土家等民族创制了14套拉丁字母形式的文字，为景颇等4个民族改进了5种文字。这些民族文字创制、改革的过程，都贯穿了1957年第63次全体会议通过并公布了少数民族文字方案中设计字母的几项原则，总的精神是以拉丁字母为基础，字母系统要清晰，便于教学、使用与交流。这个阶段少数民族文字的创制、改革是成功的，并积累了丰富的经验。

（三）改革发展阶段的少数民族语言规划。这个阶段的少数民族语言规划偏重于语言本体规划，主要是适应国家改革开放和现代化建设的需要，加强民族语言文字的规范化标准化，保持和扩展民族语言地位，推行双语教育，进一步促进民族语言发展，保护少数民族语言多样化，同时传承前一阶段的少数民族语言规划，继续保障民族语言权利，巩固少数民族语言地位，协调语言关系，完善与发展少数民族语言文字功能，使各少数民族语言规范、健康地发展，更好地为民族的繁荣与发展服务，为中华民族的伟大复兴服务。（1）恢复民族语言文字工作机构，加强民族语文规划的工作。这个阶段的初期，为恢复、发展民族语言规划，首先是恢复民族语文工作机构，全国各地原有的民族语文工作指导委员会纷纷恢复，有的地方还成立新的民族语文工作机构，全国省级民族语文工作也普遍成立省级民族语文工作委员会，国家民族事务委员会加强对民族语文工作的领导和指导，国家语委增加了少数民族语言信息处理用语言文字规范标准的管理。与此同时，先后召开了多次全国性或地方性民族语文科学讨论会和民族语文工作会议，讨论、研究民族语文规划问题，如民族语文的规范化标准化问题、新词术语规范问题、民族语文翻译问题、双语教学问题、民族语文扫盲问题等。（2）制定新时期民族

语文工作方针任务。1991年国家民委向国务院上报《关于进一步做好少数民族语言文字工作的报告》，提出新时期民族语文工作方针任务。其方针是："坚持马克思主义语言平等原则，保障民族使用和发展自己语言文字的自由，从有利于各民族团结、进步和共同繁荣出发，实事求是，分类指导，积极、慎重、稳妥地开展民族语文工作，为推动少数民族地区政治、经济、文化事业的全面发展，促进我国的社会主义现代化建设服务。"具体任务是："贯彻党和国家的民族政策，加强民族语文法制建设；搞好民族语文的规范化、标准化和信息处理；促进民族语文的翻译、出版、教育、新闻、广播、影视、古籍整理事业；推进民族语文的学术研究、协作交流和人才培养；鼓励各民族互相学习语言文字。"国务院批准了这个报告，确定了新时期少数民族语文工作方针任务。（3）加强民族语文规范化标准化。主要是制定民族语文本体的各项规范标准和语言文字信息处理用语言文字标准，还有新词术语规范标准等。信息处理用语言文字标准如《信息处理交换用蒙古文七位和八位编码图形字符集》（1987）《信息处理交换用维吾尔文编码图形字符集》（1989）《信息交换用朝鲜文字编码字符集》（1989），还有哈萨克文和藏文的编码字符集等。（4）大力推广国家通用语言普通话，同时加强民族地区的双语教育。1982年《中华人民共和国宪法》第4条规定："国家推广全国通用的普通话"。2000年的《国家通用语言文字法》规定："国家通用语言文字是普通话和规范汉字。""国家推广普通话，推行规范汉字。"国家在全国范围内，包括少数民族地区，大力推广普通话。这是个克服语言、方言障碍，使少数民族和方言地区的群众在掌握本民族语言或本地区方言之外，多掌握一种国家通用的语言，有利于社会交际与社会稳定，有利于民族地区和方言地区的发展，而不是要妨碍少数民族使用自己的语言，更不是用普通话取代少数民族语言，也不是要压制方言。在推广普通话的同时，大力加强民族地区的双语教育，提高双语教学水平，扩大双语范围，增加双语人数，为民族地区的政治经济、文化教育和科学技术等的发展，以及人才培养，在语言方面创造重要条件。（5）调查、抢救濒危语言，保护少数民族语言。语言是文化的载体，少数民族文化需要少数民族语言来保存与传播，因此保护少数民族语言有重要的意义。如同世界许多国家一样，中国也有一些弱势少数民族语言正处于濒危的状态，如满语、畲语、赫哲语、阿侬语、不辛语、普标语、拉基语、仙岛语、义都语、弄语、土家语等，有些少数民族语言，国家正采取措施进行调查、保护与抢救。其基本做法如，增加经费投入，扶植欠发达民族地区发展经济、文化，增强弱势民族语言的活力；组织民族语言工作者，深入调查各地濒危语言，记录、描写、保存这些语言资料；编写、出版刊物、濒危语言专书、词典，如近期出版的《中国新发现语言研究丛书》X本（系少数民族语言系列词典丛书》等，逐渐建立少数民族语音资料库，录制、保存弱势、濒危语言的声像资料；认真实行双语言政策，切实加强双语教育，为濒危语言的教学和使用尽量创造有利条件，延缓其消亡的时间等。这些措施的实施，开始收到一定的效果。

五 当代中国语言规划评价

对当代中国语言规划的评价，上文已有所涉及，这里从总体方面作简要回顾与评价。

（一）语言规划的制定与实施。从总体上看，当代中国语言规划的制定是符合语言规划基本原则的，无论是语言地位规划或是语言本体规划，如实行语言平等，保障语言权利，协调语言关系，加强语言接触与语言交流，缓和语言矛盾与防止语言冲突，国家通用语言文字和区域通用语言文字的确定与推行，文字的改革与创制，语言文字的规范化标准化，语言信息处理用语言文字的制定与管理，地名、术语规范化等符合科学、有效、简明、稳定性和经济性等语言规划基本原则，所以当代中国语言规划总体上进行得比较顺利，取得很大的成功。

从语言规划实施的社会效果看，当代中国语言规划的社会效果是好的。由于实行语言平等，保障民族语言权利，处理好语言关系，正确选择并大力推行全民共同语和区域共同语，进行文字改革与文字创制，加强语言文字规范化标准化，加强社会语言及信息处理中语言文字问题的管理，使当代中国的语言文字朝着规范、健康的方向发展，语言生活呈现统一、多样的特征。当代中国语言规划的实施，大力推行国家通用语的交际，对维护国家统一、民族团结、社会稳定，促进经济、文化、教育、科技发展，扩大对外交流等，发挥了重要的作用，收到显著的效果，受到国内外普遍的肯定与赞扬。

（二）语言规划成功的基本经验。综观当代中国的语言规划，其成功的基本经验是：（1）从当代中国的国情出发制定、实施语言规划。中国是一个统一的多民族国家，地域广阔，人口众多，语言方言纷繁复杂，政治、经济、文化、教育、科技不发达。新中国成立后，需要尽快发展经济、文化事业，加速现代化建设，保持社会稳定与繁荣。当代中国语言规划就是根据这些国情制定与实施的，在前一阶段偏重于语言地位规划，具体确定实行语言平等、保障民族语言权利、进行文字改革、推广普通话和加强现代汉语规范化为主要任务，后一阶段，根据国家实行改革开放和加强现代化建设的需要，语言规划偏重于语言本体规划，加强普通话、普通话和少数民族语言的规范化、加强语言信息处理的研究与管理为主要任务，任务明确，目标实际，内容具体，要求顺序渐进，语言规划声望较高，这是最重要的基本经验。（2）认真贯彻、体现国家正确、有效的语言政策。当代中国语言规划的核心是，实行语言平等，保障公民语言权利，国家推广全国通用的普通话和规范汉字，民族自治区域实行区域政策等，这些政策是正确、有效的，它对国家、民族的语言文字生活起到重要的作用。当代中国的语言规划，认真贯彻、体现了国家正确的语言政策，所以获得了成功。（3）语言规划作为政府行为，由政府主持制定与实施。中国过去的语言规划，主要是由爱国志士、社会名人、知识分子倡导、参与的社会行为，部分由政府行为，它对国家、语言方面作了不少有益的工作，有贡献，但政府行为没有完全处于主导地位，所以实施效果不大。新中国成立后，政府充分发挥其行政权威作用，并建立、健全各级语言规划专门机构，主持制定与实施语言规划，调动、协调政府各相关部门及社会团体，紧密配合语言规划工作，并动员社会各方积极参与，使语言规划得以顺利进行。（4）加强语言立法，逐渐形成语言法律、法规体系，依法管理社会语言问题及语言文字使用。《中华人民共和国宪法》及有关法律，如民族区域自治法》《教育法》等，都有关于语言文字问题的规定。2000年10月31日第九届全国人民代表大会常务委员会第十八次会议通过了中华人民共和国国家通用语言文字法》，并于2001年1月1日起实施。这是中国有史以来制定、颁布的第一部关于语言文字问题的专项法律，以法律的形式规定普通话和规范汉字作为国家通用语言文字的部门的主体地位，该法律的制定、颁布，其意义和作用是重大的。各有关部门和各地方政府还制定一系列有关法规及实行办法，形成比较完整的语言法律、法规体系，从法律方面保障语言规划的顺利实施。这些法律、法规的制定与颁布，使语言规范汉字作为有法可依，依法管理社会语言问题健康、有序地发展。（5）社会各界广泛参与，语言规划成为政府行为与社会行为相结合，并付之社会行动。语言规划最终要落实在社会，必须得到社会各界的支持，为社会大众所接受，才能顺利的完成。当代中国的语言规划在政府主持制定与实施过程中，社会团体如工会、共青团、妇联、民主党派、文联、作协等，学术机构如中国科学院、中国社会科学院、中国语言学会、语

文现代化学会等，新闻出版单位如报纸杂志社、广播电台电视台、出版社等，各级各类学校，积极配合并广泛参与，在社会上形成良好的氛围，收到很好的社会效果。(6)切实加强语言文字规范化标准化，制定并推行各项语言音规范标准，提高语言规范化程度，增强语言的社会交际功能和信息传输能力。(7)总结、吸收清末以来中国语言规划的经验，很好地继承和发扬现代语文革新运动的成效。

(三)语言规划存在的主要问题。语言规划是十分复杂、艰巨的，其难度很大。为进一步做好语言规划工作，我们在总结当代中国语言规划成功经验的同时，也要看到它所存在的主要问题。这些问题是：(1)对语言规划的长期性、复杂性、艰巨性的认识有所不足，因此有时有急于求成的表现。有些语言规划工作不够周全，如20世纪50~60年代，对汉字及其前途的认识不够全面，有些与语言规划的人士设想较快完成文字改革，早日实现汉语拼音化的，把推广、普及普通话和汉语规范化看得过于简单、容易，因此有些语言规划目标操有过高，要求实现过急。有些语言规划工作有简单化倾向。又如1986年制定新时期语言文字工作方针时，提出到20世纪末普通话要成为教学语言、工作语言、宣传语言和交际语言，也就是要在社会普及普通话，而采取的措施又不够有力，有些工作也不够细致。从时间和做法看，这个目标是不容易实现。所以1992年国家语委调整为2010年以前在全国范围内初步普及普通话。(2)对科学研究重视不够，语言规划理论较为薄弱，对社会语言生活和社会语言问题的调查、研究不够，对有些问题的论证不够充分，所以有些语言规划活动和做法科学性有所不足。如1956年经国务院全体会议第23次会议讨论通过并公布的《汉字简化方案》，及1964年中国文字改革委员会在《汉字简化方案》基础上编辑出版的《简化字总表》，是简化汉字的规范标准。从总体上评价，这批简化汉字是科学、合理的，实行效果是好的，便利千千万万人对汉字的学习与使用，对普及教育、提高文化和发展科学技术等有重要的作用，因此受到社会各界的欢迎与肯定。但是这批简化汉字中有些，其简化的科学性有所不足，主要表现在有些简化字与相近形体的字容易混淆，造成认读和识别的困难，如"儿—几，设—没，风—凤，沧—沧"有些简化字形体上与未简化的字相同，而音又有别，造成混乱，如"树叶(叶)"的"叶"与"叶韵"的"叶"，"重选(叠)"的"选"与"更选"的"选"有些简化字失去汉字形体匀称的特点，字形欠佳，缺乏美感，如"厂、广、产、习、宁"有些简化字不合原汉字的体系，特别是一些用符号简化的字，与原字形体系离得更远，给学习汉字带来不便，如"对、邓、戏、轰、汉、仅、权"。造成这些问题的主要原因是，过多考虑精简笔画数和简化字数，对汉字简化的整体化、规范化注意不够，所以简化了一些不该简化的字，对同音代替、草书楷化、符号代替的简化方法的使用有的不当，增加了一些不必要的汉字部件等。其他语言文字规范标准中，有的也不大符合科学性，如有些字音的审定，有些词形的规范缺乏理据。推广普通话的有些做法不够科学，从而影响推普效果。(3)有些语言规划工作受政治影响较大，或过分依靠行政作用，造成一定的损失。语言规划离不开政治，总是一定政治的体现，并要现行行政的组织引领导作用，但如果政治性、行政性过强，而政治有时又以政治领导代替语言规划就会违反自身的特点和规律，削弱其科学性、求实性，遭受必然的挫折，如1977年12月20日发表的《第二次汉字简化方案(草案)》，是在"文化大革命"中酝酿、制定的，因为受当时极左政治的影响，简化的字数过多，有些字的简化不科学不合理，要求试用过急，试用效果不好，

给社会用字造成混乱。国家语委经过认真、慎重的研究以后，不得不报请国务院批准于1986年6月24日正式废止。又如新疆维吾尔族长期使用阿拉伯字母为基础的察合台文，因为受政治、行政的影响，1965年主要依靠行政作用开始推行以拉丁字母为基础的维吾尔族新文字方案，1979年新疆维吾尔族自治区人民代表大会通过关于全面推行新文字、停止使用老文字的决议。新文字制订太急、太快，推行效果不好，给社会用字造成很多困难，所以1982年新疆人民代表大会又作出决议，决定恢复使用维吾尔老文字，新文字只作为拼音符号保留。(4)所制定的语言文字规范标准有的不够严谨、细致，影响了语言规划实施效果。如《印刷通用汉字字形表》(第一批异体字整理)和《简化汉字总表》中有些字有矛盾，《普通话异读词审音表》中对有些字音的审订不够恰当、可行，《关于出版物上数字用法的试行规定》中的有些规定难以实行，这都需要很好修订与完善。上述存在的这些问题，给语言规划工作造成一些损失，影响了语言规划的声望，值得认真总结与改进。

当代中国的语言规划还有许多事情要做，特别是在进一步处理好语言关系，保障人民群众的语言权利，加强社会语言生活监测与社会语言问题调查研究，加速推行和普及普通话，加强语言文字规范化标准化，进一步增强语言活力，认真实行双语政策，保护弱势、濒危语言与方言，正确对待汉语的对外影响和英语对我国的影响，保持语言生活的统一性与多样性等方面，都需要给予更多的关注与着力，借以促进我国的社会语言生活继续朝着丰富、健康、有序的方向发展。

主要参考文献

[1] 全国文字改革会议秘书处. 全国文字改革会议文件[M]. 1955.
[2] 现代汉语规范问题学术会议秘书处. 现代汉语规范问题学术会议文件汇编[M]. 北京, 科学出版社, 1956.
[3] 国家语言文字工作委员会政策法规室. 国家语言文字政策法规汇编[M]. 北京, 语文出版社, 1986.
[4] 全国语言文字工作会议秘书处. 新时期的语言文字工作[M]. 北京, 语文出版社, 1987.
[5] 周有光. 汉字改革概论[M]. 北京, 文字改革出版社, 1979.
[6] 周有光. 新语文的建设[M]. 北京, 语文出版社, 1992.
[7] 高天如. 中国现代语言计划的理论与实践[M]. 上海, 复旦大学出版社, 1993.
[8] 中国社会科学院民族研究所, 国家民族事务委员会文化宣传司. 中国少数民族语言使用情况[M]. 北京, 中国藏学出版社, 1994.
[9] 王 均. 当代中国的文字改革[M]. 北京, 当代中国出版社, 1995.
[10] 凌远征. 新语文建设史话[M]. 河南, 河南大学出版社, 1995.
[11] 于根元. 二十世纪的中国语言应用研究[M]. 山西, 书海出版社, 1996.
[12] 语文出版社. 语言文字规范手册[M]. 北京, 语文出版社, 1997.
[13] 戴昭铭. 规范语言学探索[M]. 上海, 上海三联书店, 1998.
[14] 许嘉璐. 语言文字学及其应用研究[M]. 广州, 广东教育出版社, 1999.
[15] 冯志伟. 应用语言学综论·语言规划[M]. 广州, 广东教育出版社, 1999.
[16] 郭 熙. 中国社会语言学·语言规划和语言生活[M]. 南京, 南京大学出版社, 1999.
[17] 戴庆厦. 中国少数民族语言文字应用研究[M]. 昆明, 云南民族出版社, 2000.
[18] 李建国. 汉语规范史略[M]. 北京, 语文出版社, 2000.
[19] 于根元. 应用语言学概论[M]. 北京, 商务印书馆, 2003.

二、语言学与语言规划

Einar Haugen. 1971. Linguistics and Language Planning. In William Bright (ed.), *Sociolinguistics*. The Hague, Paris: Mouton, pp.50~71. (中译文：语言学与语言规划. 林书武，译. 胡壮麟，校. 国外语言学，1984 (3): 41~53.)

【导 读】

这篇论文是美国著名社会语言学家豪根的代表作。全文从多角度论述了语言学和语言规划之间的关系。文章谈到了语言规划的性质，认为"哪里有语言问题，哪里就要求对语言进行规划"。作者给出了语言规划的定义并提出了语言规划的根本任务，谈及语言和文字的关系及各自的作用，讨论了书面语和该书面语使用者的个人言语代码之间的关系，还涉及语言中文体的问题。文章指出，语言规划的目的就是要解决信息交流与人际沟通的问题，原则上讲，哪里传递信息失败，哪里就需要语言规划。

文章阐述了语言规划者的作用以及语言规划的各种可选择的方案。作者认为，在做出任何语言规划的决定之前，必须确定语言变化的限度。语言规划者总是在某时某地展开工

作的，他首先的任务是识别要处理的语言。另外，语言规划者的方案，还受到口语传统和文字传统状况的限制。文章还逐一解释了语言规划的三条标准，即有效率、合适性和可接受性。作者认为，语言规划的执行，归根到底，是由语言的使用者决定的。文章最后论述了语言学家在语言规划中的作用。

语言学与语言规划*

〔美〕E. Haugen　　林书武译

1. 导　言

1.1. 语言的正确性问题，多年来一直是美国许多作者最感兴趣的题目。自从《韦氏新国际词典(第三版)》(下称《韦氏第三版》)问世以来，这个问题又一次提了出来。一些英语的唯美主义者，主要是自封的英语纯洁性的保卫者，已把《韦氏第三版》的方针跟结构主义语言学这个名称联在一起。批评《韦氏第三版》的一个著名人物麦克唐纳(Dwight MacDonald)对我们说：该词典处理词汇的方法，根据的是"结构主义语言学的理论。"现在，不管是在编者的说明中还是在词典的实际做法中，都没有任何证据支持这种令人惊愕的断言。然而据麦克唐纳说，该词典是一个例子，说明"结构主义语言学已渗入到不属于它的领域"。如果单单是为了保护语言学的好名声，我认为我们也应该探讨语言科学跟语言规范问题之间的关系。我们不打算反驳这里提到的对结构主义语言学荒谬的指责，只是试图给我们这代人再次系统地阐述语言规范化的性质，阐述语言学家在编制规范准则并使之具有权威性的约束力的工作中可能起的作用。①

1.2. 我们完全可以说，十九世纪以前，所有的语言学都是注重规范的。非常受人尊敬的巴尼尼，就是一个语言规则的制订者，其工作旨在保持宗教的延续性。希腊和拉丁语法学家是教科书的编写者，他们希望建立一套正确地用自己的语言写作和说话的永远不可改变的规范准则。这也许是人们总是把他们的工作，轻蔑地称为"前科学的"的原因。但甚至在十九世纪，许多杰出的新语言科学的奠基人也都深入地卷入了语言规范问题。丹麦的拉斯克(Rasmus Rask)花了许多时间，为丹麦语设计了更合理的拼写系统，并且就此题目于1826年出版了整整一部书；德国历史语言学派的奠基人，象格里姆(Jakob Grimm)和施莱歇尔(August Schleicher)，就德语的正确性这个题目写了许多文章。十九世纪下半叶，这时新语法学支配着语言学，他们对这个问题也做出了重大贡献。保罗(Herman Paul)在其《语言史原理》(*Principien der Sprachgeschichte*)一书中，用一整章来探讨标准语，而诺林(Adolf Noreen)写了一篇透彻的文章，研究语言的正确性问题。在英国，语言学伟大的奠基人斯威特(Henry Sweet)终生都活跃于"拼写改革协会"(Spelling Reform Association)。在二十世纪，梅耶(Antoine Meillet)详尽地考虑过这个问题②，而叶斯柏森(Otto Jespersen)在其《人类，民族和个人》(*Mankind, Nation, and Individual*, 1925)一书中，以两整章的篇幅讨论"正确性的标准"这个题目。叶斯柏森还积极参与国际辅助语言的工作，他本人创制了一种叫做诺维阿语(Novial)的语言。

* 原文题为 Linguistics and Language Planning，刊于 William Bright (ed.)：*Sociolinguistics*(社会语言学)，pp. 50—71，The Hague，Paris，Mouton，1971. 译文对文献目录有所删节。——译者

① 这篇论文，是我在挪威从事语言规划的副产品。

② Antoine Meillet：*Les Langues dans l'Europe Nouvelle*(新欧洲的语言)，Paris，1928.

1.3. 在美国，两位最著名的语言学奠基人萨丕尔和布龙菲尔德都对这个问题感兴趣。萨丕尔为"国际辅助语协会"工作，布龙菲尔德写了一篇文章，论述"有文化者和文盲的话"③，在其《语言论》一书中，有几页讨论将语言科学应用于语言正确性和标准语问题，以及应用于英语拼写法和国际语问题。他在结尾写道："语言研究也许能帮助我们去了解和控制人类的事态，这只是个远景，但并不是无限地遥远"(509页)。甚至霍尔(Robert A. Hall, Jr.)反对规范的看法，也表示出对规范语言学问题的严重关注。他敦促人们"让自己的语言放任自流"，或"不许干涉洋泾浜英语"，这本身就是对语言创新中相互竞争的各种方针的评价。我们在本文讨论中所建议的既不是赞成也不是反对规范，而是坚持认为语言的正确性是个语言问题；作为语言问题，它就值得语言科学的注意。反规范的态度并不自美国语言学始。现在承认的描写语言学和规定语言学之间的不同，十九世纪的语言学家早就开始加以区别了。瑞典语言学家泰内尔(Esaias Tegnér)在1874年出版的书中写道：语言学的事务不是"规定语言规则，而是描写语言规则。"然而，这两类活动之间的界限难以辨识，并且根据当代的社会科学，对于规范准则和价值以及赖于取得这些准则和价值的过程的描写，不是完全非科学的程序。我们现在的问题将是区分这两类活动，弄清语言科学和语言科学家能对这些活动作出什么贡献。即使这不是一门纯科学，它毫无疑问也是语言技术的应用，因此将划归为应用语言学的一个分支。

2. 语言规划的性质

2.1. 规范语言学或规定语言学可以看做是对语言的一种处理或操纵，其前提我将在这里称之为"语言规划"。规划是一种人类活动，来自要找到一种解决问题的方法的需要。它可以是完全非正式的，为了某一具体目的而安排的，但也可以是有组织的，经过深思熟虑的。它可以由个人进行，也可以是官方的。社会规划是我们社会中范围明确的一项活动，虽然不同国家对具体领域中的规划的喜好在程度上有所不同。如果规划做得好，这将包括如下步骤：广泛调查事实，考虑行动计划的各种可供选择的方案，做出决定以及用各种具体方法执行这些决定。

2.2. 这里提出的模式对语言规划也适用。哪里有语言问题，哪里就要求对语言进行规划。不管是出于什么原因，如果人们对某种语言情况感到不满，那么就有制订语言规划纲领的场合。我在早些时候写的一篇文章中对语言规划的定义是："为了指导构成成分不同的语言集团的人写作和谈话，编制规范的正字法、语法和词典的活动。"现在我宁可把这看做是语言规划的一个结果，是语言规划工作者所做出的决定的一个部分。语言规划的核心毋宁是我以前说过的："对现有的语言形式进行选择中作出判断。"更确切地说，我认为语言规划可以定义为对语言变化的评价。这也是印度学者拉伊(P. S. Ray)的看法。他写了一本引人入胜的书，论述语言标准化；这本书在写作这篇文章时参考价值很大。他把规定语言学说成是"对辨别语言创新过程中的合理性的探索。"④

2.3. 因为语言学自豪地宣称它自身是一门描写科学，当然也就可以否定评价和选择过程的一切科学价值。但是，如果我们不纠缠于放任主义和规定主义的问题，那么可以有把握地说语言中的选择问题远远没有解决。每个个人必须重新学习语言而从来都不是刻板地学习他老师的语言，人们在一生中可以并且的确改变着自己的语言，所有这些事实都足以保证必定有选择的余地。只要这种说法是成立的，我们可以认为，语言规划是试图影响这些选择。语言规划

③ Leonard Bloomfield：Literate and illiterate speech，*American Speech*，2(1927)，pp. 432—39

④ Punya Sloka Ray：*Language Standardization：Studies in Prescriptive Linguistics*(语言标准化：规定语言学的研究)，The Hague，Mouton，1963.

类似于其他一切评价工作，它设想存在着一些标准，根据这些标准可以对语言创新进行评价。

2.4. 然而，我们不应事先就认定我们知道这些标准是什么。语言规划不能事先承诺促进或防止语言变化的任务，也不能承诺在不同的说话人或集团之间鼓吹统一性或分化性的任务。它不能承诺抵制或鼓励语言之间互借语言成分的任务：它可以为语言纯洁化服务，也可以为语言的混合服务。它可以提倡扩展或限制语言资源。语言规划工作不能只考虑有效性而牺牲的优美，它既可以为准确性也可以为表达力服务，它甚至也不能承担保持它所规划的语言的稳定性的任务，它可以为促使这一语言变成某种其他语言而起作用。

2.5. 我们在下面系统叙述语言规划的时候，将采用决定论(decision theory)的一般方法所提出的计划。对决策工作的研究，是当代社会理论家喜爱的研究项目之一；毫无疑问，决策的一般模式对语言规划也是有用的。我并不自认为掌握了这个研究领域中的种种复杂情况，我只是想说，这里提出来的资料跟我们可以称之为决定程序的过程很适合。随便举一个定义："决策便是从社会规定的数目有限的、有问题的、可供选择的诸方案(即行动方针)中，选出一个方案，以实现决策人所设想的某种未来的状况"。我们将考虑引起语言规划的那种问题，所涉及的那种决策者，所提出的供选择的方案以及对这些方案的限制，所应用的评价原则以及方针得以贯彻的方法。这显然是个很大的题目，在本文这样的短文中，我们只能希望叙述其概要。

2.6. 在考虑引起语言规划的问题之前，重要的是确立言语和文字各自的作用。布龙菲尔德有一句名言：文字"只是利用看得见的符号来记录语言的一种方法"，这也是一般语言学家的观点。如果我们还是坚持这种观点，那么甚至是接触这个题目都不可能。上述对文字的陈述是一种有意贬低的说法，但根据布龙菲尔德论述的目的，这是可以理解的。对语言科学来说，不论从历史上说，还是从个人的学习和生活方面说，文字都从属于言语；这种认识的极端重要性谁都不能否认。然而，在语言规划的研究中，我们将不得不颠倒这种关系：把文字看成是主要的，言语是次要的。语言学家对语言规划比较缺乏兴趣，这也许是一个原因：在他们看来，语言规划把事情弄颠倒了。语言学家认为是次要的东西，它却看作是首要的；语言学家认为不过是现实的影子的东西，它却以为很有价值。之所以有这种颠倒，是因为文字有做为被时间和空间相隔的说话人之间传递信息的媒介的功能。对语言集团来说，文字的持久性及重要性，允许并且要求得到一种不同的处理，这种处理方法不同于处理自然言语的方法。文字远不只是一种记录，它是它自身的一种代码的体现，这种代码可以影响语言集团的言语。

2.7. 一种书面语跟该书面语使用者的个人言语代码之间的关系，可以分析成双重翻译过程。如果我们从任何特定的个人言语出发，语言学家便可运用其技术，用标准的语言描写的形式对这种个人言语进行分析，得出准确而详尽的记录。我们可以把这叫做说话人的个人言语字音录(grapholect)。甚至在最好的情况下，个人言语字音录之间也能察觉到有所不同。个人言语字音录不同于个人言语的地方在于：它是(1)经过编辑的，(2)经过分析的，(3)迟缓的和(4)稳定下来的。说它是经过编辑的，是指它不包含具体说话人的无数难以预料的错误话语和口误。说它是经过分析的，是说象音位或词这样的成序列的单位是分开的而不是熔合在一起的，如/wàynče télmiy/就是以我所能想象的英语文字的形式由五六个连续的单位组成：Why didn't you tell me？(你为什么不告诉我？)说它是迟缓的，是说人们把它当作第二语言来学，因而它和个人言语相比，更有更多的思考和深入理解的过程。说它是稳定下来的，是说它有更大的储存能力和运载力，从而有利于它的形式一再得到使用并保持稳定性。在把这些原则运用于个人言语的过程中，语言学家就把个人言语翻译成一种新媒介，结果技术上有所变化，信息有所丧失。个人言语字音录的使用者在学习读和写时，必须做同样的工作。

2.8. 但个人言语字音录还不是正式文字。必须进行第二次翻译，使之适应其他个人言语的需要，或简言之，在各种个人言语字音录中折衷。正如裘斯指出的⑤：理想的文字系统应该是形态音位的，从而提供某种程度的语素稳定性；它应该允许对符号做这样那样的解释，这样，不同的个人言语的读音才各有所循；它也应该是统一一致的，这样，不同的言语习惯可以翻译成这个文字系统中的文字。但这意味着标准文字在某种程度上独立于文字使用者的言语习惯，它变成自己的一种语言，并不仅仅是言语的反映。文字学习者有双重的学习问题，要学习说话和纯粹作为编码技术的文字之间的差别，以及个人言语和在文字中得到反映的那些个人言语之间的差别。第二种差别是这样一种差别，它可以导致在文字的影响下实际发生的语言变化，因为文字被人读出来就可以生成自己的言语。读者应用他所学到的翻译规则，就可以得出一个不同于他本人的个人言语。两个人的个人言语字音录有多少不同，他们的个人言语也有多少不同。不管一种语言的文字根据音位原则拼写达到何种程度，都有可能产生这种效果。实际上，完全根据音位的拼写系统将促进发音的统一，这样，根据拼写发音，德语比英语更为一致。语言学家不那么欢迎根据拼写发音；但不根据拼法发音，象高地德语这样的语言是难以想象的。

2.9. 在考虑语言规划时，语言中的文体问题也是重要的。这个问题也跟言语和文字之间的区别密切相关，它在文字发明以前很久早已存在。研究美洲印第安语的学者提供了许多材料，证明各种情况下的文体是不同的；他们使用了"非随便性的言语"(non-casual speech)这个术语，我则宁愿用传统的术语即正式的(formal)文体。我们可以确定某些话语类型，例如法律、宗教仪式和史诗用语，这些类型甚至在没有文字的社会中都要求使用正式的语言。这些类型中的语言不同于日常言语，这些语言更庄严，更清楚也更易记忆。原因就在于这些类型对语言集团的生活是如此重要，它们必须不加改变地代代相传。执法官员，教士和游唱诗人专司这些类型，他们因此成为传统的保存者，同时又是传统可能的革新者。这样从过去传下来的语言是公

众的，正式的，日常言语却不是这样。正式语言的基础是一个人对许多人说话，一个人为许多人说话；它是语言集团本身的声音。如果在没有文字的社会中情况是这样，那末在有文字的社会中情况就更是这样，因为文字极大地提高了准确性，也增加了记忆储存量。其结果是随便话语和正式语言之间的差距越来越大，以及随之而来的词汇超越时代保存下来的程度很高。如果情况不是这样，那才是最令人惊惶的事。

2.10. 为了进行语言规划，我们现已确立了文字比言语重要的观点。这样做以后，我们可以做一个总说明：语言规划主要研究正式文体，特别是书面形式的正式文体，而不是非正式文体。正式文体对非正式文体的任何影响是个次要的结果，主要的目的是通过书面表达法的改变影响正式文体。这是一切语言规划的环境和背景。

3. 语言规划中的问题

3.1. 如果我们现在考虑语言规划的第一个方面，即考虑引起语言规划的问题，那末它们都是不能传递信息这个问题的特殊情况。原则上是哪里传递信息失败，哪里就需要语言规划。但失败的只是非此即彼的概念，而是包括从完全成功到完全失败之间的不同程度。如果我们取这两个参数的两端和中间项，我们可以确立三种价值的价值状况：面对面的一级言语集团（Primary speech-community），其中说话人之间的不同只是个人的特异，用语言学术语来说，以下可

[脚注] ③ Martin Joos: Review of Axel Wijk, Regularized English (评阿克塞尔·威克的《规则化了的英语》)，刊于 Language, 36(1960)，pp. 250—62.

个人言语特点的不同；二级言语集团（secondary speech-community），其中成员可以部分懂得其他成员的语言；三级言语集团（tertiary speech-community），其中成员说话不能互通，所以需要翻译。在政治单位中，我们可以冰岛作为一级言语集团的例子，英国属于二级言语集团，瑞士属于三级言语集团。正如前面已讨论这些概念彼此相差甚者，而仅仅是相对而言；二级言语集团要求确立民族共同语的条件已经成熟，三级言语集团要求确立国际语或辅助语的条件已经成熟。这两例情况都要求语言规划给予帮助，解决语言信息的传递问题。更一般地说，其中的每一种情况都要求有共同的代码，即一种辅助语言，使那些迫切希望跟其他一级言语集团的成员进行交际的人得以交际。

3.2. 通过强调用口语以及提供语言情况的个人的重要性，语言学已挑出一级言语集团作为特别关注的对象。在这样一种集团里，语言规划是多余的，因为宣称他的需要已提供妙招正个别嘲笑现象的措施。每个学习者一有错，其他学习者就通常会用嘲笑他们的临时手段，当场纠正他；他或者用已学会的旧的模式自我纠正，直至他学会不全力和标准一样。集团的每个成员都内在化了该语言代码，就这样，它加以不懂（这叫做"代码骚音"）被减少到最小的程度。在我看来，这里提出来的以信息论为基础的模型，最充分地描写了面对面的一级言语交际的情况，这个模型也可以应用于二级至三级言语集团。在细节上作了必要的修正之后，必须通过中介进行交际的较大的言语集团，也有共同的代码为其根好地服务。这种代码给多方面情报的直接性；必须更有意识地规定其形状，而就文字而言，语言规划在这里大有用武之地。主要的问题在于：书面语没有言语所具有的自我纠正的特点，它需要一类专门的监管者，以弥补这一缺陷。

3.3. 实际上，不能预知的情景差别很大。在整个幅度的一端是一种文言，他们没有任何文字传统，也没有任何中央集权的政府，这种情况在世界范围中正透进地变得越来越多。在不少文字的地方，还可以区分若干种不同情况。弗格森（Charles A. Ferguson）提出了描写这些情况的幅度：用 W0—W2 作为描写文字的幅度，St0—St2 作为描写标准化的幅度。W2 代表这样一些语言，这些语言有单一的汇泛接受的规范，人们意到这种规范总适当的；只要把规范做些细微的修改或变更，就可以把语言应用于一切目的。甚至这些"理想的状态"也有各种各样，要求对它区分出来：例如，他认为瑞典语的 St2 的例子，但瑞典语内若干地区中有着干种根本不能互通的现用方言，据这些不同方言的人之间以相当接近标准语的人之间都不合适。对达列卡利亚地区（Dalecarlia）的说话人来说，有共同的代码为其根好地服务。不管文字或标准化的情况如何，语言规划工作者都有问题需要处理。

3.4. 如果某种语言有文字，那末这种文字的问题大不相同。如果已经有了正字法，那么对它的使用者的需要说来，它可能不适用或变得不适用了，或许可能有几种与之竞争的正字法。即使这种正字法仍适用，也许能行得很好，没有理由希望它有什么改变，但在这种标准里也还可能有变异，这些变异应加以评价；有一种自然的发音、语法、语法、语言、语言词汇。某个书面语言是否合乎需要，从而值得推广，或者这是不合乎需要，不值得推广？在这些问题上意见可能有分歧。看来从

[脚注] ③ John J. Gumperz: Types of linguistic communities (语言集团的类型), Anthropological Linguistics, 4:1 (1962), pp. 28—40.
④ Charles A. Ferguson: The language factor in national development (民族发展中的语言因素), Anthropological Linguistics, 4:1(1962), pp. 23—27.

最简单的到最复杂的语言社区都有这样的判断问题。它们甚至也不限于无文字的集团。布龙菲尔德发现：他调查威斯康星州梅诺米尼语（Menomini）时提供该语言规范的人对同族人试用的语言的性质有非常固定的意见之外。他得出结论说："一些人由于品格和地位，由于语言上的明显优越性，所有这一切使得他们和别人相比，被认为是行为和言语方面的较好的典范。"

4. 语言规划者的作用

4.1. 本节标题引导我们现在来考虑作为决策者的规划者本身。或者如同麦克格的含蓄的话来说，"如果有某种权威的话，那么，我的意思是在什么地方指导并且控制语言的变化呢？"文艺复兴时，掌管语言的权力在语法学家和修辞学家的手中。奎恩蒂利安① 在《论修辞学》中曾规定语法的功能之一是"构造正确的言语"。可以预料，希腊语法和拉丁语法在这些时代的古典时期之后很久才出现，它们在本质上对已经很多发言、语法、语言词汇标准化的。一般认识到制定这些概念互相相差甚者，而仅仅是相对而言；但仅仅是语言学家对文字中文体部分中公认的规范进行描写纯，还是把它看做是确定或者甚至是创造那种规范呢，这是有分歧之处。但随着时代的变迁，人们对编纂者的态度，他对自己的作用的想法，适用"代码"一词的意思，都发生了剧变。对那些认为语言是神祇所创造的人来说，编纂者是把上帝的其如分发给人民的权威。相继而来的是有人把代码看作是法律，把法典看作是法律颁布者；把代码看作是礼仪，编纂者便是时尚的仲裁人；把代码看作是民族象征，编纂者便是民族英雄。对美学家来说，编纂者是美的规范的维护者；对哲学家来说，则是思维法则的解释者。在语言为社会科学家，我们必须承认，上述代码的所有意义以及编纂者的所有作用在人类社会中仍然存在，并纳入语言规划的复杂的功能中。

4.2. 在十五和十六世纪，一些国家的财富增加，国力增强，同时这些国家的现代语言出现

现了第一批语法和词典。这两种现象是怎样同时出现的，值得注意。典型的例子是第一部西班牙语语法，内布里哈（Nebrija）1492 年出版的 Grammatica de la Lengua Castellana，他把这本书献给伊萨贝拉女王，称之为"御用参考书"。第一所旨在从语言中简洁不统成分的研究院，是这同一运动的组成部分，在这情况下，被的地位确立了，佛罗伦萨 及它的图斯堪（Tuscan）方言被确立为意大利语的模型。这个研究院就是 1582 年建立的克鲁斯卡研究院（Accademia della Crusca），它是由省留红衣主教（Cardinal Richelieu）1635 年建立的法兰西科学研究院的模型。这位精明的红衣主教制订了科学院的章程条例（毫无疑问这是政治上中央集权化方针的一部分）要求科学院的成员"尽可能精心勤奋地工作，制订出法语的准确规则，使法语能够纯正艺术的科学的猜罢。"其他国家纷起仿效，其中西班牙于 1713 年，瑞典于 1739 年，匈牙利于 1830 年相继建立起类似机构。这些研究院主要的可见到的成果是词典，始自第一部单语词典《克鲁斯卡研究院词汇录》（1612）。在美国，有许多十七、十八世纪的著名作家，例如弥尔顿（Milton）、德拉顿（Dryden）、笛福（Defoe）和斯威夫特（Swift）都深感不安，要求建立美语研究院，但美国人抵制加国的任何思想，特别是反对他们从中喷出权力主义气味的那种思想，最后，他们却接受了一位非官方的公民——约翰逊（Samuel Johnson）的法规，约翰逊的词典（1755）成为英语的第一个重要的裁判。美国宣布自己在语言上独立于英国，是由另一位非官方的公民韦伯斯特

[脚注] ⑤ Marcus Fabius Quintilianus，公元一世纪的罗马雄辩学家，教授雄辩学达二十年之久。他享著名的著作，就是这本《论修辞学》(De Institutione Oratoria)。——译者

（Noah Webster）来完成，他代替英国的约翰逊。

4.3. 然而，主要是由于法国和美国相继发生革命以及识字运动的开展，在十九和二十世纪对编纂者提出了最高的要求。按近群众个人教育问题，而书本是教育的工具。印刷出版物的技术上的要求需要标准化。一个人认识到每位学习一种新语言，他们实际上是自己国家的二等公民。政治混乱导致新国家的崛起，导致国家的复活；我们在一个又一个国家中看到个人、政府委员会、研究机构对语言规划和编纂典，结果各种新的语言相继确立。希腊的贺拉斯（Korais）、挪威的奥森（Aasen）、斯洛伐克的切图夫（Štur）、普罗旺斯的米斯特拉（Mistral）、波希米亚的多布罗夫斯基（Dobrovsky）、爱沙尼亚的阿维克（Aavik）和立陶宛的亚布隆斯基斯（Jablonskis），我们常想起这些名字。这些人部分是语言学家，部分是爱国者，他们的著作中有一些不能被为纯粹语言学的成分。但他们之中一些人，对语言科学的发展做出了很大的贡献，例如，奥森以是挪威方言学的集大成。所有欧洲国家都普遍实行公立学校制，由教育部控制着它们的语言的正字法和语法。在土耳其，独裁的凯末尔（Kemal Atatürk）1932 年建立了半官方的"土耳其语言学校和协会"，他委派党员和学校教师到协会中任职，委托他们规划土耳其语的改造工作；在此之前，他已正式废除阿拉伯字母，代之以罗马字母。在私人主动发起和独裁者倡导这两个极端之间，大中有各种中间机构——不管是教会、团体，还是文科和理科院校——都在为了某种语言形式从事语言规划工作。

5. 语言规划中各种可供选择的方案

5.1. 现在让我们考虑有关语言规划的一些可供选择的行动方针。我们在这里注意力将局限于二级言语集团，特别注意国家这个集团，因为弗格森不久前注意到：这个在语言学里被忽视了的实体毕竟是"通讯工具，教育制度和语言'规划'的常见基础"。还有小于国家的集团，象威尔士人，又有国家的集团，象犹太人；他们也有某种国家面临的语言问题，但因为缺少官方支持机构，他们在从事语言规划时只能尽其所需。这里所说的大部分内容，对他们也同样适用，因此我将集中注意一些国家特有的特殊情况。

5.2. 在考虑行动方针的时候，我们需要想一想语言行为的一些目的。迄今为止我们已假定这是迅速而不费力的交流信息，但交流信息的基本模式，正如比莱（Bühler）的三角可表现以发挥的。情境处理可不限于单纯表示有所指述传递信息。这种表示由由雅可布逊称为表情（emotive）功能；还有诉诸于听者的表达，他称之为意动（conative）功能。除了这些以外，还有些小功能，如交流感情（phatic），后语言（metalingual）和诗歌（poetic）等功能。从社会普遍象的角度来说，这些语言人既表示人员语言集团能够接受的东西。语言不仅仅是社会合作的手段，也是人们分解的手段。前者导致代码的一致性，后者导致多样性。实际结果必须是二者之间的某种平衡。

5.3. 因此，正象前面所说的，我们不能把语言规划的目标确定为不管何时何地都必须是一种绝对一致的代码。这是那些自然的语言规划者常抱的错误之一。他们想把一种语言固定化，什么时候都一成不变；或者是想把单一的标准强加于描写多种非常不同的方言的人们身上。但语言规划应可以设想为同一种语言代替多种语言，又可设想为用多种语言代替一种语言；可以为多样性服务，也可以为统一性服务，可以为促进变化，也可以为保持稳定性服务。又可以为统一性服务，又可以为促进变化。

[脚注] ⑦ Roman Jakobson: Linguistics and poetics (语言学和诗学), Style in Language, ed. by Thomas Sebeok (Cambridge, Mass., M. I. T. Press, 1960), pp. 350—70.

内克（Havránek）在规定标准的性质时说，标准语具有带有可变通性的稳定性。这对标准语来说毫无特殊之处，这是任何语言规范，甚至是一级言语集团所共有的。稳定性是一段时期内跟统一性相关，而可变通性是与同时期内跟多样性相关联。一种活语言的规范一方面在很大程度上是稳定而统一的，它同时也给使用者提供伸缩性和多样性的余地。正如霍尼斯瓦德指出的，一切语言变化都可定义为性质，这可以是分裂，也可以是合并，或者二者都不是。评价是跟同样的行为时，它可以决定支持多种语言而不支持一种语言，也可以支持一种语言而不支持多种语言。

6. 语言规划的限度

6.1. 但是，在做出任何这种决定之前，必须确定语言变化的限度。语言规划者总是在某时某地的情况下着手作工作的，他寄为的任务就是处理他所面临的事。当那威语言改革家奥森着手于从中世纪的遗产中重新发现挪威诗时，他不将不把这种语言确定为现存在多种农村方言中的一种规范形式。当时大多数人认为这些农村方言是方言变化的退化变体，并不多在此同时，在斯洛伐克克的切图伏进了其工作之前，该地区的所有方言为捷克语——一种文字传统长久得多的语言——的变体。语言规划者识别语言的一种方法是建立其历史。内部构拟和比较语言学相结合，这些语言学家就是用这种方法来创造这些规范形式，这些形式之超然是做为这些地区里使用的较古老的语言的直系祖先语言而存在的。语言地理和语言历史以这种方式确立起来确定能作出的可能的语言的范围。

6.2. 语言规划者的方案，还受到一个进一步的限制，即受到口语传统和文字传统状况的限制，而这些传统能是被这这些方言的诉讼需要的。如果是为一个以前没有文字的民族被出标准，那么就只需要考虑这个言语集团的诉讼形式。如果只有一个规范，那么如标准，他的问题大体上是提供一个正字法的技术问题。如果有两个以上的规范，他就面临着干种选择，这就要求考虑全部问题和我们所需要的行将讨论的评价方式。此外，如果已经存在着一个或多个正字

法，他的任务就进一步复杂化了，除非他执意依赖其中的一个文字系统，或仅是用这种那种方法把它拼凑起来。在任何有某种传统的有文字的言语集团中，关于言语和文字，有一整套信念以及证明其合理性的条条框框，对此语言规划者可能变得无能为力，除非他能把这些转而用来说明他本人的目的。不管这些条条框框是多么不合理，它们会有助于那些投入巨大精力守信社会传统的人的地位和便利。

6.3. 鉴于对这些可供选择的方案苛刻的限制，如果不是人民和社会以及他们的语言自身确实在发生变化的话，人们可能感到绝望，认为难以使事情有所变化。我们前面提出了一些问题，在评价对这些可能的解决方法时，需要有把这些供选择的方案归着的决定程序。这些供选择的方案必须是根据某种客观标准能够分类的，例如：长期的还是短期的，成熟的还是不成熟的。而这些分类的方案反过来又跟更大范围值得关注的目的联系起来，例如交流信息，自我提高或集团的稳定性。

7. 语言规划的标准

7.1. 就这个题目写了大量文章的学者已提出许多评价标准。古典论者的观点认为模式要在过去时代中寻找，机体论者的观点认为语言是一个演化着的机体，人的理性控制不了它。诺林

① Henry Hoenigswald: *Language Change and Linguistic Reconstruction* (语言变化和语言的构拟) (Chicago, University of Chicago Press,1960).

(Adolf Noreen)摒弃了这两种观点，根据他认为合理的途径，提出了一套判断"错误的"语言的标准。凡引起误解的，不能理解的，或难以理解的，以及难读难记的，不必要的冗长和复杂的，不给语言源加任何东西的创新，都是"错误的"语言。

7.2. 这些标准中的大部涉及我们可以简明概要地概括为效率标准的某些方面。我碰巧知道，最早对效率标准做系统阐述的，是瑞典语言学家斯内尔(Esaias Tegnér)。泰内尔在现代科学影响之下，早在诺林之前就做出了这种说明，他写道：最好的语言是"最容易说，最容易懂的语言"。以何最重要之处在于：它清楚地认识到说话者的兴趣照顾听话人的兴趣可能不一致。实际上，说话人说话的能力和听话人理解的能力，这二者之间存在一种不稳定的平衡，交流信息正是通过这种不稳定过程的需要。缺少劳心的直接补正，因而要求者事先预见到该者的需要，写作缺少听众的直接对正，因而要求者事先预见到该者的需要，写作缺少听众的直接对话，因而要求者事先预见到该者的些困难，如语调和手势因此必须用清楚明白的符号去弥补。对于有经验的读者甚至还可以用拼音位拼写，而这在拼写改革者和儿童中间是行不通的。

7.3. 学者和没有学过，在这里是以学者在着明显的利害冲突。对那些已学过某个系统的人来说，很简单的新系统可能也很难看懂。懂汉字的人说，读汉字比读同一个单位的拼音文字要快些，但学习汉字的代价毕竟很高。英语的拼写跟任何一种英语的发音只有不规则的关系，但正是这种完全不按音位拼写的关系，使它具有语源的同一性；而对于欧洲其他华习者来说，如果英语是按音位拼写，学起来就会更熟悉这些他珍贵的语源。因此，要学习的代价跟不学习的代价加以比较，必须以来解释效率。由于不必学习的人一般都控制社会机构，而要学习的人都是学童，显示以任何形式的变更在实事显然会受到很大的阻力。这样，一种求如果是学易用，它就是有效率的，又总原则仍然是正确的。

7.4. 有人认为短词一定比长词有效，没有格词属的语法一定比有格词属的语法有效率。我们必须避开这种表面的判断。正如拉伊(P. S. Ray)提醒我们的：使语体中经常出现的词序可能短些，学习起来的确容易，而且我们发现在自然语言中短词通常都是短词。另一方面，罕见词语有很可能被省略，因为这时词意普遍为太长词，这有效率，因为这使它们具有更多的装余信息。这样一些词也会弄得很多，因而在语法上已经常使用的词意消除。象英语这样的语言的屈折词尾虽然少，所以它一方面有极其复杂的介词系统，另一方面有严格的词序，这就要求英语的书面文体比同语系的其他语言表现在英语引进"do"和"one"这样的虚位填充词(例如: "I do say我确实说"，或"the young one这个年龄的人")。

7.5. 在确定一种语言形式比另一种语言形式更有效率这一过程中，回想关于英语从所谓的综合型语言变成分析型语言上，在十九世纪曾有两种针锋相对的看法，想到这一点足以提醒我们小心从事。浪漫派豚为之为退化，而进化论者豚之为进步。今天我们称之为变化。我们已经认识到：不能从结构中来孤立一个单个成，据此就判断它的效率如何如何，必须根据整个结构评价某一个成分；要使它这方面的看法能不仅仅是猜测意见，还有许多工作要做。

7.6. 语言规划特别关注的另一个标准，凡是它出现的场合，我称之为适合性。同拉伊称之为"语言的合理性"的说法相比，我更喜欢这个术语，这一标准也包括加文(Paul L. Garvin)遵循他弗拉内克的说法而称之为"理智化升降"的原则。这两位着家所考虑的，主要是语言作为表达所指意义的工具，它满足语言使用者的需要的能力。这是语言规划要起作用的一个场合，因为：适应现代科学的需要而创造文字。在一级言语集团，方法总是具有的：我们可以通过借用，或者是创造，把词汇扩大到满足说话人的需要。我们都知道阿拉伯人最关心骆驼，爱斯基摩人最关心雪，所以他们分别有丰富的表达骆驼和雪的词。在二级言语集团里，由于很其他成员的接触以及翻译其他民族的文件也需要。

7.7. 但还有另一种民族内孕育的适合性。这不太可能影响纯粹理性的领域，而反倒是属于诗音型语言更更密切的私人生活范围。扩大语言的适合性不仅靠增加科技和哲学词汇，而且也靠(充分发展)感情和诗歌表达的词语。斯堪的纳维亚的情况就是这样，所有斯堪的纳维亚国家的语言成过了许多年后仍然长效的，正象在弗的研究可以推动标准语的发展。适合性的规则是：一种语言形式在表达语言使用者想表达的信息时，其准确性必须达到预期的高度。

7.8. 第三个标准是可接受性。我们所说的可接受性跟拉伊提出的"语言平民化"的标准意思很相似，但这一标准从社会的角度进行评价的着标标准。我们以前研究这个题目时的学者所说的用法标准——即正确的标准。叶斯柏森曾指出：有三种类型的用法可懂性，它满足最低程度的传递信息的要求；正确性，它符合语言规范所有规的要求；优美性，它符合某些民清楚又优美的美的内外标准。这样，以清楚明确的规则则才是可能的，反过来不同实际上是指一种言语集团中另有某种可接受性的可接受性。象中二级言语集团既不是同质的又不是完全异质的，它显示出复杂的分离景象，这扩大了用法的歧异，随之使语言发生偏离规范的现象。拉伊这种规则订的术语是有用的；有一小类的语言使用者叫做"领头人"，这二级语言集团人比达值得模仿，它有声望。其他使用者可以模仿他们的用法，直到"入门"为止。这就就是使得他们的用法"散布"开来。

7.9. 这是跟某些学者对于欧洲的标准语的意见相吻合的，例如梅耶说："欧洲的标准语是杰出人物创造出来的，为之服务的。"当然，每个问题往往复杂得无比，无论是至在好几百年以人物的存在并不总是导致其语言的胜利。象希腊语、拉丁语和阿拉伯语这样的古典语言根据语人如同中海沿岸各国，并为其他言语集团，并与其他言语集团所接受。土耳其语也起过同样的作用，但正象希腊语一样，最后退到了，只限于在比较小的地区内。甚至在古代，一些地区的居民以拼音文字来支持。梅耶真奴二十世纪欧洲"语言巴尔干化①"的做法，并有根据认为：语言上的民族主义是民族主义中更有吸引力的一个方面。的确，美国年轻的一代的学者正在对民族主义本身重新估价，他们开始认识到，民族主义是朝向国际主义

① Balkanization，帝国主义国家为了推行侵略战略政策和殖民主义，把某一地区分裂成若干对立的小地区，使其互相牵制，以便从中渔利，象第一次世界大战前两方列强对巴尔干半岛各国那样政治的(用小划打小)，挑人为地分裂国治，但巴尔干地区的语言状况很复杂，导致这种复杂的原因也是多方面的。梅耶这里所说的只是一种看法——译者

前进的一步，而不是相反。首先这意味着鼓励公民个人不仅要关注个人或者当地利益，而且也要关注影响他们大社区的利益。民族主义把许多一级言语集团的人民结成二级言语集团，以此跟前者的狭隘观念和狭隘性对待。民族标准语的这种作用是使它具有民族象征的价值的理由。它成为传递信息的工具，不仅用于统治者和公民，也用于平民之间。他们成为一个大交际网的构成部分，即使他们被迫放弃某些自己的语言特点。

7.10. 在此同时，标准语是最对外部世界进行信息及交流的媒道，至少在将其它语言翻译成标准语这个方面如此。这种标准语的使用者不可能直接参与其他民族的生活，但因为他有一种翻译其他也许是更值得注意者的民族思想的语言，所以他了解其他民族的机会就比没有标准语的对手大。这样，民族标准语就经常变得从外部世界的影响，外部世界的语言甚至会不时或胁到它的独特性。民族标准语象民族一样，也有两面性：内部反对分裂而外部主张吸收。

7.11. 不管语言规划者是在确立一种民族标准语还是试图维正它，他都面临一些选择：

在他决意要使言语规范化的时候要遵循的是谁的用法。在欧洲大多数国家中，大家公认的"领头人"是是名流人物，他们的标志者是财产、权力、出身、教育程度，或者是这四点合而为一。然而，在新成立的国家或者更近的时期，流传的看法是或者名流人物根本不存在，或者被故意置之不闻。有些人主张在希腊采用德莫蒂克语(Demotike)，在爱尔兰采用盖尔语(Gaelic)，在挪威采用挪威语，这些人反对现行的名流人物把它看作是名流人物，他们的用法常是以农村方言，或者以城市日常口语为基础的。这个问题有时候被设想为：数量(采用人数最多的用法)；质量(最好、最地道的形式)；或是社会公平性(减少穷人的学习障碍)。但这些可以地理上分割的方言之间的冲突，因为每种方言都有做标准语的权利。可接受性的规则是：不管涉及到什么社会或次社会，一种语言形式都必须是"领头人"所采用或有可能采用的。

7.12. 有效率，适合性和可接受性，这三条规则在具体情况下可分可合，在某种程度上互相重叠，以不同的方式相互影响；情况不同，相关程度也不同。但是，由这三条规则应能使设计语言规划纲领的人做出某些决定。

8. 语言规划的执行

8.1. 在所有这些程序中，执行决定的时机问题。如何准确地完成规划？如果没有能保证大家接受的方法，那么手中拥有语法和词汇方案的语言学家只能是提建议而已。关于这个问题的研究，本质上是个群众宣传工具问题。要做这个工作，广告宣传家也许比语言学家更合适。归根到底，做出决定的是语言法规的执行者，这也是最后的决定。

8.2. 非官方的个人没有别的力量，只有其个人权威、或职业权威。攻击这种权威的人容易把这看做做"独裁主义"，而赞成这种权威的人倾喜欢称之为"权威性的"。有些事情太小，不能引起人们的注意，能被这些事情的偏误行去诸于权威，只有那些发音困难，字形奇特，偏离规范的拼写歌呀人们欣赏所写内容的胃口，但在某些文学形式中(例如在打油诗中)，这种偏误恰恰给人们以所希望的。没有一个规范，这样的偏误便毫无意义，只不过变成自由变异而已。在建立清楚明确的规范藉以赋予语言行为以意义之时，即象法兰西科学院式的机构，其作用是一样的。只有根据偏离规范和次规范的出现，才能理解文体的不同。

8.3. 跟非官方的个人相比，政府处于有利的地位，因为它控制着学校系统，通过这个系统可以训练或重新训练这们的书写习惯。基本上只有两种工具：(1)供读物的模型，其形式为口语的或书面的课本。这是提供语言情况的人供给的；(2)统率为语法的一套规则，这是语言学家提供的。提供语言情况的人提出语言行为的模型，你从中可以把语言学得很好，但对成年人来说，补充以清楚明确的规则则有大有用处。反过来对于语法说明的个人，你可根本学不会这种语言。因此最好的规划者就不仅要编辑语言的语法，而且还要自己编写课本。出于这个原因，研究书面语时需要写作者参加，这正象研究言语律时需要人参加一样。挪威人奥森不仅语言创出典真化，而且也写诗和散文。这就确定了使用这些法规的关键性并鼓励人参加挑拣杯标样。有关机构可提出一些奖励措施，从发给作者津贴和奖金，直到发布正式法令，清除可能破坏法规的语言对手。以达到某种方式建立的程，为那些想学习的人提供机会。要使他们得到真正的机会，以此做为促进他们学习的动力。最低限度也要通过学习，使他们在所生活的社会中成为更好和更有价值的成员，从而加强他们的自豪心。

8.4. 最简单的策略是在学校中引人改革，并让这种改革同孩子一起逐渐成熟；但这可能只会引起社会混乱。英语拼写法要改革的话，我想我们应该祈求突变而不是渐变。但那样将要求有象凯末尔那样的独裁者的行动，或者是事先获得全体居民的赞叹，而这两种情况，在不远的将来都不可能出现。

9. 语言学家的作用

9.1. 对于语言学家在语言规划中能起什么作用这个问题，我们现在尽我们所能，提供一些答案。必须承认：语言学家不一定受过从事语言规划的训练。对语言机制的作用过分神往，可能使他对对语言的功能敏感变得麻木不仁。但是虽然这么说他个人物也能爱花，就没有任何理由使语言学家受不爱用心的语言。文人须少具有关于语言模式的专门知识，不能确切说明他们是怎样使用语言的。倒不妨请求伟大的舞蹈家或小提琴家解释其艺术。能做不一定同时做到。如前面说，语言学家的独特之处不在于他怎样使用语言，而在于了解它什么，它跟语言过去和现在的结构有什么关系。十九世纪语言学的一大任务是把语言变化这个事实解释清楚：一切语言都在变化，并且变化是有规律的。规律性是如此之大，使许多语言学家变交成决定论者。另一方面，如果过分强调变化的不可避免性，语言规划总是有效引导语言向一定方向变化，需要是始终坚持决定论的观点，那一定会扼这种做法。另一方面，别的社会规章制度又常常走向僵化，以至已经无有效规划工作所改变，这一事实对那些发现自己的语言或文字不合适的人永远抱以希望。真正的问题在于评价工作有关。表达过程的媒介之体，是对于人类传递信息起作用的媒介——即语言——的性质，二十世纪语言学曾提供了宝贵的材料。只有充分了解这方面的材料，才能为有用的评价提供所必需的知识。

9.2. 也有这样的历史事实：语言学家或者作为技术顾问，或者作为首要的推动者，都曾参与过世界史中所有成功的语言规划。1963年在尼日利亚伊巴丹的大学学院举行了列弗休姆（Leverhulme）会议，会议报告特别强调了非洲发展中国家的语言学家投入语言规划工作的紧迫必要性。报告说："C在非洲迫切需要材料，据此可以采取关于语言的实际决定。……在这种情况下，语言学家对语言状况和语言问题如果仍持抗拒的、超然的、'象牙塔'的观点，他们肯定将脱离二十世纪最伟大的一些实验的过程，无法发挥其作用，他们将失去在这些领域中对本大陆的总发展做出贡献的机会，而在这些领域中，他们是可以比其他人做出更加有用的贡献的。"

9.3. 对于这个问题，语言学家可以而且必须提供的，都有哪些特殊类型的材料呢？我认为有四个方面他们可以提供帮助，可能还有其他方面被忽略了。语言学家可以作为1）历史学家，2）描写者，3）理论家，4）教师，在这四方面作出贡献。

作为历史学家，语言学家可以建立语言史。他的研究，使人们可以追溯某一集团说话或书写的延续过程，上溯到纪录或构拟形所能及的过程，他可以对语言中的本族语成分跟借用成

---

① Linné，瑞典博物学家，创立动植物种的双名法系统。——译注

分加以区别，借此看情况提出纯净化或混合化的基础。不管这种基础对传统赋予什么价值，他都能提供。一些时期，例如浪漫主义时期，因为祖先光荣，所以增强了自尊心；另一些时期，也许是比较现实，就不那么引起激情。

作为描写者，语言学家可以提供该语言集团口语和文字实践现状的准确描写。作为方言地理学家，他可以收集通用的言语中的变异和一致性的材料；作为现代社会方言学者，他可以确定各种不同形式的地位价值。他可以观察跟标准言语以及标准文字有关的现象，并加以归纳分类，这样就可以知道该语言集团的语言实践。他的研究成果，可以体现在正字法、语法和词典中。

作为理论家，他可以确定一些了解一般语言的指导方针。具体地说，他通过自己对语言分析技巧的知识，对语言类型学中共性成分的了解，可以对语言的设计作出说明。他对于言语和文字的关系的了解，使他能说明对二者之一的操作过程能期望得到什么结果。他意识到单一的结构对有效的交流信息很重要，同时能也允许有个人的变异。他研究了以前语言规划的种种方案，观察了这些方案的成功程度，这样他就能把"自然的'变化'跟'人为的'变化分开。

至于语言学家也作为教师这一方面，他注视着训练或重新训练语言使用者的过程中可能出现的问题。他的经验和所受过的训练，应使他能够判断某一规划在教学上是否可行，是否合于需要。他可以估计现在花费在学习上的努力的程度，也可以把关于学生对该规则的态度的信息反馈给本人以及其他规划者。

9.4. 人们也许认为，我们是在建议语言学完全跟语言规划等同，或建议语言规划在其方案中只用语言学家。为防止产生这种误解，我得在结尾处赶紧补充：语言学是必要的，但是不充分的。由于语言规划是一种语言政策，由于涉及什么是可能的手法以及赢得被统治者的赞许，语言规划需要政治科学的洞察力。因为它深深涉及到作为社会动物的人的行为，它需要人类学和社会学的精辟明晰的语言行为理论的支持。关于学习行为和感知方面，心理学可以在这些方面做出贡献，不管这些贡献如何，心理学在语言规划中大有用武之地。美学家和哲学家的贡献也不能忽视。即使麦克唐纳式的人物对于语言学的情况了解甚少，他说出的一个观点，如果我们不想被人称为一无所知，那也是不能忽视的。即使纯粹的或微观语言学意义上的语言学将被视线缩小到只关注语言的微观现象，宜称被包括在宏观语言学之中的应用语言学决不能忽视我们在其中实际生活、说话和书写的社会宏观现象。

（胡壮麟校）

☯ 思考题

1. 请总结分析地域方言和社会方言的差别，再列举一些教材之外的社会方言的种类和例子。

2. 请结合具体的语言实例，对比分析一下借词与意译词、仿译词的区别。

3. "语言替换"是指发生接触的语言彼此混合而产生一种新的语言吗？为什么？另外，发生语言替换有哪些必要条件？必然经过哪些中间阶段？

4. 语言规划包括哪些内容，影响语言规划的因素有哪些？

📖 拓展阅读书目

- R. L. Cooper. 1989. *Language Planning and Social Change*. Cambridge: Cambridge University Press.

- Robert M. W. Dixon. 1997. *The Rise and Fall of Languages*. Cambridge: Cambridge University Press.

- 陈保亚. 语言接触与语言联盟. 北京：语文出版社，1996.

- 李宇明. 中国语言规划论. 北京：商务印书馆，2010.